Restructuring Work and the Life Course

Edited by Victor W. Marshall, Walter R. Heinz,
Helga Krüger, and Anil Verma

Major economic, technological, and demographic forces are combining
to influence the ways in which the very structures of people's lives are
changed by the work they do. The major defining features of the life
course, including patterns of entry to and exit from work, are shifting,
as is the nature of jobs and careers. In this multidisciplinary collection
of essays, fifty contributors from seven countries examine changes in
the organization of work and their impact on people at various stages
of the life course.

In seeking to consolidate and advance life-course theory, the four
editors of this volume have sought out a wide range of approaches to
life-course theorizing, methodologies, and research designs. The contributing scholars examine the influence of economic, technological,
and demographic forces on public, corporate, and union policies concerning the organization of work. The topics covered include education, labour market change, and transitions in the early and middle
stages of the working life course; later-life transitions in relation to the
restructuring of work and retirement; and various aspects of the relationship between individual biography and social structure, with close
attention to gender and family issues over the life course.

Victor W. Marshall is Professor of Sociology, University of North
Carolina at Chapel Hill, and Director, University of North Carolina
Institute on Aging.
Walter R. Heinz is Professor of Sociology and Chair of the Life Course
Centre, University of Bremen.
Helga Krüger is Professor of Sociology and a member of the steering
committee of the Life Course Centre, University of Bremen.
Anil Verma is a professor at the Joseph L. Rotman School of Manage-
ment and the Centre for Industrial Relations, University of Toronto.

Restructuring Work and the Life Course

Edited by

Victor W. Marshall
Walter R. Heinz
Helga Krüger
Anil Verma

UNIVERSITY OF TORONTO PRESS
Toronto Buffalo London

© University of Toronto Press Incorporated 2001
Toronto Buffalo London
Printed in Canada

ISBN 0-8020-4458-1 (cloth)
ISBN 0-8020-8242-4 (paper)

Printed on acid-free paper

Canadian Cataloguing in Publication Data

Main entry under title:

Restructuring work and the life course

ISBN 0-8020-4458-1 (bound)   ISBN 0-8020-8242-4 (pbk.)

1. Work – Sociological aspects.   2. Industrial sociology.   I. Marshall, Victor W.

HD4901.R45 2001   306.3'6   C00-933052-6

The University of Toronto Press acknowledges the financial assistance to its publishing program of the Canada Council for the Arts and the Ontario Arts Council.

University of Toronto Press acknowledges the financial support for its publishing activities of the Government of Canada through the Book Publishing Industry Development Program (BPIDP).

Contents

Preface. Restructuring Work and the Life Course: Challenges for Comparative Research and Policy

The contributions gathered in this book represent research by fifty social scientists from seven countries. While the majority of these scholars are sociologists, the disciplinary backgrounds of contributors include anthropology, economics, history, industrial relations and labour studies, information sciences, and psychology. Some of the contributors focus their research gaze on youth, others on adulthood, and yet others on later life. What unites their contributions is a concern with changes in the organization of work and the impact of these changes on the life course. This includes an interest in the impact of such changes on other social institutions which, through their actions, deal with life-course issues, affect the life chances of people over the life course, and in many senses constitute or socially construct that life course.

Major economic, technological, and demographic forces are combining to influence the ways in which the very structures of people's lives are influenced by the work they do. The major defining features of the life course, including patterns of entry to and exit from work, are changing, as is the nature of jobs and work careers. Public, corporate, and union policy concerning the organization of work is ill developed, and the research foundation on which to build such policy is shaky, to say the least. Moreover, relevant research and policy developments tend to focus on one stage of the life course rather than view the life course as a whole. Thus, there is a wealth of research knowledge – and also, increasingly, policy development – around issues such as education, the transition from education to initial employment, and problems of youth unemployment; and there is a large literature on retirement itself and on the transition from paid employment to full retirement. But rarely is it recognized that such age- or stage-specific phenomena are linked. For example, the same policies that seek to reduce youth unemployment might reduce the labour-force chances of older workers, or, to take another example, the economic security of people in the retirement years is profoundly constrained by the extent to which they had stable working careers earlier in the life course.

In organizing a conference, we sought to bring together leading international experts and persons in the public, corporate, and union spheres to present a state-of-the-art overview of knowledge in this rapidly changing area and to discuss research and policy implications. Of the well over 100 contributions at the conference, we have room for fewer than one-third in this volume; but these papers, we believe, provide the beginnings of an inventory of knowledge in the area. More importantly, in the view of the editors, the unifying attempt to cast this domain in terms of life-course theory and research has allowed us to gather together important theoretical ideas and to test their applicability with data. We have been not only tolerant but encouraging of a wide range of approaches to life-course theorizing, and of methodologies and research designs. The conference presented a varied buffet table of life-course delicacies, and we have attempted to include in this book a selection of these delicacies broad enough to provide the makings of several different meals, each of them rich in insights. We hope that the book will inspire readers to contribute to the development of this new field of studies of work and the life course.

The book is organized into three major parts, preceded by a general introduction to the field by Walter Heinz. Part one, with its own introduction by Walter Heinz, brings together ten chapters dealing with various aspects of education, labour-market change, and transitions in the earlier and middle stages of the working life course. Part two, introduced by Victor Marshall and Anil Verma, includes ten chapters dealing with later-life transitions in relation to the restructuring of work. Part three, introduced by Helga Krüger, contains eight chapters that deal with different aspects of the relationship between individual biography and social structure. Many of these chapters focus on gender issues and on the intersection between work and family in relation to the life course. It should be noted, however, that gender runs through almost all the chapters in this volume, and that family concerns run through many as well. In our view this is appropriate to the theoretical, policy, and lived-world realities in this domain.

In his introduction, Walter Heinz recommends a broad-ranging methodological and theoretical approach to work in this field. Cross-cultural perspectives can lead to a more critical understanding. We should not focus unduly on any one methodological approach, such as the national-level survey, to the exclusion of more focused studies that carefully map institutional arrangements and relate life-course working trajectories to other domains such as the family and the educational system. Case studies should be linked to and contextualized in terms of larger-scale research. This is a plea not for eclecticism but for explicit methodological designs that capitalize on multiple-methods strategies and linking what Heinz calls 'local' and 'cosmopolitan' studies.

It is important to map the timing, sequencing, and duration of work-related transitions in different societies; and some patterning of these transitions will be found through such macro-level factors as welfare-state typology and degree of industrialization. However, explanations for these differences will also require theorizing at the institutional and individual levels. Thus, it appears, the central theoretical problems of the social sciences run through research in work and the life course – theoretically linking micro and macro levels of analysis, biography, and history; and methodologically drawing on holistic case studies that are rich in meaning while also linking insights from such studies to large-scale, usually quantitative, representative studies of the phenomena.

Heinz's opening chapter is not intended to introduce the specific chapters that follow. Rather, it provides a general introduction to the book, mapping the theoretical, methodological, and substantive terrain in this new field of inquiry.

VICTOR W. MARSHALL

Acknowledgments

This volume presents a small selection from the papers that originated in an international symposium, 'Restructuring Work and the Life Course,' held at the University of Toronto, Canada, in May 1998 under the joint sponsorship of the University of Toronto's Institute for Human Development, Life Course and Aging and the University of Bremen's Social Research Centre 186: Status Passages and Risks in the Life Course. This book is one of many activities reflecting a formal partnership for collaboration linking the two universities.

The conference at which earlier versions of the chapters were presented was funded by a number of sponsors, whose support we appreciate greatly. Major support came from the Social Sciences and Humanities Research Council of Canada and from four Canadian government departments: Veterans Affairs Canada; the Division of Aging and Seniors, Health Canada; Human Resources Development Canada; and Labour Canada. At the University of Toronto, additional support was provided by the Connaught Fund; the Department of Public Health Sciences; the Office of the Vice-president, Research and International Relations; and the School of Graduate Studies. Corporate support was provided by the Institute for Work and Health (Toronto); Beck's Beer (Bremen); NOVA Corporation (Calgary); and Careers: The Next Generation (Edmonton).

Victor Marshall was professor of Public Health Sciences and director of the Institute for Human Development, Life Course and Aging at the time of the conference. Original seed-grant funding for the conference was obtained through a proposal by Anil Verma when he was acting director of the Institute. The four editors of this volume planned and organized the conference. They wish to express their deep appreciation to Susan Murphy of the Institute for editorial assistance and coordination as this book became a reality.

Restructuring Work and the Life Course

1. Work and the Life Course: A Cosmopolitan–Local Perspective

Walter R. Heinz

As globalization accelerates, the world is becoming smaller and smaller. The closer societies get, the more their differences become apparent. Therefore, trusted approaches to life-course research in cross-cultural perspectives need to be re-examined and refined.

This volume aims to develop cross-cultural perspectives on work and the life course. The challenge we face is to translate the concepts and methods of cross-national research into a dynamic, temporally structured life-course framework. As we all know, single-country studies of educational level, gender, and occupational status that have focused on life-course trajectories have produced considerable results within their respective national–cultural boundaries.

Comparative life-course studies, however, have to cross these boundaries and face some difficulties that are not easily overcome. Above all, they should start by carefully mapping the institutional arrangements of work trajectories and the related life-course domains – most prominently, the family and the educational system – before analysing survey and longitudinal data. Furthermore, comparable longitudinal data have to permit intercohort and intracohort analyses of work-related transitions, and they should be linked to case studies.

I will first discuss various life-course concepts in order to extract a useful version for comparative purposes.[1] I will then explore changes in the structure and meaning of work in relation to job start, employment, family, and retirement transitions. Some remarks will follow to show how international trends in the organization of work and company restructuring are mediated by societal structures and social-policy regimes, and how these produce different life-course effects. Finally, I will take up suggestions concerning the possibility of combining standardized quantitative methods with case-oriented qualitative methods in comparative life-course research.

Cross-Cultural Variations of the Life Course

The relationship between age, social roles, and organizational participation varies between and within societies by life domains (education, work, family, social assistance, retirement) and is becoming less standardized. This change is also reflected in new ways of thinking about the life course: variations among nations in rhythms of life and in the timing of transitions are seen as resulting from differences in labour markets, educational institutions, and social policies that structure the biography from school leaving to retirement. Changes in the sequencing and duration of transitions have become a characteristic of modern, industrialized service societies: 'new time budgets' are in place not only for adulthood but also for youth and old age, and the difficulties of dividing time between work and family are increasing.

Most sociologists agree that the modern life course should be conceptualized not as a cycle or sequence of life stages but as a series of status configurations that are embedded in the structures of the welfare state (Mayer and Müller, 1986; Allmendinger, 1990). Martin Kohli (1985), for example, has pointed to a tripartition of life sequences around work: education/training, employment, and retirement. This male version, however, has to be paralleled by a more complex patterning of women's life courses into three major sequences that centre on the ambiguous relationship between family and work: education, family/household and/or employment, retirement. These models, however, are obviously an idealization because the critical question of today's life-course analysis has become the increasing destandardization of transitions from childhood to old age. In all modern societies, the average age of work commencement and family formation is increasing, while the average age at retirement is declining. Demographic data can tell us much about changes in the timing and sequence of transitions, but very little about the causes of observed age variations at the major turning-points in the life course. For example, more young persons in the United States now work parallel to their education or training, and thus participate in two domains of life simultaneously, delaying their entry into full-time employment. Many older persons remain employed after early retirement, whereas others move from a period of unemployment to retirement. Are these changing relationships between work and life-course transitions covered by current definitions of the life course?

A representative definition is suggested by Mayer and Tuma (1990, p. 3): 'the life course refers to "social processes" extending over the individual life span or over significant portions of it, especially with regard to the family cycle, educational and training histories and employment and occupational careers. The life course is shaped by, among other things, cultural beliefs about the individual biography, institutionalized sequences of roles and positions, legal age restrictions and the decisions of individual actors.' This conceptualization emphasizes that the life course consists of multiple, interdependent trajectories related to the major life domains.

Glen Elder (1995), who has played an essential role in developing the 'life-course paradigm,' highlights that the movement of individuals in time and place is conditioned by standards concerning the timing and sequencing of transitions, by human agency, *and* by 'linked lives.' Human agency refers to the individuals' active shaping of their biographies, linked lives to interrelationships of partners', spouses', parents', and children's life courses. Both notions stress that an adequate understanding of the life course requires multiple-level analysis, which ranges from structured pathways, social institutions, and market organizations to individual trajectories and social networks. For a comparative perspective it is important to look at the variations at relevant turning-points in age-structured trajectories, such as work and family careers as well as at central transitions that, taken together, shape individual and collective biographies. Furthermore, individual careers must be analysed as multiple and interlocking pathways. For instance, as Phyllis Moen (Moen and Erickson, 1995) has shown for the United States and Helga Krüger (Born, Krüger, and Lorenz-Meyer, 1996) has shown for Germany, couples tend to arrange family events by taking into account the options and restrictions of each other's work careers.

It follows that social and economic changes such as deindustrialization, extended education, and increasing labour-market participation by women have strongly affected life-course patterns. These trends have led to changes in female and male life courses in different ways, depending on the respective societal mix of labour-market dynamics, industrial relations, welfare-state institutions, and social networks.

Modern societies differ in their transition arrangements and in the range of individual options for the timing and spacing of biographical decisions: 'the cafeteria of choices' (Elder, 1995) may operate on either self-service or professionalized service with restricted or abundant supply of alternative pathways.

Life-course theorists such as Glen Elder (1995) and Andrew Abbott (1997) have started to add the concept of choice to life-course analysis in order to account for the modernization of society which has made human agency and decision making important life-course skills: 'Despite the empirical evidence on links between life transitions, the agency of individuals and their life-course choices ensures some degree of loose coupling between social transitions and life stages' (Elder and O'Rand, 1995, p. 457). In respect to the connection between work and the life course, loose coupling means that employment events do not simply add up to a certain career. Hence, an individual's work history is also a biographical accomplishment, consisting of accumulated experiences and choices between more or less restricted pathways and working circumstances. Furthermore, men's and women's work histories differ to the extent that the principle of 'linked lives' leads to an unequal distribution of employment and family roles.

To analyse work histories, then, we need data not only on the timing and sequencing of moves from one employment status to another, but also on 'the processes which move people between successive events and conditions' (Gershuny, 1998, p. 35). Such a 'recursive model of biographical action' integrates opportunity structures, institutional arrangements, and individual decisions, and also takes into account the 'linked lives' – for instance, of family members – as they affect the timing of employment and family sequences (cf Heinz, 1995).

Thus, in order to analyse life courses from a comparative, work-related perspective, we must supplement the standard dimensions of age, sequence, and duration, first, by the extent to which 'lives are linked' – formally and informally – among and within generations; and second, by the 'range of biographical choices' – that is, how people respond to the opportunities and restrictions concerning pathways in different life domains.

The Temporal Distribution of Work and the Emergent Contingent Life Course

Since Karl Marx and Max Weber, work has been a core concept for analysing social class, social conflict, and individual identity. Today, many proclaim the 'end of work' (Rifkin, 1995) and the erosion of a work-centred life course. Despite dramatic progress in technology and company restructuring, however, most people still spend their adult lives working or looking for work. Of course, the relationships between work and the life course have become more dependent on volatile labour-market dynamics, making careers and stable employment less certain. These social trends can best be analysed with an interactive conception of work which centres on the contested exchange relations between employers and employees over the life course. These exchanges concern primarily contracts with variable durations of employment and varying degrees of worker autonomy in the workplace. They are negotiated in the framework of specific institutional arrangements and industrial relations that regulate workers' and employees' rights and duties.

Such an interactive model has recently been proposed by Chris and Charles Tilly (1998, p. 264). 'The character of work under capitalism,' they observe, 'has always depended on hard bargaining within stringent institutional limits established by the previous histories of shared understandings and social relations.' The results of bargaining define the options and restrictions for individual life-course decisions in different ways, depending on the respective configurations of market rationality and welfare politics.

For comparative life-course analysis, an interactive model of work directs our attention to the temporal and contextual aspects that structure the distribution of work over the life course in different societies. We are accustomed to explaining people's varied individual voyages in work careers by social origin, gender, educational level, and occupational skills. However, employers' recruiting and promotion policies, on the one hand, and the implications of 'linked lives,' on the other, are at least as important as individual variables.

These variables have proved to be important in modelling school-to-work transitions, social mobility, and career progression in comparative research (cf Shavit and Müller, 1998; Erikson and Goldthorpe, 1992; Blossfeld and Hakim, 1997). Moreover, these studies document the enormous relevance of the respective institutional arrangements that connect individuals with work trajectories and protect them in cases of unemployment, disability, and retirement. Arguing from the North American experience, the Tillys (1998) regard social networks as a crucial factor that accounts for variations in transitions and careers.

Networks influence the nature, timing, and sequencing of employment, joblessness, and retirement more strongly in the United States than in European welfare states (Leisering and Walker, 1998) where labour markets are more regulated.

Employment opportunities are mediated by networks where internal labour markets dominate; such networks are less important in societies that have occupational labour markets, like Germany. Yet from the European perspective, which takes public systems of vocational training, occupational labour markets, and corporatist industrial relations for granted, social networks tend to be underestimated.

After the vanishing of the short-lived dream of permanent affluence (Lutz, 1984) which characterized the period of relative prosperity and employment stability from the Second World War through the mid-1970s, the last two decades have witnessed the expansion of international markets, which has led to increased competition and waves of cost reduction in the national economies and to restructuring campaigns in companies. Life-course stability has been endangered by a growing gap in contract patterns, job conditions, and earnings between the professional–entrepreneurial class and ordinary working people. In the United States, the United Kingdom, and Canada, non-standard employment is increasing, as are working hours, while in the continental European welfare states unemployment is rising (EUROSTAT data: France 12.5 per cent, Sweden 10.2 per cent, Germany 9.7 per cent in 1997) and working hours are declining. These developments will not only restrict the continuity of workers' employment trajectories but also affect the career planning of professionals.

Let us take a closer look at non-standard work: up to the 1970s, workers shared common employment histories on both sides of the Atlantic; full-time jobs and life-long employment were the rule for men. As a recent study by Felstead, Krahn, and Powell (1999) shows, part-time work, temporary jobs, multiple jobs and self-employment have increased in the United Kingdom and Canada in the period between 1989 and 1994 to more than a third of the work force. Female non-standard employment is at 50 per cent in both countries, while male non-standard work increased faster, though from a lower level. Developments in part-time work in Europe and the United States have recently been compared in a collaborative study edited by Hans-Peter Blossfeld and Catherine Hakim (1997). This study documents a wide variation in the occurrence and distribution of part-time work among countries and between genders. What is most striking for comparative life-course issues is that non-standard work has the highest growth in the age groups 15 to 24 and 55 to 64. This indicates more destandardization at the entry and exit transitions of work compared to the middle years of the employment trajectory.

Such employment trends converge into what I call the 'contingent model' of the work-related life course, consisting of variable durations of employment episodes.

The contingency of the life course derives from the declining predictability of the timing and sequencing of employment and unemployment, which vary according to the company restructuring policies and social-policy institutions at work in different societies. Social mobility and career patterns will depend more and more on the longitudinal characteristics of the different contract policies which are becoming the new 'laws of motion over time' (Tilly and Tilly, 1998, p. 91).

Another look at the increase in flexibility of retirement transitions reveals that the principle of long-term employment until retirement is waning rapidly. The departure from work is occurring earlier. (In Germany, the employment rate of the age group 55 to 64 dropped from 75 per cent to 50 per cent between 1972 and 1993; in Canada, from 76 per cent to 60 per cent). Further, the timing has become more variable, and there is a trend for women in the age group 55 to 59 to increase their labour-market participation. The interrupted work histories of women put them in a much more precarious retirement transition than men.

The case studies of North American companies conducted by an Aging Workforce Project at the University of Toronto (Marshall, 1996) show that early-retirement packages are widely used as incentives in the process of downsizing. Marshall concludes that management does not consider the life-course implications of this strategy: 'Corporate policies ... have unintended age-related consequences in that they are restructuring the entire life course and extending the duration of the retirement years' (1996, p. 29).

On the level of cultural beliefs and life-course norms, short-term contracts may reflect a low level of trust between employer and employee, whereas long-term contracts are based not only on trust but also on institutional arrangements that define both the worker's and the employer's responsibilities (cf Soskice, 1990). This relationship between trust and contract affects the extent to which individuals can anticipate and rely on temporal work arrangements and link them with family transitions. For instance, if firms do not replace early retirees with young employees, the joint responsibility for school-to-work transitions is shifting from firms to individuals. In European welfare states, which attempt to regulate and protect transitions and entire work trajectories, the emerging contingent life course is still characterized by a higher degree of trust than elsewhere, because of the engagement of third parties: contracts across the life course are embedded in a set of institutional arrangements in a framework of legal and practical agreements between the social partners. Though company restructuring and downsizing are accelerating the shift to a more contingent and episodical work pattern, the state provides support at critical transitions, such as school-to-work, retirement, or parental leave, and also for long-term unemployment.

Furthermore, from a comparative agency perspective the job applicants', workers', or professionals' expectations and decisions must also be analysed in relation to the cultural and social embeddedness of the contingent life-course model. U.S. students, for instance, tend to expect short employment episodes and look for jobs that can be combined with attending school or college, whereas German youth decide for either an apprenticeship or college and expect long-term employment after graduation (Heinz, 1999).

Biographical decisions are also affected by human-resource management. Loyalty, internal labour markets, and seniority principles that were linked to the expectation of lifetime employment and stable work trajectories are giving way to cost-cutting human-resource management strategies. These strategies create either chains of non-standard jobs or early retirement, which may be experienced, depending on the cultural context, either as an increase of individual autonomy or as a restriction of life-course agency.

Employers in the United States have moved more quickly than those in other countries from internal labour-market strategies towards contractual employment because they are less restricted by labour-market and social-policy standards. This practice is highlighted by the vice-president for human resources of AT&T, who told the *New York Times* in 1996: 'People need to look at themselves as self-employed, as vendors who come to this company to sell their skills. At AT&T we have to promote the whole concept of the work force being contingent, most of the contingent workers are inside our walls.'

Though we cannot generalize this telling description of the fluid work force to the human-resource management of all U.S. companies, small and large – and it is even more risky to generalize to the employment patterns in European societies – it is representative of management ideas of the contingent life course.

Welfare-state Variability in the Contingent Life Course

The frequency of job changes is still quite low for men in European welfare states, where career models exist and occupational markets are still operating. The spreading of labour-market deregulation and non-standard employment is contested by unions and the social democrats in Germany, France, and Italy, while in the United States and in the United Kingdom work trajectories focus on 'employability.' Applicants must show the 'skills' that match the employers' needs, mainly work habits and flexibility, which means a reduced commitment of companies to offer training and stable employment. This employability model has gained acceptance in societies where shareholder values predominate and workers have lost bargaining power, while the qualification and occupational career model still is the dominant framework for the work–life-course linkage in the continental European welfare states.

To the extent that the new employability-contingency model dominates the system of industrial relations, it affects life courses drastically. Work trajectories are turning into a series of short episodes, connected by job searching and unemployment. It may also be possible, however, to establish new sequences of employment, further education, training, and more family time. Yet the latter path would require a new social contract, a safety net of qualifications and benefits that are transportable from firm to firm and from job to job, and a system of industrial relations that sets universal employment, promotion, and retirement standards.

The transformation of employment standards into a pluralized and decentralized arrangement of precarious work trajectories is still being counterbalanced by social-policy provision and life-course support systems in welfare states. Nevertheless, there is also increasing temporal destandardization of work trajectories and a particularization of employment biographies as a consequence of company restructuring.

For a comparative analysis of the interrelationships between the restructuring of work and the creation of a contingent life course we have to ask whether there are different paths for this transformation of the life course. For example: how do regulated compared to flexible school-to-work transitions affect the timing, duration, and sequencing of employment and family transitions? How do institutional arrangements, 'linked lives,' and social networks interact in early-retirement decisions? How do gendered labour markets, social-policy provisions, and family obligations interact with male and female patterns of employment trajectories?

A closer look at case studies of the family and employment sequences and the time-bind of working mothers shows that in Germany neither the level of education nor family events seem to explain variance in female patterns of labour-market participation; the most important variable is the women's certified skills and occupation. For instance, the older women interviewed by Helga Krüger and her team (Born, Krüger, Lorenz-Meyer, 1996) at the University of Bremen looked back at their life histories and reported up to twelve job interruptions. Their biographies seemed to be unstructured when taking family events as a temporal reference point. However, examining the respective occupations revealed that the employment sequences were strongly related to the opportunities that different occupations offered in the labour market.

This occupation-driven work history seems to be less dependent on the company's family-friendly human-resource management, which was studied by Arlie Hochschild (1997) in the United States. Dual-earner couples do not seem to take advantage of the flexible work arrangements offered by 'Amerco' – a family-friendly company. According to Hochschild's controversial interpretation, the workplace is winning the contest between work and home for men and women. It may be, however, that the social rewards of working vary over the life course and by occupational qualification and job hierarchy. Moreover, family-related decisions and the timing of employment may be different in societies that have 'goodwill' firms than in societies with universal rights for parental leave and part-time work. How can we contextualize the examples that have been presented?

There have been several attempts to classify societies according to their social-policy regimes in order to construct typologies of modern welfare states. One prominent proposal distinguishes conservative, liberal, and social-democratic types of social-policy regimes (Esping-Andersen, 1990). The 'liberal welfare state' is characterized by a low level of government intervention, and by internal and flexible labour markets with high labour turnover. The life course is driven by individualized labour-market adaptation and unstable employment biographies. The 'conservative welfare state' is characterized by social partnership, occupational labour-market segmentation, and a social-security system which is based on public insurance. In a conservative welfare state, the gendered division of labour stabilizes the male life course. People with vocational qualifications have career options, while those without certified skills have bad prospects for long-term contracts at job entry and for stable employment. Finally, the 'social-democratic welfare state' focuses on reducing social inequality and promoting citizenship rights with institutional regulations and the delivery of social services to all citizens. It has an active labour-market policy in order to open new career paths, especially for women and young people, by job creation and an expansion of the public sector. The social-democratic welfare state establishes some autonomy from market forces for individual life-course transitions by maintaining a system of industrial relations that centres on social citizenship rights.

Recent changes in the international economy, however, have made it difficult to apply these ideal types as independent macro variables to comparative life-course research. Even the representatives of each type – the United States, Germany, and Sweden, respectively – now deviate from the typology, and other societies document mixtures among these types – for instance, Canada, which is categorized by Lipset (1998) as a 'liberal social-democratic welfare state,' or Denmark, which is a 'conservative social-democratic welfare state,' while even Germany seems to be moving towards a 'conservative-liberal model.'

From Occupational Mobility to Job Flexibility in Comparative Perspective

Social mobility is a core topic of sociological research which can claim to have made important contributions to cross-cultural research. Most comparative mobility research, however, is not conceptualized in terms of the life-course paradigm and rarely explores specific labour-market and social-policy contexts.

In the German school of life-course studies, Allmendinger and Hinz (1998) have made some first steps towards relating mobility and life-course studies. They emphasize that international comparisons of careers cannot look only at labour-market processes, but must also take into account the feeding institutions – education and training – as well as the respective social-policy frameworks. They observe that Germany is characterized by a stratified and standardized school and training system, the United Kingdom by a stratified school but non-regulated training arrangement, and the United States by a non-stratified school as well as an unregulated training arrangement. A comparable distinction has been developed by Müller and collegues (1997), who classify the educational systems in selected European societies as either skill-dependent or organization-dependent arrangements. In skill-dependent educational systems, schooling and training are oriented towards standardized vocational skills with reference to job descriptions. This permits relatively uncomplicated matching of applicants to jobs. Organization-dependent systems of schooling and college are not oriented towards standardized skills; instead employers offer on-the-job training, which focuses on firm-specific skills and internal labour markets. In societies which emphasize general skills in the sense of employability, companies put a premium on the applicants' educational level in recruitment processes. When skills are related to occupations and specific tasks, employers focus on occupational competence and vocational credentials (as is the case in the Netherlands, Germany, Switzerland, and Austria).

In comparing Germany, the United Kingdom, and Sweden, All-mendinger and Hinz (1998) show that societal variations in the structuring of education and training arrangements lead to employment careers with different levels of stability and social integration. The specific relationship between education, training arrangements, and employment trajectories depends on the relative strength of market forces and welfare-state regulations. An active welfare state attempts to distribute chances in the life course equally (Myles, 1995) and defines the extent to which individuals can be mobile over the life course. In European countries, comparative mobility occurs within a shifting occupational structure: manufacturing jobs declined between 1970 and 1990 in the United Kingdom from 45 to 29 per cent and in Germany from 49 to only 40 per cent. In the same period, service and public employment rose to 70 per cent in the United Kingdom, 67 per cent in Sweden, and 57 per cent in Germany. Employment opportunities for women have expanded mainly in the public sector, however, with great differences between Germany and Sweden, with 36 per cent versus 57 per cent of women working in the public sector.

This changing employment structure has life-course implications: labour-market participation varies substantially by age group and gender, for instance, at job entry versus at job exit to retirement. The 15- to 20-year-olds in Great Britain have the highest rate of labour-market participation, whereas in Germany most of the people in this age group are in either school or apprenticeship training. Looking at labour-market exits we see that employment participation starts to decline in Germany by age 55 and that only 30 per cent of the men in the age group 60 to 65 are still employed, whereas in Great Britain more than half and in Sweden more than 60 per cent still are in the labour force.

The findings on job change and occupational mobility presented by Allmendinger and Hinz (1998) support my assumption that occupational trajectories change towards a contingent life course in liberal, market or 'low-trust' societies like Great Britain, whereas changing work patterns contribute to a concentration of stable employment trajectories as well as to increasing unemployment in institutionally regulated, 'high-trust' welfare societies like Germany. In Great Britain, much as in the United States, low job stability is matched by considerable opportunities for re-employment, whereas in Germany a high degree of occupational and employment stability is achieved at the cost of excluding people with inadequate qualifications.

These results lead us to ask whether there are any converging national or international trends concerning the effects of the restructuring of work on employment trajectories and their interrelationship with family trajectories. Our examples have shown that the relative influence and interaction of causal factors vary from society to society, or at least among the different types of welfare states. This finding is also supported by the conclusion of an international research group that has studied social change in the period from 1960 to 1990 in the United States, France, Quebec, and West Germany (Langlois, 1994). With regard to divergent patterns, Germany differs most from the other societies in respect to employment patterns, particularly from the United States. For instance, early life-course transitions are more regulated and socially protected in Germany, while youth unemployment is still a major social problem in the United States and Great Britain.

Differences in labour-market participation and unemployment are usually explained with reference to the differing rates of deindustrialization and the proportions of casual jobs compared to socially protected and stable work contracts. The increase of non-standard jobs in the United States has had the effect that more people work more hours and also have more precarious and poorly paid jobs. This contrasts with Germany, where people still work in a socially protective industrial-relations framework, and where part-time jobs for women have increased while high rates of unemployment have hardly declined at all.

It should not come as a surprise that the search for divergent and convergent social trends affecting the life course in different societies yields no clear causal explanations. Micro processes of life-course change triggered by the restructuring of work are quite differently interrelated in low- and high-trust societies: 'Operating within different structures the same trends can perform quite different functions' says Langlois (1994, p. 18). With regard to the emergent contingent life course, different constellations of institutions, networks, labour-market segmentation, and welfare-state politics are creating singular contexts. Therefore, we expect that the timing, duration, and sequencing of work-related transitions will show more divergence or societal singularity than theories of modernization tend to predict.

At the same time, however, the degree of polarization of employment trajectories between core-sector workers and peripheral and marginalized workers will depend on the relative strength of government-directed programs of work creation, retraining, and social assistance for the unemployed. Despite cutbacks in social budgets, it is more likely that the continental European welfare societies will continue to build institutions that intervene into precarious life-course transitions in order to promote minimal standards of social citizenship. They may move in the direction of 'flexibly coordinated cooperatist systems' in order to protect long-term contracts and occupationally based work trajectories. The success of such systems in a period of company restructuring and mergers is difficult to predict. It depends on the level of trust among and farsightedness of government, capital, and unions as well as the implementation of a European social-policy framework. Now I should like to conclude by turning to methodology.

Comparative Strategies: Connecting Variable-oriented and Case-based Life-course Studies

Comparable data on the timing, sequencing, and duration of work-related transitions are necessary if we want to analyse life-course trajectories on the level of transition rates. The mapping of different time schedules of the life course, however, calls for explanations at both the institutional and the individual levels. Thus, it is a great challenge to connect the concepts of biographical agency, decision making, and 'linked lives' with the standard approach of comparative life-course research. This can be done if we learn to analyse micro-level mechanisms as being embedded in meso-level institutions that in turn are influenced by economic and political macro structures. Economic trends and political decisions are transformed by the institutional fabric and the labour-market structure of society into specific work-related trajectories with different linkages to education, employment, and family life. As I have shown, studying national differences in institutional arrangements is crucial if we want to understand the relationship between the changing world of work and the shape of the life course for men and women in different societies.

Hence I take up some suggestions by Charles Tilly (1997) and Karl Ulrich Mayer (1997), who argue forcefully that focusing research on a small number of theoretically significant societies is more promising than a more extensive approach involving numerous countries. The unique, historically rooted patterns of institutions, the specific relationships among state, capital, and unions, as well as the nature of labour-market segments constitute complex time- and place-dependent contexts for comparative life-course analysis. These complex societal contexts of work and the life course cannot be adequately taken into account in a research program that relies mainly on extensive, variable-based case comparisons. Though the event-history analysis promises to reveal trends in life-course patterns in different societies, we should also devote time and energy to looking at individual narratives (cf Ellwood, 1998). Event-history analysis works with a limited number of variables that cannot adequately illuminate the microsocial dynamics which link orientations, actions, and social contexts.

I would therefore like to propose a research program of cross-national comparison of life-course patterns that integrates the case-study approach with variable-oriented longitudinal studies such as the GSOEP (German Socio-Economic Panel) or the U.S. PSID (Panel Study of Income Dynamics). Case studies focus on the micro-social mechanisms that translate work conditions and their restructuring into different temporal patterns of employment-related transitions in the education–occupation–family triangle. They are very well suited to providing an understanding of how biographical decisions and 'linked lives' interact with institutions in the structuring of life courses.

Charles Tilly recommends (1997) that we construct causal stories that rest on chains of cause-and-effect relations which have to be tested by case comparison. The same strategy is proposed by Charles Ragin

(1997), who suggests linking cases to causal pathways and assessing the relative importance of different paths for life-course transitions. When we restrict our observations to a small number of comparable cases, temporal structures and interactive processes become more apparent and their interpretation can be grounded in the analysis of the institutional fabric and organizational practices as well as in biographical narratives about work – that is, event histories from the point of view of the individual. Such an approach has been practised at our research centre in Bremen (Sfb 186) for ten years by the application of quantitative and qualitative methods to comparative life-course issues. The approach presupposes substantive and theoretical knowledge about societies and issues that we want to compare and requires an explication of our concepts on both the structural and the individual-actor level.

In order to learn more about the mechanisms that restructure work and change institutional regulations that affect the life course of women and men in selected societies, it is an important first step to model the structural effects of social origin, gender, and occupation on the timing and sequencing of such life events as employment, family, and retirement transitions. However, the meaning of shifting opportunities and social expectations concerning when to graduate from school, commence work, have a child, or exit into retirement cannot be fully understood unless we study the extent to which there are institutional standards, cultural tolerance, and network support for people traversing crucial life-course transitions. Furthermore, as we have indicated earlier, societies also differ in the degrees of trust surrounding employment relations.

The ways in which biographical decisions interact over time with different institutional contexts have been neglected in the analysis of aggregate cross-national differences. Therefore, explaining variations in employment trajectories and work-related transitions also requires that we take into account the actors' temporal perspectives and their involvement in 'linked lives.' For example, in the 'contingent life course,' the effects of social origin and educational achievement on work-related transitions are likely to be modified over the life course relative to changes in employment and family trajectories. And there is evidence that 'the link between personality and social structure is not necessarily invariant over a biographical time' (Alwin, 1995, p. 223). Therefore, we expect to explain some of the variation in the relations between personality, age, and social structure by comparing transitions and life courses in different institutional settings. The findings of Phyllis Moen and her research team at Cornell University would be a good start for such a strategy: 'Daughters of mothers with few social resources have a much higher chance of having a strong sense of mastery if they themselves have achieved success in the form of a professional or a management job ... Daughters' own experiences are more important than their mothers' attitude or identity in shaping their daughters' work-role identity' (Moen and Erickson, 1995, p. 201). Does this relationship also hold in societies with a more regulated and occupationally segmented labour market, such as Germany?

The theoretical and methodological challenge for comparative life-course research, then, is to relate the structural analysis of trajectories, transitions, and turning-points to the 'agency-in-context model' (Abbott, 1997) that takes into account the individual's experiences and decisions at branching or transition points in her or his life course. The 'generalizing ambition' of life-course researchers will be limited by contextual dependency of causal variables as long as we neglect to concentrate on the explication of precisely these institutional contexts which are established by different constellations of labour markets, social-policy institutions, industrial relations, and social networks. Such a focus can be accomplished if comparative life-course researchers think as 'cosmopolitan locals' who combine variable-oriented panel studies like the GSOEP, PSID, BHPS (British Household Panel Study), and SLID (Canadian Survey of Labour and Income Dynamics) with case-based life-history analysis. Such a strategy could contribute to the gradual elucidation of how macro structural changes (the globalization of markets) affect institutional arrangements (social policy, industrial relations, labour-market segmentation) and are translated into life courses by biographical decision making and 'linked lives' (the timing and sequencing of transitions by individuals). Connecting transition-rate analysis with institutions and networks as contexts for biographical agency and 'linked lives' is a promising project that requires more and more international collaboration.

NOTE

1 I would like to thank Lutz Leisering and Victor Marshall for their insightful comments on this paper.

REFERENCES

Abbott, A. (1997). On the concept of turning point. *Comparative Social Research*, *16*, 85–105.

Allmendinger, J. (1990). *Career mobility dynamics: A comparative analysis of the US, Norway, and West Germany.* Berlin: M.P.I.

Allmendinger, J., & Hinz, T. (1998). Occupational careers under different welfare regimes: West Germany, Great Britain and Sweden. In L. Leisering & R. Walker (Eds), *The dynamics of modern society: Poverty, policy and welfare* (pp 63–84). Bristol: The Policy Press.

Alwin, D.F. (1995). Taking time seriously: Social change, social structure, and human lives. In P. Moen, G.H. Elder, Jr, & K. Lüscher (Eds), *Examining lives in context: Perspectives on the ecology of human development* (pp 211–62). Washington, DC: American Psychological Association.

Blossfeld, H.-P., & Hakim, C. (Eds). (1997). *Between equalization and marginalization: Women working part-time in Europe and the United States of America.* Oxford and New York: Oxford University Press.

Born, C., Krüger, H., & Lorenz-Meyer, D. (1996). *Der unentdeckte Wandel: Annäherung an das Verhältnis von Struktur und Norm im weiblichen Lebenslauf.* Berlin: Edition sigma.

Elder, G.H., Jr. (1995). The life-course paradigm: Social change and individual development. In P. Moen, G.H. Elder, Jr, & K. Lüscher (Eds), *Examining lives in context: Perspectives on the ecology of human development* (pp 101–139). Washington, DC: American Psychological Association.

Elder, G.H. Jr, & O'Rand, A.M. (1995). Adult lives in a changing society. In K.S. Cook, G.A. Fine, & J.S. House (Eds), *Sociological perspectives on social psychology* (pp 452–75). Needham Heights, MA: Allyn and Bacon.

Ellwood, D. (1998). Dynamic policy making: An insider's account of reforming United States welfare. In L. Leisering & R. Walker (Eds), *The dynamics of modern society: Poverty, policy and welfare* (pp 49–59). Bristol: The Policy Press.

Erikson, R., & Goldthorpe, J.H. (1992). *The Constant flux: A study of class mobility in industrial societies.* Oxford: Clarendon Press.

Esping-Andersen, G. (1990). *The three worlds of welfare capitalism.* Princeton, NJ: Princeton University Press.

Felstead, A., Krahn, H., & Powell, M. (1999). Young and old at risk: Comparative trends in 'non-standard' patterns of employment in Canada and the United Kingdom. *International Journal of Manpower, 20*(5), 277–96.

Gershuny, J. (1998). Thinking dynamically: Sociology and narrative data. In L. Leisering & R. Walker (Eds), *The dynamics of modern society: Poverty, policy and welfare* (pp 34–58). Bristol: The Policy Press.

Heinz, W.R. (1995). *Arbeit, Beruf und Lebenslauf.* Weinheim: Juventa.

Heinz, W.R. (Ed.). (1999). *From Education to work: Cross-national perspectives.* New York: Cambridge University Press.

Hochschild, A. (1997). The time bind: When work becomes home and home becomes work. New York: Metropolitan Books.

Kohli, M. (1985). Die Institutionalisierung des Lebenslaufs. *Kölner Zeitschrift für Soziologie und Sozialpsychologie, 37,* 1–29.

Langlois, S. (1994). *Convergence or divergence? Comparing recent social trends in industrial societies.* Frankfurt: Campus.

Leisering, L., & Walker, R. (Eds). (1998). *The dynamics of modern society: Poverty, policy and welfare.* Bristol: The Policy Press.

Lipset, S.M. (1998). American union density in comparative perspective. *Contemporary Sociology, 27,* 123–5.

Lutz, B. (1984). *Der kurze Traum immerwährender Prosperität.* Frankfurt: Campus.

Marshall, V.W. (1996, November 11). *Restructuring work and restructuring the life course: Lessons from North American case studies.* Paper presented at the University of Bremen.

Mayer, K.U. (1997). Notes on a comparative political economy of life courses. *Comparative Social Research, 16,* 203–26.

Mayer, K.U., & Müller, W. (1986). The state and the structure of the life course. In A.B. Sørensen, F.E. Weinert, & L.R. Sherrod (Eds), *Human development and the life course* (pp 217–45). Hillsdale, NJ: Lawrence Erlbaum.

Mayer, K.U., & Tuma, N.B. (1990). Life-course research and event history analysis. In K.U. Mayer & N.B. Tuma (Eds), *Event history analysis in life-course research* (pp 3–20). Madison, WI: University of Wisconsin Press.

Moen, P., & Erickson, M.A. (1995). Linked lives: A transgenerational approach to resilience. In P. Moen, G.H. Elder, Jr, & K. Lüscher (Eds), *Examining lives in context: Perspectives on the ecology of human development* (pp 169–207). Washington, DC: American Psychological Association.

Müller, W., Steinmann, S., & Schneider, R. (1997). Bildung in Europa. In S. Hradil & S. Immerfall (Eds), *Die westeuropäischen Gesellschaften im Vergleich* (pp 177–245). Opladen: Leske & Budrich.

Myles, J. (1995). *After the golden age: Labour-market polarization and Canadian public policy.* Tallahassee, FL: Florida State University.

Ragin, C.C. (1997). Turning the tables: How case-oriented research challenges variable-oriented research. *Comparative Social Research, 16,* 27–42.

Rifkin, J. (1995). *The end of work.* New York: Putnam.

Shavit, Y., & Müller, W. (Eds). (1998). *From school to work: A comparative study of educational qualifications and occupational destinations.* Oxford and New York: Oxford University Press.

Soskice, D. (1990). Reinterpreting corporatism and explaining unemployment: Coordinated and non-coordinated market economies. In R. Brunetta & C. Dell'Aringa (Eds), *Labour relations and economic performance* (pp 170–211). London: Macmillan.

Tilly, C. (1997). Means and ends of comparison in macrosociology. *Comparative Social Research, 16*, 43–53.

Tilly, C., & Tilly, C. (1998). *Work under capitalism*. Boulder, CO: Westview Press.

PART ONE
Education, Labour Market, and Transitions in the Working Life Course

Introduction
Walter R. Heinz

In the following section, ten contributions are presented which cover a wide range of empirically based or grounded analyses of important aspects concerning the interaction between changing occupational structures, qualification, gender, and employment throughout the life course. These chapters document that the restructuring of labour markets in North America and Europe has led to an increase of flexibility requirements for the work force at all stages for the working life course without reducing gender segregation in the labour market and without improving the quality of work. These studies come from Canada, the United States, Germany, the Netherlands, and the European Union, and the authors arrive at a rather pessimistic prediction: education-to-work transitions will become more precarious, regional disparities of employment opportunities will become more pronounced, work organizations will continue to create gendered careers, and the balancing of life spheres (family, education, and employment) will become more demanding.

In his analysis of the increasing mismatch between skill potentials and actual job requirements, based on labour-market statistics and cohort studies in Canada, Graham Lowe argues that underemployment and unemployment are characterizing labour-market entry. In the last decade, young people in Canada without a college degree have not managed to get into work careers, and college graduates tend to be concentrated in non-standard employment. There is an 'educational premium,' however; university degrees still promote access to the primary segment of the labour market. Lowe's analysis documents that transitions from education to work are becoming a long journey that is filled with stops, obstacles, detours, and dead ends. Contrary to popular typologies of the young generation (e.g., Generation X), Lowe finds that high school and college graduates want personally fulfilling and socially meaningful work and that many are feeling that they are over-qualified for the job they are doing. Lowe's results fly in the face of the rhetoric of human resource development, which does not stop emphasizing that there is a rising demand for upgrading of skills. On the contrary, Lowe finds that in the 'knowledge society' the competition for a declining number of career jobs is increasing for more and more highly qualified graduates.

Underemployment is also a feature of the restructuring that has been occurring in the Dutch labour market since the 1970s. De Witte and Batenburg analyse the relationship between levels of education and job allocation in the Netherlands. There is a substantial increase of workers who are employed below their formal qualifications, mainly women and young workers. Overeducation and displacement of the less educated are shown to be the two sides of labour-market dynamics.

Schaeper, Kühn, and Witzel discuss results from their qualitative and quantitative longitudinal study of job-entry processes in two urban regions of Germany. They argue that life-course studies should focus on the influence of space as well as on the importance of time. While the German dual system of vocational education and training provides an institutionalized transition for the majority of the non–college-bound youth, it cannot guarantee an even supply of employment opportunities for skilled young workers all over Germany. This study documents the effect of specific occupations on employment outcomes and also illuminates the extent to which good or poor regional job prospects influence career aspirations, even among skilled workers. With respect to job-search strategies, however, compared to Canada and the United States, Germany lacks a culture of mobility. Because staying in one's home region is taken for granted, a workplace as close to home as possible has first priority. Relocating is not part of the life plans of young Germans.

Karen Hughes proposes in her contribution to link the analysis of the effects of economic restructuring on work-related transitions to the question of de- and re-gendering of occupations. By looking at Canadian labour-force statistics covering a period since the early 1970s, she studies the extent of movements of women into non-traditional occupations. Are there gains, or merely adaptations to changing job openings, or even losses for women? Or is it more likely that there are divergent trends that depend on the qualification level of different occupations? Hughes documents that the overall change is quite small: in the 1990s, only one-fifth of all female workers were employed in non-traditional jobs. In addition, the wage gap between men and women in similar occupations is still obvious. If there are gains, they occur for women who are employed in technical occupations and in management. In many other less skilled occupations there is even a trend towards re-segregation.

How work organizations are creating divergent career opportunities for men and women is empirically analysed by Jutta Allmendinger and colleagues in their multi-level case study of two major German research associations. They look at the processes that produce a genderization of science by comparing individual careers of female and male research scientists through the ranks of these prominent academic organizations. There are revolving doors in operation: women who are hired get into positions that are usually vacated by women; their low representation in the higher ranks of the research organizations cannot be explained by gender differences in motivation and qualification. Career differences are a function of 'doing gender' in these research associations; individual careers are structured by implicit gender standards that permeate organizational activities.

Labour-market restructuring is also affecting the relationship between family and employment in respect to changes in the location and timing of work. Diane-Gabrielle Tremblay demonstrates with labour-market data from Canada, and more specifically from Quebec, that there has been a polarization of working hours in the last two decades: more workers do either less than thirty hours a week or more than forty hours. Like Lowe, Tremblay reports that women and youth run the highest risk of being employed in jobs with few working hours. Men tend to work more hours, and this may lead to a growing gendered division of labour between paid employment and family responsibilities. This creates difficulties for coordinating family responsibilities and labour-market participation for women with children. Tremblay argues for public work–family programs that include women and men and reduce the likelihood that flexible work means precarious employment. Such programs have become very popular in the last decade in Denmark and the Netherlands, two countries that have managed to reduce unemployment substantially.

With ongoing restructuring of work, the experience of unemployment, as spells of joblessness or as long-term exclusion from employ-ment, will become a more frequent life-course episode that affects mental health. William Avison presents Canadian data about the adap-tation of families with a history of unemployment experiences. He analyses the complex interaction among economic hardship, marital conflict, social networks, and self-esteem. The results show that, when unemployed, both men and women develop substantial levels of depression and anxiety. However, unemployed women run a higher risk of developing mental-health problems. It is alarming that wives have to cope with a 'double exposure' to job loss; their husbands' unemployment affects wives' mental health as a joint consequence of income loss and marital conflict.

Based on European Union data, Susan Yeandle shows that different regulations and definitions of employment standards make it difficult to compare social and gender divisions of employment. However, the restructuring of work and its effects on the life course seem to be trends that influence family and employment careers on both sides of the Atlantic. It seems that the societies that are included in her analysis have a limited set of strategies for improving the relationship between the different spheres of the life course. Despite some convergence of men's and women's participation rates in the labour market on the aggregate level, there is still gender inequality with respect to part-time work and precarious employment (temporary and low pay). Discontin-uous employment careers interact with destandardization of family life to increase diversity in life courses. The European labour-market and family-policy strategies still privilege the nuclear family, though other family types, most prominently those headed by single mothers, are spreading in many European societies. Yeandle argues that child care is a critical test case for societies' solidarity across generations.

The extent to which labour-market participation is an essential ele-ment of the life-course plans of women also depends on cultural tradi-tions that legitimate different 'gender contracts.' In their study, based on survey research in East and West Germany, Kreckel and Schenk have looked at the ambivalent integration of East German women into the labour market of unified Germany. After the fall of the Berlin Wall, a rapid cultural and economic modernization of the former German Democratic Republic had been expected. The differences between the east and west of Germany with respect to the labour-market participa-tion of women and work attitudes should disappear in the process of political integration. However, in the 1990s the unemployment rate in

East Germany rose to twice the rate in the west. This trend has not led to a decline of the strong work orientation among East Germany's women. The German Democratic Republic was a society where full-time work was taken for granted for men and women, and the life course was modelled according to the 'dual-earner/worker marriage.' In contrast to the west, in the east of Germany both men and women still place a high value on having full-time work. Kreckel and Schenk argue that there is a historical continuity that provides a strong attachment to the East German life-course model.

Finally, Carr and Sheridan examine the relationship between family turning-points and work transitions at midlife. They analyse U.S. data from the Wisconsin Longitudinal Study in an explicit life-course framework by asking to what extent family changes had an effect on career redirection for women and men between ages 35 (1975) and 53 (1993). This sample belongs to a birth cohort that graduated from high school in 1957. Its members experienced major changes in employment patterns and family stability by the time they reached midlife, with educational/career opportunities and divorce rates increasing simultaneously. The analysis demonstrates that family turning-points affect work transitions in different ways for women and men. Contrary to conventional assumptions, women's transitions in their working life course were not influenced by family events, because most of them had participated in the labour market since graduation. For men, however, widowhood and the 'empty nest' increased the likelihood of transitions into another occupation and, for some, the onset of life reviews as a psychological turning-point. In interpreting these results, the authors stress that historical and contextual factors are not enough to explain midlife career shifts; it is also important to look at the life goals and agency of men and women.

The papers in this section raise some more general issues at the interface between labour-market restructuring and life-course changes. When training experiences, education-to-work sequences, and career prospects are changing rapidly, the individual's competence to negotiate initial and subsequent transitions must be strengthened by basic and continuing education. This also implies the need for social policies that provide public resources to support gender equality in the division of family work and paid work. Furthermore, there are contrasting views of the effects of restructuring. Employers see skills shortages, while employees complain about meaningless and short-term jobs: the feeling of underemployment and job insecurity is widespread among individuals at different stages of their working life courses. Thus, the issue of the quality of work life must be extended to a framework that takes into account the quality of the working life course and its linkages with the family. It is obvious that we need much more comparative research into the social processes that are triggered by the restructuring of work and how they affect successful and problematic work transitions and family-employment trajectories. Some of these issues are taken up in later sections of this book.

2. Youth, Transitions, and the New World of Work[1]

Graham S. Lowe

Canada and other industrial nations have undergone two decades of labour-market turbulence that has profoundly affected employment opportunities for young people. The spread of contingent work forms, high structural unemployment, declining real incomes, and the growing gap between 'good' and 'bad' jobs have contributed to make the school-to-work transition more difficult and complex than ever. Many youth have reacted to an increasingly competitive and volatile work world by investing in further education. While this seems consistent with the human-resource-development approach to economic prosperity advocated by government and industry (Crouch, 1997), the problem of lagging productivity often gets attributed to the failure of the educational system to provide work-relevant skills. Amid debates about the nature of the postindustrial or knowledge-based economy, then, the predicament of youth symbolizes the often-incompatible agendas of human resource development, on the one hand, and the pace and direction of employer-initiated workplace change, on the other.

Using Canadian evidence, this chapter elaborates on the dominant theme in European and North American literature which suggests that 'the transition from school to work has become much more protracted, increasingly fragmented and in some respects less predictable' (Furlong and Cartmel, 1997, p. 27). I argue that human capital is actualized in the school–work transition process, with important immediate and longer-term consequences for young people and society. Given the current policy agenda of creating knowledge-intensive, technology-based economies, it is surprising that school–work transition processes are not more central to the human-resource-development policy thinking about responses to global competition. A major objective in this policy thrust should be adequate opportunities for young workers to be fully integrated into work so that they can be productive. Moreover, the pervasive influence that work contexts, especially skill requirements, can exert on a young person's working life deserves more attention from researchers into school–work transitions. The chapter also highlights how the broader national context of labour market and educational institutions shape school–work transitions. While the chapter identifies key macro-level trends that also affect segments of the youth population in other industrial nations, the details, impact, and policy responses will vary as a result of cross-national institutional, political, and economic variations.

From a life-course perspective, unemployment, underemployment, poor job quality, and barriers to life-long learning faced by youth are harbingers of work-related difficulties during their adult years (Foot and Li, 1986). Youth labour markets generally have been more volatile than adult labour markets. However, in the past two decades, school–work transitions have tended to become even more risky, protracted, and circuitous. Still, there are continuities with the past: the average high school or college graduate eventually settles into a stable work pattern and adult roles. Yet the exceptions to this general norm are increasingly numerous, the negative personal and social consequences of marginalization have intensified, and stable work in the 1990s means something very different from the standard of full-time, continuous work established in the early post–Second World War era. Harsh realities await certain groups of young people in the new world of work, re-creating ingrained patterns of inequality in new forms.

Work and the Life Course

Our starting point is the impact of work restructuring on different age cohorts. The Canadian labour force expanded by 7.2 per cent between 1990 and 1997, yet the youth labour force (15–24 years) contracted by 11 per cent (Statistics Canada, 1998a). Among 15- to 24-year-olds, full-time employment declined by a staggering 27.1 per cent during this period, a figure in no way offset by a slight gain in part-time employment. Even with a relatively smaller youth cohort, this disappearance of youth employment opportunities is unprecedented. The only other cohort to experience this process is that of 55- to 64-year-olds, many of whom are retiring early because of management cost cutting and downsizing – the same reasons that make it difficult for youth to get hired in the first place. Consequently, the average retirement age has dropped, while the average age of transition from full-time education has risen.

The restructuring of work can have the same general impact on younger and older workers – declining participation rates – but with entirely different consequences. Since the mid-1980s, the retirement age has dropped considerably, down to a median age of 62 in 1995 (Gower, 1997). Early-retirement incentives are being questioned by organizations as they grapple with the loss of corporate memory and expertise. Some older workers may realize, as well, that they are unable to afford early retirement. Still, these are different policy questions, with different social consequences, than questions about what happens to young people who face growing barriers to successful entry into the work force.

Restructuring Youth Labour Markets

Demographic patterns and shifting industrial structures have little impact on youth unemployment, because this problem mainly reflects a nation's overall rate of unemployment (OECD, 1996a). However, cross-national variations in age-specific unemployment rates are influenced by institutional factors, including the structure of the educational and training systems; social welfare, pensions, and retirement regulations; gender roles; and immigration rules. Within Canada, several groups of youth face major barriers to finding and keeping paid work: teenagers, high school dropouts, and, increasingly, those with a high school diploma, especially young males. These groups are at risk of being economically marginalized, a problem that has increased with the erosion of welfare-state provisions.

Double-digit youth (15- to 24-year-old) unemployment has been a feature of labour markets in Canada, the United States, the United Kingdom, and Australia since the mid-1970s (OECD, 1980). The recession of the early 1980s pushed up structural unemployment among adults, with direct consequences for youth as employers restricted new recruitment. In the 1990s, government deficit cutting, public-sector and private-sector downsizing, various wage-reduction and cost-cutting strategies, and persistently high structural unemployment continued to limit job opportunities, especially for youth. As in many industrial nations, Canadian youth reacted by staying longer in school or leaving the labour market to re-enter the educational system. Generally, this is a positive sign, which advances a historic trend towards higher educational attainment. But unlike in earlier decades, women more than men choose this education option. In 1996, women received 58 per cent of all university degrees granted in Canada (Statistics Canada, 1999). However, the proportion of youth with no job experience leapt from 10 to 25 per cent between 1989 and 1997. What also changed, then, is that youth face larger hurdles to gaining the requisite experience to break into the job market (Statistics Canada, 1998b). The resulting social and economic exclusion of the minority of youth who stumble badly has attracted considerable attention in some European countries, where the proportions of youth neither in school nor in work are even higher than in Canada (OECD, 1996a).

Full-time, continuous employment with a single employer represents the 'standard' job that became the (male) norm after the Second World War. The standard job is now less common among youth than among any other age cohort. The spread of non-standard employment, as employers implement flexible, lower-cost staffing regimes, is equated with 'bad' job conditions (Krahn, 1995).[2] Despite declining employment rates overall, youth have become more heavily concentrated in part-time jobs (Statistics Canada, 1998b, p. 46). By the mid-1990s, more than half of the female part-time workforce was under 25, as was 40 per cent of the male part-time work force. Because the big increase in part-time work is among out-of-school youth, involuntary part-time youth employment rose substantially between 1990 and 1995 (Betcherman and Leckie, 1998, p. 8; Krahn and Lowe, 1998a, pp 84–6). Education matters, though, and the risk of involuntary part-time employment – a form of underemployment – is below the labour-force average among university graduates. A similar story can be told about temporary work, another form of non-standard employment in which young people predominate.

Investing in Education

By acquiring more education, youth are putting the rhetoric of human resource development into practice. In the 1990s, the previous decade's rise in employment–population ratios for 15- to 24-year-olds reversed. At the same time, postsecondary enrolments grew, resulting in steadily rising educational attainment until the early 1990s when the trend began to reverse slightly (Association of Universities and Colleges of Canada, 1997, p. 14). In 1980, 20 per cent of 15- to 29-year-olds had a postsecondary degree or diploma; this percentage almost doubled by 1995 (Association of Universities and Colleges of Canada, 1997). Rising tuition fees, growing debt burdens upon graduation, and a shortage of part-time student jobs have raised concerns that postsecondary education may become inaccessible for qualified young people from less-affluent families.

In today's competitive labour market, young people without post-secondary credentials often find it difficult to making a decent living. Average youth wages relative to those of adults have been falling in all OECD nations except Sweden (OECD, 1996a). Educational credentials increasingly accentuate labour-market disparities. University graduates in Canada have obtained most of the good jobs created in the past decade. This does not mean that a university degree is a ticket to a job. Rather, in the immediate period following graduation, it reduces the chances of unemployment, part-time and temporary work, low wages, and other forms of labour-market insecurity. As a supplement to acquiring formal credentials, volunteering in the community has become a common strategy for gaining work experience among young people in Canada,[3] as well as in European countries such as the Netherlands and Denmark, and is a growing trend elsewhere (e.g., in Germany, Austria, Finland, and the United Kingdom).

Self-employment

Self-employment is the key labour-market trend in Canada during the 1990s, unlike in the United States, where this form of job creation has been far less important than north of the border (Statistics Canada, 1997b, p. 1). The vast majority of new jobs were in self-employment, but most were held by 'own-account' self-employed individuals who did not employ other workers through a small business. Indeed, the own-account self-employed comprise more than one in ten of all workers. The trend has been interpreted either as a sign of rising entrepreneurialism or as the spread of contingent work. Self-employment has visible life-course features, being far more common among older workers. This is not surprising, for these workers have the experience, networks, and financial resources needed to work independently. In fact, the largest growth in self-employment is in the 55 and older male group. In contrast, only 25 per cent of the self-employed are under the age of 35, compared with 45 per cent of all employees (Statistics Canada, 1997b). Self-employment also is gendered: it has grown more rapidly among women, who often see it as a way to balance work and family, and the male–female wage gap is greater among the self-employed than among the employed (Hughes, 1999).

Let us look more closely now at youth in Alberta (a province with a strong entrepreneurial ideology). The 1996 Alberta Graduate Survey showed that, among students in their final year of high school, very few aspired to be self-employed, listing instead a specific occupation (Lowe, Krahn, and Bowlby, 1997). The 1997 Alberta Graduate Survey, which followed up 1994 university graduates several years after leaving university, found that, among non-students in 1997, the rate of self-employment was far lower than the labour-force average, and the majority of the self-employed worked on their own (Krahn and Lowe, 1998b).[4] The trend is polarized and gendered, as women tended to be in lower-income and less-secure forms of self-employment, and to be overrepresented among fine arts and MA graduates. These data report self-employment status at a single point in time; panel data from the Edmonton School–Work Transition Study show that seven years after graduating, a slightly higher percentage of high school and university graduates had been self-employed. For some youth, self-employment is part of a repertoire of labour-market adaptations, rather than a destination of choice.

School–Work Transition Patterns

A more finely tuned overview of school–work transition patterns can be gleaned from the Edmonton School–Work Transition Study. This panel study shows that the 1985 secondary and postsecondary graduates surveyed eventually settled into the labour market, often by creating unique mélanges of work and educational experience. The crucial question is the extent to which each new youth cohort can launch meaningful and productive lives as workers, citizens, and parents.

Based on the experiences of 1985 high school and university graduates in Edmonton in the seven years after initial graduation, the answer is a carefully qualified yes.[5]

In 1985, the high school graduates in this study were in their late teens and the university graduates in their early twenties. By 1992, many of these young people had achieved independent adult status, having formed partnerships, left the family home, and started families. Yet this transition to adulthood took considerably longer than that for graduates in previous decades, and the process required difficult choices and trade-offs about school and work. Thus, young people who had stayed in school were more likely to have postponed parenthood. The challenges of balancing work and family also affected employment patterns. Among women in both samples, by 1992 part-time work had begun to replace full-time employment for many who had become parents, reinforcing more traditionally female life-course patterns (Ranson, 1998).

The Educational Premium

Consistent with national and international trends, extended educational activity was a major feature of the transition process among study participants. More than one-third of the high school sample and one-quarter of the university sample reported educational activity in 1991–2. The main reasons given for further education were work related. Many of these graduates participated in informal and formal workplace learning, especially to develop computer skills. Assuming that life-long learning is crucial in the future work world, many Canadian graduates have headed in this direction (OECD, 1996b). As one sign of this trend, almost one in five in the high school sample and one-third in the university sample exited and re-entered the educational system at some point in the seven years covered by this study.

In the context of somewhat unpredictable school–work transitions, there is a strong educational premium, with university credentials improving the chances of obtaining a 'good' job. Seven years after graduating with an undergraduate degree, more than 80 per cent of the university sample held a managerial or professional job, and those who had continued their education were doing somewhat better. (However, female university graduates were more likely than their male classmates to hold clerical and service jobs.) By contrast, only one in ten high school graduates who had not returned to school full time at any point between 1985 and 1992 had obtained a managerial or professional job.

Employers' restructuring strategies also affect the availability of better jobs in the upper-tier services sector and the goods-producing industries. The polarization between skilled, challenging, and rewarding jobs, on the one hand, and unskilled, low-wage, and insecure jobs, on the other, has come to define contemporary work. For young workers trying to find a niche in the work world, the chances of obtaining a good job depend largely on the particular segment of the labour market they enter. The part-time, temporary, and seasonal jobs in the retail and consumer services (e.g., food and beverage, tourism, and personal services) industries form a student labour market. However, students' acceptance of these conditions reflect their expectation that better opportunities await them after graduation. The challenge is having the resources to move out of this student labour market into more rewarding and stable employment that meshes with career goals.

High school dropouts most closely fit the popular image of a 'lost generation' (Cote and Allahar, 1994; Jehoel-Gijsbers and Groot, 1989). However, while many of these youth have rejected the school system once, they have not rejected the belief that an education is essential in order to succeed in the labour market (Tanner, Krahn, and Hartnagel, 1995). Many eventually return to complete high school (Frank, 1996). Mainly male and from disadvantaged backgrounds, the small group of young adults without a high school diploma risks chronic economic marginalization. Still, Canadian dropouts may differ from those in other countries by their high level of commitment to the value of education.

Unemployment and Underemployment

The provincial unemployment rate at the time the Edmonton School–Work Transition Study began in 1985 was 10.6 per cent and for 15- to 19-year-olds it was 20.1 per cent, making the mid-1980s' job market more competitive for youth than it was in the mid-1990s. University graduates were half as likely as high school graduates to be unemployed when contacted in follow-up surveys up to 1989. Unemployment among the high school graduates had dropped by 1992, in part because many were now better educated. However, for most graduates, one or more spells of unemployment were part of the transition process. Unlike in some countries, such as Britain, where long-term youth unemployment became the norm in the 1980s, unemployment has not dominated school–work transitions in Canada, except in the case of high school dropouts.

Instead, underemployment is the most noteworthy problem for young workers possessing educational credentials. When surveyed in 1992, seven years after graduation, 31 per cent of the high school graduates and 20 per cent of the university graduates reported feeling overqualified for their job. Just over one-third of employed high school respondents and only one-half of employed university sample members agreed that they were in the kind of job they had expected to have at this stage in their life. Graduates of some faculties (arts, for example) were considerably more likely to feel overqualified than were education and engineering graduates. This skills mismatch reflects the difficulties that employers face in applying the employability skills of graduates from non-professional programs.

There are clear indications of underemployment among recent university graduates. The 1997 Alberta Graduate Survey, conducted at a time of economic growth and low unemployment in the province, generally found these 1994 university graduates doing well in the labour market (Krahn and Lowe, 1998b). Members of the Class of '94 who were no longer in the educational system in 1997 reported above-average employment rates and incomes; yet sizeable numbers also felt underemployed. Of the non-students, about two-thirds were in jobs requiring a university degree, and one-quarter reported feeling overqualified for their job given their education, training, and experience. This problem is more common among women because of their over-representation in humanities, fine arts, social sciences, and some of the sciences, a factor which in turn is related to their higher likelihood of ending up in clerical, sales, or service work or in a non-standard job.

The situation is similar for other postsecondary graduates. Statistics Canada reports that in 1994, one in four community college graduates under the age of 29 felt overqualified for their job (Kelly, Howatson-Leo, and Clark, 1997). This mismatch between young, well-educated workers, on the one hand, and the requirements of their jobs, on the other, runs counter to the human-resource-development approach to economic renewal (Livingstone, 1998). As American critics of this approach argue, it has a 'field of dreams' logic, implying that if educational and training programs produce capable workers, then high-quality employment will naturally follow (Teixeira and Mishel, 1995). Even though many recent university graduates have well-paid, full-time jobs, their potential to contribute at higher levels may not be fully tapped. The obvious consequences are diminished quality of work life for individuals and a loss to the economy in terms of productivity.

Unions and School–Work Transitions

The greater diversity and risk that define the early labour-market experiences of many youth have been linked to the shift from a Fordist industrial system to the more fragmented, fluid, and diverse employment systems of a postindustrial service economy. Life-course theorists view the current era of late modernity as one in which young people actively engage in a more individualized process of becoming adults (Beck, 1992; Heinz, 1996). Social and economic structures are thought to exert less influence on young people's life course, resulting in a more individualistic stance towards working life.

Unionism provides an interesting perspective on these theoretical issues, despite having been largely overlooked in school–work transition research (Furlong and Cartmel, 1997, p. 30). One of the few studies on the topic found an individualistic identity among those Danish trade unionists who were male, young, and better educated (Madsen, 1997). But a convincing argument also could be made that union membership and attitudinal support for joining a union among the new generation of workers could indicate collectivism and greater social integration. The teenage and young-adult years are a period in which a wide range of work attitudes is formed. This underscores the importance of adopting more of a life-course perspective on workers' relationship to the labour movement. Given low rates of unionization among youth (Statistics Canada, 1998c), effective strategies to recruit more young workers are crucial to the survival of the labour movement internationally (International Labour Organization, 1997). Union orientation also would provide young workers with the basic right of collective representation and better working conditions.

In the 1996 Alberta High School Graduates Survey, we found 9.1 per cent of female and 13.5 per cent of male respondents reporting union membership in jobs they had held during the school term. As a point of reference, the province of Alberta has the lowest unionization rate in Canada (22 per cent of all employed). Yet among those grade 12 students who were not union members, 27 per cent of females and 33 per cent of males said it was likely or very likely that they would join a union if one existed in their workplace.[6] Somewhat fewer took an anti-union position, stating that it was unlikely or very unlikely they would join. Crucial, then, is the large middle group which has not yet formed an opinion for or against unions. Panel data from the 1985 Edmonton School–Work Transition Study suggest that pro- and anti-union attitudes harden over time, shaped by labour-market experiences and job quality. Expressions of latent unionism suggest that a sizeable minority do not have a predominantly individualized view of work (Lowe and Rastin, 2000).

Change and Continuity in Work Attitudes and Behaviour

The 1980s and 1990s encompass several distinct youth cohorts. This variety raises questions about how young people have adapted their work attitudes and behaviour to the new world of work. As in the case of unionism, it is useful to compare two contrasting theoretical perspectives. Postmodernists see increased diversity and individualization in how youth negotiate their way into adulthood as evidence that the institutions of industrialism are becoming less relevant. Others argue that, while young people's experience of school–work transitions has altered, there are strong continuities in the way deep-rooted structures – social class, gender, race, and region – limit or enhance opportunities along the way (Furlong and Cartmel, 1997).

A variety of Canadian evidence suggests that economic restructuring has been more evolutionary than anything else, with the institutions of education and work continuing to exert powerful influences on life-course trajectories. While there are signs that young people have created new norms governing the life course, these trends have been emerging for decades. The age of first marriage has risen steadily since the 1970s, and growing numbers of youth are opting for common-law relationships (Statistics Canada, 1997a). Living in the parental home into one's late twenties has become more common (Boyd and Norris, 1995). These trends document a longer stage of dependence and, as a result, delayed entry into key adult roles. Yet, despite these behavioural changes, a comparison of similar samples of Edmonton grade 12 students in 1985 and 1996 suggests that basic work values among teenagers have been remarkably stable over that period (Lowe and Krahn, 2000). Then as now, what high school graduates want most of all is interesting, sociable, and fulfilling work. Despite the heightened job anxieties of the 1990s, the 1996 graduates placed only slightly more priority than those in 1985 on finding a secure job and one that pays well (Lowe and Krahn, 2000).

Conclusion

I have argued that we need to rethink what it means to create work opportunities for recent high school, college, and university graduates. A major priority should be setting and achieving targets for entry-level job creation so that new graduates can get a decent start in the work world. Youth unemployment is nested in the larger economic problem of high structural unemployment, so what's also needed are macroeconomic and labour-market policies aimed at reducing unemployment *per se* by generating new jobs. Otherwise, youth unemployment will threaten longer-term social cohesion (Jenson, 1998). As 1990s youth cohorts move into their adult years, society will have to address the consequences of school–work transition problems with the inadequate policy tools of a post–welfare-state era.

Of equal concern is the inability of the economy to generate enough skilled and rewarding jobs to accommodate the rising educational levels of workers. Fundamentally, this problem stems from entrenched, rigid work systems and a lack of organizational innovation (Lowe, 2000). Priority must be placed on creating high-quality work opportunities, so that the talents and productive potential of young people can be developed continuously. This is what is best for young workers, and clearly it is what is best for national economies. Central to this agenda must be job and organizational redesign, so that the restrictions placed on human-resource development and skill use by traditional bureaucratic and Taylorist work forms can be overcome.

Policy responses have inadequately addressed the major concerns that loom large in the immediate future for youth: reducing overall unemployment and improving the overall quality of jobs by providing opportunities for skilled and meaningful work. This route to a high-skill, high-wage economy stands to benefit adult workers too. What is needed is a wide-ranging discussion of a youth-policy agenda that would meet the challenges of improving job quality, creating skilled jobs, reorganizing work, and providing more equitably distributed opportunities to earn a decent living (e.g., Rehnby and McBride, 1997).

The bleak new world of work for youth as outlined above is not inevitable. Indeed, with the right public-policy mix and a strong commitment from employers, it could be reshaped to provide real scope for the skills, learning, and knowledge now so frequently identified rhetorically as important national goals.

NOTES

1 Some of the research presented in this paper comes from the School–Work Transition Project (*www.ualberta.ca/~glowe/transition*), of which Professor Harvey Krahn and I are principal co-investigators. Major funders of this project include the Social Sciences and Humanities Research Council of Canada, Alberta Advanced Education and Career Development, and Alberta Education. Sandra Rastin provided able research assistance. Ansgar Weymann, Lynne Chisholm, Frank Trovato, Karen Hughes, and Walter Heinz provided useful suggestions on earlier drafts.
2 Non-standard work arrangements include part-time jobs, temporary work, own-account self-employment, and multiple job holding.
3 Half of the females and 40 per cent of the males in a representative sample of 1996 grade 12 (final year of high school) students in the Province of Alberta reported that they had participated in voluntary work during the current school year (Lowe, Krahn, and Bowlby, 1997, p. 47).
4 This study was part of the Government of Alberta's initiative to measure the performance of postsecondary institutions. It surveyed more than 6,000 1994 graduates from all programs at Alberta's four universities two and a half years after their graduation.
5 Almost one thousand grade 12 students and close to six hundred University of Alberta fourth-year undergraduates were surveyed just prior to graduation in the spring of that year. Follow-up surveys were completed in 1986, 1987, 1989, and 1992 (see Krahn and Lowe, 1993).
6 Respondents were asked: 'If a union existed in a workplace where you were employed, would you join?' (answered on a scale of 1 to 5, where 1 = very unlikely and 5 = very likely). Sample n = 2651.

REFERENCES

Association of Universities and Colleges of Canada. (1997, August-September). *University Affairs/Affaires universitaires*. Ottawa: Author.

Beck, U. (1992). *Risk society: Towards a new modernity.* London: Sage.

Betcherman, G., & Leckie, N. (1998). *Youth employment and education trends in the 1980s and 1990s.* Ottawa: Canadian Policy Research Networks Inc.

Boyd, M., & Norris, D. (1995, Autumn). Leaving the nest? The impact of family structure. *Canadian Social Trends, 38,* 14–17.

Cote, J.E., & Allahar, A.L. (1994). *Generation on hold: Coming of age in the late twentieth century.* Toronto: Stoddart.

Crouch, C. (1997). Skills-based full employment: The latest philosopher's stone. *British Journal of Industrial Relations, 35*(3), 367–91.

Foot, D.K., & Li, J.C. (1986). Youth employment in Canada: A misplaced priority? *Canadian Public Policy, 12*(3), 499–506.

Frank, J. (1996). *After high school: The first years. The first report of the school leavers follow-up survey.* Ottawa: Statistics Canada and Human Resources Development Canada.

Furlong, A, & Cartmel, F. (1997). *Young people and social change: Individualization and risk in late modernity.* Buckingham, UK: Open University Press.

Gower, D. (1997, Spring). Measuring the age of retirement. *Perspectives on Labour and Income,* 11–17.

Heinz, W.R. (1996). *The transition from education to employment in a comparative perspective.* Toronto: Centre for International Studies, University of Toronto.

Hughes, K. (1999). *Gender and self-employment in Canada: Assessing trends and policy implications.* Ottawa: Canadian Policy Research Networks Inc.

International Labour Organization. (1997). *World labour report 1997–1998: Industrial relations, democracy and social stability.* Geneva: ILO.

Jehoel-Gijsbers, G., & Groot, W. (1989). Unemployed youth: A lost generation? *Work, Employment and Society, 3*(4), 491–508.

Jenson, J. (1998). *Mapping social cohesion: The state of Canadian research.* Ottawa: Canadian Policy Research Networks Inc.

Kelly, K., Howatson-Leo, L., & Clark, W. (1997, Winter). I feel overqualified for my job. *Canadian Social Trends, 47,* 11–16.

Krahn, H. (1995, Winter). Nonstandard work on the rise. *Perspectives on Labour and Income,* 35–42.

Krahn, H., & Lowe, G.S. (1993). *The school–work transition in Edmonton, 1985–1992.* Edmonton, AB: Population Research Laboratory, University of Alberta.

Krahn, H., & Lowe, G.S. (1998a). *Work, industry and Canadian society* (3rd ed.). Scarborough, ON: ITP Nelson.

Krahn, H., & Lowe, G.S. (1998b). *1997 Alberta graduate survey: Labour market and educational experiences of 1994 university graduates.* Edmonton, AB: Population

Research Laboratory, University of Alberta, and Alberta Advanced Education and Career Development.

Livingstone, D.W. (1998). *The education–jobs gap: Underemployment or economic democracy.* Boulder, CO: Westview Press.

Lowe, G.S. (2000). *The quality of work: A people-centred agenda.* Don Mills, ON: Oxford University Press.

Lowe, G.S., & Krahn, H. (2000). Work aspirations and attitudes in an era of labour market restructuring: A comparison of two Canadian youth cohorts. *Work, Employment and Society, 14*(1), 1–22.

Lowe, G.S., Krahn, H., & Bowlby, J. (1997). *1996 Alberta high school graduate survey: report of research findings* (School–Work Transitions Project Rep. No. 97-1). Edmonton, AB: Alberta Education.

Lowe, G.S., & Rastin, S. (2000). Organizing the next generation: Influences on young workers' willingness to join unions. *British Journal of Industrial Relations, 38*(2), 203–22.

Madsen, M. (1997). The relationship between working life and individualisation: A study among Danish union members. *Work, Employment and Society, 11*(2), 197–217.

OECD (Organization for Economic Cooperation and Development). (1996a). *Employment outlook.* Paris: Author.

OECD. (1996b). *Lifelong learning for all.* Paris: Author.

OECD. (1980). *Youth unemployment: Its causes and consequences.* Paris: Author.

Ranson, G. (1998). Education, work and family decision making: Finding the 'right time' to have a baby. *Canadian Review of Sociology and Anthropology, 35*(4), 517–33.

Rehnby, N., & McBride, S. (1997). *Help wanted: Economic security for youth.* Ottawa: Canadian Centre for Policy Alternatives.

Statistics Canada. (1997a, October 14). *The Daily* (Catalogue no. 11-001E). Ottawa: Author.

Statistics Canada. (1997b). *Labour force update: The self-employed* (Catalogue no. 71-005-XPB), *1*(3). Ottawa: Author.

Statistics Canada. (1998a). *Historical labour force statistics 1997* (Catalogue no. 71-201-XPB). Ottawa: Author.

Statistics Canada. (1998b). *Labour force update. An overview of the 1997 labour market* (Catalogue no. 71-005-XPB), *2*(1). Ottawa: Author.

Statistics Canada. (1998c, Winter). *Perspectives on Labour and Income.* Ottawa: Author.

Statistics Canada. (1999). *Canada yearbook 1999.* Ottawa: Author.

Tanner, J., Krahn, H., & Hartnagel, T.F. (1995). *Fractured transitions from school* to work: *Revisiting the dropout problem*. Don Mills, ON: Oxford University Press.

Teixeira, R.A., & Mishel, L. (1995). Skills shortages or management shortage? In D. Bills (Ed.), *The new modern times: Factors reshaping the world of work* (pp. 193–205). Albany, NY: State University of New York Press.

3. The Dutch Labour Market since 1971: Trends in Overeducation and Displacement

Marco de Witte and Ronald Batenburg

In the last few years, the Dutch 'poldermodel' has become widely known among western European countries. The model is repeatedly cited for its achievements, such as a moderate level of wage increase, extensive schemes of direct job creation, and strategic and constructive cooperation among employers, employees, and government on the one hand and strong cuts in social-security and employment services on the other. Social-benefit funds are used in an increasingly active way, to support job creation programs, or to subsidize employers who create low-wage jobs and engage the long-term unemployed. The core of the Dutch model is the attempt to tackle socio-economic problems such as unemployment by involving all so-called social partners (employers, unions, and social-security and job agencies) in the process of policy development.

There are some negative aspects, however. One unintended consequence of the strong traditional social-security system (for example, a relatively large percentage of the Dutch labour population was on benefit from the Disablement Act [WAO] or the Sickness Benefits Act [ZW]) has largely been overcome. Another problem seems to remain more permanent. This is the imperfect fit between the educational system and the labour market. Many Dutch students who have just graduated and are starting to explore the labour market soon realize that it is not always possible to acquire the type of job they were trained for. As a result of a combination of mechanisms, this leads to the underutilization of human resources and the displacement of (less-qualified) workers. Earlier examples, dating even from the period before the Second World War, include cases of engineering graduates working as ticket collectors on tramcars. More recently, we see high school graduates working as supermarket cashiers, historians working as telephone operators, and psychologists working as kindergarten nannies. One could argue that these phenomena are just examples of short-term unemployment or a step in the transition process experienced by young people as they enter the labour market. Still, these same phenomena are also widely accepted indicators for the (in)efficiency of the job-allocation process in the labour market.

This paper builds upon earlier studies done by Huijgen on the qualitative job structure of the Dutch labour market. In the last study by Huijgen (1989), trends for the Dutch labour population were presented over the period 1977–85. In the present paper, this trend is extended to cover the period 1985–95 (see also Asselberghs, Batenburg, Huijgen, and de Witte, 1998). We largely follow Huijgen's analyses and apply his job-level measurements to replicate his findings. The main goal of this paper is to describe and analyse the job-allocation process in relation to the level of education and the job level of employees on the Dutch labour market. The lack of congruence between the employment structure and the educational system can be studied in two different ways: in terms of overeducation, and in terms of displacement. Both types of incongruence will be discussed in this paper. 'Overeducation' refers to the supply side of the labour market. The question addressed is which employees work below their educational level. 'Displacement' refers to the demand side of the labour market. Here the central question is in which labour-market segments displacement is occurring.

This paper has the following structure. First, we describe the data set and the general trends in educational level and job level of the Dutch labour population in the period 1971–95 (section 2). In section 3 the educational and job-level structures are related to each other from the employees' point of view (that is, the supply side of the labour market). Here we present our definition and measurement of overeducation. Besides the trends in the level of overeducation, we present results on how overeducation is related to a number of employee characteristics. Section 4 is devoted to the definition, measurement, and analysis of displacement. Seen from the demand side of the labour market, the mismatch between the educational levels and the job levels of employees is related to a number of sector characteristics. In section 5, the conclusions from both approaches are combined and related to research from other countries, and some policy recommendations are formulated.

Job Levels and Educational Levels in the Dutch Labour Market

The results presented in this paper are based on analysis of the largest permanent labour-market survey in the Netherlands, the Enquête Beroepsbevolking (EBB). This survey is held monthly, based on a representative sample of the Dutch population, and can be considered as the main statistical source for labour-market research and policy. The EBB survey started in 1987 as a successor of the Arbeidskrachten-tellingen (AKT) which was the most important labour-market survey in the Netherlands between 1977 and 1985. Before 1977, the census (Volkstelling) of 1971 can be used as a historical starting point for describing the educational and job levels of the Dutch labour force. All surveys were conducted under the auspices of the Dutch Central Bureau of Statistics. Since the content of the questionnaire and the method of interviewing have changed from the AKT to the EBB survey, some interpretation problems must be taken into consideration when comparing statistics over the period 1971–95.

As was mentioned in the introduction, Huijgen and his colleagues were the first in the Netherlands to code a large number of occupations according to their job level. In this system, occupations are classified at seven different levels, varying from 1 (the lowest level, i.e., unskilled jobs) to 7 (the highest level, i.e., highly specialized jobs). This coding scheme is based on the rating of occupations according to the complexity of the tasks, the required training period, and the amount of autonomy and initiative required. Although several other indicators of job level or occupational quality can be important, these three dimensions should satisfy the aim of measuring and describing the skill structure of the Dutch labour force over time. Applying this coding scheme to the occupations of respondents in the different labour-market surveys as described above (Volkstelling, 1971; AKT, 1977–85; EBB, 1987–95) we are able to describe the average job level of the Dutch labour force for a period of twenty-four years. It appears that from 1971 to 1995 the average job level of Dutch employees has increased from 3.38 in 1971 to 3.95 in 1995 (see table 3.1). This increase is due to the fact that the number of jobs in the intermediate levels decreased and the number of jobs in levels 5, 6, and 7 rose substantially. Contrary to the expectation that the number of unskilled jobs would diminish as a result of automation

TABLE 3.1
The Average Job and Educational Level of the Dutch Labour Force, 1977–1995
(means and indexes)

	1971	1977	1985	1990	1995
Job level					
Average	3.47	3.44	3.62	3.84	3.89
Index (1977 = 100)		100	105.2	111.6	113.1
Educational level					
Average	1.95	2.20	2.69	2.82	2.95
Index (1977 = 100)		100	122.3	128.2	134.1

and mechanization, the proportion of jobs in levels 1 and 2 stayed constant over time. For the late 1960s, Huijgen found that the qualitative employment structure in the Netherlands had polarized (Conen and Huijgen, 1980). After 1971 this was no longer the case. In general, there has been a strong upgrading trend, especially between 1977 and 1985. Since 1985, the upgrading trend has continued but at a relatively slow pace.

Table 3.1 also shows how the educational level of the Dutch labour force has developed between 1977 and 1995. The educational level achieved by employees is classified and coded into five categories: (1) lower (elementary training), (2) extended lower (secondary general training and first level of vocational training), (3) intermediate (advanced secondary training, high school, and second level of vocational training), (4) higher (higher vocational training), and (5) extended higher (academic training). The table shows a strong and steady increase in the average educational level of the Dutch labour force, from 1.95 in 1977 to 2.95 in 1995. Whereas the number of employees with lower and extended lower education has diminished, the proportion of employees with intermediate and higher education has increased significantly.

Both the rise in average job level on the one hand and the increase in the average educational level on the other can be compared by indexing both trends. We did this from 1977. However, table 3.1 also shows that the increase in the average job level is smaller than the increase in the average educational level. This results in a widening gap between the demand for (high) skilled jobs between 1977 and 1995 and the supply of such jobs. Despite progressive developments on both sides of the labour market, the upgrading of the job structure has not kept pace with the upgrading of the educational structure. On a macro level, we conclude that this has worsened the job-opportunity structure of the Dutch labour market over time. In the next sections, we examine the effect of this trend with reference to overeducation (section 3) and displacement (section 4).

Overeducation in the Dutch Labour Market

Definition and Measurement

In analysing overeducation, we focus on the fit between the levels of education achieved and the job levels of employees. Thus, overeducation is defined as the ratio of employees who work below a suitable job level for their level of education. This phenomenon is also called 'underutilization.' However, as some scholars have argued (e.g., Wielers and Glebbeek, 1995), the fact that workers are more highly educated than their job requires does not mean that their surplus educational qualifications are not put to effective use. In their analysis of the effects of increased educational levels, Wielers and Glebbeek emphasize that those who are overeducated for their jobs can be more productive than less educated workers and can also devise and implement innovations in the production process. However, we have restricted our analysis to the question of whether an employee is overeducated or not. Given our data, it is not possible to judge whether the surplus qualifications of overeducated employees are put to use. Therefore, we prefer to use the term 'overeducation.'

As previously mentioned, we have extended Huijgen's analysis both of the Dutch labour force and also the fit between the educational system and skill structure. Therefore, the definition and measurement of overeducation is based on the same method Huijgen (1989) applied in his 1977–85 trend study. His overeducation model is presented in table 3.2, where the (seven) job levels are cross-referenced with the (five) levels of education as described earlier in this paper.

According to this model, employees are defined as overeducated in all categories above the diagonal line. Code '1' refers to employees whose job is one level below their suitable job level, code '2' to employees whose job is two or more levels below their suitable job level. It goes without saying that this model is based on a certain interpretation of what is defined as a mismatch (overeducation) and what is not.

TABLE 3.2
Overeducation as Defined by Huijgen ('1' = overeducated by one level,
'2' = overeducated by two levels)

	Educational level				
Job level	Lower	Extended lower	Intermediate	Higher	Extended higher
1 (unskilled jobs)		2	2	2	2
2		1	2	2	2
3			1	2	2
4				1	2
5					1
6					
7 (highly specialized jobs)					

There are several other ways to draw the diagonal line. Moreover, a strong assumption is made on the scale of both job and educational level. Both are assumed to be ratio scales as we compute their means (and perform multivariate analysis later on in this paper). This assumption can be questioned. Indeed both variables are ordinal scales, but the distances between the levels are not necessarily equal. These qualifiers should also be kept in mind.

If Huijgen's categorization exercise is applied on our data we see that the percentage of workers who are overeducated by one level in the Netherlands has doubled from 18 per cent in 1971 to 37.7 per cent in 1995. Overeducation rose especially sharply between 1971 and 1985. This trend holds for all educational levels. The proportion of employees who work at two or more job levels below their educational qualifications grew from 4.3 per cent to 17.4 per cent between 1971 and 1995. This group in particular highlights the disjunction between the skill level required by jobs and the educational levels of employees. We therefore conclude that, in the Dutch labour market, job allocation in relation to level of education is far from perfect.

Who Are the Overeducated?

The previous analysis leads us to the next question: Which employees work below their educational level? or Who are the overeducated? One explanation is that particular groups which have lower expectations and/or fewer opportunities to achieve an appropriate job level are more likely to become overeducated. One such group could be young people entering the labour market without any experience who are willing to start work in jobs below their level of education in the belief that they will attain a more appropriate job level later in their career. Another such group is women, who may assume that they cannot achieve high-level jobs if they want to combine work with family life. Force of tradition thus leads women to accept jobs below their level of education more easily than men when they enter (or re-enter) the labour market.

We tested these propositions by comparing the composition and average job levels of overeducated and non-overeducated employees. To ensure a sufficiently large and coherent data set, we included data from EBB surveys of 1990 and 1995. In table 3.3, the overeducated and non-overeducated employees are distinguished by level of education, age, and gender. We performed multivariate classification analysis (MCA) in order to compare the controlled means and net effects of educational level, age, and gender on job level (as expressed by the ETAs).

As might be expected, table 3.3 shows that between 1990 and 1995 the average job level (2.31) reached by overeducated employees is considerably lower than the average job level of the non-overeducated (4.66). For both categories, education has a relatively strong effect on job level (ETA 0.55 and 0.60).

When we turn to the comparison of the age and gender composition of the overeducated and non-overeducated, we can see the following. The proportion of younger employees up to age 34 in the overeducated group (23 per cent and 36.1 per cent) is higher than the proportion of older employees within the overeducated group (22.5 per cent and 18.4 per cent). This confirms our proposition regarding 'the waiting-room effect': young employees accept jobs below their skill level because they anticipate having career opportunities in the future which will enable them to reach an appropriate job level. This hypothesis is also confirmed by the fact that the non-overeducated youngsters occupy, on average, higher job levels than their overeducated peers.

From table 3.3 it also appears that (compared to the percentage in the total sample) women are relatively overrepresented in the group of overeducated employees (42.8 per cent versus 37 per cent). This is in line with our proposition. Since the averages (and ETAs) presented in table 3.3 are the result of multivariate analysis, we can also draw the conclusion that the effect of gender is larger than the effect of age. In

TABLE 3.3
MCA analysis: Mean Job Level of the Overeducated (by One Level or More) and Non-overeducated Dutch Employees by Educational Level, Gender, and Age, 1990–95

	Total	Non-overeducated			Overeducated		
	%	%	Mean	ETA	%	Mean	ETA
Educational level				0.60			0.55
Lower	9	14.2	2.77		–	–	
Extended lower	24	18.3	4.28		34.4	1.81	
Intermediate	43	38.5	4.82		51.7	2.38	
Higher	17	20.4	5.46		9.8	3.07	
Extended higher	7	8.6	5.97		4.2	3.78	
Gender				0.10			0.04
Men	63	66.8	4.77		57.2	2.34	
Women	37	33.2	4.45		42.8	2.27	
Age				0.06			0.02
16–24	15	11.4	4.48		23.0	2.28	
25–34	33	31.9	4.40		36.1	2.32	
35–44	27	29.9	4.70		22.5	2.34	
45–64	24	26.8	4.76		18.4	2.30	
Total			4.66			2.31	

other words, youngsters are more overeducated than older employees, but overeducation in the Dutch labour market seems to be more a female than a male problem.

Displacement in the Dutch Labour Market

Definition and Measurement

Although recently the Netherlands has achieved one of Europe's lowest unemployment rates, the existence of a hard core of long-term unemployed remains a structural problem. This unemployment is not equally distributed among various categories within the population. Youngsters, immigrants, and less-educated workers have relatively high chances of becoming unemployed. Extensive research into this phenomenon often suggests 'displacement' as a key cause of the relatively high unemployment of less-educated workers. In general, displacement is described as a process by which jobs are filled from the growing ranks of more highly educated employees, while the content of the job is unchanged. When this is the case at all job levels, displacement will trickle down throughout the labour market. As less-educated employees are steadily crowded out of their jobs by the more highly educated, the unemployment rates of employees with the lowest educational level become relatively high.

Stressing the selection process at the supply side of the labour market, this theory was prominently presented by Thurow (1975). In this approach the number of jobs is a given, and it is assumed that employees primarily compete to obtain the most attractive jobs. As a result, employees line up in a hypothetical labour queue with the best educated at the front. At the end of the queue are those employees who are the least eligible for a job at a certain qualification level. Personnel managers rank potential employees in this queue according to their expected productivity, which is mainly indicated by the employee's level of education. Employees will therefore aspire to ever-higher educational levels in order to obtain an optimal relative position in the selection process for these jobs. Thus, the less-educated workers are crowded out of the jobs at lower qualification levels, or even out of employment altogether.

According to this theory, vacancy competition dominates the allocation process on the labour market. Several researchers assume that this mechanism also holds for the Dutch labour market (Wielers and Glebbeek, 1995; Dagevos, van der Laan, and Veenman, 1997; De Beer, 1996). They suggest that this is the reason why a substantial number of employees in the Netherlands apply for a job below their level of qualification. It also explains why it is extremely difficult to integrate the least educated into the labour market. The best educated become more and more successful because of their lower training costs for the firm (Wielers and Glebbeek, 1995), their positive return on investment in terms of increasing productivity and innovation power (Hartog, Mekkelholt, and van Ophem, 1988), and their social-normative qualifications (Moelker, 1992). All these arguments support the proposition that overeducation and displacement are a result of (rational) considerations of employers and their decisions at the demand side of the labour market.

Displacement can be analysed by focusing on the average educational level of workers on different job levels. Huijgen demonstrated in earlier research that there is indeed a general trend towards downward displacement, which increased substantially between 1977 and 1985 (Huijgen, 1989). The share of the least educated is pushed back at all job levels, but particularly on the lower levels of the labour market. On job levels 1 and 2, the average educational level rose strongly between 1977 and 1985. If we look at the period between 1985 and 1995, this trend continued. At the higher job levels, the rise of the average educational level was relatively strong between 1977 and 1985, but modest for the period 1985–95. We conclude that in 1995 displacement was concentrated at the bottom of the labour market. This result is consistent with the conclusions of other Dutch labour-market researchers (Teulings, 1990; Salverda, 1992; de Grip and Dekker, 1993; Webbink, van der Vegt, and Bon, 1995; de Beer, 1996; Wolbers, de Graaf, and Ultee, 1997).

Where Is Displacement Concentrated?

Next in this section we will focus on the behaviour of employers on the supply side of the labour market and address the question: Where, or in which labour segments, are employees displaced?

With the transition from an industrial to a postindustrial society, jobs in the traditional industries were reduced and work in the service sector expanded significantly. At the same time, several modern approaches of human resource management (HRM) influenced the functioning of the internal labour market of companies by, for example, the introduction of teamwork, 'business process redesign,' management development, 'sociotechnical' innovations, and so on. These approaches had the most impact on the relatively new and expanding segments of the Dutch labour market and the least impact on the traditional industries. Therefore, we expect that vacancy competition operates mainly at the academic or executive level and within the service or commercial sector. In these core segments of the labour market, the growing supply of labour (young academics) and managerial innovations considerably increased the stringency of the selection system, resulting in increased chances of displacement.

We tested these propositions by conducting a second multivariate analysis of the average job levels of overeducated and non-overeducated Dutch employees between 1990 and 1995. This analysis was conducted in these two categories in order to compare the results with these described in the previous section, in which the effects of variables on the supply side of the labour market (employee's age and gender)

TABLE 3.4

MCA analysis: Mean Job Level of the Overeducated (by One Level or More) and Non-overeducated Dutch Employees by Educational Level, Occupational Group, and Educational Field, 1990–95

	Total	Non-overeducated			Overeducated		
	%	%	Mean	ETA	%	Mean	ETA
Educational level				0.60			0.55
Lower	9	14.2	2.77		–	–	
Extended lower	24	18.3	4.28		34.4	1.81	
Intermediate	43	38.5	4.82		51.7	2.38	
Higher	17	20.4	5.46		9.8	3.07	
Extended higher	7	8.6	5.97		4.2	3.78	
Occupational group				0.39			0.29
Academic professionals	26	38.2	5.26		2.7	3.19	
Higher executives	4	6.4	5.41		–	–	
Clerical staff	20	16.5	4.24		28.4	2.60	
Commerce	9	6.0	4.74		13.6	2.22	
Service sector	10	6.9	3.98		16.9	2.29	
Agricultural	3	2.3	4.04		5.8	2.20	
Industrial crafts	27	23.7	3.99		32.6	2.06	
Educational field				0.06			0.05
General	22	24.2	4.76		16.6	2.23	
Technical	30	28.6	4.64		34.0	2.35	
Economics	20	18.3	4.76		23.7	2.27	
Care	28	20.9	4.54		25.7	2.34	
Total			4.66			2.31	

were examined. In Table 3.4, two effects of the demand side (i.e., the segmentation) of the labour market are considered. Unfortunately, the EBB and AKT data do not contain direct information on the types of organizations the employees work for. We therefore used indirect indicators for labour segmentation – namely, educational field (general, technical, commercial, and care) and occupational group (academic professional, higher executive, clerical, commerce, service, agricultural, and industrial crafts). The net effects of these two variables on the average job level of the non-overeducated and overeducated are estimated by multivariate classification analysis (MCA), holding constant the level of education.

A clear result from the MCA analysis is the strong net effect of occupational group on the average job. Field of education shows a significantly weaker relation to job level. Academic professionals and higher executives are clearly underrepresented among the overeducated. Indeed, higher executives are extremely absent from the overeducated group of employees. This shows that these jobs are not susceptible to the overeducation trend. For the service, industrial crafts, and clerical sectors, however, overeducation is significant. The proportion of these employees in the overeducated group is more than 10 per cent higher than in the non-overeducated group.

These results only partly support our earlier expectations. If we assume that academic professionals and higher executives are at the high-level core of internal labour markets, we would expect that overeducation would also be high among these employees. This is not the case. On the other hand, the characteristics of employees in the service and clerical sectors do support our proposition. As expected, they are a significant part of the overeducated labour force, segments strongly influenced by modern techniques of human resource management. This outcome is also supported by the observation that employees with degrees in economics are found more often in the overeducated group than in the non-overeducated group. The same conclusion holds for those in industrial crafts and for employees with technical training. If we assume that these labour-market segments are affected by the same managerial developments as described, this would yield an explanation for the overeducation in these areas.

Summary

Although there are still many aspects to be researched, we can draw the following conclusions from our analysis. First, the qualitative employment structure in the Netherlands has been upgraded continuously since 1971, though rather weakly between 1985 and 1995. Since 1971 the average educational level of the economically active Dutch labour force also rose steadily, but at a rather higher speed than the employment structure. This results in a serious strain in the labour market. Within the job opportunity structure, the net upgrading trend of jobs does not keep pace with the stronger increase in the average educational level of Dutch employees. Second, overeducation increases slowly but steadily, as our analysis illustrates. More and more workers are employed at one or more job levels below their qualification level. In 1995, this was the case for more than one-third of the Dutch labour force, a clear indication that the process of job allocation in the labour market is far from perfect. Multivariate analysis shows that, besides the least educated, younger employees and women are particularly likely to suffer from the overeducation trend. These groups of employees are overrepresented among the overeducated and (controlled for their level of education) achieve significantly lower job levels in comparison with their non-overeducated contemporaries. Third, the analysis of displacement showed that, through the strong increase in the average level of education at every job level, more highly educated employees elbow out those with less education. This downward displacement strongly restricts employment and career opportunities in the lower levels of the labour market. There are very few higher executives and academic professionals among the overeducated. Although it remains difficult to localize in which segments the process of trickling down is the strongest, it seems that employees in the service sector, clerical staff, and employees with an education in economics or with a technical training are overrepresented among the overeducated.

When we take the general trends in the opportunity structure of the Dutch labour market into consideration, the prospects for the less educated to acquire and keep a job at their appropriate level do not look very bright. Both overeducation and displacement keep threatening the optimal functioning of the supply and demand side of the labour market. These unintended consequences of the Dutch 'poldermodel' are similar to those in the other Western labour-market systems. We recall Livingstone's conclusion that the level of performance underemployment in both the United States and Ontario (Canada) in 1996 ranged from between 40 to 60 per cent (Livingstone, 1998). For West Germany, Büchel and Weisshuhn (1997) report that between 1984 and 1993 20 per cent of all employed persons were underemployed. We conclude that underemployment in the Netherlands is lower than in the United States and Canada and at least comparable to the level in Germany.

What do these results mean for labour-market policy? In the Netherlands labour-market participation is increasing, in absolute terms as well as by comparison with the other EU countries. The level of registered unemployment is relatively low and decreasing. Nevertheless, structural unemployment among the least educated remains high, and a significant shortage of low-income jobs persists (Salverda, 1997).

Policy makers have reacted by fiscally stimulating firms to create low-level jobs for the long-term unemployed (such as 'Melkert' jobs, named after the Dutch minister of social affairs). One can wonder if this offers even a partial solution. Our research clearly indicates that an increasing proportion of jobs is held by employees who are overqualified. These employees block the path to regular employment for less-educated workers. In this context, creating low-level jobs is just a treatment of symptoms and does not offer a structural solution to the job–skill mismatch (Kasarda, 1990). We believe that employment policies aimed at solving this mismatch should focus on the higher job levels of the labour market. That is, instead of exclusively focusing on less-skilled jobs, employment policy should also stimulate the creation of highly skilled jobs that require high educational qualifications. Doing so would ease the problem of overeducation and downward displacement.

From the perspective of overeducation, it seems a societal waste to further invest in collective training programs. This conclusion corresponds with the conventional proposals to reduce the participation in higher education. Such a view on the societal function of education is rather limited, however. Apart from the socio-economic value of education, we argue that a highly qualified labour force is an important asset for developed countries, given the current severity of international competition. In the context of the international division of labour, the human capital of a highly qualified labour force constitutes an important competitive advantage. From a macro-economic perspective, creating highly skilled jobs seems to be a more sensitive strategy than restricting the educational level of the labour force. This strategy could also lead to an increase in lower-level jobs derived from the higher-level jobs. Such a strategy could provide at least a partial solution to the problem of job–skill mismatch at the lower levels of the labour market.

REFERENCES

Asselberghs, K., Batenburg, R., Huijgen, F., & de Witte, M. (1998). *De kwalitatieve structuur van de werkgelegenheid in Nederland, deel 4* [The qualitative employment structure in The Netherlands, Part IV]. Den Haag: OSA (V44).
Büchel, F., & Weisshuhn, G. (1997). Ausbildungsinädequate beschäftigung der

absolventen des bildungssystems [Inadequate job allocation of sixth-formers]. Volkswirtschaftliche Schriften, Heft 471. Berlin: Duncker & Humblot.

Conen, J.G.M., & Huijgen, F. (1980). De kwalitatieve structuur van de werkgelegenheid in 1960 en 1971 [The qualitative employment structure in The Netherlands between 1960 en 1971]. *Economisch Statistische Berichten, 65,* 480–7.

Dagevos, J., van der Laan, L., & Veenman, J. (1997). *Verdringing op de arbeidsmarkt* [Displacement in the labour market]. Assen: Van Gorcum.

de Beer, P. (1996). Laag opgeleiden: Minder kans op een baan, meer kans op ontslag [Lower educated: Less job opportunities, more chances for retirement]. *Economisch Statistische Berichten, 81,* 908–12.

de Grip, A., & Dekker, R. (1993). Winnaars en verliezers op de arbeidsmarkt 1985–1990 [Winners and losers in the Dutch labour market, 1985–1990]. *Tijdschrift voor Arbeidsvraagstukken, 9*(3), 220–9.

Hartog, J., Mekkelholt, E., & van Ophem, H. (1988). Arbeidsmobiliteit in Nederland, 1957–1985 [Labour-market mobility in the Netherlands, 1957–1985]. *Tijdschrift voor Arbeidsvraagstukken, 4*(3), 65–75.

Huijgen, F. (1989). *De kwalitatieve structuur van de werkgelegenheid in Nederland, Deel III* [The qualitative employment structure in the Netherlands, Part III]. s' Gravenhage: OSA (V33).

Kasarda, J. (1990). The jobs–skills mismatch. In R.T. LeGates & F. Stout (Eds.), *The city reader.* London: Routledge.

Livingstone, D.W. (1998). *The education–jobs gap: Underemployment or economic democracy.* Boulder, CO: Westview Press.

Moelker, R. (1992). *Zou hij onze nieuwe werknemer kunnen zijn?* [Could he be our new employee?]. Unpublished doctoral dissertation, Academisch Boeken Centrum, De Lier.

Salverda, W. (1992). *Youth unemployment dynamics of the Dutch labour market, 1955–1988.* Groningen: Wolters-Noordhoff.

Salverda, W. (1997). *Dutch policies to increase low-skilled employment.* Paper presented at a Workshop on Contributions towards Overcoming the Employment Crisis, Rijksuniversiteit Groningen.

Teulings, C.N. (1990). *Conjunctuur en kwalificatie* [Economic developments and qualifications]. Unpublished doctoral dissertation, Stichting voor Economisch Onderzoek der Universiteit van Amsterdam.

Thurow, L. (1975). *Generating inequality: Mechanisms of distribution in the U.S. economy.* New York: Basic Books.

Webbink, H.D., van der Vegt, C., & Bon, J.M. (1995). *De werkgelegenheid naar beroep en opleiding, Deel 2 1994–1998* [Employment, occupation, and education, Part 2 1994–1998]. Den Haag: OSA (W137).

Wielers, R., & Glebbeek, A. (1995). Graduates and the labour market in the Netherlands: Three hypotheses and some data. *European Journal of Education, 30*(1), 11–30.

Wolbers, M., de Graaf, P., & Ultee, W. (1997). *Een verklaring voor diploma-inflatie op de Nederlandse arbeidsmarkt: Structurele veranderingen en gewijzigde voorkeuren?* [An explanation of credential inflation on the Dutch labour market: Structural changes and changing preferences?]. Paper presented at the SISWO-werkgroep 'Sociale stratificatie en Mobiliteit,' Katholieke Universiteit Nijmegen.

4. The Transition from Vocational Training to Employment in Germany: Does Region Matter?

Hildegard Schaeper, Thomas Kühn, and Andreas Witzel

Does Region Matter?

'Space-blindness' is a traditional feature of sociological theory in general and of life-course research in particular (cf Herlyn, 1990, p. 7; Konau, 1977, p. 6; Urry, 1981), and, with a few exceptions, space continues to be a neglected category (cf Dangschat, 1994, p. 336).

Marginalizing the spatial dimensions of social phenomena implies a belief that societies are homogeneous, unified entities. This assumption has frequently been criticized, however. In the German tradition of social-structure analysis during the 1960s, for example, it was quite common to distinguish between rural and urban areas (cf Bertram and Dannenbeck, 1990, p. 217). In the 1980s, the predominant *vertical*, occupation-based perspective on social stratification and social inequality was questioned by the discovery of new *horizontal* inequalities, including gender-specific inequality and regional disparities (cf Berger and Hradil, 1990, p. 3; Geissler, 1996, p. 320). In the 1990s, the unification of the two German nations fostered or even revitalized the sensitivity towards spatial differentiations within one society.

As far as the conceptualization of space in general sociological theory is concerned, Giddens (1979, 1984) repeatedly emphasized that time and space are constitutive for any social phenomenon and that neither human agency nor social systems can be understood without making reference to time and space. On the one hand, social systems (reproduced social practices) exist only in so far as they succeed in binding time and space so that similar social practices occur across varying spans of time and space. On the other hand, Giddens regards time and space as indispensable for the description of social action and interaction because all social action is contextual and 'all social interaction is *situated* interaction – situated in space and time' (Giddens, 1984, p. 86).

However, in view of the ongoing process of individualization and globalization, Giddens (1994) points to the possibility that space (or 'regionalization') loses some of its significance for social action. Objections to this assumption refer to the fact that human beings may not be free in their choice of social relations and places and that the continuing effects of early socialization experiences in regionally differing cultural contexts are not taken into account. Even Beck, the most prominent German proponent of the individualization debate, identifies the 'unbroken influence of regional cultural identities which are tied to the history of landscapes and places' (1983, p. 60; our translation) as an important counter-force against the process of individualization.

It is exactly this unsettled issue of the role of space we want to address from the life-course perspective. Focusing on the transition from vocational training to employment of a cohort of young adults, and taking two German regions (Bremen in the north and Munich in the south of Germany) as exemplary cases, our paper is guided by the overall question: Does region matter in the structuring of the life course and the construction of biographies?

As we will discuss in more detail in the next section, we refer to space as a contextual attribute of social action, and we concentrate on the meso level of regional opportunity contexts. In addition, our research question suggests a particular theoretical point of view. Following Giddens and other sociologists who strive to overcome the dualism of structure and action, we assume a knowledgeable and purposive actor whose knowledge is bounded and whose actions are constrained, but not determined, by sociocultural factors.

Methodologically, this framework, which comes close to the one employed by Anisef and Axelrod (in this volume), is realized by a combined use of qualitative and quantitative data. By choosing this triangulation approach we are able not only to analyse and quantify the structural impact of, for example, gender, occupation trained for, educational attainment, and region, but also to take into account the individual's aspirations, intentions, and perceptions of structural features. These subjective factors underlie and accompany career decisions and are considered as important mediators between social structures, social institutions, and individual action.

Conceptual Framework and Research Design

According to the non-dualistic conceptualization of the individual life course, our study simultaneously takes up a structural as well as a subjective perspective. As far as structural aspects are concerned, life-course research traditionally puts much emphasis on the impact of gender, race, social-class origin, educational achievement, and – this is especially true for Germany – the occupation trained for. Due to the peculiarities of the German educational and labour-market system, occupation-specific qualifications indeed play a key role in the shaping of occupational careers in Germany (for an international comparison see Shavit and Müller, 1998).

The German System of Vocational Education and Training

The most important part of the German system of vocational education and training is still the so-called dual system of apprenticeship, which combines the training for practical skills in the workplace with the learning of more formal skills in vocational schools. In the 1990s, about two-thirds of an age cohort entered an apprenticeship, typically after completion of general schooling at the lower or intermediate level (figure 4.1 roughly portrays the basic structure of the German education system). In the last two decades, however, an increasing proportion of higher-level (or grammar school) graduates, who are entitled to attend a university, opt for a vocational training in the dual system, especially for an apprenticeship in one of the more prestigious white-collar occupations. Some of them regard the vocational training as a genuine alternative to higher education; others later on decide to use their university-entrance qualification and to resume their educational career.

In Germany, 374 training occupations are officially recognized. The high number of different trades points to the fact that the German apprenticeship system is horizontally segmented and that it equips young people with more or less narrowly defined specialized skills for a particular occupation. In addition, the vocational training in Germany is highly standardized. Curricula and examinations are defined in a complex negotiation process with state authorities, employers' representatives, and trade unions and are applied nation-wide.

Figure 4.1   Basic Structure of the Education System in Germany

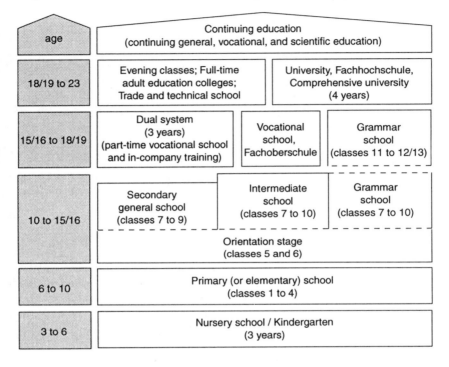

In societies like Germany, where there is a close link between vocational training and the requirements of the work sphere, employers are likely to avoid costly on-the-job-training by recruiting workers who match their demands. As a consequence, mobility between skilled occupations without the acquisition of additional formal qualifications is comparatively rare, and job opportunities depend not only on the level of qualification but also (and to a high degree) on the occupation trained for and the supply–demand ratio in particular occupational fields (cf Müller, Steinmann, and Ell, 1998).

Because of the occupational segmentation of the German labour market and its strong institutional ties with the educational system, vocational specialization, together with level of educational attainment, turns out to be a major determinant of career development. Other classical factors of social inequality – such as social background and gender – retain some significance (cf Müller, Steinmann, and Ell, 1998), but primarily affect access to the level of general education and to a certain training occupation – thereby influencing the employment career to a large extent indirectly, mediated through education.

The Concept of Region

Whereas life-course research generally pays little attention to spatial issues, Giddens (1984) considers the spatial (and temporal) organization of social life as an important frame of reference for action. Each action is situated in space – that is, each action takes place in a specific 'locale,' a physical region which constitutes the setting of action and which is used to establish its meaning. Locales are internally regionalized – divided into different zones of typical social practices. Both locales and regions, may differ in their extension and encompass a great variation in scale (see the examples given by Giddens, 1984, pp 118 ff). In our analysis we neglect the immediate setting for action, focusing instead on the nation-state of Germany and, within this locale, on regions of medium dimensions. When using the term 'region' we refer to this meso level of spatial organization.

As with occupational structure, systems of labour-market organization, and gender and class relations, regions constitute an objective structuration context (objective in so far as it pre-exists individual action and cannot be changed by the individual actor), which exhibits specific structural properties. Conceptualized as resources and rules (cf Giddens, 1984), these structural properties refer on the one hand to opportunity structures, which offer, for example, different occupational prospects and educational chances and thereby provide varying possibilities of realizing one's desires and intentions. These objective, regionally clustered sociostructural factors constitute a phenomenon that we call regional disparities. On the other hand, as the notion of rules indicates, structures include the cultural dimension (norms, values, meanings, etcetera). However, as empirical studies do not indicate any marked cultural differences between the two selected German regions (cf Bertram, Bayer, and Bauereiss 1993; Nauck, 1995), we confine ourselves to opportunity structures and operationalize the concept of region as a spatial combination of places with a similar economic structure and resource provision or – more specifically – with comparable labour-market conditions.

Region, Occupation, and the Life Course

Although our main research question focuses on the significance of region, we also have to take into account the occupation trained for, which in Germany is of crucial importance for the entire occupational life course. We neglect other factors such as gender and social-class origin, but we make sure that they do not bias our results. In part, these factors are closely linked to the selected training occupations and thereby are implicitly included in our analysis. Thus, we expect that the transition from vocational training to employment and the career patterns which follow depend on the region where the job applicants completed their apprenticeship, as well as on the occupation trained for. With respect to the joint effect of occupation and region we will consider several hypotheses in our quantitative analysis (cf Bolder, 1991, pp 27 ff). The 'cumulation hypothesis' assumes that unfavourable conditions multiply, so that occupational groups with poor job prospects are additionally discriminated against by weak economic structures. The 'disparity hypothesis' suggests that regional disparities affect all occupational groups in a similar way. And the 'hypothesis of partial indifference' claims that differing regional opportunity structures matter only in the case of advantaged graduates and remain indifferent in other cases.

Structure and Agency and the Concept of 'Self-Socialization'

When acting, actors perpetually draw upon the rules and resources embedded in the action context. Thus, structure influences (and, as Giddens points out, at the same time enables) actions and decisions by providing and restricting opportunities. Social structure, however, is not external to individuals and to a large extent does not operate directly. It mainly comes into effect after being translated into the individual's system of perceptions, interpretations, aspirations, and action strategies. Following Heinz and colleagues (cf Heinz et al., 1998), we call this process which links social structure and personality development 'self-socialization' or – with regard to the occupational pathway – 'occupational self-socialization.'

The concept of self-socialization was introduced in order to emphasize the proactive, self-reflexive, and self-monitored process of biography construction. It is based on the assumption that life-course transitions require individuals to explore alternatives self-reflexively, to assess the outcomes of decisions in view of their personal goals, to evaluate their experiences, and to adapt their aspirations to the available options and given opportunities. Occupational self-socialization, then, means 'that young people, as well as adults, have to integrate experiences of social selection and organizational participation with their aspirations and skills before and after transitions in order to shape their vocational career' (Heinz et al., 1998, p. 93). Thus, current career aspirations and action strategies result from a complex interplay between the initial aspirations and goals and the occupational context, which offers varying degrees of job opportunities, risks of unemployment, promotion prospects, and working conditions.

Biographical Action Orientations, Region, and the Life Course

As occupational opportunities depend not only on the occupation trained for but also on the regional labour market, it seems reasonable to assume that young skilled workers develop different orientations in different regional contexts. Drawing upon our qualitative data we will examine this assumption and seek to answer the question: Does the regional context exert not only a direct impact on career decisions by *objectively* widening and narrowing the range of available options, but also an indirect influence by shaping the *subjective* sphere of aspirations and orientations?

Life-course transitions and life-course events which we observe with quantitative methods can be understood as the result of an active, purposeful process of biography construction. Thus, by systematically relating the different analytical levels – that is, through the qualitative and the quantitative approach – we are able to extend our understanding of the micro foundation of life-course patterns and to explain observed life-course patterns on the basis of appropriate empirical data.

Data and Methods

According to our action model, which treats objective and subjective factors as equally important, a panel study on the occupational careers and family-related passages of young adults[1] was designed to capture both the structural aspects of the life course and the individual meanings and purposes involved.

In order to analyse and quantify the effect of structural factors on the outcomes of biographical decision-making processes on a general, representative level, we carried out a longitudinal questionnaire survey with a sample of young, skilled, blue- and white-collar workers who completed their vocational training in 1989–90 at the average age of 20.7 years. The first quantitative panel wave, carried out in 1989, included about 2,200 apprentices of six major occupations (bank employees, office workers, retail salespersons, hairdressers, car mechanics, and industrial mechanics) in the two German regions Bremen and Munich. Two more waves of this 'macro panel' were conducted in 1991 and 1994 (with approximately 1,000 respondents). In 1997–8 a fourth and last wave was undertaken. The quantitative results as presented in this paper rest on only the first three waves.

The standardized panel study was accompanied by a 'micro panel' of originally 198 and, in the third and last wave in 1994, 91 qualitative (semi-structured) interviews. These interviews were intended to gather ethnographic descriptions of occupational cultures, to investigate the ways in which actors describe, perceive, and interpret objective opportunity structures, to explore the aspirations developed by them under specific working and living conditions, and to examine the means for achieving their goals. The participants of the micro panel were chosen on the basis of the quantitative sample. The sampling criteria comprised sociostructural factors that were considered relevant for biographical agency, and for contrasting or extreme cases. In this way, the quantitative sample served as the pool for an optimal placement of the qualitative subsample.

Because of its composition, the quantitative sample (and, consequently, the qualitative subsample also) systematically takes into account gender issues and differing career prospects. Two of the selected occupations are male-dominated (car mechanics and industrial mechanics); hairdressers and office workers are predominantly female; and the remaining two occupations (bank employees and retail sales persons) are gender mixed. When the project started, car mechanics, hairdressers, and retail sales persons were exposed to a high risk of unemployment; industrial mechanics, bank employees, and office workers, on the other hand, enjoyed relatively good job prospects. As well, as will be shown below in more detail, the two selected regions also offer quite distinct labour-market opportunities.

Bremen and Munich Compared

In contrast to other research projects which included the entire territory of Germany and which identified homogeneous regional contexts by using several indicators, our study focused on two pre-selected German regions. We therefore had to prove that they represent regions as defined above. If such proof can be furnished, Bremen and Munich can be considered exemplary cases which stand for a broader range of regions with similar characteristics.

As Munich and Bremen differ largely with regard to economic structures and labour-market opportunities, there is much evidence for assuming them to be different regions. Whereas Munich is characterized by an expanding services sector, which itself offers good job prospects and in addition favours economic development in other trades and industries, Bremen is still suffering from the decline of its old core industries (especially ship building and steel manufacturing), which dominated the local economy until the late 1980s. These economic differences are clearly reflected in statistics on unemployment and training opportunities.

In 1986, the year when our cohort started their apprenticeship training, 11 out of 100 applicants in Bremen did not succeed (supply–demand ratio of apprenticeships: 89.3:100). At the same time, the supply of apprenticeships in Munich exceeded the demand considerably, even in the most prestigious occupations (supply–demand ratio: 110.2:100). Whereas Bremen school-leavers looking for training vacancies faced a fierce competition and the risk of ending up in less-attractive vocational programs, their counterparts in Munich were in a much more privileged situation. They could feel confident of being accepted for an apprenticeship and even had a good chance of gaining access to the preferred training occupation.

The same pattern of regional disparities holds when we look at the overall unemployment figures. In 1989, when the majority of our respondents completed vocational training, the risk of unemployment in Bremen was almost three times as high as in Munich (12.8 per cent in Bremen as compared to 4.6 per cent in Munich). Up to 1994, the time of the third panel wave, the situation did not change significantly (unemployment rate in Bremen: 11.9 per cent; in Munich: 5.6 per cent). All in all, Bremen – in contrast to Munich, with its prosperous economy – showed the typical characteristics of a depressed labour-market region.

The Transition from Vocational Training to Employment and the Early Occupational Career

In order to estimate the effect of occupation and region on the career development of young German adults, we analysed three indicators: the opportunity of employment with the training company after completion of apprenticeship; the risk of unemployment; and the occupational status five years after job entry.

Possibility of Staying in the Training Company

In comparison with other societies, in Germany the transition from school to work is relatively smooth. The institutional ties between vocational training and employers allow a good many young workers to enter regular employment in the training company after having successfully completed their apprenticeship. An apprenticeship does not guarantee employment with the training company, of course. Rather, the chance of being taken on depends on the trainee's performance and the labour requirements of the training company, which, in turn, partly depend on the economic standing of the particular trade and the overall and regional level of economic development.

In order to analyse the impact of the training occupation and the region of residence on the likelihood of being employed in the training company, we used a weighted least squares (WLS) method of categorical data analysis, developed by Grizzle, Starmer, and Koch (1969), also known as the GSK approach. This statistical tool is especially well suited to examine interaction effects. When dealing with small samples, however, only a few covariates can be included in the model. We therefore carried out an additional logistic regression analysis which made sure that the exclusion of other variables such as gender, class origin, school-level attainment, and size of the training company did not bias the results.

Figure 4.2 clearly demonstrates the dependence of employment chances on the occupation trained for.[2] The proportion of bank employees who were offered a job by their company upon completion of apprenticeship is considerably higher (plus 11.4 points) than the average percentage of 77.2 per cent. In marked contrast to this occupational group, a comparatively small fraction of the car mechanics report that they got the possibility of staying in the training company (18.0 points below average). The commensurate percentages in the remaining training occupations are between these extreme groups and do not differ much from the overall mean.

The estimated effect of region provides a preliminary answer to our general research question: Yes, region indeed matters. In Munich, the chances of being kept on after having passed the skilled worker's

Figure 4.2   Impact of Training Occupation and Region on the Possibility of Obtaining Work in the Training Company upon Completion of Apprenticeship (GSK model)

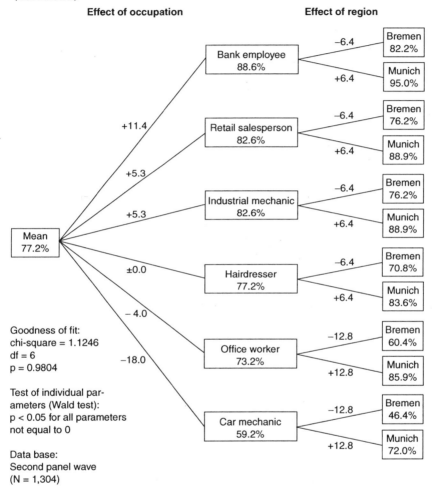

examination were considerably higher than in Bremen. The difference between the proportion of respondents in Bremen and Munich who received an offer of employment was at least 12 per cent. In addition, we observed an interesting interaction effect between training occupation and region which supports the cumulation hypothesis. In the occupations with the lowest rates of employment offers (office workers and car mechanics) the effect of region is twice as high as in occupations with more favourable job prospects.

Unemployment

Of course, whether the training company offers an employment contract or not does not determine what trainees opt for after having completed vocational training. Depending on their personal plans and preferences as well as on the working conditions offered, young skilled workers can either accept or refuse an employment offer. Those graduates of the dual system who must leave the training company have several alternatives to avoid unemployment. Consequently, unemployment rates are not as high as the proportion of respondents without an employment offer suggests. In the month following the skilled worker's examination, roughly 8 per cent of the respondents classified themselves as unemployed. During the first year after completion of apprenticeship, a total of about 12 per cent experienced at least one unemployment period of at least one month. While the occupation-specific and region-specific patterns described above also apply to the unemployment risk in the early occupational career, the situation changes when looking at later developments (figure 4.3).

Several results deserve special attention. First, the advantaged situation of those who were trained as bank employees continued to exist. The proportion of bank employees who were affected by unemployment of at least one month during a period of one to five years following vocational training (12.7 per cent) is considerably below the average of 17 per cent. Second, car mechanics, who faced the worst starting conditions, appear to have been able to compensate for this disadvantage; their unemployment rate is above average, but the deviation from the overall mean is comparatively small. Third, the favourable labour-market conditions for industrial mechanics – as indicated by the high rate of employment offers and by the low unemployment rates during the first year after completion of apprenticeship – did not continue. Their unemployment rate in the observation period is slightly, but significantly, above average. Fourth, in comparison with the possibility of staying in the training company and the unemployment rate in the first year, the effect of region decreased. For the bank employees it disappeared completely. The other occupational groups were equally affected by regional disparities. An additional disadvantage which characterized the very early occupational stage for car

Figure 4.3 Impact of Training Occupation and Region on Unemployment between One and Five Years after Completion of Apprenticeship (GSK model)

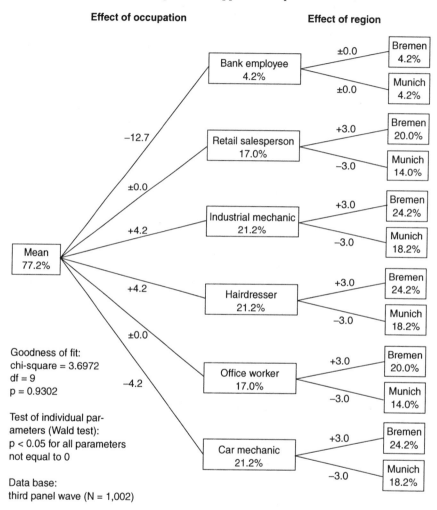

mechanics and office workers cannot be observed any longer. As far as the further career development is concerned, the cumulation hypothesis does not hold.

In view of the declining impact of region, the question arises how the disadvantaged Bremen subpopulation compensated for unfavourable labour-market conditions. At least theoretically, several possibilities come to mind. Young skilled workers may wait for an employment opportunity in the occupation trained for or try to find a job in another occupation. Depending on educational prerequisites and financial means, they can return to school, commence an additional apprenticeship, or enrol in an institution of higher education. Finally, some of the former apprentices may decide to stay at home as a housewife or, in exceptional cases, as a house-husband. In the next section we examine the different strategies in more detail. To simplify the analysis somewhat, we confined ourselves to the respondents' occupational status at the time of the third panel wave – that is, up to five years after completion of apprenticeship.

Occupational Status Five Years after Completion of Apprenticeship

To examine the respondents' occupational whereabouts at the time when the third panel wave was carried out, we distinguished among four possibilities: (1) working in the occupation trained for; (2) working in another occupation; (3) returned to school, enrolled in an institution of higher education or in a program of further education; and (4) not in the labour force (e.g., unemployed, in military service, on maternity leave, housewife/husband). As the data requirements are not fully met, we did not estimate a multi-response GSK model, but rather present the observed percentage distribution (table 4.1).

Again, the data reveal substantial differences in career patterns among the occupational groups. Office workers are predominantly still working in the occupation trained for, thus showing the most stable career pattern. In spite of the relatively scarce employment offers made by the training company and in spite of the average unemployment risk during the observation period, a majority of these respondents succeeded in finding a job in their occupation. To a certain extent, apprentices profited from a vocational training that equipped them with relatively broad skills and thereby allowed them to work in a wide range of different fields, from secretarial tasks to accounting to typewriting to personnel management.

Bank employees showed the highest propensity to re-enter the educational system or – more accurately – to study at an institution of higher education. They used their educational certificates (a large fraction of them achieved a university-entrance qualification prior to voca-

TABLE 4.1
Occupational Status Five Years after Completion of Apprenticeship (row percentages)

Training occupation	Region	Occupational status			
		In occupation trained for	In another occupation	In school, further training, or university	Other
Bank employee	all	59	4	33	4
	Bremen	59	1	38	1
	Munich	59	7	29	6
Office worker	all	74	9	8	8
	Bremen	70	10	11	10
	Munich	77	9	7	8
Industrial mechanic	all	46	18	28	8
	Bremen	44	15	28	13
	Munich	47	21	28	8
Car mechanic	all	51	24	10	15
	Bremen	52	28	8	13
	Munich	51	23	12	16
Hairdresser	all	43	34	7	16
	Bremen	47	33	2	19
	Munich	38	35	14	14
Retail salesperson	all	64	17	8	11
	Bremen	67	17	6	10
	Munich	60	17	11	11
All	all	60	14	17	9
	Bremen	59	14	17	10
	Munich	61	14	17	8

Data base: Third panel wave (N = 1,038)

tional training) in order to accumulate 'human capital' and to foster their career development. Industrial mechanics exhibited a similar tendency towards further educational investments. However, their educational careers differed considerably from those of the bank employees. Due to their lower school-level attainment, most of the industrial mechanics first had to return to school in order to acquire the formal qualifications that would allow them to enrol in an institution of higher education.

Car mechanics and hairdressers resembled industrial mechanics in their tendency to leave their occupation. Unlike industrial mechanics, however, car mechanics and hairdressers seldom engaged in further education. Rather, they took work in another occupation or left the labour force. It seems that car mechanics and hairdressers, on the one hand, and industrial mechanics, on the other, pursue different strategies when facing poor employment opportunities and working conditions.

With regard to regional differences, no overall pattern that applies to all occupational groups can be observed. In two occupations we found a higher percentage of the Bremen subgroup re-entering the educational system. With the office workers the commensurate fractions differ only slightly, but with the bank employees the difference amounts to roughly 10 per cent. The fact that far more Bremen than Munich bank employees went on to attend a university can be partly attributed to the higher proportion of the Bremen respondents who achieved a university-entrance qualification before starting their apprenticeship (when controlling for school-level attainment, the effect of region diminishes); nevertheless, it helps us to explain why the former – despite more difficult starting conditions – did not experience a higher risk of unemployment than the latter.

In three occupational groups (car mechanics, hairdressers, and retail salespersons), a larger fraction of Munich than Bremen respondents returned to the educational system. By contrast, Bremen car mechanics more often ended up in another occupation, whereas Bremen hairdressers and retail salespersons were more likely than their Munich counterparts to stay in the occupation trained for.

Bremen and Munich industrial mechanics showed the same inclination to acquire additional qualifications. However, in this case the chosen categorization conceals quite distinct educational choices. Most of the Munich industrial mechanics enrolled in upgrading training programs which provide an advanced vocational training and lead experienced skilled workers to master craftsman's or technician's qualifications. In contrast, the majority of the Bremen subgroup entered an institution of higher education.

The various results of our quantitative analysis can be summarized as follows. Our data show that the initial transition from vocational training to employment is more difficult in an economically weak region than in a prospering one, and that unfavourable regional opportunity structures affect occupational groups with poor career prospects to a larger extent than those with good employment chances. In subsequent occupational careers, however, regional differences in unemployment rates diminish, and the cumulative effect of regional and occupation-specific disadvantages disappears.

The analysis of the occupational status up to five years after completion of apprenticeship gives some preliminary explanations for the declining impact of region on unemployment rates and suggests that young skilled workers develop different strategies when dealing with the risks of the life course. Some respondents from the disadvantaged region resumed their educational career, thus trying to avoid unemployment or unsatisfactory working conditions and to attain a better standing in the labour market. Others found a job in the occupation trained for or accepted a job outside the training occupation in order to make their living.

We cannot check whether our relatively broad categorization of occupational whereabouts conceals finer regional differences. According to the concept of self-socialization, however, we assume that unfavourable occupation-specific and regional employment chances and career prospects to some extent result in low occupational aspirations, which in turn lead to the acceptance of jobs with little opportunity for promotion.

In the next section we will elaborate on this supposition by drawing upon our qualitative data. The analysis seeks to answer the question how, in what way, and to what extent the occupational and regional context shapes the individual's aspirations and orientations – thereby providing a deeper insight into the processes that underlie the career patterns observed on the quantitative level. Since a thorough discussion of all occupations in our study would go beyond the scope of our paper, we focus on four occupational groups as exemplary cases: bank employees, office workers, hairdressers, and industrial mechanics.

Aspirations, Orientations, and Action Strategies

In order to explore this subjective dimension of biography construction, we analysed our qualitative interviews with respect to the respondents' career-related biographical action orientations – that is, their occupational aspirations, strategies for realizing their goals, and assessment of the outcomes (cf Heinz et al., 1998). For the purpose of this paper we refer to two clusters of action orientations that we distinguish by the relative importance of upward career mobility. The first group represents young adults who value career advancement highly. They see work as the crucial domain in life and try hard to develop their competence and career. Their readiness to work hard and to perform efficiently is accompanied by the expectation of earning a good salary and of being promoted to a responsible position. The second group comprises young skilled workers who set less store on climbing the career ladder. Instead, they regard job security, good working conditions, a fair salary, or a pleasant climate at the workplace as most important.

The distribution of aspiration levels clearly indicates the connection between occupation trained for and the orientations developed in the occupational context, thus helping to explain the different career outcomes as observed at the time of the third panel wave. Bank employees predominantly belonged to the group with a strong orientation towards upward career mobility. They tried to realize their ambitious occupational goals either by acquiring academic degrees or by using the institutionalized promotion pathways offered by the banking sector. The office workers were distributed more evenly among the two groups, but, on the whole, a majority of them can be assigned to the second group, which places less emphasis on career advancement. Industrial mechanics were trained in an occupation that has always been regarded as one of the most prestigious occupations in the technical and industrial sector; many of them therefore developed high occupational aspirations. Their everyday job reality, however, often did not meet their expectations. Consequently, the more ambitious industrial mechanics sought to foster their career advancement by means of further education. Hairdressers, in contrast, scarcely aimed at attaining a high occupational status. As apprentices they already anticipated an occupational situation characterized by limited career prospects, low salaries, and unpleasant working conditions.

As far as the issue of region is concerned, we found only small differences between the orientations of bank employees trained in Bremen and in Munich. This finding is striking in view of the higher percentage of Bremen bank employees attending university. It can be partly attributed to the disproportionate representation of university students in our qualitative sample. To a certain degree, however, it reflects the different labour-market conditions in Bremen and Munich. The favourable promotion opportunities in Munich facilitated career advancement and the satisfaction of occupational aspirations without achieving academic degrees. As a result of their high school-level attainment and prestigious training, Bremen bank employees developed similar orientations, but, after completion of apprenticeship, they were exposed to a higher risk of unemployment and received less attractive job offers, which in addition often required geographical mobility. Under these circumstances the accumulation of extra educational credentials seems a reasonable strategy to gain an advantage in the competitive arena of the labour market.

The picture of quite homogeneous regional orientation patterns does not apply to the office workers. Office workers who were trained in Bremen showed less occupational ambition than their counterparts in Munich. An explanation for these differences can be found when looking at the economic features of Bremen and Munich and the corresponding job prospects. As our interviews indicate, the expanding services sector in Munich offered a wide range of promising options and thereby encouraged the development of a strong orientation towards career advancement.

The labour markets for office workers in Bremen and Munich differed considerably, and more than those for bank employees. When tackling the task of forming an occupational biography, young office workers made allowance for the chances and risks, opportunities and constraints, that the regional labour market offered them. In order to arrive at career decisions, they had to balance structural conditions, resources, and personal aspirations. It seems that in the depressed labour market of Bremen this process, which we term a process of 'self-socialization,' often takes the form of reducing occupational aspirations.

This also holds true in the case of hairdressers. Munich hairdressers more often aimed at higher occupational status than their Bremen counterparts, and more often saw a good chance of improving their career by re-entering the vocational education system and achieving a trade master's qualification. In response to low returns on further educational investments, Bremen hairdressers, in contrast, adapted to difficult working conditions and low wages and focused their aspirations on experiencing a pleasant social climate at the workplace.

As with bank employees, industrial mechanics in Bremen and Munich showed similar levels of occupational aspirations. With comparatively better job prospects, the industrial mechanics from Munich, however, were able to fulfil their career expectations *within* their occupation by attending upgrading training programs, whereas the Bremen subgroup had to make a greater effort in order to realize ambitious occupational goals.

The office workers and hairdressers included in our study provide an example of the socialization effect of regional opportunity structures. Our findings support the assumption that different regional occupational chances affect the level of workers' aspirations, but conflict with the findings of other studies. Rudd and Evans (1998), for instance, examined 16- to 19-year-olds in two colleges of further education in differing labour markets in England, and observed similar levels of optimism in the two regions. This may be explained by the fact that their sample had not yet experienced the realities of the labour market, whereas our respondents had already faced them when looking for an apprenticeship.

The results of our qualitative analysis also show that the regional context is only one of several factors that are associated with occupational self-socialization. As the example of bank employees and industrial mechanics indicates, occupation-specific characteristics as well as educational background must also be taken into account. In these cases, however, regional opportunity structures are decisive to the strategies young adults pursue in order to shape their occupational pathways.

Conclusion

By starting with two competing assumptions about spatial impacts on social life, our analysis was guided by the overall question: Does region matter in the structuring of the life course and the construction of biographies? We sought to answer this question by drawing upon quantitative and qualitative longitudinal data from two German regions. We examined the extent to which regional disparities affected the occupational life course of a cohort of young skilled workers and in what way training, working, and labour-market experiences influenced individual action orientations and strategies.

Our findings suggest that there is no simple and single answer to our research question. The early occupational careers show a considerable impact of region on employment opportunities, especially in the case of poor occupation-specific labour-market chances. To that extent, region indeed matters, and there is some empirical evidence for the assumption of the cumulation hypothesis – namely, that unfavourable conditions multiply. In the subsequent occupational life course, however, regional differences in unemployment rates decrease and assume a similar extent in all occupations. This observation supports the disparity hypothesis, which suggests that regional disparities affect all occupational groups in a similar way. Finally, the data on occupational whereabouts up to five years after completion of apprenticeship provide a quite heterogeneous pattern which substantiates neither the cumulation hypothesis nor the disparity hypothesis nor the supposition of (partial) indifference.

Our qualitative data shed some light on this confusing picture and suggest a more sophisticated hypothesis, which takes into account individual agency as well as the complex process of biography construction over time. Depending on individual resources and on socialization experiences associated with the occupational context and the educational background, regional opportunity structures affect action orientations and strategies in different ways. In the case of young adults who were trained in occupations of low prestige and limited career prospects (e.g., hairdressers and office workers, who often regard the chosen vocational training as a less-than-ideal solution), poor regional labour-market conditions frequently keep occupational aspirations down. As a result, career decisions are mainly guided by the principle of achieving and maintaining job security and continuity, either within or outside the training occupation. Among those trained for a relatively prestigious occupation (such as bank employees and industrial mechanics), the level of occupational aspirations seems to be quite independent of regional opportunity structures. To a certain extent, however, regional characteristics determine the strategies young adults take in order to realize their goals. Given limited regional employment opportunities and promotion prospects, young adults more often try to achieve their aspirations by acquiring academic degrees. Favourable labour-market conditions, on the other hand, increase workers' chances of climbing the career ladder *within* the training occupation – either without additional formal qualifications or after having completed company-based (bank employees) or school-based (industrial mechanics) upgrading training programs.

NOTES

1 The research project 'Managing Occupational Status and Forming a Family: Skilled Workers Ten Years after Leaving School' is part of the Bremen Special Research Centre *Status Passages and Risks in the Life Course,* funded by the German Research Foundation (DFG). In addition to the authors of this paper, Walter R. Heinz and Jens Zinn collaborated in this study.

2 Strictly speaking, our sample is not a random sample. Therefore, significance

tests are used not to infer from the sample to a population but to assess the stability of a sample value.

REFERENCES

Beck, U. (1983). Jenseits von Klasse und Stand? In R. Kreckel (Ed.), *Soziale Ungleichheiten* (pp 35–74). Göttingen: Schwartz.

Berger, P.A., & Hradil, S. (1990). Die Modernisierung sozialer Ungleichheit – und die neuen Konturen ihrer Erforschung. In P.A. Berger & S. Hradil (Eds), *Lebenslagen, Lebensläufe, Lebensstile* (pp 3–24). Göttingen: Schwartz.

Bertram, H., Bayer, H., & Bauereiss, R. (1993). *Familien-Atlas: Lebenslagen und Regionen in Deutschland.* Opladen: Leske & Budrich.

Bertram, H., & Dannenbeck, C. (1990). Pluralisierung von Lebenslagen und Individualisierung von Lebensführungen: Zur Theorie und Empirie regionaler Disparitäten in der Bundesrepublik Deutschland. In P.A. Berger & S. Hradil (Eds), *Lebenslagen, Lebensläufe, Lebensstile* (pp 207–29). Göttingen: Schwartz.

Bolder, A. (1991). *Der Übergang von der Berufsausbildung ins Erwerbsleben unter ungleichen regionalen Ausgangsbedingungen in Nordrhein-Westfalen.* Köln: Institut zur Erforschung sozialer Chancen.

Dangschat, J.S. (1994). Lebenstile in der Stadt: Raumbezug und konkreter Ort von Lebensstilen und Lebensstilisierungen. In J.S. Dangschat & J. Blasius (Eds), *Lebensstile in den Städten: Konzepte und Methoden* (pp 335–54). Opladen: Leske & Budrich.

Geissler, R. (1996). Kein Abschied von Klasse und Schicht: Ideologische Gefahren der deutschen Sozialstrukturanalyse. *Kölner Zeitschrift für Soziologie und Sozialpsychologie, 48*(2), 319–38.

Giddens, A. (1979). *Central problems in social theory: Action, structure and contradiction in social analysis.* Berkeley: University of California Press.

Giddens, A. (1984). *The constitution of society: Outline of the theory of structuration.* Cambridge: Polity Press.

Giddens, A. (1994). Living in a post-traditional society. In U. Beck, A. Giddens, & S. Lash (Eds), *Reflexive modernization: Politics, tradition and aesthetics in modern social order* (pp 56–109). Cambridge: Polity Press.

Grizzle, J.E., Starmer, C.F., & Koch, G.G. (1969). Analysis of categorical data by linear models. *Biometrics, 25*(3), 489–504.

Heinz, W.R., Kelle, U., Witzel, A., & Zinn, J. (1998). Vocational training and career development in Germany: Results from a longitudinal study. *International Journal of Behavioral Development, 22*(1), 77–101.

Herlyn, U. (1990). Zur Aneignung von Raum im Lebensverlauf. In L. Bertels & U. Herlyn (Eds), *Lebenslauf und Raumerfahrung* (pp 7–34). Opladen: Leske & Budrich.

Konau, E. (1977). *Raum und soziales Handeln: Studien zu einer vernachlässigten Dimension soziologischer Theoriebildung*. Stuttgart: Enke.

Müller, W., Steinmann, S., & Ell, R. (1998). Education and labour-market entry in Germany. In Y. Shavit & W. Müller (Eds), *From school to work: A comparative study of educational qualifications and occupational destinations* (pp 143–88). Oxford: Clarendon Press.

Nauck, B. (1995). Regionale Milieus von Familien in Deutschland nach der politischen Vereinigung. In B. Nauck & C. Onnen-Isemann (Eds), *Familien im Brennpunkt von Wissenschaft und Forschung* (pp 91–121). Berlin: Luchterhand.

Rudd, P., & Evans, K. (1998). Structure and agency in youth transitions: Student experiences of vocational further education. *Journal of Youth Studies, 1*(1), 39–62.

Shavit, Y., & Müller, W. (Eds). (1998). *From school to work: A comparative study of educational qualifications and occupational destinations*. Oxford: Clarendon Press.

Urry, J. (1981). Localities, regions and social class. *International Journal of Urban and Regional Research, 5*(4), 455–74.

5. Restructuring Work, Restructuring Gender: The Movement of Women into Non-traditional Occupations in Canada[1]

Karen D. Hughes

Since the early 1970s the life course of women in industrialized countries has been reshaped as increasing numbers have begun to enter into non-traditional occupations (that is, those in which men have historically predominated). Advocates of such change have emphasized its potential to reduce gender-based economic disparities by improving women's access to the better earnings, job security, and advancement prospects typically associated with 'men's jobs.' To date, evidence from several industrialized countries suggests that women have made important inroads, parlaying increased levels of education and labour-force participation into a diverse array of non-traditional jobs (see, for example, Reskin and Roos, 1990, in the United States; Hughes, 1990, 1995, in Canada; Crompton and Sanderson, 1990, and Scott, 1994, in Britain; Rubery and Fagan, 1995, in Europe). Yet, in documenting these trends, researchers have also raised important questions about the *pace* and *consequences* of this change – asking particularly whether non-traditional jobs offer women the genuine opportunity to improve their economic prospects that is commonly assumed.

A key reason for asking such questions is that women's entrance into non-traditional work has coincided with a period of extensive economic restructuring in most industrialized countries. Indeed, since the mid-1970s, labour markets have been profoundly changed as a convergence of forces (e.g., technological change, deregulation, globalization) has given rise to the so-called postindustrial or new economy (ECC, 1991; OECD, 1994a; 1997). The intersection of women's influx into non-traditional areas with the restructuring of labour markets and economies raises critical questions about how to interpret women's gains in specific occupations, when the nature of work and employment conditions have been altered in many industrial sectors. Whereas some researchers contend that women's growing presence in non-traditional areas represents genuine gains, others view it as a repetition of historical patterns where women have entered formerly male-dominated areas once the pay and working conditions in such occupations have been eroded. A third perspective claims that both trends are occurring, fuelling a polarization in the female work force between beneficiaries and casualties of structural change (for useful discussions in Canada, see Armstrong, 1996, 1997; Bakker, 1996).

This paper explores these issues in the Canadian context, examining women's entrance into non-traditional occupations from the early 1970s to the early 1990s. Following past life-course research that addresses structural changes in the economy and labour market (see, for example, Myles, 1992; West, 1991; Heinz, 1991), it traces out patterns of long-term change and then uses this evidence to assess debates over the consequences of women's movement into non-traditional fields (see, for example, Reskin and Roos, 1990; Wright and Jacobs, 1994). In order to situate the analysis within existing debates, the next section briefly reviews related research from the United States, Britain, and Canada. Subsequent sections then examine trends in the Canadian context, focusing on two sets of questions:

- How have changing structures of economic opportunity in Canada reshaped women's presence in non-traditional and traditional occupations from 1971 to 1991? Also, what are the general patterns of change, and what are the specific non-traditional occupations women have entered?
- How has women's entrance into non-traditional work affected their economic status (i.e., earnings, full-time job status)? And, how have women fared relative to men in the same occupations, and to female workers overall?

Gender, Non-Traditional Work, and Economic Restructuring

Much has been written on the economic and labour-market changes affecting women in industrialized countries in the past several decades. While a comprehensive discussion is beyond the scope of this paper, it is useful to highlight findings from research on women's non-traditional work in the United States, Britain, and Canada in order to illustrate the changes that have occurred and the growing complexity of this particular debate.

One important source of insight comes from aggregate-level studies of changing patterns of occupational gender segregation.[2] Overall, this research shows that women have made significant inroads into male-dominated areas since the 1970s, thus contributing to reduced aggregate levels of segregation in a number of countries (OECD, 1994b, p. 127).[3] In the United States, segregation appears to have declined most dramatically in the 1970s, with change slowing in the 1980s (Cotter et al., 1995).[4] In Britain, the widely held view until recently has been that segregation has declined since the mid-1970s, as a result of equal-opportunities legislation (Hakim, 1996, pp 152–62). Canadian research on this issue, though less extensive than that in the United States and Britain, has also identified the 1960s and 1970s as important periods of change (Fox and Fox, 1987). As in the United States, the most dramatic declines in segregation appear to have taken place in the 1970s, largely as a result of women's entrance into male-dominated occupations.

Taken together, aggregate-level studies suggest that important changes in gender segregation have occurred. Yet serious criticisms have also been made about the veracity of segregation measures, raising questions about whether existing studies overstate the extent of change (Blackburn et al., 1993).[5] Aggregate studies have also not typically addressed the dynamics underlying changes in segregation or identified the specific occupations undergoing change (Moore, 1985, p. 16; Crompton and Sanderson, 1990, pp. 25–6). Thus, as Rubery and Fagan (1995, pp. 213–19) note, while such studies are useful for establishing *levels* of segregation, they do little to illuminate what the *meaning* and *consequences* of these patterns are. As they point out, high levels of segregation have a different meaning for women in Scandinavian countries, where more egalitarian pay structures have protected women from low pay (p. 216). Given these limitations, case studies of specific occupations and disaggregated analysis are important sources of insight.

To date, several studies in the United States (Reskin and Roos, 1990; Wright and Jacobs, 1994; Jacobs, 1992), Britain (Crompton and Sanderson, 1990), and Europe (Rubery and Fagan, 1995) have developed this type of analysis, drawing on focused case studies, disaggregated occupational data, or a combination of the two. Of these, Reskin and Roos (1990) provide one of the more comprehensive analyses, drawing on census and case study data to: (i) empirically document changing patterns of occupational segregation, wages, and work status in the United States in the 1970s, and (ii) develop a theoretical model explaining the factors leading women into new occupational areas. Drawing on a queueing perspective,[6] Reskin and Roos identify three possible outcomes for women entering non-traditional occupations: (i) *genuine integration*, where women come to be proportionally represented across all occupations within a desegregated occupation and work in all industries and establishments in which the occupation exists; (ii) *ghettoization*, where women come to work in the same occupation as men but in different firms, industries, and ranks; and (iii) *resegregation*, where an entire occupation or specialty switches from a predominantly male to a predominantly female labour force. Their theoretical framework identifies a range of factors shaping these outcomes – for example, labour shortages, occupational growth, declining occupational attractiveness, and changing social attitudes (see Reskin and Roos, 1990, pp 29–90 for a full discussion of their approach).

Reskin and Roos's analysis suggests that the 1970s were an important decade of change for women's non-traditional work in the United States. They identify thirty-three occupations that had a disproportionate influx of women,[7] with roughly half in managerial/administrative, professional, and sales areas (e.g., financial managers, accountants), and the other half in clerical, service, and manual jobs (e.g., insurance adjusters, bartenders, janitors, bus drivers). Despite these gains, however, Reskin and Roos question whether women experienced genuine economic progress. Their case studies suggest that, rather than being integrated into good jobs, women were often ghettoized in jobs in distinct industries (e.g., bus driving), specialties (e.g., real estate sales), tasks (e.g., bank management), or firms (e.g., accounting). Women also found themselves resegregated into feminizing jobs such as insurance adjusting and typesetting/compositing, where they became the majority by the 1980s. While many factors underlie these changes, Reskin and Roos suggest that in many cases women's influx occurred as falling wages and deteriorating work conditions made these areas increasingly unattractive to men. Women were also drawn into occupations where employment growth was exceptionally strong.

In contrast to Reskin and Roos, other case studies in the United States come to quite different conclusions. For instance, Jacobs (1992) found little evidence of resegregation or ghettoization in his examination of women's entrance into management occupations from 1970 to

1988, arguing instead that 'the predominant trend has been towards real, if slow, progress into management on the part of women' (298). For computer specialists (i.e., systems analysts, programers), Wright and Jacobs (1994) also found little support for Reskin and Roos. While computing did rapidly feminize in the 1970s and 1980s, the entrance of women did not prompt, or follow, the exit of male workers, nor did the job earnings fall relative to those of the labour force as a whole.

In Britain, studies suggest similar patterns with respect to some of the non-traditional occupations women have entered. Crompton and Sanderson's (1990) analysis indicates that professional and management occupations such as pharmacy and accounting have seen a significant influx of women. Rubery and Fagan (1995) also point to the professions as a key site of gain for women, not only within Britain, but also among member states of the European Community. While there has been no detailed analysis in Britain of changes across the broad spectrum of occupations, Hakim (1993) has identified a wide range of male-dominated occupations that became more integrated from 1971 to 1991. These were primarily professional and managerial, but included a diverse range of jobs, such as doctors, dentists, dental technicians, dispensing opticians, pharmacists, judges, barristers, underwriters and claims assessors, property and estate managers, and buyers (299).

In Canada, studies are less extensive than in the United States, but do point to some similar patterns, at least up until the 1980s. Armstrong and Armstrong's (1992) analysis of non-traditional professions shows that women entered a wide range of areas from the early 1970s to the mid-1980s, but remained segregated within lower levels and less lucrative specializations. From the standpoint of the broad occupational structure, Hughes's (1990; 1995) analyses show women entering a range of non-traditional jobs over the long (1971–86) and short (1986–91) term, not only within management and the professions, but also within the sales, service, and manual areas.

Several case studies in Canada also explore women's experiences in non-traditional work in greater detail, focusing largely on the professions (e.g., lawyers, see Hagan and Kay, 1995; pharmacists, see Tanner et al., 1998; university professors, see Tancred and Czarnocki, 1993; engineers, see Ranson and Reeves, 1996). Overall, this research confirms the growing presence of women in the professions, but comes to a variety of conclusions about the consequences of their entrance into such work. Within law, for example, Hagan and Kay (1995) conclude that women have entered the legal profession at a time when the opportunity structure has dramatically changed and that they remain largely segregated at lower levels. In contrast, Ranson and Reeves's (1996) study of computing professionals suggests that while women have done less well than their male peers in terms of earnings and job status, this is largely due to differences in work experience.

In sum, while case studies and disaggregated analyses in the United States, Britain, and Canada suggest that women have entered a range of non-traditional occupations in the 1970s and 1980s, there are differing assessments of the extent and nature of change. Whereas some researchers feel that these shifts have been significant and meaningful, others contend that the pace of change has been slow and/or that women have entered occupations where working conditions, and benefits, have been eroded. To date, much research has focused on trends in managerial and professional work, thus providing little insight into the full spectrum of occupations. Studies have also focused largely on trends up to the early and mid-1980s, creating a need for research on more recent transitions, as well as changes over the long term.

Of the existing studies, Reskin and Roos (1990) provide one of the most comprehensive analyses of women's entrance into non-traditional occupations within the context of the economic restructuring that took place in the United States in the 1970s and 1980s. In Canada, we do not have this type of broad analysis exploring how changing economic opportunities within non-traditional work are reshaping the life courses of women. The analysis that follows seeks to develop a comparable analysis for the Canadian context. Focusing on structural changes in the economy and the labour market, it identifies long-term changes from 1971 to 1991 in (i) the pace and extent of women's movement into non-traditional occupations and (ii) the economic consequences of this change for women.

Data and Definitions

In addressing these issues, the analysis draws on published and unpublished labour-force data from Statistics Canada. The bulk of the data are drawn from occupational data from the 1971, 1981, and 1991 Canadian census, and refer to the experienced labour force. The data are strictly comparable and are classified according to the 1971 Occupational Classification Manual (see Hughes, 1995, p. 67, for a full discussion of data and definitions).

A key step in the analysis involves defining 'non-traditional' occupations for women, as the definition used clearly influences the eventual conclusions (Wootton, 1997, p. 19; Reskin and Roos, 1990). A common approach has been to use an absolute measure, defining an occupation as non-traditional if women comprise less than 50 per cent of workers. In contrast, the approach used here takes into account women's presence in an occupation relative to their presence in the labour force overall. For each occupation, a 'coefficient of representation' (*pf/PF* or *pm/PM*) is calculated. This is the percentage of women (or men) in a specific occupation (*pf* or *pm*) divided by the percentage of women (or men) in the labour force overall (*PF* or *PM*) (Hughes, 1990; 1995).

Using a coefficient of this type allows us to gauge more accurately women's movement into an occupation at a time when their presence in the labour force is also undergoing significant change. This is important in the Canadian case, where women's share of the labour force rose from 34.3 per cent in 1971 to 44.9 per cent in 1991. Without this, we have no way of knowing whether women's growing share of an occupation is due simply to a greater presence in the labour force or to a disproportionate shift into that occupation. The coefficient thus allows us to identify occupations where women were proportionally underrepresented (coefficient under 1.00) and overrepresented (coefficient over 1.00), as well as to measure the extent of change by calculating the difference in coefficients over time. Because we are interested in looking at occupations where women were a distinct minority in 1971, the analysis distinguishes between 'non-traditional' (0.00–0.49), 'intermediate' (0.50–0.99) and 'traditional' (1.00+) occupations, and focuses on the first group with respect to detailed changes from 1971 to 1991.[8]

Women's Movement into Non-traditional Occupations, 1970s to 1990s

As a starting point, it is important to note several broad changes in the Canadian labour market from the early 1970s to the 1990s that were particularly significant for women's entrance into non-traditional work. First, the Canadian economy experienced very strong growth, with the labour force expanding by 66 per cent, from 8.6 million in 1971 to 14.3 million in 1991. Growth was especially strong in the 1970s (3.9 per cent per year) compared to the 1980s (1.9 per cent per year). Second, women's participation in paid employment increased dramatically. Between 1971 and 1991, the female labour force grew by 117.1 per cent, compared to just 39.4 per cent for men. By 1991, women made up 44.9 per cent of the labour force, up from just 34.3 per cent of all workers in 1971. Finally, in addition to their growing levels of employment, women also improved their educational attainment. Whereas in 1971 fewer than one in twenty working women had some university education, by 1991 this was the case for nearly one in seven women, bringing them to near parity with men. Equally significant, women also entered into many non-traditional educational areas. Between 1975 and 1990, women in Canadian universities received a growing proportion of degrees in veterinary medicine, zoology, law, medicine, business/commerce, political science, agriculture, and dentistry, among other areas (Stout, 1992). In community colleges, women's share of diplomas also rose in non-traditional areas such as business, natural resources, engineering, and transportation (Bellamy and Guppy, 1991, pp 179, 181; Statistics Canada, 1995, p. 59).

Given these broad trends in employment growth, labour-force participation, and education, what were the consequences for women's entrance into non-traditional occupations? How extensive were their gains, and what types of occupations did they move into? These questions are examined in the following sections, focusing on two different levels of analysis: first, the broad shifts in women's non-traditional work, and second, the specific non-traditional jobs they entered.

(i) General Trends – Women's Movement into
  Non-traditional Occupations, 1971–91

In terms of broad patterns of change, table 5.1 shows the changing proportion of non-traditional occupations for women from 1971 to 1991.[9] A look at the changes over time reveals several key trends. First, from the early 1970s to the early 1990s, there was a notable decrease in the number of non-traditional occupations for women. Whereas in 1971 60.3 per cent of occupations were non-traditional (0.00–0.49), by 1991 this had fallen to 49.3 per cent. Significantly, change was faster in the 1970s, with occupations that were non-traditional for women decreasing by 3.5 per annum in 1971–81, compared to 1.8 per annum in 1981–91. While the slower rate of change does not mean that women ceased entering new non-traditional areas in the 1980s, it does mean that the extent of change was not significant enough to push these occupations into the intermediate category.

TABLE 5.1
Distribution of Women in 'Non-traditional,' 'Intermediate' and
'Traditional' Occupations, 1971–91

	1971	1981	1991
Non-traditional (0.00–0.49)			
Occupations (%)	60.3	53.1	49.3
(n)	292	257	239
Labour force (%)	8.4	7.0	5.4
Intermediate (0.50–0.99)			
Occupations (%)	12.6	18.2	23.1
(n)	61	88	112
Labour force (%)	5.9	10.9	14.6
Traditional (1.00+)			
Occupations (%)	27.1	28.7	27.5
(n)	131	139	133
Labour force (%)	85.7	82.1	80.0
Total			
Occupations (%)	100.0	100.0	100.0
(n)	484	484	484
Labour force (%)	100.0	100.0	100.0

SOURCE: 1971, 1981, 1991 Census of Canada

Despite women's inroads into non-traditional areas, it is important
to note that this change involved a fairly small proportion of the total
female labour force. As table 5.1 shows, taken together, non-traditional
and intermediate jobs accounted for just 20.0 per cent of all women in
1991, up from 14.3 per cent in 1971. After two decades, then, 80.0 per
cent of female workers continued to work in traditional areas – despite
the fact that these occupations made up just one-quarter (133 of 484) of
all those available in the Canadian economy.

*(ii) Specific Occupations – Women's Movement into
     Non-traditional Occupations*

Beyond these general patterns, what specific non-traditional occupations did women enter, and what were the economic conditions offered
by such work? Table 5.2 identifies all the non-traditional occupations
that experienced a disproportionate influx of women from 1971 to

1991, showing the change in women's percentage and coefficients of representation at various points in time. Following Reskin and Roos (1990), these occupations are defined as ones where women's representation grew at twice the rate of their representation in the labour force overall. In this case, women's representation in the labour force grew by 10.6 per cent (from 34.3 per cent in 1971 to 44.9 per cent in 1991), thus creating a cut-off of 21.2 per cent or higher among the various occupations.

As table 5.2 shows, there were 25 non-traditional occupations that saw a disproportionate influx of women in the period 1971–91. Of these, four-fifths fell into three areas: management (9 of 25), professional or technical specialities (6 of 25), and sales (5 of 25). The remainder included a diverse group of clerical, services, manual, manufacturing, transportation, and printing occupations. Although the vast majority of these occupations remained intermediate for women by 1991 (i.e., coefficients of 0.50–0.99), one in five had become traditional for women, suggesting that some resegregation had taken place in certain areas. Resegregating occupations included accountants, auditors, and other financial occupations (coefficient of 1.03 in 1991), dispensing opticians (1.25), Advertising sales (1.03), Insurance sales and agents (1.01), and Bartenders (1.28).

Looking at the trends across the 1971–81 and 1981–91 period reveals great variety in the pace of change in different occupations. Whereas some occupations attracted significant numbers of female workers in the 1970s, some saw little influx until the 1980s. Others changed more evenly over both decades. In the 1970s, several occupations saw a dramatic influx of women, with their presence growing at roughly three times the rate of the female labour force. Included here were bartenders, advertising sales, typesetters and compositors, dispensing opticians, insurance sales and agents, and production clerks. Of these, bartenders changed so rapidly that it became traditional for women by 1981. Two other occupations – dispensing opticians (0.97) and Advertising sales (0.91) – came close to being traditional for women by 1981.

In the 1981–91 period, women's entrance into non-traditional occupations was less dramatic than in the previous decade and involved slightly different occupations. Those having the greatest influx of women included optometrists; financial managers; government administrators; veterinarians; service managers; accountants, auditors, and others; dispensing opticians; lawyers and notaries; economists; purchasing officers; sales supervisors; and personnel and IR manage-

TABLE 5.2

Occupations with Disproportionate Influx of Women, 1971–1991, Canada

	Total labour force						Change 1971–91	
	1971		1981		1991			
Occupation	%F	CoF	%F	CoF	%F	CoF	CoF	%
	34.3	1.00	40.4	1.00	44.9	1.00	0.0	10.6
Management								
Financial management	8.2	0.24	23.3	0.58	43.3	0.96	0.73	35.1
Personnel and IR management	11.0	0.32	27.7	0.69	42.2	0.94	0.62	31.2
Accountants, auditors, other	15.2	0.44	29.1	0.72	46.1	1.03	0.58	30.9
Service management	9.3	0.27	21.5	0.53	38.3	0.85	0.58	29.0
Purchasing officers & buyers	8.6	0.25	22.3	0.55	36.8	0.82	0.57	28.2
Members of legislative bodies	8.9	0.26	22.2	0.55	34.4	0.77	0.51	25.5
Government administrators	10.5	0.31	19.6	0.48	36.4	0.81	0.51	26.0
Sales & advertising management	3.7	0.11	16.6	0.41	27.1	0.60	0.49	23.4
Inspectors/regulatory officers, government	4.9	0.14	15.6	0.39	26.9	0.60	0.46	22.0
Professional / Technical								
Optometrists	5.9	0.17	17.7	0.44	44.3	0.99	0.81	38.4
Dispensing opticians	16.5	0.48	39.2	0.97	56.1	1.25	0.77	39.6
Veterinarians	4.4	0.13	16.3	0.40	32.6	0.73	0.60	28.2
Lawyers and notaries	4.8	0.14	15.1	0.37	29.1	0.65	0.51	24.4
Economists	10.3	0.30	20.1	0.50	34.6	0.77	0.47	24.3
Producers/directors, Audio-Visual	14.4	0.42	28.5	0.71	36.7	0.82	0.40	22.3
Clerical								
Production clerks	16.9	0.49	35.9	0.89	40.5	0.90	0.41	23.6

TABLE 5.2-Concluded
Occupations with Disproportionate Influx of Women, 1971–1991, Canada

	Total labour force						Change 1971–91	
	1971		1981		1991			
Occupation	%F 34.3	CoF 1.00	%F 40.4	CoF 1.00	%F 44.9	CoF 1.00	CoF 0.0	% 10.6
Sales								
Advertising sales	12.7	0.37	36.8	0.91	46.3	1.03	0.66	33.6
Insurance sales & agents	12.4	0.36	33.6	0.83	45.2	1.01	0.65	32.8
Supervisor: sales (services)	8.1	0.24	22.0	0.54	35.9	0.80	0.56	27.8
Business services sales	11.1	0.32	25.4	0.63	38.0	0.85	0.52	26.9
Sales and traders, securities	8.5	0.25	22.4	0.56	31.7	0.71	0.46	23.2
Services								
Bartenders	14.5	0.42	52.6	1.30	57.3	1.28	0.88	42.8
Manufacturing/Manual								
Farm management	3.3	0.10	15.3	0.38	27.5	0.61	0.52	24.2
Transport								
Bus drivers	9.7	0.28	25.0	0.62	34.1	0.76	0.48	24.4
Printing								
Typesetters and compositors	12.7	0.37	35.9	0.89	40.7	0.91	0.53	28.0

SOURCE: 1971, 1981, 1991 Census of Canada

ment. As five of these were non-traditional for women in 1981, the entrance of significant numbers of women was an important event. Equally important, another four groups of occupations became traditional for women by 1991 (dispensing opticians; advertising sales; accountants, auditors, and others; and insurance sales and agents), with three additional occupations coming very close to this status (optometrists, financial management, and personnel and IR management).

Overall, these trends confirm that important changes occurred during the 1970s and 1980s. On a comparative note, it is interesting to draw contrasts with the U.S. trends identified by Reskin and Roos (1990). Calculating coefficients of representation for their U.S. data (1988) reveals some commonalities in terms of resegregating occupations. These include: accountants and auditors (1.03 in Canada and 1.10 in the United States), advertising and related sales (1.03 in Canada and 1.06 in the United States), and bartenders (1.28 in Canada and 1.10 in the United States). Other occupations that had already resegregated in the United States were also nearing traditional status in Canada by 1991 – in particular, typesetters and compositors (0.91 in Canada and 1.64 in the United States. Yet there were other occupations that had feminized in one country but not in the other – for instance, insurance sales, which became traditional in Canada but not in the United States (1.01 in Canada in 1991 and 0.66 in the United States in 1988).

Exploring the Nature of Rapidly Feminizing Occupations

Given the commonly held belief that women have benefited economically from entering non-traditional occupations, it is important to explore the quality of the occupations they entered. This is especially so in light of the studies discussed earlier which challenge this assumption. As Reskin and Roos (1990) show in the United States, while some women entered better-paying occupations in the expanding managerial and professional ranks, others clearly entered declining areas where earnings, status, and working conditions were being eroded. Similar questions need to be asked about the changes that have occurred in Canada.

Table 5.3 examines several aspects of the non-traditional occupations women entered from 1971 to 1991: (i) the rate of employment growth within each occupation, (ii) the percentage of women in full-time, full-year employment in 1991, and (iii) the median income for women in

1991 (in dollars and as a percentage of income for men). Employment growth is included, as it was an important factor in facilitating women's entrance into non-traditional areas in the United States (Reskin and Roos, 1990). The other two items provide an indication of job quality – specifically, the availability of *secure* rather than *flexible* forms of work, and the level of financial remuneration.[10]

Several insights emerge from table 5.3. First, with respect to employment growth, it is clear that many non-traditional occupations women entered from 1971 to 1991 expanded at above-average rates. In the first decade, four-fifths of the occupations grew at rates well above that of the labour force. Job growth was particularly dramatic in management and professional/technical specialities, suggesting a potential reason for women's increasing presence. In other occupations, growth was strong but not as pronounced – with some exceptions, such as bartenders, which grew by 163.5 per cent. A few occupations saw low or negative growth, such as sales supervisor (services), which declined by 12.9 per cent. In the 1981–91 period, growth slowed and was not as striking as in the 1970s. While strong growth continued in some areas – for example, service managers and farm managers – there were not the spectacular pockets of growth seen in the previous decade. Several occupations also saw slight declines in job numbers – for example, purchasing officers and buyers, production clerks, and typesetters and compositors.

Turning to full-time status and income, how did women fare? To what extent did entering non-traditional areas benefit them relative to the average female worker? With respect to job status and security, entrance into non-traditional occupations appears to have improved women's position within full-time, full-year employment. As table 5.3 shows, the vast majority of women in non-traditional jobs in 1991 were in full-time, full-year jobs, whereas this was the case for less than one-half of all working women (46.8 per cent). Full-time rates were particularly high within management and sales occupations (from 60.4 per cent to 81.1 per cent), and lower but still above average for professional and technical specialities (from 48.8 per cent to 67.8 per cent). Two areas, however – bartenders (31.6 per cent) and bus drivers (18.6 per cent) – had very low rates of full-time work.

In terms of employment income, table 5.3 shows the median income for full-time, full-year workers. Additional information on part-time, part-year workers is needed for future analysis, as part-time status constitutes an important dimension of gender segregation. For full-

TABLE 5.3
Job Growth, Full-Time/Full-Year, and Earnings, 1971–1991, Canada

| | Total labour force | | | | |
| | Job Growth (%) | | FT/FY 1991 | Earnings 1991 | |
Occupation	1971–81	1981–91	% F	Female	F as % of M
	39.1	19.4	46.8	$24,497	70.0
Management					
Financial management	604.9	49.6	81.1	33,932	64.7
Personnel and IR management	541.8	69.2	76.1	36,108	72.1
Accountants, auditors, other	45.0	55.8	70.1	30,818	69.9
Service management	572.8	95.9	63.8	26,342	65.0
Purchasing officers & buyers	44.1	(0.30)	75.9	30,618	79.4
Members of legislative bodies	112.0	92.5	60.4	34,543	74.9
Government administrators	62.2	63.4	77.9	38,236	74.7
Sales & advertising management	511.0	35.4	70.9	30,666	62.6
Inspectors/regulatory officers, government	54.5	34.2	70.0	35,785	87.6
Professional/Technical Speciality					
Optometrists	31.5	66.1	55.9	30,703	43.7
Dispensing opticians	134.8	45.3	56.6	21,691	67.7
Veterinarians	96.8	32.3	48.8	36,877	73.1
Lawyers and notaries	109.2	56.7	66.8	41,746	63.3
Economists	117.2	61.0	67.8	37,254	75.3
Producers/directors, audio-visual	153.4	69.6	56.4	32,622	83.6
Clerical					
Production clerks	41.2	(6.4)	64.8	25,792	74.8

TABLE 5.3—Concluded
Job Growth, Full-Time/Full-Year, and Earnings, 1971–1991, Canada

Occupation	Total labour force		FT/FY 1991	Earnings 1991	
	Job Growth (%)				
	1971–81	1981–91	% F	Female	F as % of M
	39.1	19.4	46.8	$24,497	70.0
Sales					
Advertising sales	91.8	45.6	58.2	28,274	73.8
Insurance sales and agents	58.1	36.4	73.6	25,594	69.7
Supervisor: sales (services)	(12.9)	71.3	75.1	30,912	70.0
Business service sales	102.6	24.7	60.7	30,715	83.5
Sales and traders, securities	32.0	30.4	69.1	27,255	61.0
Services					
Bartenders	163.5	17.7	31.6	12,386	73.2
Manufacturing					
Farm management	79.9	102.7	53.9	12,979	65.8
Transport					
Bus drivers	63.4	23.4	18.6	20,318	58.0
Printing					
Typesetters and compositors	7.4	(1.4)	61.8	23,472	72.9

SOURCE: 1971, 1981, 1991 Census of Canada

time, full-year workers, however, we can see that roughly four of every five non-traditional occupations in 1991 provided an income that was higher than that of the average female worker ($24,497). Significantly, about 20 per cent of the occupations women entered had earnings well below the median, ranging from $23,472 for typesetters and compositors, to lows of $12,386 for bartenders and $12,979 for farm managers. Not surprisingly, all but one of the low-income positions were concentrated among the service, agricultural, transport, and printing areas. In contrast, incomes for occupations within the management and sales groups were all above the median, though a few only narrowly so (e.g., service managers, $26,342; insurance sales and agents, $25,594).

Despite their relatively higher incomes, women in non-traditional work still earned less on average than their male co-workers. Earning differences ranged from a low of 43.7 per cent for optometrists and 58.0 per cent for bus drivers to a high of 87.6 per cent for inspectors and regulatory officers in the public sector. Slightly more than half of the occupations had an earnings gap that was narrower than that for the labour force as a whole (i.e., above 70 per cent). Beyond this, however, there appears to be no consistent pattern with respect to the earnings differential, with a fair amount of variation within the broad occupational clusters.

Discussion

In light of these findings, what conclusions can be drawn about Canadian women's entrance into non-traditional occupations in the 1970s and 1980s? To what extent did women make meaningful progress and what are the implications for gender-based inequalities? Overall, the findings suggest that important changes have taken place, though certainly not to the extent hoped for by proponents of women's non-traditional work. While women made inroads into a range of areas – with the proportion of non-traditional occupations falling from 60.1 per cent in 1971 to 49.3 per cent in 1991 – the pace of change was not constant, nor did it accelerate, as we might reasonably expect given women's steadily rising education levels. While the economic downturn of the early 1990s surely dampened the pace of change from 1981 to 1991 (Bernier, 1995, p. C-6), this is unlikely to account fully for the decline. Overall, then, the general pattern is consistent with several studies discussed earlier that point to the 1970s as a key decade of change.

In terms of the broad impact on the life course of Canadian women, the symbolic and material significance of women's gains in non-traditional occupations cannot be underestimated. Still, it needs to be emphasized that this change involved a relatively small proportion of the total female labour force. Indeed, by 1991, only 20 per cent of women worked in non-traditional or intermediate occupations, leaving 80 per cent of Canadian women in traditional jobs. In terms of key areas of opportunity, managerial and professional/technical work was particularly important, accounting for nearly two-thirds of the non-traditional occupations women entered. Yet women did not make notable inroads into these areas until the 1980s, being more likely in the 1970s to enter jobs such as bartending, advertising sales, typesetting and compositing, and insurance sales.

While further case studies are needed to identify the specific factors that encouraged women's entrance into different occupations, it is clear that employment growth played an important role. In both decades, most non-traditional occupations grew at above-average rates, suggesting, as Reskin and Roos (1990) have, that employer demand and male labour shortages were key factors in creating change. As to whether women benefited from moving into these jobs, the majority did have higher earnings and full-time, full-year status relative to female workers overall. In roughly four-fifths of the occupations, women made more than the average female worker ($24,497), and in all but two of the occupations women had higher than average rates of full-time, full-year work. However, gains were not made across the board, and several non-traditional occupations offered incomes and full-time working status well below the female average (e.g., farm managers, bartenders, bus drivers). Comparing women to their male peers also reveals significant disparities. Though slightly more than half had a narrower earnings gap than the national average (i.e., above 70 per cent), the wage gap was nevertheless a consistent feature for women entering non-traditional areas. Presumably, part of the gap is explained by the fact that women were more recent entrants into the occupations and thus had less experience and seniority. But it likely also reflects segregation within occupations (e.g., by speciality, industry), an issue that deserves attention in future research.

With respect to the debates over women's non-traditional work, what do these trends suggest with respect to integration, resegregation, and ghettoization (Reskin and Roos, 1990)? How have the lives of

Canadian women been reshaped by entering new areas of work? Several trends seem clear, though we need to keep in mind that occupational level data may mask countervailing trends at more detailed levels (Reskin and Roos, 1990, p. 320). Generally speaking, however, it appears that most occupations moved towards greater integration. There is also evidence of resegregation in several cases, with bartenders and dispensing opticians providing the clearest examples. As to whether women gained by entering non-traditional occupations, most gained relative to the average female worker. But there were also women who did not – especially those in resegregated occupations (e.g., bartenders, bus drivers). Here salaries and/or hours of work fell well below those in other non-traditional areas and below the female average, suggesting that job polarization also occurred.

Future research at a more detailed level will help to answer these questions more fully. Indeed, there are several important directions that future research should pursue. The first is to trace trends for the 1990s in order to confirm the direction of ongoing changes and identify new non-traditional areas that women have entered. The second is to undertake analysis at a finer level of detail to determine whether occupations that appear to have integrated have actually done so, or have instead seen specialities or industries undergo ghettoization or resegregation. Finally, it is necessary to develop case studies of specific occupations, and to draw on already existing materials where available (e.g., Hagan and Kay, 1995, on lawyers), in order to document the ways in which the work process and employment conditions have altered as women have entered these areas and to identify the factors that have encouraged women's growing presence. In particular, it is critical for future research to examine the links between the restructuring and regendering of occupations, so that women's entrance into non-traditional occupations is placed within the broader economic context. Doing so will allow us to evaluate whether the emphasis on women's entrance into non-traditional occupations sparked by second-wave feminism has been well placed and remains a worthy goal. While some researchers suggest that the exercise has been of limited success, these conclusions seem somewhat premature in the Canadian context. Further research will help us understand what has happened and why, and will offer vital information on how the next generation of female workers can best improve their economic prospects within a rapidly changing economy.

NOTES

1 I would like to thank symposium participants and the editors of this volume for their helpful comments on an earlier draft of this paper. I am also grateful to Michel Cote at Statistics Canada for his assistance with the data used here.

2 'Segregation' refers here to 'the tendency for women and men to be employed in different occupations from each other across the entire spectrum of occupations under analysis' (Siltanen et al., 1992, p. 6).

3 OECD analysis of aggregate data suggests that sex segregation has declined in the United States, Canada, and the United Kingdom. Yet disaggregated data for other OECD countries suggests only marginal declines (OECD, 1994b, p. 127).

4 See table 5.1 (Cotter et al., 1995, p. 5) for a useful overview of research results for the 1950s to the 1970s. For additional U.S. studies, see Bianchi and Rytina, 1986; Jacobsen, 1994.

5 See Blackburn et al. (1993) for a detailed critique and an alternative approach to measurement.

6 From this perspective, the gender composition of an occupation is shaped by a dual-queueing process – 'labour queues order groups of workers in terms of their attractiveness to employers, and job queues rank jobs in terms of their attractiveness to workers' (Reskin and Roos, 1990, p. 29).

7 From 1970 to 1980, women entered these occupations at twice the rate that they entered the U.S. labour force overall (see Reskin and Roos, 1990, pp 16–20).

8 The initial pool of occupations thus includes all those with a coefficient of 0.00–0.49 in 1971. In selecting occupations undergoing disproportionate change from 1971 to 1991, occupations with less than 1,000 employees in 1991 and those not elsewhere classified were excluded – as has been done in other studies (Reskin and Roos, 1990, p. 20).

9 As previously discussed, this is determined by calculating a coefficient of representation for each of the 484 detailed occupations in the Canadian census, and then classifying each one as either 'non-traditional' (coefficient of 0.00–0.49), 'intermediate' (coefficient of 0.50–0.99), or 'traditional' (coefficient of 1.00+).

10 Unfortunately, with respect to the data, we have no way of knowing to what extent levels of full-time, full-year workers have changed over time and how many women work full-time when they would prefer part-time work (or vice versa). We also lack data on the extent to which wages have

changed over time and how they compare for different groups of workers within these occupations (e.g., full-time, part-time).

REFERENCES

Armstrong, P. (1996). The feminization of the labour force: Harmonizing down in a global economy. In I. Bakker (Ed.), *Rethinking restructuring: Gender and change in Canada* (pp 29–54). Toronto: University of Toronto Press.

Armstrong, P. (1997). Restructuring public and private: Women's paid and unpaid work. In S.M. Boyd (Ed.), *Challenging the public/private divide: Feminism, law and public policy* (pp 37–61). Toronto: University of Toronto Press.

Armstrong, P., & Armstrong, H. (1992). Sex and the professions in Canada. *Journal of Canadian Studies, 27*(1), 118–35.

Bakker, I. (Ed.). (1996). *Rethinking restructuring: Gender and change in Canada.* Toronto: University of Toronto Press.

Bellamy, L.A., & Guppy, N. (1991). Opportunities and obstacles for women in Canadian higher education. In J. Gaskell & A. McLaren (Eds), *Women and education* (pp 163–92). Calgary: Detselig Enterprises.

Bernier, R. (1995, November). The labour force survey: 50 years old! *The Labour Force* (Catalogue 71–001), C2–C14. Ottawa: Statistics Canada.

Bianchi, S., & Rytina, N. (1986). The decline in occupational sex segregation during the 1970s: Census and CPS comparisons. *Demography, 23*(1), 79–86.

Blackburn, R.M., Jarman, J., & Siltanen, J. (1993). The analysis of occupational gender segregation over time and place: Considerations of measurement and some new evidence. *Work, Employment and Society, 7*(3), 335–62.

Cotter, D., et al. (1995). Occupation gender desegregation in the 1980s. *Work and Occupations, 22*(1), 3–21.

Crompton, R., & Sanderson, K. (1990). *Gendered jobs and social change.* London: Unwin Hyman.

ECC (Economic Council of Canada). (1991). *Employment in the service economy.* Ottawa: Author.

Fox, B., & Fox, J. (1987). Occupational gender segregation of the Canadian labour force, 1931–1981. *Canadian Review of Sociology and Anthropology, 24*(3), 374–97.

Hagan, J., & Kay, F. (1995). *Gender in practice: A study of lawyers' lives.* New York: Oxford University Press.

Hakim, C. (1993). Segregated and integrated occupations: A new approach to analysing social change. *European Sociological Review, 9*(3), 289–314.

Hakim, C. (1996). *Key issues in women's work: Female heterogeneity and the polarisation of women's employment.* London: Athlone.

Heinz, W.R. (Ed.). (1991). *The life course and social change: Comparative perspectives.* Weinhem: Deutscher Studien Verlag.

Hughes, K.D. (1990, Summer). Trading places: Men and women in non-traditional occupations, 1986–91. *Perspectives on Labour and Income, 58–68.*

Hughes, K.D. (1995, Autumn). Women in non-traditional occupations. *Perspectives on Labour and Income, 14–19.*

Jacobs, J.A. (1992). Women's entry into management: Trends in earnings, authority and values among salaried managers. *Administrative Science Quarterly, 37,* 282–301.

Jacobsen, J. (1994). Trends in work force sex segregation, 1960–1990. *Social Science Quarterly, 75*(1), 204–11.

Moore, G. (1985). Horizontal and vertical: The dimensions of occupational segregation by gender in Canada. CRIAW Papers No. 12. Ottawa: Canadian Research Institute for the Advancement of Women.

Myles, J. (1992). Is there a post-Fordist life course? In W.R. Heinz, (Ed.), *Institutions and gatekeeping in the life course* (pp 171–86). Weinhem: Deutscher Studien Verlag.

OECD (Organization for Economic Cooperation and Development). (1994a). *The OECD jobs study: Facts, analysis, strategies.* Paris: Author.

OECD. (1994b). *Women and structural change.* Paris: Author.

OECD. (1997). *The world in 2020: Towards a new global village.* Paris: Author.

Ranson, G., & Reeves, W.J. (1996). Gender, earnings and proportions of women: Lessons from a high-tech occupation. *Gender and Society, 10*(2), 168–84.

Reskin, B., & Roos, P.A. (Eds). (1990). *Job queues, gender queues: Explaining women's inroads into male occupations.* Philadelphia: Temple University Press.

Rubery, J., & Fagan, C. (1995). Gender segregation in societal context. *Work, Employment and Society, 9*(2), 213–40.

Scott, A. (1994). *Gender segregation and social change: men and women in changing labour markets.* Oxford: Oxford University Press.

Siltanen, J., Jarman, J., & Blackburn, R.M. (1992). *Gender inequality in the labour market: Occupational concentration and segregation, a manual on methodology* (Working Paper IDP Women/WP-2). Geneva: ILO.

Statistics Canada. (1995). *Women in Canada: A statistical report* (Catalogue 89–503E). Ottawa: Author.

Stout, C.W. (1992, Winter). A degree of change. *Perspectives on Labour and Income, 14–19.*

Tancred, P., & Czarnocki, S. (1993). The revolving door: Women's exit from non-traditional work. In D. Martens (Ed.), *Weaving alliances*. Ottawa: Canadian Women's Studies Association.

Tanner, J., Cockerill, R., Barnsley, J., & Williams, A.P. (1998). Gender and clinical pharmacy: The career of an occupational ideology. *Canadian Review of Sociology, 35*(4), 535–54.

West, J. (1991). Current labour market patterns in Great Britain. In W.R. Heinz (Ed.), *The life course and social change: Comparative perspectives* (pp 139–58). Weinhem: Deutscher Studien Verlag

Wootton, B. (1997, April). Gender differences in occupational employment. *Monthly Labour Review*, 15–24.

Wright, R., & Jacobs, J.A. (1994, June). Male flight from computer work: A new look at occupational resegregation and ghettoization. *American Sociological Review, 59*, 511–26.

6. Contested Terrain: Women in German Research Organizations[1]

Jutta Allmendinger, Stefan Fuchs, Janina von Stebut, and Christine Wimbauer

Science is assumed to be the hall of meritocratic principles, aiming at nothing but knowledge, achievement, and scientific progress. And, indeed, meritocracy seems to be working in some areas such as higher (tertiary) education. In 1998, every second person obtaining the immatriculation standard (Abitur) was female, the proportion of female first-year students was about 48 per cent, and 42 per cent of all university diplomas were granted to females. When we look at gender composition[2] on the academic and scientific labour market, however, the picture turns out to be quite different. In 1998, 33 per cent of all doctorates and 15 per cent of all Habilitationen (prerequisite for a professorship) were awarded to women. Moreover, as of today, only 9 per cent of all professors and 6 per cent of all full professors are women, and there are hardly any women in the upper ranks of research organizations (Statistisches Bundesamt, 1999).

It is obvious from these data that women are getting lost between leaving universities and entering the highest ranks and positions in academia and science. This 'in-between' stage is characterized by two components: the qualificational labour market (which involves *working towards* the PhD or Habilitation) and the professional labour market (which involves *working for* a research unit in universities or research organizations), both of which tasks have to be undertaken simultaneously. Concerning the qualificational part, meritocracy works because women are excellent and highly motivated scientists. Their inclusion into the academic labour market, however, is likely to fail once the academic qualification process is terminated. In short, as long as women work towards a formal degree they are included in the academic and scientific labour market. Afterwards, however, they are confronted with 'closed shops,' and meritocracy has come to an end.

What are the reasons for this phenomenon? Researchers who address the mismatch between the supply of qualified female scientists and their low representation in high-level academic and scientific jobs provide many answers, ranging from deficit to difference models. As Sonnert and Holton put it: 'The deficit model posits that women are treated differently in science, and the difference model says that women act differently in science' (1995, p. 9). Differences in the treatment of men and women in science may result from inherently gendered organizational structures such as discriminatory practices in hiring, promoting, and dismissing, and the societal value system at large. Differences in how men and women act may result from gender differences in socialization. They are manifested in 'conscious and unconscious stereotyping, prejudice, and bias related to gender, race, and ethnicity' (Federal Glass Ceiling Commission, 1995, pp 7–8) and are assumed to show in different work habits, work orientation, job involvement, and career aspirations (good overviews are provided by Etzkowitz et al., 1992, 1994; Kulis and Miller-Loessi, 1992a, 1992b; Sonnert and Holton, 1995; Zuckerman et al., 1991).

In our ongoing research project 'The Career Development of Male and Female Scientists' (described in the next section) we want to identify these barriers and develop policies to overcome them. Essentially, we try to address the 'genderization of science' (Etzkowitz et al., 1992) by linking organizational structures in academia and science to individual career trajectories. The *aggregate data* we look at are: organizational turnover, organizational demand for scientists, and the rising supply of qualified female scientists (see the section 'Institutional Variation in the Proportion of Women'). Then we analyze *individual-level data* in terms of gender differences in motivation, ability, and job involvement (see the section 'Individual Gender Differences in Work Attitudes'). Finally, we explore the genderization of organizations and investigate the way in which – via recruitment, promotion policies, mentoring, and monitoring – 'invisible colleges' and informal networks lead to a cumulation of disadvantages especially for female academics (see the section 'Gendered Organizations'). Taken together, the data will help us to understand why female participation stagnates and why equality is not in sight – despite high gains in educational attainment.

The Munich Scientific Careers Study

The Setting

This section provides background information on the organizational setting of our study. The organizations under examination are the Max Planck Society (MPS) and the Fraunhofer Society (FhS), two prestigious research organizations in Germany.[3] We will first introduce both organizations and then come to a systematic comparison.

The Max Planck Society comprises eighty-one research institutes, laboratories, and work groups with wide-ranging interdisciplinary affiliations. It covers the 'hard sciences' such as chemistry, physics, geology, meteorology, and computer science (CPT sector), biology, and medicine (BM sector), as well as various disciplines such as law, history, art history, social sciences, psychology, and linguistics (HLS sector). The annual budget of the MPS is almost entirely financed by public funds. In comparison to other research institutions in Germany, the MPS is part of the scientific élite, including an impressive list of Nobel laureates. Scientists affiliated with the MPS have considerable prestige, no teaching obligations (unless they have joint appointments with universities), and enjoy a relatively generous infrastructure. In 1997, the MPS employed a total of 10,760 people, among them 2,750 scientists, 426 of whom were women (Max Planck Society, 1998a, 1998b). The institutes are directed by the scientific members of the society, who have almost complete autonomy in decision making. In 1997, there were 220 scientific directors, with 5 of them being female. The institutes usually have more than one scientific director, the number of directors sometimes reflecting structural differentiation into departments within one institute. Once a director is recruited, he or she usually stays in that position until retirement or death, as upward mobility from this prestigious position is close to impossible. Directors are usually recruited from other scientific organizations outside the MPS itself (there is no internal career leading to this position), and on the middle level of the scientific hierarchy internal mobility is rare. Although there are quite a few tenured positions on this level, the organizational culture has changed in the last decade: increasingly, status comes from interorganizational mobility (e.g., movements to and from universities and other research facilities). Movers are seen as dynamic, while stayers are viewed as 'dead wood' and obstacles to social change and innovation.

The Fraunhofer Society encompasses forty-seven non-university research institutions organized in eight clusters. Scientists affiliated with the FhS also have considerable prestige and no teaching obligations. In 1997, a total of 2,821 scientists were employed, 290 of whom were women (Fraunhofer Society, 1998). As in the MPS, the institutes of the FhS are directed by one or more directors recruited from the outside. As of 1997, all directors were male. There are some tenured positions on the middle level, but their number is steadily decreasing.

A comparison of the MPS and the FhS shows a wide range of differences in how the organizations are run. They differ in the range of disciplines covered, with the MPS covering a wider spectrum, including the social sciences. Their budgets also differ: the MPS is financed almost entirely by public money while the FhS is financed by a mixture of public and private funds. There are also differences in the emphasis on basic research (MPS) and applied research (FhS). Whereas scientists at the MPS are expected to pursue a strictly academic career, this is not the case in the FhS. Moreover, differences in the organizational culture of the two institutions imply that innovation, social competence, organizational skills, and leadership should be relevant personality factors in the FhS; in the MPS, though, academic excellence – measured by such things as the quality and quantity of publications – should be of greater importance. Finally, the likelihood for internal mobility leading to tenured positions is somewhat higher in the FhS than in the MPS where, as of today, it is close to impossible.

Research Design

The research design employed for studying academic career trajectories was the same for both organizations. We first collected information about the institutional structures and obtained 'process-produced' administrative data. These data provide information on age, gender, position, and entry date of all scientists regularly employed in both organizations at any point in time between 1989 and 1994 (MPS) and between 1993 and 1997 (FhS). They cover about 6,600 scientists in the MPS and about 2,500 scientists in the FhS. In a second step, we selected twenty institutes (nine MPIs and eleven FhIs) for in-depth research. Criteria for selection included the size of institutes, the proportion of female scientists employed, organizational turnover, and academic discipline. A third step was to develop a questionnaire for a mail survey. Since we employed a life-course perspective, many retrospective questions (career history of respondent as well as career histories of the entire family of origin, partners, spouses, children) were combined with personality items, academic records (number and quality of publications, awards, academic networks), as well as questions on directors, the composition of the work groups, mentoring, and so on. The survey was sent to all female scientists presently working in one of the selected MPS and FhS institutes and to a random sample of male scientists working in these institutes. In addition, in order to avoid selection bias, we included all male and female scientists whose employment contract ended during the observation period. Overall, we received 318 questionnaires, 134 from women and 184 from men. In a fourth step, we conducted in-depth interviews with individuals and groups at all hierarchical levels in a selected institute (Wimbauer, 1999).

Institutional Variation in the Proportion of Women

We begin the analysis with some basic facts on the inclusion of women between 1989 and 1995,[4] using the process-produced aggregate data of both organizations. The mean proportion of women in all MPS institutes is about 17 per cent, a figure that remains almost constant over time. The proportion of women in the FhS averages at a steady 10 per cent. This aggregate stability, however, masks a great deal of variation between and within the institutes of the MPS and the FhS. While in each given year the MPS employs about 4,000 scientists, turnover is high: between 1989 and 1995, 2,780 scientists left the society while 3,331 were newly recruited. Of the total of about 6,600 persons of whom a record exists, only one-third was employed in each of the years we looked at.

Are supply and demand factors responsible for aggregate stability and institutional variation? Since we know that fluctuation is high, the question arises whether organizations fill their vacancies with women. The answer is given in figure 6.1 (y-axis). We find that the proportion of women among the scientific staff recruited between 1989 and 1995 (MPS) and 1993 and 1997 (FhS) varied between 3 per cent and 67 per cent (average 22 per cent) in the MPS, and between 0 per cent and 45 per cent (average 13 per cent) in the FhS.

The supply of female academics examined is a variable largely determined outside the organizations under study. Although the institutes offer a number of fellowships for doctoral students and thus pro-

Figure 6.1 Proportion of Female University Graduates and Proportion of Female Entries

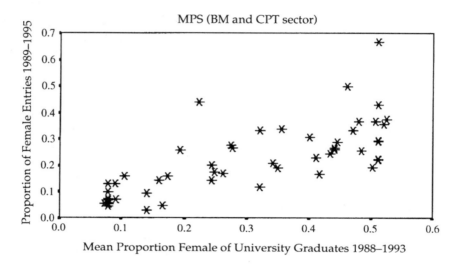

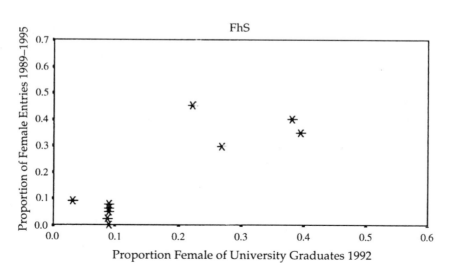

SOURCE: Survey of MPS scientists; own calculations

duce their own supply of scientists, they have to rely on a gender-segregated pool of applicants coming from the universities. According to the scientific and administrative directors of the MPS and FhS (personal communication), the supply of qualified applicants is the most important factor explaining the lack of integration of women and the variation between institutes. A look at the proportion of female university graduates across various disciplines reveals indeed large differences. Does this mean that the proportion of females in the sciences is a result of supply? Figure 6.1 shows the scatterplot of our indicator for the supply of female graduates and the proportion of female entries.[5] Overall, supply factors explain about 50 per cent of the variation in female integration. Yet, in the scatterplot we can also make out considerable variation both between and within scientific sectors: in biology and medicine, for example, the proportion of females graduating from universities is about 50 per cent; the proportion of female entries in the institutes in this sector varies from 8 per cent to 43 per cent (for more detail see Allmendinger et al., 1999).

While organizations do hire women and the pool of new applicants clearly matters, hiring women does not necessarily mean an increase in the overall proportion of women. As figure 6.2 shows, we find in both organizations institutes with a high proportion of female entrants, but no overall increase in the proportion of females. Rather, newly hired women rotate into positions vacated by other women. This suggests that organizations create work environments that function like 'revolving doors': although access is sometimes granted, subsequent exit is certain (Jacobs, 1989). In addition, there may be individual causes for this rotation of women. We will turn to individual gender differences next.

Individual Gender Differences in Work Attitudes

The conventional view on how gender differences in labour-market achievement are generated focuses on deeply rooted gender differences in work attitudes, job involvement, and labour-market attachment. With our mail-survey data at hand, we can test this set of propositions: we combine the MPS and FhS data and ask for gender differences in work attitudes, while at the same time controlling differences in the respective organizational setting.[6]

Using a life-course perspective, we start off by describing our sample of male and female scientists as they move through their career. As

Figure 6.2 Proportion of Female Entries and change in Proportion Female

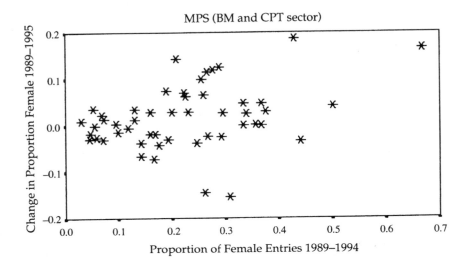

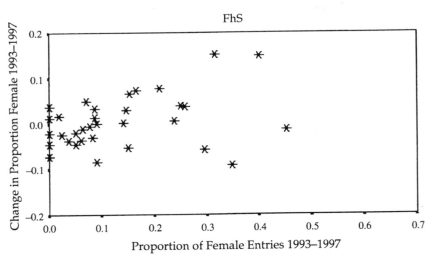

SOURCE: Survey of MPS scientists; own calculations

distinguished students, most women were already interested in their scientific subject areas when they were still in school. They shared a clear vision of their professional future: mathematics professor, physics professor, scientist. This career orientation, mostly paired with excellent degrees, does not differ between women and men and does not support any notion of female aversion to the sciences. Men and women have very similar career patterns before entering the MPS or FhS; both either actively looked for a job in the MPS or FhS, or they were pleased by corresponding offers made by the staff or the directors. At this point of entry, the MPS and FhS appear very open to hiring excellence regardless of gender: almost all men and 70 per cent of the women in our sample report that their recruitment at the MPS and FhS was all about merit, not gender. When analysing the detailed survey data on work attitudes, we were impressed by the similarities rather than the differences between both groups. Their locus of control, their motivation to achieve, their working patterns, and their self-confidence were nearly identical. Hence, gender differences in work attitudes cannot explain the low representation of women in the research organizations under study. This result is in line with findings by other researchers working on gender inequality in science (Valian, 1998).

Given that gender differences do not matter, we return to the phenomenon of revolving doors and ask whether these doors treat men and women equally. They do. Analyses of organizational exit rates of men and women based on process-produced data (personnel records) showed no gender differences (MPS) or very few (FhS) in exiting the organizations, once status is controlled (Allmendinger et al., 1999). Thus, we have to turn to the question of whether the implications of revolving doors are patterned by gender, and if so, why.

Gendered Organizations

Since Joan Acker's (1990) seminal article on gendered organizations, this expression has often been used as catchword without spelling out how exactly gender differences are generated. In the following we are more specific, and focus on three organizational aspects with gender-specific implications: (1) the principle of full availability, combined with a lack of any infrastructure to allow employees to combine family and work; (2) the lack of tenure tracks, combined with enforced mobility between organizations; and (3) the double burden of working for others (as part of a work group) while simultaneously gaining further certification.

Full Availability

Both organizations expect unlimited availability from their work force (Wimbauer, 1999). This normative orientation results in the gender-specific outcome that women do not see ways of combining work, partnership, and the education of children, while their male counterparts do. Less than one-third of the female scientists, but two-thirds of the male scientists in our sample are married; only 18 per cent of the women are mothers, but 40 per cent of the men are fathers. The older the female scientists are, the fewer children they have, while the opposite holds true for male scientists. Women see no way of combining work and family and thus delay their family formation to the (assumed) benefit of career building. They perceive an 'either children or science' dichotomy. Their arguments go in many directions: 'because I do not have children I will stay in science'; 'because I want children I will not attempt to become a professor'; and 'because I didn't get a job I decided to have children.' We suggest that exclusive dedication to science, in this stage of their life course, makes women better workers. Their availability is close to complete, even higher than the availability of their male counterparts.

However, after their fixed-term contracts are terminated, things change. Paradoxically, one reason to grant tenure after this time period is family responsibilities. Having sacrificed their family formation for reasons of occupational success, women cannot point to family responsibilities as a reason for needing tenure, and men fare much better (Wimbauer, 1999). Also, ironically, women would possibly be a lot better off with children at this point. In the eyes of the employers, there is a greater risk in employing women than men this time: women are by now in their mid-thirties, have delayed the birth of children, and are confronted with a life-cycle squeeze (Oppenheimer, 1974). At this stage, men are supposed to be more available and reliable workers. Statistical discrimination unfolds.

Enforced Mobility

Both male and female scientists usually have to leave the organization after their contract expires in order to find jobs in other research

TABLE 6.1
External and Internal Support

Support	N (252)	Men (%)	Women (%)	All Respondents (100%)
None	46	18	19	18
External only	68	26	28	27
Internal only	62	29	17	25
Full	76	27	36	30

SOURCE: Survey of MPS scientists; own calculations.

TABLE 6.2
Logistic Regression Model on Staying in Science (Persisters)

Variable	Model 1 Marginal effect	Model 2 Marginal effect	Model 3 Marginal effect
Sex	−0.21***		−0.16**
Age when finishing the PhD	−0.03*		−0.03*
Internal support		0.04	0.02
External support		0.23**	0.43***
Full support		0.16*	0.17**
Interaction sex and external support			−0.33**
N	252	252	252
Pseudo R^2	4.0	2.6	9.8
Chi^2	13.27	8.61	29.4
Degrees of freedom	2	3	6

*Significant on the 10% level; **Significant on the 5% level; ***Significant on the 1% level;
reference categories: no support; CPT sector; female
SOURCE: Survey of MPS scientists; own calculations

organizations or other settings. Successful transitions require connections, networks, mentoring, and, above all, trust. Using the MPS data, we can show that these transitions are much more difficult for women than for men.[7] Focusing on scientists when they were PhD candidates, we distinguish two forms of support: *external* support, provided by the scientific community, and *internal* support, provided by academic advisers.

As can be seen in table 6.1, 27 per cent of all men receive full support, but 36 per cent of all women do. This result comes as a surprise and should provide a solid ground for women for their career development. This, however, is not the case.

The results of a multivariate logistic regression model are shown in table 6.2. The dependent variable indicates whether a person stays in science or not, whereas the independent variables included in the models are sex and age when finishing the PhD (Model 1), the different types of support (Model 2), and all of these variables (Model 3). The marginal effects have to be interpreted as the changes in the probability of staying in science. As can be seen in Model 1, men are much more likely than women to stay in science, and the earlier in their life course, that people gain their PhD, the more likely they are to persist. Model 2 indicates that both external and full support have positive effects on the likelihood of staying in science, while internal support does not. The full model shows that – even after controlling for the different modes of support – women are 16 per cent less likely to stay than men. External support increases the likelihood of persistence by 43 per cent, full support by 17 per cent. The interaction between sex and external support shows that women cannot capitalize on their external support as much as their male counterparts. Obviously, after leaving the MPS, women find themselves in a new struggle against prejudice. This time, however, their situation is more difficult, as qualificational certification is completed and full availability is no longer assumed. Hence, the problem is not that women lack academic support; the issue is that support does not have an effect on career chances.

The Double Burden of Work and Certification

The way the German system of higher education is set up, candidates usually require labour-market exposure in order to attain a PhD and the Habilitation. It is common for young scholars to hold positions as research affiliates while simultaneously working on their academic qualification. In contrast to, for example, the United States, there is no clear division between formal academic qualification and academic employment in Germany. The double burden of performing for others as well as for oneself provides another example of structural conditions that lead to gendered outcomes. This set-up imposes continuous pressure upon all actors: young scholars bear the double burden of trying to do well for their research unit while at the same time working continuously for their own certificates, thus investing in the present and the future. Two-thirds of female and one-half of male scientists complain about a lack of advice and supervisors' indifference to their career concerns. Scientific advisers have to make sure that the goals of the organization are fully met. Consequently, they spend a limited amount of time on overseeing doctoral theses or mentoring and coaching their staff. At the same time, their priorities prove to be gendered. When working with female scientists, advisers tend to stress certification, whereas for male scientists they tend to facilitate involvement in a wide range of tasks. The statement 'I have time to focus on my own academic work' (7-point scale) averages at 4.1 for women but 2.3 for men. Women have significantly ($p = 0.001$) more time than men to pursue their certification.[8] Supervisors or mentors are 'doing gender' by emphasizing internal tasks for women instead of external challenges. In addition, men report more often that they were pushed to perform outside their institutes than their female counterparts.[9] These differences may well translate into gender differences in the achievement of external integration.

Formal certification seems almost to function as a tool to cool women out: women finish their degrees, but they do not get employed thereafter. In other words, they bear the double burden without gaining more than personal honour. In the work force they would possibly be equally well (or badly) off without the ordeal of working two shifts.

Conclusion

It has been argued that the organizations under study show considerable variation in terms of organizational structure and mission. In comparison to the FhS, the MPS includes a much wider range of disciplines and research fields. Thus, it is no surprise that the overall proportion of female scientists employed and hired by the MPS is higher than in the FhS. In addition, it could be argued that because the MPS is publicly funded, political pressure and policies aimed at increasing the proportion of woman scientists show a more direct effect there than in the market-oriented FhS.

Despite the many differences in the organizational shape of both research organizations, basic similarities prevail. Neither the effects of organizational demography nor differences in the organizational structures under study explain why women are rotating into and out of vacant positions rather than entering the MPS and FhS in larger numbers. The existence of two internal labour markets within both organizations – one for entry-level positions and one for longer-term career positions – proves to be crucial for translating academic qualification into successful academic and scientific careers. Entry into the latter type of position is possible only after scholars have successfully completed stage one and spent some time in another academic institution before re-entering the organization. It seems as if this career transition is one of the most crucial career passages for women and a heavily gendered one, too.

Our survey data indicate no individual-level gender differences in work attitudes, job involvement, and labour-market attachment. Our results clearly show that differences between men and women cannot be attributed to ability, motivation, or self-confidence; rather, structural factors must be at work. Therefore, we have to relate gender disparities in career outcomes to the organizational rationale of the two research organizations studied. Careers are not created by formal degrees and academic and scientific merit alone. Rather, careers are built upon a set of taken-for-granted prerequisites that are inherently gendered and mediated by MPS and FhS. Both stress the requirement of full-time availability, and both lack an infrastructure that could support efforts to combine work and family responsibilities. They provide almost no tenure tracks and impose the dual burden of working and qualifying work and qualify academically on their employees. While men and women are exposed to these forces to the same extent, the implications are different for male and female scientists.

Times may change. If research organizations and universities continue to restructure their work environment in a way that reduces job security, one of the few remaining reasons for pursuing academic careers may disappear and a male flight from unattractive positions may be the outcome (Roos and Jones, 1993). Our data give ample indication that this may happen. It remains to be seen whether only worsening working conditions that make jobs no longer attractive to male scientists will expand opportunities for women to join the inner circle.

NOTES

1 This research is supported by grants from the German Science Foundation and the Volkswagen Stiftung. We thank Janina Curbach for expert editing, Werner Fröhlich and Robert Hanslmaier for excellent research assistance, and Wolfgang Ludwig-Mayerhofer for valuable comments.

2 Since our data indicate the sex of scientists (male/female) and not their gender, it would be appropriate to use 'sex' rather than 'gender.' Theoretical precision aside, however, this use would often lead to awkward language and misunderstandings (e.g., 'sexism' versus 'genderization'). For this reason we will use the term 'gender.'

3 The organizations included in the analysis reported below are all in West Germany and were founded in or before 1989. Until very recently, no institutes existed in East Germany, although, shortly after unification, the MPS and FhS launched working groups aimed at founding such institutes. The development of these new institutes warrants a study in its own right, as starting conditions are very different in the East; they are therefore excluded from our analysis.

4 From the perspective of the United States, the time window might seem too short to warrant any expectations of change. Yet in Germany, the period falls in a time of intense public discussion about the integration of women in paid employment. Many public institutions, some regions, and a number of municipalities introduced legislation and policies aimed at promoting women and facilitating women's access to higher positions. Also, the turnover of scientific staff in the institutes theoretically provides ample room for social change.

5 The MPS data are based on 64 institutes; the FhS data are based on the 11 institutes selected for in-depth research.

6 There is one caveat, however. By design, our data are censored in that only male and female scientists who end up in the MPS and FhS are covered. Since we are primarily interested in the question of how and why women are getting lost after entering these organizations, this censoring works to our advantage.

7 Preliminary analyses (Wimbauer, 1999) show that the same argument can be made for the FhS.

8 This result is robust and backed by significant gender differences in responses to similar questions.

9 Answers to the respective items in our questionnaire ('I often present papers at conferences' and 'Publications are strongly supported') show significant gender differences.

REFERENCES

Acker, J. (1990). Hierarchies, jobs, bodies: A theory of gendered organizations. *Gender & Society, 4*, 139–58.

Allmendinger, J., Fuchs, S., von Stebut, J., & Brückner, H. (1999). Eine Liga für sich? Berufliche Werdegänge von Wissenschaftlerinnen in der Max-Planck-Gesellschaft. In A. Neusel & A. Wetterer (Eds), *Vielfältige Verschiedenheiten: Geschlechterverhältnisse in Studium* (pp 193–220). Frankfurt: Hochschule und Beruf.

Etzkowitz, H., Kemelgor, C., Neuschatz, M., & Uzzi, B. (1992). Athena unbound: Barriers to women in academic science and engineering. *Science and Public Policy, 19*(3), 157–79.

Etzkowitz, H., Kemelgor, C., Neuschatz, M., & Uzzi, B. (1994). The paradox of critical mass for women in science. *Science, 266*, 51–4.

Federal Glass Ceiling Commission. (1995). *Good for business: Making full use of the nation's human capital. A fact-finding report.* Washington, DC: Author.

Fraunhofer Society. (1998). Jahresbericht 1997. Munich: Author.

Jacobs, J. (1989). *Revolving doors: Sex segregation and women's careers.* Stanford: University Press.

Kulis, S., & Miller-Loessi, K. (1992a). Organizational dynamics and gender equity. *Work and Occupations, 19*(2), 157–83.

Kulis, S., & Miller-Loessi, K. (1992b). Organizations, labour markets, and gender integration in academic sociology. *Sociological Perspectives, 35*(1), 93–117.

Max Planck Society. (1998a). *Frauenförderrahmenplan.* Munich: Author.

Max Planck Society. (1998b). *http://www.mpg.de.*

Oppenheimer, V.K. (1974). The life-cycle squeeze: The interaction of men's occupational and family cycle. *Demography, 11*, 237–45.

Roos, P.A., & Jones, K.W. (1993). Shifting gender boundaries: Women's inroads into academic sociology. *Work and Occupations, 20*(4), 395–428.

Sonnert, G., & Holton G. (1995). *Gender differences in science careers.* New Brunswick, NJ: Rutgers University Press.

Statistisches Bundesamt. (1999). *Bildung und Kultur.* Hochschulstandort Deutschland: Wiesbaden.

Valian, V. (1998). Why so slow? The advancement of women. Cambridge, MA: MIT Press.

Wimbauer, C. (1999). *Organisation, Geschlecht, Karriere: Fallstudien aus einem Forschungsinstitut.* Opladen: Leske & Budrich.

Zuckerman, H., Cole, J.R., and Bruer, J.T. (Eds). (1991). *The outer circle: Women in the scientific community.* New York: Norton.

7. Polarization of Working Time and Gender Differences: Reconciling Family and Work by Reducing Working Time of Men and Women[1]

Diane-Gabrielle Tremblay[2]

As a result of major developments affecting both employment (e.g., the polarization of hours and the destandardization of jobs) and the family (e.g., the increased number of dual-earner families, a new definition of men and women's roles within some families, and new types of families), the work and family spheres are becoming less and less independent of one another. Today more than ever before, the loss of balance in one sphere directly affects the other. In the long run, conflicts within the job, family, and personal life have harmful effects on the individual, reducing personal well-being, increasing stress (Tissot et al., 1997), and negatively affecting work performance (Conference Board, 1994). The issue is very large and complex, and we cannot cover all aspects of the question here. We will therefore concentrate on the issue of working time, and on how certain aspects related to the work sphere pose problems or suggest elements of a solution. Using data from a survey we conducted on working-time arrangements and family issues, we seek to clarify the causes and implications of the difficulties of balancing work and family responsibilities throughout the life course, and investigate some means designed to alleviate the difficulties.

It will be argued that working time is central to the issue of balancing work and family. The use of strategies to restructure or reduce working time can significantly lessen the tension between the sphere of work and that of family life. Paradoxically, flexible schedules and hours are both part of the problem and part of the solution. That is, while flexible schedules imposed by the employer are often the main source of work–family balancing difficulties (Tissot et al., 1997; Tremblay and Villeneuve, 1998), flexible hours chosen by the workers themselves according to their needs and preferences can be part of the solution (Stone, 1994; Tremblay and Villeneuve, 1998). This is also the case with a reduction in working time (Tremblay and Vaillancourt-Laflamme, 2000). Restructuring and reducing working time does not necessarily solve the problem completely. It does not, for example, ensure a better gendered division of labour between men and women within the home and within paid employment. Nor does it cause men to assume a larger share of family responsibilities. However, it can alleviate some difficulties.

In the first part of the paper, we present data on the polarization of working hours and destandardization of jobs, as these appear to have increased in recent years, with a corresponding increase in the difficulties of work–family balancing. In the second part, we present our survey data on the perceptions of time and the preferences of individuals with respect to time and work–family balancing. Finally, we conclude with a discussion of the importance of working time in work–family balancing and present a few suggestions, based on both our survey results (Tremblay and Vaillancourt-Laflamme, 2000) and our general literature review (Tremblay and Villeneuve, 1998), for ways of alleviating the tension between the demands of work and family.

The Polarization of Working Hours and Destandardization of Jobs

One of the main transformations observed on the labour market over recent years has to do with the polarization of working hours. While the historical reduction of working hours is often noted, this development hides an important transformation in the distribution of hours – that is, the polarization of working hours – particularly since the recession of 1981–2. As concerns the evolution of the distribution in working hours in Canada between 1976 and 1995, the following facts emerge (full tables and figures are available from Tremblay and Villeneuve (1998), but could not be included here): the percentage of Canadian workers doing standard hours (thirty to forty hours) during one week has decreased in an important way; the percentage of workers doing short hours (less than thirty hours) has increased; the percentage of workers who have long hours (more than forty and more than fifty hours) has also increased significantly. Details will be presented below.

The situation in Québec is similar to the general Canadian situation and also presents a case of polarization of working hours. For the period from 1975 to 1994, the following observations can be made: the percentage of workers doing standard hours (thirty to forty hours) has decreased from 33.5 per cent to 31.9 per cent; the situation is slightly different from that of Canada overall with respect to relatively long hours (from forty to forty-nine), as they decrease in Québec from 42.1 per cent to 37.8 per cent; the proportion increases for short hours (less than thirty hours), from 15.6 per cent to 19.5 per cent; finally, for very long hours (fifty hours or more), the proportion increases from 8.8 per cent to 10.8 per cent.

Let us note that the polarization of working hours, while it has attracted less attention than the debate on the historical increase (Shor, 1992) or the historical reduction in working hours (Rifkin, 1995, among others), is not a phenomenon unique to Canada. It has also been observed in the United States, among other countries. In the United States, the variations observed are almost identical to those observed in Canada for the period from 1979 to 1993. Let us note that the percentage of male workers working between thirty-five and forty hours per week in their main job has decreased by about 6 percentage points, compared with 7 points in Canada. During the same period, male workers working fifty hours and more have increased by 3.5 percentage points in both countries (Morissette, 1995, p. 52). Data in Tissot and colleagues (1997) indicates that long hours pose work–family balancing problems. This particular issue, therefore, needs to be addressed in some detail, as it is often overlooked in studies using data on average hours.

Differences by Age and Gender

In general, women and youth are overrepresented in short hours, that is less than thirty hours (Sheridan, Sunter, and Diverty, 1996). Even if a relatively similar proportion of men (55.7 per cent) and women (52.3 per cent) had standard hours in Canada in 1995, 2.6 times more women worked short hours (35.7 per cent versus 13.7 per cent for men), while more men worked long hours (30.6 per cent versus 12.3 per cent for women). As for youth (aged 15 to 24), they are mainly concentrated in short hours. Their presence in the category of short hours has increased considerably, while it has diminished radically in the other categories, both of standard hours or long hours.

Polarization of working time thus concerns women and youth particularly. The percentage of different groups in standard hours diminishes from 71 per cent to 61 per cent from 1976 to 1993. During the same period, youth's share is reduced more considerably, while women are generally less numerous in the group working standard hours. The presence of all groups in short hours increases from year to year. Women are traditionally very numerous in the short-hours group, while youth see their share increase significantly.

Men are clearly more present in long hours. This has clear implications for the gendered division of labour within the family and within paid employment. It can be inferred that men have less free time for domestic work and family responsibilities (care of children and the elderly, etcetera), while women adapt their working hours in order to be able to cope with domestic and family responsibilities; this inference is also confirmed in our survey data (Tremblay and Vaillancourt-Laflamme, 2000).[3] However, as we will see later, standard, daily (nine-to-five) schedules are becoming less common, so that short hours do not necessarily solve the work–family balancing problem.

The data highlight the fact that men have to a certain extent caught up with women as concerns polarization and destandardization of working hours. From 1976 to 1995, the percentage of men doing standard hours decreased by 8.5 points, while the percentage for women decreased by 5.1 points. However, while the evolution for men is towards an increase in long hours, for women it is towards an increase in short hours. If anything, this means that the gap in the gendered division of labour between paid employment and family responsibilities can only be increasing.

It has to be recognized that women more often voluntarily accept short hours than men (Tremblay, 1997b), but it is unclear to what extent this so-called voluntary choice is constrained by men's working hours and the traditional gendered division of labour within the family, a possibility we considered in our survey. In fact, some data do indicate that women would want to reduce their hours further in order to have more time for family responsibilities: in 60 per cent of the cases of women with children and a partner, they would reduce or rearrange their working time because of family constraints, and in 14 per cent of the cases they would do so because of the partner's working hours (Tremblay and Vaillancourt-Laflamme, 2000).

Differences by Industry

Polarization also presents itself differently according to industry or sector of activity. As can be expected, there are more and more part-time workers in the service sector, while there are more and more long hours in the goods-producing sectors (Sheridan, Sunter, and Diverty, 1996).

For men working in the goods-producing sectors, the reduction in standard hours (10.1 points) is in favour of long hours (+8.3 points). As for the service sector, men have also seen a decrease in standard hours of 6.7 points, but the reduction is more equally shared between short hours (+3.7 points) and long hours (+3.0 hours). As concerns women in goods-producing sectors, the transformation of working hours is similar to the evolution observed for men in the different sectors. Standard hours have diminished, although less than for men during the same period, most likely because fewer women had standard hours already. The increase is mainly in long hours, an increase of 4.0 points between 1976 and 1995. This may partly explain the increasing difficulty in work–family balancing. As for the service sector, the reduction in standard hours is also of 4.3 points, but it is distributed differently between long hours (+2.5 points) and short hours (+1.7 points).

An important aspect has to be highlighted on the basis of this analysis – that is, that while polarization touches all sectors of activity, none is simultaneously touched by an increase and a decrease in hours. Polarization actually manifests itself as an increase in long hours in some sectors, such as transportation, storage, communications, commerce, business, education, other services, and public administration, and a corresponding unilateral increase in short hours in health and social services, as well as in hotel and restaurant services and food services.

In the case of Québec, the trend is basically the same. Short hours are more common in the service sector, while long hours are more common in the primary sectors, and in construction, transportation, and storage. The large increase in short schedules is thus a phenomenon related to the growth of the service sector over the last decades. The strong concentration of women and youth in the service sector translates into shorter hours for these groups (Tremblay, 1997a).

Differences by Occupational Group

Polarization is also differentiated according to occupational groups. The distribution in working hours is clearly dependent on various factors, including level of responsibility, qualifications required, cost of training new employees, possibility of doing paid overtime work, and possibility of promotion (which will partly explain unpaid long hours, particularly in professional and management categories). In the male categories, standard hours have decreased in all ten occupational groups. However, polarization does not manifest itself identically in all groups. Managers, professionals, and blue-collar workers are mainly concerned by an increase in hours, while office workers, salesmen, and service employees have seen a move towards short hours. For women, there is a decline in standard hours in six out of eight categories. In professional and management categories the trend is towards long hours, while there is little change for blue-collar workers, office workers, and in sales and services.

The increase in hours appears to be explained either by the possibility of promotion (managers have an increase of 8.2 points in long hours, for a reduction of 8.3 points in standard hours), or by paid overtime (blue-collar workers).

Destandardization of Work Schedules and Jobs

The destandardization in work hours translates not only into an increase in short and long hours and a decrease in standard hours (thirty to forty hours) – that is, a destandardization in *length* of working hours – but also in a destandardization of the schedules according top which these hours are done. In other words, the standard 'nine-to-five' schedule is becoming less common. One might think that this evolution in non-standard hours is due to workers' preferences, but data indicate that over 90 per cent of full-time workers who have non-standard working schedules have these schedules because of their job's requirements, while this is the case for over half (53.4 per cent) of part-time workers. With respect to forms of employment, a variety of sources indicate that a minimum of one-third of all workers have non-standard forms of employment (Tremblay, 1997a). If schedules are taken into account, the percentage increases and only one out of three workers has standard employment *and* schedule.

Atypical schedules, if chosen by the workers, can certainly contribute to reconciling the demands of work, family, and personal life; however, if imposed by the employer, they can be a source of difficulties in work–family balancing (Tissot et al., 1997; Tremblay and Villeneuve, 1998). Considering the present tendency towards a destandardization of working hours and schedules, which we have illustrated in the previous pages, and according to our own survey results, it seems that most people are short of time, and that it is more and more difficult to find time for different personal activities; we now turn to data from our survey and others which support this finding.

Perceptions of Time and Aspirations regarding Work–Family Balancing Issues

Different factors have influenced work–family balancing issues. Among the main ones are labour-market trends – mainly the new composition of the work force, where women are more important – the increase in dual-earner families, and changes in family composition. These factors all have an impact on the perceptions of time, on the difficulties people have in reconciling the responsibilities of work, family, and personal life, and on work performance. We will not go over them in detail, as we have done so elsewhere (Tremblay and Villeneuve, 1997, 1998).

For many families, the time when men worked from nine to five while women worked at home and assumed all domestic and family obligations is largely gone. As our survey and others indicate, this change translates into difficulties in balancing work and family and in the desire for a reorganization and reduction of working time.

A variety of indicators support the finding that many people have difficulty reconciling work with family and personal responsibilities. Statistics Canada published some interesting data in 1995, on the basis of the General Social Survey. The results from the survey show a trend towards work overloads that increase the conflict between family roles and work roles and have a negative impact on family and personal life.

About half of respondents in all categories are worried that they do not spend enough time with their families and friends, that they often feel they haven't done all they should during the day, and that they sometimes cut down on sleep when they are short of time. Mothers are most likely to report feeling stressed because of lack of time (69 per cent). However, more than 50 per cent of respondents in all groups report feeling short of time (Frederick, 1995). Our own data (table 7.1) indicate that some 70 per cent of women with a partner and at least one child feel that their work does not leave them enough free time, and the same is true for 67 per cent of men in the same family situation.

Fathers are proportionally more stressed than other men, according to Frederick (1995), but the difference between the groups with and without children is smaller than that between mothers and other women. In our own survey, all respondents had to have children to

TABLE 7.1
Evaluation of Time Left after Work

Evaluation of Time Left after Work		Women				Men				Total
		Other types of family	Shared care	Alone with children	Couple with children	Other types of family	Shared care	Alone with children	Couple with children	
Sufficient	No.	4	7	44	117	0	1	0	53	226
	%	21.1	38.9	40.7	27.7	0.0	33.3	0.0	29.6	30.0
Not enough	No.	11	11	61	298	3	2	1	121	508
	%	57.9	61.1	56.5	70.6	100.0	66.7	100.0	67.6	67.5
Too much time	No.	0	0	1	0	0	0	0	0	1
	%	0.0	0.0	0.9	0.0	0.0	0.0	0.0	0.0	0.1
No answer	No.	4	0	2	7	0	0	0	5	18
	%	21.1	0.0	1.9	1.7	0.0	0.0	0.0	2.8	2.4
Total	No.	19	18	108	422	3	3	1	179	753
	%	100.0	100.0	100.0	100.0	100.0	100.0	100.0	100.0	100.0

respond, and we concentrated on the differences among various family situations, as is shown in table 7.1.

Many dimensions of family and personal life, including physical and psychological health, suffer from the effects of lack of time. Other research has produced findings like those of Statistics Canada, particularly a survey conducted by the Quebec Federation of Labour (FTQ, 1995; Tissot et al., 1997). This last survey indicated that about half of the workers interviewed suffered from some form of 'psychological distress,' the percentage being twice that observed in the general population. We are clearly far away from the 'leisure society' that was expected in the 1970s.

Consequences for Work Performance

Role conflict that creates problems in one sphere usually has an impact on the other; if work sometimes has a negative influence on family life, family life can also have a negative effect on work.

In a survey conducted by the Conference Board of Canada with 385 employers, respondents said a good part of their problems with human-resources (HR) management were related to their workers' struggles to reconcile professional and family obligations (Paris, 1989). HR problems include absenteeism, difficulty in recruiting and keeping workers, lateness, and productivity and performance problems. If we combine answers saying that a quarter, a half, or more than half of various HR problems are related to work–family conflicts, we find that some 60 per cent of the employers questioned attribute at least one-quarter of all HR problems to work–family conflicts. The link between absenteeism and work–family conflicts has also been shown by other surveys. In Canada, the number of absences caused by personal or family responsibilities almost tripled between 1977 and 1990, passing from 1.9 to 5.2 days per year (Akyeampong, 1992). There is a clear difference between men and women, as women generally assume the care of children and the elderly. The number of days of women's absenteeism for personal or family reasons went from 1.9 to 5.2 per year for women working full time, but from only 0.7 to a little under 1 for men. The age of the youngest child is an important factor: in families where there was at least one child of preschool age, the annual number of days lost was on average 25.1 between 1987 and 1990. The Conference Board survey also indicated that many employers attribute more than one-quarter of their productivity problems (42.2 per cent of employers) and their performance problems (39.5 per cent of all respondents) to difficulties workers experience in balancing work and family. The Canadian survey on child care (Lero et al., 1992, 1993) presents many other aspects related to the problems working parents have in juggling child care and work. Among other things, Lero indicates that about half of parents (49 per cent) had difficulty either finding or keeping adequate child-care services during the past year. They cited the following as the main impacts on their working life: inability to do overtime as required or as desired; worries over child care while at work; reduction in professional commitment due to child-care problems; reduction in hours of work; refusal of job offers; quitting a job because of problems with child care.

Role conflicts affect not only the workers concerned, but also employers, who may have difficulty recruiting workers. The Conference Board survey indicates that some 12 per cent of workers questioned quit jobs because of work–family conflicts. Women were four times as likely as men to have done so. The Conference Board survey also indicates that 14 per cent of workers had thought about quitting their jobs because of family reasons, while 17 per cent had refused a promotion for the same reasons.

As the cost of hiring an employee becomes higher and higher – up to 93 per cent of the first-year annual wage, according to a U.S. study (Catalyst National Study of Parental Leave) – more and more employers are preoccupied by the issue of work–family balancing. Employers are thus starting to recognize that workers have family responsibilities and that the worlds of work and family have an impact on each other. The Conference Board of Canada (1994) and the Québec Employers' Federation (CPQ, 1993a, 1993b) both recognize that by implementing measures to reduce work–family conflicts, employers are acting in their own interest. However, although more and more employers are considering adopting work–family-balancing measures, many still believe that family issues are not a business concern. Of the few surveys conducted with employers, St-Onge, Guérin, and colleagues (1994) indicate that work–family-balancing programs and measures (daycare, working-time arrangements, and other measures) are not yet very numerous, with only some 25 per cent of measures identified as relatively frequent in firms. Our own ongoing survey in the private manufacturing sector (Tremblay and Amherdt, 2000) also indicates that very few firms offer many types of work–family-balancing measures. Arrangements for worker-oriented flexible work hours are quite limited, and the maximum number of measures offered is four or sometimes five out of a list of ten. Flextime is somewhat more frequent for office workers; some 50 per cent of our respondents used flextime and some 14 per cent more were offered it as an option but didn't take it. Only about one-third of our respondents could benefit from voluntary part-time work or a compressed work week. On-site day-care, information services, telework, and adapted career profiles are even less frequent, all below 15 per cent (Tremblay and Vaillancourt-Laflamme, 2000).

In such a context, it is not surprising that a good percentage of our respondents would prefer to work fewer hours (see table 7.2): about half the women (49.9 per cent) and some 45 per cent of the men would prefer to work much less, while respectively 27 per cent and 26 per cent would like to work a little less. One-quarter of the men and 18 per cent of the women would choose to work the same number of hours, and marginal percentages wanted to work more (2 per cent).

As concerns the forms of reduction preferred, table 7.3 indicates that the four-day work week was the preferred choice of the majority, some 55 per cent of women and 50 per cent of men. This is followed by a preference for time off during school holidays for 34 per cent of men and 18 per cent of women.

We also asked about workers' reasons for being opposed to various forms of working-time reorganization, including evening work and weekends, as these are often associated with reductions in working time. Table 7.4 indicates that family constraints are the main reason for being opposed to these reorganizations, followed by the partner's schedule. Family constraints and partner's schedule thus appear as the main constraining factors in working-time choices and reorganization.

Working Time and Work–Family Balancing: Options and Solutions

The previous sections lead us to an important question: Who is to assume responsibility for children, aging parents, and handicapped persons, or, to put it another way, what are the respective roles of the parents, the family, the firm, and society in this regard? We do not have enough space here for a detailed report on all the implications of our survey responses, and will thus concentrate on general principles which can be deduced from our own and other surveys (Guérin et al., 1996; Lero et al., 1993; Tremblay and Vaillancourt-Laflamme, 2000).

TABLE 7.2
Preferences regarding Working Hours

Preferences		Women					Men				
		Other types of family	Shared care	Alone with children	Coupled with children	Total women	Other types of family	Shared care	Alone with children	Coupled with children	Total men
Wants to work more	No.	2	0	4	9	15	0	0	0	5	5
	%	10.5	0.0	3.7	2.1	2.6	0.0	0.0	0.0	2.8	2.7
Wants to work the same hours	No.	2	1	33	69	105	0	1	0	44	45
	%	10.5	5.6	30.6	16.4	18.5	0.0	33.3	0.0	24.6	24.2
Wants to work a little less	No.	3	6	26	119	154	2	2	1	44	49
	%	15.8	33.3	24.1	28.2	27.3	66.7	66.7	100.0	24.6	26.3
Wants to work much less	No.	8	10	44	221	283	0	0	0	84	84
	%	42.1	55.6	40.7	52.4	49.9	0.0	0.0	0.0	46.9	45.2
No answer	No.	4	1	1	4	10	1	0	0	2	3
	%	21.1	5.6	0.9	0.9	1.8	33.3	0.0	0.0	1.1	1.6
Total	No.	19	18	108	422	567	3	3	1	179	186
	%	100.0	100.0	100.0	100.0	100	100.0	100.0	100.0	100.0	100

TABLE 7.3
Preferred Forms of Reduced Working Hours

Preferences		Women					Men				
		Other types of family	Shared care	Alone with children	Coupled with children	Total women	Other types of family	Shared care	Alone with children	Coupled with children	Total men
Four-day week	No.	12	9	58	236	315	2	1	0	90	93
	%	63.2	50.0	53.7	55.9	55.6	66.7	33.3	0.0	50.3	50.0
50% of normal schedule	No.	1	0	1	17	19	0	0	0	1	1
	%	5.3	0.0	0.9	4.0	3.4	0.0	0.0	0.0	0.6	0.5
School holidays off	No.	1	5	10	78	102	0	1	0	15	65
	%	5.3	27.8	9.3	18.5	18.0	0.0	33.3	0.0	8.4	34.9
Other form	No.	0	0	7	16	23	0	0	0	7	7
	%	0.0	0.0	6.5	3.8	4.1	0.0	0.0	0.0	3.9	3.8
No interest in reduced hours	No.	3	4	31	64	94	0	1	1	63	16
	%	15.8	22.2	28.7	15.2	16.6	0.0	33.3	100.0	35.2	8.6
No answer	No.	2	0	1	11	14	1	0	0	3	4
	%	10.5	0.0	0.9	2.6	2.5	33.3	0.0	0.0	1.7	2.2
Total	No.	19	18	108	422	567	3	3	1	179	186
	%	100.0	100.0	100.0	100.0	100	100.0	100.0	100.0	100.0	100

TABLE 7.4
Reasons for Opposition to Various Forms of Reorganized Working Hours

Reasons		Women				Men				Total
		Other types of family	Shared care	Alone with children	Coupled with children	Other types of family	Shared care	Alone with children	Coupled with children	
Family constraints	No.	7	11	73	253	1	2	1	92	40
	%	36.8	61.1	67.6	60.0	33.3	66.7	100.0	51.4	58.4
Partner's schedule	No.	2	0	1	62	1	0	0	27	93
	%	10.5	0.0	0.9	14.7	33.3	0.0	0.0	15.1	12.4
Personal constraints	No.	4	2	6	14	0	0	0	17	43
	%	21.4	11.1	5.6	3.3	0.0	0.0	0.0	9.5	5.7
Would reduce respondent's possibilities for outings	No.	1	0	1	8	0	1	0	10	21
	%	5.3	0.0	0.9	1.9	0.0	33.3	0.0	5.6	2.8
Other	No.	0	2	5	14	0	0	0	7	28
	%	0.0	11.1	4.6	3.3	0.0	0.0	0.0	3.9	3.7
No response	No.	5	3	22	71	1	0	0	26	128
	%	26.3	16.7	20.3	16.8	33.3	0.0	0.0	14.5	17.0
Total	No.	19	18	108	422	3	3	1	179	753
	%	100.0	100.0	100.0	100.0	100.0	100.0	100.0	100.0	100.0

Work–Family Balancing: Individual or Collective Responsibility?

The responsibility for establishing or re-establishing balance between work and family cannot be left to individuals, particularly in female single-parent families, of which there are many. The case for collective responsibility is strengthened when we allow for intergenerational transfers – more specifically, the fact that these mothers' children will, through social programs and transfers, assume some financial responsibility for people without children as they age and increasingly need the support of public services. Thus, from the perspective of intergenerational and social transfers, as well as that of social solidarity, it is legitimate to assume society's collective responsibility towards children in particular. A similar case can also be made with respect to the case of the elderly; here the legitimacy of collective action rests mainly on a social-solidarity rather than a financial-transfer perspective. Workers do appear to expect some form of support from their employers, and particularly from their immediate superior (Guérin et al., 1996; Tremblay and Vaillancourt-Laflamme, 2000). While some employers have started to develop daycare or programs to support family activities, those who do so are not yet very numerous (St-Onge et al., 1994; Tremblay and Vaillancourt-Laflamme, 2000; Tremblay and Amherdt, 2000). The same goes for municipalities and the school system, which have clearly not gone as far as they could, particularly in terms of diversity and flexibility of services.

In order to solve the problem, it is essential to develop a global approach, a diversified and coherent set of provisions to cover all needs, based on the different needs and preferences identified in our own and other surveys. Such provisions would include better daycare, more flexible schedules, more extensive preschool activities and programs, free daycare to cover professional-development days and school holidays that often do not coincide with parental time off, and so on. In this regard, the mandatory involvement of public services and the state would appear to be called for to design solutions for all. Firms could also be called upon to complete the support package in ad-hoc situations.

Hours and Schedules: Both Choice and Flexibility Are Essential

In different surveys, parents were asked to identify, from among a variety of options, their preferred modes of work–family balancing. A key requirement appeared to be provisions for reduced working time and more flexible hours: as our data indicate, parents would appreciate the possibility of reducing and rearranging their working hours mainly along the lines of the four-day work week or time off during school holidays. Flexibility in working hours is seen as important in work–family balancing, but while working schedules have become more flexible or variable over the years, the type of flexibility offered is not always that wanted by workers. Many workers actually suffer from variable schedules and hours that are imposed upon them by their employer, sometimes by the specific conditions of the work being done, as in restaurant work, banking, and other services, where working hours are to a large extent determined by the presence of consumers (Tissot et al., 1997; Tremblay and Villeneuve, 1997). Not only flexible work hours, but also *choice* in the scheduling of these hours are essential to make flexibility an advantage and not a problem for work–family balancing.

Of course, a range of measures is needed to address the various family-related HR problems; some are appropriate for reducing absenteeism or lateness, others for improving worker productivity and performance, others for facilitating recruitment, and yet others for reducing stress and improving employee morale (Conference Board, 1994). In other words, the measures chosen need to be tailored to specific problems and contexts.

Our review of different studies and our own surveys lead us to put forward some basic principles for facilitating work–family balancing which in our view should be considered by firms and organizations dealing with such issues. We list them quickly in the conclusion to this paper.

The first principle is that employers and governments need to think in terms of a 'work–family program.' Surveys and case studies indicate that flexible work schedules work best when accompanied by a coherent set of complementary measures designed to facilitate work–family balancing. Too few firms are adopting such a 'program' approach. Rather than adopting isolated, piecemeal measures, firms and their employees (or the employees' representatives), should take a holistic approach to the problem, considering all angles and details, including age of children, type of family (two-parent or single parent), job requirements (attendance at late meetings or out-of-town meetings), and so on.

A second principle is that solutions need to be adapted to the different situations. For example, an on-site daycare may seem like a universal ideal solution, but that will not be so for workers who are often on the move, actually working in different places or having meetings with clients in different places. Firms should therefore not just choose a few programs that *appear* appropriate to them without analyzing their employees' specific situations and needs.

A third principle is that workers' entitlement to fringe benefits, job security, opportunities for training and promotion, and medical/dental and pension benefits should not be eroded as a consequence of increased flexibility in work schedules.

This leads us to the fourth principle – which may seem to some just wishful thinking – that it is important to ensure that work–family-balancing measures are used by men as well as women, not only to ensure a better division of labour within the family, but also to ensure equality for women in the labour market. This objective is not an easy one to achieve, as it requires changes in attitudes towards the question of equal rights for all employees regardless of sex, age, or race.

To date, flexible hours, part-time work, reduced hours, and similar measures for reconciling the demands of work and family are more often imposed on women than on men, and this is particularly so for less-educated or less-qualified women. This helps to perpetuate the traditional gendered division of labour within the family, with women assuming the majority of family responsibilities, and the reduction in paid hours contributing to continuing economic and professional inequality between men and women.

NOTES

1 I would like to mention the cooperation of two research assistants in the results presented here: first, Catherine Vaillancourt-Laflamme, who worked on our survey of some 547 women and their partners (of whom 186 responded) on work–family balancing and working-time issues; and second, Daniel Villeneuve, who worked on the literature review on which our research is based. The literature review is presented in detail in Tremblay and Villeneuve (1998). The first survey results are in Tremblay and Vaillancourt-Laflamme (2000).

2 The survey was conducted in early 1998 with the following groups of female office employees – and their partners – as respondents: female members of the Syndicat de la fonction publique du Québec (the Québec public-service

union), office employees registered as students at Télé-université, and members of the Fédération professionnelle des secrétaires du Québec. The response rate was 17.5 per cent.

3 We present the general Canadian data, as they represent the whole population, but our survey, as mentioned in note 1, indicates the same trends – that is, prevalence of shorter hours for women and longer hours for men – as well as some difficulties related to this, and preference for a stronger reduction in and reorganization of working hours, to which we will turn in the second part of the paper.

REFERENCES

Akyeampong, E.B. (1992). L'absentéisme: Une mise à jour. Perspective. Ottawa: Statistique Canada.
Conference Board du Canada. (1994). *Concilier le travail et la famille: Enjeux et options.* Ottawa: Author.
CPQ (Conseil du Patronat du Québec). (1993a). Programme travail-famille: Modèle d'implantation (Dossier 93-14). Montréal: Author.
CPQ (Conseil du Patronat du Québec). (1993b). Conciliation travail-famille: Expériences québecoises (Dossier 93-10). Montréal: Author.
Développement des ressources humaines Canada. (1996). *L'avenir du travail: Tendances de la nature changeante de l'emploi.* Ottawa: Author.
Frederick, J.A. (1995). Au fil des heures: L'emploi du temps des Canadiens (Cat. No. 89-544F). Ottawa: Statistique Canada.
FTQ (Fédération des travailleurs et travailleuses du Québec). (1995). *Ré-concilier ... l'inconciliable: Recherche sur la conciliation des responsabilités professionnelles, familiales, sociales et personnelles.* Phase 2/Des faits saillants.
Guérin, G., St-Onge, S., Trottier, R., Haines, V., & Simard, M. (1996). *Pour que travail et famille fassent bon ménage.* Résultats préliminaires de l'enquête par questionnaire sur les tensions emploi–famille réalisée auprès des membres de la CSN. 19 pp.
Lero, D.S., et al. (1992). *Étude nationale Canadienne sur la garde des enfants: Les régimes de travail des parents et leurs besoins en matière de garde des enfants* (cat. 89–529F). Ottawa: Statistique Canada.
Lero, D.S., et al. (1993). *Étude nationale Canadienne sur la garde des enfants: Avantages et flexibilité en milieu de travail, tour d'horizon des expériences vécues par les parents* (cat. 89-530F). Ottawa: Statistique Canada.
Morissette, R. (1995). Pourquoi l'inégalité des gains hebdomadaires a-t-elle

augmenté au Canada? (Document de recherche no. 80). Ottawa: Statistique Canada.

Paris, H. (1989). Les programmes d'aide aux travailleurs qui ont des obligations familiales. Ottawa: Conference Board du Canada.

Rifkin, J. (1995). *The end of work: The decline of the global labor force and the dawn of the post-market era.* New York: Putnam Books.

St-Onge, S., Guérin, G., Trottier, R., Haines, V., & Simard, M. (1994, mai). L'équilibre travail-famille: Un nouveau défi pour les organisations. *Gestion,* 19(2), 64–73.

Sheridan, M., Sunter, D., & Diverty, B. (1996). *The changing workweek: Trends in weekly hours in Canada, 1976–1995.* Ottawa: Statistique Canada.

Shor, J. (1992). The overworked American: The unexpected decline of leisure. New York: Basic Books.

Stone, L. (1994). *Emploi et famille: Les dimensions de la tension.* Ottawa: Statistique Canada.

Tissot, F., Messing, K., Vandelac, L., Garon, S., Prévost, J., Méthot, A.L., & Pinard R. (1997). *Concilier les responsabilités professionnelles, familiales, personnelles et sociales: Ce n'est pas toujours la santé!* Rapport présenté à la FTQ le 19 novembre 1997.

Tremblay, D.-G. (1997a). *Économie du travail: Les réalités et les approches théoriques.* Montréal: Éditions St-Martin et Télé-université.

Tremblay, D.-G. (1997b). The 'New Division of Labour' debate and women's jobs: Results from a survey conducted in Canada from a gendered perspective. In V. Oechtering (Ed.), *Spinning a web from past to future: Women, work and computerization.* New York: Springer-Verlag.

Tremblay, D.-G., & Amherdt, C.H. (2000). *La conciliation emploi-famille: Les mesures offertes et la participation des pères.* Research Report. 99p.

Tremblay, D.-G., & Vaillancourt-Laflamme, C. (2000). *Conciliation emploi-famille et aménagement-réduction du temps de travail: Description des données d'enquêtes.* Research Report.

Tremblay, D.-G., & Villeneuve, D. (1997, juillet). Aménagement et réduction du temps de travail: Réconcilier emploi, famille et vie personnelle. *Loisir et société* (Presses de l'université du Québec), 20(1), 51–101.

Tremblay, D.-G., & Villeneuve, D. (1998). *Aménagement et réduction du temps de travail les enjeux: Les approches, les méthodes.* Montréal: Éditions St-Martin.

8. Balancing Employment and Family Lives: Changing Life-course Experiences of Men and Women in the European Union[1]

Susan Yeandle

This chapter discusses the changes being experienced by men and women as the distribution and allocation of labour changes. The changes in question represent a significant restructuring of the life course, away from its former more predictable and relatively orderly shape, towards a more diverse and fragmented experience which is polarizing the experiences of some groups while rendering more similar those of others. The chapter's focus is on changes in the social and sexual division of labour, and on the shifting boundaries between unpaid work and employment. A central concern is the extent to which formerly unpaid work, mainly done by women, has become commodified or collectivized (or both) and has emerged in the paid economy in the form of 'new jobs' in the service sector.

The term 'life course' is used here (in preference to 'life cycle') although it is from Rowntree's conceptualization of a 'life cycle of needs' that the term has evolved in social analysis (Glennerster, 1995). Glennerster's discussion of the way in which the welfare state impacts on individuals over their lifetimes has already stressed ways in which increased variability and vulnerability have emerged in the late twentieth century, citing length of schooling, labour market uncertainty and variability, marital instability and change, and rising health costs as key factors, and concluding that this increased variability is 'a cause of growing inequality between social groups and between men and women.'

In considering life-course experiences, and, in particular, the changed balance between the activities of paid work (breadwinning) and unpaid work (mainly family care and domestic labour), the chapter presents some of the main elements of change in working and family life in European countries. Here, two central questions are addressed: Are men's and women's employment patterns becoming more similar? And, are men and women developing a more similar experience of family life and sharing the tasks of family living more equitably? Both of these questions concern the possible erosion of gender boundaries. The chapter reviews developments in the delivery of care work, using the example of child care, and concludes with consideration of the significance of birth cohort for life-course experiences of paid and unpaid work (Elder, 1991).

Economic Reorganization and Restructuring: Elements of Change in Women's and Men's Employment Patterns in Europe[2]

The key elements of change in female employment patterns in Europe in the second half of the twentieth century have been widely commented upon. Emphasis has been given to the changed labour-force-participation rates of married women and of mothers, which are seen as reflecting the changed social position and status of women, their greater access to educational qualifications, changes in the occupational and industrial structure, and shifts in the demand for labour. These changes have run alongside a marked shift in some countries away from the full-time, standardized, and formal employment associated predominantly with male industrial work forces and towards the recruitment and establishment of a more diverse labour force in which the boundaries between formal and informal employment and economic activity have become less clearly marked. Here, new forms of work, including part-time employment, self-employment, insecure employment, and multiple job holding have emerged, alongside a continuing role in some states for 'family working' (Purcell and Purcell, 1998; Wedderburn, 1995; Yeandle, 1999).

The extension of non-standard employment to men is an aspect which has only relatively recently attracted attention. While it is clear that men in some occupational groups have never had the permanent, secure employment associated with mid-century skilled manual and white-collar work for men, increases in men's temporary, part-time, and casual employment, especially among younger and older male workers, have more recently become visible in some EU Member States.

Although the overall size of the labour force increased between 1984 and 1994 in most EU states (see table 8.1), men's participation rates declined everywhere, with particularly sharp reductions among younger men (partly explained by extended education) and among men over age 45, whose detachment from the labour force results from increased early retirement, higher rates of long-term sickness, and economic restructuring in key industries, notably coal, steel, shipbuilding, engineering, and agriculture.

By the mid-1990s, employment across the EU showed a strong emphasis on the service sector, with agriculture offering only a tiny proportion of employment. More specifically, within the service sector itself, employment in community, social, and personal social services, and in wholesale and retail trade, restaurants, and hotels increased (table 8.2). Such sectoral shifts in employment are linked to increased demand, triggered by demographic shifts, to changes in the availability of unpaid labour for domestic and voluntary activities, and to the developing commodification of domestic labour.

Convergence Tendencies

Part-time employment increased in most EU Member States between 1985 and 1995 and stabilized or declined only in those Scandinavian states where women's participation rates had already reached a very high level (table 8.3). Most part-time workers were aged between 25 and 49 years (ELFS). Significant percentages of employed women and of employed mothers worked part time in all states (in Belgium, Denmark, Germany, and Austria, about 25 per cent of employed mothers with a child aged 0 to 10 years worked part-time in 1993, compared with approximately 80 per cent in the Netherlands and about 10 per cent in Portugal [European Commission, 1997, pp 58–9]), but there remain major differences in the part-time working patterns of fathers and mothers (European Commission, 1997). While part-time male employment increased in most EU countries in the decade to 1995, it remained relatively insignificant in Belgium, Greece, Italy, Luxembourg, and Spain, and was not strongly linked with family responsibilities. Even in the Netherlands, where by 1995 almost 17 per cent of men worked part-time, in 1993 only about 7 per cent of fathers of dependent children were part-time workers. Where male part-time working rose sharply (e.g., among young men in the United Kingdom and among men aged 25 to 64 in France), much of this was involuntary or

TABLE 8.1
Employment in Selected Countries: Participation Rates and Sectoral Distribution

	Total labour force				Total civilian employment				
		Change since 1984 %	Female participation rate[f]			Change since 1984 %	Agriculture forestry, and fishing %	Industry %	Services %
	Thousands 1994		1994	1984	Thousands 1994				
Austria	3,876	15.3	62.1	51.5	3,737	15.5	7.2	33.2	59.6
Belgium	4,273[a]	3.3[b]	55.1[a]	48.7[d]	3,692[a]	5.4[d]	2.6[e]	27.7[e]	69.7[e]
Denmark	2,777	2.1	73.8	73.8	2,508	2.1	5.1	26.8	68.1
Finland	2,502	-2.8	69.9	72.9	2,015	-16.1	8.3	26.8	64.9
France	25,474	6.3	59.6	54.7	21,744	3.6	4.9	26.7	68.4
Germany	39,646	38.3[c]	61.8	52.3[c]	35,894	38.8c	3.3	37.6	59.1
Greece	4,193	8.4	44.6	40.9	3,790	6.7	20.8	23.6	55.5
Ireland	1,424	9.0	47.2	36.9	1,207	10.7	12.0	27.6	60.5
Italy	22,727	-2.6	42.9	40.7	20,022	-1.9	7.7	32.1	60.2
Luxembourg	213	32.3	56.5	42.2	207	31.0	2.9	......	......
Netherlands	7,184	24.4	57.4	40.7	6,631	33.2	4.0	23.0	73.0
Portugal	4,769	5.3	62.2	56.0	4,372	7.3	11.5	32.8	55.7
Spain	15,701	12.9	44.1	33.2	11,760	9.4	9.8	30.1	60.2
Sweden	4,266	-2.8	74.4	77.3	3,926	-7.7	3.4	25.0	71.6
UK	28,433	4.3	66.2	59.1	25,579	7.0	2.1	27.7	70.2

a – 1993; b – 1983–1993; c – Ex-FRG only; d – 1983; e – 1992; f – Defined as female labour force of all ages divided by female population aged 15–64
SOURCE: 'Labour Force Statistics 1974–1994,' OECD, Paris, 1996

TABLE 8.2
Contribution of Service Sector to Total Employment: Selected Countries (percentages)

Contribution to employment: % of total employment

	Wholesale and retail trade, restaurants, and hotels I		Transport, storage, and communication II		Finance, insurance, real estate, and business services III		Community, social, and personal services IV		Producers of government services V	
	1995	1985	1995	1985	1995	1985	1995	1985	1995	1985
Austria	20.7[a]	18.6	7.5[a]	7.2	7.7[a]	6.5	5.5[a]	4.6	21.8[a]	19.4
Belgium	19.1[a,b]	19.2[b]	6.4[a]	6.7	3.8[a,j]	3.9[j]	22.6[a,b,j]	17.9[b,j]	19.2[a]	20.4
Denmark	13.2[a]	13.1	7.0[a]	6.9	10.2[a]	8.8	7.1[a]	6.4	31.0[a]	29.7
Finland	15.6	16.0	7.6	7.1	9.1	6.9	6.5	6.0	25.2	20.1
France	17.5	17.0	5.7	5.8	11.3	8.7	7.2	5.7	28.0[q]	24.8[q]
Germany	..	..	5.5	6.0[e]	3.0[j]	2.7[e,j]	..	..	15.9	15.9[e]
Greece	..	15.9	..	6.9	..	3.7	..	17.2[n]	..	..
Italy	21.9[b]	21.2[b]	6.3	6.0	15.9[k]	12.9[k]	3.2[k]	2.7[k]	16.1	15.2
Luxembourg	20.6[e]	21.9	6.8[e]	6.7	9.0[e,j]	6.8[j]	20.3[e,j]	15.2[j]	10.8[e]	11.4
Netherlands	21.2[a]	18.9	6.6[a]	6.7	12.8[a]	10.1	17.1[a]	16.2	12.7[a]	14.9
Portugal	17.3[c]	15.6[h]	3.6[c]	3.9[h]	6.1[c]	3.4[h]	11.1[c]	7.7[h]	15.3[c]	13.9[h]
Spain	22.7[b,f]	20.4[b]	5.6[f]	6.2	5.2[f]	4.3	10.3[f]	8.8	15.9[f]	13.4
Sweden	14.1[a]	13.7	6.7[a]	6.7	8.9[a]	6.4	8.2[a]	6.9	32.0[a]	32.7
UK	19.6[g]	19.8	5.6[g]	5.8	11.9[g]	9.4	11.8[g]	8.6	19.4[g,r]	21.5[f]

a – 1994; b – Recovery and repair services included in the wholesale and retail trade; c – 1993; d – Restaurants and hotels included in IV; e – 1991; f – 1992; g – 1990; h – 1986; j – Real estate and business services included in IV; k – Community, social, and personal services included in III; m – Excludes sanitary and similar services; n – V included under IV; p – Refers to public administration and defence; q – Other producers included in V; r – Industries of general government included under V.
SOURCE: 'National Accounts: 1982–94,' OECD, Paris, 1996; 'National Accounts: 1983–95,' OECD, Paris, 1997

linked to other statuses, such as being a student. Variation in the average number of hours worked each week by male part-time workers should also be noted: in Portugal and Italy, male part-timers averaged around thirty hours per week, whereas in Denmark, the United Kingdom, and Germany, the average figure was between thirteen and seventeen hours per week.

A degree of convergence between states is also visible in the statistics on insecure employment. These show that the recruiment of workers for short periods, without certainty of continuous employment, is a feature of the contemporary labour market in all EU states, most notably Spain, France, Finland, the Netherlands, and Denmark (Kauppinen and Kandolin, 1996). It is well established that temporary and fixed-term contract working is more common among female than male workers (Yeandle, 1999), but, because it is differently regulated in separate countries (Cousins, 1999; Schömann et al., 1994), comparison of trends is difficult. Fixed-term employment has an important influence on how couples behave in the labour market. It can be a factor lying behind dual earning in couple-headed households, and, when permanent jobs are perceived to be scarce, individuals may choose to retain employment, combining it with caring roles, when they might otherwise prefer to interrupt their employment patterns to accommodate particular family obligations. On the other hand, fixed-term employment is often associated with those segments of the service sector which are emerging as some domestic work shifts into the market: private forms of child care and elder care, work in the catering trade, and domestic cleaning work are all available on a non-standard-employment basis (European Foundation, 1999). Meanwhile, some fixed-term employment is emerging as a by-product of women's greater attachment to the labour force – for example, as in the replacement of workers on maternity leave.

Differences within the Sex Groups

The pressures creating greater labour-force attachment among some women are strongest among those with the best earning power (and therefore with most education and higher-level jobs). Such women value economic independence, often see their work as a career, and have the means, particularly when they have a long-term marriage or partnership with a man with similar labour-force attachment, to buy some domestic services on the market. It used to seem that such

TABLE 8.3
Employment in Selected OECD Countries: Part-time Employment and Self-employment

	Part-time employment as % of total employment						Female part-time employment as % of total part-time employment		Self-employment as % of total employment	
	Both sexes		Women		Men					
	1995	1985	1995	1985	1995	1985	1995	1985	1995	1985
Austria	13.9	6.7	26.9	15.7	4.0	1.1	83.8	89.8	10.4^d	15.3^f
Belgium	13.6	8.6	29.8	21.1	2.8	1.8	87.5	86.1	14.5^e	13.7^g
Denmark	21.6	24.3	35.5	43.9	10.4	8.4	73.3	81.0	8.5^d	10.4^f
Finland	8.4	8.2	11.3	12.1	5.7	4.6	64.7	71.0	14.7^d	14.1^f
France	15.6	10.8	28.9	21.8	5.0	3.2	82.0	82.7	11.6	16.0
Germany	16.3	12.8^a	33.8	29.6^a	3.6	2.0^a	87.4	90.5^a	9.2^d	8.9^{a,f}
Greece	4.8	5.3	8.6	10.0	2.8	2.8	62.7	64.7	34.4^d	35.8^f
Ireland	12.1	6.5	23.1	15.5	5.4	2.4	72.0	74.3	21.0^d	21.7^f
Italy	6.4	5.3	12.7	10.1	2.9	3.0	70.6	61.6	24.1^d	24.6^f
Luxembourg	7.9	7.2	20.3	16.3	1.1	2.6	91.0	76.6	7.5	11.7
Netherlands	37.4	22.7	67.2	51.6	16.8	7.7	73.6	77.6	11.0^d	11.9^f
Portugal	7.5	6.0^b	11.6	10.0^b	4.2	3.4^b	69.1	65.8^d	25.5^d	32.5^f
Spain	7.5	5.8^c	16.4	13.9^c	2.8	2.4^c	75.7	71.5^e	21.9^d	23.5^f
Sweden	24.3	24.0	40.3	44.0	9.4	6.1	80.1	86.7	10.6^d	7.3^f
UK	24.1	21.2	44.3	44.8	7.7	4.4	82.3	88.0	13.5^d	11.3^f

a – ex FRG only; b – 1986; c – 1987; d – 1994; e – 1992; f – 1984; g – 1982
SOURCE: 'Labour Force Statistics 1975–1995', OECD, Paris, 1997

women were establishing a standardized life course rather similar to the male norm on which twentieth-century welfare-state policies were mainly predicated. However, as the structure, technology, and culture of work and organizations have developed, areas of strong female participation have begun to be affected by the diversification of employment experience: teachers and nurses, for example, are increasingly employed on fixed, temporary contracts. Temping and seasonal work are becoming more important features of clerical and retail occupations. In this way, commitment to one's job has become less of a guarantee of regularity or permanence of employment.

By contrast, without good qualifications, women remain concentrated in low-paid, insecure jobs. Factory work and agricultural tasks have given way to employment in the service sector, where much work is part time and low paid. Often such work is in the public, welfare, or care sectors, which have expanded through state support in some countries, and through market pressures in others. Differences in welfare-state provision, and in private demand, have produced wide differences in qualifications and status. In well-resourced public-sector services, workers in the care sector may have security of employment, approved professional status, and opportunities for career development. Elsewhere, as, for example, in the United Kingdom, most recent growth has been in the private sector: private child minders, private nursery workers, children's nannies/mother's helps, paid domestic cleaners, and other domiciliary-care workers (Gregson and Lowe, 1994). This type of work offers women little security of employment and few opportunities for advancement.

Men's situation is also becoming more polarized: between those whose 'good jobs' – with security, higher wages, and promotion opportunities – keep them linked permanently to the labour market from qualification through to (often early) retirement; and those who have suffered redundancy or unemployment or whose lack of professional skills or qualifications make it increasingly difficult for them to keep a secure foothold in work. Labour-market entry for the latter group is becoming delayed and more difficult: labour-market exit is increasingly involuntary, as downsizing, restructuring, and other major changes in the labour market produce more unemployment and economic inactivity.

In summary, then, across the EU there is some degree of male–female convergence in participation rates. The emerging dominance of the service sector is bringing some similarity of experience for men and women, but part-time employment remains much more important for women than for men, signalling a very significant difference between the sexes. Men rarely select part-time work by choice as a way of devoting more time to unpaid family and domestic work. And if many women now want what men used to take for granted – secure, long-term employment – such employment is increasingly hard to find.

Increasing Diversity in Family and Household Living

Some trends in family and household structure in Europe – growing solitarization, with increasing numbers of younger people and elderly persons living alone; more unmarried cohabiting among young people; increased childbearing outside marriage; and rising numbers of families without children – are visible throughout Europe (Rothenbacher, 1996). In most European countries the model of the two-adult, two-child 'nuclear family' fits only a minority of households, while fertility rates are low or declining towards low in all EU Member States (Eurostat, 1995), and the proportion of women living as lone parents has increased in much of Europe.

This apparent similarity means that family structure has become more diverse almost everywhere (Millar and Warman, 1996). It is these factors which underlie important aspects of the restructuring of the life course, which has historically been strongly linked to patterns of birth, marriage, and death. Different patterns of fertility and of partnership are emerging which can both shorten or prolong both the parental state and responsibility for providing for a family. For some, extended periods of living alone are emerging, especially in youth and old age, and in those countries with high rates of divorce and remarriage, family structures are becoming increasingly complex, with step-families (and same-sex partnerships) countering the simplifying tendencies which otherwise develop with declining fertility. All of these factors act to destandardize the life course. It seems unlikely that the labour market, the welfare state, or families themselves have the flexibility to respond to this increased diversity.

Debates about policies to achieve the reconciliation of work and family life now feature strongly on the EU agenda and in the social and family policies of many EU states. Here the focus is most frequently on couple-headed households with dependent children. These households have the most scope for redistribution of the sexual division of labour, both in the domestic and the labour-market spheres, and policy emphasis has been upon the reshaping of social attitudes towards housework, upon support structures for mothers/parents who wish to engage in paid employment, and, in some states, upon encouraging men to take up parental leaves. This policy thrust is geared almost exclusively towards those at the parental stage of the life course, with persons living alone or without children left almost completely outside the debate. Yet important issues affect these other family types, and most individuals experience living in a range of family and household structures across the life course. Growing diversity in family living suggests that lives are becoming more individualized, less predictable, and more strongly influenced by the personal choices made at early stages (Beck, 1992). This is perhaps particularly true of personal life and family formation.

Those experiencing (albeit often only transiently) lone parenthood, step-parenting, or living alone, whether in youth or perhaps following divorce or early widowhood, face other challenges in combining their work and domestic lives. In many of these cases, sharing either the domestic or the income-generating/employment burden with a partner is not an option – although some separated and divorced parents do make contributions to child care even when residing apart from their children. In the range of household types just described, options for redirecting self-servicing activities into services purchased in the market will be attractive, but will be affected by financial constraints. These households are more likely than couple-headed households with children to be living in poverty (Barnes, 1997).

Changes in Arrangements for the Delivery of Care Services: The Example of Child Care

With rising employment rates for mothers of young children, especially women with more education, and trends towards dual job holding in such households, there is already demand for child care services in much of the EU which is being met from outside the immediate family household. Varied arrangements for the delivery of child care in the EU are indicators of different ways in which countries are attempting to reconcile work and family life in the context of different welfare systems, different family traditions, and different boundaries between the public, private, and voluntary sectors.

In Sweden, for example, state support for child care comes in the form of comparatively generous and flexible parental leaves, publicly subsidized nurseries, and municipal child minders (Karlsson, 1995). However, around 40 per cent of preschool children in Sweden are cared for at home by a parent, and there is some continuing use of care by relatives and of private paid care (Broberg and Hwang, 1991, cited in Windebank, 1996, p. 152). By contrast, in the United Kingdom, where state support for child care has been very limited, there is a heavy reliance among women with a partner on care provided by the spouse (Windebank, 1996), by lone and some parents with partners on the informal care which their children's grandparents can provide, and on private-sector care, particularly registered child minders. The majority of child minders are self-employed; some may be working illegally or without declaring earnings. Between 1986 and 1996 (in England) day-nursery provision and the number of privately funded places with registered child minders approximately trebled, and demand for privately employed nannies also increased (Gregson and Lowe, 1994), while out-of-school care (e.g., after-school clubs and holi-day schemes for younger school-age children), supported by public subsidies and grants as well as being a cost payable by parents from their personal finances, has shown particularly rapid recent growth (Department of Health, 1996). Out-of-school-hours provision for school-aged children now offers coverage to about half of the relevant age group in Denmark and Sweden (with similar services believed to be widespread in urban Belgium), for about one-third of 6- to 10-year-olds in France, for around 10 per cent of this age group in Portugal, and for between 1 and 6 per cent in the Netherlands, the United Kingdom, and Austria. In all cases, the provision has increased during the 1990s, except in the former East Germany (European Commission Network on Childcare ..., 1995).

As these figures suggest, within the EU large numbers of children are being cared for by paid workers of different kinds. Although it is impossible accurately to estimate the number of workers involved, it can safely be assumed that in this sector it is both large and rising. A variety of measures to regulate and professionalize this form of employment are in place or in process of development in many EU states. Rising levels of parental employment, particularly of mothers, imply growing demand for workers in this field, except in those few states where there has recently been a very sharp drop in the birth rate. It is clear that additional paid jobs have been emerging in recent decades, on an upward trend. However, employment in this field is very highly gendered, with almost all nannies and child minders and the overwhelming majority of nursery workers being female (Jensen, nd). This area of work is also dominated by younger workers.

Despite this general trend, there remain marked differences between EU states in the share of child-care work which continues to be done on an unpaid basis by parents (principally mothers) and that which falls in alternative categories: the public/state/local-authority sector; the private-business sector; the voluntary sector; the self-employed sector; the paid-domestic-labour sector; and the informal unpaid sector. Where there is widespread provision of formal child care, the development of the child-care-services sector is both a support for and a source of women's labour-force participation.

Life-course Implications

So far, this chapter has outlined some of the social changes which are contributing to major restructuring of the life course in the European Union. It has emphasized that employment patterns are becoming more similar for a minority of women and men: those who are the most privileged and whose occupational security gives them the best opportunity to offset the changing demands of family life across the life course. Sexual divisions are much more marked among the least privileged, whose marginal labour-force status and poverty give them far fewer options, especially where their patterns of family living include periods of lone parenthood. Across all EU states, the responsibilities of family life have become less predictable and more complex, be it for care, for breadwinning, or for basic household maintenance. Policy responses to this diversification lag far behind.

The birth cohort (broadly defined) to which an individual belongs is a further source of differentiation which demands adjustments in social policy (Cohen, 1987; Dex and McCulloch, 1997; Rubery, Smith, and Fagan, 1995). It is to this point that the chapter now turns.

Older people – those born in the 1920s and who first entered employment in the 1940s – have mostly completed their span of working life as the century closes. Although these Europeans have witnessed enormous changes in economic and social structures during their adult lives, and may have had war-related disruptions to the early stages of their working lives, their life courses have mostly followed the pattern which they came to expect: continuous employment for most males, perhaps tailing off or becoming precarious in the latter years of working life, as European societies faced the economic restructuring of the 1970s and 1980s and the technological changes of recent decades – and with women's lives mostly dominated by the work and responsibilities of family life, and by paid work where this was needed to supplement men's wages.

For those born in the 1940s and who entered employment in the 1960s, life-course experiences have been very different. In many European countries entry to the labour market was easy, with ready access to jobs and opportunities for youth to change jobs. Work was differentiated according to gender, with equality policies in place in only a very few states, and strongly gendered educational and occupational expectations shaping young people's lives. For most, marriage came early, as did parenthood, yet cultural and socio-economic shifts placed this apparent security in some jeopardy, and in many cases the years of middle adulthood have been affected by divorce, male employment insecurity, and growing expectations of female labour-market participation. For this group, women's access to vocational training and to well-paid work has been severely limited and has kept most female workers from good jobs and independent financial security. In recent decades, however, old assumptions about the domestic division of labour may have been challenged, and anxieties about income security and welfare support in old age may now be coming to the fore.

Young workers – say, those born in the 1960s and who entered employment first in the 1980s – have had benefits scarcely dreamed of by the 1920s birth cohort when it comes to employment legislation and rights, educational opportunities, and vocational guidance. This has been especially true of women, whose statutory (if not actual) position with regard to equality of opportunity in work and training has dramatically improved during the latter half of the twentieth century. Yet these young workers are unlikely to face their future with great confidence. Most have delayed marriage and childbearing, perhaps out of choice, perhaps out of anxiety about economic security. Continuing high levels of unemployment in many European societies, coupled with the changing nature of employment opportunities, contribute to this uncertainty.

Those who are well educated have scope for career and professional development and, for both sexes, scope to support themselves independently. Marriage or cohabitation for these better-off workers may bring significant income benefits if both partners can secure and remain in full-time professional or managerial employment. Women especially may be affected by strong labour-market disincentives to withdraw from the labour force, and increasingly, with support of state, private-sector, or informal systems (depending on their nationality), couples are choosing to minimize family size and to employ domestic labour from outside the household. This is stimulating new service-sector jobs – a large-scale commodification of domestic labour, both directly into paid jobs which are mainly performed by other women (e.g., child care, domestic cleaning, laundry), and, more indirectly, into increased retail, factory, and delivery employment as ready meals and convenience foods become regular features of domestic diets.

Those younger workers who have achieved only an average or lower level of education are in quite a different position. They are increasingly likely to be experiencing some periods of temporary or part-time work, maybe involuntarily when they would prefer more secure, full-time work. The old openings in unskilled work have mostly disappeared, and establishing a steady work record or acquiring skills without prior educational credentials is increasingly difficult. This generation may find it essential for family financial security to have two earners in the household, but may still be unable to purchase domestic or child care services. In those states which take primary responsibility for child and elder care this may not matter, but in states which have taken a *laissez-faire* approach to supporting domestic labour, many people will be severely disadvantaged. Patterns of family formation and living have become more variable and diverse, with more younger people living alone and many choosing a period of unmarried cohabitation in their twenties and sometimes beyond. These shifts, creating more lone parents and more variability across the life course, carry risks for the individual's welfare and labour-market participation. Again, the welfare supports which are in place have a very significant impact on how these developments are experienced. In the United Kingdom and other *laissez-faire* systems (currently showing some signs of change) these younger workers may be forming the polar opposite of the affluent dual-career purchasers of domestic services described above. For many in this group, the domestic-labour requirements of others provide opportunities for (insecure and intermittent) employment, which may provide an essential useful supplement to irregular earnings in work or to welfare benefits.

The life courses of those younger Europeans who will live out most of their lives in the twenty-first century are likely to be even more sharply affected by the changing balance between employment and family life and its impact on other activities: if all are to be offered welfare and security, in line with the quality of social life which Europeans have come to expect, then social policies will need to adapt and change in response. There are worrying signs of increased polarization between those who have good jobs, good education, and multiple earners in stable households and those who do not. Some aspects of this polarization continue to be gendered: the time has not yet come to cease worrying about sexual divisions in poverty and affluence or in quality of jobs. But this is not just a question of sex equality: the divisions requiring most urgent change in social policy arise both from men's growing detachment from secure participation in employment and family life, and from the continuing allocation of most of society's care and domestic labour, in whatever guise, to women.

NOTES

1 I would like to acknowledge the financial support of the European Foundation for the Improvement of Living and Working Conditions, Dublin (November 1997–March 1998), and the contributions of Tony Gore, Alison Herrington, and Robert Anderson. A full report of this work appears as Yeandle, Gore, and Herrington (1998).

2 As its main information source, this section draws on the European Union Labour Force Survey (ELFS), a harmonized data set which uses common definitions in different member states. Additional information has been extracted from OECD analyses, and other European-level research reports have also been accessed and consulted.

REFERENCES

Barnes, H. (1997). Child poverty in Europe. *Cash and Care, 21*, 4.
Beck, U. (1992). *Risk society: Towards a new modernity.* London: Sage.
Cohen, G. (Ed.). (1987). *Social change and the life course.* London: Tavistock.
Cousins, C. (1999). Changing regulatory frameworks and non-standard employment: A comparison of Germany, Spain, Sweden and the UK. In A. Felstead & N. Jewson (Eds), *Global trends in flexible labour* (pp 100–20). London: Macmillan.
Department of Health. (1996). *Health and personal social services statistics for England.* London: Government Statistical Service.

Dex, S., & McCulloch, A. (1997). Unemployment and training histories: Findings from the family and working lives survey. *Labour Market Trends, 105*(11), 449–54.

Elder, G.H. (1991). Lives and social change. In W.R. Heinz (Ed.), *Theoretical advances in life course research* (pp 58–86). Weinheim, Germany: Deutscher Studien Verlag.

European Commission. (1997). *Equal opportunities for women and men in the European Union 1996.* Luxembourg: Office for Official Publications of the EC.

European Commission Network on Childcare, ... (1995). *A review of services for young children in the European Union.* Brussels: European Commission.

European Foundation. (1999). Unpublished presentations at working group meetings of the 1998–9 eight-nation study of *Employment in Household Services.* (Report [due autumn 1999] for the European Foundation for the Improvement of Living and Working Conditions). Dublin: European Foundation.

ELFS (European Union Labour Force Survey). (1985, 1990, 1995). Luxembourg: Eurostat.

Eurostat. (1995). *Women and men in the European Union: A statistical portrait.* Luxembourg: Office for Official Publications of the EC.

Glennerster, H. (1995). The life cycle: Public or private concern? In J. Falkingham & J. Hills (Eds), *The dynamic of welfare: The welfare state and the life cycle* (pp 6–20). Hemel Hempstead: Prentice Hall/Harvester Wheatsheaf.

Gregson, N., & Lowe, M. (1994). *Servicing the middle classes: Class, gender and waged domestic labour in contemporary Britain.* London: Routledge.

Jensen, J.J. (nd). *Employer des hommes dans les services d'accueil pour enfants: Un document de réflexion.* Brussels: European Commission.

Karlsson, M. (1995). *Family daycare in Europe.* Brussels: European Commission.

Kauppinen, K., & Kandolin, I. (1996). *Gender and working conditions in the EU* (Report for the European Foundation for the Improvement of Living and Working Conditions). Dublin: European Foundation.

Millar, J., & Warman, A. (1996). *Family obligations in Europe.* London: Family Policy Studies Centre.

OECD (Organization for Economic Cooperation and Development). (1996a). *Labour force statistics 1974–1994.* Paris: Author.

OECD. (1996b). *National accounts: 1982–1994.* Paris: Author.

OECD. (1997a). *Labour force statistics 1975–1995.* Paris: Author.

OECD. (1997b). *National accounts: 1983–1995.* Paris: Author.

Purcell, K., & Purcell, J. (1998). Insourcing, outsourcing and the growth of contingent labour as evidence of flexible employment strategies. *European Journal of Work and Organizational Psychology, 7*(1), 39–59.

Rothenbacher, F. (1996). Household and family trends in Europe: From convergence to divergence. *Eurodata Newsletter, 1*, 3–9 (Eurodata Website).

Rubery, J., Smith, M., & Fagan, C. (1995). *Changing patterns of work and working time in the European Union and the impact on gender divisions* (V/A/3 Equal Opportunities Unit). Brussels: European Commission.

Schömann K., Rogowski, R., & Krüppe, T. (1994). Fixed term contracts in the European Union. *European Observatory Policies* (inforMISEP, European Commission), *47*, 30–9.

Wedderburn, A. (1995). Part-time work. *Bulletin of European Studies on Time* (European Foundation for the Improvement of Living and Working Conditions, Dublin), *8*, 1–82.

Windebank, J. (1996). To what extent can social policy challenge the dominant ideology of mothering? A cross-national comparison of Sweden, France and Britain *Journal of European Social Policy, 6*(2), 147–61.

Yeandle, S. (1999). Gender contracts, welfare systems and *non-standard working*: Diversity and change in Denmark, France, Germany, Italy and the UK. In A. Felstead & N. Jewson (Eds), *Global trends in flexible labour*. London: Macmillan.

Yeandle, S., Gore, T., & Herrington, A. (1998). Employment, family and community activities: A new balance for women and men (Report for the European Foundation for the Improvement of Living and Working Conditions). Dublin: European Foundation.

9. Full Time or Part Time? The Contradictory Integration of the East German Female Labour Force in Unified Germany

Reinhard Kreckel and Sabine Schenk

East–West Differences in Germany: Time-lag or Divergent Development?

The unification of Germany in 1990 meant that the former German Democratic Republic, with the approval of the majority of its 16 million citizens, gave up its sovereignty and was merged into the Federal Republic of Germany. Unified Germany now has 82 million inhabitants. Through the act of unification, the East Germans became a minority of about 20 per cent of the total population of Germany. This minority was obliged to adapt to a fundamental transformation of its accustomed political, legal, and economic system, whereas things remained more or less unchanged for the West German majority. Thus, both by the sheer logic of numbers and by the fact that the West German institutions prevailed, a distinctly hegemonic situation was established in unified Germany.

Although the two German states were politically and ideologically separated for forty years, they shared a common cultural and historical background. In consequence, both the structural constraints of the unification process and the cultural similarity of the two parts to be reassembled seem to lead to the following common-sense hypothesis: After a period of transitory complications, the most likely outcome to be expected is the complete social, political, and economic reintegration of Germany on the basis of the predominant West German model.

Sociological modernization theory points in the same direction. From this point of view, the former German Democratic Republic, because of its one-party political system, its command economy, and its comparatively low standard of living, was a case of 'blocked modernization.' This blockage has been lifted after unification. As Wolfgang Zapf argues, on the basis of recent survey data:

> If one takes acceptance of market economy and democracy together with satisfaction with one's own economic situation as components of an *index of transformation* ... the direction seems to be obvious ... My assumption is that within five more years the East-West differences in Germany will lose their present importance. (Zapf, 1998, p. 31)

Thus, both informed common sense and modernization theory arrive at the same conclusion: The East–West differences will disappear. The only remaining question is how long this will take. Is the period of transition almost over, as Wolfgang Zapf suggests, or will it take several decades, or even generations?

Only ten years have passed since the end of the German Democratic Republic, so we are not able to draw firm conclusions about the long-term-adaptation variant of the modernization hypothesis. But there are strong indications that the process of adaptation and integration of East Germany is not proceeding as smoothly as expected.

Consider, for example, the detailed analyses of the development of the East German labour market in the first five years of German unification by Burkart Lutz and colleagues (1996). This study finds very little indication that the East German economy and employment structure are closing the gap and veering towards the patterns of the West German service society. Lutz and associates see no clear signs that sustained economic growth is taking off or that industry is recovering in East Germany. In their view, the high rates of unemployment and of unstable employment may well be lasting features of the East German labour market. They do not expect a quick closing of the gap between East and West.

Of course, it is quite impossible for a present-day sociologist to tell with any degree of precision whether West and East Germany will eventually diverge or converge, and if so, when and in what direction. In any case, when the situation is inspected again in a generation's time, what we shall find then will not be the result of deterministic mechanisms. It will have been influenced by purposeful human interventions which are hard to foresee. Therefore, we shall remain prudent in this respect. Rather, we want to tackle the question in a roundabout and indirect way, by looking at a very specific, but significant, case of labour-market development – the case of female part-time work.

Between Causation and Accusation: Female Labour Market Participation and the Rate of Unemployment

One of the salient features of the German labour market after reunification is the 'jobless growth' of the German economy and the constant rise of unemployment in East and West Germany, from 2.6 million unemployed in 1991 (6.6 per cent) to 4.8 million in February 1998 (12.6 per cent). In East Germany, the unemployment rate is twice as high as in the West. In February 1998, a staggering 21.4 per cent of the East German labour force were registered as unemployed, compared with 10.4 per cent in the West.

Both in everyday discourse and in modernization theory, the East–West difference in unemployment rates is usually accounted for by the time-lag explanation mentioned above. It argues that the East German labour market is still lagging behind and that the process of economic adjustment to the Western model has yet to be accomplished.

This is not the only explanation compatible with the paradigm of modernization theory, however. Recently, an alternative explanation has been put forward which is of particular interest for our present purpose (Schneider, 1994; Kommission für Zukunftsfragen, 1997). It holds that the higher unemployment rate in Eastern Germany is not primarily caused by major structural deficits. Rather, the enormous reduction of the East German labour market from 9.9 million jobs in 1989 to 6.0 million jobs in 1998 is considered to be the result of a process of structural normalization which is now more or less completed.

According to this view, in both East and West Germany the proportion of gainfully employed persons relative to the total population of working age is virtually identical (Institut für Wirtschaftsforschung Halle, 1995). There is no *structural* lag in this respect. Instead, the explanation of a *cultural* lag is advanced, according to which East German women adhere to a much larger extent to the social norm of full employment than their West German counterparts. This strong work orientation leads to a higher rate of economic activity among East German women. In 1996, 72.5 per cent of women of working age were economically active in East Germany. In West Germany, the female activity rate was only 57.7 per cent (Statistisches Bundesamt, 1997). It is argued, then, that women exert additional pressure upon the East German labour market.

Indeed, if one were to make the counter-factual assumption that East German women behave according to the West German model, only 57.7 per cent of them (instead of the factual 72.5 per cent) would have been economically active in 1996. That is, whereas in real life 3.7 million East German women were economically active, in our fictitiously westernized labour-market model of East Germany only 2.8 million women would have been interested in having a job – nearly 1 million fewer. In reality, the total number of women in East Germany registered as unemployed in 1996 amounted to only 821,000.

One might easily be tempted to transform this hypothetical reasoning into a causal statement. Thus, as the Kommission für Zukunftsfragen, an advisory commission appointed by the governments of the states of Bavaria and Saxony, argues in its influential report: 'If, caused by a further withdrawal of women from economic activity, the labour force potential decreases, unemployment in East Germany can also be reduced.'[1] It is not surprising that this hypothesis is strongly resented in East Germany. It attributes the main responsibility for the high unemployment rate in East Germany to the excessive demand for jobs by East German women. It implies that unemployment would be reduced to 'normal' standards if only East German women were prepared to give up their 'deviant' employment behaviour and adjust to the West German model. It also implies that the employment orientation of men is not in question.

However tempting it might be to discuss whether East German women's work orientation constitutes a cultural *advance* rather than a cultural *lag*, this is not the place for polemical controversy. Instead, we wish to explore more soberly some of the implications and consequences of the undeniable empirical fact that there are considerable differences in the labour-market participation of West and East German women, whereas the employment behaviour of men is much more similar.

East German Women's Feeling for Work

One of the most consistent empirical findings, obtained both by survey analysis and by qualitative social research is the significant difference between East and West German women's attitudes to employment. There is widespread consensus among social scientists that many more women in East Germany have a strong subjective attachment to being economically active than their West German counterparts.[2] Notwithstanding the increasing unemployment pressure for East German women, their intensive work orientation seems not to have decreased since 1990.

In fact, there are some indications that the work orientation of East German women may actually have increased in recent years. If one considers the results of the ALLBUS survey (General Population Survey) from 1991 and 1996, a stable 50 per cent of the adult population in western Germany agree that 'It is much better for all if men are fully employed and women stay at home to look after the household and the children' (see table 9.1). In East Germany, agreement with the same question was 33 per cent in 1991 and decreased to only 26 per cent in 1996. It is interesting to note that in both parts of Germany there is a negligible gender difference among the replies. This gender homogeneity of opinion gives support to the hypothesis that two divergent work ethics coexist in the two parts of unified Germany.

As table 9.1 also shows, the same data reveal structural heterogeneity with respect to age and education; every younger and better-educated generation is more likely to opt against the male breadwinner model. However, the differences by age and education are much more apparent in West Germany. That is, the youngest and the most educated cohorts of the West German respondents are most likely to be in accord with the East German pattern. This might be interpreted as an indicator that West German rather than East German women are 'lagging behind' and are in the process of 'catching up' with a more modern work ethic which favours life-long full employment for both genders.

This interpretation is still somewhat premature, however, as closer inspection suggests that the 'catching up' of West German women is not quite what it seems. As Blossfeld and Rohwer (1997) have demonstrated, the steady rise of the activity rate of West German women of working age (16 to 60) from 45 per cent in 1950 to 60 per cent in 1990 does not indicate the full inclusion of increasing numbers of women in the work force. Indeed, as table 9.2 reveals, the gradual increase in the female activity rate was generated by the simultaneous growth of female part-time employment. The newly created part-time jobs were mostly taken up by married women who would otherwise have remained full housewives. As Blossfeld and Rohwer (1997, p. 170) comment: 'The impressive increase in (married) women's labour-force

TABLE 9.1
Views on the Traditional Division of Labour between Men and Women
in West and East Germany, 1991–1996 (%)

'It is much better for all if men are fully employed and women stay at
home to look after the household and the children.'

	West		East	
	1991	1996	1991	1996
Total[a]	50	50	33	26
Gender				
Men	51	53	35	27
Women	49	47	30	26
Married women[b]				
Working	31	30	22	18
Not working	58	65	37	30
Age				
18–30	34	29	23	19
31–45	39	35	26	18
46–65	60	61	37	31
over 65	77	80	52	38
Education				
lower secondary leaving certificate[c]	64	66	44	38
intermediate leaving certificate[d]	43	43	27	19
upper secondary leaving certificate[e]	27	25	19	16

[a]German nationals only
[b]Married or living with partner
[c]Hauptschulabschluss
[d]Mittlere Reife/Polytechnische Oberschule
[e]Abitur/Fachabitur
SOURCE: Statistisches Bundesamt, *Datenreport 1997*,
p. 451, ALLBUS 1991, 1996

participation during the last thirty years in West Germany has by and
large been the result of an expansion of married women's part-time
employment. In other words, a wife's role as supplementary earner
has hardly changed.' The situation in East Germany is quite different.
The starting point in 1950 was identical, but from then on a separate

TABLE 9.2
Women's Trends in Part-time versus Full-time Employment in the
Two Parts of Germany, 1950–1989/90

	Activity rate of women aged 16–60 (%)	Part-time workers as % of employees			% female among full-time workers
		Male	Female	Total	
West					
1950	45	1	6	3	–
1960	49	2	9	4	32
1965	–	2	16	7	30
1970	50	2	24	9	28
1975		2	29	12	29
1980	53	1	29	12	30
1985	–	2	31	13	30
1990	60	2	33	14	33

SOURCE: Blossfeld and Rohwer (1997, pp 166–7)

	Activity rate of women aged 16–60* (%)	Part-time workers as % of employees			% female among full-time workers
		Male	Female	Total	
*East***					
1950	45	–	–	–	–
1960	62	–	–	–	–
1967	–	3	29	16	42
1970	66	3	33	18	43
1975	71	3	33	19	44
1980	73	3	29	17	46
1985	76	2	27	16	46
1989	78	2	27	15	45

*SOURCE: Ministerrat der DDR, Staatliche Zentralverwaltung für Statistik, own calculations
**Without the employees of the so-called x sector (military, police, etc.)
SOURCE: Statistisches Bundesamt, Zweigstelle Berlin, own calculations

development began. During the life of the German Democratic Republic, the activity rate of women aged 16 to 60 rose from 45 per cent in 1950 to 78 per cent in 1989 (table 9.2). Virtually all women, married or unmarried, were thus included in the work force. The rule was full-time employment for both men *and* women. Female part-time employment was seen as exceptional, mainly performed by older women or as reduced-hours work (see below).

Thus, at the time of the German unification two partly divergent models coexisted which attempted to bridge the structural cleavages between the sphere of productive work and the sphere of reproductive work (cf Kreckel, 1992, ch. 4). These two models imply different 'gender contracts' (Pfau-Effinger and Geissler, 1992). In simplified form, they may be summarized as follows (for references see Kreckel, 1995):

1. Both models still bear the stamp of their common predecessor, the normative model of the petty-bourgeois German 'male breadwinner family,' where the husband was supposed to be the family head and sole provider of income, whereas his wife was barred from gainful employment after marriage. She was expected to look after him, their children and elderly parents, and the household.

2. As far as the normal biography of men is concerned, the line of continuity remained largely intact in both parts of postwar Germany. To this day, the part-time employment rates of men have remained minimal in both West and East. Men were – and still are – expected to lead a life of full employment. Employers' perceptions of different career prospects of men and women are important gatekeeping devices within these processes, and part-time work is deemed to be inappropriate for any able-bodied man.

3. Household, family, and children continue to be primarily the responsibility of women in East and West Germany, whether they are fully employed or not. Although certain tendencies towards a more equal sharing of the practical and emotional tasks of domestic life have been reported from both parts of Germany, the major burden still tends to be carried by women.

4. As stated above, the normal biography of women living in the German Democratic Republic was increasingly oriented towards lifelong full employment and a full contribution to the household income. This orientation was encouraged by East German labour legislation, the social security system, and the official social policy, which tried to relieve women of parts of their responsibilities, especially in child care and education. The model of the 'dual-earner marriage' was the normative model of private life in the German Democratic Republic. Thus, life-course strategies in East Germany were strongly connected with the framework of social policy, as

pointed out in more detail by Martin Kohli (1994) and Heike Trappe (1995).

5. Women in the Federal Republic were 'lagging behind' in this respect. Interrupted employment careers, part-time work, and the role of supplementary earner are widespread characteristics of female biographies in the West German model. This model is encouraged by the organization of the social security net and the system of taxation, as well as by the absence of sufficient provision for full-time child care and education. In this way, the petty-bourgeois model of the breadwinner marriage, where the wife stayed fully at home, has been gradually replaced by the West German compromise model, which has been described as the 'modernized breadwinner marriage' (Pfau-Effinger and Geissler, 1992).

Given the hegemonial circumstances of the German unification process stated above, the East Germans are now fully exposed to the political, legal, and economic framework which was originally developed in the West German Federal Republic. This framework provides the very same structural and institutional incentives which have lead to the modernized breadwinner model in West Germany, whereas the structural conditions which once underpinned the East German dual-earner model have been superseded. In this situation it seems unrealistic to expect anything but full adaptation to the only remaining structural framework – even if, as in this case, adaptation would mean for East Germans a return to a less-modern model.[3]

As we have seen, however, the majority of East Germans of both genders have so far remained recalcitrant about following the predicted path. Their work-centred life-course projects seem to be persisting or even becoming stronger. Despite the new circumstances, every survey dealing with views on gender roles, employment, and family underlines the findings presented in table 9.1. Attitudes held about the division of labour between men and women diverge considerably between East and West Germany. For instance, while 37 per cent of West Germans agreed with the statement 'While the husband is considered to be the breadwinner of the family, the primary tasks of the wife are to look after the household and the children,' only 11 per cent of East Germans did so (Braun, 1995, p. 6). Furthermore, East Germans are less likely than their West German counterparts to worry about the negative effects on children and family life if the wife is working. In the study mentioned above, 71 per cent of West Germans agreed that

'Younger children (up to six or seven) need their mother staying at home to grow up well,' whereas only 34 per cent of East Germans did so. Finally, we also find remarkable differences between West and East German attitudes regarding the source of the household income. While there was for nearly all East Germans (94 per cent) no doubt that 'both men and women should contribute to the household income,' only 67 per cent of West Germans agreed with this statement (Braun, 1995, p. 6). These views explain why East German women are less likely than West German women to accept the compromise solution of working part-time. In fact, a considerable majority of working women in East Germany state a preference for working full-time; in West Germany, it is the other way around (see table 9.3).

Thus, we arrive at the core question of this paper, the question of the continuing unwillingness of East German women to accept part-time work. We will have to ask if it might be more than a temporary obstinacy which keeps East German women from adopting the West German model of the modernized breadwinner family.

The findings highlighted above underline what we have already noted on the basis of the results presented in table 9.1: the widespread rejection of part-time work is not a peculiarity of East German women only. It is a view which is shared by men. There is a similar corvergence of male–female attitudes in West Germany. This is the reason why we have introduced the hypothesis that two divergent work ethics as well as life-course conceptions coexist in the two parts of Germany. It implies that the part-time/full-time dilemma of married women is embedded in values shared by both genders.

If one accepts this interpretation, it follows that the strong negative feelings held in East Germany about part-time work for women cannot be treated as some kind of feminine eccentricity. Rather, the basis is a widespread social consensus.

If Ibsen's Nora had been living in modern East Germany, she would hardly have been able to provoke her husband's wrath by looking for a job of her own. She might, however, have managed to irritate him and her children if she had decided to work part time and to spend the afternoons in her 'doll's house' (1962 [1879]).

Nora's Return

The hypothesis of the two different marriage models, the dual-earner model and the modernized breadwinner model, may well explain the

TABLE 9.3
Actual Working Time and Preferred Working Time of Employees in Germany, 1995

	West				East			
	Men		Women		Men		Women	
Hours per week	Actual working time %	Preferred working time %	Actual working time %	Preferred working time %	Actual working time %	Preferred working time %	Actual working time %	Preferred working time %
40 and more	65	50	34	17	89	67	67	40
30–39	30	41	29	39	8	24	22	41
20–29	2	3	18	25	2	2	7	8
up to 20	3	6	19	19	2	8	4	6

SOURCE: Schulze Buschoff, 1997, p. 10, GSOEP, 1995

divergent work orientations of West and East German women. But it does not answer the question of whether the East German variant will be able to withstand the structural pressures of the hegemonial situation in unified Germany. In two earlier papers (Kreckel, 1995; Schenk, 1995) we sketched four paths of possible development: (1) adaptation of East Germany to the hegemonial gender contract of the modernized breadwinner model; (2) disruption of the East German gender contract whereby East German men maintain their orientation to full employment while their wives are forced out of work or into part-time jobs; (3) regressive maintenance of the exceptional gender contract and the dual-earner model in East Germany which, under economic duress, mutates to a 'dual-unemployment model' or a 'dual part-time model,' where the burdens of the labour market crisis are shared between both genders; and (4) innovative maintenance of the exceptional development path in which the strong employment orientation of the East Germans fosters creativity and productivity, generates new investments and new jobs, leads to a recovery of the East German labour market, and increases the chances of full employment for both genders.

Given the high degree of differentiation of East German society, the real development will probably contain elements of all four variants. Our question will have to be, then, whether alternatives three and four are likely to maintain enough strength to have a lasting impact.

Some empirical indicators giving support to this assumption can be found by looking more closely at the structure and development of female part-time work in East Germany. In fact, at first glance the part-time rates of women in East and West Germany just before German unification do not seem to be dramatically different: In 1988, 27 per cent of the employed women in East Germany worked on part-time contracts (Winkler, 1990). The corresponding rate in West Germany was 32 per cent (Blossfeld and Rohwer, 1997). But the following structural differences must be kept in mind: (1) On the eve of unification, the traditional breadwinner marriage was still influential in the West, but rather outdated in the East (cf table 9.3); (2) in the final years of the German Democratic Republic, part-time contracts were predominantly held by older women (cf Schuldt, 1992, p. 66) – that is, part-time work was not an element of normal family life, as in West Germany, but rather a means of gradual transition into retirement; and (3) the category 'part-time work' is not sufficiently specific. If one follows the suggestion of Hakim (1997, p. 25) and distinguishes between reduced-hours work, half-time work, and marginal work, one finds that part-time work in the German Democratic Republic was predominantly reduced-hours work, whereas the predominant pattern in West Germany was half-time work (cf Deutsches Institut für Wirtschaftsforschung, 1990, p. 265).

Meanwhile, political and economic conditions – in particular the labour-market situation – have dramatically changed in East Germany. None the less, table 9.3 shows very clearly that both the preferences expressed and the actual working-time behaviour of East German women follow very closely the pattern established in the last two decades of the life of the German Democratic Republic (cf Arnhold, 1996).

The impression of continuity emanating from these data is a very strong one. It gives support to our hypothesis that the strong attachment of the East German population to women's full employment has particular resilience because it is an integral part of a specific way of life, not an isolated element (or a 'feminine eccentricity').

Hence, it must be assumed that many East Germans are not prepared to give up their particular way of life – including full employment and economic parity for both genders – unless they are pressed to do so. In 1996, for example, 32 per cent male and 51 per cent female part-time workers in East Germany reported that they are actually working part time because they could not find a full-time job (Statistisches Bundesamt, 1997, own calculations). That is, those whose competitive position in the labour market is weakest are most likely to settle for part-time work (see table 9.4).

As table 9.4 shows, East German women make use of their education and occupational status as resources supporting their claim to full labour-market participation. If there is a chance to remain fully employed, a well-qualified women in East Germany is likely to seize this chance, whereas her West German counterpart is much more likely to accept alternative options, such as part-time work or withdrawal from the active labour force.

Certainly, the motivating power of the financial advantages of maintaining the dual-earner model are undeniable. That is, one should not be too idealistic about the East German way of life. It clearly has a strong materialistic underpinning, and there is no need to romanticize it.

In other words, and this is what sociologists should be interested in, both material interests and shared views point in the same direction in

TABLE 9.4
Women Working Part-time in East and West Germany, by
Education and Occupational Status, 1995/96 (as % of female
employees)

	West	East
*Education**		
Lower secondary leaving certificate[a]	45	26
Intermediate leaving certificate[b]	32	18
Upper secondary leaving certificate[c]	31	14
Vocational education[d]	38	22
Vocational extension certificate[e]	32	18
Higher education[f]	34	13
*Occupational status***		
Unskilled workers[g]	57	55
Skilled workers[h]	38	27
White-collar workers[i]	41	20
Professionals/managers[j]	39	11

[a]Hauptschulabschluss
[b]Mittlere Reife/Polytechnische Oberschule
[c]Abitur/Fachabitur
[d]Lehrausbildung
[e]Fachschulabschluss
[f]Fachhochschulabschluss/Universitätsabschluss
[g]ungelernte Arbeiter
[h]Facharbeiter
[i]einfache Angestellte/Beamte
[j]leitende Angestellte/Beamte
*SOURCE: Statistisches Bundesamt, 1996, own calculations
**SOURCE: Schulze Buschoff, 1997, p. 17, GSOEP, 1995

East Germany: The dual-earner model is not likely to metamorphose
into the hegemonial modernized breadwinner model. Quite the opposite may be the case. If one looks at the younger age groups of the West
German population, one gets the strong impression that the dual-
earner model is slowly making headway there (cf table 9.1).

On the basis of the data discussed in this paper, we do not see how
the propagation of women's part-time work could compensate for the
steady loss of jobs in both parts of Germany. That is, if one were to
assume that the reduction of working time could be an answer to the
endemic unemployment problem in contemporary Germany, this
reduction could not be achieved by means of a further expansion of

female part-time work. In West Germany, younger women are more strongly oriented to full-time work than older women. Therefore, the number of women prepared to opt for part-time employment is likely to decrease in the future. In East Germany, the potential for women voluntarily to opt for part-time work is even more limited.

If a further reduction of working time is going to be achieved in Germany, therefore, it will have to be done either by requiring women to give up a substantial part of the occupational terrain they have already conquered, or, if a consensual solution is sought, it will have to include both genders. In West Germany, this would seem to require a major reorganization of the gendered practice of dividing domestic and occupational work. In East Germany, the necessary reorientation might be less incisive and the transition from the dual full-time-earner model to a dual reduced-hours-earner model could be easier to achieve. For further research it might be interesting to compare the German situation with recent developments in the Netherlands, where part-time work seems to have become a reality for more and more men these days (cf Schmidt, 1997).

NOTES

1 'Zu vermuten ist, dass das Arbeitskräfteangebot in Ostdeutschland sinken wird – verursacht durch einen weiteren Rückzug der Frauen aus der Erwerbssphäre. Wenn das Erwerbspotential dadurch sinkt, kann auch die Arbeitslosigkeit in Ostdeutschland zurückgehen' (Kommission für Zukunftsfragen, 1997, vol. 2, p. 79).
2 Cf Arnhold (1996), Bauer et al. (1996), Becker (1998), Braun (1995), Engelbrech et al. (1997), Holst and Schupp (1996), Nickel (1997), Schulze Buschoff (1997), Statistisches Bundesamt (1997), and Zukunftskommission (1998). For summaries of earlier findings, see Kreckel (1995) and Schenk (1995).
    Kommission für Zukunftsfragen (1997, vol. 2, p. 78) claims a 'slow approximation of work orientations in West and East Germany,' but without providing an empirical substantiation.
3 However, if one prefers to follow the argument of Catherine Hakim (1997), one would have to say that this would be not a backward move, but a forward step towards modernity – or even towards postmodernity. According to Hakim, this modern world is characterized by individualism, structural heterogeneity and 'the coexistence of two qualitatively different work orientations among women (and men) of working age' (p. 62): One type of person

is committed to a career in the labour market and often remains childless; the other type gives priority to domestic activities and considers gainful employment to be of secondary importance.

REFERENCES

Arnhold, G. (1996). *Teilzeitarbeit in West- und Ostdeutschland: Zur Übertragbarkeit des westdeutschen Beschäftigungsmodells auf Ostdeutschland.* Halle: Martin-Luther-Universität Halle-Wittenberg, Fachbereich Geschichte, Philosophie und Sozialwissenschaften, Institut für Soziologie, Diplomarbeit (unpublished MA thesis).

Bauer, F., Gross, H., & Schilling, G. (1996). *Arbeitszeit '95: Arbeitszeitstrukturen, Arbeitszeitwünsche und Zeitverwendung der abhängig Beschäftigten in West- und Ostdeutschland.* Düsseldorf: Ministerium für Arbeit, Gesundheit und Soziales des Landes Nordrhein-Westfalen.

Becker, B. (1998). Warum ostdeutsche Frauen auf dem Wunsch nach Erwerbsarbeit beharren: Eine Betrachtung von Biographien. In H. Bertram, W. Kreher, & I. Müller-Hartmann (Eds), *Systemwechsel zwischen Projekt und Prozess* (pp 319–52). Opladen: Leske & Budrich.

Blossfeld, H.-P., & Rohwer, G. (1997). Part-time work in West Germany. In H.-P. Blossfeld & C. Hakim (Eds), *Between equalization and marginalization: Women working part-time in Europe and the United States of America* (pp 164–90). Oxford: Oxford University Press.

Braun, M. (1995). Einstellungen zur Berufstätigkeit der Frau: Steigende Zustimmung im Osten, Stagnation im Westen. *Informationsdienst Soziale Indikatoren, 95* (13), 6–9.

Deutsches Institut für Wirtschaftsforschung (DIW). (1990). *DIW-Wochenbericht* (19/90). Berlin: Author.

Engelbrech, G., Gruber, H., & Jungkunst, M. (1997). Erwerbsorientierung und Erwerbstätigkeit ost- und westdeutscher Frauen unter veränderten gesellschaftlichen Rahmenbedingungen. *Mitteilungen aus der Arbeitsmarkt: Und Berufsforschung (MitAB), 30*(1), 150–69.

Hakim, C. (1997). A sociological perspective on part-time work. In H.-P. Blossfeld & C. Hakim (Eds), *Between equalization and marginalization: Women working part-time in Europe and the United States of America* (pp 22–70). Oxford: Oxford University Press.

Holst, E., & Schupp, J. (1996). Erwerbstätigkeit von Frauen in Ost- und Westdeutschland weiterhin von steigender Bedeutung, *DIW-Wochenbericht, 96*(28), 461–9.

Ibsen, H. (1992 [1879]). *A doll's house*. Dover: Dover Thrift Edition.

Institut für Wirtschaftsforschung Halle (IWH). (1995). Data, March 1995, unpublished.

Kohli, M. (1994). *Die DDR als Arbeitsgesellschaft? Arbeit, Lebenslauf und soziale Differenzierung.* In H. Kaelble, J. Kocka, & H. Zwahr (Eds), *Sozialgeschichte in der DDR* (pp 31–61). Stuttgart: Klett-Cotta.

Kommission für Zukunftsfragen der Freistaaten Bayern und Sachsen. (1997). *Erwerbstätigkeit und Arbeitslosigkeit in Deutschland* (Vols 1–3). Bonn: Author.

Kreckel, R. (1992). *Politische Soziologie der sozialen Ungleichheit.* Frankfurt: Campus Verlag.

Kreckel, R. (1995). Makrosoziologische Überlegungen zum Kampf um Normal- und Teilzeitarbeit im Geschlechterverhältnis. *Berliner Journal für Soziologie, 5*(4), 489–95.

Lutz, B., et al. (1996). *Arbeit, Arbeitsmarkt und Betriebe.* Opladen: Leske & Budrich.

Nickel, H.-M. (1997). Der Transformationsprozess in Ost und West und seine Folgen für das Geschlechterverhältnis. *Aus Politik und Zeitgeschichte, 97*(B51), 20–9.

Pfau-Effinger, B., & Geissler, B. (1992). Institutionelle und sozio-kulturelle Kontextbedingungen der Entscheidung verheirateter Frauen für Teilzeitarbeit: Ein Beitrag zu einer Soziologie des Erwerbsverhaltens. *Mitteilungen aus der Arbeitsmarkt- und Berufsforschung (MitAB), 25*(3), 358–70.

Schenk, S. (1995). Neu- oder Restrukturierung des Geschlechterverhältnisses in Ostdeutschland? *Berliner Journal für Soziologie, 5*(4), 475–88.

Schmidt, G. (1997). Beschäftigungswunder Niederlande. *Leviathan, 96* (206), 302–37.

Schneider, H. (1994). *Arbeitsmarktperspektiven Ostdeutschlands bis zum Jahre 2010.* Halle: Institut für Wirtschaftsforschung Halle.

Schuldt, K. (1992). Arbeitszeiten als Determinante weiblicher Erwerbsarbeit. In G. Engelbrech et al. (Eds), Bedingungen der Frauenerwerbsarbeit im deutsch-deutschen Einigungsprozess. *Beiträge aus der Arbeitsmarkt- und Berufsforschung, 167,* 64–73

Schulze Buschoff, K. (1997). *Arbeitszeiten: Wunsch und Wirklichkeit in Ost- und Westdeutschland* (Discussion paper FS III, 97–410). Berlin: Wissenschaftszentrum Berlin für Sozialforschung.

Statistisches Bundesamt (Data based on the results of the Micro-Census, 1991–1996). Wiesbaden.

Statistisches Bundesamt (Ed.). (1997). *Datenreport 1997: Zahlen und Fakten über die Bundesrepublik Deutschland.* Bonn: Bundeszentrale für politische Bildung.

Trappe, H. (1995). *Emanzipation oder Zwang? Frauen in der DDR zwischen Beruf, Familie und Sozialpolitik.* Berlin: Akademie Verlag.

Winkler, G. (Ed.). (1990). *Frauenreport '90.* Berlin: Verlag die Wirtschaft.

Zapf, W. (1998). Alternative paths of societal development and the dynamics of German transformation. In Y. Yawata & H. Okamoto (Eds), *German unification and transformation of Europe* (pp 5–34). Sophia University: Institute for the Culture of German-Speaking Areas.

Zukunftskommission der Friedrich-Ebert-Stiftung. (1998). *Wirtschaftliche Leitungsfähigkeit, sozialer Zusammenhalt, ökologische Nachhaltigkeit.* Bonn: Dietz Verlag.

10. Unemployment and Its Consequences for Mental Health[1]

William R. Avison

The study of the effects of job loss and subsequent periods of unemployment on individuals' health has a long tradition in the sociology of mental health. Given the current economic climate, it is not surprising, therefore, that social scientists have redoubled their efforts to examine the impact of unemployment on the lives of individuals. The decade of the 1990s has been a period of significant economic change in the structure of national economies in North America. One important result has been an unprecedented level of restructuring of both the private and public sectors. Terms such as 'downsizing,' 'vertical cuts,' and 'outplacement' have become part of the language of the workplace. Sociologists who study mental health have been at the forefront of this research. Recent work in this area has pointed to a number of important issues that remain to be examined. First, while many studies have documented the impact of unemployment on specific disorders or on measures of psychological distress, few if any have estimated the effect of unemployment on an array of diagnoses. Second, it is clear that the loss of a job affects not only the unemployed worker but the family unit as well. Thus, it seems important to examine the impact that such economic dislocation has on spouses. This question, in turn, raises a third issue that has not been thoroughly examined in the literature: Are there significant gender differences in the impact of unemployment on individuals' mental health?

In this chapter, we estimate the impact of involuntary job loss as a risk factor for a number of different DSM-III-R – defined mental health disorders. In so doing, we are able to assess whether the mental health problems that are the consequences of unemployment are different for men and women. As well, we estimate the impact that job loss has on the mental health of the unemployed worker's spouse. Finally, we provide some tentative explanations for the gender differences that are observed.

Unemployment and Its Impact on Mental Health

Over the last two decades, much of the work on unemployment and health outcomes has been stimulated by Brenner's (1973, 1979) now famous aggregate studies. Brenner estimated that a 1 per cent increase in unemployment was associated five years later with an increase of 1.9 per cent in mortality, 4.1 per cent in suicides, 3.4 per cent in mental hospital admissions for men and 4.3 per cent for women, and a 4.0 per cent increase in prison admissions. Subsequent studies at the individual level of analysis leave little doubt that the unemployed experience more negative mental health outcomes than do the employed (cf Avison, 1999, for a review). The evidence of this correlation is most clear for outcomes such as symptoms of depression and anxiety and measures of psychological distress (Kessler, House, and Turner, 1987; Linn, Sandifer, and Stein, 1985; McLanahan and Glass, 1985; Pearlin et al., 1981; Warr, 1987; Warr, Jackson, and Banks, 1988). Of course, a major point of contention in interpreting these findings concerns whether they reflect the health consequences of job loss and unemployment or whether they represent selection effects where people with health problems lose their jobs. Studies employing longitudinal research designs have been able to address this interpretational problem. The weight of evidence from these studies appears to support the conclusion that job loss results in higher levels of mental health problems (Banks and Jackson, 1982; Dew, Bromet, and Schulberg, 1987; Dooley, Catalano, and Rook, 1988; Liem and Liem, 1988, 1990; Menaghan, 1989; Pearlin et al., 1981).

A number of interesting questions emerge from these studies. The first concerns whether the apparent impact of unemployment on symptoms of distress and mental health problems also holds for diagnosed psychiatric disorders. Evidence from the Epidemiologic Catchment Area (ECA) Study indicates that unemployment is associated with major depressive disorder (Weissman et al., 1991). As well, Catalano and associates (1993) have recently reported that job loss affects the incidence of clinically significant alcohol abuse as assessed with DSM-III criteria in the ECA Study. These findings suggest that more research is required to determine whether job loss manifests itself in elevated rates of a number of disorders.

A second question concerns whether there is any gender difference in the impact of job loss. While the majority of these studies have focused on job loss among men, there is some evidence that unemployment among women also results in increased symptoms of mental health difficulties (Banks and Jackson, 1982; Warr and Jackson, 1983), although some researchers report that the magnitude of these effects may be less among women (Cohn, 1978; Perucci, Perucci et al., 1985; Shamir, 1985). To date, however, few studies have systematically made these comparisons across different mental health outcomes. Given recent arguments that men and women differentially express the effects of stress or strain (i.e., drinking, substance abuse, and hostility among men; depression and anxiety among women) (Aneshensel, Rutter, and Lachenbruch, 1991), this is an issue that deserves research attention.

There is a third question. What of the effects of the job loss and unemployment of one family member on other family members? Elder and associates (Elder and Caspi, 1988; Liker and Elder, 1983) report evidence from their life-course studies indicating that some women whose husbands lost their jobs during the Great Depression experienced greater distress than their husbands, while others attained more power in the marital relationship and experienced increases in personal competence and psychological well-being. Cochrane and Stopes-Roe (1981) report elevated symptomatology among women whose husbands had recently lost their jobs. In their study of men's job losses due to a plant closing, Dew and colleagues (1987) document the detrimental psychological effects of husbands' unemployment on their sample of women. Recently, Liem and Liem (1988, 1990) have clearly documented elevated levels of anxiety and depression among the wives of unemployed blue-collar and white-collar workers. They have also made an important contribution to our understanding of the connections between men's job loss and subsequent distress among their spouses by proposing a dynamic model that specifies the mediating effects of the family's socio-economic characteristics, the unemployed individual's functioning, and patterns of family interaction.

Rook, Dooley, and Catalano (1991) have presented a very detailed analysis of the impact of husbands' job stressors on wives' psychological well-being. Their results clearly reveal that women whose husbands experienced job stress (including job loss) had elevated levels of psychological distress. In two recent papers, Conger and his associates (Conger, Lorenz, et al., 1993; Ge et al., 1994) report on the ways in which stressors experienced by individuals also have effects on their spouses and children. This work provides additional insights into the ways in which individuals' unemployment may have important effects on their spouses' mental health.

Mediating and Moderating Processes

It is important to understand the pathways through which unemployment influences the mental health of individuals (Avison, 1999). Studies of the factors that intervene between individuals' job losses and their health problems appear to have focused on five potential mediators. Some researchers have argued that job loss and unemployment create *financial strains* that lead to mental health problems (Kessler, Turner, and House, 1988; Voydanoff and Donnelly, 1989). Others have suggested that job loss results in a substantially *altered social support network* where the absence of support increases psychological distress (Atkinson, Liem, and Liem, 1986; Banks and Ullah, 1987; Bolton and Oatley, 1987; Gore, 1978; Warr et al., 1988). A third line of inquiry has focused on the process by which unemployment results in a *loss of self-esteem and personal efficacy* that, in turn, result in symptoms of mental health problems (cf Fryer and Payne, 1986; Pearlin et al., 1981). Fourth, some researchers have examined the mediating role of *marital and family conflict*. These studies report that unemployment leads to increasing conflicts between the unemployed worker and other family members (Liker and Elder, 1983; Voydanoff, 1990). As well, these changes in the family environment are not conducive to good health (Conger, Elder, et al., 1990; Fryer and Payne, 1986; Liem and Liem, 1990). Finally, Rook, Dooley, and Catalano (1991) have suggested that the elevated levels of distress observed among women whose husbands are experiencing job-related stress may be consistent with the costs-of-caring hypothesis that has been examined by various researchers (Kessler and McLeod, 1984; Kessler, McLeod, and Wethington, 1985; Riley and Eckenrode, 1986; Turner and Avison, 1989). This is the argument that women's tendency to be more empathetic than men results in their experiencing elevated levels of distress when someone close to them has been exposed to a stressor.

In our view, it seems unlikely that all these mediators will exert similar influences on the relationship between job loss in the family and mental health problems of husbands and wives. For example, given that husbands' salaries are often higher than those of their wives, the level of financial strain generated when husbands lose their jobs is likely to be greater than that from jobs loss among wives. Accordingly, among men, we expect financial strain to be important in mediating the impact of their own job loss on their mental health but to be less important in mediating any effect of their wives' job loss. By contrast, among women, we predict that financial strain is less likely to mediate the association between their own unemployment and their mental health but to be an important mediator of the effect of their husbands' job loss.

It also seems more likely that psychosocial resources such as mastery or self-esteem will mediate the effects of job loss on individuals' own mental health but not the effects on their spouses' health. The experience of job loss constitutes a direct challenge to one's sense of self that results in feelings of depression (Caplan et al., 1989). Almost by definition, the threat to self is personal. Accordingly, it is unlikely that the resulting erosion of the individual's sense of self-esteem or mastery will have strong, direct effects on the spouse's mental health. In addition to these mediating effects, we also expect that these psychosocial resource variables might serve important stress-buffering functions, a pattern that has often been reported in the literature (Turner and Roszell, 1994).

Because both social support and marital conflict are significantly transactional in character, it is likely that these factors mediate both the impact of individuals' own unemployment and the effect of their spouses' unemployment on their mental health outcomes. Regardless of which spouse suffers the job loss, it might be expected that the social support networks of these families will contract because of the loss of co-workers as a source of support. Moreover, we also expect that social support will buffer the effects of unemployment on mental health problems. Similarly, marital tensions may increase in families where there is job loss no matter which spouse has become unemployed. Alternatively, such conflict might also exacerbate the impact of unemployment on mental health.

The role that empathy plays in this process is perhaps less clear because of the relative absence of research on this matter. Nevertheless, it seems unlikely that empathy will have any significant role in mediating the effects of respondents' own unemployment on their mental health. Moreover, there is no compelling reason to expect empathy to operate as a mediator of the impact of a spouse's unemployment on the partner's mental health. Rather, it seems more likely that job loss occurring to the spouse might be most likely to result in mental health problems if the partner empathizes strongly with his or her spouse. Accordingly, we expect empathy to exacerbate the impact of the spouse's job loss on the partner's own mental health.

Methods

The empirical basis for our exploration of these processes is a large, community-based survey of families in which households that had experienced recent unemployment were oversampled. With relatively large numbers of both husbands and wives who had lost their jobs, we have sample sizes sufficient for analyses that can address these research questions. Although there are a number of designs that can address selection, we followed Kessler, Turner, and House (1988), who generated a sample comprising (1) currently unemployed respondents (CU), (2) currently employed respondents who were previously unemployed within a specified number of years (PU), and (3) respondents who had been stably employed throughout that time period (SE). Our approach throughout our analyses of the effects of unemployment will be to estimate these effects using the (CU + PU) versus SE con-trast because this comparison cannot be biased by selection *out* of employment.

Sampling

We first conducted a random-digit-dial (RDD) screening survey of London, Ontario, to identify a sampling pool of married or cohabiting couples with at least one child under age 18 living in the home. The screening survey determined whether either spouse was currently unemployed (CU), previously unemployed (PU), or stably employed (SE). CU refers to involuntary loss of a steady job where the worker was employed for more than twenty-five hours per week; unemployment must have been for a minimum of four weeks prior to the screening survey interview. PU refers to involuntary unemployment of at least four weeks at some time in the four years prior to the screening survey (roughly the duration of the economic recession at the time) where the individual had returned to a steady job of twenty-five hours or more per week. SE refers to steady employment of twenty-five hours or more per week with no unemployment exceeding four weeks over the last four years. Thus, when we speak of unemployment in this study, we are focusing specifically on unemployment due to involuntary job loss. Individuals who left jobs or who were unemployed of their own volition were not included. De facto, we also excluded first-time job seekers who were unable to secure employment.

Our final sample consisted of 897 families. In terms of individual employment status, of the women in our study, 532 were stably employed, 97 were currently unemployed, 90 were previously unemployed, and 178 were categorized as 'other.' This group consisted largely of women who described themselves as housewives. A very small number of these women were students, physically disabled, or retired. Among men, 560 were stably employed, 136 were currently unemployed, and 177 were previous unemployed. Only 24 were categorized as 'other.'

Measures

DSM-III-R disorders: We used the short form of the Composite International Diagnostic Interview (CIDI) that has been developed at the University of Michigan (Kessler, et al., 1994; Kessler, Andrews, et al., 1998) to obtain diagnostic information on several mental health problems: major depression, dysthymia, generalized anxiety disorder, panic disorder, and substance abuse.

Financial strains have been assessed with a multi-item scale indicating the extent to which respondents have experienced difficulties in meeting financial commitments in ten different areas. Scores can range from 10 to 40. The internal reliability of this index is excellent with a Cronbach's alpha of .88 among men and .87 among women.

Psychosocial resources: Pearlin and Schooler's (1978) seven-item measure of mastery asks respondents to indicate the extent to which they believe themselves to be in control of their lives. In our sample, Cronbach's alpha was .71 for males and .75 for females. Rosenberg's (1979) ten-item self-esteem scale also has excellent measurement properties: high test-retest reliability, and high coefficients of reproducibility and scalability. In our sample, reliability, was excellent, as indicated by a Cronbach's alpha of .86 among men and .88 among women.

Social support: We have chosen to focus solely on perceived social support. We indexed this construct with the Revised Kaplan Scale

(Turner, Frankel, and Levin, 1983), consisting of eight vignettes describing individuals with various levels of support. In this study, Cronbach's alpha was .84 for men and .86 for women.

Marital conflict: We assessed marital conflict with a six-item measure that has been used in the National Co-morbidity Study. These items index the frequency with which couples argue and aggravate each other. For men, Cronbach's alpha was .76; for women, .79.

Empathy: We employed a subset of four items from a larger eight-item measure of empathy that is under development by Hansell and Mechanic (personal communication). The four items that we employed index the extent to which respondents empathize with their spouse's difficulties or problems. Among men, Cronbach's alpha was .74; for women, alpha was .75.

Results

Two-thirds of the women in the study are between the ages of 29 and 43 (Mean = 36.2); there are no differences in age by employment category. Men in the study are a few years older on average (Mean = 38.2); two-thirds are between 31 and 46. Those who have experienced unemployment are slightly younger than the stably employed. On average, both men and women have completed fourteen years of education; those who have suffered job loss are somewhat less well educated. The mean number of children under age 19 is just under two. Stably employed families have somewhat larger families than unemployed families. The mean household income for stably employed families is $57,000 (Canadian) per year and $35,000 for families which have experienced unemployment.

One-year Prevalence Rates

Table 10.1 presents estimates of one-year rates of mental health problems for employed and unemployed men and women in this sample. In this study, we contrast those who have been stably employed over the last four years with those who have experienced any period of unemployment over that time (this group includes CU and PU individuals). For women (wives), we also contrast those who fall into the *other* category – primarily housewives.

In the left-hand panel of this table, it is clear that husbands who have experienced any period of unemployment over the last four years are

TABLE 10.1
Differences in Rates of DSM-III-R Disorders by Employment Status by Gender

	Male		Female		
Diagnosis	SE %	UE %	SE %	UE %	Other %
Major Depression	9.3**	16.1	14.6***	26.6**	15.8
Dysthymia	0.6**	4.0	1.7***	8.2**	5.8
Generalized anxiety	5.2	8.1	7.4*	12.5	8.2
Panic	2.7*	6.5	9.2*	14.7	12.3
Any affective/anxiety disorder	15.0**	22.6	23.0***	35.3	26.9
Substance abuse	2.9***	10.5	1.2*	3.8	2.9
Any disorder	15.9***	27.8	23.0***	35.9	27.6
N	442	248	513	184	170

*p ≤ .05
**p ≤ .01
***p ≤ .001

significantly more likely than stably employed men to have had a serious mental health problem in the last year. They are more likely to have had an episode of major depression (16.1 per cent versus 9.3 per cent), to have suffered from dysthymia (ongoing depressive feelings) (4.0 per cent versus 0.6 per cent), to have experienced panic attacks (6.5 per cent versus 2.7 per cent), and to have abused alcohol or other drugs (10.5 per cent versus 2.9 per cent). In total, over one-quarter (27.8 per cent) of all husbands in our study who had a period of unemployment also had experienced a significant mental health problem. This contrasts with the 15.9 per cent of stably employed men who met criteria for disorder.

Among the women in our study, those who had experienced job loss within the last four years also had significantly higher rates of all diagnosed disorders. This is displayed in the right-hand panel of table 10.1. What is particularly significant for the wives in our study is their elevated rates of depression and dysthymia associated with their unemployment. Over one-quarter of women who had job loss were also depressed in the last year; almost one in ten had experienced dysthymia. Taking all diagnoses together, more than one in every three women (35.9 per cent) who had been unemployed in the last four years had a mental health problem in the last twelve months. By contrast,

23.0 per cent of stably employed women had experienced a mental health problem during that time period. Women in the 'other' category (who described themselves mainly as housewives) fall between the stably employed and the unemployed groups.

Unemployment as a Risk Factor for Disorder

We next constructed a dummy dependent variable indicating whether each respondent had reported at least one DSM-III-R episode of any disorder in the twelve months preceding the interview. In table 10.2, we present logistic regression analyses computed separately for the women and men in our sample. We first regressed our diagnostic measure on two variables representing (a) whether the respondent had experienced unemployment, and (b) whether his or her spouse had experienced unemployment. In the second analysis, we controlled for respondent's age, age-squared, and education. In the left-hand panel, we see that women who lost jobs were significantly more likely to have had a mental disorder in the last year than women who either were stably employed or were housewives. In addition, having a husband who had lost his job also contributed significantly to the probability of having a disorder. Indeed, the effects of these two job stressors were virtually identical in magnitude.

Among men, a different pattern emerged. Their own unemployment significantly increased their odds of having a mental health problem. There is, however, no indication that the wife's job loss contributed to a husband's psychiatric morbidity.

Tests for gender differences in these coefficients are problematic. Because the data for this study are based on couples, the men and women in our sample cannot be considered independent observations. Thus, standard tests for gender interactions or tests for differences in regression coefficients are inappropriate. Typically, one computes tests for seemingly unrelated regression equations (SUR) (Conger, Lorenz, et al., 1993); however, methods for doing so involve generalized least-squares solutions for continuous data. To our knowledge, there is no comparable procedure for logistic regression. Our approach was to re-estimate these regression models using dummy variable analyses and then compute the GLS estimates. These tests reveal that the women in our study are significantly more likely than the men to be affected by their spouse's unemployment. Our results indicate that the impact of husbands' unemployment on wives' mental health ($b = .54$) is more

TABLE 10.2
Estimating the Effects of Unemployment on the 12-Month Prevalence of Any Disorder

Predictor	Females		Males		Females		Males	
	b	OR	b	OR	b	OR	b	OR
Respondent unemployed	.54**	1.72	0.63**	1.88	.51**	1.88	.57**	1.76
Spouse unemployed	.54**	1.72	▼0.21	1.23	.46*	1.58	▼.23	1.26
Education					-.09*	0.92	-.05	0.95
Age					.06	1.06	▼-.06	0.95
Age-squared					-.00	1.00	.00	1.00
Intercept	-.29		1.03		-.06		.50	

*p ≤ .05; **p ≤ .01; ▼gender difference significant at p ≤ .05; b = unstandardized parameter estimate; OR = odds ratio

than 2.5 times that of wives' job loss on husbands' mental health ($b = .21$).

In the right-hand panel, we see that controls for age, age squared, and education do not fundamentally alter this pattern. In subsequent analyses, the estimates that include these controls were used as the baseline against which we assessed the impact of the various mediating variables.

Assessing the Roles of Mediators and Moderators

Table 10.3 presents the results of analyses that estimate the impact of household income and financial strain and an array of psychosocial factors. The top panel represents the baseline estimate of the effects of unemployment on the probability of a mental disorder in the last twelve months. In the next panel, household income and financial strain have been added to the regression equation. Among women, financial strain is a significant predictor of having a disorder net of household income. While controlling for these two variables does not appear to mediate the impact of women's own unemployment on their probability of having a disorder, it results in a non-significant impact of the husband's job loss on the wife's mental health problems. By contrast, the impact of men's unemployment on their mental health problems disappears when household income and financial difficulties are controlled. Although it seems unusual that this should occur when neither financial measure has a significant effect, additional analyses clarify this pattern. We find that lower household income marginally increases the likelihood of a disorder ($p < .10$) and that financial strain is a significant risk factor for disorder. When these two variables are entered simultaneously, their effects tend to cancel each other out, a pattern that is not uncommon when two independent variables are correlated with each other. Thus, for women, financial difficulties mediate the impact of their spouse's job loss on these women's mental health problems. Among men, however, financial strain is an important pathway that connects their personal experience of unemployment with their psychiatric disorder.

In the remaining panels, the results of regression analyses that examine the impact of mastery, self-esteem, perceived social support, marital conflict, and empathy are summarized. We see that mastery has a significant inverse effect on women's likelihood of having a disorder. As well, there is clear evidence that mastery mediates the impact of both

TABLE 10.3
Estimating the Effects of Unemployment on Mental Health Net of Financial Strain and
Selected Psychosocial Factors

	Main Effects		Interaction Effects	
Predictors	Females b	Males b	Females b	Males b
Baseline				
Respondent unemployed	.51**	.57**		
Spouse unemployed	.46*	▼.23	NA	
Financial Strains				
Respondent unemployed	.49*	.39	.01	.01
Spouse unemployed	.39	.32	.00	−.01
Household income	.05	−.03		
Financial strain	.07***	.04		
Mastery				
Respondent unemployed	.30	.42	.01	−.10*
Spouse unemployed	.39	.28	.04	.09
Mastery	−.14***	▼−.09***		
Self-esteem				
Respondent unemployed	.21	.49*	.00	−.07*
Spouse unemployed	.51*	▼.29	.01	−.02
Self-esteem	−.11***	▼−.06***		
Social support				
Respondent unemployed	.32	.54**	.16**	−.05
Spouse unemployed	.47*	▼.30	.03	−.02
Social support	−.13***	▼−.05*		
Marital conflict				
Respondent unemployed	.44*	.53*	−.03	−.00
Spouse unemployed	.33	.14	−.12	−.15
Marital conflict	.15***	.19***		
Empathy				
Respondent unemployed	.50*	.58**	−.12	−.05
Spouse unemployed	.46*	▼.29	−.22**	▼−.09
Empathy	−.02	.02		

*p ≤ .05; **p ≤ .01; ***p ≤ .001; ▼gender difference significant at p ≤ .05; b = unstandardized parameter estimate
Analyses include controls for age, age-squared, and education.

women's own unemployment and their husbands' job loss. A similar pattern is observed among men for the effects of their job loss on disorder. Tests for interactions reveal only one significant modifying effect of mastery. Surprisingly, among men, the inverse association between mastery and diagnosis appears to hold only among the employed. Among unemployed men, mastery and diagnosis are unrelated.

For women, self-esteem has a significant negative association with disorder. While self-esteem mediates the influence of a woman's own job loss on her mental health, it has no such effect with regard to her husband's unemployment. Despite the observation that self-esteem also has a significant direct effect on diagnosis for men, it does not explain away the impact of men's unemployment experience on their mental health. As we observed with mastery, self-esteem appears to be negatively associated with disorder but only among employed men.

In the next panel, the significant effect of social support mediates the relationship between women's own unemployment and their mental health, but not the impact of their husbands' job loss. For men, social support also has a significant inverse effect on diagnosis but plays no mediating role. Among women, we also find that social support buffers the effect of their own unemployment on their mental health. No other interaction effects are significant.

Estimates of the effect of marital conflict reveal that this variable has a significant positive correlation with diagnosis among women. It also appears to be a pathway through which women's mental health is eroded by their husbands' unemployment. There is, however, no indication that marital conflict accounts for the impact of women's or men's own unemployment on their mental health. Nor is there any evidence that marital conflict interacts with unemployment to create stress-magnification effects.

The last set of analyses involved estimating the effects of empathy. For women and men alike, these results reveal that empathy has neither a direct effect on mental health nor a mediating role. There is, however, evidence that higher levels of empathy exacerbate the association between the husband's unemployment and a woman's experiencing an episode of disorder.

Discussion

This study provides clear evidence that unemployment is an important risk factor for a wide array of mental disorders. Men and women who had experienced a significant period of unemployment in the last four years were more than half again as likely as stably employed individuals to have had an episode of depressive illness or anxiety in the year prior to interview. Those who had suffered job loss during this time period were also more than three times as likely to report alcohol or substance-abuse disorders. These contrasts leave little doubt about the devastating consequences of job loss.

While several studies have documented the link between unemployment and symptoms of psychological distress, relatively few investigations have shown that involuntary job loss is a risk factor for diagnosable disorders. Furthermore, ours is among a very few studies that document the impact of unemployment across a wide array of diagnoses. For those researchers and policy makers who view diagnostic measures as the critical outcomes, these results should provide further evidence for the important role that the sociology of mental health plays in understanding the connections between social factors and psychiatric illness.

Of course, the cross-sectional nature of these data do not allow us to eliminate the possibility that social-selection factors may contribute to this correlation between unemployment and disorder. We are re-interviewing all 897 families some two years after their initial interviews. This longitudinal component should provide us with the ability to assess the extent to which social-selection processes are at work.

Gender, Unemployment, and Mental Health

A second major contribution that this study makes is to estimate the impact of unemployment on both men and women. Our results indicate that the mental health consequences of job loss for women are expressed primarily in terms of affective or anxiety disorders. This is hardly surprising, as a large body of research documents elevated rates of depression and anxiety among women who are exposed to various stressors. Similarly, it is not surprising to find such elevated levels of alcohol and substance abuse among unemployed men. What is remarkable, however, are the substantial levels of depression and anxiety among men who have experienced job loss. What would we have concluded about the impact of job loss on psychiatric morbidity had we employed only one diagnostic dimension, such as depressive disorder? We might have concluded that women are more affected by job loss – both their own and their husbands' – than are men. We might also have inferred that this must be attributable to some kind of differential vulnerability to the stress of job loss. Conversely, had we assessed only substance-abuse disorders, we would have drawn the opposite conclusion. Moreover, we would have underestimated the mental health consequences of unemployment among men by almost 300 per cent and for women by almost 1,000 per cent! By employing an array of measures of mental health outcomes, we find patterns that are entirely consistent with the arguments made by Aneshensel and associates that men and women may manifest stressful experience in different ways and that an accurate estimate of the consequences of stress for mental health requires us to consider a range of mental health outcomes.

Gender Differences in Mediating and Moderating Processes

A second point concerning gender differences also deserves comment. Women are in some senses in double jeopardy of experiencing the consequences of unemployment in their families. Unlike men in our study, women are at elevated risk of mental health problems both if they lose their jobs and if their husbands lose their jobs. In our view, this double exposure to job loss is an intriguing finding. Indeed, our analyses of mediating and moderating influences on this process suggest that the pathways from unemployment to mental health problems for women are much more complex than those for men.

Among men, loss of a job appears to result in increases in financial strain and declines in self-efficacy, both of which translate into episodes of mental disorders. At the same time, we observe that unemployed men with higher levels of mastery and social support are less likely to experience a disorder than are those with lower levels of resources. In some sense, this is a classic example of the stress-process model in operation.

Among women, two parallel processes appear to operate. For those women who have lost jobs, the experience erodes their self-esteem and mastery and reduces their levels of perceived social support. At the same time, there is also evidence that social support does moderate this experience. For women whose husbands have lost a job, the consequences are increased financial strain and increased marital conflict. Additionally, husbands' unemployment is more likely to result in mental health problems among women with high levels of empathy than among women with lower levels of empathy.

It seems, then, that women's own experiences of job loss manifest themselves predominantly in terms of negative evaluations of self. These include a diminished sense of control over their lives, an erosion of self-esteem, and doubts about whether they are esteemed or loved by others. In this sense, the psychic costs of women's unemployment appear to provoke the experience of mental health problems. By contrast, women whose husbands lose their jobs are at risk for mental health problems because of the financial consequences of unemployment and the emergence of marital conflict. Moreover, women who are more empathetic tend also to experience mental health difficulties when the husband loses his job.

While it seems apparent that the economic dislocations that result from husbands' unemployment increase the burden of stress for these women, it is interesting that such job loss also appears to increase marital conflict. By contrast, however, husbands report no such increases in conflict when their wives lose their jobs. This might best be understood in the context of shifting power relationships in marriages that are occasioned by husbands' unemployment. When the wife becomes the sole wage earner in a household, there may be a shift in power relations between spouses. One consequence of this shift may be marital conflict. While several researchers have examined the ways in which increases in women's power associated with their employment manifests itself in lower distress (Horwitz, 1984; Mirowsky, 1985; Rosenfield, 1989, 1992), much of this work has focused on the role that mastery plays in mediating this relationship. Our results suggest that marital conflict emanating from shifts in power relationships may partially offset the benefits to women's mental health that accrue from increases in mastery.

The 'Cost of Caring' Revisited

Our findings that unemployment in families places women at double jeopardy for mental health problems is consistent with the 'cost-of-caring' hypothesis. Initial investigations of this proposition by Kessler and McLeod (1984) and Kessler, McLeod, and Wethington (1985) were based on modest effects derived from aggregations of several large samples. Tests of this proposition by Riley and Eckenrode (1986) and Turner and Avison (1989) confirmed this pattern. More recently, however, other researchers (for example, Aneshensel et al., 1991) have failed to confirm any general pattern of differential responsiveness of women to stressors. Subsequently, stress researchers have been attracted to the argument that the apparent differential impact of stressors might actually reflect unmeasured differences in exposure.

Our results suggest that the significance of husbands' unemployment for women's mental health may partially reflect the cost of caring. To our knowledge, we may be the first to demonstrate that women who are empathetic towards their spouses are more likely to experience mental health problems when their husbands lose their jobs. Thus, the cost-of-caring hypothesis may be a proposition that deserves reconsideration in future research.

At the same time, however, it is clear that the impact of husbands' unemployment on women's mental health is a function of both the economic consequences of job loss and increases in marital conflict. In our opinion, this suggests that the gender difference in the impact of spouses' job loss cannot be attributed solely to the cost of caring. Rather, it seems that husbands' job loss generates what Pearlin (1989) has referred to as secondary stressors – in this case, financial stress and marital conflict. Because job loss among husbands is on average a greater financial blow to the family than job loss among wives, husbands' unemployment is more likely to expose families to increased economic stress. Because job loss among husbands is more likely to shift power relations in marriages than job loss among wives, it is more likely to generate marital stress.

Restructuring Work and Employment

There are two other contextual considerations that are relevant to our findings. First, it is important to consider our results in light of the growing trend towards the use of contingent labour forces in many economies. As more workers find themselves employed in limited-term contractual jobs, the prospect of repeated exposure to unemployment seems likely for many individuals. Marshall (1995) has drawn attention to the importance of this issue and suggested that the consequences of contingent labour practices across the life course are not well understood. What are the consequences of the use of contingent labour for individuals' psychological well-being? At least two competing hypotheses seem reasonable. On the one hand, our results suggest that more frequent exposure to unemployment is likely to produce increased numbers of individuals with mental health problems. Contingent labour practices should result in a higher prevalence of various psychiatric diagnoses and increased rates of recurrence of illness among those who have previously experienced a psychiatric illness. On the other hand, the predictability of job loss that results from the end of a contracted job may be less stressful than job loss from plant closings and economic downturns. Moreover, as Turner and Avison (1992) have demonstrated in their application of crisis theory to stress research, individuals who successfully come to terms with or resolve their stressful experiences are less affected by such stressors. Thus, if individuals who are employed as contingent workers have successfully coped with job loss in the past, subsequent periods of unemployment may be less threatening to their mental health than if they had no such experience of coping. The impact of contingent labour structures on workers' mental health is a topic that deserves further attention.

A second context that deserves consideration concerns the intersection of life-course contingencies. Historically, rates of unemployment have been highest among younger cohorts of our population. These are also the cohorts that have the highest prevalence of mental health problems (Wade and Cairney, 1997). More recently, attempts to reduce expenditures in both the private and public sectors have resulted in significant downsizing or outplacement of older workers. We have no studies that estimate the relative impact of job loss among younger versus older workers. Although it seems likely that job loss at different points in the life course should result in different effects on individuals' mental health, there has been no extensive examination of this issue. Indeed, it would be extremely informative if a life-course approach were to be applied to the study of unemployment and mental health. If individuals' life histories of job loss and episodes of diagnosable illness were systematically recorded, techniques such as event-history analyses have the potential to provide important insights into the interplay of unemployment and mental illness across the life course.

The impact over the life course of job loss on mental health can also be conceived as a cumulative experience. Cairney and Wade (1998) point out that the impact of unemployment among younger workers is likely to have long-term consequences for these individuals. Job loss makes saving for retirement more difficult, a problem which, in turn, may contribute to later socio-economic disadvantage that manifests itself in poorer health in old age. In this way, we might think of unemployment as having distal effects on health across the life course.

The results presented in this chapter suggest that the social and psychosocial contexts in which job loss translates into mental health problems are complex. Social scientists have only recently begun to unravel this complexity. Clearly, the study of unemployment and mental health in such social contexts presents unlimited opportunities for research.

NOTES

1 This project was supported by funds from the National Health Research Development Program (6606-5020-63B) of Health Canada and by an Ontario Mental Health Foundation Senior Research Fellowship to William R. Avison.

REFERENCES

Aneshensel, C.S., Rutter, C.M., & Lachenbruch, P.A. (1991). Social structure, stress, and mental health. *American Sociological Review, 56*, 166–78.

Atkinson, T., Liem, R., & Liem, J.H. (1986). The social costs of unemployment: Implications for social support. *Journal of Health and Social Behavior, 27*, 317–31.

Avison, W.R. (1999). The health consequences of unemployment. In National Forum on Health (Ed.), *Determinants of health: Adults and seniors* (pp 3–41). Ottawa, ON: Editions MultiMonde.

Banks, M.H., & Jackson, P.R. (1982). Unemployment and risk of minor psychiatric disorder in young people: Cross-sectional and longitudinal evidence. *Psychological Medicine, 12*, 789–98.

Banks, M.H., & Ullah, P. (1987). *Youth unemployment: Social and psychological perspectives.* Department of Employment Research Paper No. 61. London: HMSO.

Bolton, W., & Oatley, K. (1987). A longitudinal study of social support and depression in unemployed men. *Psychological Medicine, 17*, 453–60.

Brenner, M.H. (1973). *Mental illness and the economy.* Cambridge, MA: Harvard University Press.

Brenner, M.H. (1979). Mortality and the national economy: A review, and the experience of England and Wales, 1936–1976. *Lancet*, 568–73.

Cairney, J., & Wade, T.J. (1998). Reducing economic disparity to achieve better health: Modelling the effect of adjustments to income adequacy on self-reported morbidity among the elderly in Canada. *Canadian Journal of Public Health, 89*, 424–8.

Caplan, R.D., Vinokur, A.D., Price, R.H., & van Ryn, M. (1989). Job seeking, reemployment, and mental health: A randomized field experiment in coping with job loss. *Journal of Applied Psychology, 74,* 759–69.

Catalano, R., Dooley, D., Wilson, G., & Hough, R. (1993). Job loss and alcohol abuse: A test using data from the Epidemiologic Catchment Area Project. *Journal of Health and Social Behavior, 34,* 215–26.

Cochrane, R. & Stopes-Roe, M. (1981). Women, marriage, employment and mental health. *British Journal of Psychiatry, 139,* 373–81.

Cohn, R.M. (1978). The effect of employment status change on self attitudes. *Social Psychology, 41,* 81–93.

Conger, R.D., Elder, G.H., Jr, Lorenz, F.O., Conger, K.J., Simons, R.L., Whitbeck, L.B., Huck, S., & Melby, J.N. (1990). Linking economic hardship to marital quality and instability. *Journal of Marriage and the Family, 52,* 643–56.

Conger, R.D., Lorenz, F.O., Elder, G.H., Jr, Simons, R.L., & Ge, X. (1993). Husband and wife differences in response to undesirable life events. *Journal of Health and Social Behavior, 34,* 71–88.

Dew, M.A., Bromet, E.J., & Schulberg, H.C. (1987). A comparative analysis of two community stressors' long-term mental health effects. *American Journal of Community Psychology, 15,* 167–84.

Dooley, D., Catalano, R., & Rook, K.S. (1988). Personal and aggregate unemployment and psychological symptoms. *Journal of Social Issues, 44,* 107–23.

Elder, G.H., Jr, & Caspi, A. (1988). Economic stress in lives: Developmental perspectives. *Journal of Social Issues, 44,* 25–45.

Fryer, D., & Payne, R. (1986). Being unemployed: A review of the literature on the psychological experience of unemployment. In C.L. Cooper & I. Robertson (Eds), *International review of industrial and organizational psychology* (pp 235–78). New York: Wiley.

Ge, X., Conger, R.D., Lorenz, F.O., & Simons, R.L. (1994). Parents' stressful life events and adolescent depressed mood. *Journal of Health and Social Behavior, 35,* 28–44.

Gore, S. (1978). The effect of social support in moderating the health consequences of unemployment. *Journal of Health and Social Behavior, 19,* 157–65.

Horwitz, A.V. (1984). The economy and social pathology. *Annual Review of Sociology, 10,* 95–119.

Kessler, R.C., Andrews, G., Mroczek, D., Ustun, B., & Wittchen, H.-U. (1998). The World Health Organization Composite International Diagnostic Interview Short Form (CIDI-SF). *International Journal of Methods in Psychiatric Research, 7,* 171–85.

Kessler, R.C., House, J.S., & Turner, J.B. (1987). Unemployment and health in a community sample. *Journal of Health and Social Behavior, 28,* 51–9.

Kessler, R.C., McGonagle, K.A., Zhao, S., Nelson, C.B., Hughes, M., Eshelman,

S., Wittchen, H.-U., & Kendler, K.S. (1994). Lifetime and 12–month prevalence of DSM-III-psychiatric disorders in the United States: Results from the
National Comorbidity Survey. *Archives of General Psychiatry, 51*, 8–19.

Kessler, R.C., & McLeod, J.D. (1984). Sex differences in vulnerability to undesirable life events. *American Sociological Review, 49*, 620–31.

Kessler, R.C., McLeod, J.D., & Wethington, E. (1985). The costs of caring:
A perspective on the relationship between sex and psychological distress. In
I.G. Sarason & B.R. Sarason, *Social support: Theory, research and applications*
(pp 491–506). The Hague: Martinus Nijhoff.

Kessler, R.C., Turner, J.B., & House, J.S. (1988). Effects of unemployment on
health in a community survey. *Journal of Social Issues, 44*, 69–85.

Liem, J.H., & Liem, G.R. (1990). Understanding the individual and family
effects of unemployment. In J. Eckenrode & S. Gore, *Stress between work and
family* (pp 175–204). New York: Plenum Press.

Liem, R., & Liem, J.H. (1988). Psychological effects of unemployment on workers and their families. *Journal of Social Issues, 44*, 87–105.

Liker, J.K., & Elder, G., Jr. (1983). Economic hardship and marital relations in
the 1930's. *American Sociological Review, 48*, 43–359.

Linn, M.W., Sandifer, R., & Stein, S. (1985). Effects of unemployment on mental
and physical health. *American Journal of Public Health, 75*, 502–6.

Marshall, V.W. (1995). The next half-century of aging research – and thoughts
for the future. *Journal of Gerontology: Social Sciences, 50B*, S131–S133.

McLanahan, S., & Glass, J.L. (1985). A note on the trend in sex differences in
psychological distress. *Journal of Health and Social Behavior, 26*, 328–36.

Menaghan, E.G. (1989). Role changes and psychological well-being: Variations
in effects by gender and role repertoire. *Social Forces, 67*, 693–714.

Mirowsky, J. (1985). Depression and marital power: An equity model. *American
Journal of Sociology, 91*, 557–92.

Pearlin, L.I. (1989). The sociological study of stress. *Journal of Health and Social
Behavior, 30*, 241–56.

Pearlin, L.I., Lieberman, M.A., Menaghan, E.G., & Mullan, J.T. (1981). The
stress process. *Journal of Health and Social Behavior, 22*, 337–56.

Pearlin, L.I., & Schooler, C. (1978). The structure of coping. *Journal of Health and
Social Behavior, 19*, 2–21.

Perrucci, C.C., Perrucci, R., Targ, D.B., & Targ, H.R. (1985). Impact of a plant
closing on workers and the community. In I.H. Simpson & R.L. Simpson
(Eds), *Research in the sociology of work: A research annual* (Vol. 3, pp 231–60).
Greenwich, CT: JAI Press.

Riley, D., & Eckenrode, J. (1986). Social ties: Costs and benefits within differing subgroups. *Journal of Personality and Social Psychology, 57*, 651–9.

Rook, K., Dooley, D., & Catalano, R. (1991). Stress transmission: The effects of husbands' job stressors on the emotional health of their wives. *Journal of Marriage and the Family, 53*, 165–77.

Rosenberg, M. (1979). *Conceiving the self.* New York: Basic Books.

Rosenfield, S. (1989). The effects of women's employment: Personal control and sex differences in mental health. *Journal of Health and Social Behavior, 30*, 77–91.

Rosenfield, S. (1992). The costs of sharing: Wives' employment and husbands' mental health. *Journal of Health and Social Behavior, 33*, 213–25.

Shamir, B. (1985). Sex differences in psychological adjustment to unemployment and reemployment: A question of commitment, alternatives, or finance? *Social Problems, 33*, 67–79.

Turner R.J., & Avison, W.R. (1989). Gender and depression: Assessing exposure and vulnerability to life events in a chronically strained population. *Journal of Nervous and Mental Disease, 177*, 443–55.

Turner, R.J., & Avison, W.R. (1992). Innovations in the measurement of life stress: Crisis theory and the significance of event resolution. *Journal of Health and Social Behavior, 33*, 36–50.

Turner, R.J., Frankel, B.G., & Levin, D.M. (1983). Social support: Conceptualization, measurement and implications for mental health. In J. Greenley (Ed.), *Research in community and mental health*, (Vol. 3, pp 67–112). Greenwich, CT: JAI Press.

Turner, R.J., & Roszell, P. (1994). Psychosocial resources and the stress process. In W.R. Avison & I.H. Gotlib (Eds), *Stress and mental health: Contemporary issues and prospects for the future* (pp 179–212). New York: Plenum Press.

Voydanoff, P. (1990). Economic stress and family relations. *Journal of Marriage and the Family, 5*, 1099–1115.

Voydanoff, P., & Donnelly, B.W. (1989). Economic distress and mental health: The role of family coping resources and behaviors. *Lifestyles: Family and Economic Issues, 10*, 139–62.

Wade, T.J., & Cairney, J. (1997). Age and depression in a nationally representative sample of Canadians: A preliminary look at the National Population Health Survey. *Canadian Journal of Public Health, 88*, 297–302.

Warr, P. (1987). *Work, unemployment and mental health.* New York: Oxford University Press.

Warr, P.B., & Jackson, P.R. (1983). Self-esteem and unemployment among young workers. *Le Travail Humain, 46*, 355–66.

Warr, P., Jackson, P., & Banks, M. (1988). Unemployment and mental health: Some British studies. *Journal of Social Issues, 44*, 47–68.

Weissman, M.M., Bruce, M.L., Leaf, P.J., Florio, L.P., & Holzer, C., III. (1991). Affective disorders. In L.N. Robins & D.A. Regier (Eds), *Psychiatric disorders in America* (pp 53–80). New York: Free Press.

11. Family Turning-points and Career Transitions at Midlife[1]

Deborah Carr and Jennifer Sheridan

The career paths of most women (and men, to a lesser degree) are inextricably linked to their family experiences. Numerous studies reveal that child-rearing responsibilities guide occupational decisions in young adulthood, yet little is known about linkages between work and family transitions at midlife. Although midlife has traditionally been characterized as a demographically 'sparse' stage of the life course, two co-occurring trends suggest that the lives of midlife adults are now punctuated by important shifts in work and family roles (Elder and O'Rand, 1995). First, organizational restructuring has created a context where midlife workers are increasingly susceptible to displacement and may respond by forming their own businesses, seeking new lines of work, or obtaining further training and education (Farr, Tesluk, and Klein, 1998). Second, demographic patterns, including rising rates of marital dissolution and declines in mortality, mean that current cohorts of midlife adults are likely to experience important family transitions including divorce and competing demands from aging parents and young adult children. Using data from the Wisconsin Longitudinal Study (WLS), we examine whether family transitions (divorce, widow(er)hood, onset of caregiving duties, and the empty-nest transition) influence three types of midlife career transitions: returning to school to obtain a college/university degree; moving into a different occupation; and starting one's own business.

Our research is guided by the life-course paradigm, in which human lives are conceptualized as series of interlocking age-graded trajectories, such as work careers and family experiences, that are marked by sequences of events and transitions (Elder, 1994). The life-course perspective reflects the intersection of historical and personal occurrences. Its four central themes are that (1) the timing and sequencing of role transitions vary for individuals; (2) the life course unfolds differently for different birth cohorts; (3) diverse life domains, such as family and work, are interconnected; and (4) men and women make plans and choices based on the options presented to them (Elder, 1994).

Work-life Transitions

A central theme of the life-course paradigm is that transitions are embedded in rich and diverse life histories. The timing of transitions differs across individuals in terms of the social context and precursors of such transitions (Elder and O'Rand, 1995). As such, we are interested in the events and characteristics that influence the timing of three types of career transitions at midlife.

Earning a College/University Degree

Recent enrolment statistics suggest that demands for lifelong education are heightened among current cohorts of midlife adults. Students over age 40 now comprise 11.2 per cent of total higher-education enrolments in the United States (Institute for Higher Education Policy, 1997). Over the past fifty years, the progressive rationalization and bureaucratization of the economy – coupled with declining employment in the manufacturing and farming sectors – has heightened the value of educational credentials for occupational mobility (Blau and Duncan, 1967; Collins, 1979). A college/university degree is an important credential because employers use formal qualifications to screen and select, especially when job candidates outnumber job openings (Collins, 1979). At midlife, educational transitions may be linked to family transitions, as entrances to and exits from family roles represent a major shift in the economic and time resources available to an individual. Our analyses will thus address the question: To what extent do family transitions influence whether men and women return to college/university to earn a degree at age 35 or beyond?

Forming One's Own Business

Self-employment is heralded as an American ideal, promising auton-omy and self-sufficiency (Chinoy, 1955). National surveys show that more than half of Americans hope to have their own business some day (Steinmetz and Wright, 1989). Among the 35-year-old WLS respon-dents (in the 1975 interview), one-third of men and 16 per cent of women said that they hoped to be self-employed in the future. Entrances into self-employment become increasingly common after age 35 because advanced age is associated with greater work experience, accumulation of start-up capital, and the establishment of a profes-sional reputation – attributes that may be crucial to the establishment of one's own business (Aronson, 1991, p. 23; Borjas, 1986).

Linkages between family roles and self-employment have also been documented. Self-employment has been characterized as a rational choice for married men because they can ensure against the risk of unreliable employees by hiring their spouses (Borjas, 1986). For a woman, having a husband with steady earnings and benefits provides a financial cushion that increases her chances of starting her own busi-ness (Devine, 1994). Mothers of young children may choose self-employment as a flexible work option that may be combined with fam-ily responsibilities (Carr, 1996). Although the relationship between family characteristics and contemporaneous self-employment status has been explored, no studies have linked *changes* in one's family struc-ture and status over time, and the entry into self-employment. Conse-quently, in the second set of analyses we address the question: To what extent do family transitions influence whether midlife men and women form their own businesses at age 35 or beyond?

Career Change

Occupational change at midlife and beyond is a relatively common phenomenon and is expected to increase among future cohorts of midlife adults. As a result of increasing longevity and improved health later in life, older adults may delay retirement and take on 'bridge jobs' before leaving the labour force entirely (Ruhm, 1996). Demographic projections suggest that, by early in the twenty-first century, the decreasing supply of qualified entry-level workers will not meet the demands of industry (Kutscher and Fullerton, 1990). If rapid technological changes persist, older workers may be expected to retool their current job skills, or to retrain for new jobs (Tolbert, 1982).

Few studies have explicitly linked career change at midlife to family transitions. Past research on occupational change generally has followed one of four approaches. First, developmental psychologists have examined whether career change is a component of a midlife 'crisis' or turning-point (Levinson et al., 1978; Krantz, 1977; Osherson, 1980). Second, organizational and personality psychologists have examined the unique personality traits associated with career changers (Leong and Boyle, 1997). Third, sociological studies of intragenerational occupational mobility have focused on organizational structures that facilitate or constrain individual mobility (Tolbert, 1982). Finally, life-course sociologists have examined how specific career trajectories affect later-life outcomes, such as retirement and physical health (Hayward, Friedman, and Chen, 1998; Elder and Pavalko, 1993).

These four frameworks share three limitations, however. First, none explicitly links career changes with normative and non-normative family transitions. Second, an implicit assumption of the four approaches is that career change represents a *crisis* (Krantz, 1977) or is indicative of poor social and psychological adjustment (Wilensky, 1961). Because careers traditionally have been defined as orderly sequences of related jobs, with each promising more prestige, pay, and responsibility than the prior job, violations of the 'one life–one career imperative' are often depicted as the irrational acts of people with few skills or options (Sarason, 1977; Spilerman, 1977; Wilensky, 1961). Moreover, work histories distinguished by multiple job transitions have been linked to poorer physical, psychological, and economic well-being in late life (Hayward, Friedman, and Chen, 1998; Elder and Pavalko, 1993). Finally, the examination of career change has focused overwhelmingly on men. Multiple studies show that women's careers are more disjointed than men's (see Moen, 1985, for a review), yet most examinations of women's job changes have focused on the earlier part of the life course when job changes are generally interpreted as responses to child-rearing responsibilities.

We argue that changes in the nature of work – particularly organizational restructuring – have created a context where career changes are an increasingly common transition during adulthood. Guided by the life-course assumptions that work and family lives are intertwined, we will explore whether career transitions are adaptations to shifting family responsibilities. Thus, our third set of analyses will ask: To what extent do family transitions influence whether midlife men and women make a major occupational change at age 35 or beyond?

Importance of Birth Cohort

The life-course paradigm emphasizes that human lives unfold differently for different birth cohorts. In this study we examine the lives of one birth cohort: respondents in the Wisconsin Longitudinal Study (WLS), a sample of men and women who graduated from Wisconsin high schools in 1957. The experiences of the WLS sample are moulded by the historical and social conditions they faced as they came of age and as they formed families and careers. Men of this cohort were raised to believe that they would find stable careers and would be the main breadwinners of their families. Women were socialized during childhood to value family and domestic roles; careers would come later, or would be entered into only as a short-term role between finishing school and becoming a wife and mother (Baruch, Barnett, and Rivers, 1983; Coontz, 1992). Between the time the WLS participants graduated from high school in 1957 and the time they reached their thirties, major changes in family, gender, and work roles occurred. At the time that most WLS women faced reduced child-rearing responsibilities in the mid-1970s (as their children reached school age), diverse work and educational opportunities opened up to women (Bardwick, 1980). Concurrently, several demographic trends – most notably, increasing divorce rates and declining mortality rates –affected the lives of the WLS graduates (Cherlin, 1981). For the WLS cohort, divorce is not the rare event it was for earlier cohorts. Increases in life expectancy over the last fifty years mean that WLS graduates are among the first birth cohorts to see their parents survive to old age, and many may grapple with the simultaneous demands of aging parents and adult children. Decreasing mortality at younger ages, as well, suggests that few members of the WLS would have to cope with the death of a spouse; yet such an unanticipated transition may have important consequences for subsequent labour-force behaviour.

Linked Lives

The life-course concept of 'linked lives' refers to the linkages among the individual's social worlds over the life span (Elder, 1994) and includes links between adult work and family domains, and between characteristics of childhood social background and adult socio-economic prospects (Elder, 1994). In this analysis, we consider the effects on midlife career transitions of both current family roles and transitions and factors related to early social background.

Family Transitional Events

Changes in one's family roles may affect one's economic resources, or the time one has available to allocate to other tasks. Yet changes in family roles may also represent psychological turning-points, when individuals re-evaluate their values and past decisions. Accordingly, a central objective of our research is to explore whether career transitions at midlife are affected by four family transitions: divorce; widow(er)-hood; empty-nest transition; and caregiving.

Divorce and Widow(er)hood

Divorce and widow(er)hood have important economic and psychological consequences. A woman's economic standard of living may drop by 20 to 70 per cent following marital dissolution, while men's standard of living generally increases slightly, by 10 to 20 per cent (Holden, 1988; Holden and Smock, 1991). Declines in a woman's standard of living upon marital dissolution may force her to reinvest in her own education and job skills, or to seek well-paying work. Men and women who experience marital dissolution may also adapt by channelling their energies into activities that provide opportunity for self-fulfilment and personal accomplishment.

We expect that both divorce and widow(er)hood will increase the likelihood that a woman will make a career transition at midlife. Although the psychological consequences may prove devastating in the short term, the economic crises that accompany such transitions may force women to make drastic shifts in their work lives. For men, we do not expect divorce or widowerhood to increase their likelihood of career change, except perhaps an increased likelihood of returning to school for a degree in later life. An increase in standard of living and an increased desire for personal growth might be associated with returning to college or university.

Empty Nest

Early research on midlife portrayed the empty-nest transition as a crisis point when midlife women experienced depression following the loss of their role as mother; however, more recent research describes these years as a time when women seek new opportunities for self-definition (Robertson, 1978; Rubin, 1979). Financial pressures may heighten during this time, however. A 'life-cycle squeeze' may occur, where children's educational expenses coincide with a plateau in midlife parents' earnings (Moen and Moorehouse, 1983). While we expect that women's likelihood of career transition will increase following the empty-nest transition, we expect no effect for men, who (in this cohort) may have invested less time than women in the rearing of their children. Having a child leave home would not affect men's daily lives to the extent that it would affect their wives' lives. However, men may seek new jobs or may form their own businesses as a means to increase their earnings during the 'life-cycle squeeze'.

Caregiving

Women are the primary caregivers for aging parents and ailing relatives and friends (Lee, 1992; Stone, Cafferata, and Sangl, 1987). Women caregivers are more likely to leave the work force than men, and are more likely to reduce their work hours (Pavalko and Artis, 1997). Past studies have focused primarily on the effects of caregiving on labour supply, yet have not extended their analyses to career transitions among caregivers. We expect that the onset of caregiving duties will reduce the likelihood that a woman would make a career transition. We expect no significant relationship for men, given the gendered nature of caregiving duties.

Spouse/Child Characteristics

Making a career transition or pursuing educational goals at midlife may also be contingent upon the support and resources provided by other family members. We expect that respondents whose spouses do not work for pay will be less likely to make a career transition, as economic pressures may prevent a single earner from making a potentially risky career shift. Conversely, we expect that persons married to spouses with higher education and in higher-paying occupations will be more likely to make a career transition, as the spouse's resources may minimize the economic risk involved with a career change. We expect that unmarried persons and those with more children will make fewer changes, given the elevated economic pressures they face.

Characteristics of Social Background

Childhood experiences may have long-term effects on behaviour: each generation is bound to fateful decisions and events in the other's life course (Elder, 1994). Status-attainment research, for example, has documented that children whose parents have higher education, higher-status occupations, and higher family incomes tend to achieve higher levels of educational attainment and higher-status occupations (Sewell and Hauser, 1975). Young adults from more privileged backgrounds also tend to marry and bear children later and to enjoy more stable marriages (Cherlin, 1981). Characteristics of social background, based on the Wisconsin model of status attainment, will be controlled in the analysis

Planful Activity

The final assumption of the life-course paradigm is that men and women are planful and make choices among the set of options presented to them (Elder, 1994). We argue that midlife career transitions may represent the attainment of earlier occupational aspirations. We expect that men and women who sought a new line of work at age 35 will have an increased risk of career change at midlife. We expect that women whose goal was to be keeping house will be less likely to experience a career change.

Data and Methods

Analyses use data from the Wisconsin Longitudinal Study (WLS). The WLS is a long-term study of a random sample of 10,317 men and women who graduated from Wisconsin high schools in 1957. Sample members were interviewed three times: during their senior year in high school (1957), at age 35–6 (1975), and at age 53–4 (1992–3). Sample retention is high: 9,139 (88.6 per cent) of the 10,317 original sample members were re-interviewed in 1975, and 8,493 (82.3 per cent) were re-interviewed in 1992–3. This analysis is limited to the 4,512 women and 3,981 men who participated in the 1957 and 1992 interviews. We use Cox proportional hazard models to estimate the relative risk of participants' making one of three career-change transitions. Hazard models predict the probability that an event will occur at a particular time to a particular individual, given that the individual is 'at risk' at that time (Yamaguchi, 1991).

Dependent Variables

Three midlife career transitions are considered: earning a college/university degree, starting one's own business, and making a major occupational change. Each event is recorded in terms of the year and month of onset and number of months' duration. We focus on transitions that occurred between ages 35 (1975) and 53 (1993) only. This seventeen-year period is long enough to observe a significant amount of change in one's family and work roles, yet it is not so long that the larger context of surrounding labour-force patterns changed dramatically.

First, we examine the predictors of *obtaining a college/university degree* after age 35 (1975). Any respondent who was enrolled in school during the 1975 interview is excluded from the risk set; we are focusing on those who make a life change, not those who completed their degree after 1975 as the natural course of events given that they were in school in 1975. Furthermore, we include a dummy variable indicating whether a respondent was working as a teacher in 1975 (or most recent job), as many respondents who received degrees during midlife are public school teachers and are required to obtain continuing education.

Second, we examine *movement into self-employment* (including both incorporated and unincorporated businesses). We exclude those who were already self-employed in 1975, as they did not make a subsequent transition into self-employment. An additional dummy variable is coded 1 for those who ever worked in farming occupations, as we expect farmers to move more quickly into self-employment.

The third transition is the *transition from one's longest-term job* (as of 1975) into a different occupation. The subsequent job must be both (1) classified as a different major occupational group, and (2) held with a new employer. The major occupational groups, classified according to the 1970 census are: professional, managerial, sales, clerical, craftspeople, operatives, service workers, labourers, and farmers/farm workers.

This definition is used to detect substantial occupational changes, rather than promotions or minor changes in duties at one's current employer. WLS respondents who have never been in the labour force are excluded from the risk set.

Independent Variables

Family Transitions: The central objective of this paper is to assess whether family transitions trigger a career change among midlife men and women. The *empty-nest transition* is measured as the date when one's youngest child turns age 18. The WLS does not ascertain the date of each child's departure from the family home, yet the empty-nest stage is generally believed to begin when a parent's youngest child graduates from high school/secondary school (Boyd and Norris, 1995; Boyd and Pryor, 1989; Rubin, 1979). *Divorce* is measured as the month/year when the respondent stopped living with a spouse, while *death of spouse* is measured as the month/year when the spouse died. *Transition to caregiver role* refers to the date when a respondent began to provide instrumental assistance to a sick relative or friend. The WLS obtained data only on caregiving spells lasting one month or longer.

Time-varying covariates are used to capture family transitions. Dichotomous variables 'turn on,' or are set equal to one during the month that a transition is made. Irreversible events (i.e., child turning age 18 and death) are turned on when the event occurs, and stay on for the remainder of the analysis. The caregiving and marital-dissolution variables turn on when a spell begins, and are set off when the spell ends.

Characteristics of Social Background: Nine indicators of family background, based on the Wisconsin model of status attainment (Sewell and Hauser, 1975) are included in the analysis: *father's (or householder's) occupational status* (Duncan SEI score) in 1957; whether the respondent's *mother worked for pay* while the respondent was growing up (coded 1 if yes); *family income*, measured as the logged average of family income as reported on Wisconsin tax records for the years 1957–60; *father's years of completed education; mother's years of completed education; farm background* (coded 1 if respondent's father was a farmer); *family structure in 1957* (coded 1 if the family was not intact); *number of siblings*; and *respondent's mental ability*, assessed by the Henmon-Nelson test, administered during the sample members' junior year in high school.

Planful Activity: These variables represent factors associated with participants' career decisions and prospects. *Formal education* is years of schooling completed as of 1975. *Occupational education* and *occupational income of the respondent's 1975 occupation* indicate the status characteristics of the respondent's current or last job as of 1975. *Career aspirations* (1975) were elicited with the question, 'If you were free to choose, what kind of work would you like to be doing ten years from now?' Dichotomous variables indicate whether respondents hoped to be *working in a different line of work* (than their 1975 or most recent job), *keeping house, not working,* or *did not know their future goals.* The reference group includes those who wanted to continue working in their 1975 jobs.

Two conceptually and statistically distinct measures are used to capture the status characteristics of the 1975 job and the job to which one aspires: occupational education and occupational income (Hauser and Warren, 1997). *Occupational education* is the percentage of persons in an occupation category (in the 1970 U.S. Census) who attended at least one year of college/university. *Occupational income* is the percentage of persons in an occupation category (in the 1970 U.S. Census) who earned more than $10,000 (U.S.) a year. By including two distinct measures of status, rather than an averaged index such as the Duncan SEI scale, we can assess how specific characteristics of the job to which one aspires influence future work behaviour (Warren, Sheridan, and Hauser, 1998). These variables are transformed to started logit scores to make them more normally distributed (Hauser and Warren, 1997).

Linked Lives: Current work and family roles include: *number of children as of 1975; the occupational education and income of spouse's 1975 occupation; spouse's labour-force participation status in 1975* (coded 1 if spouse was not in the labour force in 1975), and *marital status in 1975* (coded 1 if respondent was not married in 1975).

Missing values for all independent variables are replaced with the sample mean (or the median, for dichotomous variables), and a dummy variable indicates that data are missing for that variable. Coefficients for the missing data flags are not presented in our tables.

Findings

Table 11.1 presents descriptive statistics by sex, and Tables 11.2 and 11.3 display coefficients from the hazard models, for women and men, respectively.

TABLE 11.1
Descriptive Statistics

	Women (N = 4512)			Men (N = 3981)		
	Mean	St. dev.	N	Mean	St. dev.	N
Career transitions						
Returned to school to receive college degree, after age 35**	Jan. 1985	58.51 mos.	278	Jan. 1982	58.04 mos.	122
Became self-employed after age 35***	June 1984	67.17 mos.	262	May 1983	69.00 mos.	361
Began job spell in major occupation category different from longest-ever job****	June 1986	54.29 mos.	849	Mar. 1985	59.63 mos.	802
Social background						
Mental ability	100.95	14.38	4512	101.45	15.18	3981
Householder's occupational status (1957)	345.98	231.85	4465	345.37	232.17	3945
Mother worked when r < 16	0.38	0.49	4488	0.36	0.48	3958
Family income (1957–60)	8.53	0.67	4218	8.54	0.69	3831
Father's educational attainment	9.67	3.36	4512	9.80	3.42	3981
Mother's educational attainment	10.31	2.84	4512	10.56	2.82	3981
Farm background	0.20	0.40	4409	0.20	0.40	3884
Non-intact family	0.10	0.30	4508	0.10	0.29	3976
Number of siblings	3.30	2.56	4495	3.19	2.55	3958
Planful activity						
Educational attainment	13.04	1.78	4512	13.88	2.47	3980
1975 occupational education*	−0.75	1.50	3199	−0.61	1.74	3892
1975 occupational income*	−2.35	1.25	3199	−0.53	1.13	3892
1975 Aspirations, occupational education*	−0.16	1.45	3168	−0.39	1.65	3223
1975 Aspirations, occupational income*	−2.04	1.28	3168	−0.42	1.06	3223
1975 Aspirations, wanted different job	0.52	0.50	4276	0.42	0.49	3737
1975 Aspirations, wanted housework	0.05	0.23	4276	0.00	0.02	3737
1975 Aspirations, wanted no work	0.04	0.20	4276	0.02	0.14	3737
1975 Aspirations, don't know	0.13	0.34	4276	0.08	0.28	3737

TABLE 11.1—Concluded
Descriptive Statistics

	Women (N = 4512)			Men (N = 3981)		
	Mean	St. dev.	N	Mean	St. dev.	N
Linked lives						
Number of children	2.88	1.52	4038	2.57	1.37	3505
Spouse's 1975 occupational education*	−0.75	1.74	3725	−0.75	1.48	1419
Spouse's 1975 occupational income*	−0.55	1.14	3725	−2.35	1.21	1419
Spouse not in labour force	0.01	0.09	3770	0.57	0.49	3338
Not married in 1975	0.12	0.32	4267	0.11	0.31	3731
Family transitions						
Youngest child turns age 18	Aug. 1986	56.59	3733	Oct. 1988	62.98	3313
Divorce	Nov. 1978	57.31	1022	Sept. 1979	63.09	956
Divorced before 1975	0.11	0.31	4512	0.10	0.30	3981
Widow(er)hood	Aug. 1983	78.79	269	Feb. 1984	72.66	84
Widow(er)ed before 1975	0.02	0.13	4512	0.00	0.06	3981
Caretaking – average start of spell	June 1989	71.69	682	July 1988	76.67	317
Caretaking – average length of spell (mos)	40.73	72.60	682	52.36	77.38	317
Other controls						
1975 non-respondent	0.05	0.02	4512	0.06	0.24	3981
Ever held elementary/secondary teaching occupation, 1975–1993	0.11	0.31	4512	0.05	0.22	3981
Any farming occupation, 1975–1993	0.02	0.15	4512	0.05	0.22	3981

*Actual percentages reported here are transformed into started logits in the multivariate analyses.
**Excluding respondents currently enrolled in 1975. N = 4344 women and 3808 men eligible for analysis.
***Excluding those self-employed in 1975. N = 3763 women and 3456 men eligible for analysis.
****Excluding those never employed after 1975. N = 4174 women and 3962 men eligible for analysis.

TABLE 11.2
Determinants of Career Transitions, Women of the Wisconsin Longitudinal Study

	Obtaining a college degree			Becoming self-employed			Changing occupation		
	Beta	S.E.	R.R.	Beta	S.E.	R.R.	Beta	S.E.	R.R.
Social background									
Mental ability	**0.03**	**0.00**	**1.03**	0.00	0.00	1.01	0.00	0.00	1.00
Head's occupational status	0.00	0.00	1.00	0.00	0.00	1.00	0.00	0.00	1.00
Mother works	0.02	0.13	1.02	*0.25*	*0.13*	*1.28*	-0.15	0.07	0.86
Family income	-0.15	0.11	0.86	0.05	0.12	1.06	0.04	0.07	1.04
Father's educational attainment	0.00	0.02	1.01	0.00	0.02	1.00	**0.03**	**0.01**	**1.03**
Mother's educational attainment	0.03	0.03	1.03	-0.02	0.03	0.98	-0.01	0.01	0.99
Farm background	-0.01	0.20	0.99	-0.20	0.20	0.82	-0.10	0.11	0.91
Non-intact family	-0.36	0.26	0.70	-0.02	0.23	0.98	-0.13	0.13	0.88
Number of siblings	0.03	0.03	1.03	0.00	0.03	1.00	-0.02	0.01	0.98
Planful activity									
Educational attainment	**0.15**	**0.04**	**1.17**	*0.09*	*0.05*	*1.10*	0.02	0.03	1.03
1975 occupational education	0.06	0.07	1.06	**-0.20**	**0.07**	**0.82**	**-0.19**	**0.04**	**0.82**
1975 occupational income	-0.08	0.08	0.93	0.12	0.07	1.12	**0.10**	**0.04**	**1.11**
1975 aspirations, occupational education	0.05	0.06	1.05	*-0.12*	*0.07*	*0.89*	**-0.14**	**0.04**	**0.87**
1975 aspirations, occupational income	0.10	0.07	1.11	**0.28**	**0.07**	**1.33**	**0.13**	**0.04**	**1.13**
1975 aspirations, wanted different job	0.17	0.16	1.19	0.14	0.17	1.16	**0.22**	**0.09**	**1.25**
1975 aspirations, wanted housework	**-2.41**	**1.08**	**0.09**	-0.62	0.59	0.54	0.23	0.32	1.26
1975 aspirations, wanted no work	-0.14	0.54	0.87	0.08	0.49	1.08	*0.58*	*0.30*	*1.79*
1975 aspirations, don't know aspirations	-0.34	0.45	0.71	-0.01	0.42	0.99	**0.64**	**0.26**	**1.90**

TABLE 11.2—Concluded
Determinants of Career Transitions, Women of the Wisconsin Longitudinal Study

	Obtaining a college degree			Becoming self-employed			Changing occupation		
	Beta	S.E.	R.R.	Beta	S.E.	R.R.	Beta	S.E.	R.R.
Linked lives									
Number of children	**0.12**	**0.05**	**1.12**	−0.04	0.05	0.96	0.05	0.03	*1.05*
Spouse's 1975 occupational education	**0.11**	**0.04**	**1.11**	0.06	0.05	1.07	0.00	0.03	1.00
Spouse's 1975 occupational income	0.07	0.08	1.07	−0.09	0.08	0.92	0.02	0.04	1.02
Spouse not in labor force	−0.29	0.61	0.75	0.43	0.62	1.54	−0.32	0.44	0.72
Not married in 1975	−0.99	1.02	0.37	−*	−*	−*	**−1.05**	**0.47**	**0.35**
Family transitions									
Youngest child turns Age 18	0.17	0.16	1.19	−0.06	0.17	0.94	−0.06	0.08	0.94
Divorce	**0.49**	**0.16**	**1.63**	0.21	0.17	1.24	0.10	0.09	1.10
Widow(er)hood	*0.54*	*0.30*	*1.71*	−0.21	0.37	0.81	*0.30*	*0.16*	*1.36*
Caretaking	0.41	0.29	1.51	−0.29	0.42	0.75	−0.09	0.20	0.91
Total N	4344			3763			4174		
Number of events	278			262			849		
−2 Log likelihood	4318.855			4160.373			13,787.794		
Degrees of freedom	37			39			38		

*Effects could not be estimated due to small number of cases.

Bold coefficients are significant at the p < 0.05 level; coefficients in *italics* are significant at the p < .10 level.

TABLE 11.3
Determinants of Career Transitions, Men of the Wisconsin Longitudinal Study

	Obtaining a college degree			Becoming self-employed			Changing occupation		
	Beta	S.E.	R.R.	Beta	S.E.	R.R.	Beta	S.E.	R.R.
Social background									
Mental ability	0.00	0.01	1.00	0.01	0.00	1.01	0.01	0.00	1.01
Head's occupational status	0.00	0.00	1.00	0.00	0.00	1.00	0.00	0.00	1.00
Mother works	0.01	0.19	1.01	0.07	0.11	1.07	0.17	0.08	1.19
Family income	0.13	0.16	1.14	-0.05	0.09	0.95	0.03	0.06	1.03
Father's educational attainment	-0.01	0.03	0.99	0.03	0.02	1.03	0.03	0.01	1.03
Mother's educational attainment	0.08	0.04	1.08	0.00	0.02	1.00	-0.03	0.01	0.97
Farm background	-0.36	0.31	0.70	0.16	0.16	1.17	0.25	0.10	1.29
Non-intact family	0.51	0.29	1.66	-0.21	0.21	0.81	0.24	0.12	1.28
Number of siblings	0.00	0.04	1.00	0.03	0.02	1.03	-0.02	0.01	0.98
Planful activity									
Educational attainment	0.10	0.05	1.11	0.05	0.03	1.05	-0.04	0.02	0.96
1975 occupational education	0.10	0.11	1.10	-0.05	0.06	0.95	-0.03	0.04	0.97
1975 occupational income	0.07	0.14	1.07	0.10	0.07	1.11	0.05	0.05	1.05
1975 aspirations, occupational education	-0.03	0.08	0.97	-0.02	0.05	0.98	-0.04	0.04	0.96
1975 aspirations, occupational income	-0.03	0.13	0.97	-0.04	0.08	0.97	0.00	0.05	1.00
1975 aspirations, wanted different job	0.20	0.21	1.22	0.35	0.12	1.43	0.26	0.08	1.29
1975 aspirations, wanted housework*	-*	-*	-*	-*	-*	-*	-*	-*	-*
1975 aspirations, wanted no work	-*	-*	-*	0.98	0.47	2.68	0.19	0.30	1.21
1975 aspirations, don't know aspirations	0.81	0.63	2.24	0.18	0.40	1.20	-0.10	0.24	0.91

TABLE 11.3—Concluded
Determinants of Career Transitions, Men of the Wisconsin Longitudinal Study

	Obtaining a college degree			Becoming self-employed			Changing occupation		
	Beta	S.E.	R.R.	Beta	S.E.	R.R.	Beta	S.E.	R.R.
Linked lives									
Number of children	0.05	0.08	1.06	0.05	0.04	1.05	0.01	0.03	1.01
Spouse's 1975 occupational education	0.21	0.16	1.24	-0.03	0.07	0.97	-0.08	0.05	0.92
Spouse's 1975 occupational income	-0.33	0.23	0.72	0.08	0.08	1.08	0.04	0.06	1.04
Spouse not in labor force	0.84	1.84	2.32	-0.45	0.81	0.64	0.65	0.58	1.91
Not married in 1975	0.70	1.86	2.01	-0.24	0.81	0.79	0.65	0.59	1.91
Family transitions									
Youngest child turns age 18	0.04	0.32	1.04	*0.29*	*0.16*	*1.34*	**0.30**	**0.09**	**1.35**
Divorce	-0.01	0.28	0.99	0.25	0.15	1.28	0.08	0.10	1.08
Widow(er)hood	-0.34	1.01	0.71	-1.30	1.00	0.27	*0.47*	*0.28*	*1.60*
Caretaking	-0.51	1.01	0.60	-0.23	0.45	0.79	0.17	0.23	1.19
Total N	3808			3456			3962		
Number of events	122			361			802		
-2 log likelihood	1863.9			5705.06			12,974.6		
Degrees of freedom	35			37			36		

*Effects could not be estimated due to small number of cases.
Bold coefficients are significant at the p < 0.05 level; coefficients in *italics* are significant at the p < .10 level.

Obtaining a College/University Degree

Women are more likely than men to obtain a college/university degree after age 35 (6.4 per cent versus 3.2 per cent). Better-educated men and women (as of 1975) are significantly more likely to return to college/university, suggesting that many adult students are obtaining advanced degrees. Career aspirations (at age 35) are related to educational pursuits only among women who wanted to be keeping house in the future; they were significantly less likely to pursue adult education than women who wanted to continue in their 1975 job.

Neither current family roles nor transitions are related to men's degree attainment at midlife, yet they are powerful predictors of women's educational transitions. Divorce and widowhood increase a woman's likelihood of receiving a degree by 63 and 71 per cent, respectively. Women with more children also are significantly more likely to return for a degree. Spouse characteristics also affect women's likelihood of returning to school for a degree. Women with spouses working in occupations distinguished by highly educated incumbents are more likely to return to college/university.

Transition to Self-employment

Men are more likely than women to become self-employed after age 35 (10.4 versus 7.0 per cent). Entrances to self-employment appear to represent the fulfilment of earlier career aspirations for WLS particpants, both women and men. The higher the occupational income score of a woman's 1975 aspiration, the more quickly she moves into self-employment, while the higher her occupational education score, the more slowly she makes this transition. Men who, in 1975, hoped to be holding a different job ten years into the future are 43 per cent more likely to form their own business, and men who did not want to be working in ten years entered self-employment 2.7 times more quickly than men who wanted to remain in their 1975 jobs. For men, neither education nor employment characteristics are associated with becoming self-employed. In contrast, higher education is positively linked to women's self-employment transitions; each additional year of schooling completed by age 35 is associated with a 10 per cent increase in the risk of self-employment. Working in an occupation requiring high levels of education (in 1975) is associated with a significantly slower move to self-employment for women. Interestingly, family transitions affected men's self-employment transitions only: the empty-nest transition raises men's likelihood of a self-employment transition by 34 per cent.

Occupational Change

Roughly one-fifth of men and women left their longest-lasting job (as of 1975) in order to enter a new occupation. Men made this transition one year earlier than women, at age 46 on average. Surprisingly, family transitions are significant predictors of men's – but not women's – movement into a new career at midlife. Both widowerhood and the empty-nest transition increase men's risk of making a major career transition at midlife. The effect of widowhood on career change for men and women is only marginally significant). Current family characteristics affected only women's career transitions. The risk of making a major job change increases 5 per cent for each child a woman has, while unmarried women are 65 per cent less likely to change occupations.

Occupational aspirations and education are linked to both men's and women's occupational changes. Men who sought a new line of work at age 35 (in 1975) have a 29 per cent greater risk of subsequently changing jobs, compared to men who wanted to continue working in their 1975 occupation. Advanced education is negatively associated with a career transition; each one-year increase in educational attainment (at baseline) is associated with a 4 per cent decline in men's risk of job change.

Among women, those who aspired to or who already worked in occupations requiring high levels of education were significantly slower (about 15 per cent slower) to make a career transition. In contrast, women who aspired to and worked in occupations with high pay changed careers significantly faster (about 12 per cent faster). Women who, at age 35, wanted to enter a new occupation were 1.25 times more likely to make a subsequent career transition than women who wanted to remain in their 1975 jobs. Women who either wanted not to be working, or didn't know what work they wanted ten years from the 1975 survey date also had a greater risk of changing jobs than those who wanted to stay in their 1975 job.

Discussion and Implications

Two important themes emerged from our research. First, both men's and women's midlife work transitions are linked to family transitions, albeit in different ways. Although linkages among women's work and family roles are widely documented, our research reveals that, at midlife and beyond, men's work lives, too, may be responsive to shifting family roles and responsibilities (Giele, 1993; Jung, 1933). Second, men and women may redirect their careers at midlife in an effort to fulfil their earlier career goals. Midlife work-life transitions may be neither an idiosyncratic response to a 'midlife crisis' (Krantz, 1977; Osherson, 1980) nor an unanticipated event which occurs among the poorly educated, the unskilled, and those with 'disorderly' lives (Wilensky, 1961). Rather, career transitions might be responses to earlier goals and shifting family responsibilities.

Work–Family Linkages

Perhaps the most surprising finding of our study is that family transitions affect men's career transitions at midlife, as well as women's. Men's work lives have traditionally been viewed as untouched by the demands of family life; Kohli (1986) has argued that for men, work is the key domain in structuring the life course. However, we find that at midlife, events such as divorce, widow(er)hood, and onset of the empty-nest syndrome are turning points for both sexes. Specifically, our analyses revealed that the empty-nest transition and widow(er)-hood significantly increased men's – but not women's – transitions into new occupations and into self-employment. This transition might be an indicator of a change in financial status; having one's youngest child turn 18 may be associated with the parental burden of paying for college/university. Likewise, the death of a spouse may be accompanied by both the loss of the spouse's income and other unanticipated expenses such as costs associated with hospitalization, funeral expenses, and medical care (Lopata and Brehm, 1986). An alternative explanation could be that after successfully launching their adult children, men may feel less pressure to play the role of breadwinner and may have greater latitude in making changes in their work lives.

Yet widow(er)hood and the empty-nest transition may represent psychological – as well as economic – turning-points. Men who have experienced the loss of an important social relationship may be particularly susceptible to a spell of life review and a desire to make changes in their lives (Umberson and Gove, 1989). Men who have invested heavily in their careers, at the expense of spending time with their children, may 'feel depressed at a sense of futility in life; they may embark on a second career, or change their life styles completely' (Rapoport et al., 1977).

We had expected that the empty-nest transition would free midlife women to invest more heavily in new work pursuits (Mayer, 1969; Rubin, 1979). Why did the empty-nest transition have no effect on women's work-force behaviour? We believe this result reflects the life course of current and future cohorts of midlife women, who no longer abandon work opportunities in young adulthood in order to fulfil family responsibilities. Nearly all (98 per cent) of the WLS women had worked at some time during their lives, and most worked while they were raising children. In the time period from 1957 to 1992–3, only 12 per cent of the WLS women had worked for fewer than ten years. Although women of earlier cohorts may have been reluctant to return to school or change their work arrangements before their youngest child reached adulthood, for most women of the WLS, work and family pursuits were blended far before they reached their empty-nest stage. The weak linkage between the empty-nest transition and women's work lives may also reflect the shifting life course of young adults. Nearly all of the children of WLS parents were aged between 21 and 35 at the time of the 1992–3 interview. As members of the late baby boom and 'Generation X' cohorts, these children are substantially more likely than prior generations to live with their parents in young adulthood, or to return to their parents' home following divorce or difficulties in the labour force (Goldscheider and Goldscheider, 1993). Thus, a child's eighteenth birthday does not necessarily coincide with that child's successful launch into adulthood (Boyd and Norris, 1995; Boyd and Pryor, 1989).

The loss of the spouse role, in contrast, is a significant and positive predictor of women's receipt of a college/university degree at age 35 or above. Widows and divorcees may return to college/university in order to develop skills and obtain the credentials necessary to support themselves financially (Collins, 1979). Returning to school may represent an adaptive strategy in the face of adversity, with women channelling their energies into self-improvement and personal growth following the loss of the spousal role. Most sociological research has focused narrowly on the economic consequences of marital dissolution for women (see Holden and Smock, 1991, for a review); other personal consequences have been largely ignored. Future research should focus on the variety of behavioural adaptations men and women make following marital dissolution, where such responses may include returning to school or making a major career transition.

Interestingly, transition to the caregiver role was not a significant predictor of midlife educational and occupational transitions. This may be attributable to the fact that we cannot ascertain how time-intensive the caregiving activity was; presumably, caregiving that requires at least ten hours a week may be a hindrance to women's labour-force transition (Ruhm, 1996). Moreover, caregiving behaviour may be associated with minor changes in one's work life, such as a reduction in the number of hours worked, but not with more extreme behaviours, such as starting a new job (Pavalko and Artis, 1997).

Purposeful Work Transitions

A second theme which emerged from our analysis is that earlier aspirations and human capital characteristics are important predictors of career change, suggesting that such midlife career transitions are purposeful – not haphazard. Traditional definitions of careers are based on the assumption that men (and women, to a lesser degree) establish themselves in a specific line of work during young adulthood (Kohli, 1986) and should subsequently receive higher pay, higher status, and more challenging work as they move upward through the ranks in their chosen profession (Spilerman, 1977; Wilensky, 1961). An implication is that major shifts in one's work life, such as movement between major occupational groups or obtaining further education in adulthood, are default actions taken by those with the fewest skills or options (Wilensky, 1961).

Our findings suggest that traditional definitions of 'career' may be less appropriate and applicable when characterizing the work lives of current cohorts of midlife adults (compared to earlier cohorts of working men). Movement between different occupations may allow men and women to fulfil their earlier career plans. For instance, men and women who reported in 1975 that they wanted to be working in a different occupation ten years in the future are significantly more likely to subsequently form their own businesses and/or enter entirely new occupations. Interestingly, aspirations for non-work roles were also linked to subsequent changes. Men who, in 1975, hoped to be not working ten years in the future had a significantly higher likelihood of subsequently forming their own business. Perhaps men who hoped not to be working were actually searching for less confining work options; self-employment can afford greater schedule flexibility and autonomy than other work arrangements (Aronson, 1991). Women who hoped to be keeping house in the future were significantly less likely to return to college/university. Apparently, women who hoped to be tending to their families may see no need to invest further in their own education.

For women, the status characteristics of the jobs aspired to in 1975 were also linked to subsequent career transitions. The higher the occupational income score of a woman's 1975 aspiration, the more quickly she moved into self-employment. Perhaps women who sought occupations with high pay believed that they could have more lucrative careers by forming their own businesses. Recent research suggests that women who hope to avoid the 'glass ceiling' in American corporations may instead turn to self-employment as a means of occupational mobility (Loscocco, Robinson, and Hall, 1991).

Men's and women's current human capital characteristics also affected midlife career change. Higher levels of education significantly reduced men's transitions into new lines of work. Similarly, women who worked in occupations with high levels of education were much slower than others both to enter self-employment and to make a career change. Those with advanced education have invested heavily in their own human capital and may have fewer incentives to find new careers at midlife. Also, more educated workers and white-collar workers can expect earnings increases well into midlife and may have fewer incentives to change careers, relative to blue-collar workers, whose earnings may plateau earlier in the life course (Featherman and Hauser, 1978).

We hope that our findings will generate future research exploring the links between family transitions and work transitions. Of particular importance is whether both macro-level economic patterns and family-level economic resources affect the relationship between family transitions and subsequent career choices. In addition, personal characteristics, such as personality, mental health, and people's values and attitudes towards work may mediate the relationship between family transitions and subsequent labour-force behaviour. Career and educational transitions will likely continue to be an important event in the lives of midlife adults. Organizational restructuring and downsizing over the past decade have created a context where workers can no longer anticipate a career with a single company; rather, multiple careers and frequent job transitions are becoming the norm (Price and Vinokur, 1995). The 'one life–one career imperative' has disappeared, and life-course sociologists must continue to identify the diverse factors associated with career redirections at midlife and beyond.

NOTES

1 This research was supported by The National Institute on Aging (AG 16545). The Wisconsin Longitudinal Study has its principal support from the National Institute on Aging (AG 9775), with additional support from the National Science Foundation (SES-9023082), the Spencer Foundation, and the Graduate School of the University of Wisconsin–Madison. A public-use version of data from the Wisconsin Longitudinal Study is available from the Data Program and Library Service, University of Wisconsin–Madison or from the Inter-university Consortium for Political and Social Research at the University of Michigan–Ann Arbor. The data may also be obtained through the Web site *http://dpls.dacc.wisc.edu*. Direct correspondence to Deborah Carr (*carrds@umich.edu*), Department of Sociology, University of Michigan, Ann Arbor, MI 48109–1382; or Jennifer Sheridan (*jsherida@ssc.wisc.edu*), Department of Sociology, University of Wisconsin, 1180 Observatory Drive, Madison, WI 53706. Both authors contributed equally to the paper; the authors' names are listed in alphabetical order.

REFERENCES

Aronson, R.L. (1991). *Self-employment: A labour market perspective*. Ithaca, NY: ILR Press.
Bardwick, J.M. (1980). The seasons of a woman's life. In D.G. McGuigan (Ed.), *Women's lives: New theory, research and policy* (pp 35–57). Ann Arbor, MI: University of Michigan, Center for Continuing Education of Women.
Baruch, G.K., Barnett, R., & Rivers, C. (1983). *Lifeprints: New patterns of love and work for today's women*. New York: New American Library.
Blau, P.M., & Duncan, O.D. (1967). *The American occupational structure*. New York: John Wiley and Sons.
Borjas, G.J. (1986, Fall). The self-employment experience of immigrants. *Journal of Human Resources, 21*, 485–506.
Boyd, M., & Norris, D. (1995). Leaving the nest: The impact of family structure. *Canadian Social Trends, 38*, 14–17.
Boyd, M., & Pryor, E.T. (1989). The cluttered nest: The living arrangements of young Canadian adults. *Canadian Journal of Sociology, 14*, 461–77.

Carr, D. (1996). Two paths to self-employment?: Women's and men's self-employment in the United States, 1980. *Work and Occupations, 23*(1), 26–53.

Cherlin, A. (1981). *Marriage, divorce and remarriage.* Cambridge, MA: Harvard University Press.

Chinoy, E. (1955). *Automobile workers and the American dream.* New York: Doubleday.

Collins, R. (1979). *The credential society.* New York: Academic Press.

Coontz, S. (1992). *The way we never were: American families and the nostalgia trap.* New York: Basic Books.

Devine, T. (1994). characteristics of self-employed women in the United States. *Monthly Labor Review, 117*, 20–34.

Elder, G.H., Jr. (1994). Time, human agency, and social change: Perspectives on the life course. *Social Psychology Quarterly, 57*(1), 4–15.

Elder, G.H., Jr, & O'Rand, A. (1995). Adult lives in a changing society. In K.S. Cook, G.A. Fine, & J.S. House (Eds), *Sociological perspectives on social psychology* (pp 452–75). Boston: Allyn & Bacon.

Elder, G.H., Jr, & Pavalko, E.K. (1993). Work careers in men's later years: Transitions, trajectories and historical change. *Journal of Gerontology: Social Sciences, 48*(4), S180–91.

Farr, J.L., Tesluk, P.E., & Klein, S.R. (1998). Organizational structure of the workplace and the older worker. In K. Warner Schaie & Carmi Schooler (Eds), *Impact of work on older adults* (pp 143–85). New York: Springer Publishing Co.

Featherman, D., & Hauser, R.M. (1978). *Opportunity and change.* New York: Academic Press.

Giele, J. (1993). Women in adulthood: Unanswered questions. In J.Z. Giele (Ed.), *Women in the middle years* (pp 1–35). New York: The Free Press.

Goldscheider, F.K., & Goldscheider, C. (1993). *Leaving home before marriage: Ethnicity, familism, and generational relations.* Madison, WI: University of Wisconsin Press.

Hauser, R.M., & Warren, J.R. (1997). Socioeconomic indexes for occupations: A review, update, and critique. In A.E. Raftery (Ed.), *Sociological methodology* (pp 177–298). Cambridge: Basil Blackwell.

Hayward, M.D., Friedman, S., & Chen, H. (1998). Career trajectories and older men's retirement. *Journal of Gerontology: Social Sciences, 53*(2), S91–103.

Holden, K.C. (1988). Poverty and living arrangements among older women: Are changes in economic well-being underestimated? *Journal of Gerontology: Social Sciences, 43*, S22.

Holden, K.C., & Smock, P.J. (1991). The economic costs of marital dissolution:

Why do women bear a disproportionate cost? *Annual Review of Sociology, 17,* 51–78.

Institute for Higher Education Policy. (1997). *Life after forty: A new portrait of today's and tomorrow's post-secondary students.* Washington, DC: Author.

Jung, C.G. (1933). *Modern man in search of a soul.* New York: Harcourt, Brace & World.

Kohli, M. (1986). The world we forgot: A historical review of the life course. In V. Marshall (Ed.), *Later life* (pp 271–303). Beverly Hills, CA: Sage.

Krantz, D.L. (1977). The Santa Fe experience. In S.B. Sarason (Ed.), *Work, aging and social change: Professionals and the one life–one career imperative* (pp 165–88). New York: Free Press

Kutscher, R., & Fullerton, H. (1990). The aging labour force. In R. Montgomery & J. Owen (Eds), *The aging of the American work force: Problems, programs, policies* (pp 37–54). Detroit: Wayne State University Press.

Lee, G.R. (1992). Gender differences in family caregiving: A fact in search of a theory. In J.W. Dwyer & R.T. Coward (Eds), *Gender, families and elder care* (pp 120–31). Newbury Park, CA: Sage

Leong, F.T.L., & Boyle, K.A. (1997). An individual differences approach to midlife career adjustment: An exploratory study. In M.E. Lachman & J. Boone James, *Multiple paths of midlife development* (pp 411–51). Chicago: University of Chicago Press.

Levinson, D.J., Darrow, C.N., Klein, E., Levinson, M.H., & McKee, B. (1978). *Seasons of a man's life.* New York: Knopf.

Lopata, H.Z., & Brehm, H.P. (1986). *Widows and dependent wives: From social problems to federal programs.* New York: Prager.

Loscocco, K., Robinson, J., & Hall, R. (1991). Gender and small business success: An inquiry into women's relative disadvantage. *Social Forces, 70,* 65–85.

Mayer, T.F. (1969). Middle age and occupational processes: An empirical essay. *Sociological Symposium, 3,* 89–106.

Moen, P. (1985). Continuities and discontinuities in women's labour force activity. In G.H. Elder, Jr (Ed.), *Life course dynamics: Trajectories and transitions, 1968–1980* (pp 113–55). Ithaca, NY: Cornell University Press.

Moen, P., & Moorehouse, M. (1983). *Overtime over the life cycle; a test of the life cycle squeeze hypothesis: Research in the interweave of social roles.* Greenwich, CT: JAI.

Osherson, S.D. (1980). *Holding on or letting go: Men and career change at midlife.* New York: The Free Press.

Pavalko, E., & Artis, J.E. (1997). Women's caregiving and paid work: Causal relationships in midlife. *Journal of Gerontology: Social Sciences, 52B*(4), S170–9.

Price, R., & Vinokur, A. (1995). The Michigan JOBS program. Supporting career transitions in a time of organizational downsizing. In M. London (Ed.), *Employees, careers and job creation* (pp 191–209). San Francisco: Jossey-Bass.

Rapoport, R., Rapoport, R., Strelitz, Z., & Kew, S. (1977). *Fathers, mothers, and society: Towards new alliances*. New York: Basic Books.

Robertson, J. (1978). Women in midlife: Crises, reverberations, and support networks. *The Family Coordinator, 27*, 375–82.

Rubin, L. (1979). *Women of a certain age*. New York: Basic Books.

Ruhm, C.J. (1996). Gender differences in employment behaviour during late middle-age. *Journal of Gerontology: Social Sciences, 51B*, S11–17.

Sarason, S.B. (1977). *Work, aging and social change: Professionals and the one life— one career imperative*. New York: Free Press.

Sewell, W.H., & Hauser, R.M. (1975). *Education, occupation and earnings: Achievement in the early career*. New York: Academic Press.

Spilerman, S. (1977). Careers, labour market structure, and socioeconomic achievement. *American Journal of Sociology, 83*, 551–93.

Steinmetz, G., & Wright, E.O. (1989). The fall and rise of the petty bourgeoisie: Changing patterns of self-employment in the post-war United States. *American Journal of Sociology, 94*, 937–1018.

Stone, R., Cafferata, G.L., & Sangl, J. (1987). Caregivers and the frail elderly: A national profile. *The Gerontologist, 27*, 280–304.

Tolbert, C.M. (1982). Industrial segmentation and men's career mobility. *American Sociological Review, 47*, 457–77.

Umberson, D., & Gove, W. (1989). Parenthood and psychological well-being: Theory, measurement and stage in the family life course. *Journal of Family Issues, 10*, 440–62.

Warren, J.R., Sheridan, J., & Hauser, R.M. (1998). Choosing an index of occupational standing: How useful are composite measures in analyses of gender inequality in occupational attainment? *Sociological Methods and Research, 27*, 3–76.

Wilensky, H. (1961). Orderly careers and social participation: The impact of work history on social integration in the middle class. *American Sociological Review, 26*, 521–39.

Yamaguchi, K. (1991). *Event history analysis*. Newbury Park, CA: Sage Publications.

PART TWO
Later Life: Restructuring Work and the Transition from Employment to Retirement

Introduction
Victor W. Marshall and Anil Verma

Just as the entry to work is being restructured, so, too, is the exit from paid work and the transition to retirement. The chapters in this section capture this process, offer hints as to the principal causes of these changes, show the diversity of new life-course transition patterns, and investigate the consequences of these changes.

The first chapter in the section reports a study by James Dowd of fifty-eight U.S. Army general officers. We begin with this chapter because it describes workers in an environment that fosters the kinds of occupational career stability that are threatened by the restructuring of work, as described in so many of the other chapters. Dowd's thesis is that the military profession is organized, especially for the officer class, in a manner that fosters in individuals the strengths to maintain stable career progression and development, and that these strengths are likely to continue following formal retirement. The chapter presents a vivid contrast to the social situations described in the remaining chapters in this section, which deal with departures from this model of stable working-life courses provided by one organization. This case can thus serve as a reference point against which to gain a better perspective on alternative ways of restructuring work and the life course.

The complexity of newly emerging transitions from work to retirement is described for Canada by Stone and Harvey with national-level Canadian data tracing the experiences of cohorts going through the work–retirement transition over the 1986–92 period. They conceptualize work as including not only paid employment, but also unpaid work, differentiated into volunteer work, work done for relatives and friends, and self-help work. They focus on important gender differences in transitions from states characterized by an emphasis on full-time paid employment to life-course states involving more work done for relatives and friends and more volunteering. The chapter presents unique national-level data acquired using a methodology that other nations might well emulate.

Two additional chapters with Canadian data follow, but these move from the national to the firm level. Chan, Marshall, and Marshall draw on a case study of NOVA Corporation (a gas-pipeline utility and petrochemical manufacturing firm) and its employees in Alberta to emphasize the importance of technological change in work restructuring. NOVA is a high-technology company undergoing rapid technological and organizational changes. Women of all ages are more comfortable with computers than men, but among men, older workers are significantly less likely to be comfortable with computers than younger workers. Nevertheless, older workers at NOVA are more likely to have experienced linear upward mobility within the company, and linear career progression is related to feelings of comfort with computers and to the employee's belief that technological change had led them to use more skills than they otherwise would have. Attitudes towards older workers are generally positive at NOVA, as is also found in other case studies and national surveys by the same research group. However, in all these studies, attitudes are somewhat less positive with respect to the older worker's ability to adapt to new technology.

The next chapter, by Singh and Verma, draws on a case study of former employees of a large Canadian telecommunications company, most of whom accepted an early retirement incentive program. These retirees are privileged in many ways: they mostly had long service in a large internal labour market, with high wages and good benefits; and they received generous incentives to retire. However, this case study shows that plans made at the time of early retirement are often unfulfilled.

The chapter by Quadagno, MacPherson, Keene, and Parham also uses a case study approach at the company level to demonstrate the effects on workers of the massive downsizing that frequently follows corporate restructuring and mergers. Job loss from restructuring has spread from the manufacturing to the service sector, and from lower-level employees to those at all levels. Accompanying downsizing has been growth in the size of the contingent labour force. Older workers who lose regular jobs face age discrimination in seeking new employment and often find work at lower wage levels and in contingent jobs without benefits. Later-life job changes can present new positive opportunities, but, for many older workers, the loss of the career job has strongly negative implications for financial security. These generalizations from the literature are brought to life in a case study of life-course trajectories of bank employees who lost their jobs following a merger.

Robin Oakley's study of occupational retrenchment and its consequences for South African migrant labourers shows that the effects of work restructuring are by no means confined to the United States or other highly developed countries. She traces the life-course experiences of four generational cohorts of workers in one community in the northwest corner of South Africa. She finds the gendered division of labour to have important consequences for later life, and she shows the value of incorporating strong elements of political economy theory into the life-course perspective.

The final four chapters in this section focus explicitly on public policy in relation to the restructuring of later-life work and its implications for income security in the post-work years. Winfried Schmähl examines the German social security system, which relies heavily on income generated from employment. This is a complex system with different types of social security arrangements for different types of workers and a complex private–public mix. Risks, Schmähl argues, are being shifted from the state and the company to the individual employee.

Takeshi Kimura and Masato Oka discuss the Japanese situation, in which a projected shortage of labour and the possibility of future fiscal problems associated with supporting a growing older population have led government to raise the pension age and to encourage older workers to remain in the labour force. Japan and the United States are interesting cases for comparative analysis because, in contrast to many European countries and Canada, for example, these countries are facing labour shortages.

A specific proposal to restructure the transition from employment to retirement is described by Peter Simoens and Jan Denys. This is the 'career break,' introduced in Belgium in 1985. This proposal allows employees the possibility of temporarily suspending or reducing the level of professional activities for up to sixty months, with a guaranteed income during the break. The vacancy is filled by an unemployed person. The career-break option is evaluated in the context of other early-exit schemes in use in Belgium and elsewhere.

The American case is presented by Sara Rix, who describes the restructuring of the working life course leading to retirement in the United States, arguing that public policy makers have hardly begun to address these issues. Rix argues that the move towards early retirement in the United States has been largely voluntary, that this trend seems to have abated, that older workers following flexible work schedules mostly do so by choice, and that many baby boomers are not accumulating the financial security to provide for a decent retirement, let alone an early one. She also points out that, while research fails to support the reservations many employees have about older workers, this research rarely deals with workers in their late sixties or older, where future growth in the population of older workers is likely to occur. It is important to place the American case in a comparative perspective. For example, unemployment rates are much lower in the United States than in other OECD countries, a circumstance which may affect both private and public policy stances.

Some general comments might be offered on the chapters in this section as a whole. Substantively, the topic of gender runs through all the chapters in this section, as it runs through the analyses in the entire book. For example, women are becoming more committed to the labour market but are more vulnerable than men if they seek re-employment following loss of the career job. The well-known disproportionate contribution of women to caring work is documented here, as it is in chapters in the next section. Gender is so important that sustained, explicit theorizing about the social processes which constitute gender relations should be encouraged. It is one thing to document sex or gender *differences* through large-scale survey research. It is quite another to theorize about the social *relations* of gender.

Several chapters, most explicitly those of Quadagno and colleagues, Oakley, and Schmähl, call explicit attention to the political economy, suggesting that the intersection between the corporate and the public sectors plays a major role in shaping work and, thereby, the life course. Although Dowd's chapter is less explicitly couched in the language of political economy theorists than the others, he emphasizes a related theoretical problem, the challenge of linking micro and macro levels of analysis – of tying biography to social structure. These theoretical issues, too, are raised throughout the book.

12. From Officers to Gentlemen: Army Generals and the Passage to Retirement

James J. Dowd

In a number of very significant ways, military organizations of the advanced industrial societies are ideal models for conceptualizing the linkages between work and retirement. The retirement system of the American military, wherein soldiers, sailors, and airmen accrue retirement benefits equivalent to 2.5 per cent of their base pay for every year on active duty, is widely considered to be one of the signature benefits of military service and perhaps the most compelling reason for a soldier's re-enlistment. Retirement benefits also include continued access to free health care at military installations, continued access to commissaries and other shopping and recreational privileges, and other benefits such as free space-available travel on military flights.

These jealously defended benefits of military service constitute the economic substructure of the bridge that spans two significant phases of life, that is, work and retirement. There is another aspect of the link between work and retirement, however, that, although less tangible than this package of retirement benefits, none the less operates to prepare the individual for the transition and enables him or her to weather the transition encounter. This often-overlooked and under-appreciated aspect is the capacity of certain work organizations to foster the structural conditions conducive to human development. The military, more than almost all other employers, structures into the careers of its soldiers (officers and enlisted men and women) continual opportunities for the acquisition of human capital. Although it is rarely credited for doing so, the military profession develops and nurtures in its members a set of characteristics that are not only advantageous for

mission-related purposes but which also are highly conducive to a satisfying and productive retirement. These characteristics include self-
confidence, optimism, a feeling of efficacy, and a sense of competence
that is manifest in a continuing desire to learn new skills and attempt
new projects. In this chapter, I will demonstrate how these same characteristics are also manifest in the approach to retirement that one typically encounters among senior officers. For them, retirement is another
challenge, or opportunity, to continue to chart a chosen developmental
course (Carver and Scheier, 1995).

The boundaries between work and retirement and between the military and the civilian worlds are, presumably, well defined in North
America. The data I will present in this chapter lead to a much different conclusion. Army generals are at the end of their military careers
and, as such, will soon be civilians. Yet their connections to the military
will, in most cases, only be loosened, rather than severed, following
their retirement. They discuss their plans for retirement in terms of a
continuation, under different circumstances, of the skills acquired and
honed during their military careers. Most will continue to think of
themselves as military men and women. Even before retirement, many
officers will already have begun to attend reunions of former units.
Almost all will also continue to visit military posts to shop, to socialize,
to obtain a variety of services, including medical and dental care, and
for recreation.

For these officers, service in the military required the development
of professional skills and competencies that are necessary for their
effective fulfilment of the range of duties they will almost certainly
encounter within any particular military career field. The young infantry officer, for example, must learn not only basic soldier skills and the
intricacies of leading an infantry unit both in garrison and in the field,
but will also almost certainly need to acquire the skills required of a
Pentagon action officer, a personnel specialist, a recruiter, an ROTC
instructor, and even a diplomat. In order to advance in rank throughout their military careers, these officers confront the challenge of
adaptating to changes in jobs and locations, acquiring new skills, and
adjusting to a continually changing series of supervisors and subordinates. The brash and bold young officer must eventually become the
judicious, experienced, even-tempered, and broad-gauged senior
leader. Those officers who are unwilling or unable to acknowledge and
correct the flaws of their youth (a lack of tact, a quick temper, or even a
tendency towards diffidence, to cite several common examples) will

almost certainly place their careers in jeopardy by this inattention. Successful military leaders are not, in other words, the unreflective organization men and women projected in many stereotypes of career military officers. They are encouraged to recognize their shortcomings and to appreciate the necessity of taking corrective action to remedy them.

The success of the fifty-eight U.S. Army officers that form the basis for the analysis in this chapter is certainly due in considerable measure to their individual talents and efforts. It would be insufficient, however, to attribute their occupational success and optimistic attitude towards retirement solely to particular individual characteristics – a tendency towards self-monitoring, for example, or the capacity to be internally engaged regardless of the nature of the external environment (what Csikszentmihalyi [1990] refers to as autotelicism). Their success must also be traced to the structural characteristics of their profession and of the military organization in which they have served for many years. At the same time, however, it would only obscure our understanding of their successful careers were we to reduce our explanation to a single-minded emphasis on their effective adaptation to either organizational or other environmental requirements. Both individual and structural characteristics are necessary for understanding the lives of these men and women. The organization in which they work is distinctive, first, in the emphasis it places on the development of leadership skills among both officers and career enlisted personnel, and second, in its valorization of the difficult act of leadership. Because of the indispensable necessity of effective leaders for successful military units, the military incorporates into its schools, field-training exercises, and everyday operations a concern with nurturing and reinforcing what is often referred to as a 'can-do' attitude among its members. In this chapter, I will examine this and related characteristics of the officers in the sample, characteristics that bode well for their pending transition to retirement and for which they are indebted to the nurturing work culture of the modern military.

The U.S. military, and specifically the U.S. Army, fosters – indeed requires – its members to engage in a career-long project of development. My specific focus is on a subset of military people, U.S. Army general officers, who, because of their successful mobility within the profession, represent an ideal case for understanding the value of a self-realizing frame of mind for successful transition to life in retirement, a period that for this group begins much earlier than for most.

The developmental effects of the military 'culture' exist for both officers and enlisted soldiers, although clearly more for officers than for enlisted members. Among officers, too, it is those who are most successful who are eligible to pursue most of the developmental opportunities the organization presents. In this paper, we look at a sample of fifty-eight army general officers, a group of individuals who are obviously successful but who are also in the twilight of their military careers and who will soon be confronting the necessity of building a life within the civilian world. The average general serves approximately five to seven years in the rank of general officer; promotion to the rank of brigadier-general, then, ironically serves to herald officers' imminent departure from military service and the dual transition both to retirement and to the civilian world. They furthermore must face this transition to civilian life while simultaneously deciding both the type of second career they might undertake and the type of retirement life they will eventually construct.

Military retirement comprises not one but a group of boundary crossings. Soldiers leaving active duty after careers that last between twenty and thirty-five years are not only crossing over from the status of 'worker' to that of 'retiree,' they are also making what for some is the far more problematic shift from military to civilian life. No longer in uniform, no longer in this communal society governed by special regulations, a unique code of conduct, and a traditional set of cultural values, they enter the larger world of autonomous, atomistic, rationally individualistic civilians. For general officers, the transition also involves an abrupt cessation of the status privileges of rank. Even if the retired general finds work in the civilian economy that remunerates his efforts at a level far exceeding that which he received while in government service, he will likely not locate a position with equivalent status honour and interactional power.

The argument of this paper is that the military profession – through its expectation that its members will commit themselves to their own personal growth and development – develops in the individual a realizing spirit that is positively linked with both a successful career and a satisfying life. By mid-career, senior non-commissioned officers (NCOs) and officers are expected to manifest generativity in their counselling and mentoring of their subordinates. I take the position in this chapter that military organizations might serve as models of how to structure, within the career path of workers, ample opportunities for the development of aptitudes and orientations that will sustain the individual through periods of change and transition, a notable instance of which is the boundary-crossing we call retirement.

Method and Sample

Between April 1993 and December 1998, I interviewed fifty-eight U.S. Army general officers.[1] These interviews were all open-ended and semi-structured. The sample includes twenty-seven brigadier-generals, twenty-one major-generals, seven lieutenant-generals, and three generals. This was the distribution of respondents by grade at the time of the interview; since the interviews were conducted, a number of generals have retired and many have been promoted to the next higher grade.[2] The sample includes two women, three African Americans, and one Asian American. At the time of the interview, the generals were serving either in the Washington, D.C., area or with a unit, school, or headquarters on posts and bases in the southeastern United States. The interviews focused initially on perceptions of the military promotion system and the characteristics of successful officers; over time, however, the interviews came to focus primarily on values, sentiments, identity, career highlights, sponsors, hobbies, family background, personal philosophy of life, cultural capital, and views on contemporary political and social issues (Dowd, 2000). Tables 12.1 and 12.2 summarize some pertinent characteristics of the members of the sample.

Analysis

Organizational Structure and Human Development

The key to my analysis is the series of links between the organization and the individual soldier that fosters individuals' own self-realizing perspectives and that provides a meaningful foundation to their lives, allowing them to withstand the more general instability that is characteristic of our time. The most salient of these links is the career structure of military officers, a structure that comprises an alternating series of work positions and educational opportunities. This alternation of work and educational opportunities is, of course, a feature of the most idealized theories of work and human development. These theories advocate a shift from traditional career patterns, wherein most formal education is completed prior to entry into the labour force, towards the

TABLE 12.1
Rank of Officer by Source of Commission

Rank	Source of commission					
	West Point	Other military school	ROTC	OCS .	Other	Total
Brigadier-general	8	3	5	8	3	27
Major-general	4	3	10	3	1	21
Lieutenant-general	4	1	2	0	0	7
General	2	1	0	0	0	3
Totals	18	8	17	11	4	58

TABLE 12.2
Rank of Officer by Primary Branch Assignment

Rank	Primary branch assignment			
	Combat arms	Combat support	Combat service support	Total
Brigadier-general	17	5	5	27
Major-general	13	5	3	21
Lieutenant-general	7	0	0	7
General	3	0	0	3
Totals	40	10	8	58

optimal pattern of a lifelong continuation of education (not simply job training but education in the more humanistic sense of individual development) in alternation with specific periods of job performance. For career military personnel, this optimal pattern has been standard procedure for at least a half-century. For army officers, for example, a typical career begins with early career branch schooling for a period of several months, followed by duty assignments lasting approximately five to six years. The officer returns to school for the three-month specialty course known as Advanced Branch Training, which is followed by another six-year period of duty assignments. At this point, the future of the officer hinges upon whether he or she is selected to attend the thirteen-month mid-career course, known more formally as the Command and General Staff Course. Those officers not selected to attend this course in residence at Ft Leavenworth, Kansas, may take the course by correspondence. Non-selection for the in-residence course, however, is a strong indicator that the officer will not be selected for battalion command and, hence, will never be promoted beyond the grade of lieutenant-colonel. Selection for this course, in contrast, is an almost certain guarantee of promotion to lieutenant-colonel and a promising sign for selection for battalion command. For those who do command battalions, the typical career pattern next places them in residence as a student in one of the year-long senior-service courses, of which the Army War College at Carlisle Barracks, Pennsylvania, is the oldest and most esteemed. The remaining steps in this model career trajectory would include promotion to colonel, selection for brigade command, a viable staff position following brigade command, and then, finally, selection as one of the thirty or so new brigadier-generals chosen annually from among the hundreds of eligible colonels considered.

The curriculum of the Army War College (and, to a lesser extent, the Command and General Staff College) is particularly interesting for its relative lack of emphasis on traditional military topics. In the basic and advanced branch courses taken earlier in their careers, the officers master the technical aspects of the operation of weapons systems, the organization of military units, and other similarly basic or practical issues. At the War College, however, the emphasis is much more on what might be described as academic, or intellectual, subjects such as military history, for example, as well as international relations, the nature of war in the next century, comparative politics and culture, civil–military relations, and so on. The pedagogical purpose of this type of instruction is quite evidently the development in senior officers of the necessary level of cultural capital to enable them to assume the more public leadership role they will soon be playing as representatives of American military policy in sites throughout the world.

A second aspect of military careers that fosters an internalized commitment to human development is the increasing responsibility over time of the jobs to which individuals are assigned. Other occupations are similarly structured, but few as thoroughly and systematically as the military. Salespeople, for example, may win vacation trips as a reward for their good work but are not typically granted paid leave of one to two years to pursue a graduate degree, as was common among the officers in my sample. University teachers may be promoted to associate or full professor, but these promotions do not carry with them the same level of increased responsibilities and power that military promotions do. Some university professors might become department heads or deans, for example, but most will continue to do at the end of their careers what they were doing at the beginning, that is, teaching, research, scholarship, and service. An army officer, however, will begin with command of a platoon of soldiers and, if successful, move to command a company, battalion, brigade, and – for a select few – division, corps, and army. In between, they might teach ROTC at a university, serve as a military attaché in an embassy overseas, work as an action officer in the Pentagon or other large headquarters, or consult on the design, testing, and manufacture of a new weapons system. These moves are qualitative shifts, not merely more of the same on a larger scale. Furthermore, the fact that the typical military position is held for only three years, after which the individual gains experience in a different assignment – oftentimes at a different post with different supervisors, colleagues, and requirements – induces in the officer an accommodative understanding of change and a degree of flexibility unmatched by civilian professionals, whose lives are typically more stable and whose occupational trajectories are marked by only a few key decision points.[3]

Military Careers and Human Development

The effects of the structural characteristics just discussed are not subtle but may be clearly seen in career soldiers' identification with military values such as teamwork and loyalty, as well as in their continual efforts to improve the performance of their unit and their commitment to fostering their own and their subordinates' development towards the ideal of the dynamic and well-rounded leader. The military, in other words, encourages human development. In this chapter, I am especially interested in three aspects of adult development that emerged with remarkable consistency across almost all of the interviews I conducted with army generals. These aspects are (1) *a desire to improve*; (2) *generativity*; and (3) *a realizing spirit*. Each of these characteristics pervades the lives of the men and women in my sample, marking them with a narrative coherence and a sense of psychological, social, and moral integration.

1. The Desire to Improve: I asked almost all of the generals in this sample to reflect upon their days as junior officers and whether they recognized early in their careers any personal deficiencies that, if left uncorrected, might have limited their chances for advancement. Almost everyone in the sample mentioned some flaw. A few of the generals recounted a particular incident in which they blundered during a training exercise or committed some other forgivable error; most, however, identified a personal limitation or behavioural characteristic that might be deemed more serious and which consequently required more continuous attention. The most common issues raised were lack of patience or tact; a volatile temper; and shyness or diffidence. The first two deficiencies are the most common and are almost expected of what senior army leaders like to call a 'hard-charger.' In other words, to be impatient in the aggressive accomplishment of one's mission is easily forgiven. If left uncorrected, however, the same behaviour that is tolerated from a lieutenant or captain would likely harm the promotability of even the most tactically accomplished lieutenant-colonel or colonel. The diffidence problem, however, operates in reverse. If the young officer does not demonstrate early in his or her career a capacity for social interaction and a skill in dealing with people, that officer would likely suffer in the comparison with his or her more outgoing peers.

In either case, however, whether the problem is impatience or diffidence, the successful officer is the one who will recognize the problem and take steps to correct it. The following interview excerpts are indicative of the way in which the patience, or tactlessness, problem was discussed by generals in my sample[4].

JD: Have there been any characteristics or qualities you have had to develop in yourself that let's say you didn't have as a young captain in order to make general officer, do you think?

No. 49: Ah, that's a great question. I don't know if I had to acquire a different skill in order to make general officer but what I found useful is a greater tolerance of people in general but maybe even of mediocrity, or of inability. Because to be a leader, you got to be ... anybody can lead a great soldier. The challenge of leadership is to take someone and make them a better soldier than they would be otherwise ... So, that's something that I had to. I think when I was a captain I didn't have much patience with people that couldn't hack the job.

JD: How were you deficient as a lieutenant?

No. 53: I had to get under control my own mouth. And I ... it was said to me just that way when I was with the Cav as a company commander. We came out of a meeting with the brigade commander, and the brigade commander was really getting pissed at me over something. After the meeting, he said, 'C'mon in here, I want to talk with you about something.' And he says, 'You know, it's really not what you're saying, it's how you're saying it. And sometimes who you're saying it to. And if I were you I'd get that under control.' Now this same brigade commander had ... about two months before sat me down and said, 'You know, you're one of the top two or three captains in the army. You got a really bright future, but I want to show you something.' He pulled out one OER [Officer Efficiency Report] signed by General [name unclear]. He said, 'If you ever see that sentence again in print,' which said I didn't have any tact, 'when you wake up and the lieutenant-colonel command list comes out and you're not on it, you heard it here first.'

Surprisingly in this sample of combat-experienced warriors, shyness was also mentioned by a number of generals in the sample, although it received far fewer mentions than did the tact/impatience issue. Those generals who mentioned this problem discussed it in the following ways, for example:

JD: As a second or first lieutenant, if some one were to evaluate you in those days, what might they have said as positive criticism, a way of constructive criticism?

No. 33: Maybe, that I should be more outgoing. Maybe that I should be more firm in my thoughts and in my actions. Those would be the things that would immediately come to mind. I had, by and large, difficulty talking in front of large groups. That definitely leads to something that I tried to correct. And the way that I set up to correct that was to teach at West Point. To get used to speaking in front of groups of people and ... So I saw that as a shortcoming that I had and something that I set out to try to fix.

JD: Looking back now, could you identify any deficiencies you had that you've had to improve upon as you have advanced throughout your career?

No. 41: Oh, absolutely – one that really stands out with me is ... back in the advanced course at Ft Knox, I was asked to be a scout leader – to be the pack leader, not just the den leader where I could work with scouts a week at a time. He asked me to take over the whole troop and run the meeting at which families were going to be present and the scouts as well. I was *petri-fied!* I was terrified of standing up in front of people and conducting this meeting. So one of my glaring weaknesses was public speaking and feeling comfortable and talking to audiences and so on. It's still not a forte today, but it's at least an area that I feel very comfortable. Now if somebody asks me to talk to a group, I can do it – if not off-the-cuff, at least with some pre-pared notes and pull it off.

So we see that the biographies of most of the general officers in this sample are replete with incidents of interpersonal conflict and turmoil that, were they to continue, would likely have derailed the promising careers of some of the army's best junior officers. Occasionally the officer himself recognized the problem and took remedial action that, although not necessarily eliminating it, rendered it manageable.

2. Generativity: In midlife, according to Erikson's intriguing view of human development, we face the challenge of being generative and of resisting the tendency to remain absorbed in our own personal ambitions and life goals. Generativity, or the 'concern in establishing and guiding the next generation' (Erikson, 1963, p. 267), logically occurs only after the adult has already met the challenges of earlier life stages in developing a sense of identity and establishing relations of love and intimacy with significant others in his or her life. According to McAdams (1993, p. 228), the generative adult 'creates things and ideas that aim to benefit and continue the social system.' A similar, though more determined, understanding of the idea has been developed by Kotre (1984) who sees in generativity a quest for leaving something behind after one's own time on earth is done. We are generative, in Kotre's view, in order to satisfy 'a desire to invest one's substance in forms of life and work that will outlive the self.'

Previous work on generativity, however, tends to disregard the orga-nizational settings that might either nurture or impede the human urge to leave something behind or to carry on a particular cultural tradition. Either generativity is viewed as a constant among human beings, as is the case when it is provided as the answer to questions concerning the impulse to have children or the tendency to believe in the existence of an immortal deity (Lifton, 1979), or it is seen as varying among indi-viduals who differ in terms of central social roles such as age, gender, and parenting (McAdams and de St Aubin, 1992). The possibility that the urge to be generative might become manifest only under favourable environmental conditions, such as in an organization that *expects* its members to be generative, has been largely ignored in this otherwise provocative strand of research. In the interviews I conducted with this sample of army generals, interviews which were not specifically intended to elicit descriptions of generative behaviour, it soon became evident that these officers worked in an organizational setting in which, were they *not* to be concerned with the well-being and future success of their subordinates, they would be failing in the single most essential aspect of their occupational role, which is 'to care for your people.'

The general officers in this sample are continually mindful of their responsibilities, both to their subordinates and to the army as an institution, to facilitate good work and to build good units. The definition of their role as senior leaders provides them with daily opportunities to demonstrate their generative concerns. These concerns are manifest through one or more of the following dimensions of their occupational role: (1) mentoring, which includes counselling but also the more tangible task of finding good jobs for one's subordinates; (2) contributing to the mission of the army by ensuring that one's best subordinates fill the most essential jobs; and (3) creating or sustaining viable, effective, and nurturing work organizations.

The key to a successful career in the military is to have a boss who actively intervenes to place you in positions of high visibility and influence. As a military career is made up of a sequence of more than a dozen jobs and schooling opportunities, the majority of which are not considered to be 'career-enhancing', it is essential that one's mentors work to find jobs that are considered to be the good, or 'hard,' jobs and that will become vacant at the time the individual is available for the new assignment. A division commander[5] described the process of mentoring this way:

> **JD:** Do you take that as a conscious responsibility of yourself in this job to sponsor people ... your really good battalion and brigade commanders?
> **No. 33:** I say yes to both. I don't think there's anything wrong with that. It means you're saying this guy is really good, and I am going to make sure he gets in the right jobs. I am going to do what I can. Not so much to help him out; it's because the right jobs are the hard jobs. And that's the kind of person we need in those jobs. I ... all the time, whenever I talk to my boss, the corps commander, the conversation invariably will come around to which one of my colonels should be a general.

JD: Oh, I see. So this is outside of the written reports?

No. 33: Oh, yeah. That's how reputations are made or not made. Another one of the responsibilities I have is finding jobs for my brigade commanders, the colonels.

JD: The jobs that they will do next.

No. 33: The jobs they go to next. Which are very, very important. Because the brigade commanders are the ones in contention for general.

JD: Did you ever request people ...?

No. 33: Yes!

JD: So people would wind up working for you that others have recommended to you?

No. 33: Correct. Happens ... happens all the time. Yeah, it happens all the time. I got a tip on the person I've just hired as the new G-3, which is a critical job ... they're all important but the G-3 is your operator ... in the division. The one I have leaves this summer. The recommendation came to me from the previous division commander. 'Hey, this guy's gonna be free and he's really good.' So I called him up and had an interview with him on the phone and hired him.

A one-star commander of a Corps-level Support Headquarters (COSCOM) reports the same understanding both of how the system works and of his role as a commander in making the system work:

JD: So you sometimes try to get people who have worked for you jobs if you know there's a job open?

No. 39: Absolutely I do that. I know a lot of people call that the good old boy network I call it taking care of the army. If I know we've got an officer in our army who's a very talented person and I see no problem with me working hard to get that person in the right job that's good for the army and good for the officer. Hopefully. See it creates a little stability, is what it does. As an example ... like I'm bringing some people in this summer who have worked for me before. I mean I went after them; I went out into the army and I'm pulling them from Leavenworth, and the Marine Corps C&GS [Command and General Staff course], and other units. And I'm bringing them in here to do specific things. That's kind of what I'm talking about.

JD: And you know you'll have those openings because of people who are in them now who are leaving?

No. 39: Right. And I negotiated those assignments with the personnel office, not those majors. Now, we talked on the phone and I said, 'Hey, you relax and I'll talk to the personnel officer and we'll get it done.'

As is evident from these quotations, the generals are somewhat sensitive to the possible criticism that, by mentoring their favoured subordinates, they are merely following the age-old tradition of looking out for one's friends, or working within the military's version of the 'old-boy network.' In their view, however, this mentoring cannot be reduced to mere favouritism. They insist that what they are doing is for the benefit of the army itself, since, after all, the jobs they are trying to find for their protégés are the army's most difficult jobs. As one general explained: 'So people who work for me, I try to provide them with opportunities. If they're good enough, I'll give them the tough jobs. [In] the army, the tougher the job that you have, the more risk it is, the higher the payoff.'

Besides working to provide developmental opportunities their subordinates, and in so doing to help the institution itself, these general officers are also looking ahead to the time when they will no longer be part of the army. As they edge closer to the time of their own retirement, they acknowledge their own dream of leaving something of themselves behind, both in the units they served and in the people they nurtured. This concern with leaving a legacy, a sign of their having made a difference, is evident in the following passages.

No. 36: Now, you know, what do I do now. I don't have a lot of time. Very little time. My average workday is fifteen hours. It just ... you have to if you're going run an organization as big as this ... Now a fifteen-hour day sounds hard to you but I also pace myself during the day ... But it's not drudgery, don't take that wrong. There's just a lot to do and it's my time. This is what I've trained for ... for all these years. And it's my chance to – especially in this information world today – this window's moving along and it's my chance to make a difference for the army. Not for ... it has nothing to do with me. What accrues back to me is irrelevant. I really don't care. I can make ... we can make such a difference for the army right at this point in time. It's what I'm trying to do.

JD: So you don't try to pick out those that are especially good, you just try to help whoever's working under you.

No. 20: They all deserve it, see. Every person deserves an opportunity to succeed ... You know, six months after I leave the army I'm an old whosits. And the only way I'm going to be remembered is by having touched subordinate leaders and taught them how to lead and motivate people and do it the right way. And instil in them some principles about taking care of people, and power down, and positive motivation, and that kind of stuff. See, that's my legacy, is them.

JD: When you look back over your career, do you have any doubts about maybe this career wasn't the right one for you or about the *value* of what you do for a living?

No. 53: No. No, I look back on what I've done and when I go to reunions and things and see other friends from other places some of whom have made substantially more money than I have, but I think that my impact has been greater than theirs or I think there's a mark that I've left. And I think – and I'll tell you why. [G]oing back to this selfless service business, I have a guiding principle of my leadership style, what I try to instil in people, is that, and I'm not talking on a religious tone here, is that we are our brother's keeper and that if we all went about life touching a few souls and trying to make just a few people better off for you having been around them, that the world would be a lot better place. So I go about trying to touch a few souls every place I go and that gives me immense satisfaction. And when I get cards and letters and phone calls that say I did, then I look back on thirty years and say, 'Good deal!'

3. A Realizing Spirit: Across any organizational group as diverse and large as the officer corps within the U.S. Army, there exists a range of personalities, talents, and local traditions. At the same time, however, different groups will, because of their mission or operating milieu, tend to cultivate or reinforce among their members a particular behavioural style and character type. Within military units, soldiers will encounter as a routine aspect of everyday life a certain degree of physical discomfort, psychological stress, hardship, and even the occasional possibility of threats to their own and other unit members' safety and well-being. For military officers, it is necessary not only to accommodate themselves to this reality but also to ensure that those for whom they are responsible also meet these daily challenges. For this reason, military organizations tend to inculcate in their members a particular spirit and approach to life. There tends to be a particular sense of humour among military people, for example, that seems most in evidence when plans go bad, situations go from bad to worse, and the fog of war sets in. There is also a sense of informality among military people that might be overlooked amid the pomp, pageantry, and precision of military parades, formations, and ceremonies. The informality is much in evidence, however, both in their interactions with others at

work and, particularly, in their gatherings away from work. They tend
to be impatient with any plan or order that wastes time, energy, or
resources or which isn't expressed clearly and simply. One brigadier-
general cites as an instance of his own impatience those occasions
when presenters 'start throwing all this babble on the table and I have
no idea what they're talking about.'

Most central to this spirit that is part of the military life is a confidence in the likely success of one's efforts and a willingness to undertake missions that would seem to have been designed to undermine
such confidence. As an example of this spirit, one among many such
anecdotes described in the interviews is the story told by a brigadier-
general who, when U.S. troops were deployed to Bosnia following the
Dayton Peace Accords, faced the prospect of crossing the Sava River
into Bosnia during winter – all under the unblinking gaze of television
cameras:

> No. 56: I've always said I do my work best in the dirt, in the dark when
> things go bump in the night. That's why people were amazed at the Sava
> River crossing. Hey, that's what I do. Me and my 2500 friends went down
> there and crossed the river. That's what we're about. As Jim Clancy, the
> reporter for CNN ... standing there with a camera rolling and his hand mike
> in my face and he says, 'Are we going to be able to cross this river?' I said,
> 'Jim, what are the options?' [JD laughs]. 'What are the options: to cross or
> not to cross it? We're going to cross it!' I mean, could I have a little better
> question than this. And he says, 'Are you going to cross the river?' I said,
> 'I'm not going to do anything. I'm just going to stand up here and look good
> and talk to you.' I said, 'All the kids out there are going to cross the river.
> They're going to make it work.' So that's what I do best, to go out there and
> do that stuff.

By a 'realizing spirit,' then, I mean to convey these officers' sense of
personal efficacy that is coupled with a faith or belief in the legitimacy
and worth of the organization to which they belong. This sense of conviction results in a determination to realize one's developmental
project and, in so doing, to further the goals of the organization and
demonstrate one's commitment to it. This spirit is not characteristic of
the 'organization man' of earlier theory, in that the retreatism and con-
formity that define the organization man are antithetical to the individual possessing a realizing spirit. Among the principal features of this

spirit are (a) a desire to contribute; (b) self-confidence, optimism, and an acceptance of challenge; and (c) playfulness and zest for life.

The desire to contribute and to make a difference can be seen in any number of ways and is an easily recognized part of military culture. One war story from the Vietnam era will suffice to describe the commitment to duty that is part of this culture.

> **JD:** When you were in those company-level commands, did you – was this something you really enjoyed doing? The idea of leading a company in combat?
>
> **No. 54:** At the time, that's all I wanted to do ... be a soldier. It was important to me ... I wanted to lead a rifle company. No, enjoying is not the word. I mean – you had such emotional rushes. The company would do well, or seven or eight soldiers would do well. And you realize this is your family. All ninety-five of you. And it becomes such a part of your life. You know everybody by name and where I was we would just walk in the jungle sometimes day after day after day after day. Long boring periods of carrying rucksacks and you get to know each other. Fresh clothes come in, dirty clothes go out. When you're done, and you're alive, and most of your soldiers are alive, and you walk away, it's a tremendous feeling that you have done something for those kids, for your country. I mean I felt that I had done my duty.

The second aspect of the realizing spirit is an acceptance of challenge. Although vulnerable to periods of disillusionment and worry, the general officers in this sample are characterized to a great degree by a sense of confidence, optimism, and efficacy. One of the generals in the sample was recently assigned, after many years away from the physical demands of an airborne unit, as the assistant division commander of an élite, light division:

> **JD:** [Commenting on his assignment with the airborne unit]: But this probably would not have been the division, if you had your choice of any division ...
>
> **No. 45:** I never thought I would come back here. Never! I've been for too long away ... so, in a way, it was the best place I could come because it pushed my nose back into an area that I hadn't studied before. It was, 'Okay, you got to prove yourself again.' This ain't going to be easy, physically. And it isn't. I do more physical stuff here than I've ever done anywhere and, at

fifty, it isn't as easy ... and you got to set the example. You got to be there. We all jump out of planes every week at night. You know, that's hard, that's not easy. With that [points to his rucksack] strapped on to you.

But the other piece of it ... that's not the important thing ... the important thing is that it forced me to learn again the air mobilé-assault techniques and the airborne assault techniques on the light side that I had gotten away from on the heavy side. So it was the best place in terms of developmental experience that I could have possibly come.

Lastly, the realizing spirit of military officers involves a sense of humour and playfulness, or what they might describe as not taking life – or the army – too seriously. In almost all of the interviews conducted as part of this research, the officer would invariably introduce an anecdote or comment whose purpose was not only to demonstrate the officer's spirit or sense of humour but also intended to enliven the interview itself. The generals, in other words, approached the interview as they would any interaction that might be considered formal: they would graciously attempt to put the other person at ease through humour and friendliness. As with the other themes developed here as indicators of the realizing spirit, this one could be exemplified with dozens of quotes. I will restrict myself to one.

The following story was told by a lieutenant general who at the time was commanding an Army headquarters and who, during the period mentioned in the story, commanded an infantry battalion on the demilitarized zone (DMZ) in Korea. Because of political considerations, the Carter administration decided to withdraw a single battalion – commanded by this lieutenant-general – from the DMZ. With nowhere else to go, the battalion, which was part of the 2nd Infantry Division, found itself garrisoned at Ft Riley, Kansas, home of the famous 1st Infantry Division, where it received somewhat less good treatment than would any of the battalions of the 'Big Red One.' The general picks up the story.

No. 25: So that battalion [was sent back to the United States] to Fort Riley, Kansas. Now, Fort Riley was the home of the Big Red One. We were still assigned to the 2nd Division, and we wore the 2nd Division patch for a year. When I brought that battalion home, we had a parade. We strutted our stuff. Second Division patch ... 'Second to none,' now at the home of the Big Red One. They put us in World War Two barracks. Everybody else was up on the hill, we were separate. They couldn't have made my life easier ...

While we were there, we gave two major parties a year. The Kentucky Derby party, you drank mint juleps, and you watched the horse race on TV and you bet and, ah, ... and you had very good food that went with this ... I just made sure you didn't drink too many mint juleps. And then we also had a very large Christmas party. Now the Christmas party was not a coat-and-tie thing. In fact what we did, it was a carolling Christmas party. We had everybody come with their wives/girlfriends and kids. And we had wassail punch, and other punch. Then we did our Christmas carolling in the neighbourhood ... And my captains picked up on this, so they had, let's see what's it called, but they were smaller functions, and more appropriate for a captain, and they had picnics, and we had Easter egg hunts. And all these things that bring units together, and it did! We had dancing lessons at Hail and Farewell ... and, you know, lieutenants went crazy. 'Noooo! We're not going to ...!' But we had a hell of a time.

Discussion

The outcome of the army's emphasis on leadership and team building is the creation of a culture in which self-realization and human development are nurtured, reinforced, and valorized. Those who spend a career in this environment face particular challenges at the end of their time in the service, not the least of which involves the anxiety of living in a highly individualistic, civilian culture. For general officers, the transition is certainly far less problematic than it might be for others, since their package of retirement benefits is highly attractive, as are the skills and experience they can offer to civilian employers. In this chapter, I have attempted to emphasize and document other, less tangible qualities that not only general officers but all senior leaders, including senior NCOs, bring with them into retirement. These individuals, most of whom have experienced the difficulty of combat, the disillusionment of life in the army during its internal crises of the 1970s, and their own personal career successes and disappointments, have acquired or have had nurtured a characteristic spirit that I describe as 'realizing.'

As a group, the generals in my sample are confident, optimistic, pragmatic, and committed to the well-being of their families and subordinates. Retirement, for them, is viewed as a new assignment, or mission. They have grown so accustomed to thinking in terms of 'Mission, Enemy, Time, and Terrain' (the oft-used METT principles) that their thinking about retirement returns, *seemingly without their willing it*, to a consideration of 'mission-essential information' such as resources, goals, time available, and so forth. They enter their post-military lives, then, with the same view that they would hold upon taking on any new assignment: they assume that there will be things to learn, some initial uncertainties, new environments to negotiate, maybe some gaps between expectations and reality, and maybe less-than-ideal conditions to work under. They will miss the friends they have made in their previous assignments, but they welcome the challenges that their new duties will provide. They are, in other words, the type of self-realizing individuals who are likely to do as well in retirement as they have in their work careers.

I asked all of the generals I interviewed about their plans for retirement. Some of them were indeed very soon to leave the army, either having already been passed over several times for promotion to major-general (and currently serving in a position widely understood to be a 'retirement billet'), or about to reach the thirty-five-year point in active service, which is the maximum time any general can serve under normal circumstances. But at least as many others of those interviewed had either just become general officers or had just been promoted to the next higher general officer rank and had a number of years of possible service remaining before reaching the thirty-five-year point. Retirement from the service, for this latter group, was only a faint blip on their radar screens. The central point, however, is that none of them indicated worry or concern that things might not work out. Regardless of their current position, they all felt confident that retirement would be an interesting experience and an opportunity to try something new.

For a significant number of these professional soldiers, this 'something new' will involve some form of community service. Given that most soldiers view their military careers as 'service to country,' the continued quest to engage in service work – to be of use to others – should not be surprising (although admittedly it is incongruent with the common view of the retired general as one who moves from a comfortable billet in the Pentagon to an even more comfortable position within the military-industrial complex). Although a significant minority of officers in my sample did mention the possibility of signing on with a civilian military manufacturing or consulting firm, many more repudiated any interest in such a Washington-type job.

Of the fifty-eight generals interviewed for this project, thirty-two indicated that they had a fairly definite idea of what they would do in retirement. Of these thirty-two generals, twenty-two (or more than two-thirds of those with a retirement plan) mentioned a form of community service as a possible retirement goal. The following excerpt exemplifies this commitment to service.

> **JD:** When you think ahead to your future after the army, have you made any plans yet for that time. Whether or not you want to go to work. Will you retire?
>
> **No. 58:** I think I'm financially very secure. I started an investment program when I returned from Vietnam with the money that I made in Vietnam and have been disciplined for almost thirty years now. And, of course, I guess I'll retire at seventy-five per cent of my base pay, so there's no financial requirement to seek employment. I think that I'll – there's lots of things in life that I wanted to do, I haven't had an opportunity to do, that have to do with *personal* growth. I'd like to read more. I'd like to write more. I'd like to listen to music more. I'd like to learn to play the piano. And then there will be a piece of that that's associated with community service. I'm sure that I'll be active in a church. I'll be happy to be active in the community. You know, I don't know if an opportunity presents itself, I'd be happy to teach in a local community college or a local college, just to share perspectives on a history that I have been a part of in some form or fashion.

Conclusions

I have argued in this chapter that the success of military leaders, not only in their work but also in their lives, must also be understood as an outcome of favourable environmental conditions, notable among which is a nurturing work culture; such organizational conditions, however, only enhance the probability that any particular individual will undertake the challenging work of constructing his or her own developmental project. Also essential to understanding their success is an awareness of the ways in which military organizations not only provide favourable structural conditions for human development but also nurture in their members a sense of efficacy, described here as a realizing spirit, that makes more likely continued success both in work and in life.

Many of the officers in this sample possess a sense of self that is unusually stable and well-grounded. The historical shift from traditional to postmodern culture is associated with an increasing uncertainty and instability in self-conceptions. Theorists of identity generally agree with Kellner (1992, p. 143) that 'as the pace, extension, and complexity of modern societies accelerate, identity becomes more and more unstable, more and more fragile.'

Social upheaval transforms not only social structures but also the cultural underpinnings of those structures, resulting in the condition described by Durkheim and others as *anomie* (Durkheim, 1951 [1897]). Disruption in the normal routines of everyday life may also exert a destabilizing effect on essential identity components, including both domain-specific feelings of efficacy and the more global themes of one's life story or narrative. Over the course of one's biography, especially during the transitions associated with later life, the stability and resilience of the self may be jeopardized (Brandtstädter and Greve, 1994). As is true of all of us, these military professionals construct identities from the materials at hand, including the tradition of the units to which they belong, the nature of the work they do, and the entire complex of biographical details that invariably shape identity. Unlike many of us, however, they also possess the conviction that their work has been important, necessary, beneficial, and successful. Their conception of self is built on the ideal of selfless service and has been oriented consistently toward the telos of rebuilding – through continual work, sacrifice, self-improvement, and critique – an institution they claim to love.

In this chapter, I have also attempted to demonstrate that some of the more idealized features of sociological prescriptions for the structure of work are present, and have been so for decades, within military organizations. I have examined the effects of this advantageous work structure on the lives of a group of men and women who have achieved high levels of success within the organization and profession. I argue that to understand their success one must appreciate their internalization of what I describe as a realizing spirit, which is the development within the individual of a enduring disposition for self-improvement. This spirit finds an especially nurturing environment within military organizations because of the demands the military places on its members. My argument, then, is essentially that theories of human development must incorporate an understanding of both individual-level characteristics *and* institutional-level properties, especially the ways in which work organizations enable or hinder the development of a realizing spirit.

I have applied this concept through an analysis of a group of successful men and women within a large organization, the U.S. Army. I have identified several properties of this organization that are particularly favourable for human development. These include: (a) its emphasis on continued, or lifelong, education; (b) the increasingly responsible and varied nature of work opportunities available to soldiers over the course of a career; (c) the emphasis on career management; (d) the informal operation of a sponsorship system, or mentoring, that complements the more formal system of career management that exists within the organization; and (e) the expectation that soldiers will acquire and demonstrate a certain level of cultural capital and a relatively cosmopolitan world view.

As the general officers are, by definition, at the end of their careers and facing an imminent transition to retirement, one wonders whether their developmental success will persist into their civilian lives as well. The generals in my sample respond to questions about their retirement plans with confidence and, occasionally, with idealism, if not certainty. Some indicate their intention of remaining within the military orbit as private consultants; many more, however, emphasize the absolute requirement that the work they take up next be meaningful, which is to say, useful. A significant minority of those in the sample expressed an intention to return to school to study in the social sciences or humanities (literature is often mentioned) or to become teachers. Given their economic security and their physical fitness, their equanimity in the face of their pending retirements is understandable. Making this group of new retirees more sociologically interesting, however, as well as eminently employable, is the commitment to continued learning and self-improvement that their time in the army has instilled and which has become for them the orienting telos of their lives.

NOTES

1 When this project began, there were more than 400 general officers serving on active duty in the U.S. Army; by the end of 1998, the number was 302.
2 The rank structure of the sample is very fluid given the twin facts of promotion and retirement. Of the fifty-eight generals who participated in this project, twenty-eight are now retired. Of those remaining on active duty (as of September 1996), eight continue as brigadier-generals; three are BG(P) – meaning that they have been recently selected for promotion to the rank of major-general; ten serve as major-generals; seven serve as lieutenant-generals; and two hold the highest rank of general.

3 Examples of such key decision points include a university's decision to promote and award tenure to an assistant professor; a law firm's decision to
invite an associate into the firm as a partner; or an investment bank's selection of an associate to advance to the more secure position of vice-president
(Roth, 2000).

4 In all of the interview segments reported in this chapter, I refer to myself as
'JD,' while the general being interviewed is identified only by a number,
which refers to the place of the interview (1 through 58) in the order or
sequence in which they were conducted.

5 The position of division commander is considered by most army officers to
be the single most desirable job in the army. A division consists of approximately 15,000 personnel; it usually consists of three combat brigades and
brigade-size artillery, aviation, engineer, combat support, and service elements. There are only ten divisions in the U.S. Army today and, consequently, only ten major-generals who command a division at any one time.
These division commanders almost always are later promoted to the three-
star rank of lieutenant-general. To be mentored by a division commander is
to be very fortunate indeed.

REFERENCES

Brandtstädter, J., & Greve, W. (1994). The aging self: Stabilizing and protective
processes. *Developmental Review, 14*, 52–80.

Carver, C.S., & Scheier, M.F. (1995). The role of optimism versus pessimism in
the experience of the self. In A. Oosterwegel & R.A. Wicklund (Eds), *The self
in European and North American culture: Development and processes* (pp 193–
204). The Netherlands: Kluwer Academic Publishers.

Csikszentmihalyi, M. (1990). *Flow: The psychology of optimal experience.* New
York: Harper & Row.

Dowd, J.J. (2000). Hard jobs and good ambition: U.S. Army generals and the
rhetoric of modesty. *Symbolic Interaction, 23*(2), 183–205.

Durkheim, E. (1951 [1897]). *Suicide* (J.A. Spaulding and G. Simpson, Trans.).
New York: Free Press.

Erikson, Eric. (1963). *Childhood and society.* 2nd rev. ed. New York: Norton.

Kellner, D. (1992). Popular culture and the construction of postmodern identities. In S. Lash & R. Friedman (Eds), *Modernity and identity* (pp 141–77). Cambridge: Basil Blackwell.

Kotre, J. (1984). *Outliving the self: Generativity and the interpretation of lives.* Balti-
more, MD: Johns Hopkins University Press.

Lifton, R.J. (1979). *The broken connection*. New York: Simon & Schuster.

McAdams, D.P. (1993). *The stories we live by: Personal myths and the making of the self*. New York: William Morrow.

McAdams, D.P., & de St Aubin, E. (1992). A theory of generativity and its assessment through self-report, behavioral acts, and narrative themes in autobiography. *Journal of Personality and Social Psychology, 62*, 1003–15.

Roth, L.M. (2000). *Making the team: Gender, money and mobility in Wall Street investment banks*. Unpublished doctoral dissertation, New York University.

13. Gender Differences in Transitions to Total-work Retirement

Leroy O. Stone and Andrew S. Harvey[1]

What are the main patterns of redistributing work effort between the market and non-market sectors as people age across the main retirement years? In the course of declining participation in the paid labour market, what are the chances that particular kinds of non-market work (such as volunteer work for organizations) will be done? What combinations of demographic and socio-economic circumstances are associated with the highest probabilities of substituting work effort in particular non-market sectors for declining participation in market sectors? What public policy issues or implications can be linked to the answers that we develop for the questions just cited?

The foregoing questions are being addressed in an ongoing study from which the present paper is derived. This paper focuses upon gender differences in the profiles of shifting work patterns during the transition to retirement from all forms of work, paid or unpaid (henceforth called 'total-work retirement' to distinguish it from the usual restriction of the use of the word 'retirement' to the process of giving up 'paid work'). With this focus in mind, the key question for the present paper is the following: What are the main gender differences in the tendency to increase time spent doing particular types of non-market work (such as family-caring work or volunteer work for organizations), as men and women experience declining market-work participation during the transition to retirement from all forms of work?

Research findings will be presented here from the analysis of Canadian data, though our ongoing study will include data from other countries. The data that are used here are derived from the 1986 and

1992 master files of the Statistics Canada Total Work Accounts System (Stone and Chicha, 1996), which are in turn based upon the General Social Survey's time-use cycles. Estimates are presented below for a set of approximate cohorts that were going through the main ages of transition to total-work retirement over the 1986–92 period.

Conceptual Preliminaries

Two concepts need to be discussed here – that of 'work pattern,' and that of 'paths among work patterns.'

Work Pattern

For this paper, 'work pattern' means the shape of the distribution of work effort over alternative classes of users (called 'destinations') of the output of the work. Examples of such destinations are parties who are expected to pay for the output (leading to the class of paid work), children who are not expected to pay for the output (e.g., child-care work), and organizations that are not expected to pay for the work outputs (e.g., volunteer work done in a hospital). A work pattern can be described statistically by means of the 'set' of proportions of the total time budget spent among the alternative defined work-output categories. (The total time budget, rather than the total working time, is used so as to allow the data to reveal declining allocation of time to work in the transition to total-work retirement.) Because of the small sample sizes and other limitations of the data sources, only a small number of such categories are designated for this project. They are as follows:

1. Users who are expected to pay for the work outputs (paid work) – called 'paid time' below and in the tables.
2. Organizations that are not expected to pay for the work outputs (including unpaid work in profit-making organizations) – called 'volunteer work' below and in the tables.
3. Relatives and friends who are not expected to pay for the work outputs – called 'relatives' time' below and in the tables.
4. Self and one's household beyond what has already been included in category 3 (these activities are restricted to ones whose outputs have a potential to be sold in the paid labour market) – called 'self-help work' below and in the tables.

Because the total time budget is the denominator of the proportions used to describe a work pattern, there is a residual fifth category, which is called 'mostly non-work time' below and in the tables.

Paths among Work Patterns

The concept of a 'path among work patterns' arises from the following considerations. Suppose we estimated a person's work pattern at ages 50, 55, 60, 65, 70, 80, and 90. We would then have a sequence of seven work patterns, which can be said to form a work-pattern path in light of the fact that the person actually assumed those patterns in a sequential manner as he or she aged from 50 to 90.

Until death, each member of the cohort will have followed a particular work-pattern path. The cohort will therefore have a distribution over all the possible paths. In that distribution, there is likely to be a modal (or most commonly used) path. The cohort may be quite distinctive in the sense that the modal path is dominant (is followed by a large proportion of the cohort members) and that several commonly used paths resemble the modal one to a significant degree. Meaningful subsets of the cohort may show systematic variation around the paths that seem typical for the cohort as a whole.

Brief Comment on the Literature

The literature on transitions to retirement 'from a cohort perspective' is sparse. Much of the existing writing views the transition in terms of the processes that individuals go through and the issues they face.

One body of thought emphasizes a process in which people compensate for major role losses by taking on new roles (Swartz, 1978). A contrasting theory predicts that new roles are not taken on after retirement. Instead, people tend to engage in the same types of activity over the life course. Thus, among those departing from paid-work activities, the volunteers will tend to be the same persons who were volunteers before that departure. (For related work, see Morgan, 1986; and Chambré, 1987.)

Selected Methodological Considerations

As noted above, a work pattern is the shape of the allocation of work time over alternative destinations for the work output. We are using only four groupings of destinations here in order to make the presentation manageable. (A much larger number of destinations for the work output can be defined by drawing upon the data resources of the Total Work Accounts System master files.)

Within each destination, a person may be seen to carry on work effort at many levels of intensity. Again for manageability, only a few levels are used in this paper. They are as follows:

1. *Paid Time* – work effort where the users of the outputs are expected to pay for the work outputs.
   Three levels are used – *high, medium,* and *low* – defined as follows:
   High – above the sixty-eighth percentile of the distribution of time spent doing paid work in the GSS time-use sample for 1992, a range that included the great majority of the distribution for those classified as having full-time jobs.
   Medium – some paid work but below the sixty-eighth percentile of the distribution of time spent doing paid work in the GSS time-use sample for 1992, a range that included the great majority of the distribution for those classified as having part-time jobs.
   Low – no time spent doing paid work on the time-use diary day.

2. *Volunteer Work* – work effort done for organizations (including informal organizations such as some unincorporated family businesses) that are not expected to pay for the work outputs.
   Two levels are cited: *some* and *none*.
   Some – some time spent, during the diary day, doing volunteer work for an organization.
   None – no time spent, during the diary day, doing volunteer work for an organization.

3. *Relatives' Time* – work effort done for relatives and friends who are not expected to pay for the work outputs
   Three levels are described: *high, medium,* and *low.*
   High – above the seventy-fifth percentile of the distribution of time spent providing help to family members, other relatives, or friends)
   Medium – from the twenty-fifth to the seventy-fifth percentile of the distribution of time spent providing help to family members, other relatives, or friends.
   Low – below the twenty-fifth percentile of the distribution of time spent providing help to family members, other relatives, or friends.

4. *Self-Help Work* – work effort done for oneself and one's household. (These activities are restricted to ones whose outputs have a potential to be sold in the paid labour market.)

    Again, there are three levels: *high, medium*, and *low*.

High – above the seventy-fifth percentile of the distribution of time spent doing work for oneself or one's household where the output is available in the paid labour market, provided that the activity has not already been classified as 'relatives' time.'

Medium – from the twenty-fifth to the seventy-fifth percentile of the distribution of time spent doing work for oneself or one's household where the output is available in the paid labour market.

Low – below the twenty-fifth percentile of the distribution of time spent doing work for oneself or one's household where the output is available in the paid labour market.

As the reader will already have noted, even these simple sets of levels give rise to a very large list of possible work patterns. One pattern, for example, would be high 'paid time,' no volunteer work for organizations, medium 'relatives' time,' and low 'self-help work.' To keep the analysis manageable, we selected a small set of work-pattern classes where each class contains a substantial subsample of persons in the 1992 General Social Survey, and where we can observe systematic gender variations in time spent doing paid work. We then added three classes of work patterns involving (1) medium paid time (mostly so-called part-time work) and some volunteer work, (2) low paid time and some volunteer work, and (3) all other patterns that included some volunteer work. (The resulting aggregates present serious issues of sampling variability in the estimates.) Through this selection process we arrived at the eleven classes of work patterns shown in the stub of table 13.1.

All the remaining work patterns were grouped into one large and very heterogeneous residual class – called 'remaining patterns' in table 13.1. No work pattern in this residual class contains any paid work or any volunteer work for organizations.

Results

Table 13.1 provides some hints as to what real cohorts might show for men. The first two columns allow us to compare the distribution, over the selected work-pattern classes, for men aged 50 to 54 in 1986 with a group for men in the age group that is *six years older* in 1992. (These are, however, not the same men, because two independent General Social Surveys are involved.) Each successive pair of columns allows us to compare an age group of men in 1986 with a group of men six years older in 1992.

A gentle fall in the weights of the patterns involving high paid-work time for the cohort aged 50 to 54 becomes a precipitous drop for the two sets of older cohorts – those aged 55 to 59 and 60 to 64 in 1986. To what extent is this profile of sharp decline in the devotion of time budgets to paid work associated with pronounced increases in the weights of work patterns that involve unpaid work for relatives and friends or for organizations?

In only one of three selected work-pattern classes that include medium or higher relatives' time is there an indication of consistent increase in men's devotion of time budgets to helping relatives and friends as they sharply reduce their time spent doing paid work (see line 7 in table 13.1). *If* the changes shown in this class for older cohorts give any useful indication of the future for the cohort aged 50 to 54 in 1986, they suggest the hypothesis that *for this cohort* the percentage with the combination of low paid-work time, medium or higher relatives' time, and high mostly non-work time will go from less than 5 per cent when in 1986 to over 10 per cent in 1996. (It is understood that applying the 1986–92 changes for older cohorts to that aged 50 to 54 in 1986 is risky; because *each cohort's behaviour pattern in a given historical period responds to institutional and other macro-level factors that may be unique for that cohort.* However, table 13.1 may be of more than passing interest once the reader appreciates that few if any countries now have time series for real cohorts with at least three observations that span more than ten years of actual historical time.)

In one of three work-pattern classes that include volunteer work for organizations we see an indication of consistent increase in men's participation in this class of work activity (see line 10 in table 13.1). An increased proportion is shown in every cohort for those who did volunteer work in combination with low paid-work time and low relatives' time. (Lines 6 and 8 involve no volunteer work.) For example, in the cohort aged 55 to 59 in 1986, the proportion with this work pattern increased from 7 per cent to 12 per cent. Even more striking is the estimated increase for the cohort aged 60 to 64 in 1986 – from 4 per cent to 13 per cent. *If* the changes shown in this class for older cohorts give any useful indication of the future for the cohort aged 50 to 54 in 1986, they

TABLE 13.1
Distributions[a] of Approximate Cohorts of Males over Selected Types of Total-work Patterns, Canada, 1986 to 1992

Work pattern class	Cohort aged 50 to 54 in 1986		Cohort aged 55 to 59 in 1986		Cohort aged 60 to 64 in 1986		Cohort aged 65 to 69 in 1986	
	1986	1992	1986	1992	1986	1992	1986	1992
1 High 'paid time' and at least medium 'relatives' time'	16	15	11	6	7	3	4	1
2 High 'paid time' and low 'relatives' time'	33	27	32	13	20	3	7	1
3 Medium 'paid time' and at least medium 'relatives' time'	6	1	6	2	3	2	1	0
4 Medium 'paid time' and low 'relatives' time'	2	3	1	3	1	3	2	3
5 Low 'paid time', at least medium 'relatives' time', and medium 'mostly non-work time'	9	6	7	6	6	8	14	11
6 Low 'paid time', low 'relatives' time', and high 'self-help work'	3	8	4	10	9	11	3	13
7 Low 'paid time', at least medium 'relatives' time', and high 'mostly non-work time'	3	4	1	6	2	8	2	8
8 Low 'paid time', low 'relatives' time', and high 'mostly non-work time'	7	8	7	12	8	15	13	17
9 Medium 'paid time' and volunteer work	1	1	1	1	1	0	1	0
10 Low 'paid time', low 'relatives' time', and volunteer work	1	7	7	12	4	13	5	11
11 Other volunteer work	2	0	0	0	5	1	4	2
12 Remaining patterns	17	22	23	28	34	31	44	32

[a]Each column adds to 100, except for rounding error.
SOURCE: Statistics Canada, General Social Survey and the Total Work Accounts System

suggest the hypothesis that *for this cohort* the percentage with the combination of low paid-work time, low relatives' time, and volunteer work for organizations will go from just over 1 per cent in 1986 to a figure of between 10 per cent and 15 per cent in 1996.

One key question here is whether the dramatic fall in the weight of high paid-work time is associated with a rise in the weight for medium paid-work time early in the stages of the transition to total-work retirement among men. The answer, by and large, is *no* (see supporting conclusions reached by Schellenberg, 1994, pp 44–6, using data from the Labour Force Survey).

The corresponding data for women show a much stronger pattern of shifting time freed from paid work into time spent doing different kinds of unpaid work (see table 13.2, where the design of columnar data is the same as in table 13.1). This is seen despite women's already relatively high devotion of time budgets to unpaid work at the start of the transitional years.

A striking gender difference is seen when we compare the first two pairs of columns for men in table 13.1 with the corresponding pairs of columns for women in table 13.2. As the younger male cohorts aged over the next six years, the falling weight of high paid-work time in their work patterns was associated with a sharply increased proportion of the cohort in the 'remaining' set of work patterns – see line 12 in table 13.1. (This set of unclassified patterns contains no paid-work time and no volunteer-work time.) No such increase is evident among the younger female cohorts – see line 12 in table 13.2.

Among the younger female cohorts, the decline in the weight of paid-work time is much more gradual (compared to their male counterparts) and that decline is made up entirely by increases in the weights of various kinds of unpaid work. Increases in the weights of the patterns that include low paid-work time and medium or higher relatives' time are more consistently shown among the younger cohorts of women than among those of men, perhaps to no one's surprise.

Like their male counterparts, the cohorts of women tend to show increased weights for the work pattern that involves volunteer work combined with low paid-work time and low relatives' time. However, there is a less striking profile of increased weights for this work pattern (see line 10 in table 13.2).

Another major gender difference is the relatively large weight of the patterns that combine medium paid-work time with medium or higher

TABLE 13.2
Distributions[a] of Approximate Cohorts of Females over Selected Types of Total-work Patterns, Canada, 1986 to 1992

Work pattern class	Cohort aged 50 to 54 in 1986		Cohort aged 55 to 59 in 1986		Cohort aged 60 to 64 in 1986		Cohort aged 65 to 69 in 1986	
	1986	1992	1986	1992	1986	1992	1986	1992
1 High 'paid time' and at least medium 'relatives' time'	13	9	8	4	4	1	2	0
2 High 'paid time' and low 'relatives' time'	14	9	9	6	3	4	1	2
3 Medium 'paid time' and at least medium 'relatives' time'	19	13	22	13	15	12	17	11
4 Medium 'paid time' and low 'relatives' time'	3	3	1	3	4	3	2	3
5 Low 'paid time,' at least medium 'relatives' time,' and medium 'mostly non-work time'	3	8	6	9	9	9	10	8
6 Low 'paid time,' low 'relatives' time,' and high 'self-help work'	1	5	3	8	7	10	10	12
7 Low 'paid time,' at least medium 'relatives' time,' and high 'mostly non-work time'	1	3	2	4	2	4	3	4
8 Low 'paid time,' low 'relatives' time,' and high 'mostly non-work time'	0	3	2	4	3	6	5	11
9 Medium 'paid time' and volunteer work	1	2	4	3	3	3	2	3
10 Low 'paid time,' low 'relatives' time,' and volunteer work	4	3	3	5	5	7	5	7
11 Other volunteer work	2	3	6	3	6	3	2	3
12 Remaining patterns	40	37	36	36	39	37	42	38

[a]Each column adds to 100, except for rounding error.
SOURCE: Statistics Canada, General Social Survey and the Total Work Accounts System

relatives' time among women. For example, in the two youngest cohorts, close to 20 per cent of the female population had such work patterns in 1986, while barely more than 5 per cent of their male counterparts did so. Also, among women cohorts the decline in the weight of these work patterns with aging is distinct but not dramatic. The 1992 value of the weight was still above 10 per cent in the female cohort was aged 65 to 69 in 1986.

In short, it seems that the years of the transition to retirement from paid work for women are largely years in which women resume the behaviour patterns that come from life-long enculturation as the primary doers of society's caring work. Although older men also show increased time spent doing unpaid work over those years, the increase is not as systematic as it is for women, when we look at the cohort-oriented data.

One implication of this interpretation is that *if* there is a major untapped pool for increased volunteering for organizations among seniors, that pool may exist much more among older men who used to hold paid jobs than among older women. The data suggest that, for both sexes, there is a modest substitution of volunteer-work time for paid-work time in the early stages of the transition to total-work retirement, and that the pattern is much sharper for men than for women.

Implications for Policy Concerns

A wide variety of topics arise when we turn to considering the policy-oriented implications of the simple data analysis and conceptual innovations presented above. The available space permits only a listing of topics that can be developed in a discussion of the findings just presented.

First, the foregoing discussion points to the need to be critical of conventional usage of the word 'retirement.' (For related discussion, see McDonald, 1996.) Related to this criticism is the need to raise the profile of the production of goods with *use value*, though perhaps little *exchange value*, in macro-economic policy making and in the evaluation of gender equity in access to compensation for total-work output in our society. (For related discussion, see Bakker, 1997.)

The supply of and demand for status-enhancing work opportunities in the voluntary-organization sector is also a key area for relevant discussion. The organizations of the civic sector can be helpful in expanding the choices among alternative activities for persons in the transition to *total-work* retirement. In turn, an increased supply of such opportunities would contribute to the strengthening of civil society.

Also relevant is the management of job–family tensions in the senior years. This is especially important for women, who, as these data show, are much more likely than men to maintain combinations of substantial paid work (even if only part-time) and family-caring work well into the late stages of the transition to total-work retirement. (For related discussion on job-family tensions, see Stone, 1994.)

Among men, the issue of late-life training and education for displaced workers is important. The abrupt fall in the weight of high paid-work time combined with no compensating rise in that for medium paid-work time is increasingly seen as being a source of significant issues in the financing of public pensions and health care, as well as in the future maintenance of an 'essential-income' safety net as cohorts reach advanced ages.

The foregoing topics are deserving of renewed discussion in light of the findings presented above. Only shortage of space prevents the display of our contributions to those discussions.

NOTES

1 Research and drafting assistance were provided by Frank Jones, Jean Randhawa, and Sharron Smith, Analytical Studies Branch, Statistics Canada.

REFERENCES

Bakker, I. (1997, May). *Integrating paid and unpaid work into economic growth and human development strategies.* Paper for the Workshop on Integrating Paid and Unpaid Work into National Policies, Seoul, Korea.

Chambré, S.M. (1987). *Good deeds in old age: Volunteering by the new leisure class.* Toronto: Lexington Books.

McDonald, L. (1996). *Transitions into retirement: A time for retirement.* Ottawa: National Welfare Grants Program, Human Resources Development Canada.

Morgan, J.N. (1986). Unpaid productive activity over the life course. In *United States, Committee on an Aging Society, productive roles in an older society* (pp 73–109). Washington: National Academy Press.

Schellenberg, G. (1994). *The road to retirement: Demographic and economic changes in the '90s.* Ottawa: Canadian Council on Social Development.

Stone, L.O. (1994). *Dimensions of job–family tensions*. Statistics Canada Catalogue No. 89–540E. Ottawa: Minister of Industry, Science and Technology.

Stone, L.O., & Chicha, M.-T. (1996). *The Statistics Canada total work accounts system*. Statistics Canada Catalogue No. 89-549-XPE. Ottawa: Minister of Industry, Science and Technology.

Swartz, E.L. (1978). The older adult: Creative use of leisure time. *Journal of Geriatric Psychiatry, 11*(1), 85–7.

14. Linking Technology, Work, and the Life Course: Findings from the NOVA Case Study[1]

Donna C. Chan, Joanne G. Marshall, and Victor W. Marshall

New technologies that incorporate computing and telecommunications are revolutionizing the way Canadians work. Information technologies can be applied in production and in information storage, retrieval, and dissemination and are key components of organizational change. The life-course perspective provides a framework within which to examine life experiences as a function of historical period and individual experience. To date, there have been few studies of the impact of technological change acting through work to restructure the life course. The purpose of this paper, therefore, is to explore the use of the life-course perspective to study the impact of technological change on life experience. Research on technology and work will be reviewed from the life-course perspective. Data from a case study of a major Canadian corporation will be used as evidence of the trends identified in the literature.

Work in the Life Course

The concept of life course refers to age-graded life patterns embedded in social institutions and subject to historical change. The life course consists of interlocking trajectories or pathways across the life span that are marked by sequences of events and social transitions (Elder, 1995; Elder and O'Rand, 1995). The life-course perspective acknowledges that aging is a lifelong process. The life course of individuals is embedded in and shaped by the historical times and places they experience over their lifetime. Historical influence can take the form of a cohort effect, when social change is catastrophic, or a period effect, when social change is relatively steady and uniform. In addition, the effect of maturation or biological aging cannot be ignored (Elder and O'Rand, 1995). Thus, in the broadest sense, the study of the life course entails understanding the context of lives.

In the past two centuries, there has been an institutionalization of the life course, centred on work (Kohli, 1986, 1988). Kohli argues that the life course can be tripartitioned into periods of preparation (education), activity (work), and retirement (leisure), and that the transitions between phases are becoming shorter and more age-differentiated (Kohli and Rein, 1991). Riley and Riley (1994) identify this as an ideal type of social structure that is the 'outdated vestigial remains of an earlier era when most people had died before their work was finished or their last child had left home' (p. 27). The tripartitioning model has been criticized for downplaying the role and impact of the family on the life course (Marshall, 1994). The model probably has never corresponded to the life-course patterns of women and marginal ethnic minorities (O'Rand, 1996). Yet it informs social policy and is culturally embedded.

On the other hand, there is evidence that greater individualization of the work life course is occurring. Changes in firm organization, the industrial structure of the economy, and pension structure are seen as reducing the tripartitioning of the work life course (Henretta, 1994). O'Rand (1996) lists other factors influencing changes in work institutions, such as globalization, increased female participation in the labour market, increased flexibility of labour through the use of contingent and part-time labour, and the slowed expansion of social welfare programs, which protected the vulnerable in poor economic conditions.

Information Technology

Within the context of working lives, information technology is playing an important role as a facilitator of change. Information Technology (IT) is a 'technological system for the storage, processing, communication and dissemination of information based on an interconnected set of technical and organizational innovations in electronic computers, software engineering, control systems, integrated circuits, microprocessors and telecommunications' (OECD, 1994, pp 132–3). The adoption of IT has led to changes in work processes and in methods of organizing work.

Information technology has evolved from the convergence of tele-communications and computers. In the past two decades the global network of computers, telephones, and televisions has increased its information-carrying capacity a million times over. Computing power has doubled every eighteen months, while the cost of computer-processing power has fallen about 30 per cent per year in real terms over the same time period (Hitchhiker's guide, 1996).

IT has also diffused rapidly – more rapidly than previous technologies. Twenty-five years ago, only about 50,000 computers existed worldwide; by the mid-1990s, there were an estimated 140 million, not including the microchips inside cars, microwave ovens, or greeting cards (Hitchhiker's guide, 1996). The rapid decline in prices and the increase in computing power encourages the adoption of computers. In addition, the lag time between innovation and application is decreasing.

IT differs from previous technologies in that it can be applied in all sectors of the economy and can affect every function within a firm. IT can be an input and a final product: it alters the production and distribution processes of industries and, at the same time, creates new products and services. IT is an agent of social change, primarily through its impact on employment. By destroying some jobs, creating new jobs, and changing other jobs, it is reshaping economies and societies.

Information Technology Use in the Canadian Workplace

The progression of IT in the Canadian economy has been traced by the Working with Technology Survey conducted for Human Resources Development Canada (HRDC) since 1980. Between 1980 and 1985, the majority of IT applications were stand-alone applications in offices rather than in the manufacturing process. Clerical and secretarial tasks were automated. From 1986 to 1991, IT applications were more sophisticated, involving data and communications networks. The focus of applications shifted to work performed by managers and professional and technical workers (HRDC, 1996b).

Other surveys of the Canadian workplace show that computer usage at work has been steadily increasing. The spread of computers into the workplace was measured by the General Social Survey (GSS) in 1994 and 1989 (Lowe, 1997, 1991). In 1994, 48 per cent of employed persons used a computer (personal computer, mainframe, or word processor) at work, up from 35 per cent in 1989. In both 1989 and 1994, young workers 15 to 19 years of age were the least likely of any age group to use computers on the job, probably because they tend to be employed in entry-level service jobs. On-the-job computer use was highest among 35- to 44-year-olds. There was an increase in the percentage of workers using computers on the job in all age groups between 1989 and 1994. The greatest increase in this time period was among those over age 45. Women were more likely to use computers on the job than men in both 1989 and 1994. The GSS also found that the amount of time spent on the computer increased from an average of sixteen hours per week in 1989 to eighteen in 1994.

NOVA Case Study

This chapter uses data drawn from a case study of NOVA Corporation, a pipeline and petrochemical firm based in Calgary, Alberta. This study was conducted as part of a larger project on Issues of an Aging Workforce in 1995. 'Key informant' interviews were conducted with senior and middle management in the various sites and divisions of NOVA. These included interviews with team leaders, practice leaders, and managers from NOVA Corporation, NOVA Gas Transmission, Novacor Chemicals, and NOVA Gas International. Eleven focus groups discussed the major themes of the research program. The NOVA sample included all employees at seven small-town Alberta sites, and a representative sample of approximately one in four employees was drawn from the NOVA head office. All grouped data referring to NOVA as a whole were weighted to compensate for this sampling strategy.

An employee survey was sent through the company mail to 1,531 NOVA employees. Some 1,107 completed surveys were returned directly to the research office, yielding a response rate of 75 per cent. Manager surveys were sent to all 201 senior executives, executives, and middle managers, yielding a response rate of 83 per cent (n = 165). However, due to a reorganization that was in progress at the time the list was developed, the final list may not have included all employees at NOVA with a leadership role. The employee sample is considered to be representative of NOVA's Alberta work force, based on age, gender, and occupational group comparisons to NOVA's human resources data. A comprehensive report of this case study is available (Centre for Studies of Aging, 1996).

The NOVA case study is cross-sectional. This type of data is not ideal for studying process and change (Ryder, 1965/1997). Age-group differences that are observed in cross-sectional data could be explained by a number of factors. These differences might reflect maturation or developmental processes occurring over time, cohort effects, or period effects. Therefore, cross-sectional age-group differences are not necessarily caused by aging. However, some interesting findings from cross-sectional data suggest the importance of technology in the work life course and indicate directions for future research.

Information Technology Use at NOVA

NOVA has implemented a range of information technologies in the workplace. Production technologies involve computerized controls, such as SAFIRE, a gas supply/demand modelling software. In 1995, NOVA installed a high-speed, high-capacity wiring system in its head office in Calgary to handle all voice, data, and video communication throughout the building. The upgraded wiring was seen as an essential foundation for the use of the Systems, Applications, and Processes (SAP) suite of integrated information systems and other components of NOVA's Information Management Architecture program. Human resource services were overhauled using information technology to reduce the number of forms and streamline processes. There are personal computers on almost every desk in the NOVA head office, and field and plant workers are increasingly using portable computers in their work.

Employee survey data suggest that most employees believe changes in technology at NOVA have been substantial. Almost three-quarters of the employees agreed when asked: 'During the last three years, have there been any substantial changes in the machinery and equipment you use in your own job (including the introduction of computers, software or automated technology)?' A middle-aged male employee speaking about the equipment used in gas control said, 'Its never stagnant. It's always evolving. We are getting retraining at a faster rate all the time. More and more stuff all the time.'

On average, NOVA respondents report spending 4.64 hours working at their computer each day. For those under the age of 35, the average is 5.11 hours, significantly higher than the average of 4.45 hours for 35- to 44-year-olds and the average of 4.28 hours for those over age 45. Administrative staff (who are primarily women) report working the

TABLE 14.1
Comfort with Computers by Age Group, Males

Comfort with computers	<35 Years %	35–44 Years %	45+ Years %
Not at all/not very comfortable	7	14	34
Comfortable	29	41	36
Very comfortable	64	45	30
Total n	214	304	215

Percentages may not add to 100 due to rounding.
$\chi^2 = 81.39$, df = 4, p < 0.001
SOURCE: NOVA Employee Survey, weighted data

highest average number of hours per day on computers (5.98 hours). Professional/technical employees spend an average of 5.13 hours using a computer; managers, 3.56 hours; and field workers, 2.90 hours. Only 10 per cent of employees report spending an hour a day or less working on the computer.

Despite the amount of time NOVA employees spend on the computer each day, there are differences in comfort level in using the computer according to age and gender. Comfort with computers varies significantly by age for men. Men over 45 are more likely to say they are not very comfortable with computers (see table 14.1). Men under 35 years of age are much more likely to be very comfortable with computers. Comfort levels are not significantly different by age for women, who are concentrated in the administrative occupations which usually use word processing and other IT office applications.

The Impact of Information Technology on Work

The widespread adoption of information technologies has led to change in the cultural and social institutions related to work. In the workplace, there have been changes in the nature of work, the skills required, where work is done, and how work is organized. This section reports, in brief, some of the changes that have been identified in the literature. This sets the context for determining the meaning and impact of work life-course events.

Information Technology and Skills

The use of IT to perform repetitive tasks and to coordinate work has led to major changes in job content. The same jobs are performed in different ways with specialized tools; the number of tasks is reduced; the nature and sequence of tasks are changed; and the total time required to carry out an activity is reduced. Not only routine tasks are automated; knowledge-based activities, too, are being computerized.

The introduction of new technologies is known to change the skill level of jobs, and a complex debate asks whether the adoption of IT leads to 'upskilling' or 'deskilling' of jobs. Changes in job duties, changes in the way jobs are performed, and changes in the organization of work are confounded in studies of change. Changes in products, services, technology, management strategy, and work design all have an effect on a job. Also, change is relative: a deskilled job for a well-educated worker may be an upskilled one for a person with lower-level skills.

'Upskilling' supposes that technological advances imply steadily more complex work tasks and therefore require a higher level of skill. Evidence for this is the change in the occupational structure of the work force, with a relative growth in non-manual occupations and a decline in manual occupations, together with skill increases within occupations. HRDC studies point to upskilling in the workplace in Canada. The third wave of the Working with Technology Survey showed, for the period 1992–4, that the requirements for professional and skilled technical jobs called for increased specialized knowledge on the part of these workers in order to carry out their jobs. Within lower-skilled intermediate and unskilled occupational groups, skill requirements related to problem solving (ability to identify and resolve problems) increased (HRDC, 1996b). Another study focused on employment by five skill measures: general educational development, specific vocational preparation, cognitive complexity, task diversity, and responsibility. For four of the five skill measures (all except responsibility), the proportion of employment at the highest skill level increased steadily from 1971 to 1991. For example, the proportion of jobs with the highest level of cognitive complexity increased from 18.1 per cent in 1971 to 21.3 per cent in 1981, and increased further to 26.8 per cent in 1991 (HRDC, 1996a)

The upskilling hypothesis has been supported by more recent findings. The GSS found that, in 1994, among workers who believed that their job had been greatly or somewhat affected by the introduction of computers or automated technology in the previous five years, 71 per cent said that their required job skills had increased. Only 2 per cent said that technological change had decreased their skills. Just over 60 per cent said that their work had become more interesting as a result of technological change, while 4 per cent found their work less interesting (Lowe, 1997). The Employee Survey at NOVA also found that 79 per cent of employees reported that technological change in the last three years had provided them with the opportunity to use more skills. Only 2 per cent reported that technological change resulted in their using fewer skills.

'Deskilling,' on the other hand, is the routinization and mechanization of work by new technologies, so that a lower level of skill is required on the part of human operators to do the same work. As part of this deskilling, workers are powerless to exercise their own judgment in carrying out their duties. Some clerical work has been subject to deskilling as information systems perform processing functions. Clerical workers are left with input functions that are governed by the technical needs of the system. Work becomes more demanding and stressful (Greenbaum, 1995; de Wolff, 1995). Other occupations have also seen deskilling of jobs. The adoption of numerical control equipment in manufacturing meant increased productivity through standardized output. Each machine produced the same product exactly according to the programmed instructions. However, for the machinist, work was reduced to monitoring the machine (Rifkin, 1995).

A third position is that both upskilling and deskilling are occurring, resulting in a polarization of skill requirements for jobs. Studies have shown that new technologies may reduce job complexity and discretion for some workers, but that they may create new, more skilled opportunities and paths of mobility for others at the same time (see Smith, 1994). These studies suggest that trends in deskilling/upskilling vary by industrial, occupational, and organizational setting.

Information Technology and Organizational Change

IT is a critical facilitator of organizational change. In order to achieve greater efficiency, effectiveness, and innovation, firms have adopted new organizational practices. IT is enabling a breakup of traditional organizational forms. Networking technologies allow multiple skills to be brought together at any time and in any location. Thus, ad-hoc teams are facilitated by IT. As these ad-hoc teams become an effective way of working, they give rise to the networking organization (Scott Morton, 1991). In this type of organization, new management systems and processes are required. As early as the mid-1980s, there was evidence that technological innovation was related to organizational innovation. Canadian firms that introduced computer-based technologies were more likely to introduce organizational innovations such as joint decision-making groups, job enlargement/rotation/enrichment, and profit sharing (Betcherman and McMullen, 1986).

The data from the employee survey at NOVA suggest that most employees believe that the changes in the organization of work at NOVA have been substantial. Seventy-two per cent of employees report that, during the last three years, there have been substantial changes in the work tasks assigned to them in their job. In the words of one middle-aged male field worker, 'It's a totally different ball game out there now with all the computer stuff.' Part of this change in work tasks includes an increase in the work load. In the manager survey, 90 per cent of managers agreed that employees must now work harder and longer to keep NOVA competitive.

The management and organizational structure of businesses have been affected by IT. IT permits the distribution of function and control to wherever they are most effective. This has revamped lines of authority and decision-making power. A flattening of the organizational hierarchy has resulted. A more recent form of IT application, the corporate intranet that allows greater sharing of internal information, promises to bring more change to the culture of organizations.

Firms have also adopted more flexible forms of organization. Flexibility in human resources is achieved both through functional strategies, such as the use of better-trained employees, multiskilling, and job rotation, and through numerical strategies, such as the use of core and contingent workers and outsourcing (Betcherman, 1997). In this environment, better-educated workers are more likely to find full-time jobs with good pay and a well-defined career path. For others, the contingent labour market with lower pay and a transitory career path are their only choice.

Linking Technology, Work, and the Life Course

Several changes in the institutionalized life course can be traced to the influence of IT on work. A major research challenge will be to identify mechanisms that link changes in information technology over time to the work life course. A review of research on technological change and work reveals that very little has been carried out using a life-course perspective. Nevertheless, existing research findings can be interpreted in light of the life-course perspective to build up a picture of the impact of technological change on the life course, individual trajectories, role transitions, and the mechanisms that link technological change and the individual.

Life-course research focuses on the complex interplay of time, historical and situational context, and biography. The effects of social selection, transitional effects, cumulative and interactional continuity, and accentuation are some of the processes studied (Elder and O'Rand, 1995). The life course reflects an individual's experience within a cohort, uniquely conditioned by prior history and social context. For example, the timing and ordering of early events has been shown to influence later-life events.

The impact of a life transition or event will depend on when it occurs in a person's life (Elder, 1997). Technological change is potentially more disruptive for older workers than for workers just entering the labour market. Technological change can lead to such things as job loss through either unemployment or redeployment within the firm, a change in work tasks, or a change in working conditions. Should technological change lead to unemployment, older workers over age 45 are more likely to experience long-term unemployment than younger workers (McDonald and Chen, 1994).

Careers in the Restructured Organization

The flattening of hierarchical organizations has been facilitated by the implementation of IT. This has important consequences for the career paths of individuals in the workplace. Linear career paths of upward progression, based on seniority, through a hierarchical organization are no longer likely. Instead, spiral career paths – consisting of lateral moves and major occupational changes – and transitory career paths – with frequent occupational changes are becoming more common (Foot and Venne, 1990; Foot and Gibson, 1994; Foot, 1996). These three types of career paths have always coexisted, but the age-structured linear path became the accepted cultural model for employment in this century (Henretta, 1994). However, this model is now eroding, and the instability of career patterns for younger workers is a significant

TABLE 14.2
Job History by Age Group

Job history	<35 Years %	35–44 Years %	45+ Years %	Total sample %
2+ jobs moving up	21	18	27	21
2+ jobs moving both up and across	43	58	52	51
2+ jobs moving across or down	16	13	12	14
Few, if any job moves	21	11	9	14
Total n	305	347	262	914

Percentages may not add to 100 due to rounding.
$\chi^2 = 30.92$, df = 6, p < 0.001
SOURCE: NOVA Employee Survey, weighted data

change from the experience of older workers, who have been most likely to experience linear career paths.

Beginning in 1994, NOVA opened several NOVA Career Resource Centres in office and field locations. These centres offer a variety of training and career development and planning tools. NOVA encourages employees to take charge of their own careers, to invest in themselves, and to develop skills that they can use at NOVA or somewhere else in the future.

With respect to career mobility at NOVA, a substantial proportion of workers (41 per cent) reported that their last job had been obtained through a lateral move. Just over half of employees (51 per cent) indicated that in their job history at NOVA they had experienced two or more jobs up and across the organization. One employee noted: 'It's a real flat management system, so there isn't really [any] progression' (younger employee, male). The following comment from a male manager shows awareness of changed patterns of mobility: 'You might like to think you were upwardly mobile in the organization, but the facts of life in this company today are that you'd better look for a lateral movement in the organization to satisfy your desire for change and new experiences because the opportunities to move up the ladder just aren't going to be there.'

Older employees are more likely to report a pattern of straight upward mobility through the hierarchy than are those in the middle-aged or younger categories, as shown in table 14.2. The importance of technology at NOVA is reflected in the significant finding that employees who felt that technological change had enabled them to use more skills were more likely to have experienced some upward mobility. The same is true for employees who felt very comfortable using a computer.

Novel human resource strategies have been adopted by NOVA. NOVA Gas Transmission is the first of NOVA's subsidiaries to adopt the Shamrock approach to human resources. In the Shamrock model, there are no longer 'permanent' or 'temporary' categories of workers. Instead, there are three designations of employees: 'core employees,' who possess skills required on an ongoing basis; 'term service providers,' who supply these same skills on an as-needed basis; and 'contractors and consultants,' who contribute expertise or equipment not typically available in-house. In NOVA as a whole, the pattern of new hires over the seven-year period prior to the study had changed from permanent full time to temporary full time or students.

The NOVA employee survey found that, of full-time workers, 86 per cent were permanent, while 14 per cent were contingent workers. These are workers who were employed full time on a permanent, part-year basis (nine or fewer months of work), temporary/casual basis (the job could end at any time), contract basis (the job lasted a specific period of time), or other kind of full-time basis. Of the contingent work force, one-quarter held temporary/contract or part-year jobs, while two-thirds were contract employees. Table 14.3 shows that these contingent workers are more likely to be under 35 years of age. The employee survey may have underrepresented contract employees, who may not have been listed in the corporate directory.

Technological Change and Training

While the effects of IT on skills may still be under debate, there is no question that, with the introduction of new technology into the workplace, the need for worker training and retraining becomes critical. In addition, the increased pace of technological change and the constant upgrading of skills suggests that lifelong learning is becoming a fact of life. At NOVA, 94 per cent of employees had taken a training course lasting one-half day or more. There were no significant age differences among those who did or did not take a training course. Of the employees who took some training, only 5 per cent reported that none of it was required as part of their regular job.

TABLE 14.3
Type of Job by Age Group

Type of Job	<35 Years %	35–44 Years %	45+ Years %	Total sample %
Permanent	75	92	91	86
Part-year (<9 months)	3	0	0	1
Temporary/casual	5	3	2	4
Contract	15	5	5	9
Other	1	1	2	1
Total n	349	394	278	1021

Percentages may not add to 100 due to rounding.
Other includes: students, secondments, gradual retirement.
$\chi^2 = 59.49$, df = 8, p < 0.001
SOURCE: NOVA Employee Survey, weighted data

There are negative stereotypes about older workers and training. The NOVA case study found that younger employees (under age 35) are more likely than workers 45 and older to agree with the statement that older workers (50 years and older) do not want to receive training. One-fifth of managers at NOVA were undecided about the statement while 13 per cent agreed and 69 per cent disagreed. Almost half of managers agreed or were undecided about the statement that older workers are harder to train. Managers are usually the gatekeepers to training opportunities. Of NOVA workers who did not take any training in the previous year, 40 per cent said that their manager did not allow them to take courses. Managers also influence training policy, so the fact that stereotypes of older workers as unwilling and unable to retrain still exist may be a problem in the larger population.

The effects of technological change can be examined through the role of co-workers in adaptations to technological change. In learning new technologies, co-workers may be the ones to whom novices turn. Older workers may act as mentors or teachers. For example, in the NOVA case study, there were significant differences by age in the percentage of workers who reported receiving instruction from co-workers. Two-thirds of workers under 35 years of age reported help from co-workers, compared to 57 per cent of workers 45 years and older.

Technological Change and the Retirement Decision

The role of technological change in early retirement is a question for further research. Research indicates that the link between technological change and job loss is weak. In 1989, the GSS included a question about job loss. Anyone who had lost a job between 1984 and 1989 was asked the reason. Less than 1 per cent cited the introduction of new technology as the reason (Lowe, 1991). Workers who had been greatly or somewhat affected by the introduction of computers in the previous five years were asked whether their job security had increased, decreased, or stayed the same. Only 11 per cent reported decreased job security. Blue-collar workers were somewhat more likely to have experienced a decrease in job security as a result of automation, compared to managerial and professional or clerical, sales, and service occupations. In 1994, 19 per cent of workers affected by technological change believed that their job security had decreased (Lowe, 1997).

The availability of training plays a mediating role in retirement decisions of workers facing technological change. Older workers in industries with high rates of technological change will retire later if on-the-job training is available. However, in industries experiencing very rapid rates of technological change, older workers opt to retire sooner because the required amount of training is an unattractive investment (Bartel and Sicherman, 1993).

The NOVA case study found that fear of future job loss was linked not to technological change but to the general climate of restructuring and downsizing that existed in the organization in the early 1990s. However, of employees who thought they would retire in the next ten years, 22 per cent indicated that they were likely to change their plans because of changes in technology.

Directions for Future Research

The life-course perspective favours longitudinal studies in order to promote a better understanding of social change and its effects. Analysis must also take into account the relative positions and experiences of different cohorts. The experiences of the leading edge of baby boomers (born in the period 1947–55) are very different from that of the Gen-Xers (born in the period 1960–6) (Foot, 1996). The heterogeneity within cohorts must also be recognized in order to gain fuller understanding of the life-course effects by cohort.

Linking technology and work within a life-course perspective therefore entails a longitudinal view of technological change. Research must take into account the different life and career stages at which individuals encounter a technology and must look at the ways in which individuals react to change. In other words, the trajectories of the life course of older workers and younger workers should be a focus of study. Transitions in the life course that result from technological change are also identified as an area of study in the life-course perspective. The relationship between technological change and retirement has not been fully studied. In addition, as spiral and transitory career paths become commonplace, the role of technological change in the transitions between jobs or between jobs and unemployment needs to be examined. The linking mechanisms that connect social change and the individual have to be explored (Marshall, 1995). O'Rand (1996) suggests that, given recent demographic and economic transformations that seem to be increasing the variability of the life course, it is time for a closer consideration of the linking mechanisms that construct the trajectories of the life course.

Conclusion

The role of technology in restructuring work and the life course has been a neglected focus in life-course studies. The impact of technology on work has been widely studied, but the consequences for the life course have not been fully explored. This paper presented findings based on cross-sectional data from a case study of an organization. These findings point to some interesting hypotheses about the linkages between technology, work, and the life course.

Technology is a facilitator of organizational change, including the flattening of traditional hierarchical structures and the erosion of traditional, rigid work practices. Organizations have adopted numerical and functional flexibility strategies that include the use of contingent workers and multiskilled workers. These strategies are already having an impact on the life course. The transition from school to work is being prolonged as graduates take longer to establish themselves in a career. The transition from work to retirement is also being prolonged because workers are starting the process in their mid-fifties. Technology itself may mediate the retirement decision. Increasingly, workers of all ages are undertaking training to upgrade their skills.

The social impact of information technology has been widely

debated in many disciplines, including sociology, management, computer sciences, and information studies. Many insights have been gained from these multidisciplinary approaches. However, there remains a research challenge to assess the impact of technology at the micro or individual level within the broader dynamics of social change. The life-course perspective offers an approach to linking the micro and macro levels of analysis. Placing case-study data on individual change within the context of ongoing organizational and technological change gives us a better understanding of the impact of information technology on work and the work life course.

NOTES

1 This paper is based on data collected by the Issues of an Aging Workforce (IAW) Project, Centre for Studies of Aging, University of Toronto, Victor W. Marshall, principal investigator, with funding from Human Resources Development Canada. The data for this paper were received from the IAW project's Research Management Committee. We thank NOVA Corporation and its employees for participating in the case study reported here.

REFERENCES

Bartel, A.P. & Sicherman, N. (1993). Technological change and retirement decisions of older workers. *Journal of Labor Economics, 11*(1, Pt 1), 162–83.
Betcherman, G. (1997). Workplace change: A synthesis of the evidence. In *Changing workplace strategies: Achieving better outcomes for enterprises, workers and society* (Report on the International Conference, 2–3 December 1996, Ottawa). [On-line]. Available: *http://www.hrdc-drhc.gc.ca/corp/stratpol/arbsite/research/change/work_e.html*
Betcherman, G., & McMullen, K. (1986). *Working with technology: A survey of automation in Canada.* Ottawa: Economic Council of Canada.
Centre for Studies of Aging. (1996). *A case study of NOVA Corporation* (Monograph Series: Issues of an Aging Workforce). Toronto: University of Toronto, Centre for Studies of Aging.
de Wolff, A. (1995). *Summary report. Job loss and entry level information workers: Training and adjustment strategies for clerical workers in Metropolitan Toronto.* Toronto: Metro Toronto Clerical Workers Labour Adjustment Committee.
Elder, G.H., Jr. (1995). The life course paradigm: Social change and individual

development. In P. Moen, G. Elder, Jr, & K. Luscher (Eds), *Examining lives in context: Perspectives on the ecology of human development* (pp 101–39). Washington, DC: American Psychological Association.

Elder, G.H., Jr. (1997). The life course and human development. In R.M. Lerner (Ed.), *Handbook of child psychology, Vol. 1: Theoretical models of human development* (pp 939–91). New York: Wiley.

Elder, G.H., Jr, & O'Rand, A. (1995). Adult lives in a changing society. In K.S. Cook, G.A. Fine, & J.S. House (Eds), *Sociological perspectives on social psychology* (pp 452–75). Boston: Allyn and Bacon.

Foot, D.K., & Gibson, K.J. (1994). Population aging in the Canadian labour force: Changes and challenges. In V. Marshall & B. McPherson (Eds), *Aging: Canadian perspectives* (pp 97–112). Peterborough, ON: Broadview Press.

Foot, D.K. (with Stoffman, D.). (1996). *Boom, bust and echo: How to profit from the coming demographic shift.* Toronto: Macfarlane Walter & Ross.

Foot, D.K., & Venne, R.A. (1990). Population, pyramids and promotional prospects. *Canadian Public Policy, 16*(4), 387–98.

Greenbaum, J. (1995). *Windows on the workplace: Computers, jobs and the organization of office work in the late twentieth century.* New York: Monthly Review Press.

Henretta, J.C. (1994). Social structure and age-based careers. In M.W. Riley, R.L. Kahn, & A. Foner (Eds), *Age and structural lag: Society's failure to provide meaningful opportunities in work, family and leisure* (pp 57–79). New York: Wiley-Interscience.

Hitchhikers guide to cybernomics. (1996, 28 September). *The Economist*, World Economy section.

HRDC (Human Resources Development Canada). (1996a). Increasingly complex jobs = higher skills. *Applied Research Bulletin, 2*(2), 8–10.

HRDC. (1996b). Working with technology – Changing skill requirements in the computer age. *Applied Research Bulletin, 2*(2), 10–11.

Kohli, M. (1986). The world we forgot: A historical review of the life course. In V.W. Marshall (Ed.), *Later life: The social psychology of aging* (pp 271–303). Beverly Hills: Sage.

Kohli, M. (1988). Ageing as a challenge for sociological theory. *Ageing and Society, 8,* 367–94.

Kohli, M., & Rein, M. (1991). The changing balance of work and retirement. In M. Kohli, M. Rein, A. M Guillemard, & H. van Gunsteren (Eds), *Time for retirement: Comparative studies of early exit from the labor force* (pp 1–35). New York: Cambridge University Press.

Lowe, G.S. (1991). Computers in the workplace. *Perspectives on Labour and Income, 3*(2), 38–50. Statistics Canada Catalogue No. 75-001.

Lowe, G.S. (1997). Computers in the workplace. *Perspectives on Labour and Income, 9*(2), 29–39. Statistics Canada Catalogue No. 75–001.

Marshall, V.W. (1994). Social research on aging: Retrospect and prospect. In J.S. Frideres & C.J. Bruce (Eds), *The impact of an aging population on society* (pp 1–21). Calgary: University of Calgary.

Marshall, V.W. (1995). The micro–macro link in the sociology of aging. In C. Hummel & C.J. Lalive D'Epinay (Eds), *Images of aging in western societies* (pp 337–71). Geneva: University of Geneva, Centre for Interdisciplinary Gerontology.

McDonald, L., & Chen, M.Y.T. (1994). The youth freeze and the retirement bulge: Older workers and the impending labour shortage. In V. Marshall & B. McPherson (Eds), *Aging: Canadian perspectives* (pp 113–39). Peterborough, ON: Broadview Press.

O'Rand, A. (1996). Stratification of the life course. In R.H. Binstock & L.K. George (Eds), *Handbook of aging and the social sciences* (4th ed., pp 188–207). San Diego: Academic Press.

OECD (Organization for Economic Co-operation and Development). (1994). *The jobs study: Evidence and explanations. Part I. Labour market trends and underlying forces of change.* Paris: Author.

Rifkin, J. (1995). *The end of work: The decline of the global labor force and the dawn of the post-market era.* New York: Putnam.

Riley, M.W., & Riley, J.W., Jr. (1994). Structural lag: Past and future. In M.W. Riley, R.L. Kahn, & A. Foner (Eds), *Age and structural lag: Society's failure to provide meaningful opportunities in work, family and leisure* (pp 15–36). New York: Wiley-Interscience.

Ryder, N.B. (1965/1997). The cohort as a concept in the study of social change. *American Sociological Review, 54*, 359–81. Reprinted from M.A. Hardy (Ed.). (1997). *Studying aging and social change: Conceptual and methodological issues* (pp 66–92). Thousand Oaks, CA: Sage.

Scott Morton, M.S. (1991). Introduction. In M.S. Scott Morton (Ed.), *The corporation of the 1990s: Information technology and organizational transformation* (pp 3–23). New York: Oxford University Press.

Smith, V. (1994). Braverman's legacy: The labor process tradition at 20. *Work and Occupations, 2*(4), 403–21.

15. Is There Life after Career Employment? Labour-market Experience of Early 'Retirees'[1]

Gangaram Singh and Anil Verma

Any study of the life course, it can be argued, must account for the labour-market experience of older workers. Past research has assumed that older workers who leave the labour force do so in a complete way and on a permanent basis (Marshall, 1995). Recent research, on the other hand, has shown that many older workers return to the labour market after early retirement from their career jobs (Monette, 1996; Herz, 1995). The period of employment between career employment and full retirement is often referred to as 'bridge employment' (Rhum, 1990; Doeringer, 1990). Bridge employment, according to the OECD (1995), is likely to have a significant impact on public policies that are central to the transition from work to retirement. Before such a conclusion is drawn, though, it is important to have a thorough understanding of bridge employment (Doeringer, 1990).

Few studies to date have examined the labour-market experience of older workers who retire early and then return to work (Doeringer, 1990; Rhum, 1990; Hayward and Hardy, 1985; Beck, 1986). In a number of ways, our understanding of bridge employment is limited. Past research has not followed a single cohort with comparable background. Moreover, cross-sectional data of a national sample make it difficult to examine the bridge-employment process at a more detailed level. Unlike past research, this paper is based on a profile of bridge employment which we developed and tested using a sample of older workers who left their career jobs before the normal age of retirement at a large telecommunications firm. Using this unique data source, we show that, indeed, many older workers do not make a smooth transition from career employment to full retirement. Instead, a period of bridge employment intervenes between career employment and full retirement. We find that people return to work for health and economic reasons but also because of their attachment to work itself. Most people are likely to end up in non-standard employment for both demand and supply reasons. We also find that managers tend to do better in bridge employment compared to workers. To the best of our knowledge, this is the first study to examine bridge employment empirically at the firm level in the context of a changing life course.

The Traditional Life Course

Individuals generally plan their lives in terms of progress through the main life-course events of school, work, and retirement (Marshall, 1995; Hareven and Adams, 1982). The traditional life course followed an orderly progression from school to work and from work to retirement. Moreover, the transition from one event to another is generally seen as being complete and final. For example, an individual who makes the transition from work to retirement does not normally return to work. It is not surprising, therefore, that the work-to-retirement transition is conceptualized and researched as a discrete event (Singh, 1998). The principal characteristics thought to be driving the decision to retire have been health and wealth. Several studies have shown that the work-to-retirement transition is related to poor health (Sammartino, 1987). In addition, many individuals make the transition to retirement because they can financially afford to do so (Fields and Mitchell, 1984; Bazzoli, 1985; Burtless and Moffitt, 1985; Pesando, Hyatt, and Gunderson, 1992; Singh, 1998). Other factors that influence the work-to-retirement transition include job characteristics, particularly where the jobs are physically demanding or require few social skills (Beck, 1983; Hayward and Hardy, 1985; Hayward and Grady, 1986). Thus, in addition to poor health and financial considerations, the decision to return to work is affected by work-related experience.

The Emerging Life Course

A number of social and economic trends give the emerging life course an increasingly dynamic pattern (Marshall, 1986; Hayward, Friedman, and Chen, 1998). North Americans have increasingly delayed the decision to enter work from school. Because students stay longer at school than they did a generation ago, the age at which the school-to-work transition is made has increased (Beuchtemann, Schupp, and Soloff, 1993). They also make the work-to-retirement transition at a younger age (Roche, Fynes, and Morrissey, 1996). We know, too, that many North Americans are working longer hours, and the two processes (that is, a shorter work life and longer hours) may indeed be driving each other (Sheridan, Sunter, and Diverty, 1996; Bell and Freeman, 1996). During the transition phases, individuals display a tendency to juggle two or more of the life-course events. Some individuals simultaneously attend school and work. Others are in a state of partial retirement in which they work on a part-time basis after leaving career employment. And another group may be juggling all three events (school, work, and retirement). School is likely to be a bigger part of our lives as life-long learning becomes the pattern. This trend may be driven by a number of demand and supply factors. Some people want to learn more and different things simply for self-fulfilment and personal growth. Others may be pushed to learn new skills as older skills are made obsolete by newer technologies. Yet others may be pursuing activities which they were not free to undertake while pursuing a career. The implication is that life-course events will increasingly overlap and that the transitions will not be seen as complete and permanent (Marshall, 1995; Hareven and Adams, 1982).

Other demand-side factors such as organizational restructuring also shape the emerging life course. The 1980s and 1990s will likely be remembered as the decades in which it became necessary to restructure organizational processes (Hammer and Champy, 1993). One critical part of organizational renewal included a drive to re-engineer processes by simplifying necessary work and eliminating activities which added little value. This, in turn, invariably reduced the number of employees needed to staff operations (Peters and Waterman, 1982). Two classes of workers emerged as a result of organizational restructuring (Feldman, 1996): 'core' employees, who fulfilled the regular functions of the organization, and 'peripheral' employees, who were used to achieve the flexible allocation of labour in a highly flexible market. This model signified a significant departure from the 'psychological contract' of traditional employment in which firms provided life-long employment in exchange for organizational loyalty (Waterman, Waterman, and Collard, 1994). Employees are now fully responsible for their employability, and employers are free to end the employment relationship should the market so warrant. Disrupted employment trajectories mean that we are likely to see more career changes, more training and retraining, and a higher incidence of early (but partial) retirement (Hayward, Friedman, and Chen, 1998).

A Model of Work After Early Retirement

Bridge employment implies that retirement is no longer a discrete event. Instead retirement should be conceptualized as a process whereby individuals gradually withdraw from the labour force over a period of time. The decision to return to work after early retirement is more prevalent among individuals who are in good health (Parnes and Sommers, 1994). Work after early retirement is also driven by inadequate financial resources (Gustman and Steinmeier, 1991; Boaz, 1987; Morrow-Howell and Leon, 1988; Fontana and Frey, 1990). Older workers who express a distaste for retirement are more likely to return to the labour market for a period of employment after career employment (Herz, 1995; Fontana and Frey, 1990). One manifestation of this distaste for retirement lies in an attachment to work itself. For many people, work provides an opportunity for creativity and self-fulfilment. One may expect that such individuals would want to return to work even if health and wealth factors were not compelling them to do so.

Individuals who returned to work in the 1990s faced a very different labour market from the market they found when they initially entered their career jobs. The labour market of the 1990s was characterized by relatively fewer full-time jobs and more part-time and contract jobs. There has also been a bias in many industries against the employment of older workers. This bias may stem from negative stereotypes which employers entertain about older workers (Mazerolle and Singh, 1999). For example, employers often assume that older workers are less likely to retrain, to remain for a long period of time in the labour market, to have good attendance, and to be productive (Canadian Aging Research Network, 1995). Several studies have shown that bridge employment is characterized by part-time employment (Monette, 1996; Iams, 1987; Rhum and Sum, 1988; Rhum, 1991) and lower wages (Doeringer, 1990; Rhum, 1991). Hence, as retirees return to the labour market, they are more likely to be found in non-standard employment such as part-time and contract work, and self-employment.

It is also likely that managers will do better than workers in terms of labour-market experience after early retirement (Verma and Singh, 1997). Skills that are more valued in an information economy are more prevalent among managers, and managers are often more educated than workers. During their career employment, managers are also more likely to develop the kinds of social and professional networks that are likely to facilitate a return to work. Given their managerial duties, they are also likely to be better informed about the kinds of skills that are in demand. Thus, managers are more likely to have more and better information, greater flexibility in skills, and better ability to plan ahead for a return to work. All these factors increase the likelihood that managers will find greater success relative to workers in finding employment after a career job.

Arguments presented in this section are summarized in the following three propositions.

1. For many early retirees, we expect a period of bridge employment between career employment and full retirement. And the decision to return to work is expected to relate to good health, inadequate financial resources, and an attachment to work.
2. A large majority of those who return to work will become employed in non-standard jobs such as part-time work and self-employment.
3. And, finally, we expect managers to do better than workers in terms of opportunities to return to work and the types of employment obtained.

Research Methods

The data for this paper are taken from a survey of former employees of Bell Canada (Canada's largest telecommunications firm). Historically, Bell Canada offered life-time employment to most of its employees. Natural attrition and financial incentives were the preferred strategy for any work-force reductions (Verma, 1999). But in the early 1980s, Bell Canada had to face competition in the long-distance market as a result of deregulation and new technology. The company responded to intensified competition with a strategy to reduce the number of employees. Between 1985 and 1995, as a result, it offered four different early-retirement-incentive plans to employees to induce them to leave. Early-exit plans were targeted at those areas where it had been determined that there was a surplus of employees (Canadian Aging Research Network, 1995). The strategy to reduce the work force by offering early-retirement incentives, it should be noted, is increasingly being used by many organizations (Davidson, Worrell, and Fox, 1996).

The population consisted of 6,846 employees who left Bell Canada between 1985 and 1995 and were entitled to a private pension. From this group, 100 per cent of those who left between the ages of 45 and 50 were selected for this study, in order to increase the probability of responses from early retirees. Fifty per cent of those who were 51 and over were randomly selected to receive the survey. This resulted in a target of 3,633 respondents (421 aged between 45 and 50 and 3,212 aged 51 and above). Nineteen were excluded because of language barrier or participation in focus groups related to the same study. Thirty-eight could not participate because of poor health, death, or relocation. The final sample, therefore, comprised 3,576 potential respondents.

Of the 3,576 potential respondents, 2,147 returned partially or fully completed questionnaires (a 60 per cent response rate). After some scrutiny, 1,805 responses were retained for analysis, as they contained the full information needed to examine the labour-market experience of early retirees. The characteristics of those in the sample are very similar to those of the general population. Two per cent of men in the population left Bell Canada at age 65 compared to 1.7 per cent in the sample. Three per cent of women in the population left Bell Canada at age 65 compared to 2 per cent in the sample. The average age in both the population and the sample was 61 years. The sample did consist of a greater proportion of managers and men than the general population. Such a bias may be related to the fact that many of the early-retirement-incentive programs were directed at middle management where it had been determined that a surplus of employees existed. The sample, nevertheless, is generally closely representative of the population from which it was drawn.

Results

Respondents were asked to answer either 'no' or 'yes' to the following question: '[h]ave you ever worked for pay since leaving Bell?' As table 15.1 shows, 40 per cent of the respondents went back to work after leaving Bell Canada. It is clear, therefore, that work remained an important part of the life course after early retirement.

In the entire sample, 20 per cent reported a health limitation. Only 17 per cent of those who returned to work reported a health limitation, while 21 per cent of those who had not returned to work reported a health limitation. Poor health, our results indicate, discourages a return to work after early retirement.

TABLE 15.1
Return to Work by Health Status, Financial Resources, and Work Attachment

Health status, financial resources, and work attachment	Sample means (%)	Return to work (%)		Chi-square
		Yes	No	
Health limitation (yes = 1)	0.20	0.17	0.21	3.79**
Full and immediate pension	0.19	0.11	0.24	
Reduced pension	0.72	0.76	0.69	
Deferred pension	0.09	0.13	0.07	49.91***
Mortgage-free home (yes = 1)	0.74	0.69	0.77	12.99***
Debt (yes = 1)	0.19	0.27	0.14	47.88***
Work attachment (above average = 1)	0.23	0.34	0.16	72.13***
Number of observations	1,805	723	1,082	

***$p \leq .01$, **$p \leq .05$, and *$p \leq .10$.

Our results also show strong associations between the decision to return to work and financial inability defined as: entitlement to a reduced or deferred pension, not owning a mortgage-free home, and owing a debt over $5,000. Eighty-one per cent of the respondents were entitled to a reduced or deferred pension, but 89 per cent of those with such a pension returned to work compared to 69 per cent of those who did not return to work. Seventy-four per cent of the respondents indicated that they owned a mortgage-free home, but only 69 per cent of those with such a home returned to work compared to 77 per cent of those who did not return to work. Nineteen per cent of the respondents reported a debt of over $5,000, but 27 per cent of those who had such a debt returned to work compared to 14 per cent of those who did not return to work. Financial inability, as indicated by our results, increased the likelihood of work after early retirement.

The results of our study also indicate a strong association between the return-to-work decision and work attachment. Work attachment was measured with a multidimensional scale. Respondents were asked the following four questions (on a Likert-type scale):

1. How often do you miss the feeling of doing a good job?
2. How often do you feel that you want to go back to work?
3. How often do you worry about not having a job?
4. How often do you miss being with other people at work?

Responses to these questions were first combined in a composite and then dichotomized by recoding above-average scores as 'one' and below-average scores as 'zero.' Thirty-four per cent of the respondents reported an above-average attachment to work. Thirty-four per cent of those who returned to work reported an above-average attachment to work while only 16 per cent of those who did not return to work did so. Work attachment, as such, improved the likelihood that an individual would return to work after early retirement.

Table 15.2 shows the types of employment people were able to find when they returned to work. Although 723 respondents returned to work, we had information on types of employment obtained from only 690 respondents. Part-time and full-time work and self-employment accounted for the types of employment obtained. Fifty-one per cent returned to part-time work, 17 per cent to full-time work, and 32 per cent to self-employment. The results, therefore, provide strong support for the proposition that the majority of individuals who return to bridge employment do so in non-standard employment. In our case, 83 per cent returned to either part-time work or self-employment. Only 17 per cent returned to standard full-time employment.

Our results indicate that health status and various measures of financial resources are not statistically significantly related at conventional levels to types of employment obtained. But a strong and statistically significant association exists between the types of employment obtained and work attachment. While 54 per cent of those who returned to full-time employment reported an above-average attachment to work, fewer (28 per cent) of those who were in part-time employment and in self-employment (31 per cent) had done so. Work attachment, according to our results, encouraged full-time employment after early retirement.

Our sample consisted of two broad occupational groups. White-collar workers (predominantly female) were represented by an unaffiliated in-house union, while blue-collar workers (predominantly male) were represented by a national union (see Verma, 1999, for details). From the total sample, we dropped 152 respondents who failed to indicate their union status, leaving a total of 1,652 usable

TABLE 15.2
The Return to Part-time Employment, Full-time Employment, and Self-employment by Health Status, Financial Resources, and Work Attachment

Health status, financial resources, and work attachment	Sample means (%)	Return to types of employment (%)			Chi-square
		Part-time employment	Full-time employment	Self-employment	
Health limitation (yes = 1)	0.17	0.18	0.17	0.15	0.78
Full and immediate pension	0.11	0.12	0.13	0.09	
Reduced pension	0.76	0.76	0.74	0.77	2.87
Deferred pension	0.13	0.12	0.13	0.14	
Mortgage-free home (yes = 1)	0.69	0.68	0.64	0.74	3.91
Debt (yes = 1)	0.27	0.27	0.32	0.25	1.80
Work attachment (above average = 1)	0.34	0.28	0.54	0.31	25.59***
Number of observations	690	349	118	223	

***p ≤ .01, **p ≤ .05, and *p ≤ .10.

responses for this part of the analysis. Panel A of table 15.3 shows a strong association between the rate of return to work and occupational status. Fifty-six per cent of managers returned to work while only 22 per cent of white-collar workers and 23 per cent of blue-collar workers returned to work. Since managers were generally better off financially compared to workers, a higher rate of return to work among managers suggests that other factors were at play. Differences among the groups, in terms of return to work, were statistically significant. Such differences were detected with the Student-Neuman-Keuls (SNK) test. SNK is better than a two-way t-test because it keeps the total amount of error (say at .05) constant across all the differences rather than allowing that error for each comparison. The rate of return for managers (shown with an 'A' in the table) was significantly different from both worker groups (shown with a 'B'), but those for the two worker groups were not different from each other. Our results, therefore, show that managers were *better* off than workers in terms of finding a job after early retirement.

Panel B of table 15.3 shows the distribution of the three occupational groups by types of employment obtained. Part-time employment was most likely to be reported by the white-collar group: 79 per cent of all white-collar workers who returned to work found part-time employment. The same figure for blue-collar workers was lower at 59 per cent and still lower at 44 per cent for managers. Each difference was statistically significant, as shown by the letters A, B, and C in an SNK test. More managers (18 per cent) found full-time employment than white-collar (11 per cent) or blue-collar workers (14 per cent), but these differences were not significant. We suspect that, since the numbers of people who found full-time employment was small (only 118 out of 690), the manager–worker difference may become significant in larger samples. Managers (38 per cent) and blue-collar workers (27 per cent) found more self-employment compared to white-collar workers (10 per cent). We speculate that this difference may be partially associated with gender, given that most white-collar workers were female. The results of our study, nevertheless, show that managers were better off than workers in terms of the types of employment they obtained after early retirement.

Policy Implications and Future Research

At the start of a new century, we are confronted with a number of

TABLE 15.3
Manager–Worker Differences in the Return to Work and Types of Employment Obtained
after Early Retirement

A: Return to Work by Occupational Status

Manager–worker status	Sample size	Return to work (%)	
		Yes	No
Managers	875	56 (A)	44
White-collar workers	313	22 (B)	78
Blue-collar workers	464	23 (B)	77
Total N	1652	661	991

F-Value = 102.39 (p ≤ .01). ***p ≤ .01, **p ≤ .05, and *p ≤ .10. Letters, A, B, or C signify
three-way statistically significant difference in means (at the 5 per cent level) based on
the SNK test.

B: Return to Part-time Employment, Full-time Employment, and Self-employment by
Occupational Status

Manager–worker status	Sample size	Return to types of employment (%)		
		Part-time employment	Full-time employment	Self-employment
Managers	471	44 (A)	18 (A)	38 (A)
White-collar workers	62	79 (B)	11 (A)	10 (B)
Blue-collar workers	102	59 (C)	14 (A)	27 (A)
Total N	690	349	118	223
F-value		16.20***	1.46	10.84***

***p ≤ .01, **p ≤ .05, and *p ≤ .10. Letters, A, B, or C signify three-way statistically sig-
nificant difference in means (at the 5 per cent level) based on the SNK test.

social and economic trends that are transforming work, workplaces,
and the employment relationship. These trends will undoubtedly continue to have a considerable impact on the life course. We addressed, in
this chapter, the issue of how older workers make the transition from
work to retirement. Most of these workers, a generation ago, would

have continued their career employment with Bell Canada (or another similar employer) until they wanted to retire or until the normal retirement age was reached. In the 1990s, and as we move into the new century, many such workers are likely to leave career employment and start another phase of their life course. In-depth analysis of bridge employment, therefore, is still required.

Our data and their preliminary analysis provide broad support for the view that work-to-retirement transitions are likely to be a phase rather than an event in people's lives. The results also provide a glimpse of the workings of the Canadian labour market. Most people who wanted to work in our sample were able to find work. The rate of involuntary unemployment in this sample at the time of the study was only 6 per cent, lower than the national unemployment rate (10 per cent) at the time (Singh, 1998). We cannot tell from these data, though, whether fewer people went into full-time employment for demand or supply reasons. Lower rates of full-time employment may be reflecting financial security. On the other hand, it may be that people took other forms of employment because not enough full-time jobs were available or because age discrimination negatively affected their chances of finding full-time jobs. Questions of this nature need to be answered in subsequent research.

Our results are revealing about the better success of managers compared to workers with respect to work after early retirement. Managers, we argued, benefited from knowledge of the labour market and targeted skills. Training for workers who want to return to work, it would seem, should be designed with the labour market and high-demand skills in mind. It should be noted, though, that we did not empirically examine why managers had done better than workers. Future studies, as such, need to explore the process that managers and workers undertook.

NOTES

1 This paper is based on data collected as part of the Issues of an Aging Workforce Project funded by the Innovations Fund of Human Resources Development Canada. Victor Marshall was the Principal Investigator. We are grateful to Bell Canada for facilitating data collection and to former Bell Canada employees for responding to our survey. Further details of this survey can be found in CARNET (1995).

REFERENCES

Bazzoli, G. (1985). The early retirement decision: New empirical evidence on the influence of health. *Journal of Human Resources*, 20(2), 214–34.

Beck, S. (1983). Position in economic structure and unexpected retirement. *Research on Aging*, 5(2), 197–216.

Beck, S. (1986). Mobility from preretirement to postretirement job. *The Sociological Quarterly*, 27(4), 515–31.

Bell, L., & Freeman, R. (1996). *Working hard*. Paper presented at Changes in Working Time in Canada and the United States, Canadian Employment Research Forum.

Beuchtemann, C., Schupp, J., & Soloff, D. (1993). Roads to work: School-to-work transition patterns in Germany and the United States. *Industrial Relations Journal*, 24(2), 97–111.

Boaz, R. (1987). Work as a response to low and decreasing real income during retirement. *Research on Aging*, 9(3), 428–40.

Burtless, G., & Moffitt, R. (1985). The joint choice of retirement age and postretirement hours of work. *Journal of Labor Economics*, 3(2), 209–36.

Canadian Aging Research Network (CARNET). (1995). *Issues of an aging workforce: A case of former employees of Bell Canada*. Toronto: University of Toronto, Centre for Studies of Aging.

Davidson, W., Worrell, D., & Fox, J. (1996). Early retirement programs and firm performance. *Academy of Management Journal*, 39(94), 970–84.

Doeringer, P. (1990). Economic security, labour market flexibility, and bridges to retirement. In P. Doeringer (Ed.), *Bridges to retirement* (pp 3–19). Ithaca, NY: ILR Press.

Feldman, D. (1996). The decision to retire early: A review and conceptualization. *Academy of Management Review*, 19(2), 285–311.

Fields, G., & Mitchell, O. (1984). The effects of social security reforms on retirement ages and retirement incomes. *Journal of Public Economics*, 25(112), 143–59.

Fontana, A., & Frey, J. (1990). Postretirement workers in the labour force. *Work and Occupations*, 17(3), 355–61.

Gustman, A., & Steinmeier, T. (1991). Changing the social security rules for work after 65. *Industrial and Labour Relations Review*, 44(4), 733–45.

Hammer, M., & Champy, J. (1993). *Reengineering the corporation: A manifesto for business revolution*. New York: Harper Collins.

Hareven, T., & Adams, K. (1982). *Aging and life course transitions: An interdisciplinary perspective*. New York: Guildford Press.

Hayward, M., Friedman, S., & Chen, H. (1998). Career trajectories and older men's retirement. *Journal of Gerontology*, 53(2), 91–103.

Hayward, M., & Grady, M. (1986). The occupational retention and recruitment of older men: The influence of structural characteristics of work. *Social Forces, 64*(3), 644–66.

Hayward, M., & Hardy, M. (1985). Early retirement process among older men: Occupational differences. *Research on Aging, 7*(4), 491–515.

Herz, D. (1995). Work after early retirement: An increasing trend among men. *Monthly Labour Review, 118*(4), 21–7.

Iams, H. (1987). Jobs of persons working after receiving retired-worker benefits. *Social Security Bulletin, 50*(11), 4–18.

Marshall, V. (1986). *Later life: The social psychology of aging.* Beverly Hills: SAGE.

Marshall, V. (1995). Rethinking retirement: Issues for the twenty-first century. In E. Gee & G. Gutman (Eds), *Rethinking retirement* (pp 31–50). Vancouver: Simon Fraser University, Gerontological Research Centre.

Mazerolle, M., & Singh, G. (1999). Older workers' adjustments to plant closures. *Relations industrielles/Industrial Relations, 54*(2), 313–36.

Monette, M. (1996). *Canada's changing retirement patterns.* Ottawa: Ministry of Industry.

Morrow-Howell, N., & Leon, J. (1988). Life-span determinants of work in retirement years. *International Journal of Aging and Human Development, 27*(7), 125–40.

OECD (Organization for Economic Cooperation and Development). (1995). *The transition from work to retirement.* Paris: Author.

Parnes, H., & Sommers, D. (1994). Shunning retirement: Work experience of men in their seventies and eighties. *Journal of Gerontology, 49*(3), 117–24.

Pesando, J., Hyatt, D., & Gunderson, M. (1992). Early retirement pensions and employee turnover. *Research in Labour Economics, 13*, 321–37.

Peters, T., & Waterman, R. (1982). *In search of excellence: Lessons from America's best-run companies.* New York: Harper and Row.

Rhum, C. (1990). Bridge jobs and partial retirement. *Journal of Labour Economics, 8*(4), 482–501.

Rhum, C. (1991). Career employment and job stopping. *Industrial Relations, 30*(2), 193–208.

Rhum, C., & Sum, A. (1988). Job stopping: The changing employment patterns of older workers. *IRRA 41st Annual Proceedings* (pp 21–8). Madison: Industrial Relations Research Association.

Roche, W., Fynes, B., & Morrissey, T. (1996). Working time and employment: A review of international evidence. *International Labour Review, 135*(2), 129–57.

Sammartino, F. (1987). The effect of health on retirement. *Social Security Bulletin, 50*(7), 31–47.

Sheridan, M., Sunter, D., & Diverty, B. (1996). *The changing workweek: Trends in weekly hours of work in Canada, 1976–1995.* Paper presented at Changes in Working Time in Canada and the United States, Canadian Employment Research Forum.

Singh, G. (1998). *Work after early retirement.* Unpublished doctoral dissertation, University of Toronto, Canada.

Verma, A. (1999). From POTS to PANS: The evolution of employment relations in Bell Canada under deregulation. In A. Verma & R. Chaykowski (Eds), *Contract and commitment: Workplace change and the evolution of employment relations in Canadian firms* (pp 182–210). Kingston, ON: Queen's IRC Press.

Verma, A., & Singh, G. (1997, June). *Do managers and workers have different labour market experiences after early retirement?* Paper presented to the Thirty-fourth Annual Conference, Canadian Industrial Relations Association, St John's.

Waterman, R., Waterman, J., & Collard, B. (1994). Toward a career resilient workforce. *Harvard Business Review, 72*(4), 87–95.

16. Downsizing and the Life-course Consequences of Job Loss: The Effect of Age and Gender on Employment and Income Security

Jill Quadagno, David MacPherson, Jennifer Reid Keene, and Lori Parham

On 13 April 1998, the front page of newspapers across the United States announced two huge banking mergers, accelerating a wave of consolidation likely to leave the financial-services industry with a few giant powerhouses (Holson, 1998). In the bigger of the two deals, Nationsbank Corporation merged with the BankAmerica Corporation, creating the first coast-to-coast bank and making the new company the largest in terms of total branches and deposits. A second merger, between Banc One Corporation and First Chicago NBD Corporation, would create the fifth-largest banking company, which would dominate financial services in the Midwest.

Although much of the media coverage focused on the financial consequences of the mergers and acquisitions, mergers also exact a human cost in the form of waves of downsizings and job losses. Even as the stock market boomed and the economy has grown, the rate of job loss, which peaked at 3.4 million in 1992, has continued to increase (U.S. Bureau of Labor Statistics, 1995). In fact, the job-loss rate in the 1991–3 period was higher than it was even during the severe recession of the 1980s. The spread of downsizing among firms is being driven by a broad set of dynamics within the business environment and within the organization, including such considerations as shareholder value, foreign consolidations, market share, productivity, employee compensation, deregulation, business peaks, institutional forces like the adoption effect and industry culture, and firm traits based on ownership status and firm size (Budros, 1997). With the expansion of global competition, the marketplace for many firms has expanded beyond the region to the nation and even to the entire world. In some industries, including banking, only a few competitors will survive consolidation and emerge as 'global gladiators' with the largest market share.

The Distribution of Job Loss

The wave of economic restructuring has been crashing down on an ever-widening spectrum of workers. During the 1980s, job loss was greatest in the manufacturing sector, and it has remained high in the 1990s (Gordon, 1996). In the 1990s, however, the locus of job instability shifted to the service sector. Although blue-collar workers still make up a majority of displaced workers, in recent years they represent a bare majority. Job loss has spread to nearly every type of employment. A survey of displaced workers conducted by the Bureau of Labor Statistics found that, although manufacturing workers accounted for one-third of the 4.5 million workers who were displaced between 1991 and 1993, there had been an increase in job loss among service-sector workers, who comprise over 75 per cent of the work force in the United States (U.S. Bureau of Labor Statistics, 1995).

Within the service sector, the first wave of worker displacement was directed at lower-level employees. Between 1990 and 1993, for example, Sears automated many of its customer-service operations and eliminated 21,000 positions (Marks, 1994). Recent mergers have eliminated jobs at all levels. The job losers of the 1990s are more educated and older than those of the 1980s. College graduates are now most likely to have a job loss because their job was abolished. In fact, the most dramatic increase in job-loss rates has occurred among managers (Farber, 1996, p. 16). Another trend associated with mergers and downsizing is a tendency for companies to rely increasingly on contingent workers. Currently, one out of every four workers in the United States is a part-time or temporary employee (Uzzi and Barsness, 1998).

Although many upper-level, white-collar employees have lost their jobs, the percentage of executive, administrative, and managerial employees to lose their jobs has continued to increase (Gordon, 1996). Research suggests that the costs of job loss and worker displacement are not distributed evenly across the labour force. Rather, the risk of income loss and downward mobility following a job loss appears to be greater for older workers and women workers than for younger men.

The Effect of Downsizing on Older Workers

One trend since the 1980s that has adversely affected older workers is a change in the main reason for the loss of a job. Since 1989 the rate of job loss because of the cutting of a position or shift has increased substantially, a change that has a big impact on older workers (ages 55 to 64), who are most likely to report a job loss for this reason (Farber, 1996, p. 13). This trend is in sharp contrast to conditions in the 1980s when seniority provisions in union contracts provided job security for older workers against a wave of plant closures (Hardy, Hazelrigg, and Quadagno, 1996). As job loss has shifted from plant closings in manufacturing industries to downsizing in non-unionized, white-collar industries (New York Times, 1996), older workers have become more at risk of losing their jobs.

Older workers who lose a job also have a more difficult time finding a new job. A survey of displaced workers in 1994 found that, although 70 per cent were re-employed, rates varied by age and by gender. The re-employment rate was highest among workers aged 25 to 54. Seventy-three per cent were working again at the time of the survey. By contrast, just over half of displaced workers aged 55 to 64 were re-employed (U.S. Bureau of Labor Statistics, 1995). Not only do older workers take longer to find a new job, they are less likely to find employment at previous wage levels (Newman, 1988).

Some older workers have benefited from the Age Discrimination in Employment Act (ADEA), which prohibits employers from firing, demoting, or reducing the salary of workers between the ages of 40 and 65 on the basis of age (Clark, 1990). In 1990, Congress amended the ADEA with the Older Workers Benefit Protection Act, which prohibits employers from treating older workers differently from younger workers if they are downsizing (Israel and McConnell, 1991). Although most of the actions taken to enforce the ADEA involve people who feel they were terminated unfairly, the downsizings often involve such massive layoffs that it is difficult to prove that age discrimination has occurred.

Some employees who lose their jobs are eligible for generous severance packages and/or have access to large lump-sum payments from their pensions, provisions which can mitigate the effects of an extended job search. Statistics show, however, that few workers (28 per cent) who receive lump-sum payments roll them over into tax-qualified savings plans (Bassett, Fleming, and Rodriguez, 1996). Indeed, only about one-third of workers over age 55 who receive a lump-sum distribution invest that money in a retirement annuity or deposit it in a savings account (Salisbury, 1993). The others presumably use it to pay expenses. Thus, downsized older workers may find themselves close to retirement age with few or no personal savings, little opportunity for re-employment at the same or a similar job, and no guarantee of a pension. These factors make restructuring and downsizing more costly for older than for younger workers.

Gender and the Consequences of Job Loss

Women may also be adversely affected by economic restructuring. In the period from 1940 to 1990, the labour-force participation of women increased from 25 to 45 per cent of the total labour force (Blau and Ferber, 1992). Before this surge of women into the labour force, women workers were generally young and single because most women usually left the labour force permanently when they married and had children (Blau and Ferber, 1992). In recent decades, however, women's labour-force participation has become more stable over the life course, even among married women with small children (Moen, 1992).

Shaw (1994) examines the persistence of married women's employment, that is, whether women who are working are increasingly likely to continue working. She finds that the number of persistent workers among both married and single women has increased dramatically: 'far fewer women drop out upon marriage, and they then continue these work habits throughout their careers' (Shaw, 1994, p. 368). Furthermore, young single women have become more persistent workers because of marriage at later ages, 'a pattern which then continues into their married years despite the birth and rearing of children' (Shaw, 1994, p. 368). Thus, while women's labour-force participation previously was intermittent, especially throughout their childbearing years, women's commitment to paid work has increased.

Farber (1995) also provides evidence that women's labour-force participation is becoming more stable. One important trend is that women are more committed to the labour market than they were twenty years ago and withdraw periodically from the labour market less frequently. Still, according to Farber, it is unclear whether women's long-term jobs are of equal quality to those of men.

Although younger women have career patterns that are more similar to those of men, no research has yet considered what consequences job loss will have on the career paths of men and women (Moen, 1996). Is the labour-force attachment of women more fragile than that of men? Are women perceived by employers as more expendable labour? The displaced workers' survey cited above suggests that older women are especially vulnerable to job loss in terms of re-employment. Among displaced workers aged 55 to 64 who subsequently found new jobs, 57 per cent of men were re-employed compared to only 47.7 per cent of women (U.S. Bureau of Labor Statistics, 1995).

There are few studies that examine the impact of mergers and downsizing on workers' subsequent employment and income security. This paper reports the initial results of a two-year longitudinal study of the career and life-course trajectories of former employees of First Interstate Bank who were among 7,500 bank employees who lost their jobs following a 1996 merger with Wells Fargo Bank.

The Banking Industry

Unlike most other industrialized nations, which have fewer than 1,000 commercial banks, the United States lacks a national banking system in which a few banks have branches throughout the country. As of 1993, the United States had more than 12,000 commercial banks, 2,000 savings and loans, and 16,000 credit unions (Marks, 1994). The presence of so many banks reflects the effect of federal regulations that have restricted the ability of these financial institutions to open branches. Each state has its own restrictions on the type and number of branches a bank can open (Mishkin, 1994).

During the 1980s, deregulation in the banking industry allowed bank holding companies headquartered in one state to purchase banks in another state. Recent changes in banking regulations allow banks to operate branches across state lines. A few large banks have taken advantage of the opportunities opened by deregulation to engage in an aggressive series of takeovers to eliminate competition and expand their asset holdings. Industry experts predict that the banking system will consolidate to only 2,000 by early in the twenty-first century (Zey, 1993). Each merger has resulted in job losses of employees at all levels, from bank tellers to bank officers.

Along with declines in employment has come a paring of employee benefits. In some cases, workers have become ineligible for any benefits. Another component of the fringe-benefit strategy has been ending the paternalism of defined-benefit plans and placing the responsibility for retirement income on the individual worker by installing defined-contribution plans instead. Health-insurance costs are another big concern of employers. In one employer survey, reducing worker health-care costs was a major priority (Marks, 1994). The emphasis on reducing health-care costs places older workers at risk of losing jobs, because they represent a higher health-care burden.

Methods and Results

In 1997, the ninth-largest bank in the United States was Wells Fargo, which initiated a series of mergers and buyouts of other banks beginning in 1986. On 23 January 1996, Wells Fargo announced plans to purchase First Interstate Bancorp (FIB) at a purchase price of $11 billion. On 1 April the date the merger was implemented, more than 1,700 First Interstate employees were notified that their positions would be eliminated. On 18 April Wells Fargo announced that it would close 25 branches throughout Orange County in Los Angeles and lay off 187 branch employees. Statewide, the bank closed 260 branches and laid off another 2,000 branch employees. By the end of 1996, another 7,200 First Interstate employees had lost their jobs through attrition and further layoffs (Press Release, 1 April 1996).

In April 1996, we mailed a short survey to 5,326 officers at FIB, immediately after the first round of layoff notices was announced. We obtained the work addresses of the officers from the 1995 FIB company phone book provided to the principal investigator by an FIB officer. A letter accompanying the survey explained the objectives of the project and asked the workers to fill out the form and return it. The main purpose of the short survey was to obtain basic demographic data and the home addresses and telephone numbers of the FIB employees. A total of 1,006 surveys were returned for a response rate of 19 per cent. The response rate is likely higher than 19 per cent, since we estimate that at least 1,000 workers did not receive the survey because they were dismissed or left FIB before the survey arrived. Among the respondents, 360 had been laid off, 482 were told they would be employed in a new job with Wells Fargo, and 164 did not yet know whether they would be laid off.

The mail survey was followed by in-depth telephone interviews with twenty randomly selected respondents. The telephone interviews provided background information on how workers were notified about the merger, what options FIB and Wells Fargo were offering workers, and how workers responded to the threatened layoff.

A second survey was mailed in mid-October 1996 to the homes of all individuals who had responded to wave 1 and who agreed to participate in follow-up interviews. The survey asked questions on current employment status, previous employment history, savings behaviour, health, and family finances. Workers were also asked to complete a financial statement concerning current salary, salary while an FIB employee, receipt of a severance package, and severance-package expenditures. A total of 750 workers completed both the first and second surveys. In addition to the mail survey, another thirty-two in-depth telephone interviews were conducted. This paper reports the results of wave 1 and wave 2.

Wave 1 Results

The subjects ranged in age from 25 to 66. Approximately 60 per cent were over the age of 40 and nearly 20 per cent were between 51 and 66. Nearly 42 per cent were male and 58 per cent were female, a distribution that reflects the feminization of the banking industry (Rich, 1995). Eighty-two per cent were white, 6.5 per cent of Hispanic origin, 4.1 per cent African American, and 2.8 per cent other. A substantial fraction of the former First Interstate Bank managers are well educated. For example, over 40 per cent of the officers had graduated from college; fewer than 10 per cent only had a high school diploma. About one-third earned more than $65,000 per year, and two-thirds earned more than $45,000 annually.

At the time of wave 1, those who were laid off differed from those who were retained by Wells Fargo on several criteria. The laid-off workers tended to be better paid, older, and more educated than those not laid off. Almost two-fifths of the retained workers were paid $45,000 or less, while only one-fifth of the laid-off employees were in this salary range. Moreoever, 22.4 per cent of those who were laid off had some graduate-level education as compared to only 16.5 per cent of those who were retained.

Wave 2 Results

As noted above, in late October 1996 we mailed out a second survey to see whether laid-off workers had found new jobs, whether those retained by Wells Fargo were still employed, and what other career options the respondents might have chosen, such as starting a business, returning to school, or leaving the labour force.

At the beginning of our study, our subjects were relatively privileged in terms of their position in the labour market. Nearly half (46 per cent) had been retained by Wells Fargo, more than one-third (36 per cent) were now employed elsewhere, 7 per cent were unemployed, and 11 per cent had left the labour force.

Among currently employed respondents, approximately 55 per cent had experienced a salary increase ranging from 10 per cent to over 25 per cent. Eight per cent experienced a small decline in salary (up to 10 per cent) and 11 per cent experienced a greater decline (10 per cent or more).

Terminated FIB workers were eligible for a severance package of four weeks of separation pay for each year of service (plus health benefits up to a total of two years). Vice-presidents were guaranteed one year of severance pay, regardless of years of service, and senior vice-presidents two years. They could take the severance package as monthly salary or as a lump sum (Wells Fargo Company Separation Pay Plan, 1996). Those who took the salary-continuation plan also received health insurance and 401(k) benefits. Terminated workers who found a new job had to take a lump sum and pay a tax penalty. Those who quit voluntarily lost all rights to severance pay. Seventy-seven per cent of the respondents received a severance package. The packages ranged from less than one-half of former salary to more than 200 per cent of former salary.

Wave 2 Results by Age Cohort

To analyse whether age had an effect on subsequent employment and job security after the merger, we divided our subjects into three cohorts: under age 37; 37 to 44; and age 45 and older. Wave 2 results suggest that age did influence both the likelihood of being laid off and subsequent income and employment. Table 16.1 reports employment by age and compares the employment status of respondents still working for Wells Fargo with those who were laid off following the merger. Current Wells Fargo employees were evenly distributed among the three age cohorts. Among laid-off workers, however, the cohort of older workers was less likely to be currently employed than the two

TABLE 16.1
Employment Status after Merger by Age Cohort

	Under Age 37	Age 37–44	Over Age 44
Employed at Wells Fargo	44	47	45
Employed, not Wells Fargo	43	35	28
Unemployed	3	7	13
Not in labour force	9	11	14

cohorts of younger workers, more likely to be unemployed, and more likely to have left the labour force.

The attractiveness of leaving the labour force was influenced by what retirement benefits were available. The in-depth telephone interviews conducted with the former FIB employees provided data on the retirement benefits, employment plans, and experiences of both downsized workers and those who remained with Wells Fargo. Former FIB employees had a generous package of benefits, including two retirement plans. Employees with at least five years of service were eligible for a defined-benefit retirement plan based on age, average yearly salary, and years of service. Regular retirement began at age 65 and early retirement at 55. The early-retirement penalty was 68.5 per cent of the full benefit (First Interstate Bancorp, 1995).

FIB employees also were eligible to contribute to a defined contribution plan (401k-type) based on years of service and prior salary after they were employed for five years (First Interstate Bancorp Prospectus, 12 November 1993). In addition, on 1 July 1979, a defined-contribution plan, called the FirstMatch Long-Term Savings Plan, was introduced. All employees who had completed at least one year of service were eligible to contribute up to 16 per cent of salary to a maximum of $9,500 according to federal regulations. Six per cent of contributions were matched by First Interstate and 10 per cent were unmatched. The matched portion of the contribution included $1 of base pay contributed by the company for every $2 contributed by the worker.

The company's share of pension contributions was invested in First Interstate Bancorp common stock. Laid-off workers who were vested would receive two-thirds of a share of Wells Fargo stock for every share of First Interstate common stock owned, the same arrangement provided for all First Interstate shareholders. However, workers were not fully vested in the company's contributions to the plan until they had been contributing for a minimum of four years. Thus, any employee who had worked for FIB for less than four years lost a portion of the company's match, with the amount of loss decreasing for longer-tenured workers (First Interstate Bancorp Prospectus, 12 November 1993).

Because Wells Fargo had terminated its defined-benefit pension in 1984, laid-off FIB employees had the following retirement options. Those who had up to nine years of service when their severance payments ended could begin receiving a pension at age 65. Those with ten or more years of service could begin receiving a pension at age 55. However, the period in which they were receiving severance pay would not count towards years for service for the defined-benefit plan. Employees who were offered jobs with Wells Fargo received a lump sum that they could convert from FirstMatch to the Wells Fargo 401(k) plan (Wells Fargo Company Separation Pay Plan, 1996).

Although workers who were not offered jobs with Wells Fargo retained their eligibility for the First Interstate defined-benefit pension, they stood to lose the years of benefit accrual while they were receiving severance pay plus any additional years out of the labour market. Thus, for many older FIB employees, retirement was a more attractive option.

Two other factors may have encouraged older workers to leave the labour force. One was that older workers fared more poorly than younger workers in regard to salary. Among all workers who were currently employed, older workers were more likely to have a lower salary (in their new jobs) and less likely to receive a large salary increase, factors which increased the attractiveness of the retirement option.

Also influencing the labour-force decisions of older workers was the severance package. Older workers were the most likely of all age cohorts to receive a severance package. Further, as table 16.2 shows, their severance packages were significantly more generous than those of younger workers, no doubt because of their longer tenure at First Interstate as well as their higher salary levels and higher positions in their former jobs. Nearly 35 per cent of workers over age 45 received a severance package that was 200 per cent or more of their previous salary.

Thus, the combined incentives of relatively generous retirement benefits, little opportunity to accrue new benefits, a large severance

TABLE 16.2
Severance pay as a per cent of 1995 salary by age cohort

	Under Age 37	Age 37–44	Over Age 44
Over 200%	3.5	7.3	34.6
150–200%	3.5	15.6	14.9
100–150%	32.2	42.2	35.5
50–100%	31.0	19.3	7.5
Up to 50%	29.9	15.6	7.5

package, and poor prospects for jobs at salaries equal to previous levels drew older workers out of the labour force.

Wave 2 Results by Gender

In comparing the effect of job loss by gender, the data show that women fared more poorly than men on every indicator. Women who were no longer employed by Wells Fargo were less likely to have a new job and more likely to have left the labour force. Although differences in salary by gender were not substantial, women were less likely than men to experience a substantial salary increase (over 10 per cent) and more likely than men to experience a small (up to 10 per cent) salary decline. Finally, women were somewhat less likely than men to receive a severance package.

Discussion

It is evident that job loss and worker displacement are not evenly distributed across the labour force. Rather, older workers and women are at greater risk than younger men of income loss and downward mobility following a job loss due to downsizing. In particular, older workers' vulnerability to financial insecurity following a job loss is linked to a larger trend taking place in our postindustrial economy: the apparent erosion of lifetime job security. As Smith and Rubin (1997) point out, workers' assumptions of long-term employment relationships have been normative in most work arenas, whether they are based on implicit or explicit contracts between employers and employees. In fact, long-term employment relationships have been a mainstay of the U.S. economy, especially for high-skilled white-collar workers (Farber, 1993). The waves of massive layoffs in the white-collar sectors of our economy are one clue that the assumption of a lifetime employment relationship is becoming anachronistic (Smith and Rubin, 1997). This trend may be problematic for older workers who experience a job loss late in their careers.

There are several ways in which the financial security of older workers may be jeopardized by job loss. Older workers may conduct a prolonged job search and remain unemployed for several weeks or months. During the job search, they may be forced to deplete their savings to pay for basic living expenses for themselves and their families. When they find a new job, they may experience a loss in income and in job status that may affect their ability to save for their retirement. They may also have to purchase health insurance in the private market or lose access to health insurance entirely. Lack of health insurance may be financially devastating should they or a family member have a major health problem. All these factors can erode retirement savings and reduce income security in old age.

In addition to financial insecurity, older workers who are downsized may be at greater risk for emotional and mental stress. Older workers who, following a merger, decide to retire before the conventional age of retirement may experience emotional anxiety. The degree of choice an individual has, as well as the amount of preparation and planning, are important predictors of how individuals experience the process of retirement as well as their satisfaction with the outcome (Hardy and Quadagno, 1995). The life-course transition to retirement has a number of possible implications for downsized older workers. One factor to consider concerns the renegotiation of familial and marital roles when older men are pushed into early retirement (Cliff, 1993). Research indicates that there are usually issues regarding the renegotiation of the domestic division of labour among married older couples when husbands leave the labour force earlier than they anticipated.

Another aspect of older workers' experiences that has been given little attention in the literature is the nature of re-employment as a life-course transition. From this research, we can speculate that there may be both positive and negative aspects to career changes later in life. On the one hand, the stress associated with beginning a new career later in life may be difficult to handle for some older workers who do not gain employment in the same field in which they spent most of their employed lives. Learning the ins and outs of a new profession – or even just a new firm – may be frustrating or difficult for some older workers. On the other hand, older workers may find a career change to be a welcome challenge after decades spent working in the same industry or firm. Further research should investigate the intricacies, including positive and negative aspects, of re-employment as a life-course transition as well as its implications for family relationships and later-life satisfaction.

Regardless of gender, an individual's life-course pattern of labour-market participation has long-term consequences for income security in retirement in both public- and private-sector benefits, because pension systems reward people with stable work histories (Harrington Meyer, 1990). In the past, these eligibility rules have placed women at a considerable disadvantage. Because of their lack of sustained labour-force participation and location in the labour market, women have had fewer opportunities than men to become eligible for pensions and have received lower benefits than men (O'Rand and Henretta, 1982; Quadagno, 1988; Pavalko, Elder, and Clipp, 1993). Thus, women's patterns of labour-force participation have made them particularly vulnerable to financial insecurity in old age.

As women's patterns of labour-force participation are beginning to resemble men's, the gap in pension coverage, especially among younger men and women, has declined. Indeed, the majority of women who are well educated and well paid have private pension coverage, regardless of where they work. Ironically, the current wave of downsizings threatens the income security of women in retirement, since they appear to be more vulnerable to job loss and premature labour-force departure.

In this study, we found that, following the merger, women fared worse than men on every indicator. Not only were more women laid off than men, but the women in our sample were less likely to have found a new job and more likely than men to have experienced a small salary decline. Our findings also indicate that women were more likely to have left the labour force altogether following the merger. Thus, an important factor to consider is the interrelationship of work and family responsibilities for women.

Although women's and men's patterns of labour-force participation seem to be converging, it is important to consider the ways in which the institutions of family and work have failed to accommodate women's entrance into the public sphere. Indeed, women are still primarily responsible for child care and the maintenance of the family, and these responsibilities are now coupled with obligations to employers (Hochschild, 1989). Thus, women's struggles to balance responsibilities in the two spheres may influence their decision to leave the labour force altogether when facing a layoff. One factor not addressed in our study is whether the presence of dependent children in the home influences women's re-employment experiences as well as their decisions about whether to remain in the labour force. Smith and Rubin (1997) found that women in households with children under age 18 experience slower rates of re-employment than do other displaced workers. While the causal relationship regarding children and re-employment is somewhat ambiguous, it is clear that future analyses need to examine how the family sphere is affected by downsizing.

It is clear, however, that job losses resulting from downsizing influence both women and men in profound ways. Further research should examine the dynamics of work and family to tease out more closely how laid-off workers' families are affected by a job loss. Our findings concerning older workers suggest that more attention should be paid to the consequences of job loss later in life as well as to the nature of re-employment as a life-course transition.

REFERENCES

Bassett, W., Fleming, M., & Rodriguez, A. (1996). *How workers use 401(k) plans: The participation, contribution and withdrawal decisions.* Unpublished manuscript. Brown University and the Federal Reserve Bank of New York.

Blau, F.D., & Ferber, M.A. (1992). *The economics of women, men, and work.* New Jersey: Prentice Hall.

Budros, A. (1997). The new capitalism and organizational rationality: The adoption of downsizing programs, 1979–1994. *Social Forces, 76*(1), 229–50.

Clark, R. (1990). Income maintenance policies in the United States. In R. Binstock & L. George (Eds), *Handbook of aging and the social sciences* (pp 382–97). New York: Academic Press.

Cliff, D.R. (1993). Under the wife's feet: Renegotiating gender divisions in early retirement. *The Sociological Review, 41*, 30–53.

Farber, H. (1993). *The incidence and costs of job loss: 1982–91.* Washington, DC: Brookings Institution, Microeconomics Section.

Farber, H.S. (1995, January). *Are lifetime jobs disappearing? Job duration in the United States: 1973–1993* (Working Paper No. 341). Princeton University, Industrial Relations Section.

Farber, H.S. (1996, March). *The changing face of job loss in the United States, 1981–*

1993 (Working Paper No. 360). Princeton University, Industrial Relations Section.

First Interstate Bancorp. (1995). *A guide to your employee benefits at First Interstate Bancorp.* Los Angeles: Author.

First Interstate Bancorp Prospectus. (1993, November). *Employee savings plan of First Interstate Bancorp FirstMatch.* Los Angeles: Author.

Gordon, D. (1996). *Fat and mean: The corporate squeeze of working Americans and the myth of managerial downsizing.* New York: Free Press.

Hardy, M., Hazelrigg, L., & Quadagno, J. (1996). *Ending a career in the auto industry: Thirty and out.* New York: Plenum Publishers.

Hardy, M., & Quadagno, J. (1995). Satisfaction with early retirement: Making choices in the auto industry. *Journals of Gerontology: Social Sciences, 50,* S217–28.

Harrington Meyer, M. (1990). Family status and poverty among older women: The gendered distribution of retirement income in the United States. *Social Problems, 37*(4), 551–63.

Hochschild, A. (1989). *The second shift.* New York: Avon Books.

Holson, L. (1998, 13 April). Major mergers expected today in bank industry. *New York Times,* pp 1A, 24A.

Israel, D., & McConnell, G. (1991). New law protects older workers. *HR Magazine, XX,* 77–8.

Marks, M.L. (1994). *From turmoil to triumph: New life after mergers, acquisitions and downsizing.* New York: Lexington Books.

Mishkin, F.S. (1994). *The economics of money, banking, and financial markets.* Reading, MA: Addison-Wesley.

Moen, P. (1992). *Women's two roles.* Westport, CT: Auburn House.

Moen, P. (1996). Gender, age and the life course. In R. Binstock & L. George (Eds), *Handbook of aging and the social sciences* (pp 171–87). San Diego: Academic Press.

New York Times. (1996). *The downsizing of America.* New York: Random House.

Newman, K. (1988). *Falling from grace: The experience of downward mobility in the American middle class.* New York: Random House.

O'Rand, A., & Henretta, J. (1982). Delayed career entry, industrial pension structure and early retirement in a cohort of unmarried women. *American Sociological Review, 47,* 365–73.

Pavalko, E., Elder, G., Jr, & Clipp, E. (1993, December). Worklives and longevity: Insights from a life course perspective. *Journal of Health and Social Behavior, 34,* 363–80.

Press Release. (1996, 24 January). *Wells Fargo and First Interstate to merge.*

Press Release. (1996, 1 April). *Wells Fargo completes acquisition of First Interstate Bancorp.*

Quadagno, J. (1988). Women's access to pensions and the structure of eligibility rules: Systems of production and reproduction. *Sociological Quarterly, 29,* 541–58.

Rich, B.L. (1995). Explaining feminization in the U.S. banking industry, 1940–1980: Human capital, dual labour markets, or gender queuing? *Sociological Perspectives, 38,* 357–80.

Salisbury, D. (1993). Policy implications of changes in employer benefit protection. In R. Burkhauser & D. Salisbury (Eds), *Pensions in a changing economy* (pp 41–58). Washington, DC: National Academy on Aging.

Shaw, K. (1994). The persistence of the female labour supply. *The Journal of Human Resources, 29,* 348–78.

Smith, B.T., & Rubin, B.A. (1997). From displacement to reemployment: Job acquisition in the flexible economy. *Social Science Research, 26,* 292–308.

U.S. Bureau of Labor Statistics. (1995). *Employment, hours and earnings.* Washington, DC: Government Printing Office.

Uzzi, B., & Barsness, Z. (1998). Contingent employment in British establishments: Organizational determinants of the use of fixed-term hires and part-time workers. *Social Forces, 76*(3), 967–1007.

Wells Fargo Company Separation Pay Plan. (1996, 14 March). *1996 benefits book.*

Zey, M. (1993). *Banking on fraud.* New York: Aldine deGruyter.

17. Generational and Life-course Patterns of Occupational Retrenchment and Retirement of South African Migrant Labourers

Robin L. Oakley

It is widely argued (Bengtson, 1989; Elder, 1997; Marshall, 1983) that a desirable feature of the life-course approach to theorizing is its reminder that the broad socio-economic environment is important to consider in relation to individual experiences. In practice, however, social and economic structures operating through time are rarely brought into life-course analyses. In this chapter I demonstrate the significance of a political-economic approach to life-course analysis through an examination of the impacts of participation in wage labour in a rural South African community. Specifically, the chapter compares the ways that oscillating wage labour has differentially shaped the life courses of four different cohorts of workers by altering certain normative trajectories across the life course. Further, it is argued that, over the past twenty-five years, unemployment and retrenchments in the mining industry have once again shifted the timing and sequence of normative trajectories. Both of these changes hinge upon varying levels of economic dependency: on the one hand, the economic dependency of the rural 'coloured' reserves[1] on the activities of the several large corporate mining companies in the region, and on the other hand, the corporate dependence upon the boom and bust of the world mineral market. In addition, the differential impact of an oscillating regional and national economy between men and women will be promulgated.

The Namaqualand Reserves: Brief Historical Background

Namaqualand is a semi-desert region located in the north-west of

South Africa in the Northern Cape Province. There are seven former 'coloured' reserves in the region, of which Steinkopf, the focus community, is the largest. The coloured reserves were set aside for the sole occupation of people classified as 'coloured' (see note 1, and also Boonzaier, 1980; Carstens, 1966; Klinghardt, 1982; Sharp, 1977; Halford, 1949). The Namaqualand reserves share economic and social similarities with industry-dependent towns found in the eastern provinces of Canada, or with the textile towns of New England in the United States. The relatively homogeneous ethnic composition, the economic dependency on institutions located outside of the community, and the ensuing social marginalization are a few of the most striking characteristics (see, for example, Cohen, 1975). As the contributions to this volume reinforce, the local effects of the global economy in work restructuring across the life course may reveal shared qualitative patterns of work entry and exit between geographically disparate but politically economic similar contexts.

Mineral Wealth and the Decline of Farming

In the latter part of the nineteenth century, Steinkopf produced a considerable agricultural surplus and people were able to re-invest it (Carstens, 1983). The high productivity enabled local farmers to resist white farmers' demands for cheap labour between 1870 and 1913 (Stitcher, 1985, pp 31–2; Browett, 1982, pp 12–13; Bundy, 1979; 1971–2). Yet, as with the majority of non-white South Africans, this relative economic florescence and self-sufficiency could not withstand the pressures of the combined effects of mineral discovery, imposed taxation (Surplus People Project, 1995, p. 11; Lemon, 1982, p. 32), and state initiatives designed to favour white over non-white farmers.

In 1850, copper, and in the 1920s, diamonds, were exploited by South African and foreign companies in Namaqualand. These companies came to rely on the rural coloured reserves to supply steady and cheap labour. The mines provided jobs to people in Namaqualand until closures after the First World War and then again in 1937 when O'okiep Copper Company replaced the Cape Copper Company (West, 1987). Declining world copper prices in the 1980s initiated a pattern of retrenchments and unemployment (Sharp and West, 1984, pp 10–15). The discovery of diamonds along the north-west coast in the 1920s further contributed to the economic dependence of the reserves. As the demand for cash increased, more and more people seeking work, both women and men, migrated temporarily to one of the regional copper or diamond mining towns, such as O'okiep, Nababeep, Alexander Bay, or Kleinzee. Migrant labour, in this case, is not the same as that for most black South Africans who historically found themselves thousands of kilometres away from their birth communities for years at a time (see Møller, 1988). For Steinkopf, migrants live in the mines for weeks or months at a time and return home frequently for visits. The gendered division of labour involves women typically employed as domestic servants and in the service sector, and men in both unskilled and skilled labour in the mining sector. Since men are formally employed, they enjoy a full range of company benefits that women, whose employment is informal, do not. These gendered patterns persist, and the wage differential in 1994–6, for example, was R 500 (CAD 230) for women versus R 1, 500 (CAD 700) for men. In the remainder of the chapter, I suggest ways that the economic dependency and wage work in the mines affected the normative life-course trajectories of four different cohorts.

Methods

The data were collected from 1994 to 1996 in Steinkopf (Oakley, 1999).[2] Research techniques included interviews and questionnaires which were incorporated into the ethnographic method of participant observation. Interviews were supplemented with a random sample of fifty-four households. The sample is compared with random household samples collected by Carstens in 1955–6 (1966) to provide a sketch of economic transformations as experienced in the household over the past fifty years. I should, however, point out that, because the data are from two different periods and were collected by two different researchers, the sample comparisons merely indicate, rather than confirm, economic change.

Economic Dependence

In comparing the household samples from the two time periods (see table 17.1), the most striking aspect to emerge is the transformation of the economic base from an agricultural to a market economy. Recall that, at the turn of the century, Steinkopf was a semi-subsistence, agriculture-based peasant community. By 1956–7, however, only 21.9 per cent of households depended on farming alone, and by 1996 there

TABLE 17.1[1]
Economic Change as Reflected in Households, 1956–7 and 1996

	1956–7 Number	%	1996 Number	%
Some stake in migratory labour	55	70.5	37	68.5
Dependent on farming alone	17	21.9	0	0
Some stake in farming	61	78.2	19	35.18

were no households which could rely on farming alone for subsistence. Households which had, on the other hand, *some* stake in farming, were 78.2 per cent in 1956–7, and had decreased significantly to 35.18 per cent in 1996.

It should also be pointed out that the population almost doubled between 1956–7 and 1994–6, from 4,000 to 7,570.[3] Along with this were ecological changes such as soil erosion and overgrazing which further reduced the viability of farming.

By the mid-twentieth century, Carstens reported that most families had at least one migrant labourer and that this was necessary to augment farming production (1966, p. 6). Interestingly, households which have some stake in migratory labour have remained relatively consistent, from 1956–7 at 70.5 per cent, to 1987 at 78.9 per cent and 1996 at 68.5 per cent. The decrease in the 1996 figure may be attributed to increases in unemployment and retrenchments.

Economic Impact of Migrant Labour on the Life Course of Different Cohorts

Arranging data into single- or multiple-year cohorts is an arbitrary method (Marshall, 1983) of organizing people by relative birth years. For the purposes of this chapter, however, the data were organized into four twenty-year cohort clusters (see table 17.2). This was determined as the optimal method of capturing historical depth and changes in the life course in response to corporate growth and decline. Predictably, as the cohorts were clustered, certain unique characteristics of each cluster emerged in a pattern in which cohorts 'cast shadows' onto previous and subsequent cohorts (Hardy and Waite, 1997, p. 7).

In this case, then, cohort organization is semi-arbitrary, as the demarcation of cohorts is defined not only by birth year but also by the objective conditions set by corporate policy. Hence, following Marshall's

TABLE 17.2
Entry, Exit, and Mean Duration of Career in Diamond Mines

Cohort birth years	1910–29	1930–49	1950–69	1970–96
Cohort size[2]	1537	2222	2801	1706
Entry into work	1930–40	1950–60	1970–90	1990+
Exit from work	1970–80	1980–90	1980–2000	1990–2000
Mean duration of work career	30–40 years	30 years	10–20 years	<10 years

[1]1956–7 samples are derived from Carstens (1966, p. 64) and are based on a sample of seventy-eight households. 1996 figures were collected by the author and are based on a random sample of fifty-four households.
[2]These birth statistics were collected from the baptismal register of the Uniting Reformed Church of Steinkopf. The sample does not represent the actual number of births, but is the most accurate historical record available.

(1983) reformulation of Mannheim's analysis of the qualitative characteristics of age organization (1952), as I have argued elsewhere, some of the single-year cohort groups may be considered a generation in terms of shared, concrete social experiences (Oakley, 1999; 1998b). Let us now turn to an examination of the four cohort clusters.

The birth cohorts in table 17.2 demonstrate the differences between birth years and their entry, exit, and duration of career in the formal diamond-mining labour force in Steinkopf from the turn of the century. The most significant finding involves the duration of years in the formal work force, which declines for those born after 1950.

Cohort A: 1910–29

Although they worked for extremely low wages, these workers were employed in the formal work force the longest of all cohorts (up to forty years). Moreover, the wages were enough to sustain relatively large households back in the reserve. During this time, most households still derived primary subsistence from farming.

Being away from the community, however, meant that people had to juggle their time and efforts between the formal sector and farming. Women became de-facto heads of households, and those who migrated for work found the only occupation open to them was in domestic service for white, often foreign, employers. The experience of both men and women in Cohort A was altered by postponing marriage and thereby having children in their mid-thirties instead of their late teens and early twenties.

Unlike succeeding cohorts, Cohort A was not provided with private retirement pensions, and the early living and work conditions were inferior. One elderly informant's comments characterize these conditions: 'When we first worked in the mines us coloured people lived behind the bushes. There were no houses for us.' Yet, while neither sex enjoyed the benefit of a company pension, both were provided with a state pension, and, more significantly, many were able to re-assume farming on the reserve after retirement from wage work. For this cohort then, the experience of retirement was blurred, since they had continued farming while employed in wage work. Overgrazing and soil erosion has largely curtailed farming activities for subsequent retiree cohorts. In short, the normative life-course trajectories of these workers was altered by participation in a wage economy and the emerging trajectories of their lives became a blueprint for subsequent cohorts.

Cohort B: 1930–49

These workers, born between 1930 and 1949, commenced their work careers in the mines after the 1950s. It was during this period that conditions improved significantly for coloured workers in terms of range of employment opportunity, training, and work and retirement benefits. As the mining towns grew and shops and services emerged, women began to move out of the domestic sphere and into the service sector. This work, while no higher in status, did offer company wages, benefits, and, later, retirement pensions. Numerous private pension schemes were introduced in the 1970s. While reaping the benefits from private pensions, fewer in this cohort were able to farm while doing wage work, or to take up farming after formal retirement. In the development of a capitalist-type economy in the reserve, they were the first (and arguably the last) to experience adult life as a 'work life' and simultaneously to experience retirement as the institutionalization of old age as a structurally distinct stage of life (see Kohli, 1988, pp. 367 and 373).

Cohort C: 1950–69

The cohort most adversely affected by changes in the world market are those who were born between 1950 and 1969 and who started working in the mines between 1970 and 1990, that is, people now between 25 and 45 years of age (Emmett, 1987, p. 69). Throughout the 1980s, retrenchments in the copper and the diamond industries were unleashed as a result of a decrease in world market demand. In 1975, world copper prices plummeted, workers were retrenched three times between 1979 and 1985, and the overall work force shrank by 23.5 per cent (Marais, 1987, p. 12). At the same time, some diamond companies were aiming to reduce operating costs and long-term capital expenditure in response to low prices and reduced sales resulting from large diamond stockpiles. The workers born after 1950 suffered several periods of retrenchment and, consequently, persistent economic instability across the life course.

In 1992 the publication of a two-volume report forecast the impact that regional mine closures would have on Namaqualand (Brownlie, 1992). It was noted, for example, that 59 per cent of households in these reserves could expect to have one retrenched employee from the diamond mines (Brownlie, 1992, p. 58). Various early-retirement packages were offered to decrease the scale of the retrenchments that were scheduled to take place in the year 2000. While the report cautioned that 'care should be taken in providing lump-sum payments as these may be squandered through ill-advised investments' (Brownlie, 1992, p. 113), workers consistently accepted large sums in retrenchment packages designed to induce early retirement. Indeed, most workers opted for these lump-sum payments because the money afforded the opportunity to build a home, although the recipients were subsequently left without savings or income. It has also been noted that numerous black workers take early-retirement lump-sum payments because they do not believe that they will live to the pension age (Møller, 1988).

Predictably, the social effects of the retrenchments on Cohort C are adverse. The people in this cohort have experienced occupational instability across the life course, with multiple periods of unemployment. As among the majority of black South Africans, this cohort can rely neither on employment in the mines nor on farming to supplement their lost wages, as the previous cohorts did (see Møller, 1988). They are too young to receive a retirement pension and, for those in their forties, are considered too old to be retrained for alternative employment.

Cohort D: 1970–90+

The current young cohort, born after 1970, who started working in the late eighties and early nineties, are aware that they will have a short career in the regional mining economy. Like Cohort C, they have already experienced retrenchments and periods of unemployment. In this cohort, the 'normal' exit time from their careers has become erratic and unpredictable. It may be the beginning of a social redefinition of 'appropriate' age boundaries or a de-institutionalization of the 'normative' age boundaries developed during the transition to a market/work economy, as Kohli and Rein have noted for the western countries (1991, p. 27).

At the same time, however, there is an emerging pattern of urbanization as people transform from semi-migrants into full migrants. In sharp contrast to past cohorts, therefore, many in Cohort D do not consider the local mines to be among their range of employment options and instead seek jobs farther afield in major cities such as Cape Town (554 km), Uppington (399 km), or Johannesburg (1,274 km). Marriage and childbearing plans are often postponed until some measure of economic security is secured. Farming, moreover, is not an option.

Longer periods of migration to more distant work locations will have significant economic and social implications for Steinkopf. Previous research on North American First Nations reserves suggests that migrants often never return to their birth communities for good, and that those who do may experience lasting difficulties in reintegrating into the community (Weibel-Orlando, 1988, pp 332 and 340). It has been argued, moreover, that the remittances so important to birth economies (and as symbols of enduring social relationships) tend to decrease and eventually cease altogether when migrants are far away for years at a time (see Philpott, 1968).

Moreover, because workers live and work on their employer's property (especially farms) until old age, it has been shown that they have no savings or family or community links to draw on when they become too old to work and are no longer permitted to live on the employer's property (Oakley, 1998a). Their period of 'retirement' is ushered in with physical decline rather than choice, and many such individuals, regardless of their age, find themselves poor, homeless, and still waiting for another chance to work.

Alternative local or regional employment is scarce. The days of the workers in Cohorts C and D, particularly those born after 1970 and still in their relative youth, are long and uneventful. Alcoholism, drug abuse, and domestic disputes, including wife battering, have become prevalent. Drinking among women is severely socially sanctioned and therefore rare; female alcoholics lose more status than their male counterparts. Yet as de-facto heads of their households, women suffer tremendous consequences as a result of male alcoholism. They note that wages are squandered, men do not contribute to the household chores, and women find themselves doing three jobs at once: informal sector wage work, household head, and garden labour as a subsistence supplement.

A final pattern in Steinkopf is that people, and entire households in Cohorts C and D, are supported by the small state pensions of individuals in Cohort A or the company pensions of Cohort B. The emerging pattern of economic dependence on the pensions of the elderly in South Africa (see Møller and Sotshongaye, 1996) has been identified in the developed world as well (Albert and Cattell, 1994, p. 117). This shift in generational exchange around the globe is related to changes in the nature of the job, as well as to unemployment, retrenchments, and early retirement. It is part of larger economic and social transformations which mean, increasingly, that adult life can no longer be considered, a priori, work life, and that the life course no longer a predictable sequence of trajectories (Kohli, 1988; Kohli et al., 1991).

Conclusion

As the above analysis of four cohort clusters demonstrates, employing a political-economic lens in conjunction with a life-course approach reveals striking qualitative changes across the life course, thereby revealing the dynamics of an otherwise elusive dialectic. It becomes apparent, moreover, that significant *generational* effects are pervasive, particularly in relation to the inherent social pathologies of an oscillating political economy.

I suggested that the corporate demand for labour has differentially affected the life course of four cohorts of workers in a South African community by producing qualitative, or generational, effects. The cohort born at the turn of the century, for example, had to postpone marriage and childbearing plans, and often sacrificed their contributions to a cyclical, agriculture-based economy to the demands of a 'boom-and-bust' wage-based one. They were, however, still able to eke out a living through agricultural pursuits and continued to rely on agriculture after retirement from wage work. Subsequent cohorts, however, became completely dependent upon wages for economic survival, and therefore were at the mercy of changes in the world mineral market. The process over the course of a century has been one of transformation from peasants into industry-dependent proletarians. Population increase, overgrazing, and soil erosion have exacerbated this dependency on wages. Yet, the life of the mines is limited, and retrenchments, unemployment, and early retirement mean that younger cohorts who cannot turn to farming have had to lengthen their period of employment migration. So far, their adult life has been one of employment instability. As this instability continues to imprint itself on the life course, the human response in Steinkopf is being dialectically transmitted and reworked by subsequent cohorts.

This dialectical nature of social change, and of generational conflict as a specific but problematic locus of change, has been widely alluded to (Bengtson, 1989; Hardy and Waite, 1997; Mannheim, 1952). I have suggested in this chapter that the 'problem of generations' (Mannheim, 1952), understood as the root of the dynamics and dialectics of social change, is fruitfully revealed through utilizing the life-course approach in conjunction with a political-economic analysis. This approach, which employs cohort analysis to reveal the effects of a boom-and-bust political-economic context, opens the way to appreciating significant qualitative (generational) changes. This, in turn, leads to an understanding of the differences between groups and individuals in relation to the larger generational unit, thereby linking social, biographical, and historical time (Hagestad, 1991, p. 23) in a concrete and methodologically rigorous manner. The dialectic of change, between the political-economic structure and the qualitative responses of different generations, consists not only of the imprints of these macro structures on lives, but also of the imprints of changing lives on the political-economic, social, and semantic structures themselves.

NOTES

1 In this chapter, as I refer to certain people as 'coloured,' I wish to emphasize that it was the term employed by the South African state under the 1950 Population Registration Act. In addition to so-called coloured people during the apartheid era, there were 'Africans,' 'Indians,' and 'whites.' While the terms are no longer jurally acceptable, they continue to be valid in an economic and sociological sense.

2 The research was conducted as part of doctoral research on the anthropology of aging and the life course.

3 The 1956–7 population is derived from Carstens (1996). The 1994–6 figures are derived from the Namaqualand Regional Services Council.

REFERENCES

Albert, S.M., & Cattell, M. (1994). *Old age in global perspective: Cross-cultural and cross-national views*. Toronto: Maxwell Macmillan International.

Bengtson, V. (1989). The problem of generations: Age group contrasts, continuities, and social change. In V.L. Bengtson & K.W. Schaie (Eds), *The course of later life: Research and reflections* (pp 25–54). New York: Springer.

Boonzaier, E.A. (1980). *Social differentiation in the Richtersveld, a Namaqualand rural area*. Unpublished master's thesis, University of Cape Town, South Africa.

Browett, J. (1982). The evolution of unequal development in South Africa: An overview. In D.M. Smith (Ed.), *Living under apartheid* (pp 10–23). London: George Allen and Unwin.

Brownlie, S.F. (1992). *Closure of de Beers diamond mines in Namaqualand: A socioeconomic impact assessment*. Cape Town: University of Cape Town, Environmental Evaluation Unit.

Bundy, C. (1971–2). *The response of African peasants in the Cape to economic changes 1870–1910: A study of growth and decay* (Societies of Southern Africa in the 19th and 20th Centuries, Vol. 3, Collected Seminar Papers 16). University of London: Institute of Commonwealth Studies.

Bundy, C. (1979). *The rise and fall of the South African peasantry*. Berkeley: University of California Press.

Carstens, P. (1966). *The social structure of a Cape coloured reserve: A study of racial integration and segregation in South Africa*. Cape Town: Oxford University Press.

Carstens, P. (1983). Opting out of colonial rule: The brown Voortrekkers and their constitutions, Part One. *African Studies Journal*, 42(2), 19–30.

Cohen, A.P. (1975). The definition of public identity: Managing marginality in outport Newfoundland following Confederation. *The Sociological Review, 25*, 93–119.

Elder, G., Jr. (1997). The life course and human development. In W. Damon (Series Ed.) & R.M. Lerner (Vol. Ed.), *Handbook of child psychology, vol. 1: Theoretical models of human development* (pp 939–91). New York: Wiley.

Emmett, A.B. (1987). *Steinkopf: A community in decline*. Pretoria: Human Sciences Research Council.

Hagestad, G. (1991). Trends and dilemmas in life course research: An international perspective. In *Status passages and the life course* (pp 23–57). Weinheim: Deutscher Verlag.

Halford, S.J. (1949). *The Griquas of Griqualand*. Cape Town: Juta.

Hardy, M., & Waite, L. (1997). Doing time: Reconciling biography with history in the study of social change. In M. Hardy (Ed.), *Studying aging and social change* (pp 66–92). Thousand Oaks, CA: Sage.

Klinghardt, G. (1982). *Social differentiation and local government in Pella, a rural coloured area in great Bushmanland.* Unpublished master's thesis, University of Cape Town, South Africa.

Kohli, M. (1988). Ageing as a challenge for sociological theory. *Ageing and Society, 8,* 367–94.

Kohli, M., & Rein, M. (1991). The changing balance of work and retirement. In M. Kohli, M. Rein, A.-M. Guillemard, & H. Van Gunsteren (Eds), *Time for retirement: Comparative studies of early exit from the labour force* (pp 1–35). Cambridge: Cambridge University Press.

Kohli, M., Rein, M., Guillemard, A.-M., & Van Gunsteren, H. (Eds). (1991). *Time for retirement: Comparative studies of early exit from the labour force.* Cambridge: Cambridge University Press.

Lemon, A. (1982). Migrant labour and frontier commuters: Reorganizing South Africa's black labour supply. In D.M. Smith (Ed.), *Living under apartheid* (pp. 64–89). London: George Allen and Unwin.

Mannheim, K. (1952). The problem of generations. In P. Kecskemeti (Ed.), *Essays in the sociology of knowledge* (pp 276–322). Boston: Routledge and Kegan Paul.

Marais, J. (1987). *O'okiep Copper Company Ltd. 1937–1987.* O'okiep: O'okiep Copper Company Ltd.

Marshall, V. (1983). Generations, age groups and cohorts: Conceptual distinctions. *Canadian Journal on Aging, 2*(2), 51–62.

Møller, V. (1988). Black South African perception of financial security and retirement. In S. Bergman, G. Naegele, & W. Tokarski (Eds), *Early retirement, approaches and variations: International perspectives* (Brookdale Monograph Series, pp 123–36). Brookdale: JDC Brookdale Institute of Gerontology and Adult Human Development.

Møller, V., & Sotshongaye, A. (1996). 'My family eat this money too': Pension sharing and self-respect among Zulu grandmothers. *Southern African Journal of Gerontology, 5*(2), 9–19.

Oakley, R. (1998a). Local effects of 'new' social welfare policy in a South African coloured community. *Southern African Journal of Gerontology, 7*(1), 15–20.

Oakley, R. (1998b, October). *A dialectical understanding of the life course: Generation and cohort in South Africa.* Paper presented at the Annual Meetings of the Canadian Association on Gerontology, Halifax, Nova Scotia.

Oakley, R. (1999). *Aging and the life course in Steinkopf, a rural South African community.* Unpublished doctoral thesis, University of Toronto, Canada.

Philpott, S. (1968). Remittances, obligations, social networks, and choice among Montserratian migrants in Britain. *Man, 3*, 465–76.

Sharp, J. (1977). *Community and boundaries: An inquiry into the institution of citizenship in two Cape coloured reserves.* Unpublished doctoral dissertation, University of Cape Town, South Africa.

Sharp, J., & West, M. (1984, April). *Controls and constraints: Land, labour and mobility in Namaqualand* (Conference Paper No. 71). Paper presented at the Second Carnegie Inquiry into Poverty and Development in Southern Africa, Cape Town, South Africa.

Stitcher, S. (1985). *Migrant labourers.* Cambridge: Cambridge University Press.

Surplus People Project. (1995). *Land claims in Namaqualand.* Athlone: Author.

Weibel-Orlando, J. (1988). Indians, ethnicity as a resource and aging: You can go home again. *Journal of Cross Cultural Gerontology, 3*, 323–48.

West, M. (1987). *Apartheid in a South African town, 1968–1985.* Berkeley, CA: Institute of International Studies.

18. Changing Working Patterns and the Public–Private Mix in Old-age Security: The Example of Germany*

Winfried Schmähl

Germany's social security system in general as well as its provisions related to old age are based to a high degree on income from work, mainly from employment (see Schmähl 1999). This type of social security arrangement is affected and challenged by many structural changes in economy, demography, and society that have consequences also for working life. Proposals have been and are still being debated for redesigning the scope and structure of social security to enable it to cope with existing or potential financing problems arising from the challenges noted above. After the collapse of former socialist economies and their integration into the world economy, discussion intensified worldwide about the proper role of the state in general, but also especially in old-age security (World Bank, 1997) and led to proposals and measures for changing the public–private mix in this area. There are strong demands for reducing state-organized social security and for increasing the privately organized part of social security arrangements. Many now believe that the state should become more a regulator and less a provider of pensions. This debate is also taking place in Germany. One of the main motives for seeking such change is to improve the international competitiveness of firms by reducing labour costs.

Changes in working patterns, labour costs, and social security arrangements result not only from political decisions but also from collective agreements and from (individual) decisions of firms (employers) and employees. Such changes include increased use of flexible

---

*In terms of legislation, this paper is based on rules in force at the beginning of 2000.

working hours and alterations in the pattern of labour-force participation among the elderly. For example, early retirement has become 'normal,' in large part as a result of incentives by public pension schemes (see Börsch-Supan and Schnabel, 1998; Schmähl et al., 1996; Viebrok, 1997; OECD, 1995a and 1995b; and Gruber and Wise, 1998, for international comparisons).

Public and private activities promoting and resulting in early exit from the (official) labour force are leading to financing problems in public pension schemes and to demands for downsizing these schemes. On the other hand, the demand is growing for supplementary (private) pension arrangements to ensure adequate pensions for the elderly in the future.

There is also an increase in the number of people not covered by public social security arrangements, in part because both firms and individuals are seeking to avoid social security contribution payments. This represents a challenge for social insurance financed by the pay-as-you-go plan and has stimulated once again proposals for disentangling employment (work contracts) and public social security (Schmähl, 1993).

There exists a complex interaction between work and social security in Germany. Some important elements are discussed in this paper, with particular focus on different types of work, structural changes in working patterns, and the link between work and old-age security, which is the most important branch of social protection in Germany. The paper starts with a short description of how different types of workers are covered by social security in Germany. It then outlines several ways in which structural changes are affecting patterns of work and the possible consequences for old-age security. Next, various changes in social security protection introduced mainly in the 1990s are discussed, with particular focus on their (potential) effects on the public–private pension mix. Finally, I discuss how reforms to the public old-age protection scheme and the possibility of increased privatization of pension arrangements are linked to the role of capital funding and to debates about the future role of employment and work as the basis for social security.

The Structure of Old-age Security in Germany and Some Developments at the End of the Twentieth Century

Germany's pension system – developed over the course of more than 100 years – is very complex. There is no uniform or universal type of pension, but the majority of the population are members of different mandatory schemes for specific categories of gainful employment. The core element in pension protection for most of the blue- and white-collar workers in the private and public sectors is the social insurance pension. This is also quantitatively by far the most important pension scheme: pension benefits are more than 10 per cent of GDP and about 70 per cent of all expenditure on old-age security (Schmähl, 1998a, pp 249–51).

Social insurance also covers some groups of self-employed persons, but there also exist special schemes for some other groups of the self-employed, such as farmers and professionals (e.g., doctors, lawyers). A specific pension scheme for civil servants exists, too. Together, these schemes build the first tier and the base of old-age security for these groups. For pensioners with low income, there is means-tested social assistance, which is separate from social insurance. However, only about 2 per cent of all pensioners take up social-assistance benefits to finance their daily living.

The second tier consists of supplementary occupational pension schemes. In principle, white-collar and blue-collar workers in the public sector are all covered by schemes based on collective agreements, while in the private sector different types of voluntary occupational pension schemes exist. These cover only about half of private-sector employees. Coverage is highly unequal, depending on industry, company size, and, in part, the sex of employees (Schmähl, 1997). As the third tier, there are several types of additional private provision for old age, such as life insurance, partly encouraged by tax incentives.

There are considerable differences between East and West Germany in occupational pension coverage and life insurance, resulting from the fact that in the former socialist German Democratic Republic old-age protection was nearly complete from state schemes. The differences between East and West Germany in the public–private mix will remain for some time.

In the 1990s, several changes in social insurance as well as in the pension scheme for civil servants were made which reduce the pension level for present and future pensioners (Schmähl, 1998a). There is a corresponding decline in coverage and in the generosity of occupational pensions in the private sector, with those who take up new jobs being particularly affected.

These downward trends and a loss of trust in the sustainability of public pensions have stimulated both public debate and increased competition among banks and life-insurance companies for a share of the emerging market for private old-age coverage.

Financing and Calculating Social Insurance Pensions and Analysing Their Link to Work

A look at mandatory social insurance reveals some interesting features of its link to and effects on employment (Schmähl, 1989). The individual contribution payment is based on individual gross earnings up to a ceiling of about 180–190 per cent of average gross earnings, only, however, if the individual gross earnings do not fall below a lower limit, which is about 14 per cent of average gross earnings. Contributions are paid half by employees and half by employers (Schmähl, 1998c). Employers' contributions are part of the labour costs. Therefore, all other things being equal (and not taking shifting of the contribution burden into consideration), labour costs for employees with earnings below the threshold for paying the obligatory contribution are relatively lower than for employees with higher earnings. This is an incentive for employers to offer lower-paying jobs. For such employees, all other things being equal, take-home pay is relatively higher than if they earned more than the threshold amount.

After the parliamentary election in September 1998, a new coalition government enacted some changes (e.g., by making these earnings in part contributory). These changes, not discussed here in detail, still lack a clear conceptual base.

In an effort to reduce the high labour costs which hamper their competitiveness, many firms now 'outsource' jobs, leading to the growth of new types of self-employment that are not covered by social insurance. The new German government therefore decided to include in social security members of the 'new self-employed' who perform work similar to that of conventional employees. The new rules are very complicated and, only a few months after being brought in, have already been changed.

Earnings from gainful employment are the most important base for the accumulation of pension claims in social insurance. Pension claims depend on the number of years of insurance and the (relative) amount of earnings of all the years of gainful employment that was covered. Besides pension claims based on covered employment, there are other activities that produce pension claims, among them child care, periods of (registered) unemployment, caring for frail (mostly elderly) people, and (some) years of schooling. In the case of unemployment, the unemployment agency pays the contribution to the pension scheme, as do long-term-care insurance funds for caregivers. From 1999 contribution payments from the federal budget will be made for pension claims by those caring for children.

Changing Working Patterns and Some Consequences, Especially for the Financial Base of Social Insurance

There was considerable concern in Germany in the nineties that changes in the structure of gainful employment, in labour-force partic-ipation, and in working-time arrangements would undermine the financial underpinnings of social insurance and thus leave many indi-viduals with inadequate pension protection in their old age.

For discussion purposes this concern can be divided into three sub-topics: 1) the impact of a decrease in the absolute and relative number of contributors compared to the number of beneficiaries because of the decreasing number of people of working age, the increasing number of low-paid jobs below the contribution threshold, high unemployment, early retirement, and reductions in the types of employment covered under the plan (the result of changes in technology and labour organi-zation, the growth of contract work, new types of self-employment, and so on); 2) the impact of a relative decline in the *share of contributory gross earnings* in national income; 3) an important *longitudinal* aspect – namely, the need to develop new ways in which people can accumu-late adequate pension claims during their working life.

The discussion that follows will examine these three aspects in turn.

Types of Work and Social Security

The type of working activity affects social security schemes as well as individual social security benefits. To understand this interaction, it is useful to start with a typology of different types of work and their rela-tionship to social insurance in Germany (see figure 18.1). As men-tioned above, because of new rules for jobs with low earnings or some new types of self-employment, this relationship can change over time.

With respect to gainful employment, it is important to determine whether these activities are in the official economy or the shadow economy, whether shadow activities are growing, and whether they are a substitute for or only a supplement to official gainful employ-ment. (Interactions of shadow activities and social security are dis-cussed in Schmähl, 1986.) At present, however, we lack sufficient data to answer these questions.

For all types of gainful employment in the official economy, the key

Figure 18.1 Types of Work and Coverage by Social Insurance

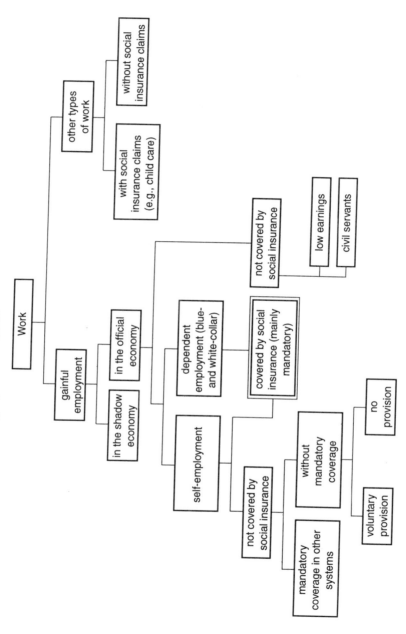

issue is whether they are covered mandatorily, either by social insurance or by other schemes, and, if not, whether adequate voluntary provision has been made.

As the discussion about so-called spurious self-employment (Scheinselbständigkeit) underlines, the distinction between dependent employment and self-employment is becoming increasingly blurred. This new kind of self-employment is an instrument used by firms to externalize risks and costs and increase their flexibility and ability to respond to emerging changes in the demand for goods and services. Although there are insufficient statistical data, there are indications that these activities are remarkably extensive. However, estimates of the number of 'self-employed' who in fact depend on an employer vary a lot, from 200,000 to 900,000.

The estimates for the number of jobs with wages below the lower limit for social insurance coverage also vary considerably, from 1.5 million to about 5 million. Such jobs may be either the sole source of income for an individual or may be held in addition to regular employment covered by social insurance. Many of those in this form of employment do have coverage for social health insurance through a spouse, but they do not accumulate claims in pension or unemployment insurance.

It is clear that, from a social-policy point of view, the shift from dependent work to some sort of self-employment may have more negative implications for old-age income security than does the growth of the number of low-paid jobs below the contribution threshold.

To cope with the problem of spurious self-employment, the new German government decided to include some groups in social insurance if specific conditions are met. However, people can be very creative in inventing new strategies to evade the new rules. In my view, it would be preferable to have a clear general rule – namely, mandatory inclusion of all gainfully employed people in social insurance except for those who are covered by another mandatory scheme (such as farmers or professionals). To ensure that the requirement does not disadvantage those starting self-employment, special rules might allow contributions to be phased in over time, or a limit might be set to the required amount of pension claims. Inclusion of, especially, those in new types of self-employment would not only broaden the financing base for social insurance, but, more importantly in my view, would help to reduce the numbers of people living in poverty or subsisting on very low income in old age.

The proposal to include all gainfully employed people in a mandatory scheme is not new. When the framework for a social insurance system was being established in Germany in the late nineteenth century, for example, the economist Adolph Wagner (originator of Wagner's law of growing public expenditure), as well as Joseph Schumpeter in the nineteen-twenties, questioned an approach that divides people into groups which need social protection and groups which do not – where self-reliance seems adequate.

Is the Financial Base of Social Insurance Eroding?

The above-mentioned trends – increases in the number of people not covered by social insurance and not contributing, and of people taking an early exit from the labour force – as well as the low increase in wage rates in recent years and high unemployment (in West and East Germany) have increased fears about serious erosion of the financing base of social insurance in Germany. On the other hand, financial markets are booming and capital income is increasing in absolute and relative terms.

The structure of factor-income shares has changed in Germany over time: a downward trend in labour-income share beginning in the early eighties was interrupted by an upward shift after German unification only because the share of capital income in East Germany until now has been lower than in West Germany, a consequence which increases the labour-income share for Germany overall. In future, if the experience of the recent past is any guide, we can expect a decreasing labour-income share in Germany.

However, this must not be looked upon as an independent development with no relationship to other trends (or other social changes). Since the early nineteen-sixties, for example, the share of wages and salaries has increased remarkably, although not steadily. Trends in the labour market are of central importance for the development of factor-income shares. Other countries such as the United States and the Netherlands, which have had a better labour-market performance than Germany in recent years, show that factor-income shares during the last ten years are relatively stable (for different approaches in labour market policy, see Schettkat, 1999).

For Germany, some structural effects may also have contributed to the downward trend in labour-income share, effects that cannot be extrapolated into the future. These include: a) reductions in paid overtime through the introduction of time (saving) accounts. This strategy reduces the sum of wages (as well as the wage costs of the firms – to reduce the latter being the motivation for introducing such time accounts); b) reductions in bonus payments at Christmas, holidays, etcetera – often voluntary payments traditionally made by firms; c) the outsourcing of some tasks into subsidiary enterprises with a lower wage level. Even if employment remains constant, labour-income share goes down because of lower average wage rates.

For contributions to social insurance, however, it is not the labour-income share that is decisive but the sum of contributory gross wages – a figure which does not include employers' social insurance contributions, voluntary social expenditures by firms, the portion of individual gross wages above the contribution ceiling, wages below the lower limit for contributions, or salaries of civil servants, who do not contribute to social security.

The assumption that the contributory labour-income share may go down even more sharply than overall labour-income share seems plausible in view of the various structural changes mentioned above. However, this assumption can be rejected empirically: since the middle of the nineteen-seventies, the percentage of all gross wages and salaries subject to contributions has remained at about 95 per cent and has developed parallel to the labour-income share. This means that there is no additional erosion of the financial base by structural changes within the factor-income share. Nevertheless, the question of how to make social security responsive to changes in the world of work remains on the agenda from a financial perspective as well as from the perspective of achieving adequate social protection for individuals. To answer this question we need to consider not only the cross-sectional view but also the life-course perspective, focusing on the effects of changing working patterns on the pension claims of individuals.

The Life-course Perspective

For individuals, income security in old age depends on both the pattern of earnings over the life course and the effects of structural changes in the employment sector on different types of social security coverage and accumulation of pension claims. Destandardization and individualization of the life course is expected to become a major source for social security. Such a longitudinal view has to take into account how different cohorts are affected by changes both in the labour market and in social security arrangements (Pfaff, 1999).

TABLE 18.1
Average Years of Insurance and Average Earnings Position in Social Insurance for Male and Female Pensioners in West and East Germany – Old-age and Disability Pensions, 31 December 1995

	Men		Women		Women/men (per cent)	
	West	East	West	East	West	East
Average years of insurance	39.46	46.37	25.11	32.87	63.63	70.89
Average earnings position (per cent)	110.04	106.51	70.95	79.40	64.48	74.55

SOURCE: Alterssicherungsbericht der Bundesregierung (Old-age Security Report of the Federal Government), Bundestags-Drucksache 13/9570 (30.12.1997), Table A4, pp. 34–5 and own calculation.

As the preceding discussion has shown, remarkable changes have taken place in social security provisions, among them lower coverage in occupational, firm-based pension schemes or reductions in the credit awarded for years of schooling in social insurance provisions. Such changes affect individual income in later years. When changes in rules or conditions potentially reduce individuals' future security, it is important to identify alternative options and strategies to compensate for the harmful effects. Differences in working life related to gender, occupation, region, etcetera, must also be taken into consideration, as these factors influence the effects of changed rules and/or conditions (e.g., in the labour market) on the individual's work, earnings, and pension. (For present and future pensioners in Germany this is discussed in Schmähl and Fachinger, 1999.)

Today's pension claims reflect past conditions, often from thirty or forty years ago. There exist remarkable differences in pension claims based on differences in numbers of years of insurance and average earnings during those years. The range of variation is evident when we compare both average numbers of years of insurance and average earnings positions for men and women in West and East Germany (see table 18.1).

There are marked differences between men and women in both variables; however, the differences are more pronounced in West than in East Germany. On average, the number of years of insurance is seven years higher in East Germany, a result of high labour-force participation in the former socialist economy. The frequency distributions of these variables also clearly show male–female and East–West differences.

Differences between East and West will level out over time (for development of working time, see Kreckel and Schenk, 2000). The high unemployment rates – higher in East than in West Germany – will affect the average earnings position of future cohorts. Other factors, such as the increase in past decades in the labour-force participation rates of (especially married) women in the West (Pfaff, 1999), will ensure that the pension claims and prospects of future cohorts of pensioners will differ markedly from those of today's pensioners.

Some Changes in Old-age Security and the Prospects for the Public–Private Mix

Prospects for the public–private mix depend on future developments in social insurance and on whether additional provisions for old age are put in place, whether by firms or by individuals.

Accumulation of Pension Entitlements in Social Insurance

For the future, pension entitlements may be increased by such changes as provision of additional credits for caregivers of children or the frail elderly or by the increasing labour-force participation of women, albeit often on only a part-time basis. Other factors, however, will reduce people's ability to accumulate pension entitlements – in particular, the growth of types of employment not covered by social insurance ('ineligible' employment). The effect of this latter trend will depend on how often individuals experience such 'ineligible' employment and for how long this category of work is also not covered in occupational pension schemes. For those not covered by existing pension schemes, their level of income after retirement will depend on whether they have been able and willing to save a portion of the income from their 'ineligible' employment.

Political decisions, as well as structural changes in employment and the rate and duration of unemployment, can limit or reduce opportunities to accumulate pension entitlements. Two such decisions are discussed here.

One is the decision to phase in deductions from the full old-age pension for those who retire before the benchmark retirement age, which will be 65 in the year 2002. The deduction is 3.6 per cent per year, and the earliest a person may take up an old-age pension will be at age 62 (for a maximum deduction of 10.8 per cent, which, incidentally, is below an actuarially fair rate).

The option of working up to age 65 will depend on general labour-market conditions, and also on such factors as the willingness (of both employers and employees) to participate in programs for retraining and further education. Another factor will be the balance between age-specific labour costs (such as wage levels tied to seniority) and age-specific productivity (which mostly is based on assumptions, not on empirical findings).

Another important element will be the design of the pension formula, which is currently under discussion. In 1997, the government decided to reduce the general pension level in stages by disentangling the development of the adjustment rate of pensions from the development of average net earnings and introducing a so-called demographic factor based on the development of life expectancy. Today, an employee with average earnings, after twenty-six years of pension contributions, receives a pension that is only as high as a full (means-tested) social assistance claim. A general reduction of the pension level would increase the number of years of contributions an employee with average earnings needs for a pension equal to a full social assistance claim (see the discussion in Schmähl, 1998a). The new federal government decided to suspend this reduction of the pension level up to the end of the year 2000, however, to allow it to work a number of alternatives. For the years 2000 and 2001, pensions will only be adjusted according to the inflation rate, which reduces the pension level (pension compared to earnings of employees) because the inflation rate is expected to be lower than the growth rate of average earnings. Taking into account demographic aging and the expected increase in the contribution rate of the social insurance pension scheme, it would seem realistic to expect further decisions aiming at a slower increase of pension expenditure. For some groups of employees this will reduce their ability to accumulate adequate pension entitlements through social insurance.

Different Approaches for Additional Provision in Old Age

The preceding discussion underlines the importance of finding ways to supplement existing financial provisions for old age. Several possibilities are under discussion. All point in the direction of a change in the balance between public and private forms of old-age protection, a change that will also lead to a shift in the method of financing, from pay-as-you-go to a system based more on capital funding. However, many different strategies and instruments for increasing capital-funded pension schemes have been proposed. The financing of pension claims can be public or private. Public financing does not necessarily require public provision of pension payments, however. Payments can also be made through the private sector. Yet another consideration is whether these activities should be voluntary or mandatory. Mandatory participation can be based on law or on collective agreements (for further discussion of methods of financing see Schmähl, 2000).

Insofar as additional pension provision is linked to employment (for example, in the case of occupational pensions) or to income generated from work in general, it is clear that having an opportunity to earn money from work is the decisive precondition for old-age provision. That means that capital-funded types of old-age pensions normally would also be based on income from work. A central precondition of self-provision, which often is demanded in the political debate, is, therefore, the improvement of labour-market conditions (also stressed by Sen, 1997).

Proposals have been made to increase the contribution rate in social insurance above the level necessary to balance the budget. Doing so would create surpluses (as has happened in the United States and, recently, in Sweden). Other proposals have been made which aim to reduce pensions in pay-as-you-go-financed social insurance, thereby lowering the social insurance contribution rate with a view to encouraging individuals to seek additional private coverage.

Taking into consideration the highly unequal coverage of employees by occupational pension schemes, an extension of coverage is politically desirable. For many years, there has been little incentive for private firms to extend coverage or to increase the generosity of occupational pension schemes. In part, this is the result of labour-market conditions (which make it unnecessary for firms to offer good occupational pension schemes to attract productive workers). In addition, reduced tax incentives and increased regulations have increased costs to employers and have made it harder to calculate future pension costs. One can expect a greater diversity among company pension plans, a greater individualization, and a shift of risks and costs towards employees. Instruments for realizing this are models of deferred compensation, time accounts, and a shift from defined-benefit plans to defined-contribution plans. However, basing additional pensions on collective agreements might have a negative effect on the voluntary occupational pension plans offered by firms.

If asked to predict the future direction of Germany's pension policy, I would suggest that in general there will be increased attempts to establish mandatory supplementary arrangements, especially if social insurance pensions are reduced further by political decisions. International comparisons indicate that most countries with scanty public pensions have introduced mandatory supplementary pension schemes.

More people – particularly those who can afford to save more (the younger cohorts especially) – will react to the long public debate about the stability and sustainability of public pension plans by investing in private plans. This will increase the amount of capital funding for old age and the number of private pensions. If this is done only on a voluntary basis, the level of income inequality among the elderly will increase in the future. There are specific problems and risks attached to increased capital funding and privatization of pensions, however, and these must be carefully compared with the risks of public, pay-as-you-go-financed schemes. (This topic cannot be discussed here in sufficient detail; see Schmähl, 1998b, and 2000, for a fuller discussion of the issue.)

Whatever system is used, however – social insurance, occupational pension arrangements, or private supplementary plans (self-help) – the key to providing social security in old age is income from work. As long as income from work remains the main source for old-age provision, the development of the labour market is crucial, even if old-age security is not linked to the employment contract or is based on capital funding instead of pay-as-you-go financing.

In light of present trends, therefore, we can expect that changing working patterns, a greater diversity in working careers, and changes in decisions by both the state and employers will combine to shift the burden of old-age security to private households, a shift that will mean greater diversity in income in old age for future cohorts.

REFERENCES

Börsch-Supan, A., & Schnabel, R. (1998). Social security and declining labor-force participation in Germany. *American Economic Review, 88*, Papers and Proceedings, 173–8.

Gruber, J., & Wise, D.A. (1998). Social security and retirement: An international comparison. *American Economic Review, 88*, Papers and Proceedings, 158–63.

Kreckel, R., & Schenk, S. (2001). Full-time or part-time? The contradictory integration of the East German female labour force in unified Germany. In this volume.

OECD (Organization for Economic Co-operation and Development). (1995a). The labour market and older workers. Paris: Author.

OECD. (1995b). The transition from work to retirement. Paris: Author.

Pfaff, A.B. (1999). Veränderte Erwerbsbiographien und ihre Auswirkungen auf die Sozialpolitik. In W. Schmähl & H. Rische (Eds), *Wandel der Arbeitswelt-Folgerungen für die Sozialpolitik* (pp 31–60). Baden-Baden: Nomos.

Schettkat, R. (1999). Soziale Sicherung und Beschäftigung: Wohlfahrtsstaaten im Vergleich. In W. Schmähl & H. Rische (Eds), *Wandel der Arbeitswelt-Folgerungen für die Sozialpolitik* (pp 107–22). Baden-Baden: Nomos.

Schmähl, W. (1986). Soziale Sicherung und Schattenwirtschaft. In H. Winterstein (Ed.), *Sozialpolitik in der Beschäftigungskrise I* (pp 137–206). Berlin: Duncker & Humblot.

Schmähl, W. (1989). Labour force participation and social pension systems. In P. Johnson et al. (Eds), *Workers and pensioners* (pp 137–61). Manchester: Manchester University Press.

Schmähl, W. (1993). Proposals for flat-rate pensions in the German debate. In J. Berghman & B. Cantillon (Eds), *The European face of social security* (pp 261–80). Aldershot: Avebury.

Schmähl, W. (1997). The public-private mix in pension provision in Germany: The role of employer-based pension arrangements and the influence of public activities. In M. Rein & E. Wadensjö (Eds), *Enterprise and the welfare state* (pp 99–148). Cheltenham, UK: Lyme.

Schmähl, W. (1998a). Insights from social security reform abroad. In R.D. Arnold, M.J. Graetz, & A. H. Munnell (Eds), *Framing the social security debate* (pp 248–72). Washington, DC: Brookings Institution Press.

Schmähl, W. (1998b). Comment on the papers by Axel Börsch-Supan, Edward M. Gramlich, and Mats Persson. In H. Siebert (Ed.), *Redesigning social security* (pp 186–96). Kiel: Mohr Siebeck.

Schmähl, W. (1998c). Financing social security in Germany: Proposals for changing its structure and some possible effects. In S.W. Black (Ed.), *Globalization, technological change, and labor markets* (pp 179–207). Boston: Kluwer.

Schmähl, W. (1999). Arbeit – Basis for die soziale Sicherung der Zukunft. In W. Schmähl & H. Rische (Eds), *Wandel der Arbeitswelt-Folgerungen für die Sozialpolitik* (pp 189–226). Baden-Baden: Nomos.

Schmähl, W. (2000). Pay-as-you-go versus capital funding: Towards a more balanced view in pension policy. In J. Stewart & G. Hughes (Eds), *Pensions in the European Union: Adapting to economic and social change* (pp 195–208). Boston: Kluwer.

Schmähl, W., & Fachinger, U. (1999). Armut und Reichtum: Einkommen und Konsumverhalten älterer Menschen. In A. Niederfranke, G. Naegele, & E. Frahm (Eds), *Funkkolleg Altern 2* (pp 159–208). Opladen: Westdeutscher Verlag.

Schmähl, W., George, R., & Oswald, C. (1996). Gradual retirement in Germany. In L. Delsen and G. Reday-Mulvey (Eds), *Gradual retirement in the OECD countries: Macro and micro issues and policies* (pp 69–93). Aldershot: Dartmouth.

Sen, A. (1997). *The penalties of unemployment* (Temi di discussione, 307, mimeo). Rome: Banca d'Italia.

Viebrok, H. (1997). *Das Arbeitsangebot im Übergang von der Beschäftigung in den Ruhestand*. Frankfurt am Main: Lang.

World Bank. (1997). *World development report 1997: The state in a changing world*. Oxford: Oxford University Press.

19. Japan's Current Policy Focus on Longer Employment for Older People

Takeshi Kimura and Masato Oka

The unprecedented rapid aging of Japanese society has posed two serious problems: a projected shortage of labour and a projected solvency crisis of the public pension fund. To cope with these, the Japanese government has decided to raise the public pension age from 60 to 65 from the start of the twenty-first century. In addition, it is pursuing a policy to secure employment for people aged 60 to 64. This chapter gives an account of how the government is pursuing this employment policy and discusses the initiative from several angles.

Older Workers in the Labour Market in Japan

In Japan, two institutional factors affect retirement, a mandatory retirement (Teinen) age, instituted by firms, and a public pension eligibility age, instituted by the government. Both have been strategic variables influencing the retirement age. Many Japanese firms have instituted a Teinen age at which they terminate employment for every employee. That marks the end of the major stage of workers' careers. The Teinen age used to be 55, but since the 1980s most firms have raised it to 60 – the same as the pension age – as a result of government and union efforts.

A remarkable feature of the Japanese labour market is a high labour-force-participation rate for males aged 60 to 64. The rate has gradually declined from about 80 per cent since the 1970s but still remains as high as about 70 per cent (Rodosho, 1997, p. 435). Neither the Teinen age nor the pension age conclusively determines the final retirement of older workers. Thus, many aged 60 and over continue to work, pursuing a second career in various forms and retiring at various ages. This pattern is significantly different from that found in Europe.

In the past, this phenomenon was explained by factors such as a high willingness to work, motivation for social participation, a high percentage of self-employed people, and a low public pension benefit. However, the situation has been changing, with fewer older people continuing to work. This is accounted for in part by a decline in the percentage of self-employed people, a decrease which has contributed to the decline of the labour-force-participation rate for the aged. However, perhaps the most important factor is a rapid rise in the generally low level of the public pension benefit since the 1970s. This rise is believed to have significantly contributed to the decline of the labour-force-participation rate of older people. Nevertheless, many older people continue to work today. The in-work pension, which is an important influence on the choice to continue working, will be discussed later.

The Japanese labour market is, broadly speaking, divided into the large-firm sector and the middle-sized/small-firm sector; there are also gender differences in the labour force of these sectors. Regular male workers in large firms, which constitute only a quarter of the Japanese labour force, are privileged to be covered by a 'lifetime employment' guarantee. In the second sector, working conditions are much worse than in the first and the turnover rate is very much higher. This sector has a large component of older workers – people who continue to work in various capacities after the Teinen age. Workers who leave large firms at Teinen usually find a second career in this sector.

Conditions for women in the labour market are generally less favourable than for men. Even those in large firms are not covered by 'lifetime employment.' In most cases they are forced to quit their firm at marriage or when they bear a child. When they return to the labour market, they usually enter in a part-time capacity.

Whatever the reason for the high participation rate, males aged 60 to 64 are extremely handicapped in the labour market. First, there has always been a much higher incidence of unemployment among them than among younger workers. Thus, in the depressed year of 1996 their unemployment rate was 8.5 per cent, while the average rate was 3.5 per cent. Second, older workers are much more likely to have to work on a part-time basis (Rodosho, 1997, p. 272). Third, even if they work full time, their pay is, on average, much lower and their employment position much more precarious than that of younger workers, especially those in large firms who are covered by long-term employment security and the age-linked system of pay raises and promotions. These inequities become evident when workers move from the larger- to the smaller-firm sector, or are transferred to a lower-paid position within the same firm at the time point of Teinen. It is this disparity in the labour market that government employment policy has been attempting to address. Although it is not explicitly stated, it is evident that the policy is designed to benefit only older male workers, since the policy, as will be discussed later, presupposes lifetime employment, from which most female workers are excluded.

The Government Employment Policy for the Aged

In the early 1960s, faced with the collapse of the coal industry, the government was forced to wrestle with massive unemployment among coal miners. Subsequently, government policy focused on middle-aged and older workers, who had suffered a higher incidence of unemployment in the midst of the booming economy. The government implemented persuasive measures to encourage employers to hire this age group up to a certain percentage of their work force (Ujihara, 1989, pp 33–6).

For a variety of reasons, employment policy in the 1970s came to be focused on males aged 55 to 59. After the Teinen age of 55, people had to pursue a second career until they reached the public pension eligibility age of 60. They were already in an unfavourable position in the labour market, and their position grew much worse during the oil crises of the 1970s. The unions began to demand that employers secure employment beyond the age of 55 by raising the Teinen age. Promoting the increase in the Teinen age became the most important objective of the government's employment policy, an objective pursued through a three-pronged strategy: Gyosei-Shido (the government's attempt to persuade the actors concerned to cooperate to pursue a policy objective); subsidy programs from the unemployment fund; and legislation. Around 1980 the government started using Gyosei-Shido to induce a number of the largest firms to raise the Teinen age to 60 and over, and by the end of the 1980s the new Teinen age was prevalent among most of the large firms. In 1986 the government enforced the Older Workers Employment Promotion Act, which made it mandatory for employers to make efforts to raise their Teinen age to 60 and over. Since by then the new Teinen age was already prevalent among the large firms, this law was intended to disseminate it to the sector of middle-sized and small firms (Kimura et al., 1994, pp 259–60). A 1994 amendment of this law made the Teinen age of 60 and over compulsory from 1998 on.

With respect to the subsidy programs, a 1974 amendment of the Unemployment Insurance Fund Act extended the existing system to assist the unemployed. The fund was renamed the Employment Insurance Fund and provided a new active manpower policy to combat unemployment. The main policy vehicle was a number of subsidy programs payable to employers who were taking measures to avoid laying off workers, and these were funded by a contribution required of all employers (Kobayashi, 1979, pp 179–92). Soon this special fund was also used for promoting the employment of the aged. Thus, the subsidy was given to the employers who raised the Teinen age or hired more than a specified number of older workers. Today the Teinen age of 60 prevails in most firms.

In the late 1980s, the focus of government employment policy started to shift to the next target group, males aged 60 to 64. Evidently, this shift was related to the intended reform of the public pension scheme. Currently, the government is attempting to secure employment for this age group in the same way in which it promoted an increase in the Teinen age. That is, it is pressing employers to continue to employ their workers in one capacity or another beyond 60 or, ideally, to raise the Teinen age further, to 65. Thus, the 1990 amendment to the 1986 act referred to the social responsibility of firms to secure employment for those aged 60 to 64 within the firm, or within a firm's group. A further amendment, in 1994, required employers to make an effort to continue to employ their workers till the age of 65. The subsidy programs also were revised to target this age group (Kimura et al., 1994, pp 303–4).

At this time the government also added a new policy vehicle. A 1995 amendment of the Employment Insurance Fund Act introduced two new benefits payable from the general Employment Insurance fund, adding to the ordinary benefit for the unemployed. One of them is a benefit for those on leave from work for child care. The other relates to older workers and is formally titled 'a benefit for the aged who continue to work' – what might be termed a 'wage-top-up' benefit. Recipients of the benefit: (1) must be aged between 60 and 64; (2) must continue to work (or must resume work after a short period of unemployment) after the Teinen; and (3) must be receiving a wage less than

85 per cent of their average wage during the six months prior to the Teinen age of 60. The sum of the benefit equals 25 per cent of the worker's wage. As a worker's wage rises above 80 per cent of his previous wage, the percentage is reduced, reaching zero at 85 per cent (Seki, 1995).

Three important points should be noted in relation to this policy. First, it assumes that wage levels will be much lower for most workers aged 60 and over, and is designed to top it up. Second, the benefit is received by the older workers themselves, whereas the previously discussed subsidies are paid to employers. Third, the policy treats older workers as semi-unemployed, since this benefit is payable from the same general fund as the ordinary unemployment benefit.

Public Pension Reforms and Their Impact on Workers' Choice

It was in the mid-1960s, when the public pension benefit level was relatively low, that it was made possible for older wage earners to draw the public pension benefit. The in-work pension was intended to top up low wages. Unless a worker's earnings exceeded a certain limit, he could receive 80 per cent of his full pension benefit (Ujihara, 1989, p. 105). At the age of 65, he became eligible for a full pension, regardless of whether he was working or retired. Until the recent reform, the earnings limit was set very low, lower than the national welfare minimum for a couple. Its effects were not clear. It is believed to have discouraged those with a higher level of benefit from continuing to work. Nevertheless, many workers received the 80 per cent in-work pension (in 1987, about 400,000 did so, out of the 1,120,000 workers in the same age range).

As a result of an amendment to the Act relating to the Public Pension for Employees in 1994, the earnings limit was substantially raised in 1995, and the barrier to work was almost eliminated for the middle and lower strata of the older population. Now, as long as the monthly total of a worker's wage and in-work pension does not exceed 220,000 yen there is no reduction of the pension. Beyond this sum, the pension equivalent is reduced to half of the excess; and beyond 340,000 yen, the reduction is equivalent to the excess (Koseisho, 1994, pp 24–8). This is expected to give a strong incentive to older workers to continue working. Moreover, for workers who also receive the top-up benefit, there is a further slight (in principle, 10 per cent of a worker's wage) reduction of the pension.

The government first proposed to raise the pension age from 60 to 65 as early as 1980 (Yamazaki, 1988, p. 105). After several failures, it succeeded in passing the amendment mentioned above. Between 2001 and 2009, the pension age for males will be gradually raised from 60 to 65. For females, it is being raised from 55 in 1993 to 60 in 2000, and is scheduled to be raised to age 65 by 2014, starting in 2006.

Roughly speaking, the public pension for employees has two parts: a fixed-sum portion, which varies only according to the length of contribution years; and an earnings-related portion. In the average benefit there is roughly a fifty-fifty split between the two portions. According to the Ministry of Health and Welfare, the average monthly benefit for new beneficiaries in 1996 was about 200,000 yen, of which about half was an earnings-related portion and the other half a fixed-sum portion for the insured and his or her spouse. Under the new system, recipients can draw the full fixed-sum portion only at age 65. An early draw is possible, but with an actuarial reduction. Thus, recipients who draw it at age 60 must accept more than a 40 per cent reduction for life.

To soften the unions' resistance, the government made a significant compromise: it allowed workers to receive an earnings-related portion at age 60 without an actuarial reduction. To take the example of the new beneficiaries in 1996, the average beneficiary receives only 100,000 yen until age 65 and 150,000 yen until his or her spouse reaches age 65 (Koseisho, 1994, pp 18–23). The effect of this provision will be to drive many people in their early sixties into the labour market.

An Overview of Government Policies

A number of important decisions that took effect from 1994 onwards have already been mentioned. The pension eligibility age was raised to 65 (policy 1). The earnings limit for the in-work pension was substantially raised in 1995 (policy 2). The Teinen age of 60 and over was to be made compulsory from 1998 (policy 3). It was made obligatory for employers to make an effort to continue employing workers aged 60 to 64 (policy 4). Finally, the top-up benefit was created in 1995 (policy 5). We can argue that these government policies, including the Gosei-Shido (policy 6) and the subsidy programs (policy 7), are intended to have effects on either the supply side or the demand side of labour. On the supply side, the public pension reforms, that is, policy 1 and policy 2, will have an enormous effect on the behaviour of older people. Policy 1 will decisively drive the middle and lower strata of the aged into the labour market. On the demand side, policy 4 and policy 6 are intended to bind employers to continue employing their workers till age 65. It is to be noted that these three policies evidently presuppose lifetime employment. Policy 7 is supposed to induce employers to do the same.

Policy 5 can be included in the latter policy group inasmuch as it encourages employers to continue employing or to hire older workers at lower wages. It is also noted that this policy does not necessarily presuppose lifetime employment.

The interrelation of government policies, summed up in figure 19.1, is viewed as a cost shift between actors and institutions: a cost shift from the Public Pension Fund to the Employment Insurance Fund resulting from a combination of the raised eligibility age for the fixed-sum pension and the wage top-up benefit; and another cost shift from firms to the government resulting from a combination of a lowered wage paid by employers and the top-up benefit.

The interrelation can also be viewed in another way as a tripartite cost-sharing system in which three participants share the cost of employment for older workers: the government supplies the earnings-related portion of the public pension and the top-up benefit; firms provide the longer, secure employment, though with a lower wage; and older people endure the loss of the fixed-sum portion of the pension.

Of these three participants, firms are in the most favourable position. They are, at most, only obliged to make an effort to continue employing older workers. Deprived of the fixed-sum pension, older workers will have very limited choices. It is likely to be the Employment Insurance Fund that shares the largest portion of the cost.

Because the burden of employing older workers will fall upon the Employment Insurance Fund, and also since the top-up-benefit scheme doesn't presuppose lifetime employment, it would be useful to determine how many people are receiving how much of this top-up benefit. However the Ministry of Labour has not made it public. In an interview with the officials of the Yamagata Office of the National Labour Exchange Agency, which administers the top-up benefit as well as the ordinary unemployment benefit, the authors obtained the number of beneficiaries and the total sum paid in the Yamagata prefecture area. In 1996, about 3,000 workers received the benefit, and the total sum amounted to 17.68 million yen. There are 30,000 workers aged 60 to 64 in this prefecture (Yamagataken, 1998, p. 36). We can conclude that each beneficiary received a miniscule annual sum of 58,933 yen. In

Figure 19.1 Interrelation of Government Policies

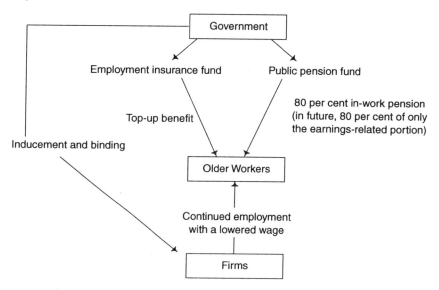

evaluating the effectiveness of this scheme, we have to take two facts into consideration. First, only one year has passed since this scheme started; second, an overwhelming portion of firms in this prefecture belong to the small-firm sector, where wages peak, on average, when workers are in their early fifties, according to official estimates. The latter fact indicates the limited effectiveness of this scheme. Older workers receive this benefit only if their wages decrease considerably at age 60. However this is unlikely to happen in the small-firm sector. In addition, if the pay scale in the large-firm sector undergoes a fundamental change, older workers in that sector also will have difficulty being eligible for the benefit.

Firms' Responses

The extent to which government policies succeed in their objectives will, of course, depend on how firms respond. To determine this, we need to look back at what happened in large firms when the Teinen age was raised to 60, and also to investigate how large firms are currently responding to present government policies.

Traditionally, the pillars of the famous Japanese tradition of 'lifetime employment' were employment security till the Teinen age, age-oriented pay raise and promotion patterns, and retirement at the Teinen age of 55 with a substantial lump-sum allowance. This lifetime employment tradition applies only to regular male workers in large firms. Large firms regularly employ many other categories of workers, such as female, part-time, and seasonal workers, who are not covered by this system. Of course, some lifetime employment features are also found in middle-sized firms. However, as the size of the firm decreases, provisions for employment security and age-oriented pay raises get weaker.

With the Teinen age raised to 60, large firms began to pursue two policies in order to cope with the aging of the work force, which meant a significant alteration in lifetime employment practices for their middle-aged and older regular workers. First, large firms began to put more of their middle-aged and older workers on Shukko – that is, maintaining the employment contract but sending them to work for subsidiaries or related firms, and paying the wage difference (between the wage the large firm is obliged to pay and the one the subsidiary, or related firm pays). According to our case studies at the end of the 1980s, large firms shed a great number of their workers aged 50 and over in this way. Second, regular workers aged 55 and over who were affected by the new Teinen age came to be excluded from the age-oriented pay raise and promotion system. That is, the wages for workers at age 55 greatly decreased (in our case studies, to about 70 per cent of previous levels), and remained the same or increased only slightly till age 60 (Kimura et al., 1994, pp 263–80).

Whether in response to the government policy or on their own initiative, many firms have instituted a 're-employment scheme' for workers who have reached the Teinen age. Generally speaking, firms re-employ such workers till age 63 and, in some cases, till age 65, with an annual renewal of contract. Most desirable from the standpoint of government policy would be a new Teinen age of 65. But as a more realizable alternative, the government seems to expect firms, especially large firms, to ensure longer employment for the older workers by this means. In reality, large firms re-employ only a very limited, select portion of such workers, and, in most cases, only in their subsidiary or related firms – part of the small-firm sector. Older workers are much more likely to be re-employed in the small-firm sector, which has to depend on an older work force, regardless of the Teinen age (Rodosho, 1997, pp 244–47).

Wages for re-employed workers are lower than those for regular workers by about 30 per cent (Rodosho, 1997). In fact, in most cases we surveyed before the pension reform in 1995, these workers' wages fell below the earnings limit for the in-work pension (Kimura et al., 1994, pp 267–9).

Government policies, especially those using legislation and Gyosei-Shido to bind firms to continue employing workers beyond age 50, are based on two assumptions: that the lifetime employment system will survive among large firms, and that large firms will be able to provide longer and secure employment in one form or another, as, so to speak, an extension of the lifetime employment policy. In the present unprecedented economic depression, however, there are signs that the tradition of lifetime employment is likely to undergo a fundamental change. First, more and more firms are replacing the existing monthly salary system with a merit-oriented annual salary system for their middle-management staff – a departure from the age-oriented pay raise system. Second, some large firms are attempting to abolish a retirement allowance and incorporate it into the wage – indicating a departure from the assumption that their workers will remain in the firm till the Teinen age (Nishikubo, 1998, pp 45–7). At present, although we cannot predict the future of the lifetime employment policy with any certainty, it seems likely that it will survive for only a handful of regular workers. Workers older than 60 will have to find marginal jobs, with marginal wages, in the labour market. Thus, only two of the government policies, the in-work pension and the wage-top-up benefit, will be effective. In addition, if the age-oriented pay raise system undergoes a fundamental alteration, the role of the wage-top-up benefit will be significantly limited.

Concluding Remarks: Perspective for the Life Course of Older People

We conclude that government policies are aiming at driving more older people to join the labour market; since the labour-force-participation rate already is high, the aim is to encourage them to work longer, in order to protect the public pension fund and ensure a secure labour supply.

We argue that, when the Teinen age used to be 55, there was a reciprocal responsibility between firms and the government; firms being responsible for providing employment till age 55 and the government being responsible for supporting people aged 60 and over through the public pension. When average life expectancy was shorter and public pension benefits were lower, the government's share of the responsibility was minimal. As longevity began to increase and the public pension benefit was raised, however, the government's role became more crucial. Even so, people had to undertake a second career up till age 60; these five years were, so to speak, the time for self-help.

The raising of the Teinen age to 60 established a new marker for the division of responsibility. None the less, many older people remain in the labour market after age 60. The conditions of their working life – that is, how many people are working for how long and at what wage – are not well known. While there are a number of reasons why older people may wish to continue working, the relationship between length of working hours, amount of pension, and motive for working is also poorly understood. We can safely assume, however, that people with a very low public pension are forced to keep on working for economic reasons, while those with an adequate pension can choose to retire, or those who seek opportunities for social participation and self-fulfilment through work can work shorter hours. Between these two extremes, a number continue to work either to augment their pension with earnings from part-time work, or for social participation, or perhaps for both purposes. The life course of older people today is more diverse than in the past, and more people have a variety of options to choose from.

The increase in the public pension age will significantly affect older people's life course. With only the earnings-related public pension provided, many will be forced to enter the labour market, or to work longer. The government is proposing to raise the age for the earnings-related pension as well, to age 65 in the 2010s. People aged 60 to 64 will be in the same position as were those aged 55 to 59 a quarter of century ago. Government policies will not likely be successful in providing more secure employment, and the role of the wage-top-up benefit will continue, though in a limited way.

REFERENCES

Kimura, T., Takagi, I., Oka, M., & Omori, M. (1994). Japan: Shukko, Teinen and re-employment. In F. Naschold & B. de Vroom (Eds), *Regulating employment and welfare: Company and national policies of labour force participation at the end of worklife in industrial countries* (pp 247–309). Berlin: Walter de Gruyter.

Kobayashi, K. (1979). *Nihon no koyo mondai (Employment problems in Japan).* Tokyo: Tokyo Daigaku Shuppan Kai.

Koseisho (Ministry of Health and Welfare). (1994). *Nenkin seido kaiseian no kaisetsu (Manual for the reforms of the public pension for employees).* Tokyo: Author.

Nishikubo, K. (1998, 13 August). Kawarihajimeta taishokukin seido (Retirement allowance system has begun to change). *Ekonomisuto (Economist).*

Seki, H. (1995, May). Koreisha no koyo to fukushi ni kansuru seisaku (Employment policies for the aged). *Rodosha Fukushi Kenkyu (Monthly Study of the Welfare for Workers)* (pp 58–81). Tokyo: Nihon Rodosha Fukushi Kyokai.

Rodosho (Ministry of Labour). (1997). *Rodo Hakusho (White Paper for Labour).* Tokyo: Author.

Ujihara, S. (1989). *Nihon keizai to koyo seisaku (Japanese economy and employment policies).* Tokyo: Tokyo Daigaku Shuppan Kai.

Yamagataken (Yamagata Prefecture Office). (1998). *Yamagataken tokei nenkan (Statistical yearbook for Yamagata).* Yamagata: Author.

Yamazaki, H. (1988). Kosei nenkin seido no bappon kaisei katei ('Fundamental' reforms of the public pension for employees). In Tokyo Daigaku Shakai Kagaku Kenshusho (Ed.), *Tenkanki no fukushi kokka (Welfare states in transformation),* Volume II (p. 105). Tokyo: Tokyo Daigaku Shuppan Kai.

20. The Career Break as an Alternative to Early-exit Schemes

Peter Simoens and Jan Denys

During the last twenty years, labour-market participation among the elderly has diminished drastically in all countries of the European Union (EU). More and more workers leave the labour market for good before reaching pensionable age. This trend, stronger in Belgium than in any other EU country, has been influenced by three factors: disability pensions, unemployment, and early-exit routes, of which the so-called bridging pension has been the most important. Only 30 per cent of the male population 50 years and over is still actively employed (against an EU average of 39 per cent). These figures are even lower for older women: 11 per cent (EU average, 19 per cent). These Belgian figures are the lowest in the European Union (Eurostat, 1997).

This early exit from the labour market can be attributed to the existence of early-exit routes (a pull factor) and to restructuring inside companies (a push factor) (Kohli and Rein, 1991). The degree to which these two factors are present in each country explains the divergences in participation rates. In Belgium both factors have been of crucial importance.

Early-exit channels have in some cases made early exit financially attractive to workers, while offering companies a socially acceptable way of reducing the labour surplus. Early exit has become a new achievement of the welfare state to which all the involved parties can consent: employers, trade unions, and government. In the course of time the expulsion of older workers from the labour market has taken on the character of a social right.

The most important early-exit route was created by the so-called bridging pension, which was introduced in Belgium in 1974. It allowed workers aged 58 years and older to leave the labour market for good after loss of a job. Such workers acquire the right to an unemployment allowance, increased by an additional allowance (paid by the employer) that is half of the difference between the last net wage and the unemployment allowance. Companies that experience economic difficulties can be given permission to lower the age limit to 52 years or, in some cases, even 50 years.

The use of the bridging pension began slowly, affecting 31,823 pensioners in 1980 but rising to 140,001 by 1990. Even at the end of the nineteen-eighties, when the labour market regained strength, the numbers didn't decline. After 1990, the number of early retirees did gradually decline, so that by 1996 there were 133,309 bridging pensioners (MTA, 1997a).

As the most important push factor, we mentioned restructuring within companies. The process of early exit can indeed be seen as a consequence of the recessions that have occurred since 1974 and of the personnel reductions linked to them. There are also more profound structural elements, such as the increasing rationalization of the production process that has stimulated the expulsion of older workers. The company reorganization, initially a one-time-only event, has become a more frequent occurrence as companies seek to achieve productivity improvements or respond to technological changes (Kerkhoff and Kruidenier, 1991).

The system of bridging pensions was an answer to the employment crisis of the early nineteen-seventies. This crisis was a consequence of three phenomena that appeared more or less simultaneously: the economic crisis in a number of traditional industrial sectors, the entry into the labour market of the baby-boom generation, and the massive entry into the labour market of women. Given these circumstances, the measure, which was considered at the time to be temporary, seemed justified. Over time, however, its drawbacks have become evident. These are discussed in the next section of this chapter. In a third section, an alternative – the career break – is discussed. We describe the development of this approach in Belgium. The final two sections review the advantages of the career-break system, as opposed to the bridging pension, and propose measures which would enable this system to be expanded in the future.

Disadvantages of Early-exit Schemes

In this section, we describe the most important disadvantages connected to the system of bridging pensions. We stress that our analysis is based primarily on an evaluation of the Belgian system, though reference is made to the international literature on the subject.

Reinforcement of Stereotypes of Older Workers

There is no doubt that the institutionalized early-exit schemes have reinforced negative stereotypes of older workers (Walker, 1997). These stereotypes hold that older workers resist change, lack creativity, reach decisions slowly, have low physical stamina, lack interest in technological changes, and are not interested in training. However, scientific research finds that, with the exception of lower physical stamina, all the stereotypes can be refuted (Rosen and Jerdee, 1985; Shea, 1991; Warr, 1997).

The consequences of these stereotypes can be illustrated through the share of recruitment of older workers: only 3 per cent of all recruited workers were older than 45 years in Belgium in 1997 (Simoens, Denys, and Denolf, 1998). This means that the chances of finding a new job are quite poor for older unemployed people.

The Trickle-down Effect: Disadvantageous Effect for the Younger Age Categories

There are also adverse effects for the younger age categories. This can be illustrated by the pattern of unemployment rates by age group, as shown in table 20.1. It is commonly known that the unemployment rate is high among young people, declines as their age increases, and grows again from a certain age on. It is commonly accepted that unemployment is at its lowest point among those aged between 30 and 35, which is considered by many to be the ideal age in the labour market. On the basis of table 20.1, we can state that this ideal age has decreased significantly since 1983: from ages 40 to 45 to ages 30 to 35 for men, and from ages 40 to 45 to ages 25 to 30 for women. This means that women over 30 years old have fewer opportunities in the labour market because of their age. There are strong indicators that institutionalized early-exit paths are connected with this phenomenon.

TABLE 20.1
Belgian Unemployment Rates between 1983 and 1997

Age	Men			Women		
	1983	1990	1997	1983	1990	1997
20–25	20.1	7.2	9.9	30.3	11.9	15.1
25–30	11.9	4.7	6.6	28.8	11.0	12.3
30–35	9.0	4.1	6.0	27.8	14.1	13.3
35–40	9.0	4.2	6.7	25.5	16.8	14.6
40–45	8.8	5.4	7.8	21.7	20.1	18.0
45–50	10.9	7.2	9.7	24.1	26.2	24.5

SOURCE: RVA (unpublished data)

The Compulsory Character of the Measure

The individual's freedom of choice is often not respected in the case of the bridging pension. Officially, in Belgium the initiative must come from the employer, as early retirement is only possible after a dismissal. This raises the question of whether the decision to retire via the bridging pension is made as a result of coercion (through restructuring and reorganization) or social pressure (for instance, from colleagues in the workplace). Trommel (1994), the Dutch specialist in this matter, adds: 'If there are no real possibilities for older workers to stay in their jobs, what choice is there for them? When we look at the early retirement channels, then it looks as if a new social automatism has been created, consisting of an institutionalized pattern of early exit. This has nothing to do with individual choices.'

This compulsory character of early retirement has been heavily criticized by specialists in the political economy of old age (e.g., Phillipson, 1982).

Inefficiency

The cost of recourse to the early-exit option in Belgium represents 0.75 per cent of the gross domestic product (GDP), which is much higher than the average of all the countries in the Organization for Economic Co-operation and Development (OECD) (see table 20.2). In absolute figures, the cost of early-exit schemes represents 53 billion Belgian francs, or 1.3 billion ECU, per year (MTA, 1997b). When taking the

TABLE 20.2
Public Costs of Active and Passive Labour Market Policy (in per cent of GDP;
period 1990–91)

	Belgium	OECD countries
Active labour market policy, with:	1.07 (28%)	0.78 (33%)
– direct creation of employment	0.54	0.08
– vocational training	0.14	0.25
Passive labour market policy, with:	2.71 (72%)	1.60 (67%)
– unemployment allowances	1.96	1.41
– early retirement	0.75	0.18
Total	3.78 (100%)	2.38 (100%)

SOURCE: Van Poeck and Van Rompuy (1995)

number of beneficiaries into account, we can calculate that the measure costs 410,000 Belgian francs (or 10,250 ECU) per full-time early retiree. In reality, the measure costs even more, because not only the cost of the unemployment allowance but also the cost of the supplementary allowance paid by the employer should be taken into account.

In addition it can be assumed that the existence of early-exit paths stimulates undeclared work, given the fact that a number of retired people over 50 are still able to produce good work. This causes an additional cost for the federal budget since no social security contributions are paid on this labour. (An increase of undeclared work can also be expected in the case of the career break.)

Ineffectiveness

The most important justification for early retirement is that it is a means of redistributing labour. It is therefore important to know whether the early retiree is being replaced effectively by an unemployed person. The total percentage of replacement in the case of the bridging pension is in reality only 31.6 per cent (RVA, 1996). This means that only one out of three early retirees is replaced by an unemployed person. This low degree of replacement can be explained by the fact that there are a lot of exceptions to this obligation (for instance, in a company that is experiencing economic problems) and by the fact that there is no control on the application of this obligation.

It is clear, at least in Belgium, that historically the bridging pension has been used more to permit enterprises to reduce numbers of workers in a socially acceptable way than to redistribute labour. International research confirms the fact that collective early-exit paths have no positive effect on the employment chances for young people (ILO, 1995; Sackmann, 1997).

Rigidity

The bridging pension is a collective, linear measure, which irreversibly cuts short the working life of many older workers. The measure hardly considers the personal situation and the individual wishes of employees. It does not provide an answer to two important labour-market trends: individualization and flexibilization.

Passivity

Both the OECD and the European Commission recommend that member states take active labour-market measures. The bridging pension is a purely passive measure: employees receive an allowance on the condition that they leave the labour market for good. The measure is in contrast with employability-increasing measures, such as training.

Loss to the Company

Finally, the early exit of older workers has many disadvantages for companies, among them loss of experience; increases in labour accidents (younger workers are statistically more likely to be involved in accidents than older ones); and labour shortages in certain sectors where the system of early retirement is frequently used (in the metal and the construction sectors, for example). In addition, the maintenance and transmission of the culture of the company are at risk when the average age of its personnel is kept artificially low; it has been argued that a mixed age composition has a positive effect on, for example, creativity within the company (Loden and Rosener, 1991).

The Career Break as an Alternative

Clearly, the many disadvantages connected to the system of early exit with bridging pensions make modifications to the system desirable. In their plea for the maintenance of the early-exit scheme, its defenders underline the role that it plays in the struggle against unemployment. In this view, the total number of labour hours in an economy is fixed; the goal is to distribute this amount fairly among those who wish to work. We argue that there are better measures than early retirement. The most important one is the generalized interruption of the professional career as a right for each employee. We argue for the career break, as it exists today in Belgium, as an alternative to early retirement.

The System

The system of career break was introduced in 1985. Belgium was the first country in the European Union to establish such a measure. Other countries, including Sweden, Finland, and Denmark, followed later (la Commission Européenne, 1997). The system of career break in Belgium offers employees the opportunity to take a temporary break from professional activities for a maximum of sixty months. Other lengths of leave – of twelve fifteen, twenty, or thirty months – are also permitted. A monthly income is guaranteed during the break, and an unemployed person replaces the career breaker. Career break is universally applicable in the public sector. In the private sector the right must be incorporated in a collective labour agreement concluded between the trade unions and the employers of the sector. The consent of the employer is required. Recently, the Belgian federal government decided to expand the number of workers eligible for a career break from 1 per cent to 3 per cent (for companies where there is no collective labour agreement on career break).

The Beneficiaries

The number of career breakers rose from just 2,019 in 1985 to 37,610 in 1989, and 56,000 in 1997 (RVA, unpublished data). Table 20.3 shows the distribution of career breakers by sector, gender, and age.

The majority of career breakers work in the public sector (53 per cent), are female (86 per cent), and are aged between 25 and 40 (52 per cent). The recognition of career break as an established right in the public sector explains the high percentage of beneficiaries. The fact that the largest number of the beneficiaries are women between 25 and 40 years old shows that the system often functions as a form of mater-

TABLE 20.3
Distribution of Career Breakers in Belgium by
Sector, Gender, and Age (in per cent; 1997)

Sector	
Public	53.0
Private	47.0
Gender	
Men	13.9
Women	86.1
Age	
−25	1.1
25–40	52.1
40–50	18.9
50+	27.9
Total	100.0
(Number)	(52,443)

SOURCE: Public Service for Labour Supply (RVA)

nity leave. It is often taken by women with one or more children in a double-income family. This can be explained by the moderate level of the allowance (12,000 Belgian francs or 300 ECU per month), which is insufficient for singles and families with one moderate main income. It should be mentioned that many 50-plus individuals use the system to partially leave the labour market. This has two additional advantages: they receive an additional allowance and they are not bound to a maximum duration of sixty months.

Advantages of the Career Break

In this section we indicate the most important advantages of the system of career break in comparison with the bridging pension.

No Age Discrimination

In the case of career break, age does not play a compulsory role. A career break can be taken at any age, if an agreement is reached with the employer in the private sector. Where no such agreement exists, 1 per cent of employees are entitled to the career break. In the public sector it is an established general right. The fact that currently the majority of users are women between 25 and 40 years old has mainly to do with the modalities of the measure.

Respect for Individual Freedom of Choice

The system of career break offers the employee the opportunity to leave the labour market temporarily on his or her own initiative. The break can be used for the care of children, training, a trip, and, since 1995, to provide palliative care.

Efficiency

Career break is much cheaper than the bridging pension. The system costs only 0.07 per cent of the GDP or 5 billion Belgian francs (125 million ECU). If we take into account the absolute number of career breakers, the system costs three times less than the early-exit scheme. Furthermore, in the case of the career break, the government doesn't have to pay an unemployment allowance to the person who replaces the career breaker. On the other hand, it should be admitted that, as in the case of the early-exit paths, an increase in career breaks will probably lead to an increase in undeclared work.

Effectiveness

The obligation to replace the career breaker is respected: in more than 80 per cent of career breaks the replacement worker is an unemployed person (MTA, 1997c). This confirms that the career break is a much more effective method of redistributing labour than the bridging pension.

Flexibility

Workers' professional careers are increasingly compressed between the ages of 25 and 50 years. The late inflow into the labour market is partially due to an extension of compulsory education from 16 to 18 years, and to an easing of the admission conditions for higher education. In addition to these factors, the increased age of entrance into the labour market is also a direct consequence of a general improvement of welfare, in combination with a generalized trend towards having fewer children. The compression of the professional career increases the risk of stress and overwork, especially when, in the same time span (between 25 and 50), people are raising children and purchasing a home.

Possibilities of Integration with Other Labour-Market Instruments

A career break offers the possibility of a better integration of family and working life. However, a career break can also be used for other purposes, such as training. This is important in a period where employability becomes a key issue. In this sense, the career break could be integrated into the system of paid educational leave. This system was introduced in Belgium in 1985 and includes the right to be absent from work to attend classes for a limited number of hours without loss of income. The purpose is to reduce pressure and fatigue for employees who follow training in combination with their full-time job.

In relation to the integration of work and family life, it is important to mention the existence of a right to maternity/paternity leave. The system was introduced in 1997 on the basis of a directive of the European Commission (96/34/EC) and was integrated into the career-break system. It entitles a parent to three months' leave following the birth or adoption of a child, for both the mother and the father. Employers have an obligation to replace the career breaker, and the career breaker receives an allowance.

The Further Extension of the Career-Break Option

In this section, we want to investigate how the existing system of career break could be extended. First, we describe a recent strengthening of the system agreed to by the social partners in the recent sectoral negotiations for the period 1997–8 and by the Flemish government. Afterwards, we discuss four possible practical new interventions.

Expansion as an Outcome of the Sectoral Labour Agreements

An analysis of seventy sectoral collective labour agreements resulting from the recent sectoral negotiations for the period 1997–8 reveals that the career break is the most frequently taken employment-stimulating measure. This is illustrated in table 20.4.

It can be seen that several sectors have expanded the right of career

TABLE 20.4
Overview of Employment-stimulating Measures in Belgium for the Period 1997–1998
(expressed in numbers of collective labour agreements concluded)

Measure	Agreements concluded	Employees concerned
Career break	51	1,180,000
Half-time bridging pension	42	860,000
Training	34	900,000
Part-time work	28	700,000
Flexible working hours	13	330,000
Reduction of working hours	9	250,000

SOURCE: MTA (1997c)

break to 5 per cent (as is the case in the maritime sector). Furthermore a new trend has emerged to give supplementary sectoral allowances in addition to the official allowances (Serroyen, 1997).

Additional Support from the Flemish Government

An employee who decides to interrupt his or her career receives monthly compensation of 5,000 Belgian francs (125 ECU) from the Ministry of the Flemish Community, which brings the total allowance to 17,000 Belgian francs (425 ECU). This premium is awarded only if the career break is taken to follow training, to take care of children, to provide palliative care, to start self-employment, or to do volunteer work. It is probable that this restricting condition will be dropped in the near future, which would further enhance workers' autonomy.

The Desirability of Supplementary Measures

Because the system of career break is likely to become more important in the future, we feel that some adjustments should be made to the system. In what follows we restrict ourselves to five possible interventions: (1) an increase in allowances; (2) a structural link with training; (3) movement towards a time-credit system; (4) the introduction of an individual savings system; and (5) the introduction of premiums for individual firms.

1. *An Increase in Allowances:* It can be assumed that the career-break system would attract even more participants if the allowances were

increased. A recent study shows that with an allowance of 20,000 Belgian francs (500 ECU) per month, instead of the present 12,000 francs (300 ECU), in eight out of ten couples one of the parents would like to remain at home for a while when a child is born (Van Haegendoren, 1998).

If the allowances were increased, the system would attract a broader range of participants than at present (we recall that the majority of career breakers are now women in two-income families with children).

The measure, as it exists today, is lucrative for the government. Reducing the scope of the very expensive early-exit schemes would create savings which could be used to raise the allowances for career breakers.

2. *A Structural Link with Training:* At the moment career breaks are seen merely as an instrument for the redistribution of labour, whereas they could also function as an instrument for managing human resources. That is, the system could be coupled to training designed to increase the employability of the worker.

In Belgium there is already a paid system of educational leave. During the training period, however, the employee is not replaced by an unemployed person. In Denmark, on the other hand, there exists a job-rotation system which provides the unemployed with the opportunity to gain work experience in the company as a replacement for an employee who is pursuing training for a certain length of time (at least a few months). About 70 per cent of the formerly unemployed replacement workers are afterwards recruited by the company. Small and medium-sized enterprises especially use this system because it is an ideal way of guaranteeing continuity in the production process. In 1996 a total of 36,000 workers were involved in the job rotation system (*Jobrotation,* 1997).

Provisions allowing career break to be linked to training in some cases (e.g., by paying additional allowances), would broaden the range of participants in the system. At present, career breaks are not used as much as they could be because the system mainly attracts older workers who want to reduce their professional activity and women in two-income families with small children. Moreover the system is criticized (e.g., by feminists) because of its role-reinforcing effect. Finally, it is possible that the measure, as it exists now, will place a heavy burden on sectors or companies which mainly employ female workers (Dehaes et al., 1997).

3. Movement towards a Time-credit System: In the long run it is desirable for the systems of early exit and career break to become integrated in one time-credit system. In such a system, at the beginning of his or her career each employee would receive a certain credit of free time that can be used, within certain limits and under certain modalities, during the career. It can be used for professional training, long holidays, care for children or parents, or early retirement. The basic legislative provisions could be supplemented by sectoral collective labour agreements.

Clearly, the introduction of such a time-credit system would lead to a so-called deinstitutionalization of the life cycle (Guillemard, 1995), moving society away from the traditional tripartite structure of the life cycle: training (for youth), work (for adults), and inactivity (for old age).

4. The Introduction of an Individual Savings System: The credit system can be supplemented by other systems on the level of the individual firm. In several companies, employees are already able to choose between a higher wage and more leisure time. Sometimes there is an option available that permits the employee to exchange an amount of his or her free time with a colleague for, say, an amount of money. In some companies, employees can even save up their leisure time for several years in order to take a sabbatical. This formula has increasingly attracted the interest of younger generations of managers. It is possible that, in the long run, new forms of career break will appear out of this new individual savings system.

5. The Introduction of Premiums for Firms: In order to compensate employers for the organizational and administrative costs associated with introducing and promoting the career-break option, the government could consider providing premiums to companies where more than 3 per cent of workers use the of career-break system.

Conclusion

The rationale behind the Belgian bridging pension system is that reducing the supply of labour can help to combat unemployment. In the last twenty years, masses of older workers have left the labour market. However, the bridging pension has many drawbacks. Not only is it expensive, it also has an age-discriminating effect in such areas as training and recruitment – the so-called trickle-down effect.

As an alternative, therefore, we urge an extension of the already existing system of the career break. In contrast to the bridging pension, it is age neutral and respects the free choice of the individual employee. At this moment the system is too selective because it is more attractive to young mothers than to other groups. To make it more broadly attractive, we suggest raising the allowances and linking the system more to other labour-market instruments such as training. In that way more men and workers in other age groups will see its advantages. In the long run, we plead for the integration of the bridging pension and the career break. In such a system each employee would get, on entering the labour market, a time credit that, under certain conditions, could be used for care, training, or early retirement. We also urge a further expansion of the 'cafeteria' system of company benefits, so that employees can opt for more leisure time instead of a higher wage and so that they can also save their credits during a certain period.

Finally, we also call for additional research on potential trouble spots in the career-break system. These would include the availability and the precarious situation of the unemployed who replace the career breaker, possible problems linked with the reintegration in the labour market of the career breaker, and organizational and administrative problems for the employer. We also call for additional research to define more precisely the groups that are eligible for a career break but that have not yet made use of the system.

REFERENCES

La Commission Européenne. (1997, 29 septembre). *Projet de la Commission concernant le rapport conjoint sur l'emploi 1997*. Bruxelles: Author.

Dehaes V., Vanzegbroeck P., Lambrechts E., & Pauwels, K. (1997). *Gezinseffectrapportage, loopbaanonderbreking en deeltijdse arbeid: Effecten van de arbeidssituatie op de gezinnen*. Brussels: CBGS.

Eurostat. (1997). *Labour force survey 1997*. Brussels: Author.

Guillemard A.-M. (1995). Paradigmes d'interprétation de la sortie anticipée d'activité des salariés vieillissants: Un bilan de la recherche comparée internationale. *Travail et emploi* (DARES), *63*, 4–22.

ILO (International Labour Office). (1995). *World labour report*. Thullen, Geneva: Author.

Jobrotation – en introduktion, K'benhavn (Brochure). (1997). Copenhagen, Denmark: Np.

Kerkhoff, W., & Kruidenier, H. (1991). *Bedrijfsleven en vergrijzing: Aanzetten voor een leeftijdsbewust personeelsbeleid*. Amsterdam: NIA.

Kohli, M., & Rein, M. (1991). The changing balance of work and retirement. In M. Kohli, M. Rein, A.-M. Guillemard, & H. Van Gunsteren (Eds), *Time for retirement: Comparative studies of early exit from the labor force* (pp 1–35). Cambridge: Cambridge University Press.

Loden, M., & Rosener, J. (1991). *Workforce America! Managing employee diversity as a vital resource.* New York: Irwin.

MTA (Ministerie van Tewerkstelling en Arbeid [Ministry of Employment and Labour]). (1997a). *Werkloosheid in België: Statistische reeksen* (maart). Brussels: Author.

MTA. (1997b). *Het federaal werkgelegenheidsbeleid: Evaluatierapport.* Brussels: Author.

MTA. (1997c). *Resultaten van de sectorale onderhandelingen 1997–1998: Informatiecampagne over 'arbeidsherverdeling.'* Brussels: Author.

Phillipson, C. (1982). *Capitalism and the construction of old age.* London: Macmillan Press.

Rosen, B., & Jerdee, T. (1985). *Older employees: New roles for valued resources.* Homewood, IL: Dow-Jones-Irwin.

RVA (Rijksdienst voor Arbeidsvoorziening [Public Service for Labour Supply]). (1996). *Maandelijks bulletin 1983–1997.* Brussels: Author.

RVA. (1997). *Jaarverslag 1996.* Brussels: Author.

Sackmann, R. (1997). Der einfluss von verrentungsprozessen und mobilitatsprozessen auf die arbeidsmarktrisiken von berufseinsteigern. *Mitteilungen aus der Arbeitsmarkt- und Berufsforschung, 3,* 675–80.

Serroyen, C. (1997). Bilan van het toekomstplan: Een overzicht van de sectorale akkoorden 1997–1998. *Nieuwsbrief steunpunt WAV, 4,* 83–8.

Shea, G. (1991). *Managing older employees.* San Francisco: Jossey-Bass.

Simoens, P., Denys, J., & Denolf, L. (1998). *Hoe werven bedrijven? 1997* (Upedi). Leuven: HIVA.

Trommel, W. (1994). Het immuunsysteem Nederland: Enige gedachten over eigentijdse vormen van pensionering. *Sociaal Maandblad Arbeid* (maart), *3,* 142–8.

Van Haegendoren, M. (1998, 7 April). Acht op tien ouders willen poosje thuis zijn. *De Standaard,* p. 8.

Van Poeck, A., & Van Rompuy, P. (1995). Knelpunten in de Belgische economie: Het arbeidsmarktbeleid en de overheidsfinanciën. *Economisch en Sociaal Tijdschrift, 1,* 31–60.

Walker, A. (1997). *Combating age barriers in employment.* Dublin: European Foundation for the Improvement of Living and Working Conditions.

Warr, A. (1997). *Age and job performance.* Unpublished manuscript.

21. Restructuring Work in an Aging America: What Role for Public Policy?

Sara E. Rix[1]

In the United States, as in most of the rest of the developed world, work and work lives underwent a dramatic restructuring over the course of the twentieth century. Men were living longer but working less. Women marched to a different drummer as growing numbers, whose life expectancy was also on the rise, entered the labour force in the postwar years and remained there longer. For both women and men, however, work beyond what might be referred to as 'conventional retirement age' – 65 when Social Security was established in 1935 and closer to 62 as the age of eligibility for benefits was lowered – became ever less common. A relatively small retired population and an expanding work force meant a low burden of old-age support for the working-age population for many decades.

Workers found retirement affordable and, hence, attractive, even though many might have preferred some type of less structured or less pressured work during their early retirement years. Employers were confronted with an ample supply of young, productive, well-educated workers in the baby boomers (born between 1946 and 1964) and saw no need to encourage older workers to stay on or return to the labour force. However, an escalating burden of retirement support, coupled with anticipated labour shortages in many fields, has sparked growing interest in the need to rethink postwar work and retirement patterns, with an eye towards developing programs and policies to restructure work over the life course in ways fostering prolonged productive labour-force attachment.

Work, Aging, and Public Policy

Public policy makers in the United States have yet to address in any systematic way the employment implications of an aging America or to assess the role that public policy might play in expanding employment opportunities for, or enhancing the productivity of, older workers. Nor do these issues seem to have generated much attention in the private sector.

Part of the explanation for this neglect may lie in the fact that age-related changes in the U.S. work force are not expected to be all that dramatic in the near future. True, the number of labour-force participants aged 55 and above – the 'older work force' for the purposes of this paper – is projected to increase by some 44 per cent between 1996 and 2006 alone (Fullerton, 1997). However, that 44 per cent translates into only 7 million more older workers and job seekers, a small addition to a work force some 138 million strong as of 1998. Moreover, most of the new older workers will be relatively young – between the ages of 55 and 64.

Furthermore, although both the median age of the work force and the proportion of workers who are old will rise, these measures of aging point to a work force that is – all else being equal – no older in 2006 than it was forty years earlier. Indeed, the proportion of the work force that is aged 55 and above will actually be lower in 2006 than it was in 1966. Thus, the short-term consequences of an aging work force are unlikely to be as momentous as many prognosticators would have us believe.

Another factor that may help explain why the older worker is not a high-priority issue in the U.S. Congress is the lack of demand for action from potential interest groups, notably older workers and their advocates. Aging organizations that might be expected to lead the fight on behalf of older workers are coping with issues of greater urgency, including the reform of Medicare and Social Security. The private sector tends to show little enthusiasm for any congressional intervention in labour matters, though it might welcome certain forms of payroll-tax relief. Furthermore, the case for intervention is perhaps not all that obvious in an economy with unemployment rates at a thirty-year low.

Work and Retirement in Twentieth-Century America

As in other industrialized nations during the past half-century, declin-

Figure 21.1 Labour-force-participation Rates of Older Men and Women in the United States, 1950–2006

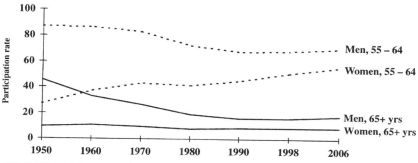

SOURCE: U.S. Bureau of Labor Statistics, *Handbook of Labor Statistics*, 1985, table 5; Howard N Fullerton, *Monthly Labor Review*, November 1997, table 4; U.S. Bureau of Labor Statistics, *Employment and Earnings*, 1991, table 3, and 1999, table 3. (Graph produced by AARP Public Policy Institute.)

ing labour-force-participation rates of middle-aged and older men in the United States (figure 21.1) reflect a restructured work life encompassing an anticipated and lengthening period of leisure in later life. Over much of this period, middle-aged women have demonstrated increasing attachment to the labour force, but not enough to offset the fall among men. As a result, at least until the mid-1980s, relatively fewer older persons were remaining in the labour force each year.

While some of the decline in the labour-force participation of older men has been occasioned by poor health or mandatory retirement (which was not officially eliminated until 1986), growing enthusiasm for later-life leisure has played a big part. Enhanced Social Security benefits and expanded private pension coverage have made retirement in dignity and comfort an achievable goal for many millions of Americans – surely one of the great success stories of the twentieth century. When early reduced Social Security benefits became available for women in 1956 and men in 1961, growing numbers of workers began to leave work early, often at the youngest possible age. With their feet, workers have demonstrated their eagerness to retire, and employers have generally wanted them to go.

Even so, many workers express interest in prolonging their attachment to the labour force, either because they like their work, want to keep active, or anticipate needing to work. For example, nearly three-fourths of preretirees (ages 51 to 61) in the first wave of the Health and Retirement Study reported that they would like to continue to work in some capacity in retirement (National Institute on Aging, 1993), with comparably high figures found in other studies (see especially Yakoboski and Dickemper, 1997, p. 4; also Farkas and Johnson, 1997). Some 80 per cent of baby boomers report that they expect to work in retirement (AARP, 1998).

Expressions of interest in continued employment are nothing new (see, for example, Louis Harris and Associates, 1979), although workers who act on that interest appear to be in the minority. In addition, as duration of retirement lengthens, interest in employment appears to wane; retirees who return to the labour force apparently do so fairly soon after retirement (Hurd, 1990; Hayward, Crimmins, and Wray, 1994). Data from the U.S. Bureau of Labor Statistics (1999, table 35) indicate that hardly more than 2 per cent of the 38 million men and women aged 55 and older who are not in the labour force actually want work, a statistic that would seem to support Schulz's (1988) observation that most people adjust quickly and well to retirement.

It is, of course, always possible that the numbers seeking work would increase if the employment options for the older worker were more attractive. Officially designated 'discouraged workers' – men and women who are neither working nor looking for work because they doubt that employers would hire them because of their age, skill level, or some other real or perceived deficiency – may be rare among the elderly in the United States, but older job seekers face formidable barriers when it comes to getting hired.

It is also the case, however, that retirement – early retirement – continues to appeal to aging workers. Fully one-third of the working respondents in the 1997 Retirement Confidence Survey contended that they would like to retire before the age of 55, although few seemed to believe that they would be able to (Yakoboski and Dickemper, 1997).

Still, anecdotal evidence suggests that some change in work behaviour on the part of older Americans is occurring. Newspaper headlines are perhaps a bit overblown – see, for example, 'Ending a Working Life: Trend Is to Labor Longer, Go Gradually' (*Philadelphia Inquirer*, 10 November 1997); 'More Americans Working beyond Traditional Retirement Age' (*Tampa Tribune*, 16 November 1997); or 'Early Retirement Becoming a Dream of the Past' (*The Nation*, 21 December 1997) – but there are other signs that the trend towards ever-earlier retirement has abated. In particular, since about 1985, the labour-force-participation rate of older persons has levelled off (figure 21.1), though, popular press reports to the contrary, it is probably premature to conclude that there has been a marked reversal in early retirement trends.

The significance of the developments depicted in figure 21.1 and elsewhere would seem to lie more in what is not happening than in what is – labour-force *withdrawal* rates at upper ages are not increasing. Moreover, the labour-force increases shown, however slight, may be harbingers of things to come.

The Baby Boomers and Retirement

The baby boomers will not begin reaching what is now conventional retirement age until 2011. Nevertheless, employers might do well to anticipate changes in work and retirement decisions as the boomers move towards age 55 or so. Early retirement may indeed be pushed back if large numbers of boomers find themselves ill prepared to maintain preretirement living standards on the Social Security benefits, pensions, and savings that they have accumulated to date. William Gale of the Brookings Institution estimates that perhaps one-third of the baby boomers are not on their way to a financially secure retirement; the security of another third could be at risk (Gale, 1997). Better educated than previous generations of older workers and perhaps cognizant of lengthening life expectancy, many may find that they want to continue working.

Boomers may also be affected by increases in the age of eligibility for full Social Security benefits. Under current law, the age of eligibility for full Social Security benefits will gradually rise from age 65 to 66, beginning with workers turning 62 in 2000. It will remain at 66 for eleven years, at which time it will gradually increase to age 67. Evidence to suggest that this change alone will have much of an impact on behaviour is scanty, but further increases seem likely in response to long-term financing problems facing the U.S. Social Security system and the shrinking ratio of Social Security contributors per retiree. Raising the age of eligibility for early, reduced benefits has also been proposed (see, e.g., Burkhauser, Couch, and Phillips, 1996).

Lengthening life expectancy is seen by some as reason enough to entertain the notion of a longer work life. Burkhauser and Quinn (1997), for example, have recently questioned whether the idealized normal retirement age established in the first half of this century is appropriate for the twenty-first century, but their concern is by no means unprecedented. As far back as 1951, then-commissioner of the

U.S. Bureau of Labor Statistics, Ewan Clague (1951, p. 71), argued that if life expectancy is prolonged 'to 90 and even 100 years ... we had better reexamine 65 as the age of retirement.'

Life expectancy at birth has yet to reach 100 or even 90, but the number of persons reaching those advanced ages is rising. Today's 65-year-old can expect to live another 17.5 years, about 5 years longer than was the case when the Social Security Act was passed (National Center for Health Statistics, 1997a, p. 31; 1997b, Table 6-4); further increases are projected. One-fourth of persons who reach age 65 can expect to live until 90, up from 14 per cent in 1960 (U.S. Bureau of the Census, 1996, figure 3-2). Up to now, these increases in life expectancy have not been accompanied by a comparable rise in the retirement age.

While many preretirees say they would like to continue working in retirement, they have no desire to be *forced* to do so. In fact, raising the retirement age is not a particularly popular option for solving Social Security's financing problems (Yakoboski and Dickemper, 1997). As former Principal Deputy Commissioner of Social Security Lawrence Thompson (1996, p. 2) has noted: 'If any consensus can be found among opinion leaders, it is that the retirement age ought to be increased. Yet few employers seem to want to keep their long-tenured employees around even longer and few individuals seem to be interested in delaying pension receipt.'

None the less, raising the retirement age will feature prominently in future debates on Social Security solvency. As a result, issues related to the older worker will achieve greater salience for public and private policy makers, who will be faced with examining the consequences of a higher retirement age for employers and workers alike. Little may be known about the effect that the recently implemented two-year increase will have, but it – like the effect of any further increase – is sure to depend on the health status and retirement income of older workers, the availability of alternative sources of labour, the nature of the available jobs, and the level of employer enthusiasm for older workers.

Preparing for an Aging Work Force

While growing numbers of older workers might begin to act on their wishes to keep working in some capacity, there is little evidence, as noted earlier, that employers are doing much to prepare for this possibility (Barth, McNaught, and Rizzi, 1993; National Council on the Aging, 1998a, 1998b; Watson Wyatt Worldwide, 1998).

In the face of the booming economy of recent years, many U.S. employers have been facing labour shortages and have become more creative and aggressive in seeking workers. They are also turning to workers whom they may have shunned in the past. In some cases, employers are attempting to entice older persons back to work with lucrative financial offers – see, for example, headlines such as 'Boeing Offering Retirees a Bonus to Return to Job' (*Seattle Post-Intelligencer*, 12 December 1997). In other cases, employers may be offering schedules that hold particular appeal to aging workers and retirees. For example, a recent article in the *Washington Post* highlights the extent to which employers in the retail trade are moving to far more flexible scheduling than even they have had in the past – two-hour shifts in the case of major retailer Sears-Roebuck (Pressler, 1998).

Similar efforts to accommodate non-traditional workers characterized the fast-food industry in the 1980s, where employers faced with a drop in the number of young labour-force entrants responded with policies designed to encourage older persons to return to work. Days Inns also began to hire and train older workers as reservations agents when confronted with labour shortages in the 1980s.

Employers certainly give every sign of valuing older workers highly when it comes to such attributes as loyalty, experience, dependability, customer relations, and the like (AARP, 1995; Barth, McNaught, and Rizzi, 1993). That being the case, the question that arises is why examples of the successful use of older workers, such as that of Days Inns, whose older workers turned out to be as productive as their younger counterparts (Commonwealth Fund, 1990), have spawned so few imitators. Though market forces have yielded labour shortages, employers maintain reservations about such workers with respect to flexibility, adaptability, technological competence (AARP, 1995), and costs that continue to discourage wide-scale efforts to retain older workers or recruit them for better jobs.

Older Americans at Work and in the Transition to Retirement

As of 1998, there were 17 million men and women age 55 and older in the labour force in the United States, the majority employed full time. Many of these older workers have simply aged on the job, but others changed careers in midstream or returned to work after retirement, proof that there are jobs for older workers. Job-tenure data reveal an increase in the proportion of workers aged 65 and over who have been employed for less than one year, another indication of job change in later life (U.S. Bureau of Labor Statistics, 1987, 1997a, 1998b).

Part-time Work

Older workers often express a preference for less than full-time work, and many older persons who remain in the labour force have found or negotiated part-time positions. About one-fourth of older Americans work part time (26 per cent in 1998), all but a handful by choice.

In general, part-time work in the United States – which employs a disproportionate share of older workers – offers lower wages, fewer benefits, and fewer challenges than full-time work. As Straka (1992, p. 23) notes in a report for the U.S. Social Security Administration, 'many or most post-career older workers [are forced] to choose between full retirement and a lesser, or at least lower-paying, job.'

Flexibility in Work Schedules

Flexible work schedules are also becoming more common as employers respond to the needs of their workers with family commitments and to the demands of consumers for greater convenience in shop hours and service delivery. As of May 1997, nearly 28 per cent of the full-time U.S. work force could vary the time they started and/or ended work. This is up from just over 12 per cent in 1985 and 15 per cent in 1991 (U.S. Bureau of Labor Statistics, 1998a).

Perhaps surprisingly, flexible work schedules are more characteristic of older men than of older women, especially in the 65-plus population. In fact, in this age group, men working full time are about twice as likely as their female counterparts to be on flexible work schedules – 38 per cent vs. 21 per cent.

The Transition to Retirement

For many workers, retirement is a process, rather than a one-time, all-or-nothing event. That process for a substantial number of eventual retirees involves transitional employment following full-time and/or career employment before leaving the labour force: perhaps as many as one-third to one-half of eventual retirees experience some form of 'bridge' employment before complete retirement (see Mutchler et al., 1997; Quinn and Kozy, 1996; Ruhm, 1990, 1994). However, very few of these bridge jobs are the result of formal phased retirement programs that might reflect employers' interest in retaining the skills and expertise of their older workers; according to the benefits consulting firm

Watson Wyatt, only 8 per cent of the 500 companies reporting to a recent Watson Wyatt query had implemented phased retirement arrangements (Watson Wyatt Worldwide, 1997). Thus, the transitional employment that acts as a bridge between career work and retirement is typically the result of a worker's own creation or job search.

The apparent downward mobility characteristic of much bridge or transitional employment in the United States (Barth and McNaught, 1989; Ruhm, 1990) may indicate that a great deal of it is involuntary, perhaps the result of job loss or premature retirement. None the less, not all older people suffer income and status losses when they secure bridge employment (e.g., Anderson, Burkhauser, and Slotsve, 1992). Ruhm (1994) has observed a surprising degree of upward occupational mobility occurring later in life, often the result of a move into bridge employment. Even so, a major concern identified by Ruhm (1994, p. 95) is the 'limited ability of many workers to either retain jobs or to obtain acceptable bridge employment,' something that formal phased retirement programs might alleviate.

Self-employment

For some older workers, the transition to retirement may be in the form of self-employment. On the one hand, self-employment can facilitate continued employment, as worker-owners have greater say over work schedules and working conditions than the non–self-employed. On the other hand, the self-employed may need to work longer (for example, until they qualify for Medicare or because pension coverage is lacking). Some workers move into self-employment upon retiring from a long-term or career job, or as a result of job loss in midlife; however, the proportion doing so seems to be small (Evans and Leighton, 1989).

Contingent Work

Although some users of the term 'contingent' include part-time work in their definition, a more restrictive but perhaps more appropriate definition would limit it to those jobs whose most salient characteristic is the lack of security, such as temporary work or contract work. A supply of contingent workers can provide the corporate world with the flexibility to respond to rapidly changing consumer demands and rising competition in the global economy; the contingent work force provides employers with flexibility to meet changing labor needs by hiring and terminating as the work load and other factors require. Contingent work may also provide retired workers with the flexibility to work when and at what they please. Because of the relative ease with which unsatisfactory contingent workers can be terminated, the growth of contingent work may actually open up opportunities to older workers who would not have been hired in the past.

In the upper age levels, contingent work (defined here as including independent contractors, on-call workers, employees of temporary-help agencies, and workers provided by contract firms) escalates in what might be referred to as the retirement-age population, that is, those aged 65 and older. The proportion of workers engaged in these work arrangements (referred to by the U.S. Bureau of Labor Statistics as workers in non-traditional arrangements) hovered around 10 per cent among workers between the ages of 25 and 64 in 1997. More than twice as many age 65-plus workers (21 per cent) could be found in such work, with the large majority reporting that they were independent contractors (U.S. Bureau of Labor Statistics, 1997b). Undoubtedly, these arrangements appeal to many of these workers because they enable them to balance their work and leisure needs and interests. For some, however, contract work may be the only option available.

Because employers typically need not pay benefits to contingent workers, such workers are generally cheaper than permanent employees, effectively vitiating one of the major arguments against hiring or retaining older workers. Unsatisfactory employees can be terminated at the end of a contract. For the retiree with pension income and no need of employee benefits, contingent work may be the perfect bridge between full-time work and retirement, or it may be the perfect retirement supplement. As it turns out, however, older workers are actually underrepresented in the contingent work force, even though older contingent workers may be viewed as something of a bargain to employers (AARP, 1995).

Issues Related to the Older Worker in an Aging America

Identifying the Older Worker

Policy discussions about the older worker are often imprecise, proceeding as if everyone knew what was meant by 'older worker,' and everyone were talking about the same person. This paper has used the convenient cut-off of age 55, a not-uncommon early-retirement age in private pension plans and the age by which many employment problems have begun to manifest themselves. But that 55-and-older population is a heterogeneous group, a fact which advocates for the older worker might do well to heed. Policies and programs that are appropriate for – and attractive to – workers between the ages of, say, 55 and 60 may be totally inappropriate for most workers above the age of 70. Employers who might be receptive to retaining more older workers in the 55 to 60 age group might well balk if faced with workers in their seventies.

Like it or not, job-performance issues will be placed on the table if a sizable older work force becomes the reality. Research undertaken for AARP, among others, indicates that age is a poor predictor of performance (Sterns and McDaniel, 1994), but little of the research applies to the age groups most likely to be affected by an increase in retirement age. Especially wanting are studies of the actual performance of workers in their upper sixties and perhaps early seventies in a wide variety of the types of jobs likely to characterize the economy in the coming decades.

Little attention has been paid to the impact of common age-associated changes and developments on work performance at upper ages. Does drug use – not abuse, but the use of perhaps multiple medications for physical conditions more common among the aged – have implications for work performance at upper ages? Again, some of these questions have been irrelevant when fewer than 9 per cent of men and women in their seventies or older are in the labour force; however, if more workers are forced to work longer, such questions may require attention, especially if the less fit cannot retire.

Older workers are less likely than their younger counterparts to be injured on the job, but their injuries tend to be more disabling and their recovery time far longer (U.S. Bureau of Labor Statistics, 1996). They are also far more likely than younger workers to suffer fatal injuries (U.S. Bureau of Labor Statistics, nd). Differences such as these are real issues for employers and cannot be dismissed easily in an aging work force. As the Bureau of Labor Statistics concludes, 'the cost implications of severe injuries to older workers are especially troublesome for the future,' given growth in this segment of the population (U.S. Bureau of Labor Statistics, 1996, p. 2). Enhanced safety standards, job redesign, and job modification may solve the problem, although the costs of some changes may also serve to deter employers from hiring or retaining older workers.

A recent survey by Watson Wyatt Worldwide (1998) provides a glimpse of what some chief executive officers (CEOs) were willing to admit anonymously about older workers, namely that they believe worker productivity peaks at around age 43. Somewhat more encouraging, at least in the opinion of U.S. and Canadian CEOs, is that peak productivity is sustained until age 60, on average. In light of rapid technological changes ostensibly affecting workers throughout the economy, more than fifteen years at peak might have been unexpected. Still, 60 is some years below what many policy makers would have as the normal retirement age.

Some scholars (see, e.g., Rebick, 1993) have suggested that the Age Discrimination in Employment Act actually works against older workers by requiring employers to pay older workers more than they are worth given declining productivity. Older workers are far more likely to be employed in Japan than in the United States, but one reason is that employers are able to hire and retain them in ways that would be against the law in the United States (Rix, 1996; Seike, 1994). Mandatory retirement is legal, so employers can divest themselves of unproductive workers at retirement age; however, employers can also retire and rehire workers they want to retain, paying them lower wages for performing the same job they did prior to retirement. Japanese employers can lower the wages of workers once they reach a certain age or transfer them to subsidiary companies at lower wages.

Similar situations may occur in the United States, when workers are encouraged or pressured to accept an early retirement incentive offer and are then rehired as consultants or contract workers (rehiring retirees for short-term projects has been common in the aerospace industry, for example); such workers probably do not collect benefits and so are paid less than they had been.

The Matter of Jobs for Older Workers

The success of efforts to promote employment opportunities for older persons will depend on more than work schedules; it will also depend on where the jobs are. The U.S. Bureau of Labor Statistics provides occupational projections for several hundred jobs in the U.S. economy, a mere thirty of which are projected to account for *nearly half* (46 per cent) of the 18.6 million new jobs that may be created in the United

States between 1996 and 2006 (Silvestri, 1997). These are, typically, service-sector jobs, and many of them are good jobs – general managers and top executives, systems analysts, and computer engineers, for example – that will demand advanced and constantly changing skills. But others require little in the way of skills and compensate accordingly; more than half pay low or very low wages. Moreover, while they may not be arduous in the sense that foundry work was, many of them can hardly be considered light work – truck drivers, food counter workers, cooks, and wait staff. Granted, these thirty occupations are not the only ones in which job growth will occur. Furthermore, attrition and retirements in existing jobs will generate employment opportunities. However, older workers and their advocates who talk about the growing demand for workers should keep in mind that much of the labour demand will be in jobs that may not attract older workers who have alternative income options.

Projections of job growth thus should introduce a note of caution to the debate on raising retirement age, whether voluntarily or involuntarily. Will older workers want or be suited to the jobs that may be available to them? What efforts need to be undertaken now to ensure that more older workers can compete successfully for the better jobs that will be available over the next ten or twenty years? The fact that baby boomers are the best educated generation in history will not help them much if most of that education ended some thirty or forty years ago.

Employment Policy for an Aging Work Force

'One of the most important issues before the U.S. Congress today is the need to find ways of expanding employment opportunities for those older men and women who want to work full or part time' (U.S. Senate, 1981).

This statement sounds as if it might have been uttered today, but the words are actually two decades old, written by Senator John Heinz, then chair of the U.S. Senate Special Committee on Aging, and Senator Lawton Chiles, ranking minority member of the committee, who were calling for consideration of and debate on a national policy on older workers. Such a policy, they contended, would 'become all the more important as our society ages, and we, as a Nation, are blessed with larger numbers of older people living longer and healthier lives' (U.S. Senate, 1981).

We are still waiting for that debate, but there is little sense of urgency in the United States about issues related to older workers. This is not to suggest that older workers have been entirely forgotten in public discourse, but merely to emphasize that there has been no concerted public effort to examine the role of older workers in an aging society or to develop a comprehensive employment policy that would address the needs and changing circumstances of older workers.

To the extent that public policy makers have focused on older workers, they have tended to do so with respect to (1) attempting to level the playing field for old and young workers by banning age discrimination in employment; (2) assisting older workers not yet eligible for retirement benefits in finding work via various publicly funded job-training programs; and (3) fostering a longer working life in response to Social Security financing problems. This last has involved the above-mentioned gradual increase in the age of eligibility for full Social Security benefits, a gradual increase in the retirement credit paid to workers who delay collecting Social Security benefits until age 70, and, more recently, a liberalization of how much workers can earn without risk of losing benefits.

Raising the Retirement Age

Ideally, U.S. policies related to the older worker in the twenty-first century will be shaped by specific and well-articulated objectives. One key concern seems to be the need to encourage longer work lives for the sake of Social Security. As stated earlier, this objective is likely to be expressed in further efforts to raise the age of eligibility for full, and perhaps early, Social Security benefits. Raising the retirement age would seem to make sense in the face of longer life expectancy, the growing aged dependency burden, rising educational levels among older workers, inadequate retirement savings on the part of millions of American workers, and projected labour shortages.

A further increase in the age of eligibility for Social Security benefits, especially if accompanied by a rise in the early retirement age and substantial penalties for early retirement, would undoubtedly suffice to keep many workers in the labour force for longer periods of time; however, it might be the *wrong* workers who stay. Older workers with alternative income sources – such as savings and investments (and many workers have realized handsome gains on their stock market investments in recent years) – may continue to retire early; these are likely to be better-educated workers in jobs where their skills and abilities are valued. Workers with fewer retirement options may be the very ones whom employers would like to get rid of. If required to retain workers longer, employers may respond by weeding out potentially unproductive workers at younger ages or continuing to offer early-retirement incentives, perhaps negating the impact of an increase in the age of eligibility for Social Security benefits. A higher retirement age also demands that policy makers pay attention to the social safety net that must be in place for those workers, many of them members of minority groups, unable to work as a result of ill health, disability, or skills obsolescence.

Alternatives to Full-time Retirement

While older workers say they would like some form of postretirement employment, it is by no means certain what they would do if actually faced with more opportunities. Many probably would take advantage of phased retirement opportunities, if for no other reason than that it would spare them the stress of a job search. It is also possible that growing numbers of employers will seek to maximize the return on their investment in certain valued workers by implementing phased retirement programs, especially if a labour shortage materializes. Much-ballyhooed skills shortages may force employers to implement strategies, such as phased retirement, to retain skilled and experienced workers longer, although few employers at present seem to see older workers as potential solutions to those skills shortages. More widespread use of phased retirement in some cases would require Congress to modify restrictions of the Employee Retirement Income Security Act (ERISA) on in-service pension distributions.

As attractive as phased retirement might be to many workers and their employers, any increase in its availability is likely to be gradual. In addition, millions of workers will never have the option of formally easing into retirement with their current employers because millions of employers will never be able or willing to introduce such employment options. It is also the case that many employers will prefer informal arrangements, working out retention opportunities on a case-by-case basis in order to maintain greater control over the workers who leave or, more likely, stay.

While one can only speculate on how the boomers will behave as they approach retirement age, the wise employer might expect that this generation, used as it is to getting its way all through life, will expect to have a say in the shaping of their final work and retirement years.

Eliminating Age Discrimination

In 1967, Congress passed the Age Discrimination in Employment Act (ADEA), making it illegal for employers and unions to base decisions about wages and benefits, hirings, firings, promotions, and training opportunities on age; subsequent amendments eliminated mandatory retirement in all but a very few occupations. Workers legally have the right to continue working as long as they are able and their job exists, and some workers have undoubtedly taken advantage of that (see Burkhauser and Quinn, 1997). Sensitivity to age issues on the part of employers has undoubtedly increased, in part as a result of some large court judgments against discriminating employers. Nevertheless, few observers are likely to claim that this legislation will succeed in eliminating age-based employment discrimination in the United States.

Better monitoring and enforcement of the Age Discrimination in Employment Act is certainly desirable, but that alone is unlikely to improve appreciably the employment prospects for older workers. In an economy with millions of small employers and where labour needs may be changing frequently, where job tenure is falling (as it seems to be doing for men), and where sizable numbers of workers are competing for contingent positions, adequate monitoring and enforcement may be unachievable.

Making Work Pay

Some proposed policy changes would seem to be givens. For example, workers should not be penalized for working longer, as they are under some defined-benefit pension plans. Kotlikoff and Wise (1987), among others, have shown how defined pension plans can penalize participants who remain on the job after some, often early, age. Workers may find that any increase in pension benefits realized as a result of delaying retirement is not enough to make up for the benefits they forego while continuing to work. In other words, delayed retirement may result in less in lifetime pension benefits rather than more, which is not an outcome designed to encourage continued employment.

Favouring the Older Worker

Fostering longer work lives through an increase in the retirement age and penalizing workers who do not conform to the higher age can be viewed as retirement disincentives (Crown, 1990). Policy makers may also want to grapple with the role that work incentives could play in effectively raising the age at which people voluntarily retire. For instance, elimination of the Social Security earnings test in 2000 has been seen as a means of encouraging more work on the part of the aged. While it is perhaps tempting to argue that the earnings limit does discourage work, the fact of the matter is that fully 88 per cent of the population aged 65 and older are not even in the labour force. They are totally unaffected by any earnings limit, as were workers aged 70 and older to whom the limit has not applied since 1984. Very few in this age group have any earnings at all.

Burkhauser and Quinn (1997) have suggested allowing workers aged 65 and above to opt out of paying Social Security taxes on all or perhaps just a portion of their earnings. Relieving employers of the payroll tax for their older workers might well encourage more of them to hire or retain workers in the relevant age group.

While care needs to be taken not to run afoul of the ADEA by singling out older workers in a negative way, positive discrimination raises its own questions. Relaxation of the payroll tax seems questionable not only in light of the growing demands on the Social Security system but also in view of the fact that many younger workers pay more in Social Security taxes than they do in income taxes. At a time when young workers worry about the ability of Social Security to pay benefits for them when they retire, policies that seem to favour older people unduly may be rejected as unfair and unwarranted.

Conclusions

As William Crown (1996, p. 391) has pointed out, 'the labor force participation decisions of older workers are enormously complex,' affected as they are by a variety of factors, only a portion of which, he goes on to say, can be influenced by the efforts of those who would sway the retirement decision. It is by no means certain that any public policy short of drastically curtailing early retirement benefits or denying Social Security benefits to workers until they reach some new, higher retirement age could do much to increase *measurably* the labour-force-participation rates of older men and women in the United States. Even with such change, employers, if they so choose, can do much to counter the impact of a higher retirement age under Social Security through pension enhancements and retirement incentives. Workers with alternative sources of income, such as pensions and savings, would, of course, be less restricted by a higher retirement age than those without such resources.

This is not to suggest that more modest changes would not encourage more older workers to rethink their early retirement decisions. However, to the extent that workers can afford to retire, much of their enthusiasm for remaining in the labour force will depend on the jobs that are available to them, and here the role for public policy is far more suspect. Congress might improve the quality of part-time jobs by requiring prorated fringe benefits, but any advantages of doing this must be weighed against the cost to employers and, ultimately, to the workers themselves. Indeed, all the benefits of keeping people working longer must be weighed against the costs of making that happen.

Advocates for the older worker have long deplored the loss to the economy of the productive contributions of older workers – an 'untapped resource' as they have been called. The question that ensues is why employers have for so long failed to recognize and take advantage of that untapped resource. Burkhauser and Quinn (1997, p. 17) stress that 'labor demand for older workers depends on the overall strength of the economy, but also on government policies that influence the net cost of hiring older workers.' Understandably, employers will balk at paying any workers more than they are worth, but has that been the problem with older workers? Would employers be substantially more receptive to retaining and/or hiring older workers if, for example, Medicare – rather than employer-provided insurance – once again became the primary payer of health care for the worker aged 65 and above? Should employers be provided with incentives to hire, train, and retain older workers? Should older workers themselves be provided with publicly funded incentives to update their job skills and/or to remain in or return to the labour force?

After three decades of attempting to enforce and improve upon a law to remove age discrimination in employment, has the time come to rethink age-neutral policies and turn to differential treatment based on age alone? Should older workers be permitted, as the Hudson Institute suggests, 'to negotiate compensation packages that involve lower salary than younger workers in comparable jobs but include more costly health care benefits,' a strategy which is now illegal (Reynolds, 1997, p. 11)? Such moves might prove fraught with danger for the very group one hopes to help with such changes.

The United States faces about ten years of relatively modest change in the age distribution of the population. However, by the second decade of the twenty-first century, the first of some 76 million baby boomers will start turning 65. If employers experience labour and skills shortages, those aging baby boomers might look quite good to them, and they just might attempt to restructure work by introducing programs and policies (such as phased retirement or better part-time employment) that would help them meet their labour demands. If the demand for labour fails to materialize – or if the available jobs fail to appeal to the baby boomers – it is by no means obvious what public policies to foster a prolongation of work life would, in the end, accomplish. It would seem that the next ten years might be profitably spent doing, as Crown (1996, p. 404) has recommended, 'some serious soul-searching about why [older worker employment] policies are being pursued in the first place.' At that point, the most appropriate policy directions – or lack thereof – for the twenty-first century might be clearer.

NOTE

1 The views expressed in this paper are those of the author and do not necessarily represent the official policy of AARP.

REFERENCES

AARP (American Association of Retired Persons). (1995). *American business and older workers: A road map to the 21st century.* Washington, DC: Author.
AARP. (1998). *Boomers look toward retirement.* Washington, DC: Author.
Anderson, K., Burkhauser, R., & Slotsve, G. (1992). A two decade comparison of work after retirement in the United States. *The Geneva Papers on Risk and Insurance, 17*(62), 26–39.
Barth, M.C., & W. McNaught. (1989). *Why workers retire early.* New York: The Commonwealth Fund.
Barth, M.C., McNaught, W., & Rizzi, P. (1993). Corporations and the aging workforce. In P.H. Mirvis (Ed.), *Building the competitive workforce* (pp 156–200). New York: John Wiley.
Burkhauser, R.V., Couch, K.A., & Phillips, J.W. (1996). Who takes early social security benefits?: The economic and health characteristics of early beneficiaries. *The Gerontologist, 36*(6), 789–99.

Burkhauser, R.V., & Quinn, J.F. (1997). *Pro-work policy proposals for older Americans in the 21st century.* Syracuse, NY: Syracuse University, Maxwell School of Citizenship and Public Affairs, Center for Policy Research.

Clague, E. (1951, June). An over-all view of the problem of older workers. Proceedings of the Problems of Older Workers Conference, University of Wisconsin Industrial Relations Center, Madison, WI.

Commonwealth Fund. (1990). *Americans over 55 at work program* (Research Reports 1 and 2). New York: Author.

Crown, W.H. (1990). Economic trends, politics, and employment policy for older workers. *Journal of Aging and Social Policy, 2*(3/4), 131–51.

Crown, W.H. (1996). The political context of older worker employment policy. In W.H. Crown (Ed.), *Handbook on employment and the elderly* (pp 391–404). Westport, CT: Greenwood Press.

Evans, D.S., & Leighton, L.S. (1989). *Small-business formation by unemployed workers* (mimeo). Washington, DC: U.S. Small Business Administration, Office of Advocacy.

Farkas, S., & Johnson, J. (1997). *Miles to go: A status report on Americans' plans for retirement.* New York: Public Agenda.

Fullerton, H.N. (1997). Labor force 2006: Slowing down and changing composition. *Monthly Labor Review, 120*(11), 23–38.

Gale, W.G. (1997, Summer). Will the baby boom be ready for retirement? *The Brookings Review, 15*(3), 4–9.

Hayward, M.D., Crimmins, E.M., & Wray, L.A. (1994). The relationship between retirement life cycle changes and older men's labor force participation rates. *Journals of Gerontology, Social Sciences, 49*(5), S219–30.

Hurd, M.D. (1990). Research on the elderly: Economic status, retirement, and consumption and saving. *Journal of Economic Literature, 28*(2), 565–637.

Kotlikoff, L.J., & Wise, D.A. (1987). The incentive effects of private pension plans. In Z. Bodie, J.B. Shoven, & D.A. Wise (Eds), *Issues in pension economics* (pp 283–336). Chicago: University of Chicago Press.

Louis Harris & Associates, Inc. (1979). *1979 study of American attitudes toward pensions and retirement.* New York: Johnson & Higgins.

Mutchler, J.E., Burr, J.A., Pienta, A.M., & Massagli, M.P. (1997). Pathways to labor force exit: Work transitions and work instability. *Journals of Gerontology, Social Sciences, 52B*(1), S4–12.

National Center for Health Statistics. (1997a). Births and deaths: United States, 1996. *Monthly Vital Statistics Report* (Hyattsville, MD: Author), 46(1, Supp. 2).

National Center for Health Statistics. (1997b). *Life tables: Vital statistics of the United States* (Hyattsville, MD: Author), 1993, II (Mortality, Part A, Section 6).

National Council on the Aging (NCOA). (1998a, 1 April). *Corporate leaders,*

NCOA launch 100,000 jobs campaign to employ older workers throughout U.S. (Press release). Washington, DC: Author.

National Council on the Aging (NCOA). (1998b, 1 April). *Study shows employers value older workers, but don't know where to find them.* (Press release). Washington, DC: Author.

National Institute on Aging (NIA). (1993, 17 June). *Health and retirement study.* (Press release.) Washington, DC: Author.

Pressler, M.W. (1998, 18 April). For retail employers, hiring is a hard sell. *Washington Post*, pp A1, A11.

Quinn, J.F., & Kozy, M. (1996). The role of bridge jobs in the retirement transition: Gender, race, and ethnicity. *The Gerontologist, 36*(3), 363–72.

Rebick, M. (1993). The Japanese approach to finding jobs for older people. In O.S. Mitchell (Ed.), *As the workforce ages* (pp 103–24). Ithaca, NY: ILR Press.

Reynolds, A. (1997). Restoring work incentives for older Americans. *Outlook, 1*(10), 1–14.

Rix, S.E. (1996). The challenge of an aging work force: Keeping older workers employed and employable. *Journal of Aging and Social Policy, 8*(2/3), 79–96.

Ruhm, C.J. (1990). Career jobs, bridge employment, and retirement. In P.B. Doeringer (Ed.), *Bridges to retirement* (pp 92–107). Ithaca, NY: ILR Press.

Ruhm, C.J. (1994). Bridge employment and job stopping: Evidence from the Harris/Commonwealth survey. *Journal of Aging and Social Policy, 6*(4), 73–99.

Schulz, J.H. (1988, November). *Job matching in an aging society: Barriers to the utilization of older workers.* Paper presented at the annual meeting of the Gerontological Society of America, San Francisco.

Seike, A. (1994). The employment of older people in Japan and policies to promote it. *Japan Labor Bulletin* [On-line], *33*(12). Available: http://www.jil.go.jp/bulletin.

Silvestri, G.T. (1997). Occupational employment projections to 2006. *Monthly Labor Review, 120*(11), 58–83.

Sterns, H.L., & McDaniel, M.A. (1994). Job performance and the older worker. In S.E. Rix (Ed.), *Older workers: How do they measure up?* (pp 27–51). Washington, DC: AARP.

Straka, J.W. (1992). *The demand for older workers: The neglected side of a labor market* (Studies in Income Distribution, vol. 15). Washington, DC: U.S. Social Security Administration.

Thompson, L.H. (1996, December). *Social security reform options.* Paper presented to the National Legislative Council of AARP, Washington, DC.

U.S. Bureau of the Census. (1996). *65+ in the United States* (Current Population Reports, Special Studies, P23–190). Washington, DC: U.S. Government Printing Office.

U.S. Bureau of Labor Statistics. (nd). *1994 census of fatal occupational injuries* [On-line]. Available: *ftp://stats.bls.gov/pub/special.requests/ocwc/osh/cftb0056.txt.*

U.S. Bureau of Labor Statistics. (1985). *Handbook of labor statistics.* Washington, DC: U.S. Government Printing Office.

U.S. Bureau of Labor Statistics. (1987). *Job tenure* (mimeo). Washington, DC: Author.

U.S. Bureau of Labor Statistics. (1991). *Employment and earnings, 38*(1). Washington, DC: U.S. Government Printing Office.

U.S. Bureau of Labor Statistics. (1996, April). Older workers' injuries entail lengthy absences from work. *Issues in Labor Statistics,* Summary 96–6.

U.S. Bureau of Labor Statistics. (1997a, 30 January). Employee tenure in the mid-1990s. *News,* USDL 97–25.

U.S. Bureau of Labor Statistics. (1997b, 2 December). Contingent and alternative employment arrangements, February 1997. *News,* USDL 97–422.

U.S. Bureau of Labor Statistics. (1998a, 26 March). Workers on flexible and shift schedules in 1997. *News,* USDL 98–119.

U.S. Bureau of Labor Statistics. (1998b, 23 September). Employee tenure in 1998. *News,* USDL 98–387.

U.S. Bureau of Labor Statistics. (1999). *Employment and earnings, 46*(1). Washington, DC: U.S. Government Printing Office.

U.S. Senate. (1981). *Toward a national older worker policy* (An information paper prepared for use by the Special Committee on Aging). Washington, DC: U.S. Government Printing Office.

Watson Wyatt Worldwide. (1997, April). Phased retirement gradually makes its way into the workplace. *Watson Wyatt Insider,* 6–12.

Watson Wyatt Worldwide. (1998). Aging workforce emerges as concern for employers worldwide [On-line]. Available: *http://www.watsonwyatt.com/homepage/gl/new/pres_rel/march98/aging-tm.htm.*

Yakoboski, P., & Dickemper, J. (1997). *Increased saving but little planning: Results of the 1997 retirement confidence survey* (EBRI Issue Brief, 191). Washington, DC: Employee Benefits Research Institute.

PART THREE
Biography and Social Structure: Stability and Change

Introduction
Helga Krüger

Systematic research on the intersection of social structure and agency, though still in its infancy, is gaining ground. The contributions in part three of this book address the most challenging aspects of life-course research, attempting to bridge the gap between personal orientations and structural contexts of biographies in a changing world. It is perhaps not by chance that these chapters predominantly focus on established or changing arrangements between labour markets, family, and gender. The majority of the authors deal with intersecting lives and consider how the life courses and status passages of significant others influence and shadow the timing of events and the stages in an individual's life. Others concentrate on constraints and chances influencing individuals' life-course decisions, which are shown to be quite complicated in female life courses.

Most of the studies in this section explicitly refer to the dynamics between structure and biography in processes of social change. The inherent complexity of analysing changing times and the interaction of decision making and context broadens the scope of the discussion. Besides offering new theoretical approaches for life-course research, the contributions also enhance our understanding of how to combine qualitative and quantitative research methods. Empirically, the findings underline the importance of considering gender as a social category. From a cross-national perspective, these findings show astonishing differences in the social gendering of life courses as well as in gender-specific ways of balancing context and biography. Methodologically, these studies bridge the gap between the analysis of qualitatively captured biographies and research at the aggregate level. Altogether, they critically revise or reject individualization theory, and they also document that life-course research and theory would benefit from cooperation by qualitative and quantitative scholars.

This section begins with three contributions that discuss several key concepts of life-course analysis. Helga Krüger deepens our understanding of how institutions mediate between personal orientations and historically consolidated cultural patterns. She argues that cultural patterns are incorporated in the organizational shape of institutions, as can be seen in the gendered segmentation of the educational system, the labour market, and family support units. Krüger demonstrates that these institutions act as a generative grammar, a role which explains national differences in the way biographies and changing individual options in the life course interact with social structure inherited from the past. Phyllis Moen and Shin-Kap Han reformulate the concept of career by arguing that it is used in life-course research as a tool for characterizing transitions and trajectories in either work or family. Their study examines how relational commitments shape choices, and they emphasize the extent to which individual biographies and institutionalized roles are clearly embedded in, and mediated through, the lives of others. Kathleen Gerson delves beneath the polarized controversy over family values and their linkage to specific family structures. She uncovers the dynamics of family forms by showing that children between the ages of 18 and 30 at the time of the interviews have experienced nearly all types of family forms at some period of their lives. The family is not declining but has become dynamic, because gender arrangements are adapting and interacting with change and social processes both inside and outside the family. Gerson argues that, for life-course research, it is more important to analyse family trajectories than to identify family forms or households as static entities. The next four contributions refer to the concept of reflexive modernity and discuss controversial theoretical propositions about the predominance of individualized living conditions which require individuals to become the managers of their own biographies. By contrasting the self-interpretations of women and men who have graduated in engineering in Alberta, Canada, between 1980 and 1990, Gillian Ranson maps out the emergence of new career trajectories and career narratives constructed in the context of economic change. Smooth transitions in the earlier cohort gave way to discontinuous careers in the later cohort. She reveals how life-course dynamics and career turning-points create new notions of one's marketability and activate the self as a 'reflexive project' (Giddens, 1991). Still in the Canadian context, Paul Anisef and Paul Axelrod follow the diverse paths of an Ontario cohort of Grade 12 students in 1973 and document to what extent personal differences matter. The ways in which economic circumstances, socially constructed gender roles, and the individual personality affect pathways from schooling to employment and to family life are discussed with reference to the concept of 'structured individualization.' Ian Procter deepens this concept, and rejects Hakim's (1998) theory that female orientations and personal preferences define women's employment patterns, by examining the multidimensional contexts and conditions of young adult women's life trajectories in the English Midlands. Two trajectories were found: the 'single workers,' who in early adulthood were single, remained childless, and were employed full time; and the 'early mothers,' who were partnered mothers with at most part-time employment – although, when leaving initial education, the two groups did not display marked differences. The interrelationship of work and family, on the one hand, and the interplay of structural context and agency on the other are the general themes of this analysis. Jane Elliott, Angela Dale, and Muriel Egerton study the role of level of education and occupational qualifications in women's family formation patterns and employment histories by the age of 33, using longitudinal British cohort data. They critically discuss different assumptions about female employment behaviour – such as the influence of occupational or organizational qualifications, of cultural traditions or preplanned personal strategies, and of the organization of working hours or personal preferences. Their findings show to what extent both the level and the type of qualification held by a woman relate to family formation and the chance of adequate labour-market participation.

The section ends with a social historian's contribution to life-course analysis. Dirk Hoerder discusses the shortcomings of life-course concepts that associate linearity, sequence normality, and the notion of work as paid work. He documents the multiple ways in which two immigrant families secured their living in Canada while having to adapt not only to a new country but also to Canada as a changing society.

All contributions theoretically *and* empirically illuminate the complexities of life courses, an approach which opens the door to new challenges for such analyses. Linked lives, different chances in the management of resources, biographically and economically induced restructuring processes of work, and personal relations shape and reflect social reality on different levels simultaneously. Individual behaviour, relations, and organizations not only reproduce the social structure of a society but also act as supporters, providers, and preservers of change. The empirical findings demonstrate the multiple ways in which orientations and contexts interplay with mediated socially structured demands and reveal how constraints and contradictions nevertheless provide new impulses for social change.

REFERENCES

Giddens, A. (1991). *Modernity and self-identity.* Stanford: Stanford University Press.
Hakim, C. (1998). Developing a Sociology for the twenty-first century: Preference theory. *British Journal of Sociology, 49*(1), 137–43.

22. Social Change in Two Generations: Employment Patterns and Their Costs for Family Life

Helga Krüger

In contrast to the United States today, where only 9.4 per cent of workers live in so-called traditional families, with a male breadwinner and a full-time female homemaker (Han and Moen, 2001, forthcoming), Germany is well known for its exceptionally low participation rates of married women in the labour force. Elsewhere in Europe, the employment rates of married women have risen notably within the last three decades, and the corresponding rates for men have declined (see Yeandle, in this volume). But for both sexes, Germany happily brings up the rear.

This fact is frequently assumed to indicate Germans' dedication to a traditional family life and to a reliable and high family orientation (Hakim, 1997) which seems to be astonishingly resistant to social change. For the United States, Gerson (1993) classified the intergenerational differences between parents in their sixties and their adult children as a 'gender revolution.' The results of our similar research revealed that in Germany one should speak not of a gender revolution but of 'suffocated social change.' Within an international perspective the differences between the countries evoke some general questions which need to be dealt with first, before our special findings in Germany are discussed.

Social Constructions of the Life Course

Generative Grammar

The definition of the life course as 'the universal escalator on which everyone rides' (Glaser and Strauss, 1971) blurs the importance of national differences. But the age boundaries of life stages, as well as the biographical preparation for and follow-up after sequences of status positions and their social and personal costs and benefits, show nation-specific patterns. These differences indicate historically rooted social constructions, in part shared, in part unique for a given society. They rely upon institutionalized social orders which complicate the international comparability of the timing and, even more so, the configuration of biographical events in life-course patterns. In borrowing from linguistics (Chomsky, 1978 [1966]), we may call these orders the 'generative grammar' of nation-specific life-course patterns which restricts or facilitates the performance of social behaviour.

The German generative grammar of the life course predominantly results from our specific welfare regime (Leisering and Leibfried, 1999), which tends to protect every citizen from the cradle to the grave. Its functioning is also consolidated by the powerful trade unions' policies in favour of one family-supporting income and one family career, the latter saving welfare costs by means of a flexible familial stand-by support for every family member's care needs. In addition, the German welfare system is complemented by a segmented education system that distributes the holders of certificates into an occupationally organized labour-market grid with horizontally and vertically framed, but also hierarchical and gendered, labour-market positions (Krüger, 1999; Heinz, 1996; Allmendinger, 1989). A German perspective on this inherited social order and on social change in life-course patterns includes the following question: To what extent do welfare arrangements and formal occupational qualifications matter?

Gender

The universal fact of belonging to a male or a female world by virtue of sex veils the variety of nation-specific social framing. In Germany, female life courses are subjected to far more institutions that determine life timetables than those of men. Hagestad (1992) refers to American female life courses and also discerns differences between male and female life sequences. She argues for analysing durations within an institutionally bounded life span and not just the sequence of events which mark the turning-points from one phase to the next. In Germany, male and female durations include differences in the accumulated costs and benefits which, again, might matter for evaluating change in an international perspective.

Agency

Deciphering the generative grammar and the social framing of gendered life courses does not preclude an analysis of options and intentions that might govern people's minds. Life-course regularities can survive only if they are adopted by social actors, but personal interpretations and long-term perspectives might influence even the consistency of the generative grammar itself in a given society. As Giddens (1984) put it, social change depends on the interlacing of individual actors and social structure. For Germany, Beck (1990) reversed Ogburn's thesis on the 'cultural lag' in social change (Ogburn, 1932) by proposing that in Germany today we witness the opposite: institutions are lagging behind personal options and innovational activities (for the United States see Riley, Kahn, and Foner, 1994). From a German perspective, people seem increasingly to take a more active, monitoring part in shaping their lives. Since people's actions in the long run might change institutional supply and demand, it might be promising to differentiate both aspects of reality in the countries compared: the norm-guided personal aspect and the organizationally mediated structural one.

Research, therefore, should take into account *both* structural boundaries *and* the actors' performance. The two may sometimes be congruent and add up; but sometimes they may be contradictory. Such contradictions, if not taken into account, may lead to false generalizations about social tendencies in change. One specific way of discovering the effects is to link qualitative and quantitative research methods – that is, to combine standardized data and in-depth interviews. When both are used in the same project we usually find qualitative methods as an initial or preliminary step for preparing the standardized survey. The possible divergence of personal options and structural constraints raises the question, however, of whether this is the best and only way of combining the mutual strengths of the two methods (see also Erzberger and Prein, 1997; Kelle, 1994). The use of appropriate methods of qualitative data collection and statistical analysis of life-course events illuminates personal meanings and decision-making processes and provides the opportunity to profit from each instrument's own empirical logic, even if the two produce contradictory results (Ross-man and Wilson, 1985). The occasionally puzzling, dissonant findings reported in the following discussion have forced us to deepen and to widen our research focus and to rethink assumptions about normality in life-course theory.

Social Change in Two Generations in Germany

At the end of our fifty-two in-depth interviews with women in their sixties, a mother of two children, married for thirty-four years, summed it up: 'When I look back at my life, I have to admit – I have got the wrong husband.' This statement was not an isolated case. On the contrary, most of the women of this generation made the same point; in contrast, their husbands, who were interviewed separately, enthused about their good marriages, their happy families, and their wonderful wives. What could cause this split between male and female perceptions of family life? Empirically, comparing fathers and sons and mothers and daughters of the same families (parents in their sixties, children in their mid-thirties) to identify the differences in self-concepts and factual employment patterns in two generations revealed the double face of family costs for men and women and of the societal context for couples' decision-making processes about how to balance family life and labour-market participation. Theoretically, these find-ings about obvious contradictions between men's and women's per-ceptions and experiences are an invitation to take the frictions produced by changing norms and non-appropriate generative gram-mars into life-course theory.

The Data

The empirical data come from the Bremen study on male and female life-course interactions. Three surveys were conducted sequentially between 1989 and 1996 in the Special Collaborative Program on Status Passages and Risks in the Life Course, financed by the German National Research Foundation (DFG). The investigations form part of a combinational research design with a stepwise theory-guided broad-ening of findings via the addition of subsamples and their systematic regrouping (see figure 22.1). In the first step, standardized data were collected on 220 women who, in 1948–9, had completed vocational training in one of the top five female occupations, and had married

Figure 22.1 The Design

The overview integrates three projects on the management of adult lives between work and family in two generations.[a]

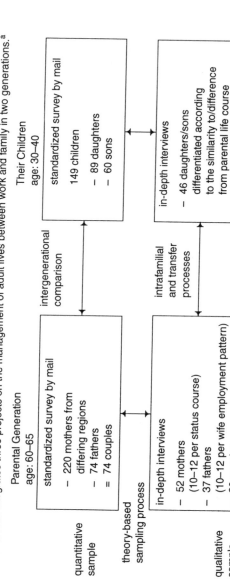

[a]The three projects form part of the Sfb 186 of the University of Bremen. They were financed by the German Research Foundation (DFG), conducted and worked out by H. Krüger and her team (C. Born, Ch. Erzberger, G. Braemer, and K. Bird) between 1989 and 1996. They are entitled:

– 'Statussequenzen von Frauen zwischen Erwerbsarbeit und Familie' (Women's status sequences between paid employment and the family), (1989–1991);
– 'Erwerbsverläufe als Innovationsprozess für Familienrollen. Zur Interdependenz von Passagengestaltungen und Verarbeitungsmustern bei Ehepartnern' (Employment careers and innovations in family roles. Interdependencies in family-employment passages and their perceptions within married couples)', (1991–1993);
– 'Statuspassagengestaltung und intergenerationales Erbe. Zum Wandel der Sequenzmuster zwischen Erwerbsarbeit und Familie im Generationentransfer' (Status passages and intergenerational effects. Social change in pattern sequencing between employment and the family in two family-linked generations), (1994–1996).

and borne children. It was assumed that milieus might have an important influence on the subjects' options and self-monitoring strategies. These women were therefore randomly selected from two culturally contrasting regions (urban and predominantly Protestant; rural and predominantly Catholic). In the next step we collected the data on 74 of their husbands' lives and career patterns and, in the next step, on their adult children (149 cases; 89 daughters and 60 sons).[1]

In-depth interviews, focusing on turning-points in the subjects' lives, were conducted with subsamples chosen on the basis of their family relations and employment patterns. Each interviewee was presented with a graph about her or his life, drawn from the data in a postal questionnaire, in order to connect the individual's personal history to life-course events and to facilitate comparisons of subjective interpretations between groups with similar and different life-course patterns.

The combination of quantitative and qualitative data collection on the same issue is always good for surprises. However, in our case we did not wait for surprises to 'emerge' by mere chance or serendipity, but systematically searched for them in order to decipher the dynamics of social change: between two generations, both sexes, and, in both these areas, between individuals' life-course patterns and their self-intentions/self-interpretations. We based our analysis on two family-affiliated generations.

The parents under investigation were in their sixties when interviewed, their children between 32 and 40 years old. Apart from their family links, with opportunities not only for the mutual validation of events but also for the inner-familial transfer of norms from parents to children, both generations are also of interest because here we have the rare situation that they also represent two distinct generations in Karl Mannheim's sense. That is, the parents belong to the German postwar generation, who shared wartime experiences in their youth and then moved on to become the generation associated with the German *Wirtschaftswunder* (the postwar economic boom). Their sons and daughters, mostly in their mid-thirties when interviewed, belong to the generation influenced by the German student movement, the 'protest generation,' with its new options, new values, and so on. In this generation we discern a sudden, significant drop in birth rates, an increase in numbers of divorces, the attainment of higher educational qualifications, and an increase in cohabitation, single parenthood, sequence marriages, etcetera (for an overview of the concentration of social change indicators in 1970s Germany see Krüger, 1997).

The postal questionnaires allowed us to identify the institutionally standardized life-course patterns and also permitted the comparison of the 220 cases to larger data sets. This comparison with representative data on these age groups (Brinkmann, 1991; Schwarz, 1988; Hofbauer, 1979) showed that the life-course patterns of our samples had no bias – that is, they showed normality for both generations with respect to employment rates identified in official statistics every ten years, marriage frequency, divorce rate, age at giving birth to first child, and average number of children.

Quantitative–Qualitative Data in Combination

The linking of the quantitative and qualitative data within and between each group under investigation opened up opportunities for internal comparisons between the sexes and the generations. The dimensions of comparison are as follows:

- intra-individual: the comparison between quantitative data about life events and the respondent's self-interpretation;
- intragenerational: the comparison between male and female patterns within each generation at both levels: their factual lives and how they think about them;
- intergenerational: the comparison between both generations as well as between and within the sexes: the changes in their lives with respect to their response to institutional demands and their norms and orientations.

Finding 1: A Puzzling Revolution

As expected, the comparison of typical quotations from the in-depth interviews demonstrates an enormous change in orientations, options, and norms between the two generations.[2] The most salient differences deal with notions of the female role in marriage. Men of the parental generation typically argued as follows: 'I still say today that a wife is a housewife. That's just the way it is – married and then she stays at home.' However, the sons' generation argued in the opposite way: '(Women's employment) I can't think of any reasons why not, only reasons for it, to get away from the children and the housework, the pension, getting qualifications, staying in touch.'

The view of the older male generation remained practically

untouched by the changes in gender roles which nevertheless took place during their own lifetimes. The sons show an astonishingly big jump ahead in men's perceptions of women's roles; this change is quite surprising in view of women's research on men's family participation, which can be summarized as: 'Men are always traditional!' (for the United States, see Gerson, 1993; for Germany see Metz-Göckel and Müller, 1985). But Gerson explained this widely shared female conviction as resulting from intragenerational comparisons, which overlook intergenerational change among men. From women's perspective, their male partners never do enough in the household.

We compared each sex in the different generations to each other. But in contrast to the intergenerational modernization on the male side, the women's self-interpretations in both generations are extremely similar: 'Going to work was just as important as my family. The two things go together' (mothers' generation). 'For me it (paid employment) is, well, part of my life, that's just as important as any other' (daughters' generation). Their statements are alike to such a degree that it is difficult even to try locating them in historical time without knowing beforehand.

Rather than shared female traditionalism, the reason that there is no change across the female generations lies in the fact that, with respect to employment, the older generation is just as modern as the younger – a result which is extremely surprising to both international and German researchers. The reason for this is that sociologists in postwar Germany idealized the postwar generation as living in the 'golden age of German normality' (Hradil, 1992) with a breadwinning male and a homemaking female – and were gender blind about females' personal options and strategies. More precisely, they generalized male definitions of female roles, which were congruent with the dominant public norms, onto women. From the quoted – and for this time very typical – male point of view, women of the older generation were supposed to be genuinely – and exclusively – family oriented, driven back to the labour market only in the case of high inner-familial economic need. There is only one quantitative study on female labour-market participation in the 1950s and 1960s that raises doubts about this model (Hofbauer, 1979), and the quantitative data on our 220 cases showed that 88 per cent of these wives participated in paid employment for periods of at least three years after having married and given birth – a quite remarkable percentage.[3] Among the fifty-two qualitatively interviewed women, only 2 per cent did not try at all to engage in paid work after marriage, and another 10 per cent tried unsuccessfully – that is, could not prevail against their husbands' resistance. The quantitative data on their husbands' labour-market careers (as well as the qualitative interviews with both) underlined that most of the women did not return to work because of tight family finances, but because of their work orientation (Born et al., 1996). The trouble is that German researchers, predominantly male themselves, did not explore women's opinions about or interest in labour-market engagement in those times and interpreted the artificially low female employment rate (see second sentence in note 3) as an indicator of adequate male incomes (for an overview see Schütze, 1986).

While the statements of both generations of women are similar and modern, the younger men have at least caught up with the female self-interpretation that we already witnessed in their mothers' generation. This also indicates changes in gender relations within each generation – a switch from patriarchal dictation to democracy. The narratives of the parental generation bring to light arguments and tensions between the couples with respect to all types of decision making involving intended or acted out labour-market participation, which women predominantly justified with the sometimes invented need for investments in home appliances. The female half felt disenfranchised; the conflict line ran between the couples – and was personalized, as summed up in the often-heard quotation: 'I have got the wrong husband.' But these women also knew that their partners' position conformed with the dominant public norms and laws of those times[4] and did not protest openly, but tried as much as possible to hide their employment arrangements from husbands' and neighbours' eyes.

In the younger generation gender relations have again changed completely. The respondents dealt very critically with notions of German 'normalities.' Women's interests and equal rights and opportunities for independently securing a living became an issue for public debate. Within our sample these new options are accepted and valued by both genders as a very important part of a satisfactory family life.

As our analysis also shows, these new public notions result not only from a generational effect, but also from the influence on the children of their parents' family life. We noted that the labour-market commitment and participation in paid work of their mothers' generation was a relatively concealed social change – not revealed in the husbands' definitions (and overlooked by researchers out of lack of interest); but it was not concealed from their sons and daughters. With reference to their mothers' lives they argue that the costs of raising a family are too high when parenthood means turning a woman into a housewife. They don't refer to the economic costs of children, but to the time-consuming effects or 'lifetime costs,' as we prefer to call them. The comparison between daughters whose mothers stayed at home for most of their lives (12 per cent of our first sample) and daughters of working mothers show the former to be even more hesitant about and critical of the role of raising a family than the latter.

> I wanted to earn my own living ... and have a partnership. I did not want to marry. There are certain things that I associate with marriage that always put me off the idea. One of these is my mother. I said to myself, you do not have to accept this role. Of course you could say that things are different today, but men and women still behave in certain ways, regardless of whether they have a modern lifestyle or not, and that always put me off the idea of marriage.

Such statements contradict the widespread thesis that mothers at home form the best resources for developing a family orientation in their children. On the contrary, Germany's traditional family patterns seem to be more likely to dampen the daughters' enthusiasm for marriage. As well, the sons are remarkable in criticizing their fathers' role and wanting to avoid repeating the pattern of their parents' homes within their own marriage. 'I really don't think it's a terribly good idea for a women to be at home all day, or either partner to be at home all day, and for it to stay that way for years ... I mean, I saw it happen to my mother, actually, that so many contacts to the outside world are lost. Then things can get difficult ...'

The generational contrast in orientation is obvious, but the proof for the sustainability of changes in norms is their effect on behaviour. The standardized data from the questionnaire on parental and children's family and employment sequences served this purpose. They included all types of employment (both official and non-official) and allowed us to compare the actual labour-market-participation patterns of both generations and both sexes.

The male employment patterns in both generations are remarkable in so far as they show only similarities: Men continued working and were successful in pursuing a career. Moreover, despite the change in male norms in the younger generation, the distance in the employment patterns between the sexes increased in proportion to the length of time spent living in their partnership.

In comparing females of both generations, in the daughters' sample we see more heterogeneity than in the mothers' (see figure 22.2). We found that the younger generation of women spent more time in education and training. This is a typical cohort effect, as the females form part of the postwar 'explosion of education,' which mainly refers to the enormous increase in the number of women in higher education (Tölke, 1989). The number of those employed part time has also increased. During the period in question for the older generation, part-time employment was possible only for office workers (after 1957), but since then it has expanded into the service sector in general, and is covered by trade-union agreements. In consequence, the percentage of women at home has shrunk. But so also has the percentage of women in regular full-time employment, despite their higher educational level. If we compare the labour-market-participation rates of both generations (not distinguishing between full time and part time) within the comparable life span, we see that, although the peak rate has shifted across age groups, the total time spent in the labour market has not changed significantly.

In comparing male and female employment patterns for both generations, it becomes clear that female life-course patterns depend less on changes in male attitudes than on the increasing availability of part-time employment – which men did not seek (only five of them had had part-time jobs and only for a short while). But these arrangements erode the percentage of women in full-time employment, leading to a vicious circle of deskilling and career interruptions (Engelbrech, 1991). Despite modern thinking and private beliefs, a traditional generative grammar seems to re-standardize differences in employment arrangements between the sexes. The lifetime costs of family life – that is, the type of time-consuming activities which hinder income accumulation – are still predominantly borne by females.

The usual way of explaining these differences is relating them to the predominance of traditional female orientations in Germany (Hakim, 1997). We showed above that this view is short-sighted even with respect to the older female generation, and particularly for the younger generation. But the new combination of the quantitative data with the qualitative material on the topic of decision making between the partners reveals that the labour-market participation of women results from the cumulative effect of a variety of influences within German society. The way in which a range of institutional policies affect women's lives has remained largely hidden until now. This fact requires further explanation.

Figure 22.2 (a) Activity from ages 16 to 41. Percentage of each age group (mothers, n = 220)

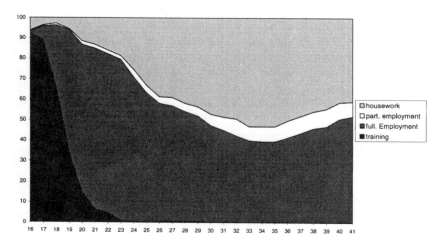

Figure 22.2 (b) Activity from Ages 16 to 41. Percentage of each age group (daughters, n = 98)

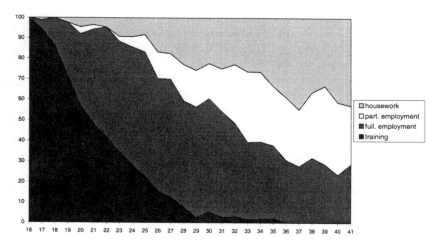

Theorizing Gender Troubles: The Double Face of Family Costs

James S. Coleman (1982) argues that with industrialization the family became anachronistic, surrounded by institutions alien to it, into which men disappear for the major part of the day. He sees women as left behind in backwaters which have become more and more meaningless for the central activities of society. This notion gives some indication of the costs of family life and the way of gendering it: into economic costs for men and lifetime costs for women, costs which may yield a small amount of economic benefit for wives in our pension system. The flaw in Coleman's argument from the perspective of life-course theory is that the social order of employment in industrial societies relies upon the existence of the family. From a gendered perspective, however, the family displays a 'double face': while supporting the integration of men into the labour market – that is, the family provides a mechanism for their inclusion – the same institution has become, for women, a mechanism of exclusion.

The exclusion–inclusion mechanism translated into life-course theory underlines that the modern life-course regime is one which counts on couples, not on individuals. Not only do specific institutions shape the individual life course as such, but gendered life-course differences are required by, and meet the needs of, institutions. This view leads deep into the analysis of the links between institutions. Institutional logics not only consistently include the labour market and the family and their supportive linkages with each other but also the arrangements surrounding the costs and timetables of kindergartens and schools, of caregiving institutions for sick and older family members, and so on. The latter create not only monetary demands but also transportation needs and management and planning requirements to an extent that Hochschild (1997) calls them a 'third shift' (besides those of paid employment and housework). They all have to be taken into account as relevant markers of life-course differences between the sexes, and their pattern suggests the gendering of family costs into monetary contributions (male) and time-consuming management (female), although the outcomes for today's women may be too much at odds with their aspirations and may produce a contradictory and conflict-laden imbalance between the sexes that puts the family (and love between partners) at risk.

The question we face is why are *gendered* solutions more common in German society than in the Anglo-American countries? Esping-

Anderson (1990) has empirically shown that, more than in other countries, the state in Germany counts on a caregiver who remains at home, and an earner in the labour force with an income sufficient to support a family. Without reflection, he takes the gendered association of the two different contributions to family life for granted and equates caregiving with females and income earning with males. But neither the welfare nor the labour-market system defines the sex of either the person at home or the person in the labour market. And our results highlight that, in both generations, women claimed to share in the monetary support of the family, while at least the younger generation of men supported this view.

The question still remains: Why does the female partner commit herself to the time-consuming regime of the institutionally determined management and planning requirements mentioned above while the male partner still predominantly engages in full-time work? Some additional historical frameworks, dating from long before changes in male norms, seem to be producing differences in the life course. Herbert Marcuse termed such mechanisms 'the frozen power of history' (1964).

Life-course Differences: When Norms Become a 'Frozen Power'

As long as both public and private male practices link female employment patterns to gendered orientations, society can avoid analysing the generative life-course grammar which remains hidden in the background. Very little research has been done which relates the division of labour in the family to the structure of vocational training and of labour-market allocation in Germany. Usually we look at the transition from school to work, not from school to work *and* family! But the debate on education at the beginning of the twentieth century was different, when the modern occupationally structured labour market developed and was supported by a transition system from school to work which defined skills and occupational titles as well as starting wages, career patterns, and chances for further training. The life-course grammar of Bismarck's welfare state and educational policies was worked out very carefully as a response to the high unemployment rates in Germany at that time, and Bismarck himself underlined that nothing would reconcile the workers better with the state, and thus lower the risk of a proletarian revolution, than the employment perspective of a stable life course with a public guarantee of material security (Ritter, 1983).

This was also the time of heated debates about the male and female 'nature-bounded' character and the consolidation of the family (Hausen, 1978) along with the need for producing a work force that was not only qualified and loyal but also healthy and stable. The historic act to stabilize the family was the discovery of occupational training as a pivot for gendered life-course differences and the construction of two types of occupations: one leading to 'existence-securing' positions and the other to 'natural vocations' – to use the nomenclature of the time (Mayer, 1992). To prevent reliance solely upon orientations and family socialization processes, this distinction between existence-securing and natural occupations was incorporated into the internal structure of vocational and educational training itself. For female youth, school-based vocational education was designed to develop skills for care-giving, nursing, dress making and repairing, and, at best, assisting in male-dominated territories, but without consideration of the market needs for securing an existence. For male youth, the dual system of skills training in work settings, with its contractually guaranteed skill protection and remuneration, was based on the structural ties to the corresponding existence-securing career. Trade unions developed their argument for a family-sustaining income with respect to the latter, and the state supported them with respect to strengthening the caregiving role of the family. This, in turn, ensured the feasibility of part-time schooling and provided care for the sick, the elderly, and preschool children under their mothers' eyes. Consequently, the market value of school-based (female) qualifications was set apart from the building blocks for an occupational career (Krüger, 1999; Kleinau and Mayer, 1996). The teaching offered to girls lacked clear occupational profiles, but corresponded to the broad areas of social support associated with family life and with private social engagement.

Historical research shows that the first German women's movement protested vehemently against this rigid structure for producing life-course difference by means of gendered educational schemes, but in vain (Kleinau and Mayer, 1996; Brinker-Gabler, 1979). Women's participation in the labour market was conceptualized as at best a pre-familial intermediary stage, with the politically motivated and thus consciously intended consequence of keeping women out of the contractually secured educational and career system (Schlüter, 1987; Nienhaus, 1982). The result was a gender-segmented labour market. The gendered norms of the early twentieth century became incorporated into the institutional order of the German state; gender relations have become social structure. The organizational patterns of work and education fixed the 'fitting' form of family life: for women in their role as homemakers, and for men in their role as breadwinners.

Times have changed, but to what extent? Male employment security is dissolving along with economic and labour-market downswings and technical change, but these changes scarcely affect the wage system. Women have caught up with men at the university level, but then have to compete in historically male-dominated areas.[5] For qualified positions below the academic level, the barriers from the early twentieth century have shrunk as a result of anti-discrimination laws, so that, in principle, girls and boys are allowed to enter all types of training in the vocational education system. But in practical terms only a third of apprenticeship places have become open to both sexes, while school-based vocational education has nevertheless grown and still functions as last chance for those who were unsuccessful in getting an apprenticeship position. More than 70 per cent of these are female (Stooss, 1997). Time has not altered the stereotyped male and female structure in the transition paths to occupations, nor the male and female occupationally structured and segmented market – the 'male' labour market with long-term career prospects and the female one with dead ends and often loosely defined job descriptions. The effects of these types of gendered educational and labour-market segmentations on the younger generation become obvious when we analyse the qualitative interviews.

Finding 2: Gendered Rational Choices

Above all, the narratives in our qualitative material show the dominance of economic calculations in inner-familial decision-making processes in the younger generation. Whereas the older generation of women had to fight their husbands, their sons and daughters all reported considerably bargaining with each other about how to organize family life and paid employment. Even so, the power of tradition still comes into play and acts out its effects: our standardized data on the younger generation show that about 70 per cent of our sample underwent preparation for work which corresponded to stereotypes for their sex. This means for females that although they sometimes had higher educational qualifications than their partners, they nevertheless had a lower economic status in the labour force, a lack of career structures, and a lower market value (Teubner, 1989).[6] The following quotation is typical: 'She doesn't earn that much – and probably won't in the future. But me ... quite promising, although not certain.' Against the background of this labour-market structure, it becomes completely 'normal' again that women overwhelmingly agreed to reduce their paid work or to quit the labour market for a while. And although these bargaining processes are repeated at each turning-point in the family history of either partner, they increasingly disfavour women as employment reductions or interruptions in Germany add up negatively (Ott, 1993). Even if we suspect a hidden element of traditional thinking behind males' arguments about who will reduce employment for the sake of family duties and who will not, the outcomes are economically convincing. When calculating the costs and benefits for the couple as a unit in order to establish the best balance between family and employment commitments, the historical calculation of the Bismarck era still works out.

Conclusions

The argument developed above tackles different dimensions. Substantively, it deepens our understanding of the low female labour-market-participation rates in Germany. The faltering nature of social change reveals that, in the postwar generation, we witnessed a high female interest in employment among married women set against the traditional and publicly shared view of their husbands on wives' conduct. In the generation of their sons and daughters, these norms had completely changed, but the bargaining processes between couples nevertheless resulted in similar traditional, gendered, life-course patterns because of women's systematically lower resources for financial independence. Norms did change, but not the gendered segmentation of the pathways from school to work and the segmentation of the labour market inherited from the early-twentieth-century period of industrialization. These segmentations connect to a welfare-state regime based on a conventional family structure, with a wage-earning husband and a home-bound, caregiving wife (whose unpaid labour significantly reduces public schooling, kindergarten, and health-care costs). Clearly, social change in gender norms has come not with a bang but a whimper.

Theoretically, the analysis highlights the problem of overemphasizing individualization approaches in life-course theory (cf Wohlrab-Sahr, 1992) – which undoubtedly is in line with our perception of a modern life course – and suggests a need, instead, for the notion of a coupled structuring of life. It is theoretically enlightening to analyse not only nation-specific differences in restructuring work and the family for men and women but also the ways in which life-course patterns are linked to institutional demands which count on dependency between the sexes. To include the social mechanisms of restructuring linked lives, in the German case, illustrates that the outcomes not only weaken the simple reference to figures in different countries when discussing female labour-market-participation rates, but also prompt a search for national differences in 'how institutions think' (see Douglas, 1987) and how they incorporate both sexes into their affairs and organizational principles.

Methodologically, the findings presented here underline the dynamics of structure and agency. But also in this context we should be aware of the fact that yesterday's norms may have become part of today's structure and that we must differentiate between the norms in people's minds and the norms incorporated into the organizational levels that standardize life-course patterns. Levy characterized social research on change in terms of near-sightedness and far-sightedness (1992), both of which produce gender blindness. He refers to the weaknesses of large-scale data sets in identifying social change in the life course as too far-sighted – and gender blind; and to qualitative research as too near-sighted – and gender biased.

In light of our findings he is right. The older female generation blamed their husbands, who were held responsible for isolating them in the home. The younger generation showed normative consensus between the sexes – and only the analysis of the quantitative data showed that the gendered norms from the early twentieth century remain incorporated in gendered labour-market resources and become all the more effective the more couples use exclusively economic criteria to balance costs and benefits for their family life. Only the combination of the quantitative and qualitative data document how the generative grammar, still active today, intertwines with changing norms between the sexes.

It is difficult to make a prediction about the effects of these frictions between people's notions of gender equality and the institutions surrounding them. It was the younger generation, however, that started to question the legitimacy of the educational and labour-market segmentation in German society, something that their parents never did. The younger generation stressed that decisions about their working hours are necessary because of a shortage of child care places, the opening hours of shops, the schooling system, the opening hours for public ser-vices, including medical services, and so on. The protest generation has lost its structure blindness, and with this generation the discussion about gendered structures, not just the more obvious gendering norms, has started to spread in Germany. The life-course grammar from Bismarck's welfare and educational policies has become an openly discussed annoyance.

NOTES

1 The initial 600 addresses for the first project were taken randomly from the final examination lists in the five occupational training schemes of interest, which are registered in the respective chambers of commerce, industry, and trade/crafts. Although most of the women had moved house and changed their name on marrying, 386 were successfully located by the German Ein-wohnermeldeämter (registration offices for residents). These women were sent a standardized questionnaire, of which 248 were returned. The data from married women with children (220) were analysed quantitatively. The questionnaire also asked for the respondent's consent to future cooperation. Of the 128 women who agreed, 52 were interviewed qualitatively. In the sec-ond project we gathered quantitative data on the still living, undivorced husbands of these 128 women (78; 4 refusals). Their children (326 in total) were later contacted, and 149 responded.

2 The qualitative analysis started with grouping generations in accordance with regional location (women/men from modern milieus [urban–Protes-tant] versus women/men from more traditional milieus [rural–Catholic]). Within these groups we then searched for the most contrasting sequences per topic in their narrations; in the next step, for the cumulation of similar quotations. The comparison with respect to the topic 'gender roles' and cor-responding sequences showed a surprising similarity between both regional groups, a finding which indicates their normative linkage to widespread general norms of the time which were not regionally differentiated. In a sec-ond step we grouped them according to gender and generation. All follow-ing quotations were chosen on the basis of their conciseness in summarizing the most frequently expressed views within each group (for the composition of the groups see figure 22.1).

3 This extremely high rate may be biased because of the selected group who belong to the lucky third that got an apprenticeship – while two-thirds of their cohort were unsuccessful in their search (Born et al., 1996). On the other

hand, the available official statistics about women's employment rates in this cohort are misleading because they do not count 'mithelfende Familienangehörige' (assisting in the family business), nor non-insured employment. Both were widespread, as Willms-Hergett (1985) witnessed. She claims that the female employment rate in Germany doesn't reflect at all the real integration rate of women into the labour market.

4 Until 1959, German husbands had the legally guaranteed final authority over their wives' decisions and activities.

5 The exception is teaching, a traditionally female occupied area.

6 The *quantitative* data showed that roughly 40 per cent of the women had undergone school-based vocational training, but apart from three exceptions, none of the men, neither husbands nor brothers, had; roughly 30 per cent of the women were trained within the dual system, and the final third had a university degree. The males' educational levels were similar: a slightly lower number with a university degree, but the others all with dual-system training, apart from the three exceptions already mentioned.

REFERENCES

Allmendinger, J. (1989). *Career mobility dynamics: A comparative analysis of the United States, Norway, and West Germany* (Studien und Berichte 49). Berlin: Max-Planck-Institut für Bildungsforschung.

Beck, U. (1990). Der Konflikt der zwei Modernen. In W. Zapf (Ed.), *Die Modernisierung moderner Gesellschaften* (Verhandlungen des 25. Deutschen Soziologentages, pp 40–53). Frankfurt: Campus.

Born, C., Krüger, H., & Lorenz-Meyer, D. (1996). *Der unentdeckte Wandel: Annäherung an das Verhältnis von Struktur und Norm im weiblichen Lebenslauf.* Berlin: Edition Sigma.

Brinker-Gabler, G. (Ed.). (1979). *Frauenarbeit und Beruf: Die Frau in der Gesellschaft* (Frühe Texte). Frankfurt: Fischer Taschenbuch Verlag.

Brinkmann, C. (1991). Arbeitslosigkeit und Stille Reserve von Frauen. In K.U. Mayer, J. Allmendinger, & J. Huinink (Eds), *Vom Regen in die Traufe: Frauen zwischen Beruf und Familie* (pp 233–61). Frankfurt: Campus.

Chomsky, N. (1978 [1966]). *Topics in the theory of generative grammer* (5th ed.). The Hague: Mouton.

Coleman, J.S. (1982). *The asymmetric society.* Syracuse, NY: Syracuse University Press.

Douglas, M. (1987). *How institutions think.* London: Routledge.

Engelbrech, G. (1991). Frauenspezifische Restriktionen des Arbeitsmarktes: Situationsbericht und Erklärungsansätze zu Phasen des Berufsverlaufs anhand von IAB-Ergebnissen. In K.U. Mayer, J. Allmendinger, & J. Huinink (Eds), *Vom Regen in die Traufe: Frauen zwischen Beruf und Familie* (pp 91–118). Frankfurt: Campus.

Erzberger, C., & Prein, G. (1997). Triangulation: Validity and empirically-based hypotheses construction. *Quality & Quantity, 31,* 141–54.

Esping-Anderson, G. (1990). *The three worlds of welfare capitalism.* Princeton, NJ: Princeton University Press.

Gerson, K. (1993). *No man's land: Men's changing commitments to family and work.* New York: Basic Books.

Giddens, A. (1984). *The constitution of society: Outline of a theory of structuration.* Cambridge: Polity Press.

Glaser, B., & Strauss, A. (1971). *Status passage.* New York: Aldine de Gruyter.

Hagestad, G.O. (1992). Assigning rights and duties: Age, duration, and gender in social institutions. In W.R. Heinz (Ed.), *Institutions and gatekeeping in the life course.* (Status Passages and the Life Course, Vol. III, pp 261–79). Weinheim: Deutscher Studien Verlag.

Hakim, C. (1997). A sociological perspective on part-time work. In H.-P. Blossfeld & C. Hakim (Eds), *Between equalization and marginalisation: Women working part-time in Europe and the USA* (pp 22–70). Oxford: Oxford University Press.

Han, S.-K., & Moen, P. (2001, forthcoming). Coupled careers: Men's and women's pathways through work and marriage in the United States. In H.-P. Blossfeld & S. Drobnic (Eds), *Careers of couples in contemporary societies: Cross-national comparison of the transition from male breadwinner to dual-earner families.* Oxford: Oxford University Press.

Hausen, K. (1978). Die Polarisierung der Geschlechtscharaktere. In H. Rosenbaum (Ed.), *Seminar Familien- und Gesellschaftsstruktur* (pp 161–91). Frankfurt: Suhrkamp.

Heinz, W.R. (1996). *The transition from education to employment in a comparative perspective.* Toronto: University of Toronto, Centre for International Studies.

Hochschild, A.R. (1997). *The time bind: When work becomes home and home becomes work.* New York: Metropolitan Books.

Hofbauer, H. (1979). Zum Erwerbsverhalten verheirateter Frauen. *MittAB* (Bundesanstalt für Arbeit, Nürnberg), 2, 217–40.

Hradil, S. (1992, July). Die 'objektive' und die 'subjektive' Modernisierung: Der Wandel der westdeutschen Sozialstruktur und die Wiedervereinigung. *Aus Politik und Zeitgeschichte* (Beilage zur Wochenzeitung Das Parlament, B-29–30/92), *10,* 3–14.

Kelle, U. (1994). *Empirisch begründete Theoriebildung: Zur Logik und Methodologie interpretativer Sozialforschung* (Status Passages and the Life Course Vol. VI). Weinheim: Deutscher Studien Verlag.

Kleinau, E., & Mayer, C. (Eds). (1996). *Erziehung und Bildung des weiblichen Geschlechts: Eine kommentierte Quellensammlung zur Bildungs- und Berufsbildungsgeschichte von Mädchen und Frauen.* Weinheim: Deutscher Studien Verlag.

Krüger, H. (1997). Familie und Generation: Der Gender Gap in den Paarbeziehungen. In J. Mansel, G. Rosenthal, & A. Tölke (Eds), *Generationen-Beziehungen, Austausch und Tradierung* (pp 31–42). Opladen: Westdeutscher Verlag.

Krüger, H. (1999). Gender and skills: Distributive ramifications of the German skill system. In P.D. Culpepper & D. Finegold (Eds), *The German skills machine: Sustaining comparative advantage in a global economy* (pp 189–227). New York: Berghahn Books.

Leisering, L., & Leibfried, S. (1999). *Time and poverty in western welfare states: United Germany in perspective.* Cambrige: Cambridge University Press.

Levy, R. (1992). Structure-blindness: A non-ideological component of false consciousness. In F. Geyer & W.R. Heinz (Eds), *Alienation, society and the individual: Continuity and change in theory and research* (pp 61–74). New Brunswick, NJ: Transaction Publishers.

Marcuse, H. (1964). *One-dimensional man.* Boston, MA: Beacon Press.

Mayer, C. (1992). ... und dass die staatsbürgerliche Erziehung des Mädchens mit der Erziehung zum Weibe zusammenfällt. *Zeitschrift für Pädagogik, 38*(5), 433–54.

Metz-Göckel, S., & Müller, U. (1985). *Der Mann: Eine repräsentative Untersuchung über die Lebenssituation und das Frauenbild 20- bis 50jähriger Männer im Auftrag der Zeitschrift Brigitte.* Hamburg: Gruner and Jahr.

Nienhaus, U. (1982). *Berufsstand weiblich: Die ersten weiblichen Angestellten.* Berlin: Universitätsverlag.

Ogburn, W.F. (1932). The hypothesis of cultural lag. *Social Change,* 200–13.

Ott, N. (1993). Zur Rationalität innerfamilialer Entscheidungen. In C. Born & H. Krüger (Eds), *Erwerbsverläufe von Ehepartnern und die Modernisierung weiblicher Lebensführung* (pp 25–51). Weinheim: Deutscher Studien Verlag.

Riley, M.W., Kahn, R.L., & Foner, A. (Eds). (1994). *Age and structural lag: Society's failure to provide meaningful opportunities in work, family, and leisure.* New York: J. Wiley.

Ritter, G.A. (1983). *Sozialversicherung in Deutschland und England.* München: Beck.

Rossman, G.B., & Wilson, B.L. (1985). Numbers and words: Combining quantitative and qualitative methods in a single-scale evaluation study. *Evaluation Review, 9*(5), 627–43.

Schlüter, A. (1987). *Neue Hüte – alte Hüte? Gewerbliche Berufsausbildung zu*

Beginn des 20. Jahrhunderts – Zur Geschichte ihrer Institutionalisierung. Düsseldorf: Schwann.

Schütze, Y. (1986). *Die gute Mutter: Zur Geschichte des normativen Musters 'Mutterliebe.'* Bielefeld: Kleine Verlag.

Schwarz, K. (1988). Umfang der Erwerbstätigkeit nach dem Zweiten Weltkrieg. *Zeitschrift für Bevölkerungswissenschaft, Heft 3,* 275–94.

Stooss, F. (1997). *Reformbedarf in der beruflichen Bildung.* Expertise im Auftrag des Ministeriums für Arbeit, Gesundheit und Soziales des Landes Nordrhein-Westfalen. In *Reformbedarf der beruflichen Bildung* (pp 47–111). Reihe: pro Ausbildung. Ausbildungskonsens NRW, hrsg. vor Ministerium für Wirtschaft und Mittelstand, Technologie und Verkehr, Düsseldorf.

Teubner, U. (1989). *Neue Berufe für Frauen. Modelle zur Überwindung der Geschlechterhierarchie im Erwerbsbereich.* Frankfurt: Campus.

Tölke, A. (1989). *Lebensverläufe von Frauen: Familiäre Ereignisse, Ausbildungs- und Erwerbsverhalten* (DJI-Forschungsbericht). Weinheim/München: DJI (Deutsches Jugendinstitut e.V.).

Willms-Hergett, A. (1985). *Frauenarbeit: Zur Integration von Frauen auf dem Arbeitsmarkt.* Frankfurt: Campus.

Wohlrab-Sahr, M. (1992). Institutionalisierung oder Individualisierung des Lebenslaufs. *Bios, Zeitschrift für Biographieforschung und Oral History, Heft 1,* 1–19.

23. Reframing Careers: Work, Family, and Gender[1]

Phyllis Moen and Shin-Kap Han

The latter half of the twentieth century witnessed dramatically changing experiences and options associated with occupational career progression. As biographies intersected with the historical events of the times (Mills, 1959), the lock-step life-course was, and is, being literally transformed. We discuss the value of a life-course perspective, leading both to (1) a dynamic approach to occupational experiences and attainment, and (2) a recasting of conventional views of occupational careers.

Mayer and Mueller (1986, p. 167) described institutional careers as the orderly flow of persons through segmented institutions. Such a framework, based on the notion of (occupational) status sequence (Merton, 1968), is how sociologists and economists have usually characterized the typical (male) biography. But women's life paths are neither orderly nor neatly segmented, as they move in and out of education, employment, and community and family roles. Given the changes over the last half-century in both men's and women's attachment to the work-force, scholars must unpack the meaning of careers for both women *and* men, in terms of biography, cultural norms, historical context, and the institutionalized opportunity structure. In this chapter we draw on life-history data on cohorts of retired workers (born 1926 to 1945) to construct typologies of alternative occupational career and family paths in order to demonstrate the ways that a life-course approach can reformulate the concept of careers.

Studying Occupational Paths

A life-course approach can contribute to our understanding of occupational careers on four analytical levels. First, it demonstrates how prior choices, institutional arrangements, and chance events so obviously shape life paths and possibilities (e.g., O'Rand and Henretta, 1982; Rosenfeld, 1980). Second, it offers insights about the links between macro-level and micro-level events and processes. Historical forces have changed options in unprecedented ways, while, at the same time, structural lags persist in constraining choices.[2] Third, the study of the relational aspects shaping choices has underscored how individual biographies and institutionalized roles and rules are clearly embedded in and mediated through the lives of others.[3] This points to the value of a growing body of work on social networks, while simultaneously moving the study of social relations into a more dynamic, temporal, and contextual orientation. Finally, a life-course approach underscores the intersecting nature of work and family roles, suggesting a broadening of the occupation career concept in ways that better reflect women's as well as men's life pathways, as they negotiate the status passages of work and family in tandem.

As to the last point, in particular, scholars have been victims of the very social institutions they purport to study, using taken-for-granted classifications and definitions to frame the focus of their research. 'Segmented lives' has come to define the subject matter of social research: occupational and organizational sociologists (as well as economists) have charted work careers (e.g., Doeringer and Piore, 1971; Granovetter, 1986; Breiger, 1995); family sociologists have concentrated on 'family' careers (e.g., Hill, 1970; Aldous, 1996); while still other sociologists have considered macro-level changes in institutions (e.g., Brinton and Nee, 1998).

By contrast, the complexity and contingent nature of contemporary life paths are forcing scholars to re-examine both the segmented life course and segmented institutions and to draw on and extrapolate from all of these bodies of work. A real contribution of the life-course perspective to sociological understanding thus has been the *reframing* of life paths, from a concentration on either work or family transitions and trajectories to considering work lives and family lives as lives in tandem.[4] This necessitates synthesizing and integrating many lines of sociological inquiry, incorporating time in order to more fruitfully capture the dynamic interplay between biography, institutions, and social change.

In our ongoing research program at the Cornell Employment and Family Careers Institute we are focusing on the utility of the concept of 'careers' to capture these dynamic connections across institutions, levels, social relations, and lives. We consider career paths as embedded not only in employing organizations but also in families, in the larger contexts of gender and age stratification, and in the changing opportunity structure (Riley et al., 1988; Moen, 1994, 1998). The 'career' concept is a fruitful one, both because it is at the intersection of the micro (individual and family) and macro (e.g., organizational and state policies and the larger economy) levels (Barley, 1989), and because it evokes *time*, the temporal nature of life-course processes.

Conceptualizing 'Careers'

The career concept is, in fact, central to understanding patterns of social behaviour. While it most frequently refers to patterns of movement across jobs, it is linked, either directly or indirectly, to just about all of the patterns and processes studied by social scientists. 'Career' is both a metaphor and an organizing principle, providing conceptual and methodological guidance to the sociology of work and occupations, organizational behaviour, the study of social stratification, roles, mobility, the economy, and the labour force, as well as the social psychology of work, motivation, and identity. We argue, however, that scholars invoke the career concept with too little rigour or reflection, typically adopting common-sense definitions and usage.

Studying women's occupational paths and passages forces attention to the embeddedness of careers – men's and women's – in the social fabric of lives, institutions, and changing societal landscapes. By incorporating women's experiences in the world of paid work, scholars can contribute to the understanding of the dynamic links between individual lives and organizations, as well as the role of mediating institutions such as family and community. They can also document social changes in the ways institutionalized and actual life paths are being reconstructed.

The issue is becoming more salient and pressing in the context of historical changes in the economy and the structure of work. A sociology of occupational careers is necessarily a sociology of time, referring to the processes of job development, mobility, and plateauing (Barley, 1989). But the notion of 'careers' is a function of historical time as well, a modern invention, emerging as a social fact only with the development of corporations, bureaucracies, and white-collar employment. As Mills (1951) pointed out, prior to the Industrial Revolution, most people worked in either agriculture or a family business. Though individual farmers, craftspeople, and family entrepreneurs may have had 'life plans,' they did not have 'careers.'

The concept embodies structure as much as process. As paid work for others, particularly in corporations and government, became a central role in contemporary society, the work career shaped life chances, life quality, and life choices in virtually every arena. But equating 'career' with occupational work history relegated *unpaid work* – whether through participating in a family business, performing domestic household labour, caring for the family, or (formally or informally) volunteering in the community – to the margins of the 'business' of society, and, consequently, the business of mainstream sociology.

Fundamental changes in the nature of work accompanied the Industrial Revolution. The shift from self- and family employment to the development of a paid labour force led to the construction of career trajectories based on the (male) breadwinner model. Given fundamental changes in the contemporary postindustrial economy, we are again witnessing profound changes in career progression and possibilities. Transformations in the structure of work, alterations in the economy and the labour force, and fundamental changes in gender roles, families, and the life course – all mean that conventional conceptualizations and operationalizations of careers may be outmoded. In point of fact, diminishing numbers of workers fit the traditional career pattern described in earlier studies.

As life-course scholars, we argue for a reassessment of 'career' as an orienting concept, pointing to its past utility and future promise as a lens with which to view both the dynamic interweave between choice and constraint and the dynamic interplay among society, organizations, and individual lives that form the basis for both social continuity and social change. We address six key issues in the contemporary study of careers, drawing illustratively on our ongoing research.

Six Challenges

1. The Need for New Typologies

In the 1970s, Spilerman (1977) described the construction of typologies based on empirical regularities in actual career lines. He pointed out the discrepancy between career characterizations and accounts on the one hand, and concrete patterns of job sequences on the other. As we move into the twenty-first century, we need empirical accounts of *contemporary* career paths – men's *and* women's. Kohli, for instance, described the segmentation of the life course into education, work, and retirement (1986). But this institutionalized pattern reflects *men's* traditional biographies. The need for new typologies, empirically derived and grounded in community and family contexts, is becoming increasingly self-evident (Kanter, 1977; Moen, 1998).

To describe various occupational career paths followed by contemporary working men and women, we use sequence analysis where the overall patterning of career pathways is both the conceptual and the analytical unit. We analyse data collected in the first wave of the Cornell Retirement and Well-Being Study (CRWB). The respondents are 458 retirees from six large manufacturing and service companies in upstate New York who were aged 50 to 72 at the time they were interviewed in 1994–5. The data on employment histories of retirees (captured through the collection of detailed life-history data) provide information on transitions and trajectories over the life course in occupation, work status, and organization from age 30 until retirement. Using yearly interval as unit-time, we transformed the data into sequence data format – that is, strings of codes. Applying optimal matching algorithm (Abbott, 1995), we empirically delineated a set of typical pathways, which we call 'occupational career pathway types,' or 'pathway types' for short.

The five pathway types obtained from the sequence analysis of the life-history data can be summarized in terms of employment history and other background variables. For easy identification and reference, we call type 1 'delayed-entry career,' type 2 'orderly career,' type 3 'high-geared career,' type 4 'steady part-time career,' and type 5 'intermittent career,' respectively (see also Han and Moen, 1999a, 1999b, 2001).

Two points are worth noting. One, there seem to be highly distinct and separate career pathways for men and women (see table 23.1). Yet the sizable presence of women in the orderly and high-geared types (2 and 3), which have been typically associated with men's careers, suggests that the gap between men's and women's work experiences may be closing. Two, men's career paths tend to be much more standardized, following only a couple of career pathways, whereas working women have travelled quite diverse paths. These findings illustrate that the issue of gendered careers cannot be addressed simply by contrasting stylized career paths of men versus women. Rather, one

TABLE 23.1
Five Pathway Types and Their Characteristics

Pathway Type	1 Delayed-entry career	2 Orderly career	3 High-geared career	4 Steady part-time career	5 Intermittent career
N	46	154	160	10	21
Gender composition**a					
(% men)	0.0	64.9	61.9	30.0	0.0
(% women)	100.0	35.1	38.1	70.0	100.0
Education**b					
(mean/years)	12.64	13.25	14.61	13.40	12.86
SEI**b					
(mean)	42.8	50.3	58.5	54.6	42.5
No. of organizations**b					
(mean)	1.5	1.2	2.8	1.7	3.7
Work status, full time**b,c					
(%)	47.4	94.6	94.4	26.2	73.7
Work status, part time**b,c					
(%)	9.3	1.5	2.3	69.6	10.6
Work status, unemployed/OLF**b,c					
(%)	43.4	3.9	3.3	4.2	15.7

Note: * denotes where $p < .01$, and ** where $p < .001$. 'a' denotes where Likelihood Ratio (L^2) test is conducted, and 'b' *F*-test. 'c' denotes where the figure is calculated on the basis of total person-years.
SOURCE: Cornell Retirement and Well-Being Study, Wave 1 (1994–5).

needs to have a more refined perspective on the differentiation between, as well as among, men and women within particular historical contexts.

2. The Male Experience as Template

Use of the career concept is heavily gendered, reflecting men's, not women's, experiences (see also Bem, 1993; Moen, 1992). Thus, 'career' commonly refers to moving through a series of (related) jobs over the life course, the typical experience of men. This can be subdivided into *organizational* careers – moving up internal ladders within a corporation – and *occupational* careers – moving up ladders within an occupation. But when women are the focus, the career concept is typically constrained to a more narrow definition, referring to their remaining in, or moving in and out of, the work force. This dual view of careers, presuming a segmented primary labour market (with internal career ladders) and a secondary labour market (with no such ladders or security), is grounded in the reality of a secondary sector with persons (frequently women) drifting between jobs (Doeringer and Piore, 1971). In their historical analysis of clerks and managers of Lloyds' Bank, Stovel, Savage, and Bearman (1995) pointed out that achievement-based careers were made possible by this ascriptive segmentation of the labour market, as women began to fill routine clerk positions in 1929.

In our study, pathway type 2 (orderly careers) seems to represent the ideal-typical career path, that is, stable, continuous, and upwardly mobile. About two-thirds of those respondents experiencing this traditional career path are men (see table 23.1 and figure 23.1). Type 3 (high geared) reflects those (disproportionately men) moving up and across ladders. They are highly educated and upwardly mobile. They start off high on the occupational ladder and engage in 'ladder hopping' across firms in order to advance their careers. But, as we have shown, there are three other pathways that could not be captured when only men's occupational experiences are the focus of inquiry. This suggests that men's life patterns can no longer be seen as the 'typical' career or life-course path.

3. The Individual as the Unit of Analysis

The pervasive gender bias in the conceptualization of careers is also reflected in an exclusive emphasis on the *individual as the unit of analysis*. Workers are defined as individuals without family responsibilities or constraints, and their careers are similarly defined as reflecting the individual's mobility patterns. When women's careers are considered, family factors are rendered immediately visible. With the increasing commonality of the two-earner couple, we would expect that family considerations are increasingly intruding on the career paths of *both* men and women, along with the demands and resources associated

Figure 23.1 Pathway 1: 'Delayed Entry'

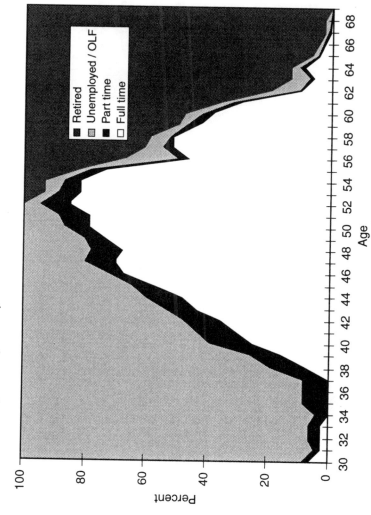

SOURCE: Cornell Retirement and Well-Being Study, Wave 1, 1994–5; see Han and Moen, 1999a, 1999b, 2001

Figure 23.2 Pathway 2: 'Orderly'

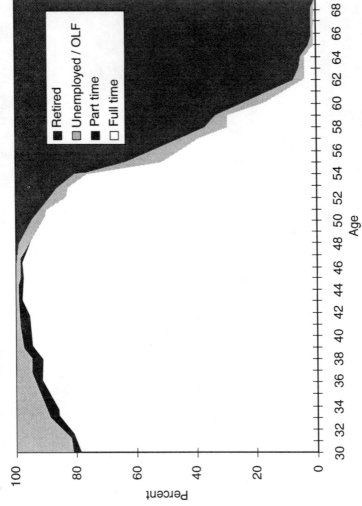

SOURCE: Cornell Retirement and Well-Being Study, Wave 1, 1994–5; see Han and Moen, 1999a, 1999b, 2001

Figure 23.3 Pathway 3: 'High Geared'

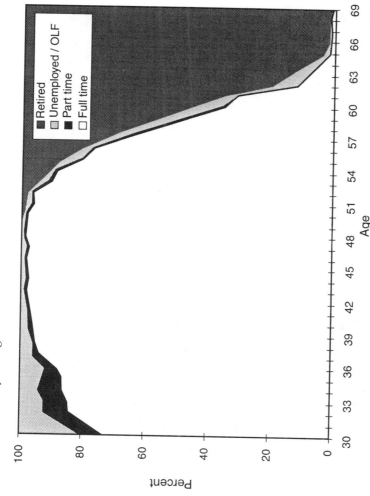

SOURCE: Cornell Retirement and Well-Being Study, *Wave 1, 1994–5*; see Han and Moen, 1999a, 1999b, 2001

Figure 23.4 Pathway 4: 'Steady Part Time'

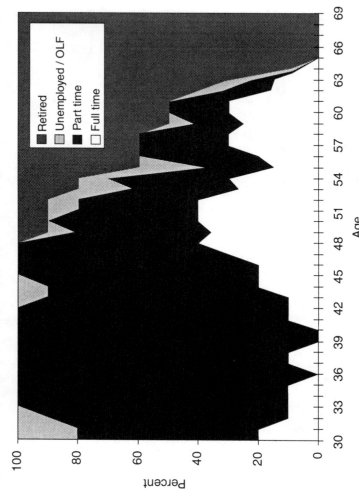

SOURCE: Cornell Retirement and Well-Being Study, Wave 1, 1994–5; see Han and Moen, 1999a, 1999b, 2001

Figure 23.5 Pathway 5: 'Intermittent'

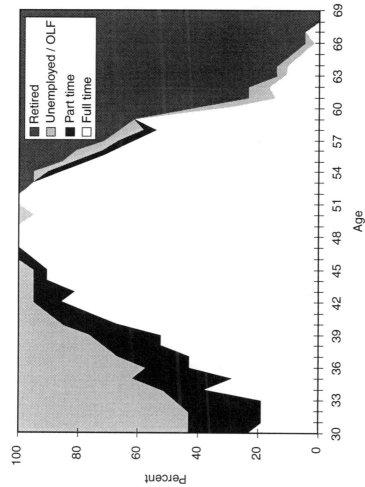

SOURCE: Cornell Retirement and Well-Being Study, Wave 1, 1994–5; see Han and Moen, 1999a, 1999b, 2001

with the spouse's career. This suggests the growing importance of the *couple*, or household, as the appropriate unit of analysis in modelling career paths.

For example, in our analysis, those following pathway type 1 (delayed entry) start working late, with an extended period of being out of the labour force early on (see figure 23.1). This group consists exclusively of women entering the labour force after their childbearing years. Although they work typically at low-prestige jobs, these jobs are relatively stable. Pathway type 5 (intermittent) in our data is another type consisting exclusively of women and is the least stable of all. Although it shares many of the characteristics of type 1 (late entry), it distinguishes itself from type 1 by a trajectory of higher mobility across organizations, mostly due to the frequent exits and re-entries (see figure 23.5). Lastly, type 4 consists of a small group of people (mostly women) working mostly part time. Yet they show a low level of inter-organizational mobility and are relatively successful in terms of their occupational prestige scores and upward mobility. All of these – late entry, part-time work, and moving in and out of the work force – reflect strategies of adaptation (Moen and Wethington, 1992) as women (as wives and mothers) juggle their multiple role obligations. Shifting the focus to couples, households, and families points to the ways family adaptive strategies typically privilege men, providing them with both a comparative advantage (e.g., Becker, 1981) and a cumulative advantage (e.g., Elder, 1998) in the occupational sphere.

4. The Hidden Value of Family

The existing study and modelling of occupational careers typically views workers as without family responsibilities. Thus, family factors are frequently disregarded while, at the same time, the institutional organization of career paths presumes that someone else – a wife – will facilitate an employee's occupational allegiance and mobility. The very notion of career is predicated on the breadwinner/homemaker template as it has become institutionalized throughout society.

This blueprint persists in shaping family strategies and preferences in ways that disadvantage women's career progression (Becker and Moen, 1999; Moen and Wethington, 1992; Curtis, 1986; Coser, 1974; Goode, 1960). In our study of men's and women's career paths (Han and Moen, 1999a, 2001), we find that being and remaining married characterizes men following both the 'orderly' and the 'high-geared' career paths. By contrast, women on those paths are the ones who experience discontinuity rather than continuity in their marital careers.

In fact, the men and women in our sample (who are all retirees who have worked for some significant portion of their prime adulthood) have quite different marital histories (Han and Moen, 1999a, 2001; Quick and Moen, 1998). In terms of marital stability, men tend to be better off by a large margin. For the women in our sample (who have spent a considerable period of time in the labour force), the likelihood of both getting married and staying married is far lower than that for their male coworkers. Men are about 50 per cent more likely to be currently married than women, whereas working women are more than seven times more likely to have never married and 34 per cent more likely to have experienced a break-up in their marriage. A marital-stability score, constructed from the detailed marital history, produces the same significant result, with men experiencing far greater marital stability than the women in our sample. There are clear differences in the relationship between occupational career pathway type and marital stability by gender. This explains why so many women who are highly successful in their careers are so often without the families and/or children that seem to be taken for granted for upwardly mobile men.

The traditional importance of family support of career attainment, hidden yet powerful, is becoming problematic for both men and women, as half the U.S. work force are married to another worker. Another fourth of the work force are single (or single parent), meaning that increasingly fewer workers have the support of a full-time homemaking spouse.

5. The Distinction between Structure and Meaning

As Barley (1989) pointed out, early sociologists acknowledged the 'Janus-like' aspects of the career concept, its 'ontological duality' embracing both its institutional character as a series of structural positions and its subjective character, as ways actors define and give meaning to the unfolding of their occupational experiences (p. 49). But contemporary sociologists have tended to ignore this dual nature of the career path, focusing exclusively on objective occupational careers. However, movement through positions also entails changing subjective self-definitions, expectations, and evaluations.[5] Contemporary life-course research is demonstrating that the meaning of work changes over the life course (e.g., Brim, 1992; Moen and Yu, 1999;

Mortimer and Borman, 1988; Tolbert and Moen, 1998). For example, qualitative research in the Cornell Couples and Careers Study shows how women (especially) shift their view of their employment as a 'career' versus a 'job,' depending on both time and energy investments in work and family demands (Becker and Moen, 1999).

6. The Confusion between Choice and Constraint

Finally, a key issue in life-course analysis is the issue of *agency* and the construction of the life course in the light of institutionalized structural imperatives (Elder, 1998; Rook, Catalano, and Dooley, 1989). On the one hand, careers are typically charted as a series of positions, a consequence of the way organizations and economies are structured. On the other hand, career moves are depicted as a series of choice points, as consequences of rational decisions based on both current and anticipated costs and benefits (e.g., Becker, 1981; Coleman, 1993). Both these formulations ignore the role of contingency and chance. Do individuals choose their career paths, do employers shape them, or do they reflect the happenstance convergence of events, social relations, and biography? The answer, of course, is all of the above.

Incorporating the Multiple Dimensions of Time

Career paths reflect pragmatic choices in constrained circumstances (Breiger, 1995). What is required are models of careers as reflecting the confluence of societal norms, organizational structures, social relations, chance events, and intentional action.

We focus in our research on three temporal dimensions of occupational careers: historical context, biographical pacing, and heterogeneity (see Han and Moen, 1999b). First, the macro-level environment – mainly the state and the labour market – and historical circumstances (such as demographic shifts) set aggregate baseline parameters around both women's and men's career progression. These external influences, consisting of long-term trends and random fluctuations, we term 'historical context.' Second, women and men, as purposive actors make decisions regarding their occupational life course. While courses of action are volitional and internal, they are also bound by a logic based on available institutional careers and cumulative contingencies. We call this 'biographical pacing.' This concept also incorporates the life-course notion of timing; *when* an event occurs in an individual's life biography has major implications for the subsequent life course (Elder, 1998; Rook, Catalano, and Dooley, 1989). For example, the timing of unemployment, downsizing, or the birth of a child can shape occupational paths both directly and indirectly.

Lastly, 'heterogeneity' refers to subgroup variations in occupational paths. Gender provides one of the most salient – easy and clear – comparative frames for occupational careers. But the structural and cultural contexts shaping gendered career paths are themselves in flux. For example, while women's work history has historically been characterized by tangential and transient ties to employment, their labour force-participation rate has continually increased and the gap between men's and women's work-force experience has been steadily closing (Tomaskovic-Devey, 1993; Guillemard and Rein, 1993; Moen, 1985, 1992; Brinton, 1988; Waite, 1981). In addition, gender reflects normative expectations (Hagestad, 1988; Hagestad and Neugarten, 1984; Neugarten, Moore, and Lowe, 1965; Henretta, 1994; O'Rand, 1995; Elder and O'Rand, 1995). But these, too, are in flux. For example, men are moving away from preferences related to promotions and income to a preference for job security, and both men and women workers value meaningful work (Tolbert and Moen, 1998). The discontinuities characterizing women's career trajectories may become increasingly evident in men's occupational experiences (Blair-Loy, 1996; Han and Moen, 1999b).

All three – historical context, biographical pacing, and heterogeneity – reflect different temporal 'clocks.' All three are contributing to the growing diversity, instability, and uncertainty regarding contemporary occupational careers, changing both opportunity and risk.

Conclusions

Barley (1989) describes the early Chicago sociologists as using the career concept as a 'lens for peering at larger social processes known as institutions,' as ways of thinking about status passages and properties, and as a mechanism for linking individuals to the social structure. Life-course scholars are reconfiguring that lens.

Heinz (1996) points out that status passages 'link institutions and actors by defining time-tables and entry as well as exit markers for transitions,' constructed by 'biographical actors, but also involving institutional guidelines' (pp 58–9). Thus, the study of career paths and passages provides a window into the dynamic interplay between institutions and individual lives. The occupational career has been a fundamental organizing force shaping both biographies and the structure of other institutions. A number of life-course scholars (e.g., Chudacoff, 1989; Kohli, 1986; Mayer and Mueller, 1986; Riley, 1987; Riley and Riley, 1994; Moen, 1994) have pointed to occupational careers as providing the organizational blueprint for the life course. But these organizational blueprints are out of step with the realities of contemporary lives.

Social science has harboured an artificial view of lives, segmenting roles and actions and treating them as independent of each other. Just as the nature and composition of the work force and of occupational careers are being transformed, so too should the study of them change. What is required is a thoughtful reappraisal of contemporary life patterns, leading to a reconfiguration of the career concept in ways that recognize the complex interplay among gender, work, and family.

NOTES

1 Support for the research reported here was provided by grants from the National Institute on Aging (grant numbers P50 AG11711 and 2 P50 AG11711–06, Karl Pillemer and Phyllis Moen, principal investigators) and a grant from the Alfred P. Sloan Foundation (grant number 96-6-9, Phyllis Moen, principal investigator).
2 Blair-Loy, 1996; Brinton, 1988; Gerson, 1985; Moen, 1989; Riley and Riley, 1994; Zhou, Moen, and Tuma, 1998.
3 See, for example, Henretta and O'Rand, 1983; Henretta, O'Rand, and Chan, 1993a, 1993b; Hertz, 1986; Hochschild, 1989; Rossi, 1985.
4 See, for example, Blossfeld and Huinink, 1991; Conger and Elder, 1994; Desai and Waite, 1991; Elder et al., 1992; Elder, George, and Shanahan, 1996; Gerson, 1985; Han and Moen, 1999a, 1999b; Hareven, 1984; Hogan, 1981; Krüger, 1996; Moen, 1989, 1992, 1996; Mortimer and Borman, 1988.
5 Clausen, 1986; Dannefer, 1984; Elder and O'Rand, 1995; Rosenberg, 1979; Swidler, 1986.

REFERENCES

Abbott, A. (1995). Sequence analysis: New methods for old ideas. *Annual Review of Sociology, 21*, 93–113.

Aldous, J. (1996). *Family careers: Rethinking the developmental perspective.* Thousand Oaks, CA: Sage.

Barley, S.R. (1989). Careers, identities, and institutions: The legacy of the Chicago school of sociology. In M.B. Arthur, D.T. Hall, & B.S. Lawrence (Eds), *Handbook of career theory* (pp 41–65). New York: Cambridge University Press.

Becker, G.S. (1981). *A treatise on the family.* Cambridge, MA: Harvard University Press.

Becker, P.E., & Moen, P. (1999). Scaling back: Dual-career couples' work-family strategies. *Journal of Marriage and the Family, 61,* 1–13.

Bem, S.L. (1993). *The lenses of gender.* New Haven: Yale University Press.

Blair-Loy, M.F. (1996). *Career and family patterns of executive women in finance: Evidence of structural and cultural change.* Paper presented at the American Sociological Association 91st Annual Meeting, New York City, NY.

Blossfeld , H.-P., & Huinink, J. (1991). Human capital investments or norms of role transition? How women's schooling and career affect the process of family formation. *American Journal of Sociology, 97,* 143–68.

Breiger, R. (1995). Social structure and the phenomenology of attainment. *Annual Review of Sociology, 21,* 155–36.

Brim, G. (1992). *Ambition: How we manage success and failure throughout our lives.* New York: Basic.

Brinton, M. (1988). The social-institutional bases of gender stratification: Japan as an illustrative case. *American Journal of Sociology, 94,* 300–34.

Brinton, M., & Nee, V. (Eds). (1998). *New institutionalism in sociology.* New York: Russell Sage Foundation.

Chudacoff, H.P. (1989). *How old are you? Age consciousness in American culture.* Princeton, NJ: Princeton University Press.

Clausen, J.A. (1986). *The life course.* Englewood Cliffs, NJ: Prentice-Hall.

Coleman, J.S. (1993). The rational reconstruction of society. *American Sociological Review, 58,* 1–15.

Conger, R.D., & Elder, G.H., Jr. (1994). *Families in troubled times: Adapting to change in rural America.* New York: Aldine De Gruyter.

Coser, L. (1974). *Greedy institutions: Patterns of undivided commitment.* New York: Free Press.

Curtis, R. (1986). Household and family theory on inequality. *American Sociological Review, 51,* 168–83.

Dannefer, D. (1984). Adult development and social theory of paradigmatic reappraisal. *American Sociological Review, 49,* 100–16.

Desai, S., & Waite, L.J. (1991). Women's employment during pregnancy and after the first birth. *American Sociological Review, 56,* 551–66.

Doeringer, P., & Piore, M. (1971). *Internal labor markets and manpower analysis.* Lexington, MA: Health Lexington.

Elder, G.H., Jr. (1998). The life course as developmental theory. *Child Development, 69,* 1–12.

Elder, G.H., Jr, Conger, R.D., Foster, E.M., & Ardelt, M. (1992). Families under economic pressure. *Journal of Family Issues, 13,* 5–37.

Elder, G.H., Jr, George, L.K., & Shanahan, M.J. (1996). Psychosocial stress over the life course. In H.B. Kaplan (Ed.), *Psychosocial stress: Perspectives on structure, theory, life course, and methods* (pp 247–91). Orlando, FL: Academic Press.

Elder, G.H., Jr, & O'Rand, A. (1995). Adult lives in a changing society. In K.S. Cook, G.A. Fine, & J.S. House (Eds), *Sociological perspectives on social psychology* (pp 452–75). Needham Heights, MA: Allyn and Bacon.

Gerson, K. (1985). *Hard choices: How women decide about work, career, and motherhood.* Berkeley, CA: University of California Press.

Goode, W.I. (1960). A theory of role strain. *American Sociological Review, 25,* 483–96.

Granovetter, M. (1986). Labor mobility, internal markets, and job matching. *Research in Social Stratification and Mobility, 5,* 3–39.

Guillemard, A.-M., & Rein, M. (1993). Comparative patterns of retirement: Recent trends in developed societies. *Annual Review of Sociology, 19,* 469–503.

Hagestad, G.O. (1988). Demographic change and the life course: Some emerging trends in the family realm. *Family Relations, 37,* 405–10.

Hagestad, G.O., & Neugarten, B.L. (1984). Age and the life course. In R. Binstock & E. Shanas (Eds), *Handbook of aging and the social sciences* (2nd ed., pp 35–61). New York: Van Nostrand Reinhold.

Han, S.-K., & Moen, P. (1999a). Work and family in temporal context: A life course approach. *The Annals of the American Academy of Political and Social Sciences, 562,* 98–110.

Han, S.-K., & Moen, P. (1999b). Clocking out: Temporal patterning of retirement. *American Journal of Sociology, 105,* 191–236.

Han, S.-K., & Moen, P. (forthcoming 2001). Coupled careers: Men's and women's pathways through work and marriage in the United States. In H.-P. Blossfeld & S. Drobnic (Eds), *Careers of couples in contemporary societies: A cross-national comparison of the transition from male breadwinner to dual-earner families.* Oxford, UK: Oxford University Press.

Hareven, T.K. (1984). *Family time and industrial time: The relationship between the family and work in a New England industrial community.* New York: Cambridge University Press.

Heinz, W.R. (1996). Status passages as micro-macro linkages in life course research. In A. Waymonn & W.R. Heinz (Eds), *Sociology and biography* (pp 51–66). Weinheim: Deutscher Studien Verlag.

Henretta, J.C. (1994). Social structure and age based careers work. In M.W. Riley, R.L. Kahn, & A. Foner (Eds), *Age and structural lag* (pp 57–79). New York: John Wiley & Sons.

Henretta, J.C., & O'Rand, A.M. (1983). Joint retirement in the dual worker family. *Social Forces, 62*, 504–20.

Henretta, J.C., O'Rand, A.M., & Chan, C.G. (1993a). Joint role investments and synchronization of retirement: A sequential approach to couples retirement timing. *Social Forces, 71*, 981–1000.

Henretta, J.C., O'Rand, A.M., & Chan, C.G. (1993b). Gender differences in employment after spouses retirement. *Research on Aging, 15*, 148–69.

Hertz, R. (1986). *More equal than others: Women and men in dual-career marriages.* Berkeley, CA: University of California Press.

Hill, R. (1970). *Family development in three generations.* Cambridge, MA: Schenkman.

Hochschild, A. (1989). *The second shift.* New York: Avon Books.

Hogan, D.P. (1981). *Transitions and social change: The early lives of American men.* New York: Academic Press.

Kanter, R.M. (1977). *Work and family in the United States: A critical review and agenda for research and policy.* New York: Russell Sage.

Kohli, M. (1986). Social organization and subjective construction of the life course. In A.B. Sorensen, F.E. Weinert, & L.R. Sherrod (Eds), *Human development and the life course: Multidisciplinary perspectives* (pp 271–92). Hillsdale, NJ: Lawrence Erlbaum.

Krüger, H. (1996). Normative interpretations of biographical processes. In A. Weymann & W.R. Heinz (Eds), *Society and biography: Interrelationships between social structure, institutions and the life course* (pp 129–46). Deutscher Studien Verlag: Weinheim.

Mayer, K.U., & Mueller, W. (1986). The state and the structure of the life course. In A.B. Sorensen, F.E. Weinert, & L.R. Sherrod (Eds), *Human development and the life course: Multidisciplinary perspectives* (pp 217–45). Hillsdale, NJ: Lawrence Erlbaum.

Merton, R.K. (1968). *Social theory and social structure.* New York: The Free Press.

Mills, C.W. (1951). *White collar.* New York: Oxford University Press.

Mills, C.W. (1959). *The sociological imagination.* New York: Oxford University Press.

Moen, P. (1985). Continuities and discontinuities in women's labor force participation. In G.H. Elder, Jr (Ed.), *Life course dynamics: 1960s to 1980s* (pp 113–55). Ithaca, NY: Cornell University Press.

Moen, P. (1989). *Working parents: Transformations in gender roles and public policies in Sweden*. Madison, WI: University of Wisconsin Press.

Moen, P. (1992). *Women's two roles: A contemporary dilemma*. Westport, CT: Greenwood.

Moen, P. (1994). Women, work, and family: A sociological perspective on changing roles. In M.W. Riley, R.L. Kahn, & A. Foner (Eds.), *Age and structural lag* (pp 151–70). New York: John Wiley & Sons.

Moen, P. (1996). A life course perspective on retirement, gender, and well-being. *Journal of Occupational Health Psychology, 1*, 131–44.

Moen, P. (1998). Recasting careers: Changing reference groups, risks, and realities. *Generations, 22*, 40–5.

Moen, P., & Wethington, E. (1992). The concept of family adaptive strategies. *Annual Review of Sociology, 18*, 233–51.

Moen, P., & Yu, Y. (1999). Having it all: Overall work/life success in two-earner families. In T. Parcel (Ed.), *Research in the sociology of work* (Vol. 7, pp 107–37). Greenwich, CT: JAI Press.

Mortimer, J.T., & Borman, K.B. (Eds). (1988). *Work experiences and psychological development throughout the life span*. Boulder, CO: Westview Press.

Neugarten, B.L., Moore, J., & Lowe, J.C. (1965). Age norms, age constraints and adult socialization. *American Sociological Review, 54*, 635–47.

O'Rand, A.M. (1995). The cumulative stratification of the life course. In R.H. Binstock, L.K. George, V.W. Marshall, G.C. Myers, & J.H. Schulz (Eds), *Handbook of aging and the social sciences* (4th ed., pp 188–207). San Diego, CA: Academic Press.

O'Rand, A.M., & Henretta, J.C. (1982). Women at middle age: Developmental transitions. *The Annals of the American Academy of Political and Social Science, 464*, 57–64.

Quick, H.E., & Moen, P. (1998). Gender, employment, and retirement quality: A life-course approach to the differential experiences of men and women. *Journal of Occupational Health Psychology, 3*, 44–64.

Riley, M.W. (1987). On the significance of age in sociology. *American Sociological Review, 52*, 1–14.

Riley, M.W., Foner, A. & Waring, J. (1988). Sociology of age. In N.H. Smelser (Ed.), *Handbook of Sociology* (pp 243–90). Newbury Park, CA: Sage.

Riley, M.W., & Riley, J.W., Jr. (1994). Structural lag: Past and future. In M.W. Riley, R.L. Kahn, & A. Foner (Eds), *Age and structural lag* (pp 15–36). New York: J. Wiley.

Rook, K.S., Catalano, R., & Dooley, D. (1989). The timing of major life events: Effects of departing from the social clock. *American Journal of Community Psychology, 17,* 233–58.

Rosenberg, M. (1979). *Conceiving the self.* New York: Basic Books.

Rosenfeld, R.A. (1980). Race and sex differences in career dynamics. *American Sociological Review, 45,* 583–609.

Rossi, A.S. (1985). Gender and parenthood. In A.S. Rossi (Ed.), *Gender and the life course* (pp 161–92). New York: Aldine.

Spilerman, S. (1977). Careers, labor market structure, and socioeconomic achievement. *American Journal of Sociology, 83,* 661–93.

Stovel, K.W., Savage, M., & Bearman, P. (1995). Ascription into achievement: Models of career systems at Lloyds Bank, 1890–1970. *American Journal of Sociology, 102,* 358–99.

Swidler, A. (1986). Culture in action: Symbols and strategies. *American Sociological Review, 51,* 273–86.

Tolbert, P.S., & Moen, P. (1998). Men's and women's definitions of 'good' jobs: Similarities and differences by age and across time. *Work and Occupations, 25*(2), 168–94.

Tomaskovic-Devey, D. (1993). *Gender and racial inequality at work: The sources and consequences of job segregation.* Ithaca, NY: ILR Press.

Waite, L.J. (1981). *U.S. women at work.* Washington, DC: Population Reference Bureau.

Zhou, X., Moen, P., & Tuma, N. (1998). Educational stratification in urban China: 1949–1994. *Sociology of Education, 71,* 199–222.

24. Children of the Gender Revolution: Some Theoretical Questions and Findings from the Field

Kathleen Gerson

As a new century commences, it is clear that fundamental changes in family, work, and gender arrangements have transformed the experience of growing up in American society. Only several decades ago, an American child was likely to grow to adulthood in a two-parent home with a mother who worked outside the home either intermittently or not at all. No such common situation unites children today. With fewer than 14 per cent of American households containing a married couple with a breadwinning husband and homemaking wife, children living in a 'traditional family' now form a distinct minority (Ahlburg and De Vita, 1992; Gerson, 1993). Regardless of race, ethnicity, or class, most younger Americans have lived, or will live, in a family situation that departs significantly from a pattern once thought to be enduring. Many have grown up in a two-parent home in which both parents have pursued strong and sustained ties to work outside the home. Others have lived through marital disruptions and perhaps the remarriage of one or both parents. Still others have been raised by a single mother who never married the father of her children. Most of these children have experienced shifting circumstances in which some substantial change occurred in their family situation before they left their parents' home.

This revolution in the experience of childhood has provided an unprecedented opportunity to unravel the processes of human development and better understand the consequences of growing up in diverse family situations. We are living through a natural social experiment that makes it possible to assess the effects of family arrangements as well as other social and cultural institutions on the lives of children. As the recipients of widespread gender and family change, this generation is ideally positioned to shed light on a number of important theoretical questions.

First, what is the relationship between family composition and children's welfare? Is family structure, as measured by the household's composition and gender division of labour, the most consequential aspect of a child's developmental environment, as has been generally assumed, or is family form mediated by other factors, such as interactional processes within the home and contextual factors outside it? Second, what are the links between parental choices and children's reactions? How do children make sense of their family situations and their parents' circumstances, and what strategies do they develop to cope with their situations? Are children inclined to adopt their parents' choices and beliefs, and when and under what circumstances are they more likely to reject or modify them?

Third, what part do institutions outside the family, and especially community, educational, and labour-market structures, play in shaping a child's outlook and developmental trajectory? And, finally, as new generations of women and men respond to widespread cultural changes outside the home and shifting dynamics within it, what personal, social, and political strategies are they developing to cope with the new contingencies wrought by the family and gender revolutions? What do the experiences of this pivotal generation portend for the future of gender – as a cultural belief and a lived experience?

The 'children of the gender revolution' have grown to adulthood in a wide range of circumstances, and their experiences offer a window through which to glimpse both general processes of human development and historically embedded social shifts. By taking a careful look at the developmental paths and personal conflicts of this generation, we can untangle the role that family structure plays in children's lives and discover the other processes and factors that either mitigate or explain its effects. And since members of this generation are now negotiating the transition to adulthood and thus poised to craft their own work and family strategies, they offer important clues to the future course of the transformation in family, work, and gender patterns begun by their parents.

Changes in Children's Lives: Contending Theoretical Approaches and the 'Family-values' Debate

The diversification of family forms has produced disputes among American social scientists (as well as among politicians and ordinary citizens) about the effects of family and gender transformations on the welfare of children. These debates have been framed in 'either/or' terms, in which those who decry the decline of the homemaker–breadwinner family have clashed with those who defend and, to some extent, celebrate the rise of alternative family forms.

Analysts concerned that family and gender transformations threaten children's welfare and undermine the larger social fabric have developed a perspective that emphasizes 'family decline.' (See, for example, Blankenhorn, 1994; Popenoe, 1989 and 1996; Whitehead, 1997.) This approach tends to view the 'traditional family,' characterized by permanent heterosexual commitment and a clear sexual division of labour between stay-at-home mothers and breadwinning fathers, as the ideal family form. The rise in divorce, out-of-wedlock parenthood, and employment among mothers thus represents serious family breakdown that is putting new generations of younger Americans at risk. From this perspective, 'non-traditional families,' such as dual-earner and single-parent households, are part of a wider moral breakdown, in which the spread of an individualistic ethos has encouraged adults to pursue their own self-interest at the expense of children.

While compelling, the 'family-decline' perspective contains both logical and empirical deficiencies. First, it treats family change as if it were a cause rather than an effect. Yet new family forms are inescapable reactions to basic economic and social shifts that have propelled women into the workplace and expanded the options for personal development in adulthood. By idealizing the mid-twentieth-century homemaker–breadwinner household, this perspective also tends to downplay the positive aspects of change, and especially the expansion of options for women. We now know, however, that family life in the past rarely conformed to our nostalgic images and that many homemaker–breadwinner families were rife with unhappiness and abuse (Coontz, 1992).

In response to the critique of family change, less pessimistic analysts have responded that family life is not declining but rather adapting, as it has always done in response to new social and economic exigencies. These analysts point out that a return to family forms marked by significant gender inequality is neither possible nor desirable and would not solve the predicaments parents and children now face (see, for example, Skolnick, 1991; Stacey, 1990 and 1996; Coontz, 1997). The roots of the family and gender revolution extend deep into the foundations of the economy, the society, and the culture. Single parents and employed mothers have thus become scapegoats for social ills with deeper economic and political roots.

Despite the polarized nature of the American family-values debate, both perspectives have tended to focus on family structure as the crucial arena of contention. Yet research suggests that family structure, taken alone, cannot explain or predict outcomes for children. While children living with both biological parents appear on average to fare better than children in one-parent homes, most of the difference can be traced to the lower economic and social resources available to single parents as well as to factors such as high family conflict that promote parental break-up in the first place (Cherlin et al., 1991; McLanahan and Sandefur, 1994).

In the case of employed mothers, circumstantial factors also appear to trump family structure. Despite the persisting concern that children are harmed when their mothers work outside the home, decades of research have yielded virtually no support for this claim. Instead, the critical ingredients in providing for children's welfare are such factors as a mother's satisfaction with her situation, the quality of care a child receives, and the involvement of fathers and other supportive caretakers (Barnett and Rivers, 1996; Hoffman, 1987). Even comparisons between oft-labelled 'traditional' and 'non-traditional' families show that diversity within family types is generally as large as differences between them (Acock and Demo, 1994).

The focus on family structure has thus obscured a number of more basic questions about the short- and long-run consequences of these complicated and deeply rooted social changes. While it is clear that a return to a world marked by a clear sexual division of labour, an unquestioned acceptance of gender inequality, and the predominance of patriarchal families is neither desirable nor possible, it is less clear what new social forms will or should emerge. To understand this process, we need to delve beneath the polarized controversy over family values to clarify the consequences of diversifying family forms, increasing female autonomy, and shifting adult commitments onto those who are the most direct recipients of change. How has the generation born during this period of rapid and tumultuous change experienced, interpreted, and responded to the gender revolution forged by their parents?

Understanding the Children of the Gender Revolution

To answer these questions, I have interviewed a group that can be considered to be the 'children of the gender revolution.' These late adolescents and young adults, between the ages of 18 and 30 are members of the generation that is young enough to have experienced the dynamics of family change at close hand, yet old enough to have a perspective on their childhood circumstances and to be formulating their own plans for the future. Since family change may have been experienced differently in different economic and social contexts, the group has been drawn from a range of racial and ethnic backgrounds and a variety of poor, working-class, and middle-class communities. Of the 120 people interviewed, approximately 56 per cent are non-Hispanic white, 20 per cent are African-American, 18 per cent are Hispanic, and 6 per cent are Asian. They were randomly selected from a range of urban and suburban neighbourhoods in the New York metropolitan area. (Most respondents were selected by a random sampling procedure as part of a larger study of the children of immigrants and native-born Americans. To ensure that the parents of my respondents had been born and grown up amid the changing family circumstances of American society, my sample was drawn entirely from the native-born group. See Mollenkopf et al. [1997] for a description of the study and sampling techniques.)

To illuminate how these children of the gender revolution have made sense of their childhoods and are formulating strategies for adulthood, in-depth life-history interviews elicited information on their experiences growing up, their strategies for coping with past and present difficulties, and their outlooks on the future. Most lived in some form of non-traditional family arrangement before reaching age 18. About a third lived in a single-parent home at some point in their childhood, and an additional 40 per cent grew up in homes in which both parents held full-time jobs for a sustained period of time. Even the remaining group, who described their families as generally traditional, were likely to grow up in homes that underwent some form of notable change as mothers went to work or marriages faced crises. As a whole, this diverse group experienced the full range of changes now emerging in U.S. family and gender arrangements.

The experiences of these strategically placed young women and men call into question a number of long-held assumptions about the primacy of family structure in human development. Their life paths and outlooks point, instead, to the importance of processes of family change, the shape of opportunities outside the family, and children's active strategies to cope with their circumstances amid inescapable but uncertain social shifts.

Family Structure or Family Trajectories?

Despite the theoretical focus on family structure, which generally refers to the composition and division of labour in the household, these young women and men offer a different view of how they formed their sense of self and their outlook on the future. From their perspective, what matters instead are more subtle family processes and pathways. Indeed, simple family typologies, based on differences among homemaker–breadwinner, dual-earner, and single-parent homes, mask important variations within such family forms. Regardless of the apparent structure of the household, most children experience some form of change in their family life over time. While a minority can point to stable, supportive family environments marked by few noticeable changes, the more common experience involves transitions, sometimes abrupt and always consequential, from one family environment to another. Surprisingly, this experience of change applies to many whose parents remained married and not just to those whose households underwent a break-up. More important than household structure at one point in time are the *trajectories* that families follow as they develop throughout the life of a child.

From the time a child is born to the time she or he leaves home, the family environment can develop in different ways. From the point of view of the child, these family experiences assume the form of family trajectories or pathways that can either remain stable or move in different directions. A stable trajectory may remain relatively harmonious, supportive, and secure, or it may remain chronically conflictual and unsupportive. A changing trajectory may become more stable and supportive as family conditions improve over the span of childhood and adolescence, or it may become more conflictual and insecure as family conditions deteriorate.

These trajectories are important, but they are not closely linked to prevailing notions of traditional and non-traditional family structures. While classical theories might predict that traditional households would be more stable and harmonious than non-traditional ones, the experiences of these young women and men reveal no such clear relationship. For example, a number of apparently stable traditional households are actually marked by chronic conflict or some kind of less readily noticeable change. In one case, a family's outward stability masked chronic parental addictions and abuse that never improved, despite their status as a two-parent home. In another case, a drug-addicted, distant father moved out of the family home in response to his wife's demand that he break his addiction or leave. Several years later, after a successful recovery, he returned to become a supportive, involved parent. This outwardly stable but internally riven traditional family thus became more harmonious and secure over time.

A comparable diversity of processes and practices can be found in non-traditional households. While all children undergo some kind of change if their parents separate or divorce, the transition can bring improvement or deterioration. One young woman, for example, felt relieved when her father divorced her neglectful, emotionally abusive mother, and she found stability and support when he remarried a nurturing, economically successful woman.

Static categories of family type thus offer limited clues about the dynamics between parents and children or the unfolding nature of family life. Children rarely perceive their families as fixed arrangements; rather, they experience them as a range of situations in flux which either offer or deny them support over time. These processes are important in providing for a child's welfare, but they are not simple reflections of family structure. A breadwinner–homemaker arrangement does not guarantee a stable or supportive home, and those with dual-earning, single, or step-parents are clearly able to provide support and care.

Employed Mothers and Other Parents

If family process is more important than family structure, then a mother's well-being is also more important than whether or not she works outside the home. While most of these young women and men grew up in homes in which their mothers were strongly involved in earning a living, the fact of working or not working mattered less than whether or not mothers (and fathers) appeared satisfied with their lives as workers and parents.

Young women and men reared by work-committed mothers generally agreed that the ensuing benefits outweighed any hypothetical losses. In many cases, a mother's job kept the family from falling into poverty, and in some it helped propel the household up the class ladder. A mother's employment also gave both parents increased autonomy and appeared to enhance parental equality. While some worried that their mothers and fathers had to toil at difficult, demanding, and low-paying jobs, no one felt neglected simply because a mother worked. To the contrary, they were appreciative of their mothers' efforts to provide for their own and their family's welfare. Working outside the home thus provided a way for mothers as well as fathers to become 'good' parents.

Those whose mothers did not pursue independent avenues outside the domestic sphere expressed more ambivalence. While some were pleased to have their mothers' attention focused exclusively on home and family, others were concerned that the choice had been an unnecessary sacrifice. In these cases, when a homemaking mother seemed frustrated or unhappy, the child's reaction was more likely to centre on guilt and minor resentment than on gratitude.

More important than the choice to work or stay home, however, is the child's perception about why the choice was made. When a parent, whether mother or father, appeared to work for the family's welfare as well as her or his own needs, the child accepted these choices as unproblematic. If, in contrast, a mother's choice appeared to contradict her family's needs or her own desires, the child responded with concern and doubt. Children felt supported when parents made choices that provided for everyone's needs and did not pit the wishes of mothers against the needs of children. They fared better, however, when contextual supports helped working parents resolve the conflicts between family and work. Most important were reliable, neighbourhood-based child-care resources, involvement from committed fathers, and satisfying and flexible jobs for both parents.

Beyond Family Structure: Family Processes and Opportunity Contexts

How did children from these diverse family situations fare as they negotiated the challenges and dangers of childhood and adolescence? Their diverse fates ranged from successful young adults who were able to launch promising college and work careers to those who became entangled in less-felicitous patterns, such as school failure, involvement in crime, and early parenthood. Why were some able to negotiate the risks of adolescence while others were propelled down perilous paths? While it may be tempting to attribute these disparate outcomes to family structure, that does not appear to be the explanation. Not only were people from all types of families, including traditional ones, socially and emotionally sidetracked, but many from nontraditional households were able to avoid or overcome the dangers they faced.

Several important, interacting factors influence individual trajectories. First, processes within the family either provided or denied emotional and social support to the child. Second, social and economic resources outside the family, including neighbourhood-based resources such as peer groups and schools and class-based resources such as economic stability, provided or denied financial and social capital to either avoid or escape dangerous situations. Structural and cultural contexts outside the family thus influenced children's outlooks and trajectories, regardless of the kinds of families in which they lived.

School experiences, for example, ranged from academic involvement and success to minor alienation to school failure. Those who fared poorly were likely to have parents who lacked either the will, the skills, or the money to make a special effort to hold the child to reasonable standards, to fight for a child in the face of an indifferent bureaucracy, or to make financial sacrifices (such as choosing a parochial or private school). Those who succeeded, on the other hand, were fortunate in a variety of ways. Most possessed either class-related resources that provided access to good schools or the social pressures and expectations of school success. In the absence of class resources, the support of only one person who believed in and would fight for the child could made a crucial difference. Yet single mothers, many of whom were poor, and dual-income parents with time-consuming jobs were just as likely as traditional families to provide these pressures and supports. For example, one young man attributed his college and graduate degrees to his struggling but feisty single mother, who fought against a school bureaucracy determined to consign him to the category of 'learning disabled.'

Experiences outside of school also ranged from engagement in constructive activities, such as organized sports and social service, to involvement in dangerous pursuits, such as crime, drugs, and sexual risk taking. While opportunities to experiment in risky ways were more prevalent in poor and minority communities, there were inducements in all types of neighbourhoods. Those who fell prey to more dangerous lifestyles were not more likely to live in non-traditional homes, but they were more likely to become integrated into peer groups that countered a family's influence. Indeed, avoiding risky behaviour often required resisting local temptations, such as a street culture centred on illicit activities. Neighbourhoods matter and can thwart the efforts of parents to protect their children from the influences of a burgeoning youth culture outside the home. Class resources, however, offer a consequential buffer. Middle-class children were more likely to be shielded by their parents and their communities while they passed through a stage of adolescent experimentation, whether it involved drugs, sex, or petty crimes. Poor and minority children were more likely to 'get caught,' to become ensnared in a punitive system, and to pay a higher long-term price for youthful indiscretions. In all of these ways, class resources and family processes (especially in the form of parental support) provide the context for family life and tend to supersede family structure as crucial shapers of children's life chances and developmental trajectories.

Children's Interpretive Frameworks and Coping Strategies

Family processes and class resources form the context for children's experiences, but these contexts are always sifted through a child's interpretive framework and personal coping strategies. These strategies and frameworks represent active efforts on the part of children to give meaning to the actions of others and to craft their own choices amid the uncertainties of changing circumstances.

As this strategic generation has confronted the ideas, opportunities, and models of work and family institutions in flux, most have had to cope with a world in which high hopes and aspirations are colliding with subtle fears and constricted realities. Regardless of race or class position, most women and men strongly support those aspects of change that have opened up opportunities for women and created new possibilities for redefining gender. Yet these hopes coexist with concerns about the difficulty of combining work and family, the dangers of economic insecurity, and the lack of institutionalized supports for non-traditional choices. Whether the issue is work, family, or how to combine the two, the men and women emerging from the gender revolution perceive both new opportunities and a new set of dilemmas with few clear resolutions. While most hold egalitarian and pluralist ideals, at least in the abstract, they are less sanguine about whether or how these ideals can be achieved. (In a study of children living in gender-equal families, Risman [1998], also finds a gap between children's egalitarian ideals and their identities.)

Work

Among women and men of all classes, almost all aspire to better jobs than their parents secured or than they have yet been able to find.

However, if the desire for a good, well-paying, white-collar job or career is nearly universal, the expectation of achieving it is not. Rather, these young women and men are divided in their optimism about the future. These divisions reveal blurring gender boundaries even as class boundaries persist. Women and men alike thus hold high aspirations for work careers, although those with constricted opportunities are less confident about reaching them. Optimism seems well founded for some (e.g., college-educated whites) and ill-founded for others (e.g., young, single mothers and high school drop-outs). Most are hoping to find satisfying jobs, willing to settle for economic security, and not confident that they will be able to achieve either.

The scepticism about long-term economic prospects is reflected in men's and women's expectations of each other. Both groups view their economic prospects in individualist terms. Since men generally do not expect to earn enough to support wives and families alone, and women do not expect to be able to rely on male breadwinners, both groups believe their economic fate depends on their own achievements in the job market rather than on forging a lasting commitment with one partner. Women are thus as likely as men to express high job aspirations, and men are as likely as women to long for respite from the demands of earning a living. Despite these shared aspirations, women remain aware that their opportunities are more constricted than men's. A common refrain is, thus, 'Women have it better today than in the past, but men still have it better and probably always will.'

Marriage

If economic security and job options remain a concern, most nevertheless believe it is easier to shape their own labour-market fate than to control the fate of their personal relationships. The vast majority of women *and* men view egalitarian marriage as the ideal, not only because dual-earner marriages appear to provide the best economic alternative but also because they offer the best hope for balancing personal autonomy with mutual commitment. These are high standards for defining a 'good marriage,' and many are sceptical they will be able to achieve it.

Gender provides a lens through which similar expectations are experienced differently. While women and men are equally sceptical of creating lasting commitments, women are more aware of the consequences for work and family. They are more likely to see the possibility of raising children alone and more likely to link this possibility to the need for economic autonomy. Yet women agree with men that it is better to go it alone than to become enmeshed in an unhappy or narrowly confining commitment. Even the minority – mostly men – who view traditional marriage as the ideal are more wishful than certain. In the face of these ideals, however, women remain sceptical that men can be counted on to shoulder their fair share, and men doubt they will have the job flexibility to do so.

Parenthood

Changing views of marriage provide the context for shifting orientations towards parenthood. For most women and men, the best parenting appears to be equal parenting. The rise of employed mothers and dual-earning couples thus appears to be good for children – bringing in more family income, fostering happier marriages, and providing better examples of women's autonomy and gender justice. Most (though not all) have concluded that 'ideal mothers' and 'ideal fathers' are fundamentally indistinguishable, and, across races and classes, the majority are wary of family arrangements based on rigid or insurmountable gender differences.

Regardless of their own family experience, moreover, everyone agrees that a committed partnership and happy marriage provide the best context for raising a child. The problem, however, is that a happy marriage is difficult to achieve. Most also agree, therefore, that in the context of a deteriorating or chronically conflictual marriage, a child cannot thrive. The key for this generation is that both parents remain involved and supportive even if they find they cannot sustain a commitment to each other.

Views of Gender

Larger cultural shifts, and especially the rising acceptance of and need for women's economic independence, have permeated everywhere, leaving children from all classes and family situations exposed to changing definitions of gender and new work and family options. Most support these changes, arguing that while women have gained considerable opportunities, they have not done so at men's expense.

Women as well as men place a high value on autonomy, and men are equally likely to espouse egalitarian ideals at home and at work. These ideals clash, however, with institutional options that put many of them out of reach. If egalitarian ideologies, support for diversity, and a desire for personal choice predominate, behavioural strategies may stray far from these ideals.

Despite the desire to span the perceived gap between goals and opportunities, few can envision effective social, institutional, or political resolutions to these intractable dilemmas. When asked whether employers or the government can or should help families, most reply that individuals in American society are on their own. The protracted political battle over family values has left this generation with little faith that political action can make a difference or that personal problems can have social causes and institutional solutions.

Self and Society amid the Gender Revolution

A diverse and shifting set of experiences are sending these children of the gender revolution in a variety of new and unclear directions. Most hold high aspirations for the future but are also sceptical about the possibilities for achieving their fondest dreams. And because they do not generally see the link between their own seemingly intractable dilemmas and the larger social-structural forces that are shaping the contours of change, they lack a vision of the possibilities for social solutions to what are experienced as very personal problems.

Prepared to face a gap between ideals and options, they are determined to exercise some choice over which trade-offs to make – between work and family, parenthood and career, marriage and going it alone. If their work and family ideals prove to be false promises, they reserve the right to change their circumstances. Despite the uncertainty ahead, however, most agree that the future will not and should not bring a return to the idealized past of separate spheres for men and women. From their perspective, the era when unhappy marriages were inescapable, women stayed home with children, and men wielded unquestioned power is irretrievable and undesirable.

Beyond the 'Family-values' Debate

The emergence of diverse family arrangements in the United States offers a unique opportunity to develop a better theoretical grasp of the link between the institutions of child rearing, the experiences of growing up, and the long-term trajectories of children. While debate has focused on the importance of family structure, the developmental trajectories of those who have grown up amid these changes reveal a more complicated picture. The lessons gleaned from these lives suggest expansions to and reformulations of prevailing theoretical frameworks.

First, family processes and trajectories matter more than family structure. Not only can conflict and neglect be found in all types of families, including those that may appear outwardly stable and secure, but processes of nurturance and support also emerge in a range of family contexts. More important than a family's structure at one point in time are processes of family change over time. Does a child's family context involve increasing support and declining conflict or, in contrast, declining support and continuing or rising conflict? From the child's perspective, what matters in the long run are emotional and economic sustenance, mutually respectful dynamics within the home, and caring bonds with their parents and other caretakers. Traditional families cannot guarantee these conditions, and non-traditional ones are often able to provide them.

Similarly, the employment status of mothers matters less than the overall context in which mothers (and fathers) create their lives. Across classes and gender groups, children are less concerned about whether their mothers work outside the home than about why their mothers work (or do not work), how their mothers feel about working (or not working), and what kind of caretaking arrangements their mothers and fathers can rely on. On balance, children see their mothers' employment as a benefit on many levels. Mothers' jobs offer families greater economic security and increased resources, enhance mothers' satisfaction and autonomy, and provide an example worthy of emulation. Children do worry, however, about their mothers' and fathers' ability to obtain jobs with good economic prospects, supportive working conditions, and enough flexibility for combining work with family life. Given the varied and ambiguous influence of family structure, it is time to focus theoretical attention on the institutional arrangements and social processes that matter for children, regardless of the form of family in which they happen to live. Community and economic resources are crucial, providing the context for family life and either opening opportunities or posing risks and dangers. Resources such as educational and work opportunities, child-care services, and personal networks of adults and peers help shape parents' strategies for rearing their children and children's ability to cope with difficult circumstances.

Finally, children are not passive recipients of parental and social influences. They actively interpret and respond to their social worlds, often in unexpected ways. As social actors facing unforeseen contingencies, they must make new sense out of received messages and develop a variety of innovative coping strategies. They are crafting these strategies in a changing social and cultural context, where new views of gender and shifting work and family opportunities are as likely to influence their outlooks as are immediate family experiences. The trajectories and experiences of these children of the gender revolution suggest that a search for one *best* family form provides neither a fruitful theoretical avenue nor a useful practical agenda. Instead, the challenge is to understand how children experience and respond to family conditions that are usually in flux and always embedded in wider institutions. Regardless of a child's family circumstance, contextual supports are essential for enabling parents and children to cope with change in a satisfying way.

For those who have grown to adulthood during this era of fluid personal paths and family arrangements, the fundamental aspects of change appear irreversible and, on balance, desirable. The dismantling of the homemaker–breadwinner ideal has widened options that few are prepared to surrender. These changes in family life and women's options have not, however, been met with comparable changes in the organization of the workplace and community life. And although most have adopted non-traditional, egalitarian ideals, few can envision support for achieving their goals from employers or the government. Lacking faith in work or political institutions, they are resolved to seek individual solutions to unprecedented social dilemmas and to develop new ways of negotiating adulthood. The experiences and responses of this new generation are especially important in this era of irrevocable but incomplete transformation. These young women and men may be the inheritors of change, but their strategies for responding to their parents' choices and their own dilemmas will shape its future course.

REFERENCES

Acock, A.C., & Demo, D.H. (1994). *Family diversity and well-being*. Thousand Oaks, CA: Sage.
Ahlburg, D.A., & De Vita, C.J. (1992, August). New realities of the American family. *Population Bulletin, 47*(2), 1–44.

Barnett, R., & Rivers, C. (1996). *She works/he works: How two-income families are happier, healthier, and better off*. San Francisco, CA: Harper.

Blankenhorn, D. (1994). *Fatherless America: Confronting our most urgent social problem*. New York: Basic Books.

Cherlin, A., Furstenberg, F.F., Jr, Chase-Lansdale, P.L., Kiernan, K.E., Robins, P.K., Morrison, D.R., & Teitler, J.O. (1991, June). Longitudinal studies of the effects of divorce on children in Great Britain and the United States. *Science, 252*, 1386–9.

Coontz, S. (1992). *The way we never were: American families and the nostalgia trap*. New York: Basic Books.

Coontz, S. (1997). *The way we really are: Coming to terms with America's changing families*. New York: Basic Books.

Gerson, K. (1993). *No man's land: Men's changing commitments to family and work*. New York: Basic Books.

Hoffman, L. (1987). The effects on children of maternal and paternal employment. In N. Gerstel & H. Engel Gross (Eds), *Families and work* (pp 362–95). Philadelphia: Temple University Press.

McLanahan, S., & Sandefur, G. (1994). *Growing up with a single parent: What hurts, what helps*. Cambridge, MA: Harvard University Press.

Mollenkopf, J., Kasinitz, P., & Waters, M. (1997, October). *The school to work transition of second generation immigrants in metropolitan New York: Some preliminary findings*. Paper presented at Levy Institute Conference on the Second Generation, Bard College, New York.

Popenoe, D. (1989). *Disturbing the nest: Family change and decline in modern societies*. New York: Aldine de Gruyter.

Popenoe, D. (1996). *Life without father: Compelling new evidence that fatherhood and marriage are indispensable for the good of children and society*. New York: Free Press.

Risman, B.J. (1998). *Gender vertigo: American families in transition*. New Haven, CT: Yale University Press.

Skolnick, A. (1991). *Embattled paradise: The American family in an age of uncertainty*. New York: Basic Books.

Stacey, J. (1990). *Brave new families: Stories of domestic upheaval in late 20th century America*. New York: Basic Books.

Stacey, J. (1996). *In the name of the family: Rethinking family values in a postmodern age*. Boston: Beacon Press.

Whitehead, B.D. (1997). *The divorce culture*. New York: Alfred A. Knopf.

25. Engineers and the Western Canadian Oil Industry: Work and Life Changes in a Boom-and-bust Decade

Gillian Ranson

At the level of local labour markets and work organizations, economic restructuring in effect restructures employment opportunities and the career trajectories of workers. This study explores some of the effects of restructuring during the 1980s in a particular industry – the western Canadian oil and gas industry, centred in the province of Alberta and largely managed from the city of Calgary – on a particular professional group, namely engineers.

In the sense that it examines a particular and (relatively) bounded system (Stake, 1994), this is a 'case study' of the social and economic relations of engineering work in a particular regional context and during a period of relatively dramatic change. Stake would further describe it as an 'intrinsic' case study, in that it seeks a better understanding of this particular system. But it also engages with larger debates, both methodological and theoretical. It is not merely a case, but a 'case of' (Ragin, 1992, p. 6). In this sense, it is an 'instrumental' case study in that it 'provides insight into an issue or refinement of theory' (Stake, 1994, p. 237). Specifically, this study illuminates a particular theoretical perspective on the life course which will be articulated shortly.

The Social and Economic Context

An important part of the social context of engineering work in Calgary, and by extension the environment in which all the graduates in the study were trained, is the relatively high proportion of engineers in the community, and the high status of engineering as a profession. Census data for 1991 indicate that the province of Alberta has, per capita, double the number of engineers of any other province, and the city of Calgary is reputed to have the third-highest concentration of engineers of any city in the world. The designation 'professional engineer' (characterized in Canada by the letters 'P.Eng.' after the name) belongs to a university graduate who has fulfilled specific post-degree licensing requirements including an extended period of supervised engineering work experience. At least until relatively recently, about half the registered membership in the Association of Professional Engineers, Geologists and Geophysicists of Alberta (the provincial professional association) worked in the oil and gas industry, a proportion which was estimated to represent most of the industry's professionals (Human Resources Study Steering Committee, 1992).

Thus, engineering graduates in Calgary have traditionally entered a fairly clearly defined labour market, with more or less specialized educational backgrounds targeted to a particular kind of employment. During the 1970s, when world oil prices made Alberta energy highly competitive, post-graduation careers seemed assured. However, a National Energy Program, introduced by the federal government in 1980 with the intention of increasing Canadian ownership of what was then an immensely valuable resource, had the effect of discouraging U.S. investment and beginning an economic downturn. This was exacerbated by the downward spiral of world oil prices, beginning in 1981 but culminating in the early months of 1986 (Petroleum Monitoring Association, 1986). Oil companies, formerly the major employers of engineering graduates, reduced their recruitment of new graduates during the 1980s to levels of about one-third that of previous years (Human Resources Study Steering Committee, 1992). Reduced recruitment was accompanied by major downsizing in most companies.

Theoretical Framework

The life-course perspective is a useful theoretical tool to orient the analysis of work experiences described by the engineering graduates in the study during a period in which conventional engineering workplaces were undergoing major restructuring. As a means of viewing the flux and flow of individual lives in a holistic way, this approach recognizes that individual life courses are constructed 'at the intersection of families, educational and social institutions, and labour markets' (Heinz, 1992, p. 9).

While some theorists (for example, Kohli and Meyer, 1986; Meyer, 1986) argue that the progress of modernity has led to life courses structured to the point of institutionalization, others (for example Beck, 1992) see the life course as becoming increasingly a 'biographical project' of individual actors in a era in which the institutions of modernity are beginning to fragment. Elements of this individuation thesis are contained in Giddens's (1991) analysis of 'high modernity' and the post-traditional order. But in the context of this study, it is Giddens's (1991) discussion of the self as a 'reflexive project' that is most helpful.

Giddens points out that transitions in individuals' lives have always required some psychic reorganization, often given ritual recognition in traditional cultures as *rites de passage*. In conditions of modernity, however, 'the altered self has to be explored and constructed as part of a reflexive process of connecting personal and social change' (Giddens, 1991, p. 33). Giddens would recognize the kinds of change experienced by many of the individuals in this study as representing 'fateful moments,' or times when individuals stand 'at a crossroads' in their existence; when 'the protective cocoon which defends the individual's ontological security' is threatened; when 'the "business-as-usual" attitude that is so important to that cocoon is inevitably broken through'; and when individuals may be forced to change habits and readjust projects (Giddens, 1991, pp 131–2). More specifically, '[t]he reflexive project of the self, which consists in the sustaining of coherent, yet continuously revised, biographical narratives, takes place in the context of multiple choice as filtered through abstract systems' (Giddens, 1991, p. 5).

Engineering work, as Zussman (1985) has demonstrated, is a variety of professional work best understood through an emphasis on career rather than through models of professionalization or proletarianization. 'Career' is seen as a source of integration at the workplace, the point at which 'biography and social structure intersect,' linking past, present, and future (Zussman, 1985, p. 228). And Grey (1994), building on Giddens, suggests that the concept of career as an organizing or regulative principle is a part of the 'project of the self' (Grey, 1994, p. 481). As Evetts (1996) has pointed out, this draws on an older interactionist tradition which explores 'subjective careers' as individuals' own changing perspectives towards their careers. Thus, in times of change, when global events like economic restructuring threaten 'business as usual' in a literal sense, what must be reflexively explored and reconstructed is the narrative of the career. The career narratives constructed in the context of economic change by the engineers in the present study are examined from this perspective.

Methodology

This study is part of a research project which examined the work histories and family circumstances of women and men who graduated from the Faculty of Engineering at the University of Calgary during the 1980s. The project has involved tracking all the women who graduated between 1980 and 1990, together with a comparable number, randomly sampled, of the male graduates in those years. Findings reported here are drawn from information from a total of 315 engineering graduates (162 women and 153 men) who took part in either structured telephone interviews (N = 218) extensive, semi-structured face-to-face interviews (N = 62), or who completed self-administered questionnaire versions of the telephone survey (N = 35) between July 1997 and August 1998.[1] In each of these categories of data collection, comprehensive work-history information from the time of graduation to the present was gathered, together with a family history which took account of changing domestic circumstances and other dimensions of adult life around which career decisions may have had to be made.

Findings

There are two general categories of findings presented here. The first concerns some specific effects of restructuring in the Alberta energy industry during the 1980s on the work experiences of the engineering graduates surveyed. Here the study addresses cohort differences in the experience of the transition from university to the anticipated career in engineering; the acknowledgment of contract and consulting work as a legitimate career option; and the institutionalization of mobility and the multi-employer career.

The second category of findings links more directly to the broader debates about work and the life course by suggesting how these facts about restructured work are experienced and interpreted by the graduates surveyed. Using the issue of mobility and the multi-employer career as a focus, the study examines the way survey participants reflect on their own career paths and discursively organize their experiences as part of a 'reflexive project of the self,' to use Giddens's (1991) term.

TABLE 25.1
Proportion of Graduates with Jobs Lined Up on
Graduation

	Total interviewed	% with jobs lined up
1980	20	75
1981	27	78
1982	26	73
1983	32	47
1984	36	50
1985	34	53
1986	29	48
1987	30	63
1988	24	54
1989	27	44
1990	30	70
	N = 315	

Effects of Restructuring

i) *Cohort Differences:* The effects of the National Energy Program, as noted above, first began to be felt (along with some softening of world oil prices) in 1982 and 1983. The sharp drop in world oil prices occurred in early 1986. Thus, different cohorts of graduates were differently placed to encounter the adverse labour-market effects of these changes. These differences are most easily seen by reference to table 25.1, which shows the proportion of graduates in each cohort year who had jobs lined up at graduation. Interviews with graduates suggest that these years have come to be identified as 'good years' and 'bad years' in terms of job prospects. The 'good years' – notably 1980 and 1981 – reflect the end of the energy boom. Oil companies carried out active campus recruitment campaigns, and many graduates were able to weigh several job offers. 'Bad years' occurred in the mid-1980s, when engineering graduates faced dramatically diminished prospects.

The clear university-to-work transition evident in the older cohorts was replaced for many graduates in the younger groups by other patterns. For example, nine of the twenty-nine graduates surveyed from the 1986 cohort did not start their first jobs until at least a year after graduation. Five of them, in fact, remained at university to complete master's degrees, temporarily opting out of the competition for jobs.

ii) The Legitimation of Contract and Consulting Work: A second major effect of the restructuring of the Alberta energy industry in the 1980s is the acknowledgment of contract work as a legitimate career alternative. In the words of one male engineer, where during boom times consulting or contract work was the lot of those who 'couldn't get a real job,' now it has achieved legitimacy for the many engineers who, indeed, *couldn't* get a real job and turned to contract work to survive.

Numbers of those currently doing contract or consulting work are difficult to gauge, partly because of the way the work is organized, and the way individual contract workers choose to describe the terms of their employment. Some consulting companies actually hire engineers as employees; other companies subcontract work to engineers with whom they have long-standing arrangements, who look like employees but are actually self-employed. In the present study, about 17 per cent of the women in the study who were still working in engineering were self-employed contractors or consultants. About 15 per cent of the men indicated they were consultants, but this proportion does not take into account the number working under the subcontracting arrangements described above – or, indeed, the proportion who had done some contract work earlier in their careers.

iii) The Institutionalization of Mobility: When they were interviewed, the earliest of the cohorts surveyed – the 1980 group – had been in the labour market for seventeen years, and the most recent cohort for seven. Clearly, the length of time in the labour market and the presence or absence of other factors (notably family responsibilities) also played a part in defining the shape of the work career. But one of the most significant effects of 1980s restructuring on Alberta engineering careers, once launched, appears to be the institutionalization of multiple-employer careers.

Only about 19 per cent of the graduates currently working in engineering or engineering-related jobs have had only one employer. In this group of currently employed engineers, the mean number of employers (including self-employment) is 2.95. That this mobility is affected by time in the labour market is suggested by the fact that about 54 per cent of those who had only one employer are members of the three most recent graduating cohorts. Yet even in the most recent cohort (1990), 50 per cent have had two employers, and 20 per cent have had three to five employers.

In all cohorts, those who have had multiple employers can be further divided into those whose mobility can best be described as reactive or involuntary (in other words, involving a layoff or company failure), and those whose mobility is proactive and voluntary, involving a strategic move to achieve some sought-after end. Of all of those interviewed, 23 per cent reported having experienced a layoff at some point in their careers, and 4 per cent reported accepting a voluntary severance package. Nearly 21 per cent of all first jobs ended in layoff, voluntary severance, or the end of a short-term contract, and a further 7 per cent ended for a variety of reasons related to instability of employment.

Making Sense of Change: Reflections on Paths Taken and Not Taken

Not only is the traditional one-employer career no longer the norm for the engineering graduates studied, but there are signs that mobility is coming to be perceived as an important sign of career progress in engineering. In other words, a variety of employment experience is coming to be seen as the preferred career path for those whose focus is their career.

Those who have made, or been forced to make, job changes, and whose career paths reflect the mobility described earlier, speak in a particular way about their choices and experiences. Testing oneself (or being tested) and taking control are the terms in which mobility comes to be described, however tentatively and cautiously the move is made. For example, one male engineer, after sixteen years with a major oil company, had just made a shift to another, smaller, energy company. He first began to think about moving a couple of years earlier, he said, because, ironically, he was concerned about long-term security. Until that time, he had 'never really thought about working anywhere else' and had anticipated staying with the company until he retired.

> But because of the layoffs and, you know, looking at what the future [might bring], made you change your way of thinking. You know, if you wanted to have at least some say or input or control over, sense of control over your destiny or over your career, then you'd have to take a little bit more active role in it. I looked at ... what I could offer, where I was marketable.

Those who are veterans of many moves see themselves differently still – as survivors, perhaps even adventurers, and proud of it. They see job change, even job loss, as a virtue and not a failure. They see themselves as more marketable, perhaps even better engineers than those who have not moved at all. At any rate, they are engineers who are very sure of themselves. One 1980 graduate whose entrepreneurial career has culminated in his present position as vice-president of a small energy company talks of his sympathy for laid-off former colleagues at the oil company where he first went to work, who have been 'schooled in bureaucracies as opposed to the physical realities of getting things done.' A woman who graduated in 1981 and who has been recruited to a succession of jobs with small companies commented that a lot of people who have come through big companies need to be 'coddled': 'There were people that I worked with at [large company] for years who had never ever looked for a new job because they were afraid they wouldn't be marketable and they were just scared to go out in the big world. It's too bad and some of them ended out there regardless.'

Another male engineer commented, 'I don't think I would have been happy in an organization where you do the same thing day in and day out.' This man, an adventurous entrepreneur whose present small-company involvement will, he hopes, allow him in five years to 'sell his options and move to Bermuda,' looks at the contrast of his own career:

> A lot of people I don't think realize how transferable skills are. I mean, what I do now, I specialize in, if there's anything I do that is a specialty, it's project management, which is a very broad and general concept and idea. What is a project manager? I have the ultimate confidence. I can build anything. I don't even have to know anything about it. You give me some plans, a schedule and a budget and I'll build it for you because I know the steps, the processes involved.

Another man, laid off by his first employer and then rehired a total of three times, echoes this exuberant confidence: 'The best thing that ever happened to me was getting laid off three times. Oh, yeah, by far. I mean, I have all the confidence in the world [in] what I can do now.'

In other words, the mobile, multiple-employer, varied career path is discursively constructed as giving the individual more practical skills and knowledge and more confidence, thereby creating a more marketable engineer.

In contrast, the value of the single-employer career is described in terms of the benefits extrinsic to work that it makes available. For example, one 1980 engineering graduate who has worked for the same large oil company all his working life has relinquished his goal of being a vice-president in his present company by age 40, but he has no aspirations outside the company either: 'Is it worth the sacrifice? ... Like right now I'm comfortable and I think that people get into a comfort zone that's hard to get out of. And right now our lifestyle is pretty good.'

The women with children in this single-employer path had usually been able to intersperse full-time employment with maternity leaves, sometimes negotiating periods of part-time employment to accommodate the needs of infants and preschool children. Some spoke of careers on hold and promotions delayed or declined through their childbearing years – but most also spoke of a shift in their priorities from career to family, and the need to achieve balance between work and family life. A woman who has been employed with the same major oil company since her graduation in 1985, through two maternity leaves and another health-related leave, commented: 'I think if somebody was to offer me a promotion of some sort, I would have to think about it very, very carefully, and think about what it could mean, especially to the flexibility I have while my kids are still fairly young ... I mean I figure that where I am right now is just exactly where I need to be.'

These comments collectively suggest a pragmatic taken-for-grantedness about careers that offer extrinsic benefits and do not demand sacrifice. Conspicuous by their absence are any comments about the 'professional' value of the single-employer career, or any sign of aspirations to reach the top of the career ladder at work. In other words, the stable, single-employer path is discursively constructed as one which accommodates an individual who is less career-centred than some others.

Discussion

The economic cycles of the energy industry in western Canada have had serious implications for engineering graduates attempting to establish careers. Those who survived the 'bust' did so in a variety of ways. A minority were survivors in the sense that they were able to remain with a single employer through periods of downsizing. Others were laid off, or 'saw the writing on the wall' and moved voluntarily to new employment, sometimes on more than one occasion. Others relished the opportunities created by the reorganization of engineering work and took an entrepreneurial approach to their careers. A single historical contingency, centred on Alberta, shaped an array of biographies. These biographies are not institutionalized, in the sense that they are by no means all the same. But at the same time they are not so individual that patterns are not discernible.

The major pattern emerging from a consideration of the work experiences described here is the shift from the single-employer career to careers defined by mobility and discursively constructed as producing individuals with more confidence and more marketable skills. But while this shift, and the others noted earlier, might well be purely local responses to restructuring, there are much broader theoretical links. What these engineers have experienced constitute, in Giddens's (1991) terms, threats, in a whole series of 'fateful moments,' to the ontological security of business – and careers – 'as usual.' As part of the reflexive project of the self, their ideas about careers and acceptable career paths have come to be redefined, in the wake of these changes, very much along the lines Giddens's discussion of the life course in the post-traditional order would suggest.

In other words, they have been required continuously to revise their career narratives as they negotiate options in rapidly changing and unpredictable economic circumstances. The coherence these narratives *do* achieve is testimony to the work that has gone into them, the sense-making required to create local and individual order and meaning out of events whose reach is global.

NOTES

1 Though the interest in this paper is in mapping the emergence of new career trajectories and employment options, rather than in statistically determining their representativeness, it should be noted that the number of engineers surveyed represents about 69 per cent of the 240 women and 62 per cent of the sampled 248 men who graduated in engineering between 1980 and 1990. It represents approximately 84 per cent of the women and 76 per cent of the men for whom current addresses could be obtained.

REFERENCES

Beck, U. (1992). *Risk society: Towards a new modernity.* London: Sage.

Evetts, J. (1996). *Gender and career in science and engineering*. London: Francis and Taylor.

Giddens, A. (1991). *Modernity and self-identity*. Stanford: Stanford University Press.

Grey, C. (1994). Career as a project of the self and labour process discipline. *Sociology, 4*(2), 479–97.

Heinz, W.R. (1992). Introduction: Institutional gatekeeping and biographical agency. In W.R. Heinz (Ed.), *Institutions and gatekeeping in the life course* (pp 9–27). Weinheim: Deutscher Studien Verlag.

Human Resources Study Steering Committee. (1992). *Changes, challenges, choices: Human resources in the upstream oil and gas industry*. Ottawa: Employment and Immigration Canada.

Kohli, M., and Meyer, J.W. (1986). Social structure and social construction of life stages. *Human Development, 29*, 145–9.

Meyer, J.W. (1986). The self and the life course: Institutionalization and its effects. In A.B. Sorensen, F.E. Weinert, & L.R. Sherwood (Eds), *Human development and the life course: Multidisciplinary perspectives* (pp 199–216). Hillsdale, NJ: Lawrence Erlbaum Associates.

Petroleum Monitoring Association. (1986). *1985 monitoring survey* (Cat. No. N27–22/1986E). Ottawa: Minister of Supply and Services.

Ragin, C. (1992). Introduction: Cases of 'what is a case?' In C.R. Ragin & H.S. Becker (Eds), *What is a case?* (pp 1–17). Cambridge: Cambridge University Press.

Stake, R.E. (1994). Case studies. In N.K. Denzin & Y.S. Lincoln (Eds), *Handbook of qualitative research* (pp 236–47). Thousand Oaks: Sage.

Zussman, R. (1985). *Mechanics of the middle class*. Berkeley: University of California Press.

26. Baby Boomers in Transition: Life-course Experiences of the 'Class of '73'[1]

Paul Anisef and Paul Axelrod

This chapter is based on a panel study that closely charts the life-course pathways of an Ontario cohort of Grade 12 students in 1973 ('the Class of '73') to the leading edge of middle age in 1995. It employs a life-course theoretical perspective to assess the relative importance of structure and agency in the multiple school-to-work and life transitions made by one baby-boom cohort. Like other life-course researchers represented in this volume, we note that there have been tremendous social and economic changes over the past several generations (Heinz, 1999; Chisholm and Du Bois-Raymond, 1993; Evans and Heinz, 1994; Krüger, 1998). These changes – as we found in the case of the Class of '73 – affected the values and directions taken by young people as they moved along uncharted pathways, constructing life scripts that were influenced by social-structural factors and individual circumstances. We anticipate that our findings will provide benchmarks for comparison with younger generations.

Our research is driven by two basic questions:

1. To what degree do social structural forces beyond the individual's control determine pathways to adulthood?
2. In what ways do agency and personal choices affect such outcomes?

In addressing these themes, this chapter draws on longitudinal survey data and personal interviews and focuses on the themes of social mobility, occupation, gender, and family life.[2]

Structure, Agency, and the Life Course

Theorists and researchers who address the human agency–social structure debate vary in their approaches to the subject (Wyn and Dwyer, 1999). Some, like Lyotard and Baudrillard, contend that structural analysis has lost its validity and that the world has now entered a new postmodern epoch where patterns of behaviour and individual life chances have become less predictable than formerly (Furlong and Cartmel, 1997, p. 1; Chisholm, 1999). Beck argues that the influence of class, family, and gender on individual experience has diminished in modern industrial societies. Traditional social bonds and barriers, including social stratification, are weakened in a social and economic environment that is less enduring and less certain than in the past. 'The tendency is towards the emergence of individualized forms and conditions of existence, which compel people – for the sake of their own material survival – to make themselves the centre of their own planning and conduct of life.' (Beck, 1992, p. 88). Others, such as Jones and Wallace (1992), are more cautious in interpreting social change. While they acknowledge a greater degree of uncertainty and a weakening of traditional ties in Western societies, they contend that life chances and experiences can still be predicted by knowing a person's location within social structures. Thus, while class effects may not be as strong in Britain today as they were in the past, 'pathways out of school are still structured by factors such as social class, family background, academic achievement ... and opportunities in the local labour market' (1992, p. 45).

Roberts and colleagues (1994) compare youth transitions in Germany and England and conclude that a pattern of 'structured individualization' reflects the situation in both countries, whereby the movement to goals, the aims themselves, and the individuals' ability to realize them were products of their structural location (p. 51). Though agreeing that young people do face new risks and opportunities in the modern world, Furlong and Cartmel (1997) assert that the 'risk society is not a classless society, but a society in which the old social cleavages associated with class and gender remain intact; on an objective level, changes in the distribution of risk have been minimal' (p. 7).

Our study finds evidence of the *combined* influence of structural forces and individualized decision making. We maintain that personal agency is present in the transition from youth through to adulthood. Young people do make distinctive choices about their education and career pathways. These decisions are influenced by such individual-ized traits as interests, ability, personality, and ambition. But such deci-sions are not made in a vacuum. Structural factors – social class, gender, ethnicity, and location – play an important role in shaping the context in which personal choices are made. For example, our data demonstrate that youth from higher socio-economic strata are more likely than the less advantaged to pursue postsecondary education, and our interviews explore how young people – both those who pur-sue postsecondary education and those who do not – explain and understand their decisions.

Though the social structures within which young persons grow and mature operate 'above their heads,' they should not be thought of as necessarily constraining. In fact, social structures are simultaneously constraining and enabling. Though they may preclude the possibility of making certain choices, they also offer the very possibility of human choice (Hays, 1994, p. 65). For members of the Class of '73, social life was fundamentally structured as they made school-to-work transi-tions, and the choices they made usually tended to reproduce these structures. As Hays (1994) observes, 'That reproduction process, how-ever, is never fully stable or absolute and, under particular circum-stances, the structured choices that agents make can have a more or less transformative impact on the nature of structures themselves. Human agency and social structure, then, have a simultaneously antagonistic and dependent relationship' (p. 65).

As one ages, structure and agency continue to affect the life course, though not always evenly. Our data indicate that the importance of class and residence diminish once students enter higher education; their occupational pathways are affected more by the amount and type of education they obtain. At the same time, it is important to explore how individuals come to understand and then negotiate their location and social-class position as they pursue their educational and occupa-tional aspirations. This effort itself is strongly influenced by individual traits, including clarity of choices, strength of commitment to life goals, and personal priorities and values (Anisef et al., 2000).

With regard to gender, occupational segregation continued from the 1970s through to the 1990s (Phillips and Phillips, 1993). Notwithstand-ing the growing participation of women in higher education, there were clear distinctions between the subsequent occupational profiles of men and women, and, individually, women made different deci-sions about the ways they would manage work and family life. As a number of researchers have noted, domestic responsibilities, orientations to marriage and family, and personal experiences can affect educational attainment, employment, and career opportunities, normally influencing the lives of women more than they do the lives of men (Wotherspoon, 1998, p. 168). We found that personality, interests, family matters, even health concerns influenced the varied decisions of members of the Class of '73. Structure and agency worked reflexively in their transition to adulthood, and personal choices were continuously being made and remade in the context of changing structural conditions (Anisef et al., 2000, especially chapter 7).

With Heinz (1995), we believe that it is important to interpret the meaning attached by individuals to conventional social forces (such as class) and their actual use. For this reason we conducted a micro life-course analysis for a selected number of respondents in the Class of '73 that charts separate trajectories and then links them with transitions and turning-points in the lives of individuals (Anisef et al., 2000, chapter 8). Furthermore, although the Class of '73 grew up in a society where status passages were governed by clear and explicit expectations, as they moved into their twenties and thirties they encountered instances of greater risk and uncertainty. We contend that there is no standard biography and that each person plays a critical role in writing her or his own life script. We therefore examine the type of individual decisions that were formulated in the various transitions between schooling, work, marriage, and parenting.

Our earlier work, which employed human-capital and status-attainment theories, has thus been enriched, we hope, by our use of life-course theory (Anisef et al., 1980; Anisef et al., 2000). Human-capital theory posits that through individual effort and investment in education, skills acquisition and credentials are normally converted into employment and career prospects (Livingstone, 1999, p. 162). The status-attainment model, though incorporating social-structural factors and individual traits, de-emphasizes social, economic, and historical contexts in analysing school-to-employment transitions (Boyd et al., 1985; Wotherspoon, 1998, p. 21). Useful as they are, these theories fail to capture the complexity of the transition process, the uncertainty flowing from a period of turbulent economic change, and the means by which individuals seek to assert control over their environment. For this reason we have turned to life-course theory.

Life-course theory, which attempts to explain the dynamic relationship between the individual and social order, allows researchers to examine a cohort's collective experience without reifying it and to remain attuned to individual differences without ignoring social context (Buchmann, 1989). More specifically, as Elder has noted, 'the life course refers to the pathways through the age-differentiated life span, to social patterns in the timing, duration, spacing, and order of events; the timing of an event may be as consequential for life experiences as whether the event occurs and the degree and type of change' (Elder, 1978, p. 21). Within this framework, school-to-work transitions are seen as constructed and negotiated by individuals within the context of social forces, educational selection, work experiences, and employment options. Decisions made by people are seen as both time dependent and more complex than is suggested by either the human-capital or the status-attainment model (Heinz, 1996, p. 7).

In our view, the concept of 'structured individualization' (Rudd and Evans, 1998, p. 61) best captures the theoretical model we have employed. The model indicates how structure and agency both shape the life course, intersecting continuously, as individuals construct their life 'scripts' in the context of conditions that are beyond their control (the state of the economy), and those which depend upon personal choices (marriage, having children, and seeking further education). The individual does her or his utmost, while at the same time recognizing that there is a kind of 'system' that might affect the available options and outcomes (Rudd and Evans, 1998, p. 61).

Class, Education, and Occupation

The analysis of findings in all phases of the study make it clear that structural factors, including class and region, have played a most significant role in shaping educational choices developed during the high school years. Our data show that those of high socio-economic origins were virtually four times as likely to obtain university degrees by 1979 as respondents with low socio-economic origins. Though the majority of respondents entered first jobs that were either skilled or unskilled, those who obtained postsecondary educational qualifications were more likely to begin their careers as professionals, semi-professionals, or mid-level/high-level managers.

For those lower-class youth who obtained higher education, the importance of class and region diminished with time. They achieved considerable success in the labour market as professionals, semi-professionals and managers, entering careers that were indistinguishable from those achieved by upper-class youth who had also pursued postsecondary education. Class mattered, but its impact on occupational attainment was tempered by the amount and level of education, clearly reflecting the underlying influence of agency.

While young people with high and low socio-economic origins started out with roughly similar occupational distributions with respect to first-entry jobs, they ended up with significantly different occupational distributions in 1995, differences that favour individuals from the high socio-economic group in terms of occupations concentrated in managerial and professional categories. While this shows that the impact of socio-economic origins was substantial, so too were the effects of educational attainment over the long term. By 1995, almost half of the university graduates were in high-level management and professional positions. Middle-management, semi-professional, and technical occupations drew heavily from all backgrounds including Class of '73 members with only high school education. Very few university graduates were found in either skilled or unskilled employment, whereas these sorts of occupations drew heavily from among those with community college or no more than high school education.

We also sorted 1973 high school region of origin into urban and rural and found that region of origin had a modest effect on first jobs, with the urban location favouring entry jobs in the two higher-status occupational categories. Having rural origins was strongly linked to the number of respondents starting out as farmers. By 1995, the occupational distributions of participants from cities and rural areas differed substantially, with even higher percentages of those with city origins ending up with occupations in the two higher-status occupational categories. We found that by 1995, for youth who started out with unskilled first jobs (white-collar and blue-collar), those with city backgrounds had been upwardly mobile into the managerial and professional ranks, while those with rural backgrounds had either been upwardly mobile into skilled occupations (white-collar and blue-collar) or remained in the unskilled occupational category.

Notwithstanding the impact of region on occupational destinations, the degree of occupational mobility for the Class of '73 was high. In all likelihood, this was the combined result of stability and growth in particular occupation sectors between the mid-1970s and the early 1990s and the personal attributes and circumstances of individuals. After beginning their careers in low-level jobs, large numbers of employees were evidently still able to 'work their way up' the company or organizational ladder. The pathways forged by individuals varied significantly, however, as the following case studies indicate.

Navigating the Life Course

Neither of Jennifer's parents went to university or college, but they encouraged her to pursue higher education. 'I guess they wanted us to do better than what they had done themselves,' she said. Her mother was a secretary and her father a district fire chief. After finishing high school, Jennifer took a university degree in administrative studies. She then worked in secretarial jobs for which she was overqualified. But set as she was on paid employment, she 'took the first thing [she] could get.' After a year she was hired by a bank in a position where she was able to apply her university training. She eventually moved into a managerial position, where she remained in the early 1990s. The combination of parental encouragement and personal persistence (agency) and expanding opportunities in the service sector (structure of the economy) influenced Jennifer's life course.

By contrast, Frank, the youngest of five children of an Italian-immigrant working-class family, dropped out of Grade 13, worked as a surveying assistant, a job he disliked, and left. He then completed a Manpower retraining program in painting and decorating and worked briefly as a painting contractor, but quit following a dispute with his employer. For several years, he drifted, occasionally working with his mother at a laundromat, at times collecting unemployment insurance. He moved out of the family house at age 27 to marry, and has since worked as a maintenance man for a utility company. There have been many layoffs in the organization, and his job in 1994 was neither well paying nor assured, though he was hopeful that his seniority would secure his position. In Frank's case, the lack of postsecondary education limited his occupational options, though he was able to obtain some skilled training and employment. His commitment to assisting his mother and his difficulty in finding work that could sustain his interest contributed to the largely unrewarding vocational state. The recession of the early 1990s lurked in the background as an added source of pressure.

Frank's experience was quite different from Sam's, whose parents were also working-class Italian immigrants in a small Ontario town. His father worked as a garbage collector and his mother as a cook. Sam was a successful high school athlete and won a sports scholarship to an

American university. Because he missed his family, he returned home, and then transferred to another American university. He played hockey while at college but did not pursue it professionally. Clearly, his interest in sports stimulated his pursuit of higher education, and he eventually received a bachelor's degree in business. He worked in hotels during the summer, where he met his then-future (now current) wife. Her father owned a restaurant/hotel in which Sam began to work. He 'moved up the ladder' and now manages the hotel. In the mid-1990s, he hoped one day to be the proprietor of his own hotel.

In Sam's case, the support he received from his parents to pursue his schooling, his special aptitude for sports, and his selection of a marriage partner all affected his career progress, facilitating to some degree his ability to surmount social-structural barriers. Elsewhere in our study, we document the particular determination of immigrant families to help improve the social status of their children (Anisef et al., 2000, chapter 6). This factor, too, affected Sam's outlook.

Consider also the case of Kelly, who grew up in a central-Ontario farm close to a small town. One of ten children, in a family that struggled financially, she finished high school and then a nursing program at a community college in another Ontario city. She did this despite the fact that her father did not value education highly. She was determined not to be a 'farmer's wife because farm women work too hard and they get no credit for it.' Still, she cherished country living, and resolved both to avoid the 'big city' and to live near her family. She moved back to the outskirts of her home town and has since worked part time in the local hospital, where secure full-time employment has been difficult to obtain. She married a builder/carpenter, who works irregularly; they have two children. Their very modest family income situates them at the low end of the socio-economic scale, though the mortgage on their house (which Kelly's husband built) is almost paid off. In 1995, Kelly remained very satisfied with rural life, which she considered superior to the frenetic pace of urban living. However, she was concerned about the future for her children, given the high level of youth unemployment, especially in economically deprived areas. She wanted them to continue living close by; however, with the gradual erosion of rural life in Ontario and the uncertain economy, she wondered how they would eventually support themselves.

In Kelly's situation, one can clearly see the combined impact of structure and agency. Like many other rural Ontarians, she did not attend university. In addition, she chose a traditionally gender-specific field of employment. But by undertaking college education away from home, she asserted her independence and increased her self-confidence. Employment conditions then limited her ability to work full time, but this was offset to a significant degree by the priority she placed on life-style and family concerns. The family lived modestly, but managed financially and revered its quality of life.

These examples illustrate the varied experiences of those from modest backgrounds. Status-attainment literature correctly notes that those who are born into more privileged families have a 'head start,' and generally maintain or improve their social status. Our study certainly supports this theory, but we explore as well individuals' particular experiences and perceptions, which are diverse, distinctive, and largely unpredictable.

Walter, for example, whose father was a professional and who grew up in a middle-class neighbourhood, recalled that 'there was never any decision to be made as to whether you would go to postsecondary education. It was more a function of when you would go ... [University was] a natural progression of events.' Still, his educational and occupational pathway was not entirely linear. He enrolled in science but performed rather poorly and did not complete his degree. He began to work part time for a large company as a computer operator, a skill he mostly learned on the job. He then took an auditing position with a bank. The job proved to be less interesting than advertised, and he was dissatisfied with his promotion prospects. He returned to university to complete a degree in economics and computer science. A subsequent job as an information-centre consultant for an insurance company lasted for a decade. But the 'shakeup of the industry,' which involved the 'elimination of huge layers of middle management,' led him to consider other possibilities. He left his job voluntarily and now works with a small reinsurance-facilitation company. He valued the autonomy he had gained in his work and the time it allowed for an active family life.

Coming from a middle-class background, Walter thus had the 'cultural capital' that enhanced his prospects for higher education. Although he did not initially complete his degree, he was interested in and able to find work in two areas of employment in which opportunities were expanding: computers and financial services. He eventually obtained his degree, inspired more by personal than by economic factors. He felt it important to finish a task that he had begun. The financial-services industry in which he worked has been subjected to major structural changes, though his experience and particular skills enabled him to work continuously and happily.

Gender, Family, and the Challenges of Working Life

Throughout the 1980s and early 1990s, members of the Class of '73 traversed their ways through the world of employment – a world in which opportunity and uncertainty coexisted. Without question, economic policies beyond the control of individuals affected their working lives (Krahn, 1996). Inflation, recession, free trade, the growth of the service sector, corporate downsizing, and public-sector deficit cutting all affected the availability and conditions of employment throughout the period. So, too, did the individual's social background, educational attainments, and gender. By 1995, the participation of women in the labour force had grown significantly – dual-income families were now the norm in Canada – but males and females still constructed their lives in distinctive, gender-specific ways.

However daunting the social and economic challenges, the men and women of the Class of '73 sought to ensure their personal autonomy and assert control over their working lives. Family life was a particularly important priority, and they were determined – women especially – to reconcile the demands of work with those of home and children.

As they looked back over the period from the perspective of our 1995 survey, the majority of respondents – 66 per cent – declared themselves to be satisfied or very satisfied with 'the way things have turned out' with respect to *work or career*. Some 22 per cent were neither satisfied nor dissatisfied, and almost 12 per cent were dissatisfied or very dissatisfied. By contrast, more than 85 per cent were very satisfied or satisfied with their *family life*, and 5.7 per cent were dissatisfied or very dissatisfied. Some 83 per cent were similarly content with their *personal life* and slightly less than 5 per cent expressed dissatisfaction. Thus, in 1995, most respondents were positive about, or at least reconciled to, the reality of their working lives. But family life was a far greater source of fulfilment. Given the economic vagaries of the previous two decades, this attitude was understandable.

Overall, the respondents appeared to enjoy their work, with women experiencing a slight edge in job satisfaction. By 1995, job satisfaction bore no clear relationship to educational attainment, but those respondents who held high-level management/professional positions and middle-management/semi-professional jobs were more likely to express strong satisfaction than respondents who held skilled or unskilled jobs. (Anisef et al., 2000, chapter 4).

Interviewees described, often in considerable detail, the conditions that both enriched and diminished the quality of their working experiences. The virtues of autonomy, diversity, flexibility, and creativity were highlighted by numerous people working in a variety of occupations. Where one or more of these conditions was absent, respondents might well have made changes, including voluntarily leaving their positions, in order to improve the quality of their work and their lives.

Ray, a chartered accountant, gave up a well-paying but 'boring' job with a large firm to start his own company. This was a 'risky' venture in the mid-1980s, given the fluctuations in the economy, but with the assistance of his wife, who helped with the books, he succeeded. He came to realize that accountants are employable in both good and bad economic times and that, to some degree, the profession is 'recession proof.' As a self-employed person, he came to cherish the control he gained over his hours and conditions of work.

Some, like Aaron, found it possible to fulfil their aspirations within a large organization. He dropped out of high school but later enrolled in university part time where he studied economics. Employed for several years by a major gas company, he had done economic forecasting and worked in both 'regulatory' affairs and policy development in the area of 'rate design.' He anticipated that he would refuse any promotions which reduced his independence and creative opportunities on the job.

While working as an occupational therapist, Jessica ran a small catering service at the hospital where she was employed. Entrepreneurial ambitions led her and her husband into the real-estate field where they worked successfully during the housing boom of the mid-1980s. In one three-week period, they sold eleven houses. Her husband did the marketing and she worked closely with clients, a facet of her job with close parallels to her work in occupational therapy. In both fields she was required to 'hold [the client's] hand' and provide emotional support under stressful circumstances. She left the job to raise her children. Her husband continued in the real-estate business full time, while she worked with him 'in the background.'

Many women, as our survey shows, left paid employment, either temporarily or permanently, to bear and raise children. Some 81.5 per cent of women not employed in 1994–5 identified family responsibilities, including pregnancy and problems arranging child care, as reasons for being out of the labour force in 1994–5. Employed women frequently described the challenges of reconciling family and occupational demands, and those who successfully managed this were the most fulfilled. Others wrestled with the problem on a daily basis.

Stephanie, for example, enjoyed her current employment as a music teacher, which took her many years to obtain. But in 1995 she was experiencing stress. The mother of three children, her teaching job required her to offer programs in two schools, and she was feeling 'burned out' by the competing demands on her time. Having regularly banked a portion of her salary, she was preparing to take a year off from her job, though she 'remain[ed] passionate' about her career.

Our quantitative and qualitative data revealed that, within the household, married and cohabitating women still shouldered a greater burden of family responsibilities, including looking after children, cooking meals, cleaning the house, and shopping for groceries. Men and women shared responsibility for household finances and for disciplining children.

To realize their occupational aspirations and cope with labour-market pressures and family demands, women chose a variety of strategies. Laura, the mother of three sons, was married and living in suburban Toronto in 1995. She had switched to occasional relief work from the full-time secretarial position she had held at a utility company. But when her employer laid off its part-time staff, Laura was forced to register with a temporary-employment agency. She found travelling to downtown Toronto and looking after three children very stressful, and she decided to stay home full time. She was very involved in her children's school and sports teams, and although she found having primary responsibility for child rearing difficult at times, she derived considerable satisfaction from it. She described herself as 'Ms Chauffeur,' claiming to be much busier than when she was working now that her sons had so many activities. 'But I enjoy it,' she added.

Judy, whose job in the food industry required her to be at work very early in the morning, relied on her husband to feed and dress their two children, aged 7 and 3, and drive them to school. As her job ended at 1:30 p.m., she was able to take over child-care responsibilities for the afternoon. This reorganization was possible because her husband was unemployed for six months. During that time, as her workload increased, he took on more of the domestic duties. Although he eventually obtained full-time work, he continued to share many of the household tasks.

The concept of sharing such duties reflects the high proportion of respondents in dual-income families. However, female respondents were more likely than males to adapt their occupations to family needs by entering occupations long associated with the traditional female sphere – such as nursing and teaching – as well as various support services – such as clerical and secretarial work. Women in the Class of '73 were more likely to have married in their early twenties than men. However, it also true that many did not marry until their late twenties, and most waited to have children until they had been in the labour force for a number of years. Finally, unlike their parents, very few had more than three children, and most had two.

It is interesting to speculate on the extent to which these women's responses reflected their commitment to work and career rather than merely their need to adjust to the realities of their situations. Typically, with the birth of their second child, women made compromises with respect to the work setting and their place within it, even when they continued to work full time. This, of course, must be taken in the larger context of women's situation in the labour market, particularly with respect to their (lower) earning capacity. Given these practical but important matters, family decision making which accommodated the work and careers of men over those of women could be seen as rational and of general economic benefit to the family household. Extending this argument even further, not having children, or having only one child, would have paid greater dividends to women from a career standpoint. To fully understand the commitment of Class of '73 women to have and raise children, one must consider the combined influence of personal priorities, the intrinsic satisfaction attached to family formation, and the continuing impact of cultural pressures in reinforcing women's traditional domestic roles.

Conclusion

Both this chapter and the larger study from which it is drawn have sought to demonstrate the interactive role of structure and agency in shaping the life course. Employing the concept of 'structured individualization,' we argue for the importance of agency and, more specifically, individual traits, for understanding the choices and experiences of young people as they move from adolescence to adulthood. A close examination of personal biographies among members of the Class of '73 revealed important personal differences. Some articulated a clear vision of the future in their adolescent years, while others drifted through adolescence and early adulthood, giving little thought to the conscious pursuit of life goals. Those who drifted were more likely to succumb to the constraining aspects of social structures which operated around them, while those who articulated a clear vision and sought to enact their dreams were able to take creative advantage of the enabling aspects of these same social structures.

An examination of individual lives accentuated the unique ways in which people construct and negotiate their way within the context of existing social structures and the social and economic realities of the historical period within which they grew up. We have traced the ways in which the vagaries of the economy, socially constructed gender roles, and the importance of individual personality affected pathways from schooling to employment and to family life. Individuals found themselves in historical moments that shaped the context of their lives. Yet many were determined, through the choices they made, to determine the texture and substance of their daily experiences. For the most part, they believed they had succeeded. This final quotation reflects typical attitudes expressed in a distinctive voice.

> Despite what you may gather from this survey, I'm very happy with the outcome of my life: marriage, children and work. At some time, many of us wish for a better life! But I'm not complaining, considering the economy as such. Remember, to be fairly successful in life, no matter how much education or how many diplomas you acquire, you have to chase the dream whether it be happiness or wealth or both. Mind you, a great education helps immensely, and a good attitude toward life doesn't hurt either.

NOTES

1 This research was made possible by the Social Sciences and Humanities Research Council of Canada under the Strategic Grants Program, Education and Work in a Changing Society. We would also like to acknowledge the contributions of other members of the Ontario Life Course Project Team to the development of ideas expressed in this paper.

2 Those surveyed and interviewed graduated from Grade 12 in Ontario high schools in 1973. They were surveyed six times. The last survey occurred in 1994–5 and included 788 of the original sample of 2,555. In 1995, they were in

their early forties with some twenty years of labour-market experience. They were able to review their school-to-employment and adolescent-to-adulthood transitions, and to reflect on their current family circumstances. This chapter reports selectively on the survey data and personal interviews.

REFERENCES

Anisef, P., Paasche, G., & Turrittin, A.H. (1980). *Is the die cast?: Educational achievements and work destinations of Ontario youth: A six-year follow-up of the critical juncture high school students*. Toronto: Minister of Colleges and Universities.

Anisef, P., Axelrod, P., Baichman, E., James, C., & Turrittin, A. (2000). *Opportunity and uncertainty: Life course experiences of the class of '73*. Toronto: University of Toronto Press.

Beck, U. (1992). *The risk society: Towards a new modernity*. London: Sage.

Boyd, M., Goyder, J., Jones, F.E., McRoberts, H.A., Pineo P.C., & Porter J. (1985). *Ascription and achievement: Studies in mobility and status attainment in Canada*. Ottawa: Carleton University Press.

Buchmann, M. (1989). *The script of life in modern society: Entry into adulthood in a changing world*. Chicago: University of Chicago Press.

Chisholm, L. (1999). From systems to networks: The reconstruction of youth transitions in Europe. In W.R. Heinz (Ed.), *From education to work: Cross national perspectives* (pp 298–318). Cambridge: Cambridge University Press.

Chisholm, L., & Du Bois-Raymond, M. (1993). Youth transitions, gender and social change. *Sociology, 27*(2), 259–79.

Elder, G.H., Jr. (1978). Family history and the life course. In T.K. Haraven (Ed.), *Transitions: The family and the life course in historical perspective* (pp 17–64). New York: Academic Press.

Evans, K., & Heinz, W.R. (1994). Transitions in progress. In K. Evans & W.R. Heinz (Eds), *Becoming adults in England and Germany* (pp 1–16). London: Anglo-German Foundation.

Furlong, A., & Cartmel, F. (1997). *Young people and social change: Individualization and risk in late modernity*. Buckingham: Open University Press.

Hays, S. (1994). Structure and agency and the sticky problem of culture. *Sociological Theory, 12*(1), 57–72.

Heinz, W.R. (1995). *Status passages as micro-macro linkages in life course*. Bremen: University of Bremen, Special Research Centre 186.

Heinz, W.R. (1996). *The transition from education to employment in a comparative perspective*. Toronto: University of Toronto, Centre for International Studies.

Heinz, W.R. (Ed.). (1999). *From education to work: Cross-national perspectives.* New York: Cambridge University Press.

Jones, G., & Wallace, C. (1992). *Youth, family, and citizenship.* Buckingham, U.K.: Open University Press.

Krahn, H. (1996). *School-work transition: Changing patterns and research needs.* Ottawa: Human Resources Development Canada, Applied Research Branch.

Krüger, H. (1998, May). *Social change in two generations: Employment patterns and their costs for family life.* Paper presented at the International Symposium on Restructuring Work and the Life Course, Toronto.

Livingstone, D.W. (1999). *The education–jobs gap: Underemployment or economic democracy.* Toronto: Garamond Press.

Phillips, P., & Phillips, E. (1993). *Women and work: Inequality in the Canadian labour market.* Toronto: James Lorimer.

Roberts, K., Clark, S.C., & Wallace, C. (1994). Flexibility and individualization: A comparison of transitions into unemployment in England and Germany. *Sociology, 28*(1), 31–54.

Rudd, P., & Evans, K. (1998). Structure and agency in youth transitions: Student experiences of vocational further education. *Journal of Youth Studies, 1*(1), 39–62.

Wotherspoon, T. (1998). *The sociology of education in Canada: Critical perspectives.* Toronto: Oxford University Press.

Wyn, J., & Dwyer, P. (1999). New directions in research on youth in transition, *Journal of Youth Studies, 2*(1), 5–21.

27. Becoming a Mother or a Worker: Structure and Agency in Young Adult Women's Accounts of Education, Training, Employment, and Partnership

Ian Procter

This chapter is concerned with women's transition to young adulthood. Its focus is a comparison between two groups of women interviewed[1] between 1992 and 1996 when in their early to mid-twenties.[2] The women had many things in common, but the key difference between them was that in one group the women were single, childless, and employed full time while in the other the women were partnered mothers with, at most, part-time employment. The paper seeks to explain how the women came to be in these contrasting social locations. The argument will be that at the point of exiting initial education little differentiated the two sets of women, and that their experience of training, employment, and personal relationships with men led them down these two different paths of transition.

The theoretical context of this comparison picks up a feature of recent debate on youth transitions in Britain. British sociologists have been cautious about a claim by their continental European colleagues (Buchmann, 1989) that the social structuring of the transition to adulthood has become much more individualized than previously. As Beck classically puts it, 'Decisions ... no longer can be made, they must be made' (1992, p. 135). British sociology responded to this claim with a re-emphasis on the structural determination of paths of transition in terms of class, gender, and ethnicity (Banks et al., 1992; Bates and Riseborough, 1993). A sharp example of this is the idea of 'structured individuation' (Roberts, Clark, and Wallace, 1994) in which 'Even when individuals had moved consistently toward pre-formulated goals, these aims themselves, and the individuals' ability to realize them, were products of their structural locations' (1994, p. 51).

A feature of this debate is that structural determination and human agency become polarized into mutually exclusive alternatives, a characteristic which contrasts with developments in general social theory in which agency and structure are features of *all* human action. In Giddens's theory of structuration, for example, the 'duality of structure ... expresses the mutual dependence of structure and agency' (1979, p. 69), and 'By the duality of structure I mean that the structural properties of social systems are both the medium and the outcome of the practices that constitute those systems' (1979, p. 69). Note that here agency and structure are not *alternatives* but constituent features of social reality. So, if youth transition is heavily *structured*, the transition still occurs through the agency of young people (and many others). Alternatively, if youth transition is more open, then choices are made in structured contexts. In Giddens's theory, agency and structure are one – that is, any given act is simultaneously the purposeful action of an individual, an expression of structure, and a reconstitution of that structure. Archer's (1995) recent development of social theory criticizes this preoccupation with the 'interpenetration' (1995, p. 15) of agency and structure. For her this plays down the 'vexatious fact of society' (1995, p. 1) – how social structure has an emergent reality of its own which confronts people as an external fact that either constrains or channels them. Yet this is not a return to structural determination. Archer argues for the 'analytical dualism' of agency and structure in the sense of the interplay of two irreducible aspects of social reality. It is this emphasis on the relationships between the structural contexts of training, employment, and boyfriend relationships and the agency of young women making their own lives that will be the main theoretical theme of this chapter.

The Problem: Becoming a Worker or a Mother

The chapter draws upon the experience of seventy-nine young adult women. When first interviewed they were aged between 18 and 27, and resident in the Coventry and Warwickshire area of the English Midlands. They form two groups. The first are called the 'single workers.' They were all single, childless, and employed full time. The second are the 'early mothers,' who were all partnered mothers with, at most, part-time employment. The focus of this paper is how these women came to be in these contrasting positions in work and family. A crucial point is that, a few years prior to our research, at the point of leaving initial education the two groups did not display marked differentiation. This claim is substantiated in terms of educational qualifications, experience of schooling, and retrospective memory of family aspirations at the time of leaving school.

At the time of leaving initial education[3] the groups included similar proportions of women with different levels of educational achievement. About 50 per cent left with 16-year-old school-leaving qualifications, about 20 per cent with vocational certificates, and around 30 per cent with 18-year-old or higher qualifications. Insofar as educational achievement is an indicator of labour-market potential, the women were very similarly placed as they exited education. The interviews collected retrospective data of the women's experience of education. They were asked whether they had enjoyed school, whether they achieved a balance between schoolwork and their social lives, whether they chose the right subjects to study, whether they achieved their potential, and whether they were supported by their teachers. The general trend of responses to each question was similar for both the single workers and the early mothers. For example, a majority of each group felt that they had not achieved their potential at school, and around half of each group felt they had devoted too much time to socializing rather than school work. There are some differences: for example, more of the single workers enjoyed school as compared to the early mothers. But these differences do not all tend in the same direction: for example, more early mothers than single workers had devoted more time to school work than to sociability. The crucial point is that these recollected school experiences do not mark a clear distinction between the two groups such as that the single workers were positive about their educational experience and the early mothers were negative.

A third point is the women's memory of their expectations for future family when they left school – in particular, their anticipation of whether they would form partnerships and at what age. This evidence indicates some differences. Some of the single workers but none of the early mothers had not planned to form a partnership at all and, when they indicated an age range, the single workers tended to specify an older age than the early mothers. However, these data are not consistent: many more of the early mothers remembered anticipating partnership in the *distant future*. Again the crucial point is that the two groups do not neatly differentiate into single workers who anticipated late partnership on leaving school and early mothers who expected to partner early as they left school.

In this section the possibility that the two groups were already differentiated at the point of leaving school has been considered. If educational qualifications are taken as an indicator of labour market potential, then the two groups had similar employment prospects. The school experience of the single workers does not seem to have given them a competitive edge over the early mothers in, for example, choosing suitable specialisms or achieving their potential. Finally, although the early mothers had in fact partnered much earlier than the average, they had no more anticipated doing this at the time of leaving school than the single workers.

If little distinguished the two groups at the time of leaving education, then the significant differences in their current status must be accounted for by factors which come into play after education. In the following sections the women's experience of training, employment, and relationships with boyfriends are examined.

Training

A remarkably high proportion of the single workers were vocationally qualified by the time of our first interview. Forty-two of the fifty-four had successfully completed some kind of vocational qualification. This included fourteen with first-degree or postgraduate certificates. Six of the women had pre-degree but still advanced qualifications such as bilingual secretarial and public-sector accounting. Seventeen of the women had intermediate qualifications in areas such as clerical skills, veterinary nursing, business and finance, computing, and hairdressing. Three women had pre-nursing certificates and two had dance qualifications. It is clear that the interval between leaving school and the interview had seen these women gaining vocational skills. The single workers covered a broad span of occupations, from near-qualified professionals, managers, and a wide range of technical and clerical jobs, to hairdressers and care assistants. But in their various occupational niches they had, in the main, secured training and qualifications.

It is important to note here that the path to gaining these skills and certificates had not always been a smooth one. There are many reasons for this, including examination failure, misleading careers information, and broken promises by employers, but examples are offered which illustrate a theme to be developed as this chapter progresses. Diana held a junior management position in a French-owned firm which paid for her to develop her French-language competence to a high level. However, her monolingual line manager used her as a French-speaking secretary and also blocked her promotion, because, she suspected, no one else in this primarily technical department spoke French. A second women successfully completed a Youth Training Scheme (YTS) in motor-vehicle parts, a course in which she was the only woman and in which she had to struggle against the sexism of her fellow trainees.

> *Jade Louise*: I was at college with twelve of the lads who at sixteen did not appreciate a female being there ... if I got something right I was a prude, if I got something wrong I was sick 'cause I was female, I had all these sexist jokes. I used to hate going to college after school definitely.

These two examples are picked out because they illustrate these women's struggles against sex typing in a wide range of their experience, a theme to be developed through the chapter.

Turning now to the training experience of the early mothers, a very different picture emerges. Twenty of the twenty-five early mothers had undertaken some post-school education and training, including ten who started YT schemes. However, only seven of the twenty successfully completed their program of study and training. The success rate is relatively high among those taking courses outside YTS, with some women gaining qualifications such as nursery nursing, legal secretary, and MSc in toxicology. On the other hand, there are also many cases of women not completing training, dropping out of courses in teaching, engineering, insurance, and horticulture. Paula Carty's ambition was to be a computer programmer, but her examination results prevented her from doing a degree course. She opted for a Higher National Diploma (HND) but her interest in higher education diminished when she found the course quite different from her expectations:

> *Paula Carty*: It didn't take long to realize it wasn't for me. Because it was working in workshops and things with big boots and overalls and that wasn't me. I wanted to do computers ... The description of the course was completely different to when we actually went.

Among the women who took a YTS, this pattern of lack of completion becomes striking. Only two of the ten YTS trainees finished the course, and one of them dropped out of employment immediately. Numerous studies of YTS castigated it for lack of training, use of cheap labour, and sex typing (Cockburn, 1987; Lee et al., 1990). Among the early mothers this characterization immediately rings true. Michelle, for example, wanted to become a police officer in order to work with dogs. She was not able to do this, but took a YTS in a pet shop. Despite enjoying this scheme, Michelle found that three months before its completion she had no guarantee of continued employment; so when a job came up in a completely different area and requiring no training, she took it. Jacqueline was a full-time trainee in a kennels but found she earned less than part-time employees doing exactly the same work for a half-day shift. She left the scheme to earn more money on half the hours doing the same thing. As Mizen (1995) argues, for these women YTS was a way of getting into work at both entry to the scheme and (early) exit from it. Entry allowed women access to employers (not necessarily employment); early exit was to employment and its relatively greater rewards but at the cost of training rather than on the basis of training.

Both the single workers and the early mothers left school with similar employment potential. In the former, post-school vocational education and training strengthened their position in the labour market. On the face of it, the early mothers also had experience of training, but for the great majority this amounted to very little. We thus see a differential opening up between the groups in this respect.

Employment

This section considers the employment experience of the two groups of women over the time between leaving initial education and the close of the research period. The single workers were all in full-time employment at the beginning of the research. Over the next three and a half years, however, this status changed for some of them – notably, in this context, six left the labour market for full-time training or education. The outstanding feature of the employment experience of the remaining forty-eight is that they established themselves in the primary labour market. To demonstrate this, three criteria are used: first, the degree to which employment had been secured in large public or private organizations or with smaller employers in specialist fields such as consulting engineers or a patent agency; second, whether employment experience over time was marked by 'job development,' that is, increasing levels of skill, responsibility, and remuneration; third, insofar as jobs did not develop in this way, whether they were marked by security of employment in large organizations or specialist employers. By reference to these three criteria, all but four of the single workers had located themselves in the primary labour market by the end of the research period. In illustrating this, examples are used which once again pick up the theme of resistance to sex typing introduced in the discussion of training above.

Jackie Kennedy completed a four-year apprenticeship as an engineering technician in a large manufacturing company selling in international markets. At the completion of her training she hoped to be placed in sales and service in a post which would involve overseas travel. However, she did not obtain this post, as the company felt that a woman would not be acceptable as an engineer in many of their overseas markets. She was thus placed in a job she did not enjoy. However, over the next two years she continued to apply for the position she wanted and was eventually successful.

At the close of the research period, Toni had achieved her longstanding ambition to become a police officer. In this she had faced initial caution from her parents, who insisted that she obtain an alternative training prior to applying for the police at the minimum age. This she did, joining a computer studies course alongside nineteen young men. Her first job after this was in the retail sector, taken in order to improve her interpersonal skills. Again, her parents were not impressed, and she moved to a computing job where she immediately encountered scepticism about her abilities from her male boss. After two years she secured her appointment as a police constable despite parental doubt about her career moves and having to prove herself both in training and employment.

These examples illustrate the types of hurdles faced by single workers attempting to establish themselves in the primary labour market. The process was not without effort and frustration. Many kinds of constraints threw up difficulties for them, and among these were the gender-linked structures of work, which are highlighted here for the purposes of this discussion. The early mothers' employment experiences were very different. The pertinent period of comparison here is the time between leaving education and the first pregnancy. During this time only seven of the early mothers had been employed by a large organization. The majority of the twenty-five had worked in small offices, pubs, nursing homes, shops, and hairdressing salons. Further-more, those women who had worked for large firms rarely experi-enced promotion. There was a type of promotion for two women, but the experience of Daisy is instructive. Her employment with a large chain store had involved movement between stores and some promo-tion. However, the main reason for this movement was not job spiral-ling; rather, she was following the migration of her boyfriend, who also worked for the company. He was spiralling, she was making the best of the moves. As well as working for small employers, most of the early mothers worked in low-skill/low-status occupations. There were a few exceptions, such as a fully trained hairdresser, but typical occu-pations were clerical assistant, factory operative, cleaner, care assistant, waitress, and catering worker.

The examples of employers and occupations discussed so far sug-gest that there was a disparity between the education and/or training that at least some of these women acquired and the employment they followed. Four women took A-level examinations, but this path led to only casual and part-time work. Seven women completed a post-school course in education or training. However, these qualifications generally failed to ensure access to jobs with skill requirements or to promotion ladders. Julia was trained as a legal secretary but became a temp doing general clerical work, and Anne had no employment after her MSc. Thus, even those with some achievement in either education or training found little opportunity to establish themselves in the pri-mary labour market.

At the time of leaving education, little differentiated the single work-ers and the early mothers. However, moving forward just a few years has revealed a widening gap between the two groups. The great major-ity of the single workers acquired some measure of training and estab-lished themselves in jobs with some degree of skill, responsibility, or future prospects. At a similar juncture in biographical time, the early mothers had typically left uncompleted training. A minority had been unable to implement the education/training potential they had devel-oped. Almost all were in jobs requiring little skill or responsibility or offering little future potential.

Boyfriends

To the best of our knowledge, all the women who participated in this research were heterosexual. In the post-school period considered here, the great majority had at least one relationship with a boyfriend. Indeed, for the early mothers this was a given, as all were partnered. The issue to be addressed in this section is the effect these relationships had on the main trajectories of the women's lives – in the case of the single workers, towards full-time employment; in the case of the early mothers, towards giving priority to family responsibilities.

Three aspects of the boyfriend relationships of the single workers will be considered. In each, the focus of concern is whether boyfriends presented a constraint on the woman's educational and employment prospects. The argument developed here is that, while this was potentially the case for many of the single workers, they acted to maintain their independence from traditionally defined female roles.

The first area of study was the presence and significance of boyfriends as the women were coming to the end of their schooling. Research on adolescent girls has emphasized their increasing preoccupation with their own sexual identity as women and their relationship to boys. In particular, pressures to form a relationship with a 'steady' boyfriend to avoid the risk of being negatively labelled as either 'slag' or 'drag' have been identified, so that the constraining impact of boyfriends has been highlighted (Griffin, 1985; Lees, 1993). This did not seem to be the case in these women's retrospective memory of relationships with boyfriends. Thirty-two of the fifty-four women told us that when they were leaving school they did not have a steady boyfriend. Of the twenty-two who did have a boyfriend at that time, only a minority of seven remembered them as a discouragement to their studies and work. On the other hand, there were a similar number of instances of women receiving some support from their boyfriends. However, the most common view expressed was that relations with boyfriends was about *socializing*, which they saw as segregated from schoolwork.

Among the single workers there are some instances in which boyfriends were a factor in the woman's decision making about educational and employment options. In a few instances, boyfriends represented a marked constraint on the woman's action, but it was far more typical for the relationship to be one contributory factor in a complex decision. An example here is Tamsin, who studied at a Welsh university and received two job offers as she graduated, one in the town in which she had studied, the other in Birmingham. Even though her boyfriend was remaining in Wales for a further year, she declined the Welsh job and took the one in Birmingham. However, she decided to live in nearby Coventry because her boyfriend's parental home was located there. Thus, boyfriends have played a part in decision making but generally as a contributory rather than a constraining factor.

The third aspect of boyfriend relationships considered here is cohabiting relationships and the problems the women encountered. None of the single workers were living with a partner at the first interview. However, nineteen of them had previously cohabited but encountered problems in the partnership. Although a variety of problems were cited, a recurring theme among the single workers is disputes about the woman's working life and her domestic role. Alannah began her cohabitation at 17. Her partner was unhappy about her meeting men at work, an inevitable outcome given that she worked in engineering. He discouraged her from taking further qualifications, wanting to start a family and have Alannah stay at home.

> *Alannah:* ... he wanted to get married, three kids, family, and I suddenly went ohhh, err, not yet and I don't know how long he would have waited, and it just didn't seem fair. I was putting a lot of work into the house that we had and working all day, coming home, sorting everything else at home for tea, etc., and he came and ate and sat down.

When she was a student, Hannah Best had cohabited with a man who 'was very negative in anything I wanted to do. I think he thought I should stay at home and have children really. That was his opinion. It was very old fashioned.' Marie, too, found herself doing all the housework; otherwise it simply did not get done. In her case she was also paying all the bills, so that the supposed reciprocity between breadwinner and homemaker did not apply and she had both roles. In these instances, the relationship had ended. They illustrate tension about the balance of work and domestic roles between the cohabitees. In the case of the single workers, the women had opted for a greater degree of independence from traditionally defined female roles than their former partners expected.

The early mothers experienced a very different relationship with boyfriends. This can be initially explored by considering relationships started while the woman was still in education. Prior to entering the labour market, nine of the twenty-five early mothers had boyfriend relationships which led to partnerships. Cohabitation or marriage occurred soon after they left education or training. Indeed, these women hardly entered the labour market. Insofar as they did, partnership formation coincided with deterioration in their labour-market position. Three were pregnant and withdrew from training or employment, and others moved from training or education into part-time or casual work. Sarah Marsh had trained as a nanny but worked for only six months part time in that field, combining this work, and eventually replacing it, with waitressing. She indicated the link between this change and her cohabitation: 'If I hadn't met him, or it hadn't worked out, then I would have gone out to work full time.' In these cases – about one-third of the early mothers – there is clearly a very direct association between relationships started prior to labour-market entry and lack of training and employment progression. Indeed, these women never properly entered the labour market before forming partnerships. This does not apply to the remaining early mothers, but here again early partnership and motherhood are features.

The average age at which the early mothers had first cohabited was 19.4 years. Seventeen of them were married and their average age at marriage was 21.2 years. This was also the mean age at which the women's first baby was born. Nationally, the mean age at which women first married in Britain in 1993 was 26.2 years,[4] and the mean age at which first babies were born in 1994 was 26.5 years (Armitage and Babb, 1996, p. 9). One other feature of the group is striking. In fifteen of the twenty-five cases the first pregnancy was not intended. 'Falling' pregnant came as a shock to many of these women, perhaps especially the nine who at the time were neither cohabiting nor married. Yet all these women continued with their pregnancy. Perhaps it is this which differentiates the two groups. The single workers were either lucky or more careful, the early mothers were 'caught' in the age-old trap despite modern contraceptive methods. This, however, cannot be an adequate explanation. At least eight of the single workers had had an abortion, and most of the early mothers could have terminated their pregnancies legally. They decided not to, for, as one of them said with concise perception, these babies were 'not intended but not unwanted.' This phrase focuses the issue of why the early mothers opted for partnership and motherhood. This can be explored by turning to the remaining sixteen early mothers, who all entered the labour market before starting relationships with boyfriends which led to partnership and pregnancy. The sequence of the latter leads to two rather different chains of events. In seven cases the women started work, became pregnant, and then formed partnerships. The other nine also began work, but became pregnant after either cohabitation or marriage.

Where pregnancy preceded partnership, a number of points are salient. First, this was not planned. These women had anticipated conventional family futures in which partnership came before family formation. Second, none of these pregnancies occurred in casual relationships; the women may not have been partnered but they were in serious relationships. Third, in all but one case, the relationship, continued after the birth of the child. Three were married prior to the birth, while the others continued to cohabit and in most cases had further children with their partner. As well as the positive attraction of the boyfriend relationship, the negative features of the women's work situation should be noted. Most had had only short periods of employment and low-status/low-skill jobs. None of these women seriously considered an abortion, despite the unintended circumstances of their pregnancy. None of them faced being lone mothers; all had the agreement of the fathers to carry the pregnancy through and form a partnership. On the other hand, their working lives provided no counter attraction to partnership and family formation.

Nine women entered the work force but then formed relationships at a relatively early age. The relationship altered job opportunities for some women. Laura Lucas made several job changes between factory and office work, moves linked to her relationship. On her engagement she left an office job for the higher wages of factory work because the couple needed to save for a mortgage. This lasted a year, and she left her next job because she had to give up her car to work locally, again because of her impending cohabitation and house purchase. Aside from cases in which there is a direct impact of partnership on employment, first pregnancies occurred at an early age and quite soon after partnership formation. Again, we can look at the woman's work situation as the backdrop to this. With one exception, none of these women had achieved promotion, and their job changes were haphazard. Besides training in horticulture and a degree course (both incomplete), Ellis had had jobs as an *au pair*, in a fish-and-chip shop, as a shop assistant, and as an office worker.

This discussion has drawn out how the early mothers came to the two statuses of being partnered mothers. In all cases, partnership and pregnancy occurred early by comparison with national trends, but nevertheless followed distinct pathways. In the first group of cases, nine women hardly entered the labour market at all before becoming a partner with responsibility for a child or, at least, for running their household. Sixteen women did enter the labour market. Seven left when they became pregnant and went on to form partnerships with their boyfriends. The remainder left employment on becoming pregnant in an established partnership. A significant number of all these pregnancies were unintended at the time. However, we have explored why they were not *unwanted*. Establishing a family was an attractive option in itself, as all these women had willing partners. On the other hand the world of employment offered them little.

Conclusion

The women in this study fell into two very distinct groups – the single workers, who in early adulthood were single, childless, and employed full time, and the early mothers, who were partnered mothers with at most part-time employment. Yet on leaving education little had differentiated them as far as qualifications, school experience, and family aspirations are concerned. After initial education, however, differentiation becomes apparent in training, employment, and relationships with boyfriends. The single workers became trained and established themselves in the primary labour market. In their relationships with boyfriends they maintained a distance from traditional female roles, which was also apparent in their training and employment experience. The early mothers generally lacked successful training and had been located in the secondary labour market. For many of them, early relationships with boyfriends had led to pregnancy or at least the adoption of traditional domestic responsibilities.

In drawing this together, we need to stress a number of points. The first is the interrelationship among the three contexts discussed here: training, employment, and personal relationships. To comprehend the transition the women made to early adulthood necessitates taking the three in conjunction. The single workers' working lives are not independent of either gender discrimination against working women or their relationships with boyfriends. The early mothers' formation of partnerships and families are not separate from their training and work experience. Second, this interdependence cannot be simply represented in terms of the values of variables. It is not just that the single workers received training, worked in rewarding jobs, and had weak relationships with men. Neither are the early mothers simply those with lack of training, dead-end employment, and strong relationships with men. Rather, third, the essential link mediating these structural contexts is the woman's own agency. Many of the single workers had to exert their own control over their training and employment and break relationships with men which threatened to define them in traditional ways. Conversely, the early mothers had to take a life-shaping decision to complete a pregnancy when they could have done otherwise. However, fourth, such agency does not imply choice in a sense abstract from the concrete situations faced by the women. The single workers were 'career oriented' not in the abstract but in the context of real training and employment opportunities. The early mothers were not 'family oriented'[5] outside the specific context of a weak labour-market position and the real possibility of partnership when they fell pregnant. The interrelationship of work and family, on the one hand, and the interplay of structural context and agency, on the other, are the general themes of this analysis. An explanation of the different life-course transitions of the two groups of women involves both of these interconnections.

Within British sociology these linkages are often not displayed. Illustration of this oversight can be taken from two recent interventions in debates around women, work, and family. Hakim (1996) has developed a controversial[6] theory suggesting that the female population is fundamentally divided between two underlying 'work orientations,' one to career and one to family. She emphasizes the agency of women in choosing one of these early in adult life, with long-term consequences. Yet this act of choice is not situated in the interaction of agency and structure emphasized here. Conversely, a concern in the literature on young women's transition to adulthood is to identify the social processes which generate marriage as an *inevitability* for adult women. Leonard lists the pressures which impel young women into courtship, such as restrictions on their unescorted mobility, the break-up of girls' peer groups, their low earnings, and the dangers of being labelled as sexually promiscuous, and concludes: 'They are therefore impelled to accept courting relationships and even marriage with men to whom they are (initially at least) less than totally attracted ...' (Leonard, 1980, p. 263). This theme of women having to buckle to social definition of adult womanhood grants little place to women's agency in the face of these structural pressures. This paper has sought to show the fallacy of both these positions in giving an explanation which shows women living in the real world of education, work, and personal relationships yet making their own lives. It has stressed the interconnection of training, employment, and boyfriend relationships on the one hand, and the interplay of structural contexts and the women's agency on the other.

NOTES

1 I am grateful to the Leverhulme Trust for research funding. Dr Maureen Padfield acted as research fellow, and I wish to acknowledge her overall contribution to the project.
2 A full discussion of the research and arguments advanced can be found in
   Procter and Padfield (1998a). This includes (chapter 2) an outline of our
   methodology which is not given here. See also Padfield and Procter (1996)
   and Procter and Padfield (1998b).
3 In the late 1980s, when these women left education, the minimum school-
   leaving age was 16. At that point students took either the General Certificate
   of Education (GCE Ordinary level) or the (inferior) Certificate of Secondary
   Education. A minority remained within school until age 18 and took the
   GCE Advanced level; again, a minority of these went on to higher education.
   The majority left school at 16, but by this time few went directly into
   employment. Vocational training was again hierarchical. Those with appropriate qualifications took recognized courses in the further education sector;
   those without were left with the Youth Training Scheme whose general character is portrayed later in the chapter.
4 Population Trends 85, 1996, page 76, table 21.
5 The reference here is to Hakim's two forms of work orientation, which will
   be mentioned shortly.
6 See the recent interchange between Hakim (1998) and Crompton and Harris
   (1998a; 1998b)

REFERENCES

Archer, M.S. (1995). *Realist social theory: The morphogenetic approach*. Cambridge:
   Cambridge University Press.
Armitage, B., & Babb, P. (1996). Population review: (4) Trends in fertility. *Popu-
   lation Trends, 84*, 7–13.
Banks, M., Bates, I., Breakwell, G., Bynner, J., Emler, N., Jamieson, L., & Rob-
   erts, K. (1992). *Careers and identities*. Milton Keynes: Open University
   Press.
Bates, I., & Riseborough, G. (Eds). (1993). *Youth and inequality*. Milton Keynes:
   Open University Press.
Beck, U. (1992). *Risk society: Towards a new modernity*. London: Sage.
Buchmann, M. (1989). *The script of life in modern society*. London: University of
   Chicago Press.

Cockburn, C. (1987). *Two-track training: Sex inequalities and the YTS*. Basingstoke: Macmillan.

Crompton, R., & Harris, F. (1998a). Explaining women's employment patterns: 'Orientations to work' revisited. *British Journal of Sociology, 49*(1), 118–36.

Crompton, R., & Harris, F. (1998b). A reply to Hakim. *British Journal of Sociology, 49*(1), 144–9.

Giddens, A. (1979). *Central problems in social theory: Action, structure and contradiction in social analysis*. Basingstoke: Macmillan.

Griffin, C. (1985). *Typical girls? Young women from school to the labour market*. London: Routledge and Kegan Paul.

Hakim, C. (1996). *Key issues in women's work: Female heterogeneity and the polarisation of women's employment*. London: Athlone.

Hakim, C. (1998). Developing a sociology for the twenty-first century: Preference theory. *British Journal of Sociology, 49*(1), 137–43.

Lee, D., Marsden, D., Rickman, P., & Duncombe, J. (1990). *Scheming for youth: A study of YTS in the enterprise culture*. Milton Keynes: Open University Press.

Lees, S. (1993). *Sugar and spice – sexuality and adolescent girls*. Harmondsworth: Penguin.

Leonard, D. (1980). *Sex and generation: A study of courtship and weddings*. London: Tavistock.

Mizen, P. (1995). *The state, young people and youth training: In and against the training state*. London: Mansell.

Padfield, M., & Procter, I. (1996). The effect of interviewer's gender on the interviewing process: A comparative enquiry. *Sociology, 30*(2), 355–66.

Procter, I., & Padfield, M. (1998a). *Young adult women, work and family*. London: Mansell.

Procter, I., & Padfield, M. (1998b). The effect of the interview on the interviewee. *International Journal of Social Research Methodology, 1*(2), 123–36.

Roberts, K., Clark, S.C., & Wallace, C. (1994). Flexibility and individualisation: A comparison of transitions into employment in England and Germany. *Sociology, 28*(1), 31–54.

28. Returning to Work after Childbirth: A Longitudinal Analysis of the Role of Qualifications in Mothers' Return to Paid Employment[1]

Jane Elliott, Angela Dale, and Muriel Egerton

Qualifications provide a way of formalizing the type and level of education received. They may provide employers with 'signals' as to the ability of a job seeker, or they may provide specific training for a particular occupation and thereby play an important role in gaining entry to the labour market. Various studies have demonstrated the value of qualifications to young people when seeking work in difficult labour markets (Bynner and Roberts, 1991; Payne, 1991), while Layder, Ashton, and Sung (1991) have attempted to operationalize the role of both structure and agency in entry to specific labour-market segments. Certain types of qualifications have a particular value in being closely related to a specific occupation and therefore providing a clear route into employment (for example, secretarial qualifications or hairdressing). Higher-level occupationally specific qualifications are often associated with a profession (e.g., medicine, law, architecture) or a semi-profession (teaching, nursing, pharmacy) which may require membership of a national professional association in order to practise. Other qualifications may be directly related to an occupation (e.g., social work, librarianship) without being formalized as a profession.

Occupational and Organizational Labour Markets

The degree to which a particular qualification relates to a specific occupation, therefore, has important implications for the employment prospects of those who possess it. This is recognized in the labour-market segmentation literature in the distinction between occupational and organizational labour markets. In the former, the labour market is available to those who hold a specific occupational qualification and mobility is typically between employers; in the latter, entry is to an organization, and any training or further qualifications are obtained after entry, with mobility usually within the organization (Doeringer and Piore, 1971). This conceptualization has been further refined to distinguish, for both organizationally and occupationally based labour markets, those with promotion prospects from those without them. For example, a hairdresser and a doctor both have occupationally specific qualifications, but the latter has greater scope for upward mobility than the former, as well as a much higher level of education (Althauser and Kalleberg, 1981; Dale, 1987a). Within organizational labour markets, similar distinctions may be made between those who have career paths, often dependent upon gaining further qualifications, and those who do not.

Crompton and Sanderson (1986; 1990) have developed a career typology based on Brown (1982) which makes similar distinctions between occupational and organizational qualifications, but with a much more specific gender dimension. In particular, they identify two different tracks among those with occupational qualifications – 'careerists' and 'practitioners.' They suggest that 'careerist' routes follow an upward linear progression, usually involving mobility between employers, and are typically filled by men. By contrast, practitioners are not on career paths, mobility is sideways, and jobs are often part time and held by women.

Occupational and Organizational Labour Markets and Motherhood

Because of the external recognition accorded to occupational qualifications, it is expected that they will facilitate re-entry to employment for women who experience a geographical move as a 'trailing wife' or who have a period away from the labour market. For example, Glover (1994) found that, in Britain, women teachers with children were much more likely to be in paid work than white-collar managers and clerical workers. She interprets this by stating that 'It is probable that we are seeing here the effect of the difficulty of re-entry for women in *organizational* occupations such as banking' (p. 91).

This chapter focuses on women with occupationally specific qualifications but makes a distinction between qualifications at different levels of educational attainment. This also reflects a distinction, noted by

Crompton and Sanderson (1986), which relates to the degree of professionalization associated with the qualification, with medicine and law at one end of the spectrum and typing at the other. We do not, however, attempt to make, either conceptually or empirically, a distinction between careerists and practitioners. To do so would require assumptions about future career progression on the basis of women's past or current employment. It also raises a question as to whether women have made a choice about following a particular trajectory.

The transition to motherhood is widely recognized as a time when women's employment is likely to be disrupted, although in recent decades there has been greatly increased continuity of employment. Maternity-rights legislation in Britain gives women who have worked for the same employer for at least two years the right to return to the job which they held prior to childbirth. Women who have been employed for six months with the same employer are entitled to eighteen weeks' flat-rate statutory maternity pay, while those who have worked for the same employer for at least two years are entitled to receive 90 per cent of their salary for the first six weeks of their maternity leave. In addition, certain employers allow women to take additional unpaid leave as long as they return to work within a year (McRae and Daniel, 1991).

In the following discussion and analysis, the phrase 'women who take a break from employment' is used to describe women who have left the labour market for a time, in contrast to those who have taken maternity leave and returned to the same employer. The National Child Development Survey, on which our analyses are based, asked women who took maternity leave to record a period of continuous employment on their work histories. We have therefore made the assumption that women who recorded continuous employment during the period when they had a child had taken maternity leave. The empirical focus of the chapter is on the speed with which women who leave the labour market return to employment after having children.

The sharp rise in women's educational attainment in recent decades is reflected in their increasing attachment to the labour market. This is evident through an increased likelihood of taking maternity leave and faster returns to employment for those who do take a break, particularly for the most highly qualified (Martin and Roberts, 1984; McRae, 1993; Macran et al., 1996; Joshi et al., 1996). In this context, it is of particular importance to examine the role played by occupational qualifications, independent of level of educational attainment.

If occupationally specific qualifications facilitate re-entry to the same occupation following a period out of the labour market, we may expect women with these qualifications to feel less pressure to maintain a continuous profile than women who have followed an organizational career. They may therefore be more likely to have children, and more able to leave the labour market for a time if they do have children. Alternatively, women with these qualifications may feel a greater level of commitment to continuous employment (Desai and Waite, 1991), particularly where they have chosen to follow a vocational route. However, if continuity of employment is related to level of education rather than the possession of a specific qualification, then we would not expect differences in employment behaviour among women at the same educational level (e.g., degree or above) by the type of qualification.

It is not sufficient, however, for an occupation to provide entry on the basis of a qualification; other factors may also come into play in facilitating women's re-entry (Dale, 1987b; Desai and Waite, 1991). One of the most important of these is the organization of working hours. In some occupations, working hours are much more family-friendly than in others; teaching is the clearest example, where hours in school fit reasonably well with child care – particularly in terms of cover during school holidays. In other occupations – such as nursing – the availability of part-time jobs facilitates combining child care with paid work. Alternatively, the ability to work on a self-employed or free-lance basis (for example, a locum pharmacist or a self-employed physiotherapist) may provide a basis for regulating hours of work. An additional factor that has been shown to have an independent and positive effect on women's employment behaviour during family formation is earnings ability (Dex et al., 1996). This may be because, if working hours do not accommodate child care, the alternative is usually to pay for child care – an option available only to those with sufficient earnings. Also, from a rational economic perspective, women with higher earnings potential have more to lose than other women from taking time away from the labour market. However, the level of a partner's earnings may work in the opposite direction with high earnings, removing the imperative for two salaries. (Brannen [1987] cites evidence of the importance of meeting mortgage repayments in the decision to return to work of women with an unplanned pregnancy.)

Cultural factors are also likely to influence women's decisions to take paid work while their children are young. The 1991 British Social

Attitudes Survey showed that almost 50 per cent of men and women under 40 agreed that a women should stay at home when her child is under school age (Scott et al., 1993); this view was more likely to be held among older age groups. Women are therefore still likely to encounter negative views towards working while their children are young.

A factor that may have an important influence on how a woman decides to combine employment and motherhood is her own mother's employment behaviour (Sanders, 1997). As Duncan and Edwards (1997) have argued, decisions about how best to combine motherhood and employment are unlikely to be made solely on economic grounds. The values which underpin women's employment behaviour are socially formed and negotiated, and the values and behaviour of their own mothers may make an important contribution to this process.

A question of considerable interest is whether some women choose a particular occupational route in the belief that it will allow them to combine paid work with child care. From an economic perspective, Becker (1981) argues that women choose occupations in which discontinuity will not incur a penalty; Polacheck (1979) suggests that women choose occupations which facilitate time out while children are small; others cite the choice of family-friendly occupations such as teaching and nursing by women who wish to combine paid work with children.

However, qualitative research has cast doubt on whether women do, in fact, make these kinds of choices. In a case study of women engineers and scientists in Britain, Devine (1994) found that choices had been based on subject preferences at school rather than well-formulated career plans. Crompton (1997) cites interviews with pharmacists and professionals in the finance industry to suggest that decisions over continuity may have been either opportunistic or a response to changes in family circumstances rather than the result of a pre-planned strategy. There is some evidence that, having made an initial choice of occupation, women may then make further decisions on the basis of combining work and family. For example, within the medical profession there is evidence that women choose specialties that can be accommodated to having children.

Although we cannot entirely disentangle the complex influences on the type of qualifications which women hold and the way in which these impact upon family formation and paid work, we can go some way towards assessing the role of occupational qualifications in women's family formation patterns and employment histories. We use data from a longitudinal British cohort study to examine the differences in family-formation patterns for women by the age of 33 in 1991 in relation to level and type of qualification. While we cannot arbitrate between the alternative processes discussed above on the basis of the data presented, we are able to identify the extent to which there are distinctive family-formation patterns associated with particular types of qualification. We use event-history analysis to assess the independent effect of qualifications versus other factors on the 'hazard' of returning to work after the first birth and after the second birth and also on the competing risks of returning to work full time or part time after a first birth.

Data

Analyses have been carried out using data from the National Child Development Study (NCDS). This is a British cohort study of all individuals born in the first week of March 1958. Data were collected at birth and then at ages 7, 11, 16, 23, and 33. The data used in the analyses reported here have mainly been taken from the fifth and final sweep of the study, carried out in 1991 when 11,407 cohort members were interviewed. As part of this sweep, cohort members were asked to complete a life history. The life history includes retrospective information about each job the respondent has held since leaving full-time education. The start and end dates (to the nearest month) of each job are recorded, together with whether the job was full or part time. In addition, these retrospective life histories include information about the start and end dates of all cohabiting and marital relationships, and about the dates of birth of any children.

Qualifications

A variable with eight categories was constructed to indicate both the level of qualifications gained by cohort members and whether those qualifications were occupationally specific. The derived qualifications variable was based on a cohort member's highest qualifications by age 33. A check was made to ensure that this qualification had been obtained prior to the birth of any children. This meant that qualifications could be treated as an exogenous variable in the event-history analyses.

Detailed information about the subject of the highest qualification at age 33 was used to determine whether these high-level qualifications were occupationally specific or not (Dale and Egerton, 1997). Degrees which were classified as occupationally specific included medicine and dentistry, social work, law, librarianship, and architecture, with the majority being degrees in education probably leading to a career in teaching.

A variable with eight categories was constructed as follows:

1. Occupationally specific degree and higher degree including degrees in education
2. Degrees in other subjects (e.g., English, classics)
3. Technical, business, and teaching qualifications below degree level (Higher National Certificate [HNC]/Higher National Diploma [HND])
4. Nursing qualifications below degree level
5. A-levels (typically taken at age 18 as entry requirements to university)
6. O-levels (typically taken at statutory school-leaving age)
7. Clerical and commercial (plus O-levels in some cases)
8. Apprenticeships, other unclassified qualification, and no qualifications

Analysis

Combining Work and Motherhood

As an approach to analysing information about women's work histories in conjunction with information about the birth of children, the life-history data from the National Child Development Survey were conceptualized in terms of episodes. Completed episodes may then be characterized by an origin and a destination. It is important to note that the unit of analysis has therefore shifted from the individual to the episode. This means that women who have two periods out of the labour market while caring for their first child will contribute two episodes to the analysis. The length of an episode was therefore treated as the duration until an event of interest.

Cox proportional hazards models were used first to examine the effect of different types of qualifications on the length of episodes before returning to work: (a) following the birth of a first child, and (b) following the birth of a second child. The role of qualifications in the process of returning to work part time or full time following the birth of the first child was then examined using competing risks models. A key variable, which was included as a covariate, was the age of the cohort member when she first became a mother. In addition, the presence of a partner (cohabiting or married) and the age of the first and (if appropriate) second child were also included in the model.

One of the advantages of the National Child Development Survey is that it includes information about the cohort members at different stages of their development. Of relevance to the current study is a variable we were able to include indicating whether the cohort member's own mother worked during the cohort member's early childhood (that is, before age 7). At age 16 cohort members were asked about their career aspirations. A dummy variable indicating whether women reported wanting to follow a professional or managerial career was also included in the model.

The results reported below should be interpreted with some caution. The numbers in some of the categories are relatively small, particularly when we try to distinguish between returning to work part time or full time. The numbers of episodes included in the event-history analyses are given in table 28.1.

Results

Timing of Motherhood and Qualifications

Women with degree-level qualifications were much less likely to have had children by age 33 than women with other qualifications, or with no qualifications. Only 47 per cent had had a child by this age, by comparison with 84 per cent of women with no qualifications. There was very little difference between those with occupationally specific degrees and those with degrees in other subjects.

Approximately a quarter (27 per cent) of all women in the NCDS recorded continuous employment at the birth of their first child. In other words, we can assume that they took maternity leave and remained with the same employer. The propensity to take maternity leave was found to be strongly related to level of qualifications. While 55 per cent of those with occupationally specific higher qualifications reported continuous employment, this compared to only 24 per cent of those with O-levels, and 19 per cent of those with no qualifications.

TABLE 28.1
Number of Episodes Used in the Cox Proportional Hazards Models

Transition from	Mother not in paid employment, with one child					Mother not in paid employment, with two children				
Transition to	N	Ft	Pt	2nd child	Cens.	N	Ft	Pt	3rd child	Cens.
Qualification										
1	92	12	38	33	9	48	7	19	5	17
2	133	9	37	71	16	81	6	21	14	40
3	134	17	48	57	12	83	10	40	15	18
4	233	25	81	113	14	161	18	85	28	30
5	359	40	79	204	36	278	27	114	51	86
6	1544	193	395	842	114	1200	127	593	235	545
7	161	13	48	89	11	130	5	70	27	28
8	1367	160	317	779	111	1106	126	475	291	214

Those with non-occupational degrees were found to be slightly less likely to take maternity leave than those with occupational degrees (49 per cent versus 55 per cent).

Women with occupationally specific higher-level qualifications (such as those with nursing qualifications; technical, business, or teaching qualifications [below degree level]; or occupationally specific degrees) were also found to be more likely than women with non-occupational degrees to return to part-time work between the births of a first and a second child (39.5 per cent versus 30 per cent). This also suggests that occupationally specific qualifications may enable women who wish to do so to re-enter the labour market relatively quickly after becoming mothers.

Event-history Analyses

In order to focus explicitly on the role of qualifications in facilitating women's return to the labour market, a series of multivariate event-history analyses were conducted. Tables 28.2 and 28.3 present the results of these analyses. The coefficients can be interpreted in a manner analogous to ordinary least-squares regression and enable us to assess the relative impact of a number of different categorical and continuous covariates on a woman's chances of returning to work (Allison, 1984).

Returning to Work after One Child

Table 28.2 shows a clear relationship between level of qualifications and a mother's speed of returning to work after the birth of a first child but before a second birth. The women included in these analyses have all recorded a break from employment although it did not always fit neatly around the birth of their child. Women with continuous employment are omitted.

Having an occupationally specific, degree-level qualification dramatically increases the speed of returning to work, whether after the first child or the second child. Other occupationally specific qualifications, such as HND, BTEC, teaching, or nursing qualifications, also have a substantial effect. Having a non-occupational degree has a rather smaller effect, and, for the second child, is not significantly different from having no qualifications. The importance of qualifications is clearly observable (except for women with A-levels), even once

TABLE 28.2
Cox Proportional Hazards Model, Returning to Work after Motherhood

Variable	Returning to work (one child)			Returning to work (two children)		
	B	S.E.	Exp (B)	B	S.E.	Exp (B)
Occupation-specific degree (including teaching)	1.1969	0.1580	3.31**	1.31	0.4088	3.7145**
Non-occupational degree	0.3267	0.1610	1.39*	0.1513	0.4367	1.1633
Technical/business/teaching	0.7500	0.1382	2.12**	0.7271	0.3408	2.0692*
Nursing qualification	0.6265	0.1135	1.87**	0.5209	0.2665	1.6835*
A-levels	0.1614	0.1066	1.17	0.1428	0.2210	1.1535
O-levels	0.2969	0.0631	1.34**	0.1557	0.1288	1.1684
Clerical/commercial	0.4176	0.1369	1.52**	−0.7739	0.4571	0.4612
None/apprenticeship	ref cat.		ref cat	ref cat		ref cat
Age at motherhood (months)	0.0013	0.0007	1.0013*	−0.0023	0.0019	0.9977
No partner	0.1265	0.0647	1.13*	0.2066	0.1572	1.2295
Own mother worked < age 7	0.2355	0.0644	1.26**	0.1772	0.1397	1.1939
Aspirations at 16	0.1479	0.0607	1.15*	0.2657	0.1328	1.3043*
Age first child	0.0122	0.0009	1.0123**	0.0016	0.0031	1.0016
Age second child	na	na	na	0.0168	0.0032	1.0169**

'B' = the parameter estimates (i.e., the coefficients for the model)
'S.E.' = Standard Error
'Exp (B)' = the exponential of the coefficient
* indicates a statistically significant coefficient (p < .05)   ** indicates p < .001
Model for return after first child: improvement (−2LL):307.229; df = 12; p < .0001
Model for return after second child: improvement (−2LL):345.29; df = 13; p < .0001

TABLE 28.3
Cox Proportional Hazards Model, Returning to Work after Birth of First Child

Variable	Returning to Work (Part Time)			Returning to Work (Full Time)		
	B	S.E.	Exp (B)	B	S.E.	Exp (B)
Occupation-specific degree (including teaching)	1.1508	0.1827	3.1609**	1.2984	0.3162	3.6634**
Non-occupational degree	0.3481	0.1816	1.4146**	0.2112	0.3538	1.2352
Technical/business/teaching	0.7253	0.1621	2.0653**	0.7992	0.2658	2.2237**
Nursing	0.6594	0.1317	1.9336**	0.5366	0.2259	1.7102*
A-levels	0.0321	0.1305	1.0327	0.4482	0.1844	1.5655*
O-levels	0.2533	0.0769	1.2882**	0.3889	0.1100	1.4754**
Clerical/commercial	0.5188	0.1561	1.6800**	0.0790	0.2897	1.0822
None/Apprenticeship	ref cat	ref cat	ref cat	ref cat	ref cat	ref cat
Age at motherhood (months)	0.0037	0.0008**	1.0037	−0.0040	0.0012	0.9960**
No partner	−0.1809	0.0857	0.8345*	0.6513	0.1037	1.9191**
Own mother worked < 7	0.3554	0.0757	1.4267**	−0.0407	0.1230	0.96
Aspirations at 16	0.1789	0.0726	1.1959*	0.0659	0.1104	1.0681
Age first child	0.0111	0.0012	1.0112**	0.0130	0.0013	1.0131**

'B' = the parameter estimates (i.e., the coefficients for the model)

'S.E.' = Standard Error

'Exp (B)' = the exponential of the coefficient

* indicates a statistically significant coefficient (p < .05)   ** indicates p < .001

Model for return full time improvement 211.971; df = 12; p < .0001

Model for return part time improvement 206.4; df = 12; p < .0001 other salient factors such as age at motherhood and presence of a cohabiting/marital partner have been included in the model.

Thus, for women who have experienced a break from employment, an occupational qualification is clearly associated with a faster return to work than that achieved by women with degree-level qualifications not directly linked to an occupation.

Age at motherhood is also significantly associated with the speed of returning to work after a first child, with older mothers being likely to return more quickly. The absence of a cohabiting/marital partner also appears to increase slightly the probability that a woman will return to work after the birth of her first child, but this only just reaches significance (p = .03). Career aspirations measured at age 16 and having a mother who worked in early childhood both also have a positive effect on the speed with which a mother with one child returns to work. As would be expected, the age of the child at the start of the episode is significantly associated with the mother's probability of returning to employment, such that the older the child, the greater the probability of the mother's return.

In order to understand how the hazard rate, or probability of returning to work, varies over time, it is necessary to examine the gradient of the cumulative hazard plots. To facilitate interpretation, the classification of qualifications has been greatly simplified so that a three-way distinction is made between those with higher-level occupational qualifications (categories 1, 3, and 4), those with non-occupational degrees (category 2), and those with lower qualifications (categories 5, 6, 7, and 8).

In the case of returning following the birth of a first child (figure 28.1) there is a clear distinction between those with occupationally specific higher-level qualifications and those with lower-level qualifications. For the first eighteen months of being out of the labour market with a child, the hazard of returning to work is higher for those with occupationally specific qualifications. However, after this point the cumulative hazard lines become virtually parallel, suggesting that there is little difference in the hazard of returning to work for the two groups. Those with non-occupational degrees appear to be very similar to those with lower-level qualifications.

Figure 28.2 suggests that the process of returning to work might be rather different for women once they have two children. In this case, the type of qualification makes relatively little difference to women's observed behaviour with respect to returning to work in the first year.

Figure 28.1 Cumulative Hazard of Returning to Work after the Birth of a First Child

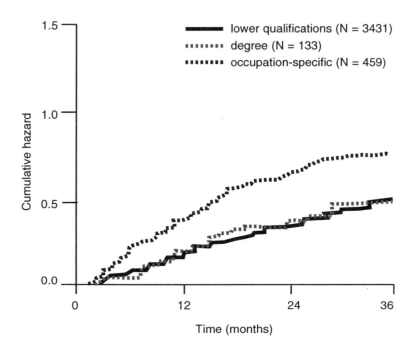

However, after this point, the probability of returning to work for women with non-vocational degrees reduces to a very low level; while women with high-level vocational qualifications continue to have a relatively high probability of returning, and those with lower qualifications fall between these two groups.

Returning to Work Part Time or Full Time
Following the Birth of a First Child

Table 28.3 shows some interesting differences in the process by which women return to work part time or full time after the birth of a first child. Again, the analysis is restricted to women who recorded a break from the labour market.

Figure 28.2 Cumulative Hazard of Returning to Work after the Birth of a Second Child

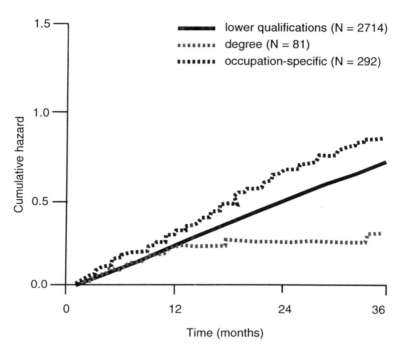

The effect of degree-level occupational qualifications is distinctive from that of other qualifications for speed of return to both full-time and part-time work. Coefficients are, again, lower for women with non-vocational qualifications than for those with non–degree-level teaching and nursing qualifications and, for return to full-time work, are not significantly different from those for women with no qualifications. While being older at motherhood increases a woman's probability of returning part time, it decreases her probability of returning full time. The absence of a cohabiting or marital partner substantially increases a woman's probability of returning full time but has the opposite effect on returning part time.

Once again the graphs of the hazard rates against time were plotted for women returning to part-time work and for women returning to full-time work. They show that, for the first eighteen months, women

Figure 28.3 Cumulative Hazard of Returning to Work Part Time after the Birth of a First Child

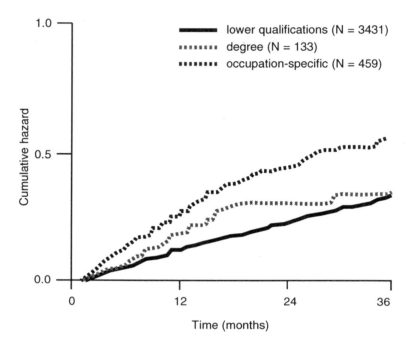

with occupationally specific qualifications have a higher probability of returning to part-time work than women with lower-level qualifications. However, after the first eighteen months the lines become approximately parallel, and therefore the hazard of returning to work would appear to become similar for the two groups. Women with non-occupational degrees have a probability of returning to work which lies between these two groups for the first eighteen months. After this point there are very few women returning to work, and interpretation of the graph is problematic.

Figure 28.4 suggests that the hazards of returning to full-time work are very low for all women; however, once again it is those women who have occupationally specific qualifications who have the highest probability of returning to work.

Figure 28.4 Cumulative Hazard of Returning to Work Full Time after the Birth of a First Child

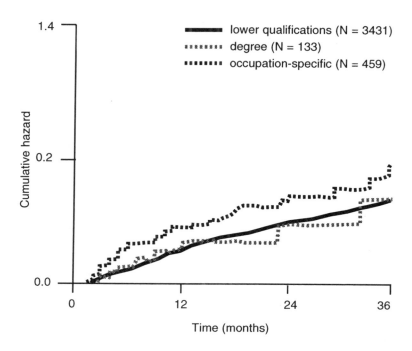

Discussion and Conclusions

The results of these analyses suggest that, among women with degree-level qualifications, those with occupationally specific qualifications are clearly differentiated from women with non-occupationally specific degrees. The former group are distinctive in the speed with which they return to work – after both a first and second child.

By comparison, for women who have degrees which are not directly linked to a particular occupation and who leave the labour market at motherhood, their speed ('risk') of returning to work after either their first or second child is substantially lower, not only than that of the occupationally qualified degree-level women but also than that of those with lower occupationally specific qualifications. Similarly, the speed of return to either full-time or part-time work is lower than for women with other tertiary qualifications.

These results suggest that women with a degree-level *occupational* qualification show very strong commitment to the labour market and, if they have a break for childbearing, are quick to return. These women are not, therefore, having children sooner or taking longer breaks than women who may find it harder to return to employment – in fact, the reverse is the case. However, where these women leave the labour market they do seem able to make a rapid return to work, although we are not yet able to establish the occupation into which they are returning.

Women with non-occupational qualifications behave in a way that is quite different and consistent with an organizational career. While a substantial proportion of women retain continuity at childbirth, for those who take a break, re-entry to employment takes considerably longer than for women with occupationally specific qualifications – whether degree-level or lower. However, we cannot tell whether a delay in returning to work is caused by the difficulty of the work hours expected by employers and the pressures of the job or because this group of women have chosen to spend more time as mothers.

From these results we can conclude that there are differences in child-related employment behaviour not only by level of qualification but also by whether or not it is occupationally specific. We can also conclude that having an occupationally specific qualification appears to facilitate re-entry to employment. However we cannot establish whether this apparent difference is explained by a high commitment to work by women who have chosen these qualifications or by the fact that the qualification itself provides a ready pathway back to work.

It is noteworthy that, in this cohort of women, a large number of women with non-occupational degrees went on to take a further qualification in education and are thus recorded as having an occupationally specific qualification (Dale and Egerton, 1997). Is this a response to difficulty in obtaining a job with their first degree? Is it the result of a desire for a teaching career? Or is it a wish to move into an occupation which is more accommodating of employees with children?

As always, it is likely that all these explanations play a part in explaining the observed patterns. What we can say from these results is that there are, in this cohort of women, clear differences in employment behaviour which are closely related to both the level and the type of qualifications held.

NOTE

1   The research on which this article is based was funded by the Economic and Social Research Council, Grant Number R00023 6549. We wish to thank Peter Shepherd and the NCDS user support group at the Institute of Education, London University, who gave advice on use of the data set. We particularly acknowledge the valuable statistical consultancy supplied by Professor Richard Davies and Dr Rob Crouchley at the Centre for Applied Statistics, University of Lancaster.

REFERENCES

Allison, P.D. (1984). *Event history analysis: Regression for longitudinal event data.* Beverly Hills: Sage.

Althauser, R.P., & Kalleberg, A.L. (1981). Firms, occupations and the structure of labor markets. In I. Berg (Ed.), *Sociological perspectives on labor markets* (pp 119–45). New York: Academic Press.

Becker, G. (1981). *A treatise on the family.* Cambridge, MA: Harvard University Press.

Brannen, J. (1987). *Taking maternity leave: The employment decisions of women with young children.* London: Thomas Coram Research Unit.

Brown, R. (1982). Work histories, career strategies and class structure. In A. Giddens & G. Mackenzie (Eds), *Social class and the division of labour,* Cambridge: Cambridge University Press.

Bynner, J., & Roberts, K. (Eds). (1991). *Youth and work: Transition to employment in England and West Germany.* London: Anglo-German Foundation.

Crompton, R. (1997). Paid employment and the changing system of gender relations. *Sociology, 30*(3), 427–46.

Crompton, R., with Sanderson, K. (1986). Credentials and careers: Some implications of the increase in professional qualifications among women. *Sociology, 20*(1), 25–42.

Crompton, R., & Sanderson, K. (1990). Credentials and careers. In G. Payne & P. Abbott (Eds.), *The social mobility of women: Beyond male mobility models.* London: Falmer.

Dale, A.M. (1987a). Labor market structure in the United Kingdom. *Work and Occupations, 14*(4), 558–90.

Dale, A. (1987b). Occupational inequality, gender and life-cycle. *Work, Employment and Society, 1*(3), 326–51.

Dale, A., & Egerton, M. (1997). *Highly educated women: Evidence from the national child development study* (Research Paper No. 75). London: Department for Education and Employment.

Desai, S., & Waite, L.J. (1991). Women's employment during pregnancy and after the first birth: Occupational characteristics and work commitment. *American Sociological Review, 56*, 551–66.

Devine, F. (1994). Segregation and supply: Preferences and plans among 'self-made' women. *Gender, Work and Organisation, 1*(2), 94–109.

Dex, S., Joshi, H., McCulloch, A., & Macran, S. (1996). *Women's employment transitions around childbearing* (Discussion paper series, No. 1408). London: Centre for Economic Policy Research.

Doeringer, P.B., & Piore, M.J. (1971). *Internal labor markets and manpower analysis.* Lexington, MA: D.C. Heath.

Duncan, S., & Edwards, R., (1997). Lone mothers and paid work – rational economic man or gendered moral rationalities? *Feminist Economics, 3*(2), 29–61.

Glover, J. (1994). Women teachers and white collar workers: Domestic circumstances and paid work. *Work, Employment and Society, 8*(1), 87–100.

Joshi, H., Macran, S., & Dex, S. (1996). Employment after childbearing and women's subsequent labour-force participation: Evidence from the British 1958 birth cohort. *Journal of Population Economics, 9*, 325–48.

Layder, D., Ashton, D., & Sung, J. (1991). The empirical correlates of agency and structure: The transition from school to work. *Sociology, 25*(3), 447–64.

Macran, S., Joshi, H., & Dex, S. (1996). *Employment after childbearing: A survival analysis* (NCDS working paper). London: Department for Education and Employment.

Martin, J., & Roberts, C. (1984). *Women and employment: A lifetime perspective.* London: HMSO.

McRae, S. (1993). Returning to work after childbirth: Opportunities and inequalities. *European Sociological Review, 9*(2), 125–38.

McRae, S., & Daniel, W.W. (1991). *Maternity rights: The experience of women and employers.* London: Policy Studies Institute.

Payne, J. (1991). *Women, training and the skills shortage.* London: Policy Studies Institute.

Polacheck, S. (1979). Occupational segregation among women: Theory, evidence and a prognosis. In C. Lloyd, E. Andrews, & C. Gilroy (Eds), *Women in the labor market* (pp 137–59). New York: Columbia University Press.

Sanders, K. (1997). Mothers and daughters in the Netherlands: The influence of the mother's social background on daughters' labour-market participation after they have children. *The European Journal of Women's Studies, 4*, 165–81.

Scott, J., Braun, M., & Alwin, D. (1993). The family way. In R. Jowell, L. Brooks, & L. Dowds (Eds), *International social attitudes: The 10th BSA report* (pp 23–47). London: SCPR and Dartmouth.

29. Reconstructing Life Courses: A Historical Perspective on Migrant Experiences

Dirk Hoerder

Life Courses: Models and Experiences

Traditional life-course models conceptualize a linear development from birth to death through education, work, and retirement, or pre-work, work, and post-work stages (Kohli, 1985; Kohli et al., 1991). While it was the achievement of Kohli (1986) to reintroduce the concept of the life course into social sciences dominated by structuralist and institutional approaches, his concept of work refers to waged or salaried employment without reference to unpaid work in reproduction. A so-called normal biography emerges which, however, excludes large segments of any population from consideration. First, life-course models based on remunerative productive or administrative work are male oriented and thus neglect the other half of any society. Second, such linear life-course models exclude risks and assume similar access to social resources by men. Third, non-linearity, formerly called 'fate,' needs to be introduced – that is, the disruption of life courses by natural catastrophes or war, or by illness or the sudden death of near kin.

As regards productive and unproductive labour, Kohli's differentiation is part of 'liberal economic theory,' as it has come to be designated. Its father, Adam Smith, offered but an inquiry into the wealth of nations under the circumstances of 1776. He lived in the male part of a gendered world and offered a critique of the gentry class's creation of an unproductive servant class detrimental to the common wealth. Probably taking his Scottish home town to Glasgow as the example, he proposed a program for new socio-economic priorities at the historic conjunction of change from a regime of agricultural family production in hierarchicized societies with a non-productive, consumption-centred gentry class to a regime of middle-class male-centred commerce, production, and accumulation in Britain (Smith, 1976 [1776], pp 330–1). His economic model lost both the gendered and intergenerational aspects of labour in an agricultural economy. Work spheres of husband and wife and inheritance of land by children in return for taking care of aging parents were restructured in commercially oriented middle-class households and in manufactories. In the economic development from industrious families to industrial factories after 1776, the value of accumulating as many children as possible along with the integration of productive and caregiving labour were replaced by the goal of accumulation of material wealth, including capital. In most European societies, daughters had to be married off with the help of a dowry payment. In societies which valued women's work differently – African societies, for example – men had to pay a bride price to compensate the bride's parents for the loss of her industry. 'Work, whether paid or unpaid, is better defined as having utility for the user of the output.' This encompasses both paid employment and unpaid family labour, including the 'burdens of caring' (Stone et al., 1998).

As regards unequal access to societal resources, recent research has incorporated institutionalized stratification, gatekeeping, regional disparities, and other causes. Institutional regimes may also provide cushioning effects, if willed politically (Heinz, 1991), but research on supportive payments or services – as epitomized in the modern welfare state – disregards risks that are outside the realm of particular institutions that soften disruptions in the lives of individuals.

Disruptions resulting from societal and natural disasters made linear life courses almost impossible to achieve in Europe for the generations born since the 1870s and living to the 1980s. Most of the European and part of the North American populations lived through two world wars as well as the decade-long major depression of the 1930s, and other shorter ones. For these age cohorts, no construction of linear life courses was possible. Individual actors could not achieve undeviating job careers and straightforward family-formation patterns. They had to rechart directions in each depression and, after wartime loss of breadwinning or support-giving members, had to reconfigure emotional relationships and income-generating strategies. In the present, the same holds true for the masses of men, women, and children involuntarily departing from refugee-generating polities.

If actual life courses are not usually linear, construction of linearity serves two important purposes – identity creation, and access to institutionalized transfer payments for material security in old age. Unless embittered, most men and women, when looking back on their lives, see an identity-preserving coherence, even continuity, in which coping strategies evolved in reaction to major breaks or proactively as means to expand limited options. Individual decisions include migration between economic regions, polities, or continents. They also include a selective memorizing of the past to shut out debilitating events (a selective forgetfulness) and a compartmentalization of spheres of life to shut out spaces/episodes/statuses in which powerlessness was experienced or assumed. This construction of continuity – usually – does not depict rigidly delimited one-way streets; rather, it suggests a high degree of – assumedly purposeful – flexibility. It reflects multiple identities of active insertion into different cultures, as well as transcultural skills (Schiller et al., 1992, pp 1–24; Schiller, 1996, p. 2).

Continuity of life courses is also required to achieve entitlement to material security in old age after the end of income-generating work. Sufficient savings have to be accumulated, either by means of the material competency of nineteenth-century skilled artisans, or through children in intergenerational intra-family customary support systems, or through long-time membership in institutional social security systems.

The achievement of coherent life courses across status passages, debilitating social inequalities, and the outside interference of factors like war or paralysing illness demands flexibility on the part of the individual actors, including – on the societal level – the absence of restraining customs. It demands flexibility and transparency of institutional arrangements as well as flexible labour markets and responsibility-sharing arrangements of reproductive work. The need for coping strategies has been emphasized by Glen Elder in his ground-breaking study of people living in the Great Depression (1974). Recent criticism of bureaucratized social security systems misses the point that free labour markets under conditions of long-term recession constrain options and that lack of transparency in employer decisions to hire and fire as well as in bureaucratized social security systems prevents individuals from making informed choices. Continued gendered access to paid productive work and allocation of burdens of unpaid reproductive work further limits the options of women. Allocation of funding to or away from educational institutions by national administrative and political institutions structures options available to youths. Neoliberal-ist stances in modern mass societies overlook the obvious: In Adam Smith's model for mid-sized eighteenth-century urban societies, actors had near-perfect access to information and freedom to act. Hierarchici-zation by class and monopolistic concentrations of economic power were (considered to be) absent; only the state seemed to interfere.

My critique of Kohli's model of linear life courses through educa-tion/training to work in the paid labour force is based empirically on a qualitative study of a representative sample of Canadian immigrant life writings between 1840 and the 1990s (Hoerder, 1999) and on a model of acculturation concentrating on the status passages involved in migration (Hoerder, 1996, 1997). This concept of a meso level of action between the macro level of nation-states and the micro level of individuals and families includes subnational regional economies which mediate global economic cycles and developments for indi-vidual economic performance, as well as the local village or urban neighbourhood social customs, and organizations like clubs and asso-ciations. Life-course research has to measure up to the following agenda:

– A *gendered approach* includes the social construction of gendered
  spheres and family-related status passages and risks: traditionally,
  women's paid work before and immediately after marriage, often
  followed by a period of unpaid reproductive work from the birth of
  the first child on, a possible re-entry into the paid labour force once
  children may take care of themselves or have left the home, and
  another period of reproductive work when women take care of
  aging parents. These ideal-type stages vary over time, across space,
  and from family to family. The different strategies of reproductive
  life-course planning, including full-time life-long work for women
  with the hiring of caregivers, expand the 50 per cent models of the
  world based on men's lives to comprehensive ones (Hareven, 1978b;
  Kammen, 1979; Krüger, 1995, based on the recent work of numerous
  other women scholars).
– A *childhood-focused approach* distinguishes between infancy, preschool childhood, schooling, and vocational training/secondary–tertiary education as stages of the development of a person's human
  capital. If most individual development options are socialized in the
  first years of life, familial investments in early childhood ('quality
  time') and societal ones in educational facilities pay off in terms of

adolescents' human capital. In contrast to economists' restricted view of human capital, I include emotional resilience, all coping strategies, decision-making capabilities, adeptness in establishing relationships, as well as skills acquired by education and training. (See also Cunningham, 1998.)

- A *community-focused approach* incorporates the social group into which individuals are born, and their social relations. This involves, first, a critical analysis of power relationships. For example, although according to political theory/Western ideology all men – that is, individual men and women – are born equal, empirically, they begin their life courses by being born into unequal power relationships with unequal access to resources. Second, this approach involves the analysis of strategies for forming relationships through which to gain access to communities and their organizations, relationships which permit individuals and families to develop social capital. Access to social relations/capital influences satisfaction (health, transactional capabilities) during particular stages of the life cycle.

- Finally, a *historically grounded approach* incorporates career and family breaks caused by war and economic cycles, changing modes of production, or particular processes of production. Late-nineteenth-century mechanization and Taylorism, for example, dislocated millions of skilled craftsmen and their families and destroyed home economies in which women produced cloth, clothing, and food ('surplus' populations). The social space of dislocation and the social space of new options (in contemporary ideology, 'unlimited opportunities') were geographically separate worlds – rural and urban – or even on different continents.

In short, the linear life-course model has little relationship to lived lives and needs to be replaced by a *historico-societal life-course model* in which men and women actively structure their lives in 'participational passages' (Heinz, 1991, p. 19) as long-term projects and in response to short-term exigencies, and in which childhood human-capital formation is part of the analysis. This model recognizes conditions of unequal access to societal resources and the ongoing process of intra-familial negotiations about income-generating and family-care strategies. It relates multiple options and multiple constraints to major macro-level disruptions (war, depression) or enhancements (economic boom periods) on a meso level of regional economies and communities by flexible adaptive skills and coping strategies (Elder, 1974; Hoerder, 1996). The French approach to economic self-determination on the shop floor, *'autogestion,'* offers a research strategy. It combines a sociography of institutions and associations with a study of workers' agency as circumscribed by degree of information, attitudes, and aspirations and as expressed in decision making in relation to other actors (bosses, social institutions, families).

Case Study of Two Polish-Canadian Families

I will contrast the simplifying male-continuous work-life model with the complexity of experienced lives by taking as examples Walter F. Chuchla, born in Poland in 1904, who immigrated to Canada in 1926, and Anne K. Pieronek, born to immigrant parents from Poland in 1915 as the eldest of eight children. The two met in Albera in the late 1920s and married in 1931.

Walter was born in Austrian Poland to a smallholding peasant family. He was considered a 'fast learner' by his father and was sent to school. In 1914, at age ten, the macro-level declaration of war interrupted both the micro-level family economy and Walter's education. The father and an older brother were drafted into the Austrian army and returned sick; another brother, drafted into the Polish army in 1920 for the Polish–Soviet War, returned injured. After Polish independence, Walter joined the Peasant Party, wrote articles for its newspaper, and, by self-education, upgraded his skills. Various life-course options were ruled out – peasant farming because of insufficient land, further education because of insufficient money, full-time politics because of insufficient connections. However, the Polish culture of world-wide migrations and the existence of a Polish diaspora suggested other possibilities (Bobinska and Pilch, 1975; Morawska, 1989).

After considering Brazil, Walter opted for Canada and emigrated in early 1926, just before Pilsudski's coup forced his co-nationals to reconsider life-course strategies at home. There were risks initially associated with departure. Walter and his family assumed a U.S. $180 debt and severed all face-to-face social-emotional ties. A seemingly minor hygienic measure – all passengers had their heads shaved before embarkation at Gdansk – was experienced as identity threatening: 'We looked like prisoners.' On board, he recreated social ties by consorting with other young Poles who encouraged each other but dispersed after arrival to prearranged jobs or to segmented labour markets. Walter, who 'had nobody in Canada,' faced social risk and had to rely on his human capital in flexible but unrewarding labour markets. Social capital and stable work relationships had to be reconstructed (W. Chuchla, 1978, pp 63–4).

Circumstances were adverse for the re-establishment of social capital. From the perspectives both of income generation and of emotional stability, Walter's life took a further downward course: jobs on isolated Alberta farmsteads; employers with whom he had no common language; the struggle to stake a homestead in a marginal northern district. His first job ended because of 'homesickness' arising out of his lack of contact with other Poles. The next two jobs improved his micro-level integration by small steps. The fourth – well-paying work with a harvesting crew – came to a premature end when early rains interrupted his project of re-establishing economic security and cast him back into unemployment. He decided to move west, stopped in Calgary for an in-town job, and continued to the mining community of Coleman, where a Polish merchant sent him and two Ukrainian men to clear land. Their lives were reduced to a survival economy in a lonely shack in a bitterly cold winter.

At this time, Coleman's community, which included about 150 Polish families, experienced a disastrous mining accident. Walter attended the funeral and thereby introduced himself to the community. Most of the families and single men came from his region in Poland. His readiness to share their grief changed his tenuous tie to Coleman's Poles and, with his human capital, he managed to achieve a multiple-level community integration. He joined a drama club and, in early 1927, moved permanently from male bush camp to the gendered community. Activating the political experience he had gained in Poland, he became recording secretary of the local mutual-aid society. Intentionally avoiding an individualist strategy, he never returned to his northern homestead, so distant from markets and communities. Instead he quickly developed his social capital: volunteer work in the Polish community, connections to the mutual-aid society's branches in other towns, and contacts with the U.S.-based Polish immigrant newspaper and the Winnipeg-based Polish consul.

His economic base remained tenuous. He had an outstanding debt from his initial emigration expenses. The work available was mostly odd jobs, obtained through acquaintances, or unskilled mine labour. His lack of skills made better-paying work hard to find. Though raised in a peasant family, he decided to join the labour union. With his wages and the strength of his arms he built a two-room house. This increased his social standing and chances of attracting a promising marriage partner. In 1929, the Great Depression interrupted the reachieved continuity/linearity of his life course. Since he, like all immigrants, lacked access to socio-political macro levels to demand welfare benefits or unemployment insurance, he had to rely on his own immediate coping strategies and quickly adjust long-term projects for his life.

The family of Anne Pieronek had been part of Polish emigration culture for two generations. Her paternal grandfather had moved back and forth across the Atlantic three times while the grandmother stayed in Poland. An uncle brought her father, Martin, over to Canada. Her maternal grandfather had migrated to Canada with his daughter, Frances, while this grandmother, too, remained behind. Frances and Martin, who had been next-door neighbours in Poland but had not seen each other for years, married within a year of Frances's arrival. In these life courses spanning two continents, emotional relations continued to function and economic bases were secured by the spreading of risks across different economies. Migrants always looked for both economic stability and emotional support. Otherwise the psychic cost of migration would have outweighed the benefits for the family (Massey et al., 1993, 1994; Massey and Espinosa, 1995; Hoerder, 1996).

In 1919, when the Pieronek's first daughter, Anne, was 4 years old, Martin decided to end his stint as a miner and to fulfil his dream of tilling the land. His non-linearity, from farm in Poland to mine work in Alberta, remained a deviation, side-tracking his intended way of life. The move to a run-down and therefore affordable farm sixteen miles outside the town of Coleman was meant to re-establish linearity in his life project, but it interrupted that of Frances, who lost her community relations. In scholarship epitomized by F.J. Turner's frontier thesis, the move to the land was a type of nationalized life-course model to establish an independent existence as producers. But, under macro-level industrialization and urbanization, family farms had to compete with corporate agribusiness. Martin Pieronek's charted life-course also did not fit the regional meso-level economy. His decisions were informed about land prices but based on an unrealistic vision/expectation. With insufficient starting capital, the farm did not provide a secure economic base; Martin frequently returned to mine work to keep the family supplied with cash or to finance the purchase of farm machinery. Thus, the family unit was often disrupted, with the mother frequently left alone with the children. The move – at age 4 for Anne – involved her transition to family labour. She took care of her younger siblings when her mother worked in the fields. After the onset of the Depression, when Anne was 14, family clothing was made from flour sacks and sugar bags. Anne had to leave school to work in a restaurant and help feed the family. When she met Walter, he was an itinerant farm labourer. She joined the same theatre group. Their decision to marry involved an adjustment of two life-course projects to each other. Even where the model of linear life courses is applicable, marriage implies changes for both partners (A. Chuchla, 1979).

In the second year of the Great Depression a five-month strike interrupted Walter's wage income. Eventually, he and some eighty other miners were fired. Feeling that their social capital was spent and employment opportunities nil, the couple moved to Edmonton. Walter found a mining job, and Anne took in boarders. Their first and only child was born, a daughter. When demand for coal fell further, Walter became unemployed again. For a couple of years he worked on farms and at odd jobs wherever he found work. Anne kept the home base going, caring for their child and running her boarding-house business. In 1935, the family returned to Coleman. Walter again found a mining job and, with the help of a skilled miner, rose from an unskilled to a semiskilled position – another attempt to give direction to their lives in an economy in which many people were set adrift. Despite their hardships, the Chuchlas were better off than their relatives in Poland, whose lives were shatteringly disrupted by the Second World War. In 1944, a mine accident partially disabled Walter. The family then moved to Calgary, where Anne worked in several restaurant jobs while Walter became a custodian for the school board. Only then did their lives achieve linearity. They remained in their jobs till Walter's retirement in 1970. No care of aging parents is mentioned in the memoirs, and their daughter left home to pursue a career of her own.

Their lives spanned two continents, two wars, and a depression decade. Each decision to adjust micro-level family life to macro-level outside forces ruled out other options. Walter and Anne both had a high amount of human capital and a capability to convert their skills into social capital. Thus, they began with better assets than many others, migrant or non-migrant.

Structuring/Negotiating Life Courses

Approaches to life-course research which focus on social and human capital link the micro level of individuals and families, through the meso level of identity-supporting community and material life-supporting economic regions, to national frameworks and global migration options. The meso level is the arena in which men and women receive their socialization, have to come to terms with larger socio-economic forces, and live, act, and feel as community and family members. Here non-migrants and migrants act out aspirations and values, adapt to customs, or choose innovative strategies. This level comprises, first, family economies as well as kin and friendship networks in which information is digested, decisions are made, and interests of group members are weighed and, ideally, balanced (Tilly and Scott, 1978, p. 12 passim). Such negotiating processes depend on the power hierarchies that separate and connect genders and generations ('kinscripts,' Stack and Burton, 1991). The goal is not equilibrium or equal rights and benefits but a fair deal, a compromise among individual interests that satisfies the local moral economy within the framework of socially allocated status. Second, in meso-level village or urban neighbourhoods and in regional economies, potential migrants have to find a way to earn a living. There they look for jobs, expect to become independent of their families-of-birth, and, usually, establish their own families. Thus family strategies and regional job markets are closely entwined. Goals are not restricted to income maximization but include a search for independence and for human dignity within a framework of specific norms and values. Thirdly, information flows about potential options elsewhere connect meso-level economic regions. With earlier migrants acting as informants, social relations provide access to information flows and permit an accumulation of social capital.

The concept of family economies and social capital as well as the inclusion of non-measurable emotional and spiritual factors avoids, on the one hand, a reductionist neoclassical economic approach to wage differentials between societies and, on the other, the reductionist linear wage-labour-oriented life-course model. Family economies combine the income-generating capabilities of all family members with reproductive needs and consumption patterns to achieve the best results possible according to traditional norms and within the framework of macro-level restrictions or opportunities. Allocation of resources depends on the stage of the family life cycle and of individual life courses, as well as on gender and generational power hierarchies, and has to be negotiated in terms of maximization of benefits for each: of income or leisure, child care or work outside the home, education or wage work for children, traditional networking or individualist separation from the community. The Chuchlas and Pieroneks remained in survival economies, their lives focused on strategies to prevent poverty rather than upward-bound projects to increase material security. They had been climbing up a downward escalator.

This comprehensive, holistic, material-emotional approach integrates economic and emotional, material and spiritual aspects of individual lives and considers individuals as making conscious choices about perceived opportunities. Decisions about life courses involve a complex of traditional cultural norms and practices, of actual emotional and spiritual needs, and of economic rationales. Immigrant women workers wanted 'bread and roses, too' – that is, community beyond cash, emotional rewards beyond economic survival. This complexity results in a methodological problem for the researcher: neither the loss of relationships, sadness, and homesickness (which I prefer to call network-deprivation) nor happiness and the benefits of emotionally sustaining social contacts can be measured on a numerical scale as wages and consumption expenditures can be. Rather, such factors enter individual decision making as subjectively weighed factors within a community culture.

Anne's *autogestion* of her life was bound by family ties as long as she had to hand over her own wages to her family of birth to be allocated in what the parent generation considered the interests of all, including younger non–wage-earning siblings. Walter's self-determination, ironically, was hampered by his success in Coleman: women who had competed for his attention to their daughters turned hostile when he chose Anne; when, as treasurer of the union, he gave relief funds to industrious families regardless of ethnic origin and bypassed Polish families because of intemperance, a segment of the Polish community turned hostile. His and Anne's social capital became a liability in a community that neither shared nor valued their flexible resourcefulness. Their departure to Edmonton was a reaction to the push of hostility. The intricate connection between economic and emotional factors is shown in migrants' timing of decisions to leave. A slump in either economic conditions or emotional circumstances, stemming from family or community relations, influences the timing of departures from home communities, jobs, and social networks. Departure is, at the same time, a striking out into new directions (Hoerder, 1996, 1997).

Increasing Options

Walter and Anne pursued life-course strategies that increased their options. This could not be achieved by trying to homestead or farm in locations cut off from markets and supportive neighbours. The ability to rely on casual wage labour as a survival and improvement strategy was premised on the existence of functioning labour markets with year-round job openings. In Canada, winters undercut the self-sufficiency of agricultural and outdoor urban labourers. An absence of societal relief systems during wars and depressions undercut income-generating strategies. Individual bad luck, such as Walter's accident in the mine, also demanded coping strategies and networks of support.

The options of individuals and families thus depend, first, on their own human capital, the parameters of which are set in childhood and youth by identity-formation, education, and training. Second, they depend on social capital, the support of communities and institutions, the availability of jobs, and projects for the near and distant future. Third, macro-level political processes, economic cycles, and societal frameworks determine the limits of individual decision making.

Current neoliberal policies and programs, with their emphasis on individual initiative, overlook both the complex interactions among these factors and the fact that certain prerequisites must be fulfilled if individual strategies are to succeed. Independent lives demand flexible and open labour markets as well as flexible but reliable social security systems with cushioning effects. The rise of institutionalized, bureaucratized social security occurred parallel to a decline of informal, community-based social security. The blanket provisions of state social security ignore the importance of individual, network-based life projects and the multiple interests individuals in family or non-traditional relationships have to negotiate. All of the factors – individual–community relationships, labour markets, intergenerational family emotional-economic systems, and social security regulations – are manageable and negotiable for individual men and women only as long as they are sufficiently simple to be understood.

The holistic material-emotional approach combines a systems approach to macro-level societal frameworks with micro-level analysis of individual life courses. The meso level of individual experience is formative for migrants' and non-migrants' choices in the present, as it was in the past, whether nineteenth century or the Middle Ages. On the meso level, risk diversification, access to resources, and opportunities for entry into segmented labour markets are all important. On this level, migrants develop both their human and social capital and evaluate the emotional, material, and spiritual benefits accruing to themselves and their immediate kin in terms of projected life courses. Societal parameters and structures have to remain flexible so that men and women may shape, create, construct, and negotiate their life courses with a certain amount of identity-providing independence.

REFERENCES

Bobinska, C., & Pilch, A. (Eds). (1975). *Employment-seeking emigrations of the Poles world wide, XIXc and XXc*. Krakow: Panstwowe Wydawn.

Chuchla, A.K. (1979). The Martin J. Pieronek family. In J. Matejko (Ed.), *Polish settlers in Alberta: Reminiscences and biographies* (pp 140–4). Toronto: Polish Alliance Press.

Chuchla, W.F. (1978). My first steps in Canada: Coleman and my work in the Polish community. In J. Matejko & Tova Yedlin (Eds), *Alberta's pioneers from Eastern Europe: Reminiscences [and biographies]* (2nd ed., pp 63–72). Edmonton: University of Alberta. See also Chuchla, W.F. (1979). Personal experiences from 1904 till 1978. In J. Matejko (Ed.), *Polish settlers in Alberta: Reminiscences and biographies* (pp 49–79, 265–9). Toronto: Polish Alliance Press.

Cunningham, H. (1998). Review essay: Histories of childhood. *American Historical Review, 103*, 1195–1208.

Elder, Glen H., Jr. (1974). *Children of the great depression: Social change in life experience*. Chicago: University of Chicago Press.

Hareven, T.K. (1978a). Cycles, courses and cohorts: Reflections on theoretical and methodological approaches to the historical study of family development. *Journal of Social History, 12*, 97–109.

Hareven, T.K., (Ed.). (1978b). *Transitions: The family and the life course in historical perspective*. New York: Academic Press.

Heinz, W.R. (1991). Status passages, social risks and the life course: A conceptual framework. In W.R. Heinz (Ed.), *Theoretical advances in life course research* (pp 9–22). Weinheim: Deutscher Studien Verlag.

Hoerder, D. (1996). Migrants to ethnics: Acculturation in a societal framework. In D. Hoerder & L. Page Moch (Eds), *European migrants: Global and local perspectives* (pp 211–62). Boston: Northeastern University Press.

Hoerder, D. (1997). Labour markets – community – family: A gendered analysis of the process of insertion and acculturation. In W. Isajiw (Ed.), *Multiculturalism in North America and Europe: Comparative perspectives on interethnic relations and social incorporation* (pp 155–83). Toronto: Canadian Scholar's Press.

Hoerder, D. (1999). *Creating societies: Immigrant lives in Canada.* Montreal: McGill University Press.

Kammen, M. (1979). Changing perceptions of the life cycle in American thought and culture. *Proceedings of the Massachusetts Historical Society, 91,* 35–66.

Kohli, M. (1985). Die Institutionalisierung des Lebenslaufs: Historische Befunde und theoretische Argumente. *Kölner Zeitschrift für Soziologie und Sozialpsychologie, 36,* 1–29.

Kohli, M. (1986). The world we forgot: A historical review of the life course. In V.W. Marshall (Ed.), *Later life: The social psychology of aging* (pp 271–303). Beverly Hills: Sage.

Kohli, M., Rein, M., Guillemard, A.-M., & van Gunsteren, H. (Eds). (1991). *Time for retirement: Comparative studies of early exit from the labor force.* Cambridge: Cambridge University Press.

Krüger, H. (1995). Statusmanagement und Institutionenregimes: Die Kategorie Geschlecht zwischen Leistung und Zuschreibung. Unpublished research paper, Universität Bremen.

Massey, D.S., Arango, J., Hugo, G., Kouaouci, A., Pellegrino, A., & Taylor, J.E. (1993, September). Theories of international migration: Review and appraisal. *Population and Development Review, 19,* 431–66.

Massey, D.S., Arango, J., Hugo, G., Kouaouci, A., Pellegrino, A., & Taylor, J.E. (1994, December). An evaluation of international migration theory: The North American case. *Population and Development Review, 20,* 699–752.

Massey, D.S., & Espinosa, K.E. (1995). *What's driving Mexico–U.S. migration? A theoretical, empirical, and policy analysis.* 1995 paper presented January 1996 at the Social Science Research Council Conference, Becoming American/American Becoming: International Migration to the United States, Sanibel Island, Florida.

Morawska, E. (1989). Labor migrations of Poles in the Atlantic world economy, 1880–1914. *Comparative Studies in Society and History, 31,* 237–72.

Schiller, N.G. (1996, January). *Who are these guys? A transnational reading of the U.S. immigrant experience.* Paper presented at the Social Science Research Council Conference, Becoming American/American Becoming: International Migration to the United States, Sanibel Island, Florida.

Schiller, N.G., Basch, L., & Blanc-Szanton, C. (1992). *Towards a transnational perspective on migration: Race, class, ethnicity and nationalism reconsidered.* New York: New York Academy of Sciences.

Smith, Adam (1976/1776). *An inquiry into the nature and causes of the wealth of nations* (Vol. 2). In *The Glasgow edition of the works and correspondence of Adam Smith* (6 vols). Edited by R.H. Campbell, A.S. Skinner, & W.B. Todd. Oxford: Oxford University Press.

Stack, C.B., & Burton, L. (1991). Kinscripts. In W.R. Heinz (Ed.), *Theoretical advances in life course research* (pp 115–29). Weinheim: Deutscher Studien Verlag.

Stone, L.O., Harvey, A., & Jones, F. (1998, May). *Work transitions in later life: A view from the total-work perspective.* Paper given at the symposium entitled Restructuring Work and the Life Course, University of Toronto.

Tilly, L.A., & Scott, J.W. (1978). *Women, work and family.* New York: Holt, Rinehart and Winston.

Contributors

Jutta Allmendinger is professor of sociology at the University of Munich and president of the German Sociological Association.

Paul Anisef is a professor of sociology at York University in Toronto and an associate director of CERIS, a federally funded centre of excellence for research on immigration and settlement.

William R. Avison is professor of sociology at Florida International University.

Paul Axelrod is a professor in the Division of Social Science at York University.

Ronald Batenburg is assistant professor HRM at Nijmegen University, Nijmegen Business School, and senior researcher at Utrecht University, Department of Sociology.

Deborah S. Carr is an assistant professor of sociology at the University of Michigan, and as an assistant research scientist at the Survey Research Center and Population Studies Center, within the Institute for Social Research.

Donna C. Chan is a doctoral candidate in the Faculty of Information Studies, University of Toronto.

Angela Dale is professor of quantitative social research and director of the Centre for Census and Survey Research at the University of Manchester.

Jan Denys (labour sociologist) is now a manager of strategic labour-market policy for Randstad Belgium.

Marco de Witte is assistant professor, labour and organization, at the Faculty of Management and Organization, University of Groningen (section HRM), and a management consultant at Wagner Consultancy.

James J. Dowd is a sociologist at the University of Georgia, where he teaches courses on aging, film, culture, and the military.

Muriel Egerton is a research fellow at the Centre for Longitudinal Studies, Institute of Education, London University.

Jane Elliott is a lecturer in sociology at the University of Liverpool. She was formerly a research fellow at the Cathie Marsh Centre for Census and Survey Research at the University of Manchester.

Stefan Fuchs is a doctoral candidate in sociology and research affiliate at the University of Munich.

Kathleen Gerson is professor of sociology at New York University, where she is currently serving as department chair.

Shin-Kap Han is assistant professor of sociology at the University of Illinois at Urbana-Champaign.

Andrew S. Harvey is professor of economics at Saint Mary's University.

Walter R. Heinz is professor of sociology and social psychology and chair of the Life Course Research Centre (Sfb 186) at the University of Bremen. Professor Heinz has also been the visiting chair for German and European studies at the University of Toronto (1995–6).

Dirk Hoerder teaches North American social history and history of migration at the University of Bremen, Department of Social Sciences.

Karen Hughes is an associate professor of women's studies and adjunct professor of sociology at the University of Alberta.

Jennifer Reid Keene is a doctoral candidate in sociology at Florida State University.

Takeshi Kimura is professor at the Faculty of Humanist and Social Sciences, Yamagata University.

Reinhard Kreckel is professor of sociology and the rector of the Martin-Luther-University Halle-Wittenberg.

Helga Krüger is professor of sociology of family, socialization, and work at the University of Bremen and a member of the steering committee of the Bremen Life Course Research Centre (Sfb 186).

Thomas Kühn (psychologist) is researcher and PhD candidate in the Life Course Research Centre, University of Bremen.

Graham S. Lowe is director of the Work Network at Canadian Policy Research Networks Inc., and professor of sociology at the University of Alberta, where he recently held a McCalla Research Professorship.

David MacPherson is professor of economics and research associate of the Pepper Institute on Aging and Public Policy at Florida State University.

Joanne G. Marshall is dean and professor, School of Information and Library Science, University of North Carolina at Chapel Hill. She was coordinator of the NOVA case study while a professor in the Faculty of Information Studies at the University of Toronto.

Victor W. Marshall is director of the University of North Carolina Institute on Aging, professor of sociology, and adjunct professor of health behavior and health education at the University of North Carolina at Chapel Hill.

Phyllis Moen is the Ferris Family Professor of Life Course Studies and professor of human development and of sociology at Cornell University. She is also the founding director of the Bronfenbrenner Life Course Center at Cornell and director of the Cornell Employment and Family Careers Institute.

Robin L. Oakley is a lecturer in the Department of Anthropology at the University of Toronto.

Masato Oka is professor at the Economic Research Institute, Yokohama City University.

Lori Parham is a graduate student in the Department of Sociology at Florida State University.

Ian Procter is senior lecturer and chair of the Department of Sociology, University of Warwick.

Jill Quadagno is a professor of sociology and a research associate in the

Pepper Institute on Aging and Public Policy at Florida State University. She holds the Pepper Eminent Scholar Chair in Social Gerontology.

Gillian Ranson is an assistant professor in the Department of Sociology at the University of Calgary.

Sara E. Rix is a senior policy adviser with the Economics Team of the Public Policy Institute of AARP (formerly the American Association of Retired Persons).

Hildegard Schaeper is senior researcher in the Life Course Research Centre at the University of Bremen.

Sabine M. Schenk is a researcher at the Department of Sociology at Martin Luther University Halle-Wittenberg.

Winfried Schmähl is professor of economics, University of Bremen and former chair of the Social Advisory Board on Pension Policy to the German federal government.

Jennifer T. Sheridan is a doctoral candidate in sociology at the University of Wisconsin-Madison.

Peter Simoens has been based at the universities of Leuven and Ghent. He is now a sociolinguist in the worldwide headquarters of Lernout and Hauspie (Ieper).

Gangaram Singh is an assistant professor in the Department of Management at San Diego State University.

Leroy O. Stone is an associate director-general in the Analytical Studies Branch of Statistics Canada and an adjunct professor, Department of Demography, at University of Montreal.

Diane-Gabrielle Tremblay is professor of labour economics and sociology of work, as well as director of research at the Télé-université of the University of Québec.

Anil Verma is professor of industrial relations and human resource management at the Rotman School of Management and the Centre for Industrial Relations, University of Toronto.

Janina von Stebut is a doctoral candidate in sociology and research affiliate at the University of Munich.

Christine Wimbauer is a doctoral candidate in sociology and research affiliate at the University of Munich.

Andreas Witzel (psychologist) is senior researcher in the Life Course Research Centre, University of Bremen.

Susan Yeandle is professor of sociology at Sheffield Hallam University, conducting research in the Centre for Regional Economic and Social Research (CRESR), and teaching in the School of Social Science and Law.